CORPORATE POWER
AND RESPONSIBILITY

Issues in the Theory
of Company Law

J. E. PARKINSON

CLARENDON PRESS · OXFORD

This book has been printed digitally and produced in a standard specification
in order to ensure its continuing availability

OXFORD
UNIVERSITY PRESS

Great Clarendon Street, Oxford OX2 6DP

Oxford University Press is a department of the University of Oxford.
It furthers the University's objective of excellence in research, scholarship,
and education by publishing worldwide in

Oxford New York

Auckland Bangkok Buenos Aires Cape Town Chennai
Dar es Salaam Delhi Hong Kong Istanbul Karachi Kolkata
Kuala Lumpur Madrid Melbourne Mexico City Mumbai Nairobi
São Paulo Shanghai Singapore Taipei Tokyo Toronto

Oxford is a registered trade mark of Oxford University Press
in the UK and in certain other countries

Published in the United States
by Oxford University Press Inc., New York

© John Parkinson 1993

The moral rights of the author have been asserted
Database right Oxford University Press (maker)

Reprinted 2002

ISBN 0-19-825989-1

Front cover photo: *Factory site in Prescot, Lancashire, circa 1930.*
Back cover photo: *Same factory site today.*

CORPORATE POWER AND RESPONSIBILITY

*Issues in the Theory
of Company Law*

To my family

Preface

Large businesses are keen to stress their credentials as good corporate citizens. They wish to be seen as caring employers, playing a part in supporting the communities in which they operate and behaving responsibly towards the environment. Much of this concern can probably be explained in terms of public relations, but whether it can or not company managements are undoubtedly required to make decisions that involve genuine ethical and social-policy choices. In an economy dominated by a comparatively small number of large enterprises the way in which managers make these choices affects us all. Whether decision-making in public companies should be guided purely by considerations of profit or should take account of the interests of third parties and social welfare more generally has been debated at least since Berle and Means raised the issue in 1932. In recent years there has been a resurgence of interest in this and related questions, manifested, for example, in a growing literature on corporate social responsibility, the creation of a number of chairs in corporate responsibility in British business schools, and the foundation of organizations such as Business in the Community to encourage social involvement. Of the numerous explanations for this growth in interest three stand out. The first is an awareness of impending ecological crisis. It may be that merely strengthening regulatory controls will be an insufficient response to the problems of environmental degradation. A shift in attitudes towards the environment on the part of management, involving a reassessment of company objectives, may be necessary as well. Second, changes in the structure of the economy, resulting in part from technological advance and increased international competition, have contributed to persistent unemployment, particularly in large urban areas. The ability of business to make a direct impact on unemployment has focused attention on the possibility of private solutions to this and other economic and social problems, especially against the background of a government ideology unsympathetic to state intervention. Finally the collapse of communism in Eastern Europe, as well as pointing up the merits of the market system, has also raised some questions about the virtues of corporate capitalism. It has created opportunities for western businesses to expand their empires, but whether this is the most appropriate response to the challenges presented is subject to dispute. There may also be implications at home. With the abatement of the 'external threat' we may feel more comfortable about re-evaluating capitalist institutions, questioning the legitimacy of private power, and demanding increased accountability on the part of corporate leaders.

Issues of corporate social responsibility aside, there has also been a debate in the last decade or so about the effectiveness of large-scale business enterprises in meeting their economic objectives. It has been argued that public companies suffer from a failure in the mechanisms of corporate governance (the means by which executive management is controlled and corporate objectives are set) resulting chiefly from the inadequacy of the incentives for shareholders to exercise a supervisory role. A contrast is often presented between the lacklustre performance on the one hand of the British and American economies, and on the other of those of Germany and Japan, where corporate governance is not in general perceived to be a problem. A different view holds that the market for corporate control is a more than adequate substitute for direct shareholder involvement, but to others take-overs are a part of the problem facing our economy rather than one of the solutions.

Identifying appropriate modes of control over management demands that we first decide what the objectives of companies should be. These questions of means and ends form part of the subject-matter of many disciplines, including moral and political philosophy, economics, and management studies. They are also part of the subject-matter of law. Whether one emphasizes the role of the state or of contract in corporate existence, companies are creations of law, their objectives are defined by law, and the law is a major source of the practical constraints on management behaviour. The purpose of this book is to consider what approach company law should take to the regulation of corporate conduct. It aims to provide a framework for addressing the debate between those who advocate pursuit of the traditional profit goal and those who favour a reorientation of corporate ends. It examines the role and effectiveness of law in obliging managers to comply with the profit objective and its potential as a technique for introducing a wider range of considerations into company decision-making.

In writing this book I have been helped by many friends and colleagues. I am grateful in particular to Chris Clarkson, Della Evans, David Feldman, Michael Ford, Nigel Furey, and Keith Stanton who have read parts of the book in draft. I should also like to express my thanks to Richard Hart of OUP for his patience and encouragement.

J.E.P.
Bristol
March 1993

Preface to Paperback Edition

Popular and academic interest in questions of corporate control has remained very much alive since the hardback edition of this book was completed in the early part of 1993. The debate over the recommendations of the Cadbury committee on corporate governance, for example, is continuing, and it has been proposed that the committee be reconvened next year to review the operation of its 'Code of Best Practice', and possibly also to examine broader issues of governance than those touched on in the original report.[1] Our understanding of the available structures of governance is in the meantime being enriched by a growing body of comparative literature on the subject. This literature is not only illuminating the details and relative advantages and disadvantages of variations in governance forms internationally, but is also revealing that these different systems of governance reflect, and are central features of, different systems of capitalism.

A particular focus of attention has been Michel Albert's *Capitalism against Capitalism*,[2] the English edition of which was published in 1993. Albert has identified two diverging forms of capitalism (accepting that there are variations within the categories): the 'neo-American' model, practised in Britain as well as the USA, and the 'Rhine' model, operated in parts of western Europe and also to an extent in Japan. At the centre of the first model is a belief in the benign effects of the pursuit of individual self-interest in unfettered markets. The other in contrast places a greater emphasis on the advancement of collective well-being and provides a richer institutional framework to achieve that end. One illustration of the differences of approach can be seen in attitudes to the welfare state. The Rhine variant celebrates an active role for the state in cushioning the impact of economic change and dispersing the benefits of increased wealth more widely than is likely to result from the market alone. This may be contrasted with the more restrictive, 'safety-net' approach to state provision and regulation espoused by the other model, which sees social protection and other forms of market interference as obstacles to growth.

Turning to the corporate sphere, the direct concern of this book, a key

---

[1] Committee on the Financial Aspects of Corporate Governance, *Report* (London, 1992).

[2] M. Albert, *Capitalism against Capitalism*, trans. P Haviland (London, 1993). See also the essays on related themes in C. Crouch and D. Marquand (eds), *Ethics and Markets* (Oxford, 1993).

characteristic of Rhenish institutional arrangements is that they are said to promote mutually beneficial cooperative long-term relationships, for example, between enterprises and their suppliers and customers, which may be harder to establish in the more aggressively market-oriented neo-American system. While companies remain formally independent within such relationships, it has been claimed that the resulting groupings take on the character of hybrid forms of enterprise in which the division between firm and market modes of interaction is less absolute, enabling the business to benefit from the positive features of both.[3] Among the advantages of these high-trust relationships are lower transaction costs, improved information flow, and a willingness of trading partners to make transaction-specific investments. Companies collaborate as well in highly developed trade associations, capable of producing collective benefits, for example, in relation to training and the development of new technology.[4] Cooperative relations exist furthermore not just between, but also within enterprises. The belief is that where employees are allowed a say, for example, in the management of technological change and are given a share of the benefits, they are likely to make a more constructive response to the problems of restructuring, as well as being more positively motivated generally in the pursuit of enterprise goals. The argument is, then, that this inclusive, consensual style of corporate ordering has advantages both in terms of efficiency and also in fulfilling wider social objectives.

What may be of particular importance in providing a setting conducive to cooperation is the absence of an active market in corporate control in the countries embracing the Rhine model. The issue is disputed, but there is at least a possibility that the threat of take-over forces management to concentrate on short-term profitability, reducing the scope for the 'give and take' necessary to maintain cooperative relationships, the returns from which accrue only over the longer term. This is thus a further element in the short-termism debate, to be added to the charge that share-price pressure discourages investment, among other things, in research and development and training. Whatever the truth may be as regards that version of the argument, it is clear enough that long-term relationships are disrupted by consummated hostile take-overs, and that where the threat of take-over is prevalent, there is likely to be a reluctance to enter into such arrangements in the first place.

Among the more positive factors encouraging cooperation in Rhenish economies are reciprocal customer-supplier shareholdings, and significant

---

[3] See W. C. Kester, 'Industrial Groups as Systems of Contractual Governance', in (1992) Vol. 8 No. 3 *Oxford Review of Economic Policy: Corporate Governance and Corporate Control* 24; M. J. Roe, 'Some Differences in Corporate Structure in Germany, Japan, and the United States', (1993) 102 *Yale L J* 1927; R. J. Gilson and M. J. Roe, 'Understanding the Keiretsu: Overlaps between Corporate Governance and Industrial Organization', (1993) 102 *Yale L J* 871.

[4] See e.g. C. Crouch, 'Co-operation and Competition in an Institutionalised Economy: The Case of Germany', in Crouch and Marquand, *Ethics and Markets* (above, n. 2) 80.

equity stakes held by banks.⁵ These create a mutuality of interest, and will tend to reduce the incentive to engage in opportunistic behaviour in trading relationships, since the resulting gains are liable to be partially off-set by lower investment returns. They also mean that companies have shareholders with stakes large enough to justify active monitoring of management performance. The 'separation of ownership and control' is in consequence rarely an issue in these economies and the associated problems of weak management accountability are correspondingly diminished. There is the further advantage that the shareholders who are involved in monitoring have an interest in stability and long-term growth, rather than a preoccupation with the level of dividends and share prices, as tends to be the case with investors whose participation is purely financial and who more actively trade their shares.

In some countries links with trading partners and banks are reinforced through representation on the board, and in Germany this practice in extended and formalized by requirements for employee membership of the supervisory boards of public companies. It is generally agreed that the system of co-determination, which depends for its effectiveness on plant-based works councils and trade union bargaining rights as well as board representation, has not brought about a radical transformation of the traditional profit-seeking goal. Nevertheless it has been suggested that it has converted labour from a variable into a relatively fixed factor of production. The significance of this is not merely that employees have greater job security because reducing the size of the workforce is more difficult, but rather that the interest of the employees in continuity of employment must be given much greater weight in enterprise planning.⁶ On a more abstract level, the acceptance of the institutional constraints on management freedom of action that co-determination represents reflects a conception of corporate enterprise which differs from that widely held in this country. From the neo-American perspective companies are essentially the property of the shareholders, or at least, as is the preferred position in some quarters, the contract to which the shareholders are a party gives them the right to insist that the company be run for their benefit. This is not the viewpoint adopted by Rhine capitalism. In the German version the company is a community of interests, none of which should take precedence over the others. Profit-making remains an important goal of the organization, but one that ought to

⁵ For a discussion of the position in Germany, see T. Baums, 'Takeovers versus Institutions in Corporate Governance in Germany', in D. D. Prentice and P. R. J. Holland (eds), *Contemporary Issues in Corporate Governance* (Oxford, 1993) 151 and 'Banks and Corporate Control in Germany', in J. McCahery, S. Picciotto, and C. Scott (eds), *Corporate Control and Accountability: Changing Structures and the Dynamics of Regulation* (Oxford, 1993) 267. For a more general discussion of governance arrangements internationally, see J. Charkham, *Keeping Good Company: A Study of Corporate Governance in Five Countries* (Oxford, 1994).
⁶ See W. Streek, *Social Institutions and Economic Performance* (London, 1992) ch 5.

be balanced against the welfare, among other things, of employees and the local community, and the quality of the physical environment. The Japanese go further in relegating the interests of shareholders, seeing the company as existing primarily for the benefit of employees.[7] The German and Japanese are of course still capitalist systems, with capital largely in private hands and enterprises operating in more or less competitive markets, but they are systems in which there is less confidence in the 'invisible hand', both to create wealth and also to limit the adverse social consequences of economic activity.

There are no doubt drawbacks with the Rhine variant as well as advantages. The greater asset mobility to be found in relatively unconstrained Anglo-American markets seems likely to be more conducive to allocative efficiency and rapid adaptation to changes in technology than the conditions provided by the rival system. For example, whatever the inadequacies and adverse side-effects of reliance on hostile take-overs as a form of management discipline, it has been suggested that enforced ownership transfers may have an advantage over internal monitoring in correcting *ex ante* failure. This describes the situation in which the company may have performed acceptably, such that the removal of management by an internal control mechanism might be hard to justify, but in which a bidder anticipates that still higher returns could be achieved by redeploying the company's assets, and this necessitates a change in control.[8] Concern has also been expressed that monitoring banks are subject to conflicts of interest arising from their split role as provider of loan capital and other financial services on the one hand, and as shareholders on the other, with the possibility that the agency-cost problem of managerial opportunism is simply replaced by one of subordination to the interests of dominant banks[9]. Mechanisms to protect employment, furthermore, may actually be damaging to employees, in that if there are serious obstacles to reducing the size of the workforce it will inevitably make companies more reluctant to take on staff in the first place. This is liable to be a serious problem in periods of low or negative employment growth in the economy as a whole, creating the danger of a sustained division between a relatively prosperous employed group and a group of welfare-dependent outsiders.

Whatever the merits of the arguments, governance structures perceived to be too protective of management and as implicated in inadequate returns to investors are increasingly coming under attack. The growth in overseas holdings of American institutional investors and greater competition in

[7] See R. Dore, 'What Makes the Japanese Different?', in Crouch and Marquand, *Ethics and Markets* (above, n. 2) 66.

[8] See J. Franks and C. Mayer, 'European Capital Markets and Corporate Control', in M. Bishop and J. Kay (eds), *European Mergers and Merger Policy* (Oxford, 1993) 162, at 184-91.

[9] See J. C. Coffee, 'Liquidity versus Control: The Institutional Investor as Corporate Monitor', (1991) 91 *Colum L Rev* 1227, at 1300-1; Baums, 'Banks and Corporate Control in Germany' (above, n. 5), at 285-6.

international capital markets are, for example, sources of pressure for change towards the Anglo-American model. The same can be said of the European Community programme for lowering institutional barriers to take-over, though shareholding patterns in most European countries mean that regulatory changes to make possible a market in control are likely to have a very limited effect. More generally in Europe there are growing calls for deregulation, particularly to help reduce labour costs, in the face of increased international product-market competition.

It can be argued, notwithstanding these developments, that 'what the Anglo-American tradition sees as distortions, impeding free competition, [can be viewed] as the necessary conditions of competitive success'.[10] Relational contracting allows firms to concentrate on their core strengths, to have flatter organizational structures, and to be closer to their markets. All of these are likely to be of importance in a future in which high quality and adaptability to customer preferences will be needed to meet growing competition from low-cost producers overseas. Similarly, in relation to mechanisms for the protection of employee interests, it has been observed that in a sophisticated economy, human capital holds the key to competitive power; and the more important human capital becomes, the less appropriate is the model of economic behaviour drawn from the Anglo-American tradition'.[11] Economic success is likely, in other words, increasingly to depend on the skills and committment of the workforce, and in turn on striking a new balance in the relationship between labour and capital.

The contrast between different forms of capitalism affords another perspective from which to view the issues raised in this book. There is now little room for doubt that capitalist arrangements of one sort or another will be with us for the foreseeable future. It is, however, clear that we have a choice not just about the precise mix of the mixed economy – whether industries should be in the private or public sector or the forms and levels of welfare spending – but also about the dynamics of corporate enterprise itself. It is true that some of the elements of the different systems are not readily transferable. The German situation, in which there are large inter-corporate holdings and major stakes under bank control, would, for example, be difficult to reproduce in the UK, even if it were thought desirable. There is, nevertheless, considerable scope for institutional re-design. The half-hearted efforts to inject a genuinely independent element into British boards might, for instance, be transformed into something more radical. The pressure from the threat of take-over could at the same time be relaxed by modifying the rules constitutive of the market for control. To add a more explicit social dimension to corporate thinking, the permissible ends of managerial

[10] Crouch and Marquand, *Ethics and Markets* (above, n. 2) Introduction, at 1.
[11] Ibid. at 2.

decision-making could be altered, and measures might be introduced to shape the manner a discretion broadened in this way is exercised. These might include mechanisms for enabling employees to participate in determining enterprise policy. Or we might prefer to do none of these things, and instead trust to market pressure or increased institutional activism to bring about such changes as might seem necessary.

So one way or another company law plays a central role in determining how well the economy works, and how the economic and social systems inter-relate. The purpose of this book is to examine some of the existing rules of company law, and some of the ways in which the rules might be changed, against this background. The text is unaltered from the hardback edition, save for the correction of typographical errors.

Bristol.   June, 1994

Contents

Table of UK Cases

Note: Principal references are shown in bold type

Table of Commonwealth Cases

Table of US Cases

Table of UK Statutes

Note: Principal references are in bold

European Community Legislation

Regulations

Directives and Proposed Directives

UK Statutory Instruments

Legislation From Other Jurisdictions

What is a Company? → Slide of logo —

Familiar yet v. different → Legal creation → Neam of contracts

Ask what is the purpose of Company → Diff. Model → Market driven

Socio-legal → Companies exercising social power

Introduction

The traditional focus of study in company law is on the rules and principles that safeguard the interests of the company's members and creditors. The members, being often uninvolved in the day-to-day operation of the business, need some assurance that management will run the company for their benefit, and minority shareholders need protection from the possibility that their interests will be sacrificed to those of the majority. The creditors, because of the company's limited liability (or, more properly, the limited liability of the shareholders) are exposed to a greater risk that their debts will go unsatisfied than when dealing with an unincorporated business, and hence the law attempts to minimize the scope for abuse. A different approach to company law starts by noticing that the way companies are run affects not only their members and creditors, but also their customers, suppliers, employees, and neighbours, and also society in a more general sense. Thus decisions made in companies are a major determinant of employment levels, regional development, the pace and contours of technological change, and the condition of our physical, and even cultural, environment. The point is not just the obvious one that companies 'affect' society, but that their decisions constitute exercises of significant social power: companies are private forums or contexts in which social planning is carried on, and carried on in accordance with their own, presumably self-serving, decisional criteria. From this second perspective, therefore, a study of company law is a study of the rules that sustain and regulate a mode of decision-making that rivals the market and the democratic process as a mechanism of social choice.

Chapter 1 will defend the claim that corporate social decision-making power must be exercised in the public interest. The 'public interest' is not, of course, capable of objective definition, and so to make this claim is only to establish a framework for further enquiry, both about what the relevant public interest is and how company behaviour can be made to conform with it. One theory holds that companies serve the public interest where they seek to maximize their profits, subject to the general legal constraints in force at any particular time – the rules of employment law, consumer law, and environmental law, for instance. The justificatory assumption on which the theory relies is that profit maximization leads in general to the maximization of social wealth. In those cases in which maximizing profits has economically sub-optimal effects (because of market failure) or conflicts with social values distinct from those that support aggregate wealth maximization (values requiring, for example, the protection of individual rights or community interests), the theory supposes that the constraints needed to align the public and private good can be adequately expressed through the medium of external regulation. The theory holds, therefore, that the role of company law is to provide a set of rules conducive to profit maximization; if the pursuit of that goal leads to socially undesirable results, the appropriate response is not to modify the profit objective, but to strengthen the regulatory framework within which profit maximization is carried on. Chapters 2–8 discuss some of the existing rules of company law on the assumption that this approach should shape their design.

It is possible, on the other hand, that corporate decision-making will adequately serve the public interest only if it explicitly takes account of social welfare considerations. It may not be sufficient, in other words, in order to align private action with the public good, merely to strengthen the background legal constraints within which businesses operate. It may also be necessary to alter companies' decision-making processes to permit or require them to take account of non-profit interests, or even to change their goals. Company law itself in these circumstances becomes an instrument of broad social policy, to be used perhaps to construct a 'corporate conscience', or to make the organization more 'open textured' and hence more responsive to its social environment. The means that might be adopted to bring about these results are examined in Chapter 11. Before that Chapter 9 will review the extent to which departure from profit maximization is already permitted, or at least possible, within the existing framework of company law. That chapter will also explore the use that companies make in practice of such freedom as they have to carry out social policy. This will lead on to the discussion in Chapter 10 of whether the public interest *would* be better served if companies moderated profits in favour of social policy objectives. Should companies attempt to minimize environmental damage, for instance, or give financial or other support to community projects, in either case not merely because, and to the extent that, such behaviour is required by law or is a precondition of profitability in the long term, but because it seems a worthwhile end in itself, to be engaged in even though a sacrifice of long-run profits may be involved? The chapter will consider some of the arguments bearing on these and other examples of profit-sacrificing social responsibility.

Finally, it is arguable that the existence of corporate power is unjustifiable, regardless of whether it is exercised with a view to profit maximization or in accordance with alternative social-welfare criteria. If so, this indicates a need for a more radical alteration of the structure of productive enterprise, with a view either to dispersing power, or at least to locating it within organizations that can be shown to possess it legitimately, in a way that companies as currently constituted, *ex hypothesi*, cannot. The relevant arguments and some of the alternatives to existing business forms will be examined in Chapter 12.

1

Corporate Power

Our style of life is largely determined by the activities and style of business; and the style of business is largely determined by the activities and style of our companies.

Confederation of British Industry, 1973.[1]

The purpose of this chapter is to describe some of the ways in which companies exercise power and to examine the relevance of the possession of power to the concerns, or what should be the concerns, of company law. The chapter will cover the following ground. It will begin with a brief survey of the corporate economy. This will provide a background for the consideration of the nature and scope of corporate power[2] that will follow in section II. Section III will support the claim that the possession of power by companies is justifiable only in so far as they promote the public interest, and accordingly that society is entitled to demand that corporate policies serve that interest. The claim will be defended in particular against the argument that the company should be seen as a private vehicle which may legitimately be employed for the exclusive pursuit of the purposes of its members. The final section will set out a provisional theory explaining how companies best further the public interest and the implications of that theory for company law.

I THE CORPORATE ECONOMY

The next section will examine in more detail what is meant by 'corporate power', and the different areas in which it has an impact. The purpose of the present section is to bring to mind the shape and scale of the corporate economy in which this power is located. The possession of power by

---

[1] Confederation of British Industry, *The Responsibilities of the British Public Company* (1973), at 8.

[2] Throughout this chapter the term 'corporate power' will be used without enquiring who within (or outside) the firm actually possesses it. Some light will be shed on this issue in Ch. 2, where the arguments about the effectiveness of shareholder control over management and (briefly) problems of top management control over lower levels within the organization will be considered.

companies is principally an attribute of size, and so the companies with which this book is concerned are large, in absolute terms and usually also in relation to the industry or industries in which they operate. There is, however, no need for a precise definition of 'large' since nothing turns on any particular size threshold being crossed. The companies we shall be discussing are public companies with publicly listed shares. (There is also a small number of very large companies that are private.) They often have a broad product range, operating in more than one industrial sector, and they sometimes show a high degree of vertical integration, having control of their sources of supply at one end and the chain of distribution at the other. They have professional management and normally a complex organizational structure. For convenience these enterprises will mainly be discussed as though they were single companies, though in fact they are normally composed of a parent company and several layers of subsidiaries. In many cases some of these subsidiaries are based overseas. Conversely, a significant proportion of the companies operating in this country are offshoots of enterprises whose head offices are situated abroad.

Large companies constitute a very small proportion of the total population of firms ('firm' refers to all forms of business organization, not only those that are incorporated). In manufacturing, for example, firms with fewer than 100 employees accounted for 95 per cent of all firms in 1981.[3] As far as companies are concerned, in 1992 there were well over 1 million on the register in Great Britain, but of these only a little more than 1 per cent were public companies.[4] But while large companies are only a small percentage of total businesses, they dominate the economy, such that 'a large proportion of economic activity in present-day capitalist economies is concentrated in a relatively small number of absolutely large firms'.[5] As Hannah points out in his historical study of the development of the corporate economy, during the course of the present century British industry was transformed from 'a disaggregated structure of predominantly small, competing firms to a concentrated structure dominated by large, and often monopolistic, corporations'.[6] This transformation came about as companies expanded to take advantage of mass-production methods and associated economies of scale and integration, and also as they strove to limit the competitive forces to which they were subject. Some of this expansion was through organic growth, but the increase in concentration is mainly accounted for by a series of merger waves beginning towards the end of the nineteenth century.[7]

[3] P. J. Devine, et al. *Introduction to Industrial Economics* (4th ed., 1985), at 86. This is calculated from the 1981 Census of Production, as are the other figures quoted below in relation to 1981.
[4] DTI, *Companies in 1991–92* (1992).
[5] Devine et al., *Introduction to Industrial Economics* (above, n. 3), at 85.
[6] L. Hannah, *The Rise of the Corporate Economy* (2nd ed., 1983), at 1.
[7] See L. Hannah and J. Kay, *Concentration in Modern Industry* (1977), ch. 1 and generally, and

UK's Biggest C's
World's biggest?
Theme Big v. Small
Shift from Big → small
Small become big quicker

Large absolute size was in turn facilitated by improvements in financing and management techniques and developments in organizational structure.[8]

To gain an impression of the size of individual enterprises on a global scale, the world's ten largest companies (by number of employees) employ a total of 4.3 million, and it has been estimated that when the dependants of those employees are taken into account the welfare of up to 21 million people, a figure approaching the population of the Scandinavian countries, is *check* directly affected by their decisions. In 1989 their assets totalled US $560 *figure!* billion, equivalent to the GNP of Canada.[9] As regards the UK, in 1985, 165 companies in the UK employed over 10,000 people, 36 over 50,000, and 11 over 100,000.[10] A composite picture of the position of large companies within the economy is presented in a study of statistics relating to the 'top 100' manufacturing companies published by the Department of Industry in 1976. This reveals that these companies accounted for about 40 per cent of manufacturing industry's net assets, employment, and inward direct investment from overseas (excluding oil company investment), 40–50 per cent of visible exports, 70 per cent of expenditure on industrial scientific research and development, and about 75 per cent of direct investment by UK companies (excluding oil) in manufacturing overseas.[11] In the same vein, the Bullock Committee in 1977 noted that the 'last 20 years have seen the growth of the giant industrial enterprise and the concentration of economic power in the hands of fewer and fewer such companies. For example, in 1953 the 100 largest manufacturing enterprises in the UK accounted for 25 per cent of the total net output; in 1971 the corresponding figure was 40 per cent'.[12] By 1981 328 companies accounted for over 50 per cent of manufacturing employment, and a mere 66 companies for 30 per cent.[13] Changes in the structure of British industry, including the contraction of the manufacturing

S. J. Prais, *The Evolution of Giant Firms in Britain* (1976). For a brief history of merger activity in the UK see also J. Fairburn and J. Kay (eds), *Mergers and Merger Policy* (1989), at 2–8.

[8] Particularly the transition from the U-form to the M-form enterprise: see Ch. 2, below. More fundamentally, there is a substantial literature explaining the movement towards coordination of productive activity within hierarchical organizations, rather than through discrete transactions in the market, in terms of transaction cost reduction: see R. H. Coase, 'The Nature of the Firm', (1937) ns 4 *Economica* 386; A. D. Chandler, *The Visible Hand: The Managerial Revolution in American Business* (1977), at 6–8; O. E. Williamson, *Economic Institutions of Capitalism* (1985); R. A. Posner, *Economic Analysis of Law* (3rd ed., 1986), at 367–8; O. Hart, 'An Economist's Perspective on the Theory of the Firm', (1989) 89 *Colum L Rev* 1757. For commentaries see D. A. Hay and D. J. Morris, *Industrial Economics and Organization: Theory and Evidence* (1991), at 281–285; M. C. Sawyer, *The Economics of Industries and Firms* (2nd ed., 1985), at 198–204.

[9] See A. Demb and F.-F. Neubauer, *The Corporate Board: Confronting the Paradoxes* (1992), at 3.

[10] Hay and Morris, *Industrial Economics and Organization* (above, n. 8), at 273–4.

[11] Department of Industry, 'The Importance of the Top 100 Manufacturing Companies', *Economic Trends* no. 274 (1976), at 85–8.

[12] *Report of the Committee of Inquiry on Industrial Democracy* (Cmnd. 6706, 1977), at 20, para 2.

[13] DTI, 'Report on the Census of Production 1981', Summary Tables, *Business Monitor PA* 1002 (1984), at 258.

base over the last decade, seem to have done little to reduce overall concentration. Peacock and Bannock point out that while there was a slight fall in manufacturing concentration between 1970 and 1988, it is likely that this trend has since been reversed in view of the recent merger boom.[14] They also point out that the quoted company sector is becoming more concentrated in terms of market capitalization, the share of the 100 largest companies having risen from 65.2 per cent in 1984 to 67.3 per cent in 1990.[15]

Within the set of large companies there is a tendency towards dominance by the very largest. Thus in 1982 the top 100 quoted companies accounted for well over half the turnover, profit, and capital employed of the top 1000 companies, and within the top 100, the top ten accounted for over a quarter of turnover and capital.[16] The figures for concentration overall indicate the degree of centralization of decision-making in the economy as a whole. The level of concentration within a particular industry casts light on the competitiveness of the industry and hence on the scope for the exploitation of economic power (though the globalization of business and difficulties in specifying product markets, given the availability of substitutes, make the figures an uncertain guide). It is clear that in a number of sectors concentration is significantly higher than in the economy generally. The share of total output of the five largest companies in chemicals, vehicles, electrical engineering, and drink, for example, average around 70 per cent.[17] Large parts of the service sector, which now contributes a higher proportion of GDP than manufacturing industry, are similarly characterized by high concentration ratios. Retail banking, insurance, property, shipping, communications, and retailing, for example, are all dominated by a small number of giant enterprises.[18]

Corporate power is not merely a matter of the resources and market share of formally independent entities. It also results from coordinated activity *between* companies. As Herman explains,

Collective action may result from structural ties between firms that integrate their interest and facilitate coordination between them—such as a common ownership interest—or it may arise out of a recognized common interest or mutual business interdependence with minimal personal contact and communications among the

[14] See A. Peacock and J. Bannock, *Corporate Takeovers and the Public Interest* (1991), at 24. They explain that while spin-offs accompanied the 1980s merger boom, it is likely that a large proportion of them involved sales of subsidiaries between large groups. This is liable to increase concentration rather than reduce it, i.e. where diversified groups dispose of unrelated activities to companies which already have a high market share in the relevant sector.

[15] Ibid. at 25.

[16] R. I. Tricker, *Corporate Governance: Practices, Procedures and Powers in British Companies and their Boards of Directors* (1984), at 47.

[17] Hannah, *The Rise of the Corporate Economy* (above, n. 6), at 144. See also Hannah and Kay, *Concentration in Modern Industry* (above, n. 7), ch. 6.

[18] D. F. Channon, 'Corporate Evolution in the Service Industries', in L. Hannah (ed.), *Management Strategy and Business Development* (1976).

companies and their officials. In between these extremes is a wide spectrum of linkages, such as interlocking directorates; common membership in trade associations, government advisory bodies, and public affairs groups; and personal connections of officials through clubs and other social bases of contact.[19]

All of these relationships are integral features of the British economy,[20] though assessing their practical significance in terms of reduced competition or the pursuit of common purposes is far from straightforward.

It is important to note finally the international character of corporate enterprise. As regards the presence of outposts of overseas companies in this country, it has been observed that though 'the British economy is not dominated by foreign investment, the foreign presence in Britain is highly visible and statistically important. Roughly one in seven of British workers work in foreign companies, which [incidentally] tend to be more efficient than their British competitors'.[21] Conversely, most of the 100 largest UK companies also operate abroad. A significant feature is that for many of these companies their overseas activities are more important than their domestic ones. It has been pointed out, for instance, that in 1983 the largest 70 British manufacturing multinationals had a foreign output of around £100 billion, whereas their home production was £70 billion.[22] As compared with foreign multinationals, for British multinationals a notably higher proportion of production and employment is located overseas.[23]

While the parent company in a multinational group will necessarily be registered in a particular country and the group headquarters and a preponderance of shareholders may also be located there, in the case of some multinationals it is scarcely any longer appropriate to regard them as having national loyalties. Thus it has been suggested that

although we think of IBM and General Motors as American, and Unilever and Shell as British (or, more exactly, Anglo-Dutch), firms as large and diverse as these plan their operations on a global scale in their own interests. In terms of sheer size they are sometimes bigger than the countries in which they operate; they are estimated to control over a quarter of world output; and their 'inter-firm' shipments of goods from one country to another account for nearly one-third of recorded trade.[24]

Clearly, controlling such organizations is beyond the regulatory capacity of national governments. Attempts to regulate the global activities of

---

[19] E. S. Herman, *Corporate Control, Corporate Power* (1981), at 194–5.

[20] E.g. on interlocking directorships see J. Scott, *Corporations, Classes and Capitalism* (2nd ed., 1985), at 95–102.

[21] J. M. Stopford and L. M. Turner, *Britain and the Multinationals* (1985), at 4–5. See also ch. 6.

[22] Ibid. at 3.

[23] See H. Ramsay, *1992 — The Year of the Multinational? Corporate Behaviour, Industrial Restructuring and Labour in the Single Market*, Warwick International Papers no 35 (1990), at 3.

[24] P. Donaldson and J. Farquhar, *Understanding the British Economy* (1988), at 162.

Problems of regulating
multi/trans national corps

multinationals, particularly in relation to employment and developmental issues in the Third World, have evoked an intergovernmental and 'world-organizational' response.[25] A consideration of the form and effectiveness of this response falls outside the scope of this book, but it should be emphasized that the international context in which large companies operate is of central importance to the control of companies domestically, which is the concern here. The ability of enterprises to transfer investment from countries in which the regulatory environment threatens to become uncongenial, and the damage to international competitiveness that may result if domestic industry is subject to a more stringent regulatory regime than rival firms abroad, are liable to circumscribe severely the capacity of national governments to establish an appropriate control framework. Purely national solutions to problems of corporate control are likely, therefore, to be unavailing.

II THE NATURE OF CORPORATE POWER

Power is a contested concept. For our purposes there is no need to explore all the different conceptions of it, though some of them will emerge during the course of the discussion.[26] A widely accepted understanding of power is that it is the ability of A to cause B to behave in a manner intended by A that B would not have done without A's intervention. Implicit is the idea that A has some form of control over B, or at least a strong bargaining position that enables A to score a 'victory' over B.[27] Companies sometimes have power of this kind over suppliers, as might be the case when the company is one of only a limited number of buyers of a firm's goods or services,[28] and even to an extent over governments, manifested, for example, in negotiations over subsidies or in successful attempts to dilute the content of regulation. (We will return to the issue of corporate influence over government below.)

The context in which power in this sense most conspicuously occurs, however, is in regard to employees. Companies may have power in setting the terms of the employment relationship arising from a possible asymmetry in bargaining positions, but they also possess power within the relationship. Indeed, the position of authority in which the company stands towards its

---

[25] For a brief summary of attempts to regulate multinationals at a supra-national level see F. P. McHugh, *Business Ethics* (1988), at 43–8; T. Donaldson, *The Ethics of International Business* (1989), ch. 3.

[26] For an examination of the different conceptions of power see S. Lukes, 'Power and Authority', in T. Bottomore and R. Nisbet (eds), *A History of Sociological Analysis* (1979), reprinted in S. Lukes, *Moral Conflict and Politics* (1991), ch. 6.

[27] G. K. Wilson, *Business and Politics: A Comparative Introduction* (2nd ed., 1990), at 6.

[28] P. Davies and P. Kelly, *Small Firms and the Manufacturing Sector: Bolton Committee Research Report, no. 3* (1971), report that over a third of small manufacturing enterprises sell a quarter or more of their output to a single customer.

employees is a central feature of the standard definition of the firm. According to Coase, firms are 'islands of conscious power' in a sea of market transactions.[29] This idea of an authority relation, giving the employer a special power of direction over employees not found between parties transacting in the market, has, however, been disputed, notably by Alchian and Demsetz, who argue that the employer/employee relationship does not differ in substance from any other relationship founded in contract.[30] An employer has no more power to give orders to an employee than a customer has to demand that a grocer supply goods at a certain price: all a discontented employer can do in practice, just like a customer, is terminate the relationship. In neither case is there any additional disciplinary power with which employers or customers are able to impose their will. From this perspective, therefore, employers do not have power over employees; they do not give them instructions, but rather are involved in a process of constant renegotiation of the employment contract.[31] But this is surely to misdescribe the social reality of the employment relationship. Dismissal imposes costs on the employee, in terms of lost income, severance of social relationships at work, and the inconvenience involved in finding another job, that the employee will wish to avoid and which have no equivalents when relationships between customers and grocers break down. And in periods of high unemployment, and especially in areas or occupations in which the current employer is in a dominant position, the threat of discharge is a potent weapon. The attempt to assimilate the employment relationship to one of continuous contractual renegotiation is therefore unconvincing.[32]

Decision-Making Power

The possession of power over employees is not unique to large companies (though as just mentioned, size may create a position of dominance and

---

[29] Coase, 'The Nature of the Firm'(above, n. 8).

[30] A. Alchian and H. Demsetz, 'Production, Information Costs, and Economic Organization' (1972) 62 *Am Econ Rev* 777. The idea that employers have no coercive power over employees is a common theme in market liberal literature: see e.g. F. A. Hayek, *The Constitution of Liberty* (1960), at 135–7.

[31] Alchian and Demsetz, ibid. at 777–78, contend that '[t]o speak of managing, directing, or assigning workers to various tasks is a deceptive way of noting that the employer continually is involved in renegotiation of contracts on terms that must be acceptable to both parties. Telling an employee to type this letter rather than to file that document is like telling my grocer to sell me this brand of tuna rather than that brand of bread'. This analysis is not legally correct. The employer is entitled to give instructions within the scope of the employment contract. It may be true that employers are unlikely to sue for damages where their orders are not carried out, and therefore that since the only effective sanction is dismissal, each 'instruction' can be counted as a contractual renegotiation (the employee has the option of accepting or leaving). As argued in the text, however, this does not correspond with the realities of the situation.

[32] See also R. A. Dahl, *A Preface to Economic Democracy* (1985), at 113–16; C. Perrow, *Complex Organizations: A Critical Essay* (3rd ed., 1986), at 226–7.

Power to make decisions

hence accentuate power), but rather is inherent in the employment relationship itself. We turn now to a type of power that is more specifically an
attribute of large companies, and which is our central concern. This is power
in the sense of *decision-making power*. Power of this kind can be defined as 'the
scope of significant choice open to [an actor] . . . his power over others is the
scope of his choices which affect them significantly'.[33] It is distinguishable
from power in the sense just discussed (though the two forms may exist side
by side) in that it does not rely on any idea of direct control over others or
coercion. The key elements are instead *discretion* and *significant effects*.[34] The
point at issue is, then, that companies are able to make choices which have
important social consequences: they make private decisions which have
public results.[35] It is possession of this kind of power that gives rise to a
distinct need for justification, and which forms the basis for the claim that
companies must be required to act in the public interest. We should note
that in recognising that companies have power, it is not suggested that their
power is anything like absolute. Corporate decision making is constrained by
governments, unions, customers, other companies, and community pressures
of both diffuse and organized kinds. These constraints limit and shape
corporate power, but the discretion that lies within them, although variable,
is nevertheless real.

Power and the Market

In the economist's model of perfect competition firms have no capacity to
exercise significant choice: they have no option but to obey the signals of the
market. It is because markets are not perfect in reality that companies have
power, though in adopting this perspective it is important to guard against
the tendency to view divergences from the model as temporary and aberrant
rather than as a standard feature of market systems. In the perfect competition model the number of producers is sufficiently large that all firms are

[33] C. Kaysen, 'The Corporation: How Much Power? What Scope?', in E. S. Mason (ed.), *The Corporation in Modern Society* (1959), at 85.
[34] For a consideration of what constitutes affecting someone 'significantly' such as to denote the existence of power, see S. Lukes, *Power: A Radical View* (1974), esp. chs 5 and 6. For some other discussions of corporate power along similar lines to those in the text, see A. A. Berle, *Power without Property* (1960), esp. at 82–7; R. Nader, M. Green, and G. Seligman, *Taming the Giant Corporation* (1976), ch. 1; G. A. Steiner and J. F. Steiner, *Business, Government, and Society: A Managerial Perspective* (3rd ed., 1980), ch. 9.
[35] See e.g. J. K. Galbraith, 'On the Economic Image of Corporate Enterprise', in R. Nader and M. Green (eds), *Corporate Power in America* (1973), at 6:
General Motors sets the prices for its cars (and, in conjunction with the other automobile companies, for all cars) with public effect. And it negotiates wage contracts with public effect. And it designs cars and incorporates or rejects safety features with public effect. And it decides on engine design and emissions with public effect. And it persuades the public to its designs with public effect. And it powerfully influences highway construction with public effect. The public decisions of General Motors in the course of any year are far more consequential than those of any state legislature. So with other large firms.

'price-takers'. A firm cannot, in other words, charge more for its goods than the current market price. Because firms have no discretion over prices but must passively accept the price prevailing in the market they have no 'market power'. They can make profits only at the level that justifies the continued employment of their assets in their existing use and are unable to effect a transfer of wealth from customers to themselves. Competitive conditions also ensure that firms have no discretion over the quality of goods supplied, since failure to match the quality or provide the features demanded by the market (the model assumes that market participants possess full product information and knowlege of alternative opportunities)[36] would mean that a firm would lose all its business to competitors. Furthermore, since all firms are bound by an exogenously determined price, a firm with production costs higher than those of rivals would not survive. This, together with perfectly competitive markets for labour and other inputs and the assumption that all firms are fully informed about the most profitable factor combinations, has the effect that discretion over production methods is also ruled out. Where the requirements of the model are satisfied it can thus with some truth be said that there is an 'utter dispersion of power'.[37]

In reality many companies operate in conditions which are to a greater or lesser extent uncompetitive. Although technical monopoly may be a rarity, markets are commonly dominated by a small number of large producers.[38] In such circumstances by colluding or in virtue of the structural properties of oligopolistic markets, companies are able to obtain variable degrees of protection from competitive pressures.[39] In addition to the relatively small number of producers, other requirements for perfect competition are also unlikely to be met in practice. Thus an uncompetitive market structure may be maintained indefinitely because of barriers to entry and exit; products are not, as in the model, homogeneous, but have differentiating characteristics which enable producers to raise prices without causing a total shift in demand to their rivals; and finally, purchasers lack perfect information and hence may pay higher prices than they would if aware of alternative,

[36] If the perfect knowledge assumption is dropped, then in certain circumstances market forces in a competitive market will 'impose a regime of misrepresentation and degradation of product quality': see W. J. Baumol, '(Almost) Perfect Competition (Contestability) and Business Ethics', in W. J. Baumol and S. A. B. Blackman (eds), *Perfect Markets and Easy Virtue: Business Ethics and the Invisible Hand* (1991), 1, at 7 (emphasis omitted); i.e. the market will still eliminate producer discretion, but in a way unfavourable to customers.
[37] G. J. Stigler, 'Competition', (1968) 3 *International Encyclopedia of Social Science* 181, quoted in A. Etzioni, *The Moral Dimension: Toward a New Economics* (1988), at 218.
[38] For a consideration of the extent of market power in the British economy see J. Fairburn and P. Geroski, 'The Empirical Analysis of Market Structure and Performance', in Fairburn and Kay, *Mergers and Merger Policy* (above, n. 7), ch. 6.
[39] See R. G. Lipsey, *An Introduction to Positive Economics* (7th ed., 1989), ch. 14; Etzioni (above, n. 37), at 218–20, and literature cited therein.

cheaper sources of supply.[40] The effect of these various imperfections is to cede to companies a zone of discretion in relation to products and prices and the wide range of factors connected with the production process. The ambit of this discretion will now be reviewed in more detail.

The Theory of Consumer Sovereignty

It will be convenient to examine corporate discretion over products and prices by exploring the weaknesses in the 'demand side' corollary of the theory of perfect competition, the theory of consumer sovereignty.[41] This holds that through their actions in the market consumers oblige companies to produce the goods they require in the largest quantities at the lowest possible price. As well as making claims about the efficiency of markets, the theory denies the existence of producer power, at the same time drawing a reassuring analogy with democratic control in the political sphere: corporate behaviour is no more than a reflection of the popular will, expressed not through the ballot box, but via individual purchase decisions.[42] Once the reality of some degree of uncompetitiveness in markets is acknowledged the consumer's sovereign status is inevitably diminished. It must be accepted, however, as Lindblom has pointed out, that it is by no means wholly destroyed, since 'monopoly weakens responses to popular control, but it neither eliminates a response or leads to a perverse one ... Rare, even bizarre, circumstances aside, it never profits a monopolist to do more when customers are signaling for less, or less when they are signaling for more'.[43] In the same vein, Winter explains that 'if consumers prefer yellow widgets to blue ones or widgets with safety features to plain ones, and if they will pay the true cost of such improvements, the monopolist ignores their tastes only at a financial cost. Even in the case of a clear monopoly, therefore, markets do constrain corporate behaviour, although output is restricted and resources misallocated'.[44] But we should be careful to note that inherent in this finding of inefficiency is also an acknowledgement of the existence of power. A company's ability to raise the price of its goods above the competitive level affects the demand for its products (and, through the effect on relative prices, the pattern of demand throughout the economy). From this it follows that a degree of decision-making power about how society's resources should be

---

[40] See further F M Scherer, *Industrial Market Structure and Economic Performance* (2nd ed., 1979), ch. 2; Lipsey (above, n. 39), ch. 12.

[41] For a further discussion of consumer sovereignty, see N. C. Smith, *Morality and the Market: Consumer Pressure for Corporate Accountability* (1990), at 33–42.

[42] The analogy between voting and market behaviour is, of course, weak, not least because of the unequal distribution of market 'votes' that inequality in purchasing power represents. For a partial defence of the analogy see C. E. Lindblom, 'Democracy and Economic Structure', in W. N. Chambers and R. H. Salisbury (eds), *Democracy Today: Problems and Prospects* (1962), at 80.

[43] C. E. Lindblom, *Politics and Markets* (1977), at 149.

[44] R. K. Winter, *Government and the Corporation* (1978), at 60.

Consumer choice?

used has been transferred from the market to the enterprise. The sovereignty of consumers has therefore become at best a shared sovereignty.

A separate source of unresponsiveness to the consumer 'electorate' derives from the fact that since companies have control over the goods and services made available to the public, consumers cannot positively 'vote' for the production of goods with the particular characteristics that best suit their requirements, but can only 'veto' the products they are actually offered. Products which do not meet consumer desires will fail the market test, but whether products come onto the market in the first place is a matter entirely in the hands of business. Companies have in this sense the power to shape the 'structure of opportunities' available in society.[45] A practical instance is cited by Lindblom, who notes that

For twenty-five years after World War II, the automobile industry in the United States demonstrated that industry response to consumer wishes can be extremely slow. Until the last few years the entire auto industry was so fixed in its opposition to small cars as to leave the market for them to foreign firms. Clearly corporations exercise substantial discretionary controls over the timing and fullness of their responses to consumer demands, including the possibility that for a decade or more they may ignore them'.[46]

As this excerpt itself implies, the dynamics of competition may in due course bring producer behaviour into line with the wishes of consumers, since there are clear opportunities for profit in being the first to satisfy unmet demand. Where these opportunities are ignored by domestic companies they are likely to be exploited by those from overseas, particularly in an increasingly global market. Nevertheless, as the quotation also illustrates, companies can have substantial vested interests in the viability of current products and production processes. Once the assumptions of the perfect market model are dropped it becomes clear that they have the capacity to safeguard these interests, manifested in a sluggishness of response, if not outright resistance, to changes in what consumers actually want, or might want if they were aware of the full range of possible alternatives.

It has so far been assumed that, while the corporate sector's response to consumer demand may be imperfect, that what is responded to is at least an authentic expression of consumer tastes. If, however, those tastes have been generated by companies in the first place then the idea of consumer sovereignty is overthrown. Far from companies being part of a productive apparatus under the ultimate control of consumers acting through the market, the position is reversed and consumers are instead the manipulated subjects of producer domination. It follows in virtue of this control that companies have power not only in the sense of discretion over the allocation

[45] See generally, T. Parsons, *The Social System* (1966).
[46] Lindblom, *Politics and Markets* (above, n. 43), at 153.

of resources between different uses, but also in a more invasive sense of an ability to influence individual desires and conduct. These ideas are particularly associated with Galbraith, who refers to the process whereby consumers are managed in the corporate interest as the 'revised sequence'. Instead of instruction flowing in one direction—from the consumer to the market to the producer (the 'accepted sequence')—'the producing arm reaches forward to control its markets and beyond to manage the market behaviour and shape the social attitudes of those, ostensibly, it serves'.[47] Such management, which is effected through advertising and other forms of promotional activity,[48] is necessary, Galbraith argues, to minimize the risk inherent in modern, large-scale, capital-intensive production methods. Without the assurance that there will be a market of sufficient size for the company's products when they eventually come on stream (a considerable period may elapse between product conception and realization), projects requiring major capital investment would be too hazardous to undertake.[49] Want creation is thus an essential part of a modern, technologically based economy. Galbraith's views have been widely criticized, most frequently on grounds of exaggeration,[50] though it should be noted that he does not suggest that the revised sequence has replaced the accepted sequence, but that there is a complex interaction between the two. It is undeniable that consumers have the capacity to resist the blandishments of advertisers, as borne out by the failure of many products brought onto the market. And again, companies that produce goods that customers 'really' want can be expected to out-perform, and ultimately replace, those who merely manipulate demand. Nevertheless, the view that consumer tastes are in part the result of corporate influence and do not originate exclusively in the autonomous individual will is a persuasive one.[51]

We should note finally a separate strand in Galbraith's argument, to the effect that advertising and associated activities serve the purpose not only of promoting the products of individual companies, but also of shaping the 'attitudes necessary for the performance and prestige of the industrial system'.[52] These attitudes involve, he suggests, a high regard for material

---

[47] J. K. Galbraith, *The New Industrial State* (2nd ed., 1972), at 217.

[48] See Galbraith, ibid. at 208: 'The management of demand consists in devising a sales strategy for a particular product. It also consists in devising a product, or features of a product, around which a sales strategy can be built. Product design, model changes, packaging and even performance reflect the need to provide what are called strong selling points. They are as much a part of the process of demand management as an advertising campaign.'

[49] Ibid. especially chs 2 and 3.

[50] For a discussion of some of the criticisms, see Smith, *Morality and the Market* (above, n. 41), at 34–6. See also Hannah and Kay, *Concentration in Modern Industry* (above, n. 7), at 30–1.

[51] For a suggestion that the implications of this are nevertheless rarely serious, see D. Miller, *Market, State and Community* (1989), ch. 5, and D. Miller, 'Why Markets?' in J. Le Grand and S. Estrin (eds), *Market Socialism* (1989), at 38–42.

[52] Galbraith, *The New Industrial State* (above, n. 47), at 215. See also R. Miliband, *The State in Capitalist Society* (1969), at 211–18, where the same issue is discussed from a Marxist perspective.

goods and consumer services in general, as distinct from non-commercial leisure activities and forms of human association that do not depend on commercial products, and also from publicly provided services. Without corporate efforts to reinforce the importance of traded goods and services the sustainability and growth of the industrial system would be at risk. Advertising and its related arts are thus necessary to 'develop the kind of man the goals of the industrial system require—one that reliably spends his income and works reliably because he is always in need of more'.[53] The extent to which the desire for the products of industry, beyond necessities, results from the processes of want creation as distinct from pre-existing materialistic tendencies is obscure, but there is some plausibility in Galbraith's picture of a corporate system whose power includes an ability not only to stimulate demand for particular goods but also to shape prevailing social values.[54]

Discretion in Making Delegated Decisions

We have so far considered corporate decision-making power in the sense of discretion over what to produce, in what quantities, and at what price. Our conclusion was that control over these matters is not located entirely in the market, as the theory of consumer sovereignty holds, but is divided between companies and the market in an uncertain and complex way. Corporate power is not, however, limited to decisions about products. In a useful distinction, Lindblom refers to the discretion that exists also in making (often more important) 'delegated' decisions. These are the 'decisions instrumental to production: among others, on technology, organization of the workforce, plant location, and executive prerogatives'.[55] As he points out, 'even in an idealized market system, consumer control over them ranges from weak to non-existent, except to impose least-cost decisions'.[56] Thus, even on the unrealistic assumption that consumers acting through the market are able to force managements to produce at the lowest possible cost, companies nevertheless retain a discretion within that constraint over such issues as plant location, appropriate levels of automation, and policy on research and development, since these and other delegated questions do not yield *unique* least-cost solutions. Further, the concept of least cost is not in any case self-applying, but depends on the exercise of choice over production variables

[53] Galbraith, ibid.

[54] For an alternative analysis of why the economy might fail to supply what we 'really want', see F. Hirsch, *Social Limits to Growth* (1977), esp. at 39–41 and 107–10. Hirsch's thesis is that the corporate sector is unable fully to match consumer desires because of market failure – a failure of the price mechanism to accommodate social preference as a result of the 'tyranny of small decisions': see further Ch. 10 below. Hirsch's analysis differs from that of Galbraith in that the former does not depend on the view that producers interfere with consumer preferences, so much as that the price mechanism is incapable of adequately reflecting them.

[55] Lindblom, *Politics and Markets* (above, n. 43), at 154.

[56] Ibid. Cf. Winter, *Government and the Corporation* (above, n. 44), at 58–63.

and the time-frame. As Lindblom observes, a 'least-cost location for a new plant, for example, depends on the range of products that might be produced, the flexibility built into the plant, and the period over which costs and revenues are estimated'.[57] The scope of corporate discretion in making delegated decisions is obviously extended substantially once the unrealistic perfect-competition assumption is dropped. Weaknesses in the corporate governance structure and slackness in the other markets that constrain management behaviour[58] also mean that despite the existence of these additional controls managers will often have considerable latitude to depart from the requirements of least cost. Whether managers fully exploit the pocket of discretion created by product-market imperfections and the inadequacy of other constraints depends on the intensity of their commitment to profit maximization. A number of theories maintain that managerial self-interest is better promoted by the pursuit of objectives other than profit maximization, and it is also argued, perhaps with less plausibility, that managers may seek to further some sub-profit-maximizing conception of the public good. We will explore in due course whether these objectives are pursued to any significant extent in practice.[59] For the moment the point is that in the conditions that many companies face managements have a discretion to make delegated decisions not only within the least-cost constraint but also to some extent outside it.

If companies have discretion in making delegated decisions, in what ways might the exercise of that discretion significantly affect others, demonstrating the existence of power? One group conspicuously affected by corporate decision-making is the company's employees. It was mentioned above that employees are subject to company power in the sense of being in an authority relationship with the employer. One aspect of company power of the different kind that is in issue here lies in the company's ability to shape the terms of that relationship. As far as wage levels are concerned, this is self-evidently an area in which corporate discretion is not unbounded, particularly in view of the countervailing power of trade unions. The strength of union bargaining power is, however, variable, being dependent on such factors as levels of unionization, the regulatory controls to which unions are required to conform, the ease with which the employer can transfer operations to another country, and not least the state of the employment market. An area of corporate discretion traditionally less constrained by bargaining relates to the nature of the work experience: whether, for instance, employees are allowed to participate in decision-making at appropriate levels in the organization; whether attempts are made to enrich otherwise boring jobs by rotation of tasks; or whether the introduction of new technol-

---

[57] Lindblom, ibid. at 155.
[58] See 113-32, below.
[59] See Chs 2 and 9 below.

ogy leads to deskilling or instead prompts investment in the acquisition of new competencies. These and similar decisions not only affect how a substantial proportion of the population spend their working lives, but also influence the level and distribution of skills within the workforce, which in turn is a determinant of national economic success.

Corporate decision-making, of course, affects not only what employees do at work, but sometimes whether an employee has a job at all. As Hannah and Kay observe, 'the elimination of inefficient productive capacity is now less frequently achieved through the action of bankruptcy in a competitive market *process*, but more commonly emanates from decisions to 'rationalise' made by a bureaucratic *organization*'.[60] They go on to say that large firms 'are constrained in some way [in making these decisions] by the requirement to make profits and serve consumers', but it is nevertheless appropriate to stress that companies will usually have *options* about how to manage the impact of changed market conditions or technology: the company is not merely a passive instrument of the market. Responses which may be open to the company range from plant closures and mass redundancies, through scaling-down operations with some job losses, to investment in alternative productive capacity with partial or full retention of the workforce. It is also important to note that the option chosen will often affect not only the employees directly involved, but may also have a significant impact on the local economy. Large-scale redundancies, particularly where the company employs a sizeable proportion of the workforce, are liable to result in a substantial reduction in local purchasing power; this may in turn have a knock-on effect on other local businesses and on local tax revenues and hence municipally provided services, and the ensuing high level of unemployment is likely to contribute more generally to a weakening of community relations.[61]

Turning to the impact of corporate discretion on communities more generally, it is clear that decisions about the location of company activities can have major implications for the economic, environmental, social, and cultural well-being of urban centres and entire regions. As Kaysen notes, 'Where new plants are placed both in regional terms and in relation to existing centers of population affects the balance of regional development and the character of urban and suburban growth'.[62] These decisions are not, needless to say, left wholly to companies. The system of planning controls imposes limits on their freedom to locate operations where they will or to increase the scale or change the nature of the activities carried on at a particular site. And national or local government may offer subsidies for businesses to set up in favoured areas. Nevertheless, negative planning

---

[60] Hannah and Kay, *Concentration in Modern Industry* (above, n. 7), at 29–30 (emphasis in original).
[61] See J. W. Singer, 'The Reliance Interest in Property', (1988) 40 *Stan L Rev* 611, at 717–20.
[62] Kaysen, 'How Much Power?' (above, n. 33), at 93.

controls and the positive inducements of regional policy leave the basic
initiative about locational decisions with the company. It should be noted
further that these decisions affect not only the physical character of an area,
including its infrastructure requirements and the condition of the local
environment, but also the range and type of other economic activities that
are carried on there. The construction of a large production plant may, for
instance, attract an influx of other manufacturers to supply it. Of particular
significance is the siting of company head offices, research and development
facilities, and various other executive functions. These create a demand for a
mix of local support services such as those of financial institutions, lawyers,
and technicians, and whose availability may attract into the area additional
users of these services, strengthening its economic base.[63] A region dominated
by branch assembly facilities and devoid of senior decision-makers, in
contrast, is likely not only to suffer from a sense of remoteness from those
who control its destiny, but will also tend to lack social diversity and cultural
vitality.[64]

The consequences of corporate discretion in the field of research and
development are worldwide and pervasive. Kaysen has pointed out that:

Decisions as to the technical areas which will be systematically explored by research
and development divisions and decisions as to what scientific and technical novelties
will be translated into new products and processes and tried out for economic
viability have very deep effects. Ultimately, the whole material fabric of society, the
structure of occupations, the geographic distribution of economic activity and population are all profoundly affected by the pattern of technical change.[65]

Research is, of course, carried on outside the corporate sector in universities
and other institutions of learning; even so, these bodies are increasingly
dependent on commercial sponsorship, and corporate funds tend to flow
more readily into projects identified by, or otherwise of interest to the

---

[63] It has been suggested that the presence of indigenous banking and other financial services
are of prime importance in retaining local decision-making power: Scott, *Corporations Classes and
Capitalism* (above, n. 20), at 214. See also *Guinness PLC and the Scottish Economy* (1987; report of a
conference sponsored by the City of Edinburgh District Council), where the loss of decision-
making autonomy in the Scottish economy is discussed in general, and in particular the issues
surrounding the breach of the undertakings given by Guinness during the take-over of Distillers
to site the enlarged group's headquarters in Scotland are considered.

[64] The tendency for decision-making authority to be centralized was noted by the Bullock
Committee, *Report of the Committee of Inquiry on Industrial Democracy* (Cmnd 6706, 1977), at 20:

As companies have grown in size and complexity, they have also tended to become remote
from the people whom they employ. Major decisions about the nature of a company's or a
plant's organization, affecting closely the future of the local community or the jobs of the
employees, may often be taken far away from the site by the directors of a parent or holding
company, sometimes by the management of a parent company overseas.

See also CBI, *Investing for Britain's Future: Report of the City/Industry Task Force* (1987), para 127,
and the discussion of the impact of take-overs on regional diversity and development at 126-7,
below.

[65] Kaysen, 'How Much Power?' (above, n. 33), at 93.

sponsor. And it is industry that usually has control over which developments are taken up and marketed.

This list of areas affected by corporate discretion could go on, taking in decisions about the environment, the employment and promotion of women and members of racial minorities, and issues of mainstream business policy not so far touched on. Decisions of the latter kind, about whether to import components or obtain them locally, for instance, or about investment policy in a recession or pay restraint, can have major implications for national economic performance. Mention should also be made of the importance of large corporate organizations as disseminators of news, entertainment, and cultural values, bringing an ability to influence perceptions of political and social issues and prompting Goyder to ask whether 'spiritual and intellectual values [can] be safeguarded when the channels for their transmission to the masses are cut in commercial grooves for commercial ends'.[66] But by now the basic point is clear. Corporate freedom of action is bounded by law (the rights of employees, environmental controls, and so on) and constrained by markets, but within these limitations there is a core of real business discretion. It is with the legitimacy of this discretion, and particularly with the form that the rules of company law should take in order to control it in the public interest, that this book is principally concerned.

Political Power

Arguments that companies possess political power, defined here as the ability to influence government policy and law-making, should finally be noted.[67] A recurrent theme in the literature is that the position of business in relation to government differs from that of other interest groups by virtue of the possession by companies of 'real' power—social decision-making power as it has been termed above. Marsh and Locksley, for instance, contend that business 'is different from other interests because it exercises power or influence in two ways—directly through interest groups and structurally because of the crucial role boards and managers exercise over production, investment and employment decisions which shape the economic and political environment within which Governments make policy'.[68] To elaborate, busi-

[66] G. Goyder, *The Responsible Company* (1961), at 54.

[67] For completeness, attempts by companies to protect their interests through *unlawful* interference in the government process should also be mentioned, graphic examples being the participation of the American company United Fruit in the overthrow of the government of Honduras in the 1950s and the more recent bribing by the Lockheed Corporation of the prime minister of Japan. For a discussion of the (not necessarily unlawful) involvement of British companies in international affairs, see Stopford and Turner, *Britain and the Multinationals* (above, n. 19), at 210–14.

[68] D. Marsh and G. Locksey, 'Capital in Britain: Its Structural Power and Influence Over Policy', (1983) 6 *West European Politics* 36, at 59, discussed in W. Grant, *Business and Politics in Britain* (1987), at 19. See also Herman, *Corporate Control, Corporate Power* (above, n.19), at 184:

ness, like other interest groups, makes representations to government in order
to influence government policy.[69] But company decision-making also shapes
the economic context in which policy is formulated and hence constrains the
available policy choices. And further, the crucial role of companies at the
structural level substantially enhances the bargaining power of business in its
dealings with government, giving it a special influence which other interest
groups lack. Important to this analysis is the fact that the electoral prospects
of democratic governments are substantially dependent on the overall
performance of the economy, something that is at least partially under
business control. This being so, it is essential for government to retain the
confidence, and hence the cooperation, of the business sector by maintaining
the conditions for its profitability. In an increasingly internationalized
economy particularly, governments must be sensitive to how their policies
will be perceived by business interests, since an adverse reaction can lead to
rapid and massive capital outflows and consequent economic destabilization,
or the relocation of productive capacity to more hospitable environments
with an equally obvious effect on jobs and growth.

One concrete result of government dependence on business, as Lindblom
has noted, is the corporate sector's ability to extract 'inducements in the
form of market and political benefits',[70] for example, tax concessions and
subsidies. Another is that governments must be cautious in their regulatory
policies, avoiding 'excessive' regulation that might damage profitability;
governments that 'go too far' may be subjected to direct pressure from
industry to dilute regulatory regimes.[71] It has been suggested further that

'capitalism as a system imposes constraints on government, and these constraints are fixed
mainly by the requirements of business. This results first and automatically from the strategic
position of business in carrying out basic economic functions, and thus in making key decisions
on production, investment, and employment that are crucial to community welfare.' For a
comparison of pluralist, neo-pluralist, and Marxist analyses of corporate influence over the
democratic process see D. Held, *Models of Democracy* (1987), ch. 6.

[69] For a discussion of the role of company government relations departments, see Grant, ibid.
ch. 5, and see chs 6 and 7 on the representation of sectoral and industry-wide interests by trade
associations and the CBI.

[70] Lindblom, *Politics and Markets* (above, n. 43), at 173.

[71] Devine et al, *Introduction to Industrial Economics* (above, n. 3) at 98, suggest that this is
illustrated by the way in which recommendations of the Monopolies and Mergers Commission
have been dealt with: 'typically the government has entered into negotiations with the firms in
question, and the outcome has usually been agreement on a course of action that has fallen well
short of that recommended by the Commission but has been more acceptable to the firms'. A
recent example is the treatment of the MMC report on the brewing industry; after intense
lobbying by the industry the controls adopted were much less stringent than those originally
proposed: see the *Financial Times*, 12 July 1989. See also M. Jacobs, *The Green Economy:
Environment, Sustainable Development and the Politics of the Future* (1991), at 41 (pressure by oil
companies and the motor industry during the 1970s and 1980s to prevent and then delay
legislation enforcing unleaded petrol). And note D. L. Engel, 'An Approach to Corporate Social
Responsibility', (1979) 32 *Stan L Rev* 1, at 70–5. While in general opposed to departure from the
goal of profit maximization for 'socially responsible' purposes, Engel accepts that companies
should voluntarily forebear from interference in government processes. There is a substantial

corporate ambitions extend beyond influencing the detail of regulation, with Reagan, for instance, claiming that

Corporations are not only much concerned to protect their own immediate legislative interests, but are reaching out in an attempt to create a business-oriented political and social framework within which all public decision-making would be constrained. Instead of the society channelling business decisions within the bounds of public interest, the corporations seek to channel public-interest decisions within business-interest bounds'.[72]

An example might be business efforts to create a climate unsympathetic to high levels of corporate and personal taxation, with the consequences this entails for the public provision of services in areas such as health and education.[73] Cohen draws attention to the structural limitations on government freedom of action by pointing to the difficulties that a government might face in attempting simultaneously to increase growth and to redistribute income, given that high taxation would weaken the incentives of companies to invest.[74] Whether or not we accept these points, their importance for the present discussion is clear. They indicate a need for a measure of caution, first, about the ability of the state to constrain the self-interested exercise of corporate decision-making power through external regulation. Second, they call into question the capacity of the state to reorder corporate objectives by intervening in the internal governance processes of companies or to make more fundamental changes to productive arrangements should conventional regulatory techniques appear inadequate.

III CORPORATE POWER AND THE NEED FOR A PUBLIC-INTEREST JUSTIFICATION

As stated earlier, the purpose of this book is to examine certain aspects of company law from a particular point of view, one which takes the relevant rules to be part of the machinery by which power, and particularly what we

---

literature on the separate issue of the 'capture' of regulatory agencies by the companies they regulate: see e.g. G. Richardson, A. Ogus, and P. Burrows, *Policing Pollution: A Study of Regulation and Enforcement* (1982), at 63–4 and refs. See also L. Hancher and M. Moran, 'Organizing Regulatory Space', in L. Hancher and M. Moran (eds), *Capitalism, Culture and Regulation* (1989), 271, at 274–6, doubting the coherence of the notion of autonomous spheres of regulators and regulatees.

[72] M. D. Reagan, *The Managed Economy* (1963), at 129–30. See also the discussion of the role of social reponsibility as a means of heading off public policies damaging to business interests, Ch. 9 below.

[73] Ibid. at 130–1.

[74] See M. Cohen, 'The Economic Basis of Deliberative Democracy', in E. F. Paul, F. D. Miller, and J. Paul (eds), *Socialism* (1989), 25, at 28, and references cited therein. For a discussion of the concept of power as involving the restriction of choice in the political sphere, see Lukes *Power: A Radical View* (above, n. 34), ch. 7.

have called social decision-making power, is sustained and regulated. The
legal duties and control structures imposed or sanctioned by company law
shape the criteria by which companies exercise social decision-making power.
Some advocates of corporate social responsibility (the term is deeply ambiguous, as will be seen in Chapter 9) maintain that companies should allow
their decisions to be influenced not only by profit, but also by social policy
factors. This causes them to argue for a loosening of the legal duties that
define the objectives of management decision making, which currently
emphasize the maximization of shareholder wealth,[75] to enable a broader
range of purposes to be pursued. And in some cases there is support for more
elaborate reforms to ensure that social-welfare considerations are given
appropriate weight in decision-making and are not left merely to managerial
discretion. Critics of these views, on the other hand, insist that the public
interest is properly served only where companies pursue the traditional goal
of profit maximization. These positions have in common that they express a
view about how company law should regulate corporate power in the public
interest: by introducing social-welfare considerations as explicit decision-
making criteria, or by excluding them and relying instead on the benign
effects of the invisible hand, guided where necessary by external legal
controls. The merits of the respective arguments will not be considered until
Chapter 10. In this section the object is to examine in some detail the
important preliminary issue of why the debate should be one about the
public interest in the first place, and why company law should not be seen
instead as being solely concerned with the furtherance of the interests of
shareholders and the protection of creditors. It should also be emphasized at
this point that references to the 'public interest' are not intended to imply
that there is a consensus about what constitutes the public good or that it is
objectively determinable. The discussion in this chapter and throughout the
book is less concerned with what the public interest actually is (though the
issue cannot be ignored) than with appropriate mechanisms for securing it.
Nor in referring to the 'public interest' is it necessarily intended to suggest
that there is an interest that should be served that transcends the interests of
the individuals who are affected by corporate activity. Rather the term is
meant to refer to some defensible balancing of the interests of affected groups,
be they for example employees, customers, suppliers, the local community, or
the community at large on the one hand, with on the other those of the shareholders and creditors that are the more traditional concern of company law.

A well-established approach denies that the public interest is the relevant
standard, or at least the primary standard, by which company law should be
assessed. It sees companies as purely private organizations, existing for
whatever purposes their members intend. There is no assumption that they

[75] See Ch. 3, below.

Basic Question - should O's have any obligation to consider public interest
y/s
-> Although arguments that

should serve the public good, though the approach recognizes that their operations are, in fact, highly beneficial to society. From this perspective proposals to redefine corporate decisional criteria in the public interest are misplaced. External regulation, at least in a form that applies to all citizens equally, is legitimate, but state intervention beyond that constitutes an illicit curtailment of individual freedom. The point then is not that reforms will necessarily fail in their objective of furthering the public good (though this is normally supposed), but that interference in company affairs for that purpose is morally impermissible. We intend to reject this approach, and instead to embrace Dahl's claim that 'every large corporation should be thought of as a *social enterprise*; that is, as an entity whose existence and decisions can be justified only insofar as they serve public or social purposes'.[76] The reason large companies should be viewed as social enterprises relies, it is suggested, on a political theory about the legitimacy of private power. That theory holds that the possession of social decision-making power by companies is legitimate (that is, there are good reasons for regarding its possession as justified)[77] only if this state of affairs is in the public interest. Since the public interest is the foundation of the legitimacy of companies, it follows that society is entitled to ensure that corporate power is exercised in a way that is consistent with that interest. To describe companies as social enterprises is thus to make a claim about the grounds of their legitimacy, and its practical significance is to hold that the state is entitled to prescribe the terms on which corporate power may be possessed and exercised.[78]

[76] R. A. Dahl, 'A Prelude to Corporate Reform', (1972) *Business and Society Review* 17 (emphasis in original). And see A. A. Berle and G. C. Means, *The Modern Corporation and Private Property* (1932, rev. ed. 1967), book 4, ch. iv; A. Chayes, 'The Modern Corporation and the Rule of Law', in E. Mason (ed.), *The Corporation and Modern Society* (1959), 25; G. Goyder, *The Responsible Company* (1961); K. W. Wedderburn, *Company Law Reform* Fabian Tract 363 (1965), and generally, W. W. Bratton, 'The "Nexus of Contracts" Corporation: A Critical Appraisal', (1989) 74 *Cornell L Rev* 407, at 437–8.

[77] i.e. a normative, as opposed to an empirical, concept of legitimacy is being adopted. Cf. M. A. Eisenberg, 'Corporate Legitimacy, Conduct, and Governance – Two Models of the Corporation', (1983) 17 *Creighton L R* 1, at 4, who suggests that it is appropriate to view the legitimacy of corporate power as an empirical question, referring to the 'widely accepted conception under which the legitimacy of an institution depends on its popular acceptance, so that legitimacy is an empirical rather than a deductive phenomenon'. In one sense this still relies on a normative concept in that popular acceptance is taken to be a good reason for regarding the company as legitimate. The significance of popular acceptance is however problematical: what weight should be given to it (assuming that it exists) in the absence of detailed popular knowledge about, and an effective choice between, alternative arrangements?

[78] There has been some recognition in the company law reform process in the UK of the 'public' status of companies: P. Bircher, 'Company Law Reform and the Board of Trade, 1929–43', (1988) 18 *Accounting and Business Research* 107, at 116–9, in discussing the background to the formation of the Company Law Amendment Committee (the Cohen Committee) in 1943 notes the attitude during the Second World War, linked to a change in social attitudes generally, to the effect that companies were bodies existing primarily for the public good. A more limited connection between the company and the public interest (i.e. interests other than those of the members and creditors) is made in the White Paper, *Company Law Reform* (1973, Cmnd. 5391),

It should be stressed at the outset that maintaining that large companies
are social enterprises involves no necessary finding that the root principle
beneath the current rules of company law, that companies exist to make
profits for the benefit of shareholders, is unsatisfactory. It is quite possible
that that arrangement is the one that is most conducive to the public good.
But the point is that making profits for shareholders must now be seen as a
mechanism for promoting the public interest, and not as an end in itself. It
follows that society is entitled to insist, for example, that companies are
equipped with governance structures adequate to enforce a commitment to
profits on the part of management and to promote the efficient operation of
the business.[79] And the detailed rules of company law must be tested, not just
to see how well they serve the interests of shareholders, but also how well
they serve the interests of society in having an efficient and productive
economy. A separate dimension of the social enterprise perspective is that if
we view the company as a public or social body, albeit under private
control, then its directors and managers should be held to requirements of
disclosure and standards of ethical conduct appropriate to those carrying out
public functions. Galbraith has described the denomination of corporate
enterprise as '*private* enterprise' as 'a formula for hiding public business
behind the cloak of corporate privacy'; it is a device for diverting the eyes of
government and the general public 'from things like executive compensation,
lobbying, political activity by executives and employees, profits, and
bureaucratic error or nonfeasance'.[80] If we reclassify companies as *social*
enterprises such issues are then not only matters of legitimate public concern
about which the public has a right to information, but also matters in which
the state is entitled to intervene in order to safeguard the public interest and
to ensure compliance with publicly acceptable ethical standards.

It may be, on the other hand, that profit maximization within the law is
too limited a formula for aligning corporate decision-making with the public
good. Without examining at this stage the measures that might be necessary
to improve the responsiveness of companies to the interests of the various
groups that make up 'the public', we should note that the social enterprise
perspective supplies a justificatory foundation for the relevant programme of
reform. That foundation is analytically stronger than one relying on the
casual observation that since companies possess power, they must use that
power 'responsibly'. Rather, because the public interest is taken to be the

which, at 5, acknowledges that companies 'have a manifest obligation towards all those with
whom they have dealings': see the discussion in D. Imberg and P. MacMahon, 'Company Law
Reform', in (1973) 1 *Social Audit* 3.

[79] See C. Graham, 'Regulating the Company', in L. Hancher and M. Moran (eds), *Capitalism,
Culture and Regulation* (1989) 199. For arguments to the effect that optimal governance structures
evolve through the process of contracting by corporate participants and the impact of market
forces, and without the need for external intervention, see 177–90 below.

[80] Galbraith, 'On the Economic Image of Corporate Enterprise' (above, n. 35), at 5–6.

root of corporate legitimacy, compliance with whatever 'social responsibility' demands is seen as a prerequisite, a defining condition, for the possession of power.[81] It follows that changes to the legal framework that are deemed necessary to encourage or induce the desired behaviour should be viewed as permissible even though a substantial curtailment of shareholder rights may be involved. Social responsibility is thus not merely a matter of the voluntary adoption of changed standards. Further, because the public interest is the foundation of corporate legitimacy, demands for responsibility need not be confined to the avoidance of obvious forms of social harm, such as might result from pollution, dangerous products, or false advertising, but potentially embrace all exercises of social decision-making power by companies, for example, in relation to plant closures or policy on research and development, and the various other manifestations of corporate discretion that were considered earlier.

The Concession and Contract Theories of the Company

The idea that companies should be viewed as social enterprises does not depend on a theory specifically about the nature of the corporate form, but, as has been mentioned, on a theory about the circumstances in which power may legitimately be held. In arguing that large companies are social enterprises there is therefore no intention to revive the concession theory of the company, at least in its traditional form. That theory and its antithesis, the contract theory, share a common assumption that whether or not society has a right to demand that companies serve the public interest depends on whether the state can be depicted as playing some special role in corporate existence, different in kind from its role in sustaining unincorporated businesses. It is worth spending some time in showing that this assumption is false, and why the theories that employ it should be rejected. If the assumption is false, then the contract theory, while currently popular in some quarters, cannot in itself immunize the company from public-interest demands, nor explain why the state may not intervene in companies' 'internal affairs' in order to enforce those demands.

The concession theory regards the company as owing its existence to an exercise of state power.[82] More specifically, in allowing certain individuals

---

[81] For a brief discussion of the relationship between corporate power and responsibility, see T. F. McMahon, 'Models of the Relationship of the Firm to Society', (1986) 5 *J Bus Ethics* 181.

[82] The concession theory is often coupled with, but should be distinguished from, the fiction theory. The latter is one of three ontological theories concerned with the nature of corporate personality; it regards the company as an artificial entity distinct from its human participants. This fits well with (though is not necessitated by) the concession theory, which explains the creation of this new being by reference to an exercise of state power. The contract theory, on the other hand, would find the existence of a separate person difficult to account for, a problem which is avoided by treating the company as being no more than an aggregation of its

the benefits of incorporation the state is viewed as having made a concession or having bestowed a privilege on them.[83] This favourable treatment is explained and justified on the basis that the corporators are required to perform public functions in addition to serving their own private interests. In contrast, the contract theory sees the company as the result of a purely private initiative. It is the outcome of a series of contracts between, among others, the founding shareholders and managers: in so far as the state has a role in corporate creation it is not materially different from its role in enforcing contracts in general.[84] Given, therefore, that the company has come about essentially through private means, it must be understood as a private body, to be run by the corporators for their own self-selected purposes, and without any obligation to further the greater good.

The importance of the concession theory is that it establishes a theoretical framework sympathetic to state intervention; the company is a creature of the state, existing to promote the public welfare, and as such the state has the right to interfere in its internal affairs and need not confine itself to external, general-law regulation. The state may thus mould the company's constitution so as to protect the interests of parties directly involved, for instance the interests of shareholders against abuse of position by management, but it also has a much broader right of intervention, allowing it, if

individual members. A third ontological position, the natural entity theory, views the company (somewhat mysteriously) as a *real* entity, distinct from its members, and with an existence independent of the state. M. J. Horwitz, 'Santa Clara Revisited: The Development of Corporate Theory,' (1985) 88 *W Va L Rev* 173, suggests that this theory, popular in the United States during the period of the rise of the management corporation, was relied on to legitimate that form of organization. Cf. D. Millon, 'Theories of the Corporation', [1990] *Duke L J* 201, at 241–2, who argues that there is a more complex, two-way relationship between theories of what companies are on the one hand and legal doctrine and social practice on the other. As a matter of *legal analysis*, the nature of the corporate body is unproblematical – it is a separate, artificial entity with some of the attributes of a natural person, as defined by law: see J. Dewey, 'The Historic Background of Corporate Legal Personality', (1926) 35 *Yale L J* 655; H. L. A. Hart, 'Definition and Theory in Jurisprudence', (1954) 70 *LQR* 37. It is proposed to treat the ontological debate as subsidiary to the political/justificatory one, and so it will not be explored further here in its own right. For the theory of corporate legal personality generally, see R. W. N. Dias, *Jurisprudence* (5th ed., 1985), ch. 12; see also the discussion of the ontological theories in W. W. Bratton, 'The New Economic Theory of the Firm: Critical Perspectives from History' (1989) 41 *Stan L Rev* 147; Millon, 'Theories of the Corporation', above; J. C. Coates, 'State Takeover Statutes and Corporate Theory: The Revival of An Old Debate' (1989) 64 *NYULR Rev* 806, and see W. H. Simon, 'Contract Versus Politics in Corporation Doctrine', in D. Kairys (ed.), *The Politics of Law: A Progressive Critique* (rev. ed., 1990), 387, at 389–91.

[83] One variant of the theory dates from the Middle Ages, its function being to support the claim of centralizing state authorities to be entitled to control groupings that might grow into rival sources of power: see Dewey, ibid.

[84] Contractual theories of the company have been invoked during different historical periods, for different purposes. The concern here is with the role of contract in establishing the private nature of the company in opposition to the claims of the concession theory. Ch. 6 will explore the modern 'nexus of contracts' theory, the origins of which lie in economics. It has been relied on to combat the theory of *management* power *vis-a-vis* investors, and the view that companies as a result of that power are inefficient, and accordingly in need of structural reform.

appropriate, to redefine corporate objectives to secure compliance with favoured social goals. As might be anticipated, the contract theory denies that companies have any special relationship with the state that would justify such a right. Companies are merely voluntary associations of individuals joined together by contract, and correspondingly the state has no greater standing to intervene in corporate affairs than it has in the individual affairs of the citizens who make up the company. In short, the debate turns on two overlapping questions. First, has the state conferred special benefits on the corporators such as to justify a right of intervention of a kind that does not exist in regard to other business forms? Second, is it appropriate to regard the state as bringing companies into existence on the understanding that they are to carry out public purposes, and hence similarly justifying a right of intervention?

Few would now give a positive answer to these questions. It is widely accepted that attempts to apply the concession theory in modern conditions are inapposite.[85] There is no longer any 'privilege' involved in obtaining corporate status and the source of companies' 'economic energy' undoubtedly lies in individual initiative and not in the state.[86] Historically there *was* a 'privilege', and it took a number of different forms. First, incorporation itself was a privilege in the sense that it was an advantage that was not available to all, being dependent on an exercise of state discretion by way of the grant of a royal charter or a specific Act of Parliament. But with the enactment of general incorporation statutes, corporate status, and then limited liability, became freely available to any applicant on registration,[87] and hence the element of differential treatment on which the concession theory partly rests disappeared. Second, a range of collateral benefits have in different periods

---

[85] See e.g. M. Stokes, 'Company Law and Legal Theory', in W. Twining (ed.), *Legal Theory and Common Law* (1986) 155, at 162–5; N Barry, *The Morality of Business Enterprise* (1991), ch. 2. Bratton, 'The "Nexus of Contracts" Corporation' (above, n. 76), at 343–436, suggests that the theory has no modern proponents and is merely set up by contract theorists for the ease with which it can be knocked down. The language of the concession theory is, however, still in current use, though not necessarily with any intention to rely on a technical concession argument: see, e.g. R. A. Dahl, (above, n. 76, emphasis omitted), who asks 'why should we, through our government, grant special rights, powers, and privileges, protections and benefits to any firm except on the understanding that its activities are to fulfill our purposes?' And see Wedderburn, *Company Law Reform* (above, n. 76), at 2 -3; Graham, 'Regulating the Company' (above, n. 79), at 200.

[86] See W. W. Bratton, 'The New Economic Theory of the Firm' (1989) 41 *Stan L Rev* 1471, at 1475. See also T. Donaldson, *Corporations and Morality* (1982), ch. 3, and E. M. Hartman, 'Donaldson on Rights and Corporate Obligations' in R. E. Freeman (ed.), *Business Ethics: The State of the Art* (1991) 163, at 170–72.

[87] In 1844 and 1855, respectively. And see *Canada National Fire Assurance Co v Hastings* [1918] AC 451, at 456, per Sir Walter Phillimore: companies 'are formed by contract . . . under memorandum and articles of association to which the Registrar of Joint-Stock Companies necessarily assents if the documents are in regular form'. For a brief history of the development of the corporate form and references to more detailed source material, see L. C. B. Gower, *Principles of Modern Company Law* (5th ed., 1992), chs 2 and 3.

also accompanied incorporation. Commonly, these took the form of monoploy rights,[88] possessed by such early incorporated bodies as the medieval guilds,[89] and later by the overseas trading companies, for example the Merchant Adventurers and the East India Company.[90] In the nineteenth century incorporation of utility and railway companies was also generally accompanied by other inducements and special powers deemed necessary for the success of the undertaking, such as rights of compulsory acquisition of land.[91] Today, of course, corporate status carries no implication that the business has in some other way been favourably treated by the state, and so in this respect too the idea of privilege is now inappropriate.

In the past the company's status as a body responsible for the performance of public functions, and the idea that public benefit was a prerequisite of incorporation, were also evident. The craft guilds, for example, supervised the quality of their members' work and imposed standards of fair dealing in the public interest.[92] Similarly, with the state lacking means of its own to regulate the conduct of business by its subjects overseas it was convenient to

[88] The idea that companies were anti-competitive *per se* lingered on into the nineteenth century: see P. S. Atiyah, *The Rise and Fall of Freedom of Contract* (1979), at 563–4. In the United States fear of market domination and associated economic and political power resulted in the imposition of restrictions on the capital, duration and objects of companies even after incorporation became freely available: see J. W. Hurst, *The Legitimacy of the Business Corporation in the Law of the United States 1780–1970* (1970), ch. 1; Bratton, 'The New Economic Theory of the Firm' (above, n. 86), at 1486; Coates, 'State Takeover Statutes' (above, n. 77), at 811–18; Nader, Green, and Seligman, *Taming the Giant Corporation* (above, n. 34), ch. 2; Lord Wedderburn, 'Trust, Corporation and the Worker', (1985) 23 *Osgoode Hall L J* 203, at 206–207; D. Millon, 'Theories of the Corporation', [1990] *Duke L J* 201, at 207–11. In this country restrictions on the scope of the company's business by way of the *ultra vires* doctrine were viewed more as a means of protecting members and creditors than of limiting corporate influence; see e.g. the speech of Lord Hatherley in *Ashbury Railway Carriage & Iron Co v Riche* (1875) L R 7 H L 653.

[89] These bear little resemblance to the modern corporate enterprise, being made up of individual craftsmen and merchants who traded on their own account and not by means of a joint fund. The function of the corporate body was to hold the legal charter which conferred on the members a territorial or occupational monopoly and various other privileges: see C. A. Cooke, *Corporation, Trust and Company* (1950), ch. 2.

[90] Originally the companies, some of which date from the fourteenth century, were composed of traders operating on their own account under the umbrella of the chartered body, in the manner of the guilds. During the course of the seventeenth century, however, the practice developed of the company itself trading with a joint stock contributed by the members, and ultimately the members were forbidden to trade on their own account: see Gower, *Principles of Modern Company Law* (above, n. 87), at 21. As well as possessing a monopoly of trade with a specified region, the members of the companies also enjoyed exemption from various statutes imposing penalties for 'unlawful assembly, illegal oaths, and leaving the country with ships, goods, gold and men': see Cooke, ibid. at 49–50.

[91] See Cooke, ibid. at 118–23; for a discussion of the similar position in the United States see Hurst, *The Legitimacy of the Business Corporation* (above, n. 88), at 23–4, and 60–1.

[92] See Cooke, ibid. 27. Comparing guilds with municipal corporations, Cooke explains that

The corporate form in both was applied to a public purpose in which the widest considerations of social welfare and the social good were put before the interests of the members of the corporation. Both gild and borough remained for some centuries organs of government in adjacent fields; the link between them was this common purpose of government, and they shared the end of control on behalf of the community of which they were organs.

delegate this function to the great trading companies, which also assumed responsibility for general colonial administration. The companies thus provided 'the requisite amount of public law for local government, trade organization, control of the customs and foreign policy',[93] as well as serving national commercial interests by gaining access to natural resources and expanding overseas trade. Cooke notes that this equation of incorporation with public service continued into the eighteenth and early nineteenth centuries, with the general theory of corporate form still dominated by 'the concept of the corporation as a public body, an institution created by specific act of Parliament or the Crown for purposes approved as being in the national interest'.[94] In accordance with this concept incorporation was, for example, much easier to obtain in the case of transport and utility undertakings, such as canals, railways and waterworks, than for ordinary trading ventures.[95] Here the public interest in encouraging the private provision of a transport infrastructure and the other prerequisities of industrial development were manifest, and the comparative willingness of the state to provide a business vehicle that would facilitate the accumulation of the vast sums of capital required is readily comprehensible in that light.[96] Since in these cases incorporation and public benefit were intimately linked, it was also accepted that there should be a measure of state control to ensure that private interest was not allowed to predominate over the public good. In the case of the railways this included a power to revise fares where excessive profits were made and even in some circumstances an express right to take the undertaking into state ownership.[97] Again, however, with the arrival of general

[93] Cooke, ibid. at 49. See also Hurst, *The Legitimacy of the Business Corporation* (above, n. 88), at 4.

[94] Cooke, ibid. at 78. Petitions for incorporation were scrutinized in the light of public policy criteria: ibid. at 92 and 118. See also Hurst, ibid. ch. 1.

[95] In other cases obtaining a charter remained problematical, in part because of the fear of economic crisis arising from speculation in shares which persisted beyond the South Sea Bubble affair and the passage of the Bubble Act of 1720. A. B. Dubois, *The English Business Company after the Bubble Act, 1720–1800* (1938), at 12, notes that 'not only were the operations of unincorporated joint stock companies restricted by the [Bubble] Act, but the Act was used as an expression of policy to restrain the formation of business corporations.' For a similar reluctance in the United States to grant charters of incorporation to manufacturing enterprises, see P. I. Blumberg, 'Limited Liability and Corporate Groups', (1986) 11 *J Corp L* 573, at 587–91.

[96] As A. Chayes, 'The Modern Corporation and The Rule of Law' in Mason, *The Corporation in Modern Society* (above, n. 76), at 34, puts it: 'the objects pursued are beyond the reach of the members as individuals. The needed amounts of capital are too great, the risk is too high, the duration of the enterprise too long'.

[97] See Cooke, *Corporation, Trust and Company* (above, n. 89), at 135–7; Atiyah, *The Rise and Fall of Freedom of Contract* (above, n. 88), at 562. (There are some obvious parallels in the modern regulatory controls over privatized utilities, though these are of course not linked to corporate status: see generally, C. Graham and T. Prosser, *Privatizing Public Enterprises* (1991).) Similar provisions applied in the case of American utility companies. For example, the charters of transport companies provided for the regulation of tolls and made the provision of services over specified routes a condition of the right to operate: see Hurst, *The Legitimacy of the Business Corporation* (above, n. 88), at 39. Note also the position in Germany, where until general

incorporation on registration the idea of public benefit as a specific precondition of corporate status disappeared. Instead, consonant with the prevailing economic orthodoxy, the public interest became at most a background justification for the free availability of incorporation and limited liability. This would serve the general welfare by facilitating the development of large-scale business enterprises, which, if left alone to pursue their own interests, would also further the interests of society. There was no longer any understanding that in making available advantages to private individuals the state was at the same time imposing a 'trust' that the business be conducted for the public good.

In modern conditions the only remaining peg on which to hang the concession theory's claim that the state has a special right of intervention in company affairs is the idea that since separate personality and limited liability are benefits conferred by the state, the state is entitled to intervene to safeguard the public interest as a quid pro quo. But that argument is difficult to sustain. For one thing, it is not at all clear that in offering the facility of doing business in corporate form the state is performing a service materially different from the service it provides in making available and enforcing the rules of contract, which supports no such argument. But in any event, the argument makes a disproportionate claim, or may even involve a *non sequitur*. Thus, while the conferment of limited liability undoubtedly warrants the imposition of statutory safeguards to prevent its abuse, it does not provide an adequate foundation for a *general* right of intervention in corporate affairs, unrelated to creditor protection.[98] Nor do the other attributes of incorporation suggest a basis on which a more extensive right of intervention on public-interest grounds could be justified in the case of a company, than of, say, a partnership, *simply in virtue of their respective legal characteristics.*

The answer to all of this is surely that it is not the legal qualities of limited liability or separate personality in themselves that justify intervention, but the concentration of power in private hands that has come about partly as a result of their existence.[99] The right to intervene does not, in other words,

incorporation became available in 1870, the government had a right to place a representative on the management body: see D. Vagts, 'Reforming the 'Modern' Corporation: Perspectives from the German', (1966) 80 *Harv L Rev* 23, at 50–51.

[98] Cf. Lord Wedderburn, 'The Social Responsibility of Companies', (1985) 15 *Melbourne U L Rev* 4, at 9: 'the crucial question for our company law' is still '[w]hat are the modern ... conditions on which private capital in a mixed economy can be allowed the privilege of incorporation with limited liability'. See also Wedderburn *Company Law Reform* (above, n. 76), at 2–3 and 19.

[99] For a view questioning the conventional wisdom that limited liability has been of central importance in the development of the company, see R. E. Meiners, J. J. Mofsky, and R. D. Tollison, 'Piercing the Veil of Limited Liability', (1979) 4 *Del J Corp L* 351. Cf. P. Halpern, M. Trebilcock, and S. Turnbull, 'An Economic Analysis of Limited Liability in Corporation Law', (1980) 30 *U Toronto L J* 117; F H. Easterbrook and D. R. Fischel, 'Limited Liability and the

depend on any particular characterization of the state's role in corporate creation. Nor is it determined by contemporary attitudes towards the terms on which corporate status is made available. It relies instead on a political theory about the legitimacy of private power and the conditions subject to which that power may be exercised: a theory contending that power may be legitimately held only for the purpose of furthering the public good. The reason for this somewhat laboured refutation of the concession theory is to emphasize that the social enterprise concept does not in any way depend upon it. It shows further that since the social enterprise concept does not rely on a special characterization of the role of the state in corporate existence, then even if the contract theory provides a more descripively accurate account, no threat to the concept is entailed. It thus does not follow from the inappropriateness of the concession theory in modern conditions that we must accept the normative conclusions of the contract theory. It should instead be recognized that the concession/contract debate is a distraction, artificially confining the discussion to the company's supposed public or private origins. In truth, the fact that a position of power might be attained as a result of 'private'[100] contracting in itself says nothing about the legitimacy of the possession of that power, and hence, even if the company could be

Corporation', (1985) 52 *U Chi L Rev* 89, reproduced with revisions in F. H. Easterbrook and D. R. Fischel, *The Economic Structure of Corporate Law* (1991), ch. 2. See also J. Hicks, 'Limited Liability: the Pros and Cons', in A. Orhnial (ed.), *Limited Liability and the Corporation* (1982) 11.

[100] Even where the company is understood as constituted entirely through contract the state is still profoundly implicated in corporate existence (as it is in all business forms), since the viability of the company depends on state enforcement of the constitutive contracts and support for the underlying private property regime. Viewed from this perspective, our question about the legitimacy of private power can be rephrased as a question about the justifiability of the state's upholding a system of private power. Whichever way the question is posed, the need for justification is not dependent on regarding the state as playing some 'special' part in corporate creation. For a similar idea see the discussion of the 'sovereign coercion theory' in Bratton, 'The "Nexus of Contracts" Corporation', (above, n. 76) at 438–439. This holds that since all contracts ultimately depend on state coercion, they are never fully private, but represent an exercise of delegated state power. This will frequently be of little significance, but where contracting leads to an accumulation of power in private hands the delegation has public consequences and the state is accordingly entitled to demand accountability. See also Millon, 'Theories of the Corporation' (above, n. 88), at 261. A consequence of this approach is that, since it views the state as already bound up in private power structures, state intervention cannot be depicted as an alien interference, but should be seen instead a modification of the terms of the original delegation. For a general discussion of the possibility of 'pure' contract, that is, binding agreement based entirely on consent and without state intervention, see G. M. Hodgson, *Ecomomics and Institutions* (1988), at 156–167. See also the discussion and references in M. J. Horwitz, 'The History of the Public/Private Distinction, (1982) 130 *U Pa L Rev* 1423, and G. E. Frug, 'The Ideology of Bureaucracy in American Law', (1984) 97 *Harv L Rev* 1276, at 1363–4. On the public/private distinction generally, from a critical legal studies perspective, see K. E. Klare, who argues that 'the social function of the public/private distinction is to repress aspirations for alternative political arrangements' in 'The Public/Private Distinction in Labor Law', (1982) 130 *U Pa L Rev* 1358, at 1361. See also R. H. Mnookin, 'The Public/Private Dichotomy: Political Disagreement and Academic Repudiation', ibid. at 1429.

explained in purely contractual terms this would, without more,[101] have little impact on the question of the propriety of state intervention.

As it is, the company cannot in any case be accounted for as a wholly contractual phenomenon. The distinctive attributes of the company, separate legal personality and limited liability, are beyond the reach of private agreement.[102] Furthermore, while the corporate constitution has a partially contractual basis, there are also significant mandatory elements, and many of those ingredients which are attributable to private ordering are more accurately described as resulting from management imposition than a process of contracting.[103] We will see later that a model of the company infused with the imagery of contract, suggesting negotiation and mutually beneficial exchange, or at least optimal, market-induced equilibria, supports a different analytical and evaluative approach to current corporate governance arrangements from one which views those arrangements as partially shaped by management power, but that is a different debate from the one in which we are currently engaged. The scope of the present debate will now be expanded by examining whether there are more substantial grounds than those so far considered for regarding companies as 'private' bodies.

Shareholder Rights and Corporate Legitimacy

Under this heading some arguments will be considered to the effect that

[101] It may be an element in a more substantial argument: see below.

[102] This has presented contract theorists with some difficulty. As Posner explains, limited liability can be achieved without the assistance of statute as against contractual creditors by writing appropriate terms into all contracts. Since parties are (theoretically) free to refuse to enter into contracts with limited liability companies, they can be regarded as consenting to the company's status and hence the conferment of limited liability by statute can be seen simply as a device to minimize transaction costs. Posner admits, however, that 'the contract analogy breaks down' as regards tort liability (above n. 8), at 372. R. Hessen, *In Defense of the Corporation* (1979), at 18–21, attempts to provide a 'private' explanation of limited liability for torts by invoking the aggregate theory of corporate existence: it is a mistake to view a company as an entity distinct from its members, and hence where an employee commits a tort (on this view the company itself cannot behave tortiously, or in any other way, since it does not exist) it is not the entity that is vicariously liable, but the shareholders. Since passive investors have no control over employees, however, they should be immune from action and it is this that accounts for their individual limited liability. Whatever the rhetorical force of this argument it is incorrect as a piece of legal analysis. No shareholders, passive or otherwise, are *vicariously* liable in tort (a shareholder involved in management may be *personally* liable), and *all* shareholders are indirectly liable up to the nominal value of their shares. See also D. R. Fischel: 'The Corporate Governance Movement', (1982) 35 *Vand L Rev* 1259, at 1274. While acknowledging that with respect to tort 'corporations have attributes that would not exist absent state statutes' he insists that 'this does not make corporations creatures of the state. Limited liability in tort cases is more accurately viewed as a subsidy to encourage a certain type of private conduct, forming corporations . . ., than as a creation of the conduct itself'. Surely the most straightforward explanation is the best: limited liability is a state-conferred benefit (as Fischel admits) but this does not have the normative implications for which the concession theory contends.

[103] See M. A. Eisenberg, 'The Structure of Corporation Law', (1989) 89 *Colum L Rev* 1461, at 1471.

corporate power can be legitimated by reference to the rights of the corporators. If this proposition is valid, our insistence that companies should be regarded as social enterprises is undermined. The idea that society is entitled to take whatever steps may be considered necessary to ensure that companies serve the public interest depends on the theory that the only basis on which companies can be allowed to possess power, which effectively means the only basis on which large companies can be allowed to exist, is that they produce consequences beneficial to society. The theories now examined offer an alternative, non-consequentialist justification of corporate power, and argue that the exclusive concern of company law should be to protect the rights of the relevant rights-holders.

A Revised Contract Theory

A possible response to the dismissal of contract as a ground of corporate legitimacy is that it pays insufficient attention to the moral significance of contract. Is not the act of contracting an exercise of the parties' moral rights, with the effect that the outcome of the contracting, the company, is legitimated by reference to those rights? Put another way, in so far as companies have power, is not that power justifiable on the basis that those who exercise it can claim a moral right to do so? Expressed in these terms the contract theory does not merely (irrelevantly) emphasize the company's non-state origins, it also offers a political justification for the possession of private power. Arguing along these lines, Hessen asserts that 'men have a natural right to form a corporation by contract for their own benefit, welfare, and mutual self-interest'.[104] More particularly, he contends that a company is the result of an exercise of freedom of association and freedom of contract.[105] On this basis it could be argued that companies should indeed be regarded as purely private organizations, and that state intervention in their internal affairs constitutes an improper interference with the moral rights of the participants. It is suggested, however, that corporate power cannot be legitimated merely by reference to the rights cited by Hessen. The foundation of a company's power is its control over property, and the claim of the members to be entitled to exercise that power or to delegate it to representatives rests on their rights as owners.[106] Without access to property, the freedom of the parties to associate with one another and to make agreements would be of little practical significance in this context.

A Property Rights Theory

A credible justification of corporate enterprise in terms of rights must,

---

[104] Hessen, *In Defense of the Corporation* (above, n. 102), at 22.

[105] Ibid. at xiv.

[106] It is theoretically possible for a company to function without an initial endowment of equity capital and instead to rely entirely on borrowings, but property rights (in this case those of the lender) nevertheless remain central.

therefore, be based on rights of ownership.[107] A property rights justification might take the following general form. While shareholders are not the owners of the company's assets as a matter of strict law,[108] they are in substance the owners by virtue of being the contributors of the company's capital.[109] Owners are entitled to use their property in whatever ways they wish. It follows that the power that results when shareholders pool their resources in corporate form is legitimate, because in possessing and exercising it they are doing only what they have a right to do. Accordingly it is not necessary, in order to establish that corporate power is legitimate, to show that the existence of companies is conducive to the general welfare, and the state has no right to intervene in their affairs in the name of the public good other than by the traditional means of altering the background legal constraints within which all businesses and citizens must operate. Before evaluating this argument two preliminary objections will be noted.

The first is that the corporate constitution does not provide that the *members* shall decide how the business is run, but vests decision-making power in the directors and managers. Not only that, if we accept that there has been a divorce between ownership and control in the typical large company,[110] then management has escaped effective shareholder supervision and hence possesses a broad discretion as to the ends for which the company's power shall be used. The objection therefore is that since power and property

---

[107] See Eisenberg, 'Corporate Legitimacy, Conduct, and Governance' (above, n. 77) at 5, who suggests that 'in our society control soley by virtue of ownership — hands-on or hands-off — is a fully legitimating principle.' It should be noted, however, that in making this statement he adopts an empirical, rather than a normative, concept of legitimacy (see note 77, above), and hence avoids consideration of the justificatory force of a property rights argument.

[108] For a consideration of whether corporate assets should be classified as a form of private property of the shareholders see J. Waldron, *The Right to Private Property* (1988), at 57–59.

[109] It can be argued that it is a mistake to regard shareholders as owners at all: they are mere investors, and in so far as company law gives shareholders rights akin to those of owners it fails to reflect the complex reality of the modern large company, ignoring in the process the claims of such groups as employees, consumers and the local community to have a voice in decisions about how the company is run. Because these interests are excluded., the argument runs, corporate power is exercised illegitimately. There is no need for an attempt to resolve this issue here, since it will be suggested below that even if the shareholders can be regarded as the company's owners, their legal rights of property do not in themselves provide an adequate moral foundation for their position within the company. For a non-radical version of the 'shareholders are not owners' argument, see Goyder, *The Responsible Company* (above, n. 66), ch. 12. It is interesting to note in this connection that the German Constitutional Court has held that the shareholders' rights are rights of membership in an organization and not direct rights over property (with the effect that the statutory rights of participation in management granted to employees do not infringe constitutional guarantees of private property): see T. Hadden, 'Employee Participation - What Future for the German Model?' (1982) 3 *Co Law* 250, at 252. Advocates of the modern 'nexus of contracts' theory of the company also do not regard the members as owners, though in their case this proposition is not usually relied on to downgrade the members' right to have the company operated exclusively in their interests: see the discussion in Ch. 6 below.

[110] See Ch. 2 below.

have separated, the legitimating link between them has been broken. As against this, it is possible to argue that corporate power, as exercised by management, is still ultimately rooted in, and hence legitimated by, property rights, on the ground that the structure that gives rise to it is created with the consent of the shareholders.[111] The members' rights of ownership entitle them not only to make decisions personally about how their property is to be used, but also to delegate that power to others, and they are free to stipulate what degree of control they require over the discretion ceded by them. The validity of this reasoning ultimately depends, it is suggested, on the genuineness of the shareholders' consent to the resulting situation. If the reality is that. through the inadequacies of the governance structure and of other pressures for conformity the directors have effectively wrested power to pursue goals which diverge from those preferred by the shareholders, then the necessary legitimating connection with property rights is not made out. Whether corporate boards have escaped shareholder control will be considered in Chapter 2 below.

The second objection is that the ownership justification erroneously assumes that property rights are absolute. The justification supposes that so long as a person is possessed of a right, that right may be exercised regardless of the consequences for others. But it can be argued that we should not view rights in this way, and that when their use has adverse effects on third parties, rights should not be treated as signifying a moral entitlement in the right-holder to bring about those effects. The harm resulting from corporate discretion might lie in its impact on particular individuals or groups, or it might exist at a more abstract level, in the social disfigurement that the concentration of power in a small number of hands represents. If the position of power that comes about when shareholders combine their property in a company is damaging in either of these ways, then an invocation of ownership rights will not constitute a conclusive justification. Now the purpose of relying on a rights-based argument is frequently to claim an entitlement to act irrespective of the consequences for others, and so if the idea of rights is to be coherent we must accept that a freedom to act in the face of at least some adverse social outcomes is entailed.[112] If this is so then the issue should be formulated as one of whether the existence of corporate power is sufficiently objectionable to defeat the prima facie justificatory force of a rights' claim.

---

[111] See, e.g. Hessen, *In Defense of the Corporation* (above, n. 102), at xiii. It should be noted also that there is a second-order legitimacy question concerning the legitimacy of the exercise of shareholder rights by the controllers (who are not themselves owners) of institutional funds, which now hold a large proportion of British equities: see further 166–7, below.

[112] See R. Dworkin, *Taking Rights Seriously*, (2nd ed., 1978), ch. 7. See also A. Sen, 'The Moral Standing of the Market', in E. F. Paul, F. D. Miller and J. Paul (eds), *Ethics and Economics* (1985) 1.

It is not clear how this issue could be resolved, other than by stipulation,[113] and hence rather than attempt to reach a conclusion we will proceed to the more fundamental question of whether the shareholders should, in the first place, be considered to have a moral right to decide how companies should be run in virtue of their ownership of corporate property.[114] If the fact of ownership does not carry with it a moral right of control, then the property rights justification of corporate power collapses and the objection in the previous paragraph (and the one before) becomes irrelevant. Much of the theoretical literature in company law treats property rights as though they were unproblematical; they are the unquestioned starting points of analysis rather than artefacts whose existence and distribution themselves demand justification. This truncated approach is unsatisfactory, and so the discussion that follows will explore the grounds on which ownership of corporate property might be thought morally to entitle shareholders to exercise power, and, more realistically, to delegate that right to management. Needless to say, a full-scale review of the moral justification of private property will not be undertaken, but enough will be said to indicate that there are substantial difficulties in the way of providing a satisfactory justification of corporate power by reference to the shareholders' supposed moral ownership rights.

Historical Entitlements

A well-established tradition holds owners to be morally entitled to their property when they have obtained it by way of an uncoerced transfer from someone who received it in a similar manner, subject to the property having been originally taken into private ownership by a legitimate process of acquisition. The latter requirement necessitates showing that the person who first removed the property from the 'common store' was entitled to do so; it must then be demonstrated that subsequent transfers have been consensual. Locke explains how property rights are intitially obtained by reference to the labour expended on the property by the acquirer.[115] Nozick, the most recent exponent of entitlement theory,[116] does not discuss the precise requirements for a morally just acquisition, but asserts that since taking property into private ownership will not in general prejudice the interests of others (he argues that their welfare will be increased owing to the greater efficiency of

---

[113] The issue is not whether the use of property conflicts with clearly recognized 'background constraints' (e.g. ownership of a knife does not entitle the owner to stab someone with it: see Waldron, *The Right to Private Property* (above, n. 108), at 32–33), but a more intractable one of identifying when otherwise acceptable exercises of rights become unacceptable because of the position of power that is thereby created.

[114] I.e. it will be assumed that the shareholders do in substance own the assets employed in the business.

[115] J. Locke, *Two Treatises of Government* (1690).

[116] R. Nozick, *Anarchy, State and Utopia* (1974).

an economy based on private property),[117] a taking will normally be morally legitimate.[118] The problem faced by all versions of entitlement theory, however, is in demonstrating why acquirers should be rewarded for their efforts with full rights of private ownership.[119] We might accept, for instance, that labouring on property should give the labourer some preferential interest in it (for example, a right to the value added by the work done), but it is not self-evident that any particular set of more extensive rights is warranted. The success of entitlement theory depends, however, on showing precisely that. Since historical entitlement theorists make original acquisition the root of all subsequent entitlements, it is essential that they demonstrate that acquisition is an event of sufficient moral significance to bestow on the acquirer all the incidents of private ownership, including the right to transfer the property at will and to confer the same package of rights on all subsequent transferees. Some quality of original acquisition must, in other words, provide a justification for the perpetual privatization of property and the consequent denial of its use to third parties. But rather than meet this challenge, entitlement theorists simply take for granted that if original acquirers deserve any rights they deserve the full rights of liberal ownership, and hence they assume, rather than demonstrate, the legitimacy of that which has to be justified: the institution of private property.[120] Entitlement theory therefore offers no satisfactory justification of private property in general, and hence, for the purposes of our more limited enquiry, establishes no moral basis for shareholder control over corporate property in particular.

Property Rights and Freedom

A different way of justifying private property is by reference to a supposed

---

[117] For a cogent criticism of this proposition, see G. A. Cohen, 'Nozick on Appropriation', (1985) 150 *New Left Rev* 89.

[118] Where there has been an injustice in acquisition or transfer, Nozick accepts the need for 'rectification', that is, return of property to the rightful owner, or descendant thereof, or the payment of appropriate compensation: see Nozick, *Anarchy, State and Utopia* (above, n. 116), at 150–3. If taken seriously, such a right would entirely destabilize current property holdings, given historic irregularities in transfers. Wholesale rectification does not, of course, take place and hence it would seem to follow that most property holdings, including holdings of corporate property, should on this view be regarded as morally impeachable: see R. A. Dahl *A Preface to Economic Democracy* (1985), at 77.

[119] For an analysis of these rights, see A. Honoré, 'Ownership', in A. G. Guest (ed.) *Oxford Essays in Jurisprudence* (1961), 107.

[120] See e.g. A. Honoré, 'Property, Title and Redistribution', in Honoré, *Making Law Bind* (1987); C. C. Ryan, 'Yours, Mine and Ours: Property Rights and Individual Liberty' in J. Paul (ed.), *Reading Nozick*, (1981) 323; Waldron, *The Right to Private Property* (above, n. 108), chs 6 and 7. J. Gray, *Liberalism* (1986), at 63, a sympathetic commentator, writes that '[i]t can fairly be said that no adequate theory of initial acquisition exists . . . '. The same difficulties are not faced by justifications of private property that do not make original acquisition carry the whole weight of justification. The utilitarian account of ownership, for example, relies on original acquisition to set the system in motion, but regards private property's welfare-maximizing consequences as its legitimating basis.

dependence of individual freedom on the existence of a private property system. Hayek claims, for instance, that 'a people averse to the institution of private property is without the first element of freedom'.[121] The point is not that *everyone* needs property to be free; some people have little or no property but are not necessarily any the less free as a result. The freedom that a private-property system brings is not the freedom *to* do things with property,[122] but freedom *from* coercion, and this does not depend on property being owned by all. The connection between the existence of a system of private property and freedom is that the former enables each individual to construct a 'private sphere', rendering him or herself safe from coercive interference by others. Where there is private property the actions of individuals cannot be 'shaped at will by another'[123] because the individual is able to form a coherent plan of action in the knowledge either that he has control, through ownership, of the material objects necessary to implement it, or that he can enter into enforceable contracts with a range of other people enabling him to have access to those objects. What is crucial, then, is not that a particular individual should necessarily own property himself, but that 'property should be sufficiently dispersed so that the individual is not dependent on particular persons who alone can provide him with what he needs or who alone can employ him'.[124] The chief virtue of a private property system is that it achieves this dispersal and is therefore structurally antagonistic to coercion.

The problem with this reasoning is that even if we accept the narrow definition of freedom on which it relies,[125] a system of *private* property, and in particular private ownership of productive assets, is not the only property system that is capable of bringing about the required dispersal of control over material goods. Monolithic state ownership is not the sole alternative to private property; productive assets can, for example, be owned in common by the members of a cooperative, no individual member having a transferable property right in them.[126] In such systems it is entirely feasible for there to be

---

[121] Hayek, *The Constitution of Liberty* (above, n. 30), at 140, quoting Lord Acton, *The History of Freedom and Other Essays* (1907), at 297.

[122] Hayek denies that this positive characterization of freedom is a form of freedom at all; rather, it is a confusion of freedom with the ability to act. Furthermore it is, according to him, a dangerous confusion, since it 'leads to the identification of liberty with wealth; and this makes it possible to exploit all the appeal which the word "liberty" carries in the support of a demand for the redistribution of wealth': ibid. at 17. Justification of property by reference to what ownership allows an individual to do is of obvious appeal. As the quotation makes clear, however, this route is not open to Hayek, since it begs the question of why the benefits of ownership should be unevenly distributed.

[123] Ibid. at 21.

[124] Ibid. at 141.

[125] The concept of freedom is a highly contested one; for an introduction to some of the arguments see A. R. White, *Rights* (1984), ch. 9.

[126] For further discussion, see Ch. 7 below. For a discussion of some other examples of non-private ownership involving dispersed holdings, see Honoré, 'Property, Title and Redistribution' (above, n. 120).

a plurality of owning or controlling groups, thus preventing any particular group from having a monopoly over goods or employment opportunities that would enable it to exercise coercion. Private property and freedom are not uniquely connected in the way that Hayek suggests, therefore, and if private property is to be justified in terms of freedom some further argument is required that the dispersal theory does not supply.[127]

Rights Protecting Interests

Rather than justifying private property by reference to its role in creating a 'free society', emphasis can be placed on the part played by ownership in securing vital human interests. This latter approach, unlike the previous one, depends on all individuals actually owning some property, and not merely the background existence of private property as an institution. Waldron refers to a justification of property along these lines as a right-based argument for private property, which he defines as 'an argument which takes an individual interest to be sufficiently important in itself to justify holding others (especially the government) to be under duties to create, secure, maintain, or respect an institution of private property'.[128] We might claim, for instance, to have a right to life because we each have an interest in being alive that is of sufficient importance to justify holding others to be under a duty to respect our lives, and the government to be under a corresponding obligation to reinforce that duty by enacting appropriate laws. Similarly, we might claim to have a right to private property on account of having interests which crucially depend on private ownership. One such interest might be autonomy, the rights of exclusive use and alienation inherent in private property enabling individuals to organize their affairs without the need to obtain the permission of others. Alternatively, private ownership might be necessary for our full development as moral agents, for instance, in

---

[127] A utilitarian justification of private property, postulating optimal efficiency from an economic system founded on private property and thus the maximization of welfare, may be easier to sustain. It is suggested, however, that a utilitarian theory of individual property rights cannot provide a stable basis for a justification of corporate power. It does not follow that because the individual ownership of assets is justified by virtue of its consequences that an institution in which those assets are pooled (a company) would similarly be justified. It may be, for instance, that where assets are aggregated the efficiency which justifies individual property holdings is fatally diminished (perhaps because of the need to employ non-owning managers), or that the positive consequences in terms of efficiency are outweighed by the negative effects of the resulting accumulation of power. In other words, a consequentialist argument will be persuasive only where it is targeted directly at the institution that is to be justified. A consequentialist justification of the company will be considered below.

[128] Waldron, *The Right to Private Property* (above, n. 108), at 115. The theories of Locke and Nozick discussed above are right-based, but take the form of what Waldron calls a special-right-based argument (see ibid. at 116). This is an argument which takes an interest as being sufficiently important to justify holding others to be under a duty, etc., on account of the occurrence of some particular event, in the case of the theories of Locke and Nozick, original acquisition. The discussion that follows is concerned with general-right-based arguments, which focus on the nature of the interest itself.

order to foster a sense of responsibility and prudence.[129] These arguments are attractive, and might well justify private property in personal possessions, and also such productive assets as may be needed for the satisfactory fulfilment of an individual's human potential. It is difficult to see, however, what interests we might have of the necessary importance whose realization depends on owning corporate property. And once we take notice that in reality individual holdings in companies, other than in exceptional cases, give the holder negligible rights of control, it becomes clear that ownership of corporate property could make no distinctive contribution to the realization of whatever individual interests might be specified.

Conclusion: Back to Social Enterprises

This brief survey reveals some of the difficulties of establishing that shareholders are morally entitled to control companies by virtue of their legal property rights, and hence of attempting to legitimate corporate power by reference to those rights. If shareholders cannot be shown to have an antecedent moral right to the control over corporate property that their legal rights give them, then the property rights justification of corporate power must fail, and with it the project of explaining companies as private shareholder domains. It should be added that it does not follow from this conclusion that shareholders do not have *any* interest in the company that merits protection on the basis of moral rights. In arguing that shareholders do not have moral rights of control, it has not been necessary to contend that they have no rights at all. The right to a return (not necessarily the highest possible return) on their investment may, for example, be supportable on the basis of moral rights. Nor does the rejection of justificatory theories of corporate power based on antecedent rights signify that the full set of legal rights in the company possessed by the shareholders, including the right to exercise ultimate control and to have the business operated in their interests, are not morally defensible. If, as will be considered in the next section, companies serve the public interest by seeking to maximize their profits, then the shareholders' rights may be justifiable on *functional* grounds, that is, by virtue of their role in securing the efficient operation of the business.[130] But the significance of a

---

[129] See S. R. Munzer, *A Theory of Property* (1990), ch. 6.

[130] This idea of the contingent status of shareholder rights also appears in E. M. Dodd, 'For Whom Are Corporate Managers Trustees?' (1932) 45 *Harv L Rev* 1145, at 1149 (part of the celebrated Berle-Dodd debate), where Dodd observes that 'business is permitted and encouraged by the law primarily because it is of service to the community rather than because it is a source of profit to its owners.' He goes on to state that if businesses continue to be allowed unregulated profits 'it will be as a matter of legislative policy because the lawmakers regard the competitive conditions under which such businesses are carried on as making regulation of profits unnecessary, and not because the owners of such enterprises have any constitutional right to have their property treated as private in the sense in which property held merely for personal use is private'.

justification in terms of consequences rather than rights is that the shareholders' position is dependent on a positive evaluation of consequences. If, therefore, the single-minded pursuit of profits (as constrained by external regulation) is liable to damage the public interest, then this will require a modification of the existing set of shareholder rights and the framework of company law that upholds them. Since, according to the argument above, the rights of the shareholders are not foundational, the necessary reforms may legitimately be undertaken.

Now that the objection based on shareholder rights to viewing companies as social enterprises has been removed, we can proceed to a provisional account of the objectives companies should be required to adopt if they are to serve the public interest. If the existence of companies should be regarded as premised on 'the understanding that their activities are to fulfill *our* purposes',[131] some idea of how 'our purposes' should be understood is needed.

IV COMPANIES AND THE CREATION OF SOCIAL WEALTH

What criteria should guide corporate decision making if companies are to serve the public interest? A useful starting point is to note the traditional justification of capitalism in terms of consequences (as distinct from rights). This is that capitalism, and now its modern form of large-scale corporate capitalism, is the most efficient (practically realizable) system for the creation of wealth.[132] According to economic theory, with some reservations that will be examined shortly, companies contribute to the maximization of society's total wealth when they seek to maximize their own profits. If, therefore, we were to equate the public interest, so far as relevant to the operation of business, with the maximization of the wealth of society as a whole, it would follow that in order to serve the public interest companies should be required to pursue the goal of profit maximization: maximum profitability should be the sole criterion that guides management discretion and the exercise by companies of social decision-making power.

Unconstrained profit maximization is not, however, conducive to the public interest, or at least any easily defended conception of it, for two reasons. First, while the efficient creation of wealth may be regarded as a high social priority, we also recognize individual and collective interests and values that ought not to be sacrificed in its pursuit. Such recognition is reflected, for instance, in the enhancement by statute of the rights of employees against dismissal, which from an aggregate wealth viewpoint may be depicted as

---

[131] Dahl, 'A Prelude to Corporate Reform' (above, n. 76), at 17 (emphasis in original).
[132] See e.g. P. L. Berger, *The Capitalist Revolution* (1987), ch. 2.

inhibiting factor mobility and hence on occasion as being wealth-reducing. Second, because of defects inherent in the operation of markets, the strict maximization of profits will in any case frequently fail to lead to the maximization of aggregate wealth. An example is the problem of 'externalities'. This is the problem that behaviour which is privately profitable will not be wealth-maximising overall where an actor can ignore the costs that its activities impose on others, for example, when a company without cost to itself can emit into the atmosphere the noxious by-products of its production methods.[133] Society seeks to rectify the effects of this divergence of private and social interests by imposing limits or prohibitions on certain kinds of emissions or on the use of polluting processes; other techniques, such as taxing the production of harmful wastes, are also available to force companies to 'internalize' the full costs of their activities.

The imposition of legislative constraints on profit maximization can, therefore, be viewed as a procedure for adjusting, in the public interest, the terms on which wealth is created. If this procedure is the most appropriate way of correcting market failure and of otherwise setting the requisite 'sociopolitical limits on the exercise of economic rationality'[134] then it would seem to follow that the goal of companies should continue to be profit maximization, within the relevant constraints. To the extent that maximising profits conflicts with the public interest, the solution from this perspective is not to modify corporate objectives, but to strengthen the limiting conditions within which companies are required to operate. In this way society benefits from the most efficient means of producing wealth, consistent with the protection of non-aggregative social values. It follows from this reasoning that a company law focused on the public interest should define management duties exclusively in terms of profit maximization and should more generally provide a legal framework orientated towards that end.

Dissatisfaction with the 'profit maximization within the law' formula is at the centre of the debate about corporate social responsibility. It can be argued that the interests of the various groups affected by company decision-making—employees, local communities, consumers, and all of us, through our interest in the environment, for example—are invested with a moral significance that cannot be adequately captured within the relatively finite external legal controls that are currently relied on to regulate the terms on which wealth is created.[135] Accordingly, obedience to the demands of 'profit

---

[133] Externalities and other examples of market failure will be examined in more detail in Ch. 10 below.

[134] K. E. Goodpaster, 'Ethical Imperatives and Corporate Leadership', in Freeman, *Business Ethics: The State of the Art* (above, n. 86), at 98.

[135] Ch. 10 below will examine why. A different aspect of the social responsibility debate, also considered in Ch. 10, is concerned not with action to safeguard the interests of groups affected by the way the company runs its business, but with corporate involvement in community

maximization within the law' prevents the full range and texture of third-party interests from being taken into account or given sufficient weight in corporate decision-making. For example, whether or not a company should relocate its head office, creating unemployment and inflicting wide-ranging economic and social damage on the community from which it proposes to exit, is not an issue that is resolvable by conventional regulatory techniques. It is true that ethical values are to some extent also transmitted through markets, with the effect that a company committed to profit maximization cannot afford to ignore the impact of its activities on others. Some minimum level of compliance with societal expectations is, in other words, built into the profit goal. A business may, for instance, spend more on anti-pollution measures than is necessary to satisfy the relevant legislation, perhaps to avoid adverse publicity which may damage sales. But so long as the company's objective is maximum profits, a concern with the welfare of third parties is necessarily an instrumental one: it is a means of protecting profitability in the long term. The concept of social responsibility, in contrast, demands that affected interests be treated as ends in themselves, and this will at times require a deviation from long-run profit maximization.[136]

From the standpoint of advocates of social responsibility, therefore, it should be a function of company law to facilitate the reception and proper weighting of third-party interests in corporate decision-making, even though this may require the adoption of policies which are not privately profit-maximising. As compared with a 'profit maximization within the law' regime, this may in some areas lead to outcomes which are more efficient from a social point of view, as when a company takes voluntary action to internalize external costs. In other respects it may in principle result in conduct which is wealth reducing overall, as when a company keeps open an unproductive plant or retains corparatively expensive local suppliers in order to protect the host community. Mechanisms by which third-party interests might be more fully integrated into the corporate decision-making process will be discussed in Chapter 11.

For the time being these issues will be held in suspense, and the following chapters will examine those aspects of company law which bear on management decision-making on the assumption that their aim should be to promote profit maximization subject only to external legal constraints. Whether this objective *should* underlie company law, viewed from a public interest perspective, or whether the alternative approach just discussed is preferable, will be

---

projects (e.g. charitable donations and secondment) which are not directly related to the conduct of the company's ordinary business affairs.

[136] The term 'social responsibility' may, however, also be used without any implication that there is a conflict between the interests of society and long-run profit maximization: see Ch. 9 below.

considered in Chapters 9 and 10. Thus, Chapters 2–8 will, among other things, describe and evaluate the controls on goal selection, the controls relating to the efficiency with which permitted goals are pursued, and the controls designed to prevent the diversion of corporate assets to management.

Three issues remain for consideration in this chapter. First, it is necessary to look more closely at the relationship between profit maximization and aggregate wealth maximization, and to introduce an additional reservation. Second, it will be examined why, granted the profit maximization objective, the profits should accrue to the shareholders, as opposed, for example, to the employees: if considerations of efficiency underscore the shareholders' current position of pre-eminence, then this may be thought to provide a justificatory foundation for shareholder rights within a public-interest framework. Finally, it has so far been taken for granted that satisfaction of a social objective of efficient wealth creation is capable of legitimating the existence of corporate power. The capacity of wealth maximization to legitimate power, however, requires some elaboration.

The Relationship between Profit Maximization and Wealth Maximization

It will be assumed for present purposes that society's wealth is maximized when production takes place at the lowest possible cost, thus avoiding the waste of scarce resources (the goal of 'productive efficiency' is satisfied), and goods and services are produced in the quantities and are of the quality demanded by consumers (the goal of 'allocative efficiency' is satisfied). There is an obvious connection between profit maximization and productive efficiency. A company committed to maximizing its profits will strive to minimize its costs, and will thus aim to use the resources at its disposal in the most productive way. The link between profit maximization and allocative efficiency, on the other hand, is more complex, since profit maximization can lead to different outcomes depending on the structure of the market in which the company operates. A profit-maximizing firm under conditions of perfect competition will expand production up to the point at which the additional cost of producing the last unit of output ('marginal cost') is equal to price. Once this point has been reached increased production will make no further contribution to profits. Output at this level is optimal not only for the firm, but also for society, because the type and quantity of goods produced will match the demand for them, at least in so far as demand is represented by the willingness and ability of the consumer to pay.[137] Where this situation prevails in all industries throughout the economy (that is, price equals marginal cost for every firm) the distribution of resources between competing

---

[137] There is no uniquely optimal pattern of output, only patterns which are optimal relative to existing demand, which is a function of the distribution of wealth: see further below.

uses is allocatively efficient: the total value of output could not be increased by distributing resources in some other way.[138] The pursuit of profits and the social interest are therefore coincident.

However, as was mentioned earlier in the chapter, the model of perfect competition does not present an accurate picture of reality. Many industries are dominated by a small number of large companies; because of their relative share of the market, the existence of barriers to entry, and the differentiated character of their products, these companies are not pure price-takers, but have the ability to increase their prices above marginal cost. Where firms maximize profits in uncompetitive conditions the effect is that consumers are denied goods which they would have been willing to buy at the competitive market price. Output is accordingly lower than it would have been under conditions of perfect competition, and resources are diverted to alternative, less valuable uses. Another result is that firms make 'supernormal' profits (profits in excess of those necessary to induce them to remain in the industry) at consumers' expense. In short, the outcome is allocatively inefficient: a rearrangement of resources would produce a net increase in the satisfaction of wants.[139]

It does not necessarily follow from this, however, that an economy in which large firms predominate is inefficient on balance. In many cases the large size of a company, which is the source of its market power, may enable it to make cost savings which, although not fully passed on, more than compensate for the distorting effects of an uncompetitive market structure.[140] It may therefore be that while a perfectly competitive market composed of producers big enough to benefit fully from economies of scale would be the ideal, something like the existing state of affairs, particularly against a background of merger control and regulation of anti-competitive practices, is the best realizable outcome.[141] But though this may quell doubts about the

[138] For a more detailed explanation, see Scherer, *Industrial Market Structure and Economic Performance* (above, n. 40), ch. 2; Lipsey, *Positive Economics* (above, n. 39), ch. 12; F. H. Stephen, *The Economics of the Law* (1988), ch. 4. Under conditions of perfect competition productive efficiency is also assured; since all firms are price-takers, those that have higher production costs than their rivals will be driven out of business.

[139] See Scherer, ibid. ch. 2; Lipsey, ibid. chs 13 and 14; Stephen, ibid. ch. 4. Lack of competition also gives rise to doubts about productive efficiency: given the weakening of competitive pressure in companies' product markets they are no longer forced to adopt the most cost-effective production methods or management techniques. Cf. M. Olson, 'On the Priority of Public Problems', in R. Marris (ed.), *The Corporate Society* (1974), 294, at 294–300.

[140] See O. E. Williamson, 'Economies as an Anti-Trust Defense: The Welfare Trade-Offs', (1968) 58 *Am Econ Rev* 18, discussed in A. Hughes, 'The Impact of Merger: A Survey of Empirical Evidence for the UK' in Fairburn and Kay, *Mergers and Merger Policy* (above, n. 7) 30, at 31–2.

[141] It is also possible, contrary to the traditional view which argues that vigorous competition provides a strong incentive for companies to innovate, that a market structure which offers some shelter from competition is more conducive to technological progress, given the costs and risks associated with research and the development of new products and techniques: see Scherer, *Industrial Market Structure* (above, n. 40), at 14 and 22.

benefits of the existence of large-scale enterprise, it does not bear on the point that where competition is attenuated a policy of profit maximization may not be wealth-maximizing: society might be better served if companies were to lower price and increase output, even though this would be less profitable from the company's point of view.[142] This point will, however, be ignored until Chapter 10, and in the meantime it will be assumed that profit maximization is in the social interest regardless of the particular market structure within which the company operates.

Profit Maximization and Shareholder Rights

The fruits of a policy of profit maximization accrue to the shareholders as dividends and increased share values. What is the logic that dictates that the shareholders should be entitled to the corporate surplus, rather than to a fixed return on capital, with profits being distributed to the employees, or even to management?[143] The possibility of a functional justification of the rights of shareholders was referred to earlier. It is sufficient for present purposes to note one such justification, the incentive-residual rights theory.[144] Alchian and Demsetz characterize the firm as involving a team use of inputs together with the occupancy of a central position by a party whose function is to monitor the outputs of the team members and the other factors of production employed in the firm.[145] Monitoring is necessary in order to limit the tendency of team members to 'shirk', that is, to increase leisure and reduce effort 'on the job'. (They explain the existence of the firm by reference to the superiority of internal monitoring through observation of the

---

[142] See D. Helm, 'Mergers, Take-overs, and the Enforcement of Profit Maximization', in Fairburn and Kay, *Mergers and Merger Policy* (above, n. 7), 133.

[143] See e.g. Berle and Means, *The Modern Corporation* (above, n. 76), at 301: 'one cannot escape the conclusion that if profits have any influence as a motivating force, any surplus which can be made over a satisfactory return to the investor would be better employed when held out as an incentive to action by control [management] than when handed over to the "owners" who have surrendered control.' Remuneration schemes linking rewards to corporate performance capitalize on this incentive effect: see 114–16 and 221–6 below.

[144] See L L Dallas, 'Two Models of Corporate Governance: Beyond Berle and Means', (1988) 22 *U Mich J L Ref* 19, at 53–68. An alternative approach, associated principally with Williamson, points to the asset-specific character of the shareholders' investment, such that investment is likely to be forthcoming only on terms that the firm will maximize profits for the benefit of shareholders: Williamson, *The Economic Institutions of Capitalism* (above, n. 8), at 52–61, explained and criticized in Dallas (above), at 69–80. The shareholders' role as risk bearers is also frequently cited as justifying their position, see e.g. E. F. Fama and M. C. Jensen, 'Separation of Ownership and Control', (1983) 26 *J L and Econ* 301, at 302–3: because the shareholders' entitlements arise only when all contractual claimants have been satisfied, they require a higher return when the company is successful. It is not, however, self-evident that their reward needs to be the whole of the residual: see Goyder, *The Responsible Company* (above, n. 66), ch. 16. And see Dahl, *A Preface to Economic Democracy* (above, n. 32), at 79–80, dismissing the argument that investors are morally entitled to a reward for sacrificing the use of their money.

[145] Alchian and Demsetz, 'Production, Information Costs, and Economic Organization' (above, n. 30) .

behaviour of team members over monitoring of teams by market competition.)[146] The central monitor, in turn, is given an incentive not to shirk in performing the monitoring function by giving him or her a right to the residual, that is, a right to the surplus that remains after all the other factors of production have been paid at the market rate. Since the size of the residual depends on the efficiency of the firm, the monitor has an interest in ensuring that the firm is run as efficiently as possible. In the classical firm the central monitor is the owner/entrepreneur. In the large company with professional management the monitoring role is performed by the occupants of various levels in the management hierarchy, culminating with the board, but with the board itself ultimately monitored by the shareholders. Shareholder monitoring may be depicted as taking an owner-like, internal form, involving scrutiny of management and replacement of under-performing directors via the company's democratic channels, or an external form, whereby dissatisfied shareholders dispose of shares in the market, possibly triggering the removal of the board via the market for corporate control.[147] In either event, it is argued that the residual rights of the shareholders create an appropriate incentive for them to activate the relevant disciplinary mechanisms. As well as the shareholders having the proper incentives to prevent shirking, it should be added that they also have incentives to press management to make decisions that will maximize profits. Since the shareholders, standing last in line but with an unlimited right to the surplus, gain most from top quality performance, they have a powerful reason to hold managers to the profit-maximization objective.[148]

As Chapter 3 will discuss, the legal duties imposed on management are directed towards shareholder benefit. They do not consist of an abstract duty to maximize profits or otherwise to act in the interests of society. Similarly, ultimate rights of control over the company are legally vested in the shareholders, giving them, at least in theory, the ability to shape the company's purposes for their own ends. The members' status as residual claimants suggests that they have in fact the same interest in profit maximization as we have postulated for society as a whole, and the incentive to enforce profit

---

[146] Ibid. 779–80.

[147] See 119–31 below. The active role of the shareholders in the market for control partly undermines Berle and Means' claim in *The Modern Corporation and Private Property* (above, n. 76), at 312, that 'by surrendering control and responsibility over the active property [i.e. the company's assets], [the shareholders] have surrendered the right that the corporation should be operated in their sole interest, — they have released the community from the obligation to protect them to the full extent implied in the doctrine of strict property rights'. From the social enterprise perspective, however, in order to show that the company need not be operated in the shareholders' interests exclusively it is not necessary to establish a 'surrender' by the shareholders of their rights or a functional attentuation of their role, but rather that a policy of profit maximization fails to serve the public interest: see further 265–6 below.

[148] See Easterbrook and Fischel, *The Economic Structure of Corporate Law* (above, n. 99), at 67–8.

maximization in both their own and the social interest. This therefore suggests a unity between the fundamentals of the existing structure of company law and the interests of society, as they have been provisionally defined. Chapter 12 will examine the challenge to the notion that the shareholders are uniquely qualified to be holders of residual rights, and the argument that a form of productive organization in which the trading surplus accrues to the employees rather than the providers of capital is capable of operating no less efficiently, at least as far as the control of shirking is concerned,[149] than the existing corporate form. In the meantime the discussion will largely remain within the shareholder-centred conception of business enterprise, and during the course of the next seven chapters it will be considered whether in practice the mechanisms of shareholder control, particularly against a background of widely dispersed holdings, are adequate to promote satisfactory levels of corporate efficiency.

The Justificatory Force of the Maximization of Social Wealth

In the foregoing discussion the interest of society in the efficient creation of wealth was recognized. If it is assumed that the system of corporate enterprise is the most efficient system for the creation of wealth,[150] should it therefore be concluded that corporate power is legitimate? In other words, does the system's putatively superior wealth generating capacity justify the concentration of decision-making power that is entailed? Putting the question this way makes clear that a justification in terms of wealth relies on a trade-off: corporate decision-making power should be accepted as the price of efficient wealth creation. The point is not that companies are ideal mechanisms for making decisions which have important social effects (in the sense that we would choose them for this purpose, other considerations being equal). Rather, it is that if we want the benefits of efficient wealth creation it must be acknowledged that companies will inevitably possess power.

In order to be persuaded by this justification one would need to be satisfied that the price is worth paying, that is, that alternative arrangements in which power was more widely diffused would not be preferable, even though this might mean that the system produced less wealth overall. This is clearly a matter for moral or political evaluation and can have no objective answer. It is, however, important to be a little clearer about the moral

---

[149] Apart from the question of shirking it is argued that enterprises under worker control will adopt a goal of maximizing the income of current workers rather than of profit maximization, and will accordingly adopt sub-optimal employment and investment policies: see 428–33, below.

[150] A systematic assessment of whether this assumption is valid is beyond the scope of this book (and the capacity of the author). Some consideration will, however, be given to the relative efficiency of worker-controlled enterprises in Ch. 12.

significance of wealth maximization. That the aggregate wealth of society is as high as it can be is of no moral value in itself; what counts is the effect of increases in total wealth on the welfare of the individuals who make up society.[151] The maximization of social wealth is not however the same thing as the maximization of total or average welfare. An economy may be highly efficient, in the sense that goods and services are produced with the minimum of waste and are allocated in accordance with the demand for them, while at the same time the basic needs of many go unsatisfied. What is in issue here is 'demand' that includes an ability to pay, and that is a function of the distribution of wealth. As Veljanovski points out, 'if wealth is concentrated in the hands of a few rich landowners who buy Rolls Royces and caviar, then allocative efficiency will be consistent with the poor starving and the economy's productive capacity channelled into the manufacture of these luxury items. If wealth were distributed more equitably, less Rolls Royces and caviar and more necessities of life would be produced'.[152] The plausibility of a justification of power in terms of wealth cannot therefore be separated from questions about how wealth is distributed. The issue of the legitimacy of corporate enterprise can, however, be saved from being swallowed up in this wider debate if the assumption is made that alternative patterns of distribution can be secured through state action should the prevailing one be considered morally unappealing. In other words the justification for corporate enterprise lies in its ability to create wealth against any given background distribution. If the existing distribution is unsatisfactory that is not an objection to corporate enterprise but results from the failure to rectify distributive injustice. Of course, against this position, it is possible that corporate power is itself a barrier to changes in distribution.[153] Furthermore, corporate capitalism is actually a generator of substantial inequalities in primary incomes, and it is arguable that such inequalities are a precondition for the effective functioning of the system, with the consequence that the scope for redistribution is in practice limited.[154]

A different way of questioning the justification of corporate power in terms

[151] For a discussion of these issues, see R. Dworkin, 'Is Wealth a Value?', (1980) 9 *J of Legal Studies* 191, reprinted in R. Dworkin, *A Matter of Principle* (1985) 237. And see the reply by R. A. Posner, *The Economics of Justice* (1981) 107–15, reprinted as 'Dworkin's Critique of Wealth Maximization', in M. Cohen (ed.), *Ronald Dworkin and Contemporary Jurisprudence* (1984), 238, and Dworkin's response, ibid. 295. See also R. A. Posner, 'Utilitarianism, Economics, and Legal Theory', (1979) 8 *J of Legal Studies* 103, at 119–136; J. L. Coleman, *Markets, Morals and the Law* (1988), at 112. And see J. Rawls, *A Theory of Justice* (1972), e.g. at 71: 'the principle of efficiency cannot serve alone as a conception of justice'.

[152] C. G. Veljanovski, 'The New Law-and-Economics: A Research Review', in A. I. Ogus and C. G. Veljanovski (eds), *Readings in the Economics of Law and Regulation* (1984), 12, at 22.

[153] See 19–21, above.

[154] See R. A. Dahl, *A Preface to Economic Democracy* (above, n. 32), at 102–3; Miller, *Market, State and Community* (above, n. 57), at 14–15.

of wealth maximisation[155] is to argue that at least beyond a certain level of prosperity, increases in wealth do not compensate for, cannot be traded-off against, the accumulation of power. The corollary of the possession of power by companies is that the individuals, interest groups, and communities affected by it suffer a lack of control over the conditions which determine how they live their lives. The power to make decisions that is located within companies could in principle be vested in, or at least shared with, the affected groups. An alternative vision of human flourishing to that which underlies wealth maximization as a social goal ranks autonomy above continued increases in material well-being, and thus calls into question the legitimacy of non-participative organizations. Some of the measures discussed in Chapter 11, designed to induce socially responsible behaviour on the part of companies, involve the empowerment of affected groups *vis-à-vis* the company, and consequently a reduction of corporate power over them. Chapter 12 will consider more comprehensive arrangements for participation in decision making by the group whose interests are most intimately bound up with the company, the employees. More radical demands for participation argue against the legitimacy of the capitalist corporate form altogether. A suggested alternative, the worker-controlled enterprise, will be discussed towards the end of the chapter, and in particular whether worker-controlled firms can be designed in such a way that participation is not bought at the price of rendering the economy as a whole substantially less efficient.

---

[155] There are of course other ways, e.g. the Marxist objection to the exploitation of labour by capital.

2

Ownership, Control, and the Pursuit of Profit

The previous chapter provisionally accepted that it is beneficial for society as a whole that companies should attempt, within the general law, to make the highest possible profits. It assumed that pursuit of that goal is conducive to the maximization of wealth overall: profit maximization leads to the most efficient use of scarce resources and the greatest satisfaction of human wants. The purpose of the present chapter is to examine the threat to the wealth-creating potential of large-scale corporate enterprise resulting from the organizational phenomenon generally referred to as the 'separation of ownership and control'. The response of company law to that threat, and the response that a reformed company law might usefully make, will be considered in succeeding chapters.

I DELEGATION AND THE PROBLEM OF CONTROL

In all but the smallest companies efficiency necessitates the delegation of authority to manage the business to a specialized management team. As noted by the European Commission, efficiency demands that the contributors of capital 'hand over the management of the company's affairs to a smaller group capable of relatively quick and continuous decision making. This also permits the company's affairs to be placed in the hands of those who are equipped with the special abilities and skills which are necessary for effective management and which many shareholders may not themselves possess.'[1]

But while delegation is a prerequisite of corporate efficiency, it also carries with it the risk, common to all agency relationships,[2] that the managers[3] will act in their own interests at the expense of the shareholders, thereby reducing the expected gains, not only for the shareholders but also for society as a

[1] EC *Bull Supp* 8/75, at 16. See also F. H. Easterbrook and D. R. Fischel, 'Corporate Control Transactions', (1982) 91 *Yale L J* 698, at 700.

[2] Technically, the directors are not agents of the shareholders, though they do act as agents of the company. See *Automatic Self-Cleansing Filter Syndicate Co Ltd v Cunninghame* [1906] 2 Ch 34, CA.

[3] The terms 'director', 'manager', and 'management' will be used as equivalents except where the context otherwise requires.

whole.[4] Thus, Eisenberg explains that all agents have a potential interest 'in working at a slack pace and in avoiding the effort and discomfort involved in adapting to changed circumstances, such as the emergence of new technologies. This is the problem known as *shirking*. All agents have a potential interest in diverting the principal's assets to their own use through unfair self-dealing. This is the problem of *traditional conflicts of interest*'.[5] A third problem is what Eisenberg refers to as that of *positional conflicts of interest*. These are conflicts that exist because managers' interests are only indirectly and imperfectly linked to profit maximization, with the result that they are liable to adopt divergent goals more focally connected with increasing the benefits attached to the occupancy of managerial office. The behaviour that pursuit of management self-interest might entail is examined below.

Shirking and the pursuit of managerial goals are generally regarded as forms of behaviour that are socially inefficient, since the former involves the sub-optimal use of resources and the latter, on the assumptions discussed in Chapter 1, produces allocatively inefficient outcomes. Traditional conflicts of interest too are liable to have adverse efficiency effects. The solution to these problems is conventionally seen as lying largely in the oversight function performed by the shareholders. The principal instrument of shareholder control is their power to remove the directors from office. Either through the use of this power, or the background threat of its use, the members are in principle able to induce management to conform to the demands of profit maximization. Company law also assigns to the members the ultimate right to make decisions in certain key areas, for example with regard to changes in the corporate constitution or increases in capital,[6] again in order to ensure that the business is run in accordance with their, and not the directors', interests. Similarly, the directors are bound by a fiduciary duty to advance shareholder welfare, (imperfectly) enforceable by the members.

The idea that compliance with profit maximization should be enforced through shareholder supervision and control lies at the centre of what we will refer to as the 'ownership model' of the company. The model is so

---

    [4] The insight that companies are prone to inefficiency as a result of the management of the business being in the hands of non-owners has a long history: Adam Smith observed that
> The directors of such [joint-stock] companies, however, being the managers rather of other people's money than of their own, it cannot well be expected, that they should watch over it with the same anxious vigilance with which the partners in a private copartnery frequently watch over their own ... Negligence and profusion, therefore, must always prevail, more or less, in the management of the affairs of such a company.
An Inquiry into the Nature and Causes of the Wealth of Nations, book II (1776), at 233. Similar concerns have been voiced by, among others, Marx, Alfred Marshall, and Keynes: see N. J. Mitchell, *The Generous Corporation: A Political Analysis of Economic Power* (1989), at 26–7; M. A. King, *Public Policy and the Corporation* (1977), ch. 2.
    [5] M. A. Eisenberg, 'The Structure of Corporation Law', (1989) 89 *Colum L Rev* 1461, at 1471.
    [6] See further 163–66, below.

named because it describes a mechanism designed to compel managers to act in the shareholders' interests which depends on vesting owner-like rights in the shareholders to appoint, monitor, and replace the most senior tier of management and to make certain other fundamental decisions. A recognition of the failure of this mechanism, consequent on the massive growth in the capitalization of companies in the twentieth century, the corresponding increase in the size of their membership that this growth has required, and the shareholder passivity that inevitably results, underlies much modern company law scholarship. The breakdown of the control apparatus is widely perceived as liberating managers to pursue economically sub-optimal goals, and as causing insufficient pressure to be imposed to promote managerial vigour and to ensure the competence of the management team. A desire to strengthen the disciplinary framework has prompted a search for ways either of restoring integrity to the model or of installing functional equivalents for owner control. With regard to traditional conflicts of interest, which are also liable to be efficiency-reducing, there is little reason to think that the separation of ownership and control has contributed significantly to the scope for management self-dealing, but it does pose problems for the effectiveness of the mechanisms that regulate it, the design of which is premised on shareholder involvement. These issues are considered in Chapter 7.

Before examining the separation of ownership and control and the inefficiency to which it allegedly gives rise, it should be noted that from a different analytical perspective the supposition that the absence of effective shareholder control over management is a problem which existing or improved governance mechanisms might or might not solve appears highly tendentious.[7] Writers with a preference for market over regulatory solutions (whom we will refer to generically as 'market theorists') insist that management and shareholder interests are adequately aligned by market forces, and therefore that the lack of shareholder participation in the internal processes of control need give no cause for concern, and certainly does not indicate the necessity for any kind of external intervention. Supporters of the nexus of contracts model of the company go further, seeking to deprive the 'problem' of weak shareholder control even of its status as a problem, and thereby to legitimate the replacement of control by means of shareholder democracy with control through markets. The failure of the shareholders to behave in an owner-like way is problematical only if they are appropriately categorized as owners. From the nexus of contracts perspective the shareholders are not owners, but simply one of the several parties who make a contract with management to provide a factor of production (in their case, capital) for their common benefit. As economically rational actors, the shareholders will

---

[7] For a discussion of the implications of adopting different models of the company in setting an agenda for the study of company law and surrounding issues, see L. L. Dallas, 'Two Models of Corporate Governance: Beyond Berle and Means', (1988) 22 *U Mich J L Ref* 19, at 27.

ensure that the contract contains the terms necessary to safeguard their interests against management abuse. The resulting 'optimal' control structure finds no place for active shareholder involvement, and hence the fact that the shareholders do not participate is a non-issue. Chapter 6 will return to the contractual model of the company, where the conclusion will be reached that it is dangerously misleading. For the time being, having noted the rival analysis, the issues will be approached through the framework of the traditional model and it will accordingly be assumed for the purposes of analysis that weak owner control at least raises a presumption that there is a problem about the adequacy of management discipline. The following section looks in some detail at its parameters.

II THE SEPARATION OF OWNERSHIP AND CONTROL

Since the publication in 1932 of Berle and Means' study of American capitalism, *The Modern Corporation and Private Property*, it has been the orthodoxy that in the majority of large public companies managements have escaped effective shareholder control. That shareholder control had become severely attentuated was certainly accepted in Britain by 1945. In that year the Cohen Committee succinctly explained how this state of affairs had come about:

The illusory nature of the control theoretically exercised by the shareholders over directors has been accentuated by the dispersion of capital among an increasing number of small shareholders who pay little attention to their investments so long as satisfactory dividends are forthcoming, who lack sufficient time, money and experience to make full use of their rights as occasion arises and who are, in many cases, too numerous and too widely dispersed to be able to organize themselves.[8]

The weakness of shareholder control results, in short, from the 'logic of collective action':[9] while the shareholders as a group would benefit if their rights of control over management were exercised, it is rational for the members individually to remain passive.[10] It is unlikely that voting by a single shareholder will make much difference to the success of a resolution

---

[8] Company Law Amendment Committee, Cmd. 6659 (1945) para 7 (e). The Jenkins Committee reporting in 1962, was of the view that the position was much the same in that year as it had been in 1945, though they considered the description of 'the control theoretically exercised by the shareholders' as 'illusory' to be 'perhaps now something of an overstatement': *Report of the Company Law Committee*, Cmd. 1749 (1962), para 106.

[9] The phrase derives from M. Olson, *The Logic of Collective Action: Public Goods and the Theory of Groups* (2nd ed., 1971). See also D. R. Fischel, 'The Corporate Governance Movement', (1982) 35 *Vand L Rev* 1259, at 1276-8; F. H. Easterbrook and D. R. Fischel, *The Economic Structure of Coporate Law* (1991), at 66-7.

[10] For some empirical support see K. Midgley, *Companies and Their Shareholders—The Uneasy Relationship* (1975), at 37-58, who reports derisory shareholder participation in general meetings and use of other statutory control rights, and CBI, *Pension Fund Investment Management* (1988), at 64-6, noting that more than half the pension funds questioned never or only rarely voted. It

either way, and so it is not worthwhile for shareholders to evaluate proposals put to the general meeting. They will do better either to abstain from voting, or to vote with management as a low-cost 'rule of thumb'. It is true that the shareholders would make an impact if they were to agree to vote in the same way, but this will usually involve the costs of educating and obtaining the cooperation of other shareholders being borne by individual activist members, and these are likely to outweigh the benefits that will be captured by them, since any increase in the value of the company attributable to intervention will be distributed among the shareholders as a whole. The state of shareholder inactivity that results from these factors, it is argued, enables managers to pursue objectives of their own choosing. These are likely to be self-serving, but, in Berle and Means' view, the possibility is also opened up that, rather than furthering their own interests, or those of the shareholders as currently required by law, management might act in the interests of society as a whole, evolving into a 'purely neutral technocracy balancing a variety of claims by various groups in the community and assigning to each a portion of the income stream on the basis of public policy rather than private cupidity'.[11]

This, then, is the outline of the theory of managerial autonomy ('the managerialist thesis').[12] There are a number of variants of the theory, with different positions taken on how managers are likely to use their discretion,

should be noted that shareholders in large, bureaucratically complex organizations face considerable problems in exercising control, quite apart from the separation of ownership and control issue. See Dallas, 'Two Models of Corporate Governance' (above, n. 7), at 21, who observes that 'Berle and Means could have attacked the traditional ownership model by focusing exclusively on the size and complexity of the modern corporation. Responsibility for and control over corporate operations even by an owner-manager is largely attenuated in such a corporation' (footnote omitted). For a consideration of the problem of 'control loss' in large organizations, see D. A. Hay and D. J. Morris, *Industrial Economics and Organization* (2nd ed., 1991), at 285–6.

[11] A. A. Berle and G. C. Means, *The Modern Corporation and Private Property* (rev. ed., 1967), at 312–13. See also A. A. Berle, *The 20th Century Capitalist Revolution* (1954) at 61–115; 164–88. The extent to which this possibility has been realized will be considered in Ch. 9 below.

[12] The idea that economic power is wielded by employed managers rather than by the property-owning class has created problems of assimilation for the Marxist class analysis of society. One solution has been to hold that 'the "owners" and "managers" of the large corporations, taken as a whole, constitute different strata or segments—when they are not merely agents—of the same more or less unified social class': M. Zeitlin, 'Corporate Ownership and Control: The Large Corporation and the Capitalist Class', (1973–4) 79 *Am J Sociology* 1073, at 1078. For evidence of a community of interest between the owners of capital and management, see P. J. Devine et al, *Introduction to Industrial Economics* (4th ed., 1985), at 115–16. For a different view, see R. Dahrendorf, *Class and Class Conflict in an Industrial Society* (1959), who argues that class is defined by the possession of authority rather than by ownership (with the dependence of authority on ownership being a historically bounded phenomenon of industrialization), and see generally J. Scott, *Corporations, Classes and Capitalism* (2nd ed., 1985), at 16–27 and ch. 8. See also H. J. Perkin, *The Rise of Professional Society: England Since 1880* (1989), at 302–3:

Managerialism as a theory has always been resisted by Marxist intellectuals because they fear that it undermines their interpretation of the exploitative nature of industrial capitalism and the egalitarianism of post-revolutionary society. So it does, but not in quite the way they suppose. It certainly changes the exploiters, from the owners of the means of production to the controllers of corporate bureaucracies. To the workers, however, there is no particular

but they share a common structure. This is made up of three propositions. First, dispersal of shareholdings has led to effective control over the company being ceded to management. Second, directors and managers have interests or aspirations which differ from those of the members, and hence their objectives are likely to diverge from the goal of maximizing profits. And third, managements are able to pursue divergent objectives, not only because of lack of shareholder control, but also because of weak competitive conditions. These propositions will now be examined in turn.

The Location of Control

The issue of who controls the company is of fundamental importance, since on it depends, as Herman points out, '[w]hether the profitability goal is preserved, and the intensity with which it is sought'.[13] 'Control' in this context has been defined by most commentators as the ability to appoint the board.[14] Where the board can effectively determine its own composition it has generally been assumed that it becomes immune from direct shareholder influence and hence that control has shifted from the owners to managers. The point is not merely that decisions about the day to day operation of the business or even long-term strategy have been taken out of the shareholders' hands—this is the intended, central advantage of the corporate form—but that the shareholders are no longer able to shape the purpose for which the business is run, that is, they are unable to oblige management to maximize profits.

The Role of the Board

Before examining the evidence on the location of control, a brief digression to clarify the role of the board and its relationship to management may be helpful. The Companies Act provides that companies must have directors[15] but does not define their functions. This is left to the articles, where the almost universal practice is to vest in the board all the powers necessary for the management of the business, bar those reserved by the Act to be exercised by the shareholders in general meeting.[16] From the board powers

gain in being exploited by professional managers rather than by old-fashioned capitalists, and indeed there may well be loss.

[13] E. S. Herman, *Corporate Control, Corporate Power* (1981), at 4.

[14] See e.g. Berle and Means, *The Modern Corporation* (above, n. 11), at 66: 'control lies in the hands of the individual or group who have the actual power to select the board of directors'; Herman, *Corporate Control, Corporate Power* (above, n. 13), at 54: 'the basic question of establishing who has power over key decisions, as a practical matter, revolves ultimately on determining who has the power to name the top executives of the corporation'.

[15] CA 1985, s 282.

[16] See e.g. Table A, art 70. This provides that the shareholders may give the board 'directions' by special resolution, a power which it is extremely unlikely will be used in a company with dispersed shareholdings. The powers vested by the Act in the shareholders are considered in Ch. 6, below at 163–6.

are frequently delegated to committees of directors or to individual board members, and thence down the managerial hierarchy. As to the functions retained by the board itself there is no consistent practice. The Bullock Committee found that

The role of a board varies from company to company and is constantly changing with the requirements of business. It may be related to the size, complexity and nature of the company's operation and therefore to the organizational structure which has been developed over many years. It may depend on the philosophy of management in the company or on the personality of the chief executive.[17]

What is clear is that the scale of a large company's business and the fact that the board meets only periodically, perhaps monthly or even quarterly, mean that it is only the most important decisions that are made at board level.[18] The board will usually have responsibility for long-term strategic planning, for example, concerning investment in new production facilities and products, merging or making a bid for another company, closing down existing plants or pulling out of unprofitable markets. Another important function of the board, at least in theory, is to monitor the performance of senior executives, and also the performance of the company's operating divisions and subsidiaries. The latter, as separate legal entities, are also required to have boards of their own. In some cases these will have only a pro forma existence, with decision-making power lying higher up in the group and the organizational structure bearing little correspondence to the legal one.[19] In other groups subsidiaries or divisions may have a considerable degree of autonomy in operational matters; in these cases the role of the parent board is that of an allocator of capital, rewarding successful operating units with funds for expansion and curtailing or restructuring the activities of those whose performance is weak. Our interest lies chiefly with the main board since it is here that investor pressure or the lack of it has its main significance. Whether

[17] *Report of the Committee of Inquiry on Industrial Democracy*, Cmnd 6706 (1977), at 64–5. And see R. I. Tricker, *Corporate Governance* (1974), ch. 10; A. Demb and F.-F. Neubauer, *The Corporate Board: Confronting the Paradoxes* (1992), esp. at 50–2.

[18] Note also that the extent to which the board constitutes a decision-making forum in its own right has been questioned. A study of the operation of British boards concluded that in practice the role of even the most active boards was largely to act as gate-keepers—evaluating management proposals, letting some through and rejecting others. (Some companies were identified as having entirely non-functioning boards, which at most ratified management decisions and had no effective discretion.) Furthermore, even the gate-keeping function was capable of being subverted through managements' ability to select the information on the basis of which boards make their decisions and by limiting the range of alternative courses of action. These manipulative strategies have the capacity considerably to enhance the power of executive directors and senior management at the expense of the board as a whole. See R. E. Pahl and J. T. Winkler, 'The Economic Elite: Theory and Practice', in P. Stanworth and A Giddens (eds), *Elites and Power in British Society* (1974), 103.

[19] See the *Bullock Committee Report* (above, n. 17), at 65–7; T. Hadden, *The Control of Corporate Groups* (1983), ch. 2; Tricker, *Corporate Governance (above, n. 17), ch. 5*.

managers lower down the hierarchy pursue the profit goal depends in large part on organizational structure and the values imposed from above, though this is not to underestimate the problems of organizational design or the difficulties involved in ensuring compliance with those values.[20]

The main board will normally be made up of a chief executive, who will hold the office of managing director, or possibly chairman, or both, and will include a number of 'heads of department', for example, the finance director, personnel director, technical director, and so on. As well as these full-time directors, most large companies also appoint (usually a minority) of part-time, non-executive directors to their boards. Their function is in general to supplement the skills and experience of the management team, often by bringing a more dispassionate understanding to bear on strategic and operational matters. It is also said that they are able to exercise an element of independent supervision over inside management. In some companies this role has to a degree been formalized through the creation of audit committees made up of non-executives, their function being to review the effectiveness of the company's auditing procedures and to liaise with the auditors. Non-executives may also staff a remuneration committee responsible for top management appointments and for setting the level of their salaries and other benefits.

Chapter 6 will consider the effectiveness of non-executive directors and that discussion will not be duplicated here. We should, however, briefly note that because of their dependence on inside management for their tenure of office, their likely minority position, and the absence of a legal specification of the monitoring function and the powers necessary to perform it, the potential for non-executive directors to exercise meaningful control over the executive members of the board will usually be slight.[21] Furthermore, since the board is dominated by the most senior representatives of management (this term will be used, except where the context requires otherwise, to refer to the executive directors and senior managers) it can hardly be regarded as a body providing independent supervision of management on the shareholders' behalf. The absence of an effective internal mechanism for regulating the conduct of management means, of course, that the inability, if such it be, of the shareholders to exercise effective control is of increased significance. We now turn to consider the extent to which management control is a reality in the modern large company.

Management Control

Berle and Means concluded that 44 per cent of the largest 200 American

---

[20] A little more will be said about organizational structure and its effect on the selection of goals below: see 68–9.

[21] Other 'outside' directors, representing e.g. specific shareholders or providers of loan finance, may have greater influence, dependent on and strengthening that of their sponsor.

corporations were subject to management control in 1929.[22] By 1963 Larner claimed that the figure had risen to 84 per cent,[23] and in his major study conducted in the mid-1970s, Herman found that 82.5 per cent of the top 200 non-financial corporations were controlled by management.[24] In Britain, where the matter has been less extensively researched, Florence reported in 1961 on the basis of data from 1936 that two thirds of the 'very largest' companies were controlled by management and that the tendency towards the dispersal of shareholdings was increasing.[25] However, in a more recent study Nyman and Silberston cast some doubt on the growth of management control, reporting that as high a figure as 56.25 of the top 250 companies in the UK were still controlled by shareholders, and concluding that 'the extent of managerial control is more limited than has been thought and may not have an inexorable tendency to increase.'[26]

The disparity in the results revealed by these and various other surveys is in part accounted for by the use of different definitions of 'owner control'. The percentage shareholding necessary to give control is problematical since, as the degree of dispersal increases, effective control can be exercised with a decreasing proportion of the votes, and certainly with considerably less than the 50 per cent required for a member or members to have the right to remove the board. Berle and Means considered that a member with 20 per cent of the votes would have minority ownership control of the company. Larner set the figure at 10 per cent, and in his later study, with the process of dispersal having become even more marked, Herman acknowledged that a holding of 5 per cent or more 'begins to approach non-negligibility from the standpoint of corporate power'.[27] It has even been suggested that a member

---

[22] Berle and Means, *The Modern Corporation* (above, n. 14), at 109. These findings have been much criticized. See e.g. Zeitlin, 'Corporate Ownership and Control' (above, n. 12), at 1081–2, who claim that Berle and Means 'had information which permitted them to classify as definitely under management control only 22% of the 200 largest corporations, and of the 106 industrials, only 3.8%!'

[23] R. J. Larner, *Management Control and the Large Corporation* (1970), at 21.

[24] Herman, *Corporate Control, Corporate Power* (above, n. 13), at 66. There is also, however, 'an undercurrent of research muddying these social scientific waters': see Mitchell, *The Generous Corporation* (above, n. 4), at 29–35, where a number of studies challenging the dominant view are discussed, and see further below.

[25] P. S. Florence, *Ownership, Control and Success of Large Companies* (1961), at 85. For the evolution of management control in Britain, see L. Hannah, *The Rise of the Corporate Economy* (2nd ed, 1983), ch. 5, and A. D. Chandler, 'The Development of Modern Management Structure in the US and UK', in L. Hannah, *Management Strategy and Business Development* (1976), 24.

[26] S. Nyman and A. Silberston, 'The Ownership and Control of Industry', (1978) 30 *Oxford Economic Papers* 74. See also J. Cubbin and D. Leech, "The Effect of Shareholder Dispersion on the Degree of Control in British Companies: Theory and Measurement', (1983) 93 *Economic Journal* 351. They found that 47 out of a sample of 85 large UK companies were under management control and the rest were owner-controlled.

[27] Herman, *Corporate Control, Corporate Power* (above, n. 13), at 63. Though he does not regard 5 per cent as in itself giving rise to a control position: see 61–2, below.

could exercise control with as little as 1 per cent of the votes. Thus Beed has claimed that 'since ownership is very widely dispersed . . . either it could mean, with Berle and Means, that no one individual or small group could gain sufficient votes for control, *or*, contradicting Berle and Means, that only a few per cent of votes was required for control.'[28] Beed's preference for the latter alternative is, however, misplaced, since as Herman explains, it involves 'a confusion between *who* controls and *how* control is obtained and maintained'.[29] *Management* can exercise control with a very small proportionate holding, but their control does not depend on their ownership stake, but on the position of power that results from executive office. A member with a holding of a similar size will be quite unable to present a credible challenge to the board because in any contested vote the bulk of shareholders who bother to participate can be relied on to support the incumbent management team.

It is clear, however, that whatever percentage holding is regarded as indicating minority control, the figure selected will be somewhat arbitrary. The approach of classifying control on the basis of fixed percentages is, therefore, likely to produce misleading results in some cases. Instead of using a fixed percentage, Cubbin and Leech argue that a shareholder or group of shareholders can be regarded as having control when it is likely that they would win a contested vote, but that this can be determined only by examining the degree of dispersal of shareholdings within the individual company concerned.[30] The results achieved by Cubbin and Leech applying this method were similar overall to those obtained in their parallel study using traditional fixed percentage criteria, but there were different outcomes in respect of a significant number of individual companies within the sample. Nyman and Silberston, while making use of fixed percentages, also insist that the location of control can only be discovered by a case by case approach. They argue that 'for many firms there is an effective locus of control connected with an identifiable group of proprietary interests' which crude statistical tests may fail to reveal.[31] A company may be 'related to other

---

[28] C. S. Beed, 'The Separation of Ownership from Control', (1966) 1 *J Economic Studies* 29, at 32.

[29] Herman, *Corporate Control, Corporate Power* (above, n. 13), at 24–5.

[30] Cubbin and Leech, 'The Effect of Shareholder Dispersion' (above, n. 26), at 355–63. It should be noted, however, that all approaches based on analyses of the structure of shareholding within companies are indirect methods of determining control. They do not prove that a particular group exercises control, but provide the basis for an inference that they do, given the structural position. In order to establish that a group actually exercises control in a given company, it would be necessary to examine the outcome of disputes between groups competing for control. This would, however, produce only a partial picture; where, e.g. management goes unchallenged, this may either be because they have control, making a challenge pointless, or because they are acting consistently with the wishes of a controlling shareholder group. See Nyman and Silberston, 'The Ownership and Control of Industry' (above, n. 26), at 81.

[31] Nyman and Silberston, 'The Ownership and Control of Industry' (above, n. 26), at 80. See also A. Francis, 'Families, Firms and Finance Capital', (1980) 14 *Sociology* 1.

corporations, banks, financial institutions, and family owners via complex patterns of shareholdings, interlocking directorates, and kinship networks'[32] which must be investigated before applying a control classification.[33] Employing this methodology Nyman and Silberston, as already noted, find a significantly higher occurrence of ownership control than is generally assumed.

Scott argues further that insufficient attention has been paid to the potential for collaborative action on the part of shareholders, which he regards as indicating the possibility of a form of ownership control despite the absence of minority holdings large enough in themselves to amount to a control position.[34] The growth of institutional investment is regarded as being of particular significance in this respect. As will be considered further in Chapter 6, the large value of institutional holdings, the comparatively small number of institutions, and their mutual accessibility, make joint action more feasible than it is in the case of individual shareholders. Scott contends that the growth of investment institutions has given rise to a distinct mode of control, namely 'control through a constellation of interests'. This is said to exist where a company has a number of large shareholders who engage in limited cooperation to protect their common interests, but are insufficiently cohesive and lack the necessary coordination to give rise to majority or minority control. He goes so far as to claim that this form of control is now 'characteristic of the majority of enterprises in the USA and Britain',[35] thereby denying the predominance of the management control form. It is suggested, however, that to attribute control to a temporary and unstable alliance of members who intervene spasmodically to defend their interests in the face of emergent threats pays insufficient attention to the circumstances in which power is exercised on a continuous basis. In the absence of a reasonably permanent alliance, the possibility of shareholder collaboration is better understood as limiting management freedom of action, but not as in itself amounting to a control position.

Exaggerating the significance of passive ownership stakes or the potential for collaborative action, sometimes ideologically inspired, is unhelpful, in that it draws attention away from the crucial issues of management motives and competence, and the adequacy of the mechanisms of accountability. From this point of view Herman's approach of adopting a restrictive definition of minority control, but recognizing the importance of sizeable ownership interests as a constraint on management power, is much more attractive.

---

[32] At 78.

[33] See also the company-specific factors taken into account in attributing control by Herman, *Corporate Control, Corporate Power* (above, n. 13), at 304–6.

[34] Scott, *Corporations, Classes and Capitalism* (above, n. 12), chs 2 and 3. It has been suggested that failure to give proper weight to shareholder collaboration, owing to the absence of firm evidence as to its extent, has resulted in serious exaggeration of the extent of management control: see M. Zeitlin, 'Corporate Ownership and Control' (above, n. 12), at 1088–9.

[35] Above at 83.

Herman generally regards a company as under minority control where there is a holding in excess of 10 per cent together with board representation. A large shareholding (for example, the Solvay group's 9.7 per cent stake in Allied Chemical) is not regarded as giving control in the absence of regular participation in management. Rather, it is treated as evidence of latent power, which serves as a constraint on management freedom of action.[36] The result is significantly lower figures for ownership control than with a methodology such as that of Nyman and Silberston, discussed above. The virtue of this control/constraint approach is that, while laying due emphasis on the significance of management power, it also makes clear that management control is not an absolute. Management control does not entail a state of decision-making autonomy, but rather is consistent with the possession of considerable influence by shareholding and other groups. Moreover, as Herman explains, the boundaries between control and constraint are overlapping, since

A constraint is a form of control even if only negative in exercise, as it shapes the decisions made by limiting the scope of choice. In many cases the power of veto is accompanied by the power to consult and a positive say in what is to be done. A constraint also merges into control when it extends to the power to displace the active management. But constraints usually involve power over only one or a narrow range of corporate activities, so that they amount to partial control rather than control over the entire spectrum of major decisions.

He goes on to conclude that in large companies management frequently possesses power over a wide range of decisions, subject to constraints or partial control exercised by others in some decision areas.[37] Thus, by accepting in appropriate cases the existence of management control subject to constraints, the continuing significance of ownership interests can be captured without misrepresenting the nature of ownership involvement in the management process. Precise classification of control type itself then also becomes less important, and attention can be shifted to more fruitful enquiries about the source, scope, and intensity of the factors that constrain management power.

The foregoing discussion has juxtaposed management and owner control, but there is, of course, a range of other influences that set limits to managerial autonomy. Of particular importance are providers of debt finance, who, through powers contained in loan agreement covenants, may prevent the directors from disposing of particular assets, for example, or restrict their ability to raise further debt or to pay dividends.[38] Some writers have also

---

[36] Herman, *Corporate Control, Corporate Power* (above, n. 13), at 21.
[37] Ibid at 19–20.
[38] See R. Sappideen, 'Fiduciary Obligations to Corporate Creditors', [1991] *JBL* 365, at 377–9. For a consideration of the possibilities of creditor intervention to improve managerial efficiency see V. Finch, 'Company Directors: Who Cares about Skill and Care?', (1992) 55 *MLR* 179, at 189–95.

seen financial interests as exercising a more general control over companies, notably through networks of interlocking directorships.[39] Other limiting factors include unions, large customers and suppliers, and government. Again without wishing to underestimate the significance of these and other influences, however, it seems more illuminating to regard them as sources of constraint rather than as contradicting the assumption of management control.

Managerial Motives

The second component of the managerialist thesis holds that because of the weakness of ownership control managers are able to, and do, engage in forms of behaviour that fail to maximize shareholder wealth and which are inefficient from the point of view of society as a whole. As already mentioned, one aspect of this behaviour is 'shirking'—expending insufficient effort to ensure the maximum profitability of the business. It seems intuitively likely that in the absence of effective shareholder control or other forms of external discipline some managers will shirk, though the importance of a sense of professionalism and self-esteem should not be overlooked. The problem generally classified as 'shirking' also extends to incompetence, since, if the shareholders are for practical purposes unable to replace management, the company may suffer from inept leadership quite separately from questions of managerial diligence. The other form of inefficient behaviour that may be attributable to the separation of ownership and control is the pursuit of goals that diverge from profit maximization. What these 'managerial' goals might be requires some elaboration. The discussion here will be confined to self-interested goals; consideration of 'socially responsible' motives will be deferred until Chapter 9, which will conclude that sacrificing profits for socially responsible ends does not occur on a scale sufficient to raise serious doubts about the commitment of managers to profitability (or whatever other, self-interested goals may predominate).

The goals commonly attributed to management, in no particular order, are status, power, salary, and security. It is assumed that these are not linked to profit maximization, but depend on the size of the enterprise. The predominant management goal therefore becomes one of growth, and in particular growth of sales.[40] It should however be noted that while profit

---

[39] For theories of financial control see Herman, *Corporate Control* (above, n. 13), ch. 4; Scott, *Corporations, Classes and Capitalism* (above, n. 12), ch. 4; M. C. Sawyer, *The Economics of Industries and Firms* (2nd ed., 1985), at 172–3. See also R. Minns, *Pension Funds and British Capitalism: The Ownership and Control of Shareholdings* (1980), chs 1 and 2; J. Coakley and L. Harris, *The City of Capital* (1983), at 105–17; T. Schuller, *Age, Capital and Democracy: Member Participation in Pension Scheme Management* (1986), at 95–9.

[40] See R. Marris, *The Economic Theory of 'Managerial' Capitalism* (1964); W. Baumol, *Business Behavior, Value and Growth* (rev. ed., 1966), and see generally Hay and Morris, *Industrial Economics and Organization* (above, n. 10), ch. 9.

maximization is not regarded as a goal, it is accepted in managerial theories that there is a profits constraint, either because a minimum level of profitability is a condition of survival of the enterprise, or necessary to protect management from loss of office through take-over.[41] Furthermore, growth itself is more difficult without a respectable profits record, and conversely in a dynamic economy continuing profitability frequently demands growth. The mutual dependence of profitablity and growth, as we shall see, makes the assessment of management motivation particularly problematical.

The connection of status and power with size, rather than with high profits *per se*, seems fairly self-evident. Prestige is derived from holding executive office in a large, and hence well-known, organization. And the bigger the company is, the more important are the decisions made by its managers likely to be, affecting a greater value of assets and a larger number of employees. The scope for discretionary action may also be increased, given the connection between size and market power.

The existence of a relationship between increased remuneration and profits on the one hand or growth on the other is capable of less impressionistic assessment, and indeed has been subject to detailed research. It should be noted, however, that at best the results can establish only that managers have a reason for pursuing one or other goal, and not that they actually do pursue it. For one thing, if, as will be considered shortly, employment income is in some cases only a small proportion of a manager's return from the company, then even with a significant correlation between remuneration and growth the growth motive might be cancelled out.[42] For another, the overall effect depends on the relative importance of income and other motives as determinants of management behaviour: a positive relationship between income and profitability may not counteract a growth motive inspired by a quest for prestige or security. Even with these reservations, in fact no very clear picture emerges from the studies.[43] Two British ones agree

[41] See e.g. Marris, ibid.

[42] Similarly, managerial labour-market implications must be taken into account, e.g. if a manager improves his 'marketability' by increasing company profits, this may counter the incentive towards growth: see further Ch. 4 below. The 'neoclassical' explanation of income determination also argues against a growth motivation. This explanation postulates that

managers vary in ability, with that of a particular manager fixed and easily ascertained, and the more able the manager the higher the income he can command. Managers with more ability are required for larger firms because of the greater problems involved in running a larger firm. Then we would expect to observe a positive association between managerial income and firm size. But this would not create incentives to the manager to increase the size of the firm. For if the size of the firm increases, the degree of managerial ability required increases and the present manager is replaced by a more able and more highly paid manager.

Sawyer, *The Economics of Industries and Firms* (above, n. 40), at 179 and 183. See also Herman, *Corporate Control, Corporate Power* (above, n. 13), at 96-8.

[43] See Herman, ibid. at 96-8; Sawyer, ibid. at 179-85; Hay and Morris, *Industrial Economics* (above, n. 10), at 299-302.

that both profitability *and* size affect remuneration, one finding size to be the major determinant,[44] the other that profitability was at least as significant as growth.[45] The results of the American surveys are also equivocal.[46] The most recent British survey on the other hand concludes that directors' pay is strongly correlated with corporate growth, such that a 50 per cent increase in sales leads to a 10 per cent increase in remuneration.[47]

The argument that size and security are related has taken two forms. The first is that the risk of insolvency diminishes with increased size. Coffee has argued that this is evident particularly in the case of conglomerates, with growth being attributable to the desire of managers to reduce the risk of collapse by diversification.[48] He posits a difference in the attitude to risk on the part of management on the one hand and shareholders on the other, the former being much more averse to risk than the latter, given the effect of insolvency on managers' jobs and on the value of their shareholdings in the company (which often constitute a considerable proportion of their total wealth), together with the possibility of personal liability in the event of winding up. The shareholders, in contrast, at least as far as large and sophisticated investors are concerned, have no interest in increased diversification *within* the firm, since they will already have spread the risk associated with investment in a particular company or industry by holding a diversified portfolio. Under the influence of excessive aversion to risk managers are liable to cause the firm to grow to an inefficient size and to engage in other forms of behaviour which are sub-optimal from the shareholders' point of view, such as making low dividend payouts and an inadequate use of the company's borrowing capacity. Coffee regards risk aversion as being responsible for the construction of bloated, inefficient mega-firms in the

---

[44] A. Cosh, 'The Remuneration of Chief Executives in the United Kingdom', (1975) 85 *Econ J* 75.

[45] G. Meeks and G. Whittington, 'Directors' Pay, Growth and Profitability', (1975) 24 *J Ind Econ* 1.

[46] Herman, *Corporate Control, Corporate Power* (above, n. 13), at 96–8, suggests that the different outcomes depend, at least in part, on the width of the definition of income. Where unearned income, i.e. dividends and capital gains on shares, is included, it is more likely that income will correlate to profits rather than size: 'it is possible that compensation narrowly defined is primarily related to size, or growth in size, whereas compensation extended to include owner-based income of management is primarily related to profitability.'

[47] P. Gregg, S. Machin, and S. Szcmanski, *The Disappearing Relationship Between Directors' Pay and Corporate Performance*, LSE Centre for Economic Performance Working Paper no 282 (1992), at 8. See also M. C. Jensen and K. J. Murphy, 'Performance Pay and Top Management Incentives', (1990) 98 *J Pol Econ* 225, indicating a low correspondence between pay and company performance.

[48] J. C. Coffee, 'Shareholders Versus Managers: The Strain in the Corporate Web', in J. C. Coffee, L. Lowenstein, and S. Rose-Ackerman (eds), *Knights, Raiders, and Targets* (1988), 77. See also A. Shleifer and R. W. Vishny, 'Value Maximization and the Acquisition Process', (Winter 1988) 2 *J Econ Persp* 7.

1960s,[49] in turn creating the setting for the wave of 'bust-up' take-overs of the late 1980s. As he points out, the difference between the asset value and the depressed share price of the conglomerates concerned gave bidders an opportunity to make a profit by disposing of ill-fitting activities or otherwise increasing efficiency by reducing the scale of operations (though in fact the record of take-overs in increasing efficiency is mixed and not all take-overs are explicable as moves to reduce inefficiency in the target).[50] This reasoning seems plausible, though it is also possible that policies which, as it turned out, led to non-profitable growth, might at least in some cases be accounted for simply as failed experiments in increasing profitability. Furthermore, the extent to which the underlying cause of inefficient diversification should be attributed to growth inspired by risk aversion, as opposed to growth resulting from other managerialist motives, is unclear.

The other possible connection between growth and security is that large size offers a degree of protection from hostile take-overs and hence against loss of office. There is some empirical support for the proposition that the likelihood of attack decreases with size.[51] As just mentioned, however, there may in some cases be an offsetting increased risk of take-over as a result of unprofitable growth causing a depression in share price. Assessing the magnitude of these conflicting variables and their impact on management motivation is clearly problematical.

An alternative (though partially overlapping) motivation to that of growth is Williamson's concept of 'expense preference'.[52] The idea is that managers derive utility from spending the company's funds to an extent beyond that necessary for profit maximization. They thus obtain status and other 'psychological' benefits at the shareholders' expense, and increase their rewards from office in a more tax-efficient way than through regular remuneration. The types of behaviour to which this motivation is said to lead include employing a larger staff than is required for the purposes of the business, lavish expenditure on office accommodation, transport, and various forms of entertainment, and on image-building (but not cost-justified) advertising, and charitable giving. Casual observation gives grounds for suspicion that excessive spending under these heads does take place, though establishing definitively the absence of an underlying profit justification is obviously difficult.[53]

A different approach to management motivation from that considered so

[49] On which see M. E. Porter, 'From Competitive Advantage to Economic Strategy', (May-June 1987) *Harv Bus Rev* 43, at 45.

[50] See Ch. 4 below.

[51] See 128 below.

[52] O. E. Williamson, *The Economics of Discretionary Behavior: Management Objectives in a Theory of the Firm* (1964).

[53] For a rigorous treatment of expense preference and other non-profit-maximizing models of the firm, see Hay and Morris, *Industrial Economics* (above, n. 10), at 317–24.

far is adopted by the behavioural school, whose members insist that it is inappropriate to regard the company as engaging in maximizing behaviour of any kind, be the end to be maximized profits on the one hand, or growth, or some other determinant of management utility, on the other. Simon argues that as a result of 'bounded rationality' individuals do not maximize, but 'satisfice'.[54] This behaviour has two facets. Because of the vast range of the information potentially bearing on a decision individuals do not attempt to collect and assess all of it before deciding, but settle for a more manageable sample. Further, rather than engage in an extended search for the maximizing solution, they follow a truncated search process, accepting a solution which produces a merely satisfactory outcome. When attention moves from behaviour at the individual to the organizational level, it is argued that since organizations are not unitary actors, but are made up of individuals and groups with competing interests and objectives, companies cannot be understood as pursuing a single goal, but rather a range of conflicting goals.[55] Company behaviour must then be understood as the outcome of a continuous bargaining process whereby management attempts to meet the demands of the various interests within the organization. Compromises are possible, among other reasons, because objectives are expressed in satisficing rather than maximizing terms, and by making use of organizational slack. The latter idea is that organizations have spare capacity that can be brought into play so as to enable the company to comply with the demands of one group without requiring a damaging transfer from another.[56] The validity of the behaviouralist analysis and the impact of the conduct it portrays on profitability is uncertain. As Scherer concludes, 'we know far too little about the methods of goal formation and conflict resolution within large organizations. What *is* clear is that business managers are pulled in many directions and that they must and do make choices among alternative objectives'.[57]

The Continuing Pull of Profits

We have so far considered reasons why the interests of managers may not be best served by pursuing the goal of profit maximization. There are, however, other factors that suggest that management and shareholder interests are more closely aligned than the managerialist thesis assumes. One concerns the proportion of a manager's income that is derived from holding shares in the company in comparison with the proportion that depends on being an

[54] H. A. Simon, 'Theories of Decision-Making in Economic and Behavioral Sciences', (1959) 49 *Am Econ Rev* 253.

[55] R. A. Cyert and J. G. March, *A Behavioral Theory of the Firm* (1963). And see Devine et al. *Introduction to Industrial Economics* (above, n. 12), at 119–22; Hay and Morris, *Industrial Economics* (above, n. 10), at 288–92.

[56] See F. M. Scherer, *Industrial Market Structure and Economic Performance* (2nd ed., 1980), at 34–5.

[57] Ibid. at 34 (emphasis in original).

employee. Research conducted in the United States discovered that for the top five executives from a sample of 50 of the largest companies three times as much income came from shares as from employment.[58] As Hay and Morris point out, 'with regard to managerial objectives, it [may be] less important what proportion of a company's shares is owned by the management, but much more vital what proportion of the managers' remuneration depends on stocks and shares'.[59] Another factor that may bring the position of managers closer to that of the shareholders is the use of performance-related pay and share-option schemes. But while such inducements presumably have some positive effect, later discussion will note that management control over their terms casts doubt on the extent to which they secure an identity of interests with shareholders. There is a danger that they may create pressures for short-term increases in accounting profits or merely permit management to extract for themselves an increased proportion of company revenues.[60] The other market incentives/deterrents that might be expected to align management and shareholder interests will be briefly noted at the end of this chapter and examined in some detail in Chapter 4.

A different factor to which great significance has been ascribed in maintaining the pre-eminence of the profit objective is the evolution of the multi-divisional ('M-form') enterprise, which is the form of organization now adopted by the bulk of large companies in the UK.[61] In the traditional unitary form ('U-form') enterprise, the business is organized as a single unit with administrative functions, such as production planning, sales, and personnel, centralized in a head office. As the organization grows there will be a partial delegation of these functions to branches, but because the business is still run as a single unit (even though it may produce a wide variety of products at many separate locations) responsibility for operational matters, as well as long-term strategy, remains with top management. Such an organizational structure entails long chains of command, with the consequence that there is great potential for the distortion of instructions from senior managers as they pass down the hierarchy. Effective monitoring of compliance with instructions and control of sub-goals are also inhibited. In the M-form enterprise, in contrast, the company is organized into separate

[58] W. Lewellyn, 'Management and Ownership in the Large Firm', (1969) 24 *J Finance* 316, at 320, concluding that '[a] separation of ownership and management *functions* clearly exists; it seems that a significant separation of their pecuniary interest does not.'

[59] Hay and Morris, *Industrial Economics* (above, n. 10), at 300. Cf. Eisenberg, 'The Structure of Corporation Law' (above, n. 5), at 1493–5.

[60] See 114–16 and 221–6 below.

[61] By 1970, 72 per cent of the largest 100 manufacturing companies had adopted the M-form structure: D. F. Channon, *Strategy and Structure of British Enterprise* (1973), at 236. The relevant work on organizational structure is associated with A. D. Chandler, *Strategy and Structure: Chapters in the History of American Industrial Enterprise* (1962), and O. E. Williamson, 'Managerial Discretion, Organisational Form, and the Multi-division Hypothesis', in R. Marris and A. Wood (eds), *The Corporate Economy* (1971) 343.

product divisions, each with responsibility for many of the administrative operations formerly performed by the head office and its sub-offices. This enables each division to be treated as a separate profit centre, facilitating 'the imposition of standardized financial goals on the various divisions, in place of ad hoc evaluations of the performance of noncomparable functional parts'.[62] The chief significance of this from the 'separation of ownership and control' viewpoint is that it is said to restore 'integrity to the goal-specification and policing process'[63] that is lost through the attenuation of shareholder control. Indeed, superior control might be obtainable because 'control is now internal and by informed managers rather than external and by uninformed shareholders.'[64] Two objections, however, may be made to this reasoning. First, while tighter control over operating units and the exclusion of sub-goals may be achieved, it is not self-evident that the M-form organization will affect pursuit of divergent objectives at the level of top management, though Williamson does suggest that formalized goal and capital allocation procedures educe 'a profit preference at the top as well.'[65] Second, it may underestimate the capacity of lower-level managers to transmit upwards inaccurate or self-serving information, particularly when they have the advantage of technical expertise not possessed by the head office.[66] By exaggerating operating difficulties or temporary adverse market conditions, for instance, managers can shape board decision-making, providing some leverage against the imposition of rigorous profit-maximizing targets, or may attract funds for divisional growth to a greater extent than is justified by the profit potential.

A final pro-profit influence is what Herman describes as the 'subtle ideological impact' of ownership.[67] The suggestion is that profitability is the pervasive criterion of success, providing the standard for self-assessment and for judgements of management performance made within the company and

---

[62] Herman, *Corporate Control, Corporate Power* (above, n. 13), at 105.

[63] Williamson, 'Managerial Discretion' (above, n. 61), at 370.

[64] Hay and Morris, *Industrial Economics* (above, n. 10), at 309.

[65] Williamson, 'Managerial Discretion' (above, n. 61), at 380.

[66] See Pahl and Winkler, 'The Economic Elite' (above, n. 18). And e.g. B. W. E. Alford, 'The Chandler Thesis—Some General Observations', in L. Hannah, *Management Strategy and Business Development* (1976), at 55:

> although on the face of it McGowan [the chief executive] exercised dictatorial control over [ICI] he admitted to knowing little about technical matters and was, therefore, usually willing to assent to projects wrapped up in technical language; and even though at any given time McGowan imposed overall limits on expenditure, in many cases these limits would have been substantially pre-determined by previous technical commitments.

For a consideration of the possibility that central financial control leads to a stifling of worthwhile investment opportunities because of lack of operational knowledge at the centre, see P. Marsh, *Short-termism on Trial* (1990), at 60–3. For a review of the evidence on the comparative performance of M-form and other types of organization see Hay and Morris, *Industrial Economics* (above, n. 10), at 310–311.

[67] Herman, *Corporate Control, Corporate Power* (above, n. 13), at 102. See also J. Fidler, *The British Business Elite: Its Attitudes to Class, Status and Power* (1981), at 119.

in the business community as a whole. It is not inconsistent with this interpretation that managerialist goals are sometimes pursued, but it argues that such conduct should be seen as aberrant behaviour, contrary to the dominant management culture. As against this view, however, Jensen and Murphy suggest with some plausibility that

there are strong political and organizational forces that tend to define success in dimensions other than shareholder wealth and exert pressures for actions that reduce firm value. Managerial conformance to pressure to maintain employment, peace with unions, or major contributions to communities by keeping unprofitable plants open can easily become synonomous with success.[68]

Here, as elsewhere, therefore, no conclusive view of the relative importance of potential motives seems possible.

Market Constraints

The final ingredient of the managerialist thesis is the absence of strong competitive pressure. Lack of competition is a prerequisite for the survival of inefficient managements and the pursuit of non-profit objectives, since without some degree of monopoly power failure to maximize profits would in the long run lead to collapse. Chapter 1 noted that competitive conditions in many product markets are such that they are likely to be tolerant of managerial ineffectiveness and in some substantial deviations from the profit goal will not be incompatible with enterprise survival. Over the past two decades, however, market theorists, accepting the oligopolistic character of the product markets in which many companies operate, have elaborated theories that locate the company and management within other markets which, they argue, exert a more powerful disciplinary effect. It is held that the market for corporate control in particular enables shareholders to set strict performance standards on management, not, in the terms of Hirschmann's much-quoted distinction, through 'voice' (through the company's internal control mechanisms), but through 'exit' (selling their shares).[69] In order to avoid repetition, description and evaluation of these theories is mainly postponed until Chapter 4. For the moment it is sufficient to note that while the managerialist picture of management discretion unbounded by market pressures is unquestionably a serious distortion, the more extreme claims made for the constraining power of these additional markets also give rise to considerable doubts.

---

[68] M. C. Jensen and K. J. Murphy, 'Performance Pay and Top-Management Incentives', (1990) 98 *J Pol Econ* 225, at 252.

[69] A. O. Hirschman, *Exit, Voice and Loyalty: Responses to Decline in Firms, Organisations and States* (1970).

Conclusion

The consideration of the consequences of the separation of ownership and control in this section has inevitably been somewhat impressionistic. There is, however, no shortage of studies attempting to assess the impact of weak owner control on company performance. Many of these have involved a comparison of rates of return on equity in owner- and management-controlled companies. Herman refers to 14 such studies, but notes that the results are inconsistent, with nine of them finding that owner-controlled companies performed better than those subject to management control.[70] The inconsistency of the results is partly accounted for by the different methods used for adjusting for other variables, such as disparities in size and monopoly power between control types,[71] but clearly these studies do not bring a definitive answer much closer. Similarly inconclusive are studies that have attempted to evaluate the managerialist hypothesis through surveys of management attitudes based on questionnaires. Of the two British studies, neither finds strong support for the managerialist view,[72] but this is perhaps unsurprising given that there is likely to be an under-reporting of what respondents consider will be perceived as deviant behaviour. There may also be a degree of self-deception, or at least lack of clarity, on the crucial issue of the distinction between means and ends: is growth seen as a means to long-term profitability, or are profits required as a precondition of growth?

Whatever the evidence, there is undoubtedly a widespread belief that the absence of effective supervision of management is an important factor (though by no means the only one) in the weak performance of the British (and the American) economy as compared with those particularly of Germany and Japan, where management accountability is not in general regarded as a problem.[73] This chapter has suggested that in the majority of large public companies the separation of ownership and control is a reality, and that this opens up the possibility that in some of them, subject to the variable constraining influence of market forces, managements will pursue deviant goals and/or shirk. In others, even though managers may be conscientious and committed to furthering the interests of the members, weak shareholder control may ensure the survival of boards which are incompetent or simply

[70] Herman, *Corporate Control, Corporate Power* (above, n. 13), at 111–2. His own study, relying on more recent data, supported the five studies which discovered no such superiority.

[71] See Scherer, *Industrial Market Structure* (above, n. 56), at 38–41. The results may also reflect other characteristics which distinguish owner- and manager-controlled companies. E.g. Herman, *Corporate Control, Corporate Power* (above, n. 13), at 107–8, speculates that well-informed owners may gradually dispose of interests in companies with an unpromising future, with the effect of disproportionately increasing the number of 'has beens' in the management-controlled sector.

[72] See Fidler, *The British Business Elite* (above, n. 67), ch. 5; A. Francis, 'Company Objectives, Managerial Motivations and the Behaviour of Large Firms: an Empirical Test of the Theory of "Managerial" Capitalism', (1980) 4 *Cambridge J Econ* 349.

[73] See 170–2 below.

just 'average'. Of course, it need not be supposed that management control has detrimental effects in all companies, since that would be to ignore the significance of management values, and in any case the extent to which managers benefit from pursuing non-profit goals is unclear. In short, while accepting that no conclusive view on the effects of the separation of ownership and control is possible, it is important to enquire what contribution the law and structural reform might make to closing the disciplinary gap. Such an inquiry is undertaken in the next four chapters.

3

The Legal Control of Management Discretion

Chapter 2 considered how shareholder passivity in large public companies with widely dispersed shareholdings creates the possibility that managers will pursue self-interested ends, divergent from the goal of profit maximization. This chapter will examine the role of law in overcoming that problem through the imposition of legal duties which limit the purposes for which managerial discretion may legitimately be exercised. The relevant duty is the duty to act bona fide for the benefit of the company. Chapter 4 will describe and evaluate the legal response to shirking and managerial incompetence, the other problems we have assumed to be exacerbated by the separation of ownership and control, by way of the duty to exercise diligence, care, and skill. Chapter 4 will also examine the impact of market mechanisms on those problems, a discussion which is relevant as well to the control of management goals under consideration in this chapter. A third duty bearing on the consequences of the separation of ownership and control, the duty to act for a proper purpose, is the subject of Chapter 5. That duty plays an important, indirect, role in shaping corporate objectives and in imposing pressure for high quality performance by protecting from management interference the company's governance structure and the operation of the market for corporate control. Chapter 6 will consider the control of managerial discretion through the mechanisms of shareholder democracy, the possible revitalization of those mechanisms as a result of increasing institutional dominance, and the merits of governance reform.

The control of managerial discretion by means of legal duties (sometimes hereafter called 'duty-based controls') relies ultimately on the use of an external agency, the courts, to monitor management conduct. Two important issues arise from this reliance. The first, which is one of the main concerns of this chapter, and a recurrent concern of the rest of the book, is with the role and effectiveness of rule-based standards, and judicial monitoring of compliance with them, as a technique for shaping management behaviour. The second issue relates to the mechanisms by which management conduct is brought before the courts for review. Frequent judicial intervention is not essential for duty-based controls to be effective, and would if it took place prove extremely costly, but it is necessary that there be a realistic prospect of enforcement. Whether or not a suit is brought mainly depends on the shareholders, but the collective action problem which underlies the separation of ownership and control also militates against shareholder participation in enforcement proceedings. The question of enforcement is the subject of Chapter 8. The remainder of this chapter is divided into two sections. The first will examine the way in which the law has defined the ends for which the directors must exercise their powers. The second will consider the effectiveness of the law as a control technique in holding directors to the ends so specified.

I THE CONTENT OF THE DUTY TO ACT BONA FIDE FOR THE BENEFIT OF THE COMPANY

The Legal Model

A distinction should be drawn first of all between limits on the discretion of the directors that result from the company's objects clause, and limits that depend on fiduciary duties. As to the former, the objects clause in the company's memorandum of association sets out the activities for which the company has been formed, though these activities may subsequently be altered by special resolution.[1] As a result of changes effected by the Companies Act 1989[2] the objects clause no longer limits the company's capacity, or at least, the validity of an act may no longer be 'called into question on the ground of lack of capacity'.[3] The right of shareholders to restrain directors from entering into transactions that fall outside the company's objects is preserved, however, and the directors remain liable to the company for any loss that may result from entering into such transactions,[4] and to that extent the doctrine of *ultra vires* survives. Furthermore, the objects clause continues to limit the directors' authority (as distinct from the company's capacity), though this will only affect a third party who is not in good faith, a requirement which is generously defined.[5] The objects clause is of little relevance to the containment of conduct inspired by self-interested 'managerial' motives. The activities specified in it invariably extend to virtually every conceivable form of business, and so no basis is provided, for example, for restricting the ability of the company to diversify. And so long as a transaction falls within the scope of an activity set out in the objects

---

[1] CA 1985, s 4.
[2] CA 1989, s 108, inserting ss 35–35B into CA 1985.
[3] CA 1985, s 35 (1).
[4] CA 1985, ss 35 (2) and (3), respectively.
[5] See CA 1985, s 35A (2)(b); as well as knowing that the directors are exceeding their powers, to be in bad faith it would seem that the third party must know that the transaction is contrary to the company's interests.

clause ('manufacturing', 'property development', and so on) it will be authorized. The purpose for which the transaction is entered into, be it to secure the maximum contribution to profits or to further some divergent managerial interest, is not an issue that arises as far as questions of authorization are concerned. The *ultra vires* doctrine has, on the other hand, been used to curtail management 'generosity' to non-shareholder groups in the form of gratuitous payments. There is a substantial overlap here with the fiduciary controls and so this issue will be considered below, and in more detail in Chapter 9, where the extent to which the legal rules are tolerant of expenditure for 'socially responsible' purposes will be examined.

The fiduciary controls on managerial discretion provide that it is the duty of the directors to act in the interests of the shareholders. This coincides with the view provisionally adopted in Chapter 1 about how the *public* interest is best served. It is not suggested however that directors' duties, which are largely of judicial creation, are shaped by a theory that regards the purpose of the company and company law as being to further the public interest; it is not suggested that the 'social enterprise' perspective has influenced the development of the law.[6] Rather, the focus on shareholder interests results from a private conception of the company and company law. The underlying theory views the shareholders as having an entitlement that the company be operated for their benefit (or for whatever other purposes they may choose)[7] by virtue of their position as members or owners. The law respects the right of the shareholders to determine the objectives of their association through contract and accepts that by virtue of their capital contributions they should be regarded as the owners of the company. By reason of their ownership rights, and given the 'traditional logic of ownership',[8] it is taken that the shareholders are entitled to have the company run in their interests: it is *their*

---

[6] i.e. it is not suggested that the objective of social wealth maximization is an operative consideration within company law or in the reasoning of the courts. Cf. the claims of descriptive law and economics, e.g. to the effect that legal rules in general 'tend to look as though they were chosen with a view to maximizing social wealth (economic output as measured by price) by judges subscribing to a certain set of ("microeconomic") theoretical principles': F. I. Michelman, 'A Comment on Some Uses and Abuses of Economics in Law', (1979) 46 *U Chi L Rev* 307, at 308.

[7] The corporate form is, e.g., used by charities. For a consideration of the effect on the content of directors' duties of the presence of non-commercial objects in the objects clause of an otherwise commercial company, see 278–9, below.

[8] See A. A. Berle and G. C. Means, *The Modern Corporation and Private Property* (1932, rev. ed. 1967), at 294, who go on to explain that

the stockholder in the corporation has posed both as the owner of the corporation and the owner of its assets. He was removed slightly from legal ownership of the assets in that he did not have legal 'title' to them—that was vested in the corporation; but collectively the stockholders, through their participations were entitled to the whole of any corporate profits which could be made. The corporation was theirs, to be operated for their benefit.

For the view that shareholders should not be regarded as owners, but as parties to a 'nexus of contracts', see 177–90, below.

company.[9] This conception of the company as a private association will be referred to as the 'legal model'.[10] In recent years the model's exclusive focus on shareholder interests has to an uncertain degree been modified. The main objective of the following discussion is to ascertain the extent to which the duty of the directors *is* to maximize profits, and hence is consonant with the putative social interest in profit maximization. This demands an examination of how the courts have interpreted shareholder interests, and a consideration of the theoretical and practical consequences of the modifications to the model.

The Interests of the Company

The standard formulation of the duty of the directors in running the business is expressed not in terms of benefiting the members, but of benefiting the company.[11] This does not, however, mean that the directors must use their powers to promote the welfare of the legal entity,[12] though technically the duty is *owed* to the entity (this has important implications for enforceability).[13] A requirement to benefit an artificial entity, *as an end in itself*, would be irrational and futile, since a non-real entity is incapable of experiencing well-being.[14] Indeed, it is doubtful that an inanimate entity can meaningfully be

---

[9] It was argued in Ch. 1 above that ownership rights do not of themselves justify the shareholders' favoured position. For the view that an object of company law is to confer legitimacy on companies see M. Stokes, 'Company Law and Legal Theory', in W. Twining (ed.), *Legal Theory and Common Law*, (1986), 155, and for a detailed discussion of the legitimating role of company law from a Critical Legal Studies perspective see G. E. Frug, 'The Ideology of Bureaucracy in American Law', (1984) 97 *Harv L Rev* 1276, especially at 1279–86: '[legal theories] comprise ... a series of assurances that the legal system can overcome the perennial concerns about bureaucratic organizations' (at 1284). The object in this book is not to lay bare the legitimating role of law, but to discover whether good reasons exist for regarding companies as legitimate social forms and to consider how their behaviour might best be made to conform with the general interest.

[10] Although the distinction is not pressed in the text in order to avoid unnecessary complexity, this term has a different meaning from the 'ownership model' introduced at the beginning of the chapter. The latter is a normative device: it states how managers should be controlled (by shareholder governance) and the rights that shareholders should have in order to perform a governance function. The legal model on the other hand is a descriptive model, in that it describes the content of directors' duties, regarding that content as flowing from the premise of shareholder ownership.

[11] See, for example, *Re Smith & Fawcett Ltd* [1942] Ch 304, at 306.

[12] Cf. *Re Halt Garage Ltd* [1982] 3 All ER 1016, at 1035; *Dawson International PLC v Coats Paton PLC* [1989] BCLC 233, Ct Sess; R. Instone, 'The Duty of Directors', [1979] *JBL* 221; F. G. Rixon, 'Competing Interests and Conflicting Principles: An Examination of the Power of Alteration of Articles of Association', (1986) 49 *MLR* 446; J. D. Heydon, 'Directors' Duties and the Company's Interests', in P. D. Finn (ed.), *Equity and Commercial Relationships* (1987), 120; L. S. Sealy, '"Bona Fides" and "Proper Purposes" in Corporate Decisions', (1989) 15 *Mon L R* 265, at 270.

[13] See Ch. 8 below.

[14] See P. L. Davies and Lord Wedderburn of Charlton, 'The Land of Industrial Democracy', [1977] *ILJ* 197, at 199.

said to have interests, or if it could, what they would be. Is it in the interests of a corporate entity to be as profitable as possible, for example, or very large, or socially responsible? Given that these questions seem incapable of being answered, it would be impossible to assign any definite content to a duty framed in terms of benefiting the enterprise as such. This becomes feasible only when the purpose of the enterprise is taken into account, and the enterprise's purpose can be understood only in terms of serving human interests or objectives.[15] The correct position is thus that the corporate entity is a vehicle[16] for benefiting the interests of a specified group or groups. These interests the law has traditionally defined as the interests of the shareholders.[17] The duty of management can accordingly be stated as a duty to promote the success of the business venture, *in order* to benefit the members.

For the most part, what is good for the business will also be good for the shareholders and so speaking of a duty to benefit the business will often be accurate enough. It is important, however, to stress the instrumental character of the prosperity of the business as far as the shareholders are concerned, since otherwise a discontinuity between the 'enterprise interest' and the interests of the shareholders is liable to be concealed. That the welfare of the shareholders and the fate of the company are not coextensive is evident in the situation that arises where a take-over bid is made for the company.[18] With the offer price necessarily in excess of current market value a member's best course may be to sell, depending on an estimation of what

[15] It is difficult, in the light of this, to make sense of the proposal of the New Zealand Law Commission to establish a statutory hierarchy of interests, with a fundamental, overriding duty to act 'in the best interests of the company', with 'the company' being equated with 'the enterprise itself': *Company Law Reform and Restatement*, Report No 9 (1989), para 194.

[16] See *Brady v Brady* [1988] BCLC 20, CA, at 40: '[t]he interests of a company, an artificial person, cannot be distinguished from the interests of the persons who are interested in it': per Nourse L J. An earlier, though now too simplistic, way of looking at the matter was to regard 'the company' simply as a synonym for 'the members'; e.g. L. S. Sealy notes that: 'in the Victorian lawyer's eyes "the company" was regarded as the associated members rather than the legal entity: the company was "they" and not "it"'': 'Directors' "Wider" Responsibilities— Problems Conceptual, Practical and Procedural, (1987) 13 *Mon L R* 164, at 165. See also P. Ireland, I. Grigg-Spall, and D. Kelly, 'The Conceptual Foundations of Modern Company Law' in P. Fitzpatrick and A. Hunt (eds), *Critical Legal Studies* (1987) 149, at 150–1.

[17] See *Greenhalgh v Arderne Cinemas Ltd* [1951] Ch 286, CA, at 291, [1950] 2 ALL ER 1120, at 1126, where Evershed MR states that 'the phrase "the company as a whole" does not (at least in such a case as the present) mean the company as a commercial entity as distinct from the corporators.' This was in the context of an exercise of shareholder voting power in general meeting, but it is widely accepted as equally applicable to the duty of directors: see, e.g. *Parke v Daily News Ltd* [1962] Ch 927, at 963, [1962] 2 All ER 929 at 948. See also *Kinsela v Russell Kinsela Pty Ltd* (1986) 10 ACLR 395, CA, NSW, at 401: 'the proprietary interests of the shareholders entitle them as a general body to be regarded as the company when questions of the duty of directors arise', per Street C J. For a consideration of the effect of CA 1985, s 309 (duty to have regard to the interests of employees), see 82–7, below.

[18] Another example is where it would be in the interests of the shareholders for the company to be liquidated rather than continue in business. Presumably, a duty to act in the interests of the enterprise would involve an obligation to ensure its survival.

the company's future performance under existing management is likely to be and the possibility of a higher offer. It is of no concern to a member who does sell[19] (at least from a financial point of view) that the bidder, having gained control, may go on to operate the company less efficiently than the previous management or in some other way that is damaging to its business. The law recognizes that the shareholders' interest lies ultimately in the value of their shares and not in the business as such,[20] or at least, it recognizes that it should be the shareholders who determine the outcome of a bid, and hence (as we shall see in more detail in Chapter 5) prohibits certain forms of defensive action on the part of the target company board which could have the effect of depriving the members of an opportunity to dispose of their investment on favourable terms. This is regardless of the character of the bidder or the possibly depressing prospects for the company under the new management.[21] A duty founded on exclusive shareholder benefit affords no protection to management action designed to avoid such damage to the business.

Of course, a rule permitting the directors to defend the company from a poorly managed predator would be perfectly coherent (and might be desirable),[22] but this would not be because the entity has an intrinsic significance that merits protection, but rather because the rule would serve the rational purpose of protecting the interests of groups other than the shareholders who

[19] Shareholders who stay on as a minority will suffer if the company is subsequently mismanaged, but the law, consistent with the principle of majority rule, gives precedence to the majority's wishes: in the words of Lord Wilberforce in *Howard Smith Ltd v Ampol Petroleum Ltd* [1974] AC 821, PC, at 837–8, [1974] 1 All ER 1126, at 1136: 'the right to dispose of shares at a given price is essentially an individual right to be exercised on individual decision and on which a majority, in the absence of oppression or similar impropriety, is entitled to prevail.' See also *Heron International Ltd v Grade* [1983] BCLC 244, CA, per Lawton L J at 265: 'The directors owe no duty to the successful bidder or to the company after it has passed under the control of the successful bidder. The successful bidder can look after himself, and the shareholders who reject the bid and remain as shareholders do so with their eyes open ...' The shareholders who remain will, of course, have the benefit of the usual minority protection remedies, and in addition members who do not accept an offer have a limited opportunity subsequently to change their minds and sell to the bidder on the same terms as other members: CA 1985, s 430A. A successful bidder also has limited rights to buy out a dissenting minority: CA 1985, s 429.

[20] Though it should be stressed that the shareholders do not have an individual right to compensation where otherwise actionable management conduct causes the value of their shares to fall: *Prudential Assurance Co Ltd v Newman Industries Ltd (No 2)* [1982] Ch 204, CA, at 222–4, [1982] 1 All ER 354, at 366–7; cf. *Heron International Ltd v Lord Grade* (above, n. 19).

[21] Cf. *Cayne v Global Natural Resources PLC* (unrept. 1987), discussed 153–4, below. And see *Dawson International v Coats Paton* (above, n. 12) which appears to envisage a separate entity interest. Lord Cullen, at 8, holds:

I do not accept as a general proposition that a company can have no interest in the change of identity of its shareholders on a take-over. It appears to me that there will be cases in which its agents, the directors, will see the take-over of its shares by a particular bidder as beneficial to the company. For example, it may provide the opportunity for integrating operations or obtaining additional resources. In other cases the directors will see a particular bid as not in the best interests of the company.

[22] See Ch. 5, below.

would be adversely affected by a change in control. These groups might include, for instance, the company's employees, customers, or suppliers. Defensive measures might also be justifiable as being for the good of society as a whole (i.e. because society has an interest in the efficient operation of the business that might be damaged if the company is taken over). A duty to act in the interests of the enterprise could, therefore, be understood as a duty to protect the business for the benefit of those groups, in addition to the shareholders, whose interests are likely to be affected by its success. If the success of the business is equated here with commercial success, it should be noted that while this might permit defensive action in a take-over context, it would otherwise have little impact on the content of directors' duties. Furtherance of the company's commercial success will nearly always be in the interests of the shareholders, but the conduct it will sometimes require, for example, plant closures or the use of environmentally damaging production processes, will often be harmful to other affected groups.[23] A duty to act in the interests of the enterprise could however permit trade-offs between the interests of affected groups if the duty were understood rather differently as a duty to benefit a range of corporate 'constituencies', permitting the directors to balance the various interests as they see fit.[24] But expressing such a duty as a duty to further the interests of the enterprise would be unhelpful, since the formulation has very limited information content: it fails to identify the relevant constituencies and gives no indication of what priority should be given to them *inter se*. These issues will be considered again later in the book. For the moment it is sufficient to note that, while various different meanings can be imputed to a duty to act in the interests of the enterprise, they all require reference to underlying human interests. Historically the legal model has excluded all non-ownership interests,[25] and 'enterprise' formulations are

---

[23] See O. Kahn-Freund, 'Industrial Democracy', (1977) 6 *ILJ* 65, at 76–7.

[24] See C. M. Schmitthoff, 'Employee Participation and the Theory of Enterprise', [1975] *JBL* 265; Sealy, 'Directors' "Wider" Responsibilities' (above, n. 16), at 174; F. Kübler, 'Dual Loyalty of Labor Representatives', in K. J. Hopt and G. Teubner (eds), *Corporate Governance and Directors' Liabilities* (1985) 429, at 439–41; R. R. Drury and P. G. Xuereb (eds), *European Company Laws: A Comparative Approach* (1991), at 8–15 and generally.

[25] Though it may be noted that the protection afforded to shareholder interests by fiduciary duties is imperfect. This is evident in the rule that the directors are at liberty to issue shares at a price below their market value, thus diluting the value of the holdings of existing members: see *Hilder v Dexter* [1902] AC 474, HL; *Lowry v Consolidated African Selection Trust Ltd* [1940] AC 648, HL, but see Lord Wright's dissenting speech at 679 (and a remedy for unfair prejudice may also be available pursuant to CA 1985, 459). Such a ruling would be impossible if directors' duties were unequivocally predicated on shareholder welfare: see A. A. Berle's classic article, 'Corporate Powers as Powers in Trust', (1931) 44 *Harv L Rev* 1049. The situation where shares are issued at a discount on market value to outsiders is distinguishable from that where they are issued to a section of the existing members. The issue in the latter case is one of fairness between different groups of members rather than of a failure to respect the interests of the owners as a class, and differential treatment is thus more consistent with the legal model: see e.g. *Mutual Life Insurance Co of New York v The Rank Organisation Ltd* [1985] BCLC 11. The problem of dilution has now been partially addressed by statutory rights of pre-emption. These were introduced by CA 1980

in any event a less than ideal way of broadening the scope of management duties.

Present and Future Members

It is often suggested that 'the members' as the beneficiaries of directors' duties means 'the present and *future* members'.[26] It is difficult, however, to see why the directors should have to take account of the interests of the as yet unidentifiable persons who might acquire shares in the company at some future date. Such an obligation would be particularly hard to justify, given that those who join in the future will do so on financial terms that reflect the company's situation at the time they acquire their shares. The point is of some significance because a duty to balance the interests of present and future members would involve an expansion of the directors' discretion, in effect, allowing them to justify their actions by reference to the well-being of the enterprise even though they are contrary to the interests of the existing members.[27] It is surely more consistent with the legal model to hold, not

(though were already required by Stock Exchange rules), pursuant to the EEC Second Directive; see now CA 1985, ss 89–96. The dilution issue still creates periodic friction between managements and institutional investors, however, arising from the desire of the former to issue shares by private placement (see e.g. the *Financial Times*, 18 April 1987, regarding the proposed placements by Fisons and Barclays). This involves an offer to a small group of investors, often clients of the company's merchant bank. Raising equity by this method reduces the company's transaction costs, but tends to involve a transfer in value from existing members to placees: see C. C. P. Wolff, 'Pre-emptive Rights versus Alternative Methods of Raising Equity on the London Stock Exchange', (1986) 80 *Investment Analyst* 3. For the latest guidelines setting limits to the proportion of a company's equity that the institutions are prepared to tolerate being issued free of pre-emption rights, and the size of permissible discounts, see the *Financial Times*, 22 October 1987.

[26] The advice of counsel to the directors in the Savoy Hotel affair, referred to by the inspector appointed by the Board of Trade to investigate it, is frequently cited in support of this view: see the Board of Trade, *The Savoy Hotel Ltd and The Berkeley Hotel Company Ltd: Investigation under Section 165(b) of the Companies Act 1948: The Report of E Milner Holland QC* (1954), and see L. C. B. Gower, 'Corporate Control: the Battle for the Berkeley', (1955) 68 *Harv L Rev* 1176. The directors had reorganized the company to make it impossible for a future controller to change the use or dispose of a hotel that the company owned. This conduct can be classified as a breach of duty either by reference to the 'proper purpose' doctrine (see below, Ch. 5), or because of the adverse effect on the value of the *current* shareholders' investment resulting from the company being deprived of the ability to control the hotel's destiny. It is quite unnecessary to rely on the adverse effect on the interests of future shareholders as a ground of decision. See also *Heron International Ltd v Lord Grade* (above, n. 19), at 265; S. Lofthouse, 'Competition Policies as Take-Over Defences' [1984] *JBL* 320, at 324; C. Baxter, 'The True Spirit of *Foss v Harbottle*' (1987) 38 *NILQ* 6, at 25, n. 79. Cf. *Gaiman v National Association for Mental Health* [1971] Ch 317, at 330; *Dawson International PLC v Coats Paton PLC* (above, n. 12), at 243.

[27] Berle and Means, *The Modern Corporation and Private Property* (above, n. 8), at 295, warn of the consequences. Thus (writing of the United States), sometimes 'the courts, shielding themselves behind a consideration of the advantage of the "corporation as a whole", have overlooked the fact that apparent advantage to the mythical corporate entity may mean staggering loss to its separate owners; and that it is often necessary to trace *what group within the corporation* receives the ultimate advantage' (emphasis in original).

that the directors must take account of the interests of future shareholders, but rather that they have a discretion concerning the time-scale over which existing members may be benefited. The directors are accordingly not obliged to maximize current profits in order to satisfy short-term demands for dividends at the expense of a growth in profitability over a longer period. They are entitled, in other words, to regard the members' interest in the company as being in general a continuing one.[28]

The Exclusivity of the Members' Interests

The effect of the duty introduced in the Companies Act 1980 to have regard to the interests of the company's employees, and of certain recent decisions in relation to creditors, will be examined in a moment. These developments aside, the legal model has traditionally regarded the shareholders' interests as exclusive, in the sense that other groups may be benefited only to the extent that this furthers the interests of the members. Thus the interests of employees, customers, or the local community, for example, may be served only as a means of increasing shareholder wealth and may not be treated as ends in their own right. The directors may, for instance, make gifts to the employees, but only where this can be regarded as 'an inducement to them to exert themselves in future, or as an act done reasonably for the purpose of getting the greatest profit from the business'.[29] A graphic illustration of the purely instrumental status of employee interests can be found in the American case of *Dodge v Ford Motor Co*.[30] There Ford's management (dominated by Henry Ford) declared that they proposed to limit dividends in order to lower the price of cars and increase employment, so as to spread 'the benefits of this industrial system to help [the employees] build up their lives and their homes'.[31] Such a policy, the court held, was improper, since a

business corporation is organized and carried on primarily for the profit of the stockholders. The powers of the directors are to be employed to that end. The discretion of directors is to be exercised in the choice of means to attain that end, and does not extend to a change in the end itself, to the reduction of profits, or to the nondistribution of profits among stockholders in order to devote them to other purposes.[32]

But while promoting non-shareholder interests is not a permissible management objective, the (limited) satisfaction of third party expectations is often a

---

[28] Whether the members' short- and long-term interests conflict in any case is considered below at 89–92.

[29] Per Cotton L J, *Hutton v West Cork Railway Company* (1883) 23 Ch 654, CA, at 666. See also *Hampson v Price's Patent Candle Company* (1876) 45 LJ Ch 437.

[30] 170 N W 668 (1919).

[31] Ibid. at 683.

[32] Ibid. at 684.

prerequisite of maximizing profits, and hence consideration of them is not precluded by the legal model.[33] A company will be adversely affected if it suffers from low employee morale, for example. Similarly, a reputation for inflicting environmental damage will be harmful to profits, and conversely the company may be benefited if it is associated in the public mind with 'good works'. Given an objective of long-term profit maximization, it is evident that a broad range of concessions to third party interests that do not promise immediate financial returns may be advisable, and therefore that managers must be allowed considerable scope for discretion in such matters.[34] That the propriety of expenditure is premised on the possibility of an eventual return to the shareholders is, however, made starkly apparent in a number of cases concerning companies that are ceasing to trade. In this situation, the basis on which 'altruistic' acts can normally be supported, their putative contribution to long-term profits, no longer obtains.[35]

The Interests of Employees: Section 309 of the Companies Act

Section 309(1) of the Companies Act 1985 provides that 'The matters to which the directors of the company are to have regard in the performance of their functions include the interests of the company's employees in general, as well as the interests of its members.' What effect does this have on the legal model? The section is open to at least two interpretations. According to the more ambitious it is now the duty of the directors to operate the business in the interests of the employees in addition to those of the members. If this is so, the legal model of the company as so far described needs to be rejected in favour of one which does not explain the rules of company law exclusively in terms of the rights of owners, but which instead regards members and employees as joint stakeholders, each with legitimate demands that the company be run for their benefit. Clearly, there is a substantial community of interest between shareholders and employees. Improvements in the prosperity of the company that lead to higher dividends or rising share values may also result in increased wages and job security. But there is inevitably also a conflict of interests. Each of the groups has an obvious, competing, interest in maximizing its share of the surplus generated by the company's business activity. And there is also a potential conflict in respect of the way the surplus is generated, and its size. Shareholders have an interest in profits being as high as they can be. The employees would prefer profits to be lower if maximizing them involves plant closures or the introduction of job-destroying

---

[33] For a more detailed consideration of this issue see Ch. 9 below.

[34] In practice the discretion is difficult to police, and hence management, if so minded, will frequently be able to benefit third parties even though there is not even the prospect of a long-run return to the company: see Ch. 9 below.

[35] *Hutton v West Cork Railway Company* (above, n. 29); *Parke v Daily News Ltd* (above, n. 17). As regards gratuitous payments to employees the situation is modified by CA 1985, s 719 (see below).

technology. Since employee interests will not always be best served by a policy of profit maximization, it is follows that section 309, on this first interpretation, will sometimes require, or at least permit, management behaviour to diverge from that which in Chapter 1 was *provisionally* accepted as best serving the general interest.

The argument in support of this interpretation is that section 309 changes the definition of 'the interests of the company'—it adds the employees to the shareholders as the persons whose interests the directors are required to serve. The section gives no indication that the interests of employees and shareholders are to be given a different weighting, and hence the duty of the directors in running the company would appear to one of balancing the respective interests.[36] Even if this interpretation is correct, however, the section is not likely to have very much effect on the way companies operate in practice. This is because, first, the duty would appear to be effectively unenforceable. Section 309(2) provides that the duty is owed 'to the company (and the company alone) and is enforceable in the same way as any other fiduciary duty owed to a company by its directors'. In other words, an action complaining of breach of the duty must be brought by the company (i.e. by the directors whose conduct is being challenged). In certain circumstances proceedings for breach of other fiduciary duties may be commenced by a member on the company's behalf in derivative form.[37] This raises the possibility of an employee with a shareholding being allowed to enforce the section 309 duty derivatively. Fitting such a claim into the requirements for a derivative action would, however, demand greater judicial creativity than can perhaps in the circumstances be realistically expected.[38]

[36] The Committee of Inquiry on Industrial Democracy (the Bullock Committee) which advocated a section similar to the one eventually enacted seems to have regarded this as being its effect: *Report* Cmnd. 6076 (1977), paras 38–40. And see Davies and Wedderburn, 'The Land of Industrial Democracy' (above, n. 14) at 198–203. The crucial difference, of course, is that Bullock intended the section as complementary to the appointment of employee directors: see further Ch. 12 below.

[37] See Ch. 8 below.

[38] It would presumably be necessary to establish that the breach is unratifiable and that there was 'wrongdoer control' (see Ch. 8 below). In that the duty is for the protection of employees it is conceivable that breach of it might be held to be incapable of ratification by the shareholders: see *Fulham Football Club Ltd v Cabra Estates* [1992] BCC 863, CA. There is also an analogy here with the apparent non-ratifiability of certain breaches which are damaging to creditors: see below. As to 'wrongdoer control' it is not at all clear what meaning should be given to this requirement in a context which is quite different from the one in which it has been developed. Presumably, non-employee shareholders would not be regarded as wrongdoers simply by virtue of benefiting from the impugned act; if they were, a company with a majority of non-employee members would always be under wrongdoer control for these purposes. If the requirement is merely that there be an absence of a majority sufficiently independent of the putatively wrongdoing management to enable a 'proper' decision about the merits of bringing an action to be made, then it would be unlikely that the requirement would ever be satisfied. And as Sealy, 'Directors' "Wider" Responsibilities' (above, n. 16), at 184, has pointed out, recent rulings 'effectively bar any derivative action that does not have the approval of a majority of shareholders other than those who are defendants' (i.e. *Taylor v NUM* (*Derbyshire Area*) [1985] BCLC 237; *Smith v Croft* (*No 2*) [1988] Ch 114, [1987] BCLC 355).

The second reason for regarding the section as likely to have only a limited impact is that the relevant duty, like the duty to act bona fide for the benefit of the company, is a subjective one.[39] The directors must act in accordance with what they believe to be an appropriate balancing of the sometimes conflicting interests, but the court cannot intervene merely because it disagrees with the way in which the directors have weighted those interests. The court cannot, in other words, review the substantive merits of the directors' decision. This means that a management policy that is injurious to employee interests can be attacked only on the grounds that the directors lacked good faith, meaning that the directors did not honestly believe that the policy constitutes an appropriate balancing of interests, or that they have altogether disregarded the impact of their decision on the employees. The prospects for establishing bad faith are very limited, however, given that virtually any policy that is premised on increasing profits but which will be damaging to employees, such as a plant closure, can be portrayed as being beneficial to the employees in general, for example, by making other jobs in the company more secure, thus supporting the claim that employee interests have been sufficiently considered.

The effect of the section on this first analysis is, therefore, despite its mandatory language, to give the directors a *discretion* to act in the interests of the employees where they consider it appropriate in preference to those of the shareholders; they do not have a practicably enforceable obligation to further employee interests. Another way of putting it, and this may be the section's true significance, is that the section provides the directors with a defence in the event of their making a decision that favours the employees at the shareholders' expense. In that the directors are often likely to be better disposed to the workforce than are the shareholders this may be of some practical importance. In general, however, the pressures on management are orientated towards shareholder rather than employee welfare. The fact that the directors' discretion is not reviewable, therefore, means in short that the section is likely to have little causative impact: it does not compel the directors to do anything they would not otherwise have been inclined to do.[40]

According to the second interpretation even this may substantially overstate the effect of the section. One of the leading practitioner's texts on company law, Gore-Browne, argues that while the directors are now required to take employee interests into account, they are never permitted to subordinate the shareholders' interests to them. This view is supported on the basis that the section does not affect the definition of 'the interests of the company', which continues to mean 'the interests of the company as a

---

[39] See 93–4, below.
[40] Cf. P. G. Xuereb, 'The Juridification of Industrial Relations Through Company Law Reform', (1988) 51 *MLR* 156.

commercial entity as judged by reference to the interests of the shareholders'.[41] Thus in deciding, for example, whether to close down an unprofitable factory and make those working in it redundant, the directors are required to consider the effect of closure on the employees, but they are nevertheless under a duty to shut the factory if they believe this to be in the interests of the shareholders. On this interpretation, 'having regard' to the interests of employees means literally that. The duty is merely a procedural one, having no substantive content. This does not perhaps leave the section totally without point, in that by directing the board to consider the employees it might expand the cognitive basis of decision-making and so might on occasion lead to a superior accommodation of employee interests within the traditional framework of shareholder supremacy. But it is difficult to believe that directors do not give at least some consideration to the impact of their decisions on employees in any event, regardless of the section.[42]

It is not clear which of the two analyses the court would adopt in a case in which there was a clash between shareholder and employee interests, and there was evidence that the board had favoured the latter.[43] The decision of the Court of Appeal in *Fulham Football Club Ltd v Cabra Estates*[44] provides some support for the first view. The main issue in the case was whether the directors had improperly fettered their discretion by giving an undertaking as part of a commercial transaction to support a planning application affecting the company's land. It was held that the directors had not acted in breach of duty in giving the undertaking, but the court went on to hold, without giving detailed consideration to the issue, that if the directors had acted improperly it would have made no difference that the agreement into which the company had entered enjoyed the unanimous assent of the shareholders. The court observed that 'the company is more than just the sum total of its members. Creditors, both present and potential, are interested, while section 309 of the Companies Act 1985 imposes a specific duty on directors to have regard to the company's employees in general.'[45]

This suggests that the court considered that section 309 expands the meaning of 'the company as a whole', in keeping with the first analysis. For reasons suggested above, this is unlikely to have much impact on management behaviour, though as the case itself demonstrates, the conclusion that section

[41] A. J. Boyle, *Gore-Browne on Companies* (44th ed, 1986), paras 27.4. and 27.4.1.

[42] L. S. Sealy, 'Directors' "Wider" Responsibilities' (above, n. 16), at 177, has described the section as 'either one of the most incompetent or one of the most cynical pieces of drafting on record'.

[43] In *Re a Company, ex p Burr* [1992] BCLC 724, at 734, an application under CA 1985, s 459, Vinelott J held that the directors were entitled, in deciding to acquire new premises in the company's current neighbourhood, to take account of the interests of the employees in retaining their jobs, but there was no evidence that the interests of the shareholders were thereby prejudiced. *Re Welfab Engineers Ltd* [1990] BCLC 833 is similarly inconclusive.

[44] See above, n. 38.

[45] Ibid. at 876.

309 modifies the legal model has additional technical implications. As well as being unable to regularize a fettering of directors' powers, it is conceivable that the shareholders would no longer be competent to authorize or ratify any other breach of duty that might adversely affect the employees, for example, a breach of the duty of care. Further, the restrictions on management action taken to defend the company against take-over, discussed in Chapter 5, which are predicated on a model of the company in which only the shareholders' interests count, becomes questionable if the directors also have an obligation to safeguard employee interests. Whether the court would be inclined to apply the reasoning in *Fulham Football Club* after a more detailed consideration of the implications is, however, unclear. An ambiguously worded provision, patently lacking adequate means of enforcement, may be too slender a ground on which to anticipate that the courts would sanction a derogation from the ownership rights of the shareholders, lying as they do at the foundation of the legal model of the company.

Chapter 11 will consider proposals to extend further the list of groups whose interests management should consider in running the company, with a view to limiting the harmful effect of corporate activities on them.[46] The present discussion of section 309 exposes the difficulties inherent in such a strategy. An objective duty to balance potentially conflicting interests would present the courts with a near-impossible task and hence it is impracticable to impose one: not only would the court need to assess the likely impact on each group of a contested business policy, in both the short and long term, but also it would have to evaluate the policy in accordance with a theory which stipulated when one set of interests should prevail over the others. Even if the courts had the resources to perform the first of these tasks, the latter involves value judgements of a kind inappropriate to the judicial function. If the duty is framed in subjective terms, as we have seen, the practical effect is not to impose a duty but to confer a discretion and hence a management which is not disposed to sacrifice profits (or otherwise depart from its chosen course) in order to advance other interests will not be compelled to alter its behaviour. It seems to follow that if an objective of changing corporate policy is to be effective it will be necessary to look further than the modification of directors' duties, though this is not to say that some form of modification of duties would not be needed as well.

Before leaving employees, a limited situation in which it is permissible for the directors to give priority to the interests of employees should be noted. The Companies Act empowers a company to make payments to employees or former employees on the cessation or transfer of the business (in effect, voluntary redundancy payments), notwithstanding that the exercise of this power is not 'in the best interests of the company'.[47] This provision overcomes the difficulty mentioned above that where a company is ceasing to trade there is no justifying rationale for such payments because there is no future flow of profits that present 'generosity' to employees might help increase.[48] Consent of the shareholders by ordinary resolution is required, unless the articles permit the board to sanction payments without shareholder approval, or provide that a resolution passed by more than a simple majority of shareholders must be obtained. The requirement for shareholder consent, either by resolution or, formally, by their consent to the delegation of final decision-making power to the board, maintains the surface integrity of the legal model based on shareholder ownership, though certainly at least in the latter case, shareholder consent is more hypothetical than real.

The Interests of the Creditors

A number of English and Commonwealth decisions have recognized a duty (owed to the company) to take account of the interests of creditors where the company is insolvent or on the verge of insolvency.[49] The decisions mainly concern the situation where creditors' interests have been prejudiced as a result of a gratuitous or non-commercial transfer of the company's assets to a director or to some person with whom the directors are connected. On the facts of most (though not all) of them breach of duty could have been established on the conventional ground that the directors had failed to act in good faith for the benefit of the company.[50] Their main significance is that, by predicating the breach on damage to the interests of creditors and thus expanding the corporate constituency, it no longer automatically follows that the breach should be ratifiable by the shareholders. This is of practical importance, particularly in the case of closely held companies or wholly-owned subsidiaries where the conduct complained of may well have received unanimous shareholder assent, which would otherwise have the effect of regularizing the transaction and hence preventing the liquidator from taking remedial action in the absence of some other ground of attack. The notion of a duty to respect creditor interests gives rise to a number of conceptual and

---

[47] CA 1985, s 719. See also Insolvency Act 1986, s 187 (payments by liquidator).

[48] The section overcomes the difficulty that payments might not be sanctioned by the company's objects clause, with the result *inter alia* that a shareholder could obtain an injunction to prevent a payment from being made; see CA 1985, s 35(2). Even with that problem overcome, a gratuitous payment to employees in these circumstances would still be a breach of fiduciary duty, hence the stipulation that the power may be exercised 'notwithstanding that its exercise is not in the best interests of the company' (s 719(2)).

[49] See e.g. *Walker v Wimborne* (1976) 137 CLR 1, H Ct of Australia; *Nicholson v Permakraft (NZ) Ltd* [1985] 1 NZLR 242, CA, NZ; *Kinsela v Russell Kinsela Pty Ltd* (above, n. 17); *Re Horsley & Weight Ltd* [1982] Ch 442, CA, [1982] 3 All ER 1045; *Winkworth v Edward Baron Development Co Ltd* [1986] 1WLR 1512, HL, [1987] 1 All ER 114; *Brady v Brady* [1988] BCLC 20, CA, at 40, reversed on different grounds, [1989] AC 755, [1988] BCLC 579, HL; *West Mercia Safetywear Ltd v Dodd* [1988] BCLC 250, CA.

[50] See Sealy, 'Directors' "Wider" Responsibilities' (above, n. 16), at 172.

practical difficulties (e.g. should present and future creditors be afforded different protection?).[51] These issues will not be pursued further here, however, since in addition to the limitation of the duty to cases of insolvency or near-insolvency, the authorities as they stand do not suggest a need for behaviour at variance with the demands of profit maximization.[52] A *duty of care* founded on creditor interests, in contrast, if held to exist while the company is solvent might in theory constrain the pursuit of maximum profits, since it is in the interests of creditors that the company should undertake low-risk, but sub-profit-maximizing projects, given an entitlement to a fixed return. The existence of such a duty has, however, been denied by the Court of Appeal[53] and any development in that direction seems unlikely.[54]

The Interests of the Members and Profit Maximization

It is possible that some of a company's shareholders will have interests, for example, as employees or customers, that are distinct from their investment interest in the business. Others, while having a relationship with the company only in the capacity of member, might prefer the directors to take account of such issues as the environmental or social consequences of the company's activities, and where there is a conflict to modify the profit instinct accordingly. Some may even consider that the company has positive obligations to secure the well-being of employees, the local community, or other non-shareholder groups. Thus, although the legal model may prevent directors from regarding third party interests as ends in their own right, it is arguable that it is consistent with the directors' obligations to the shareholders for the company to sacrifice profits in order to protect them, given these possible relationships with shareholder utility. The problem with such a view is that, as between the members in general, the various non-profit interests and aspirations are likely to conflict and members will undoubtedly differ in the extent to which they are prepared to forego profits in order to see them fulfilled.[55] It would be impossible, therefore, to construct a rule that would

---

[51] See Sealy, ibid. at 176–82; see also R. Grantham, 'The Judicial Extension of Directors' Duties to Creditors', [1991] *JBL* 1; D. A. Wishart, 'Models and Theories of Directors' Duties to Creditors', (1991) 14 *NZULR* 323.

[52] This is not to deny that there are various ways in which shareholder and creditor interests may conflict: see R. Sappideen, 'Fiduciary Obligations to Corporate Creditors', [1991] *JBL* 365, at 367–72.

[53] *Multinational Gas and Petrochemical Co Ltd v Multinational Gas and Petrochemical Services Ltd* [1983] Ch 258, CA, [1983] BCLC 461; cf. *Nicholson v Permakraft* (above, n. 49), at 249, where Cooke J contemplated a duty owed directly to creditors in tort.

[54] See Sealy, 'Directors' 'Wider Responsibilities'' (above, n. 16), at 181.

[55] The interests of institutional shareholders are, as a matter of law, likely to be construed as purely financial, given the duties of their trustees/managers to the beneficiaries/investors: see *Cowan v Scargill* [1985] Ch 270, [1984] 2 All ER 750; on the position of charitable trusts, see

frame the ambit of management discretion in such a way as to ensure that
the members' varying expectations were uniformly satisfied. The only
practicable alternative, of allowing the directors themselves to decide when a
departure from the profit goal is justified, would involve a substantial
abandonment of the duty-based control mechanism and would offer no
guarantee that *any* member would be satisfied with the particular balance of
interests that the directors might choose to strike.[56] While this issue has not
been expressly considered, it seems fair to assume that, rather than incur the
risks inherent in giving the board so wide a discretion, and relying on the
usually well-founded assumption that the shareholders' dominant purpose is
to increase their individual wealth,[57] the court, at the price of some distortion,
would define the interests of the members exclusively in terms of their
personal financial well-being.[58]

The Maximization of Shareholder Wealth

To summarize the position so far, it would seem, subject to whatever the
correct interpretation of section 309 may be, and except where the company
is insolvent or on the verge of insolvency, that the directors are required to
further the interests of the shareholders exclusively, and that those interests
should be defined purely in financial terms. The law does not provide any
more specific guidance however on how the furtherance of the shareholders'

Harries v Church Commissioners for England [1993] 2 All ER 225. On 'ethical investment' see 376–7
below.

[56] The abandonment need not, however, be total: see 371 below.

[57] This idea is captured in the formulation 'the members as a whole in their capacity as
associated persons': see H. A. J. Ford, *Principles of Company Law* (4th ed., 1986), para 1507,
quoted in Sealy, 'Directors' "Wider" Responsibilities' (above, n. 16), at 166. A company is free
to state in its objects clause that it also has non-commercial objectives: see *Re Horsley & Weight
Ltd* (above, n. 47), and 278–9, below. From the failure to specify non-commercial aims it
might be inferred that the members' interests should be understood in purely financial terms.

[58] In *Cowan v Scargill* (above, n. 53) at 761, in the context of the scope of the discretion of
pension fund trustees, Sir Robert Megarry V-C explained that

> the benefit of the beneficiaries which a trustee must make his paramount concern [does not]
> inevitably and solely [mean] their financial benefit, even if the only object of the trust is to
> provide financial benefits. Thus if the only actual or potential beneficiaries of a trust are all
> adults with very strict views on moral and social matters, condemning all forms of alcohol,
> tobacco and popular entertainment, as well as armaments, I can well understand that it
> might not be for the 'benefit' of such beneficiaries to know that they are obtaining rather
> larger financial returns under the trust by reason of investments in those activities than they
> would have received if the trustees had invested the trust funds in other investments. The
> beneficiaries might well consider that it was far better to receive less than to receive more
> money from what they consider to be evil and tainted sources. 'Benefit' is a word with a very
> wide meaning, and there are circumstances in which arrangements which work to the
> financial disadvantage of a beneficiary may yet be for his benefit.

He goes on to state, however, that these circumstances will be rare. This will clearly be the case
if the test is that *all* the beneficiaries must share the relevant moral views. Applied to a
company, with a multitude of shareholders, it is inconceivable that this requirement would be
met and hence the presumption that the members' interests are exclusively financial would
never be displaced.

financial interests should be understood. The standard formulation of the proper objective of management in the economics literature is that managers should seek to maximize the value of the firm, that is, the value of the residual after all fixed claims, such as those of the providers of loan finance and of employees, have been met. This corresponds with the concept of profit maximization that has so far been employed above, save that the latter concept contains an ambiguity about time-scale: it does not specify the period over which profits are to be maximized. A goal of *short-term* profit maximization implies conduct different in important respects from that required by a *long-term* profit goal. Long-term profitability may depend on investing in research and development, capital equipment, and training, for example, expenditure which will be avoided where the objective is to maximize profits only in the short term.

Maximizing the value of the firm, on the other hand, does not entail any kind of trade-off between short- and long-term profits, since it is assumed that the firm's *present* value will reflect the *future* proceeds of current investment. Thus the value of the firm is equal to the total value of its expected future stream of cash flows, discounted to take account of the 'time value of money' ('a pound tomorrow is worth less than a pound today') and risk. It follows that undertaking an investment project that will produce only a delayed return may nevertheless contribute to the maximization of the firm's present value. That maximizing the present value of the firm will in practice also maximize shareholder wealth depends on the validity of certain assumptions about the efficiency of the stock market ('the efficient market hypothesis'). The hypothesis holds that the stock market takes account of all relevant information in valuing a company's shares, with the result that the underlying realities of the company's business are fully reflected in share price.[59] The company's expenditure on training, for example, should have an impact on the price at which its shares are currently traded. Maximizing present value ought, furthermore, at least in theory, to serve the interests of all shareholders, notwithstanding that some shareholders might have preferences for high dividend payouts rather than capital growth.[60] Since maximizing the value of the firm will have the effect of maximizing the value of each member's holdings, members with a demand for income need simply sell a proportion of their now more valuable shares in order to unlock their investment.[61] Of course, if no value-increasing projects are available to the company profits should be distributed to the shareholders.

[59] See further 119–20 and 129–31, below.
[60] That there is an investment policy that is optimal from the point of view of all shareholders (because of capital market liquidity) has been hailed as explaining the viability of the large public company whose shareholders inevitably have conflicting expectations about income and growth and different attitudes to risk: see R. A. Brealey and S. C. Myres, *Principles of Corporate Finance* (4th ed., 1991), at 22, and ch. 2 generally.
[61] According to the theory first advanced by M. Miller and F. Modigliani: 'Dividend Policy,

It would seem to follow from this analysis that the most appropriate content to ascribe to the duty to act in the interests of the shareholders is that the directors should attempt to maximize the present value of the company. It would appear, furthermore, that the policy of maximizing firm value is ideal, not only from the point of view of the shareholders but also from that of society as a whole, since, by giving proper weight to projects with a future pay-off, it strikes an optimal balance between production for present consumption and growth.

There is, however, a problem with this theoretical account, which is that it depends, as mentioned, on the validity of the efficient market hypothesis, that is, it assumes that the underlying value of the company's business is accurately reflected in the market price of its shares. Whether or not this assumption is well founded turns on the rationality of stock markets and their ability to absorb and evaluate information about a company's prospects. It has been observed that there are failures in both these respects and that '[e]mpirical analyses consistently show that fluctuations in the stock price can be only modestly related to economic realities'.[62] Thus, if fads and limited access to, and comprehension of, information on the part of the market lead to a divergence between underlying value and the market value of a company's shares, then the maximization of underlying value will no longer necessarily maximize shareholder wealth. Should this be the case, it

Growth and the Valuation of Shares', (1961) 34 *J Business* 411, discussed in Brealey and Myres, *Principles of Corporate Finance* (above, n. 60), ch. 16, in the absence of transaction costs, taxation, and market imperfections, share price will not be affected by dividend policy (e.g. shares of companies that make 'generous' distributions will not trade at a higher price for that reason) and hence shareholders should be indifferent to whether investment projects are financed by borrowings or retentions. There is, however, evidence that in practice investors do prefer high payouts and therefore that share price is not independent of dividend policy. A possible explanation is that there is a belief on the part of shareholders, given the separation of ownership and control, that retained earnings will be invested in projects that will produce a lower return than would dividends invested elsewhere: for this and other explanations, see D. A. Hay and D. J. Morris, *Industrial Economics and Organization: Theory and Evidence* (1991), at 404–19. Whatever the 'correct' basis for dividend decisions may be, the courts have little contribution to make in controlling dividend policy. Given the intractable nature of the issues, the court is unlikely to interfere with management discretion. In *Re a Company (No 00370 of 1987) ex p Glossop* [1988] BCLC 570, at 577, Harman J contended that the court would permit a challenge to a dividend decision if persuaded that the directors were motivated by an intention 'to keep moneys in the company so as to build a larger company in the future and without regard to the right of members to have profits distributed so far as was commercially possible', but the position of a private company with a small number of shareholders and where there is a clear conflict of interest between members involved in management and those who are not is distinguishable from a company with shares traded on the market. For a similar distinction revealed in the American cases see V. Brudney, 'Dividends, Discretion, and Disclosure', (1980) 66 *Va L Rev* 85, at 101–3. For a radical solution to the perceived problem of excessive retentions see A. Rubner, *The Ensnared Shareholder: Directors and the Modern Corporation* (1965), recommending the compulsory distribution of all profits.

[62] H. T. C. Hu, 'Risk, Time, and Fiduciary Principles in Corporate Investment', (1990) 38 *UCLA L Rev* 277, at 357.

would seem to follow that a strict concern with shareholder interests would dictate that managers should instead attempt directly to maximize share price, and that directors' duties should be framed accordingly, and not as just suggested.

Whatever advantages there may be to the shareholders in the adoption of one or other of these goals as the object of directors' duties, liability rules, as will be shown in more detail in section II, are too unsophisticated a control technique to make it possible in practice to discriminate between them.[63] That capital market imperfections might create discrepancies between share price and underlying value is a significant point, however, because it indicates a possible divergence between the shareholders' interests and the general interest in economic efficiency in the long term. If this is so, there are important practical implications, since while there may be no legal pressures, there would appear to be *market* pressures on managers to focus on share price.[64] A central element in the charge that companies are 'short-termist' is that the stock market undervalues projects with a long-term pay-off, and therefore that companies may be deterred from investing to the extent that is socially desirable for fear of an adverse effect on the market value of their shares. If these short-termist pressures exist (whether they do or not is controversial), the solution would appear to lie in addressing the market and institutional conditions that generate them, rather than the precise formulation of directors' duties. A clarification of what society expects of directors might nevertheless be of some value in combination with other measures. The issue of short-termism is considered in more detail in Chapter 4.

II THE EFFECTIVENESS OF THE DUTY TO ACT BONA FIDE FOR THE BENEFIT OF THE COMPANY

As the courts have not articulated more precisely the content of the duty to act in the interests of the company we will continue to describe directors as being under a duty to maximize profits. While this terminology may be ambiguous, it is however clear that the duty excludes the various managerialist objectives considered in Chapter 2, and hence to that extent is consistent with the general interest, as so far understood. Having examined how the law defines the ends for which directors must use their powers, we are now in a position to consider the law's capacity to ensure that they act within the bounds laid down. It is suggested that the controls constitute a necessary

---

[63] It is arguable in any case that it is inherently unlikely that managers are able to devise policies that would allow them to exploit market irrationality and information deficiencies to the shareholders' net advantage: see Hu, ibid. at 357–61. The phenomenon of short-termism may, however, belie this suggestion.

[64] Principally, those generated by the market for corporate control: see Ch. 4 below.

conceptual framework, and presumably have some practical impact on behaviour by providing a normative code for the guidance of management and a public standard for the evaluation of their conduct by others, but that as an enforceable control mechanism their effectiveness is very limited. We will not for the moment consider the suitability of the procedures for bringing complaints of breach of duty to court,[65] though the existence of well-informed plaintiffs with standing and motivation to sue is clearly an essential part of any system of control that is ultimately dependent on judicial sanctions. Our current interest is rather in the inherent feasibility of controlling management objectives by means of legal duties.

The core of the difficulty faced by duty-based controls lies in the fact that 'profit maximization', even ignoring questions of time-scale, does not refer to behaviour with any definite, objectively identifiable, content. In the economist's model of perfect competition management behaviour is uniquely determined, since there is only one set of responses consistent with the survival of the enterprise. In more realistic conditions, however, managers are faced with a complex series of questions in the resolution of which they must exercise choice, for example, about plant location, production methods, employment levels, output, advertising, investment, research and development, and so on. Furthermore, companies operate in an environment in which market conditions, consumer tastes, technological knowledge, and the behaviour of competitors, are in a state of constant change. In order to maximize profits a firm would need both complete information about present and future states of the world and the capacity to digest and evaluate that information. Given that in practice managers, like everyone else, suffer from 'bounded rationality', that is, inadequate information and computational skills, it is apparent that the conduct required for profit maximization can only be a matter for judgement: there is no practically discoverable, uniquely correct, profit-maximizing course of action.

The Subjectivity of the Duty

Against this background it is not surprising that the duty to benefit the company should be framed not as a duty to take specific actions or to achieve determinate results, but is instead concerned only with ensuring that the directors act in accordance with proper objectives. The duty is thus a subjective one, requiring the directors to act 'bona fide in what they consider—not what a court may consider—is in the interests of the company'.[66] In fact, there is no necessity for the courts to abandon a concern with substantive outcomes entirely since, despite the problems just noted, a

---

[65] See Ch. 8 below.
[66] Per Lord Greene MR, *Re Smith & Fawcett Ltd* (above, n. 11), at 306. See also *Lee Panavision Ltd v Lee Lighting Ltd* [1992] BCLC 22, CA, at 29.

judicial evaluation of the likely profit consequences of a particular course of action would not be impossible, within fairly broad limits. The court could, for instance, intervene prospectively where a member was able to demonstrate that a proposed business policy would produce a manifestly inadequate return. There are, however, few attractions in making the court an *ad hoc* part of the corporate decision-making machinery. Lord Wilberforce has insisted that '[t]here is no appeal on merits from management decisions to courts of law: nor will the courts of law assume to act as a kind of supervisory board over decisions within the powers of management honestly arrived at.'[67] Subjecting proposals to scrutiny by a body distinct from management may well be desirable, but this is clearly a function for an *actual* supervisory board,[68] and not one for the court. Apart from the unwieldiness of the procedure and the inevitably sporadic character of the intervention, judges are not obviously well qualified to make substantive evaluations of business policy. Chapter 4 will show that the courts do, or at least could, play a part in controlling the quality of management decision-making by laying down and enforcing appropriate standards of care and skill, but requiring judges to determine whether managers have complied with what are essentially procedural decision-making criteria is quite different from asking them to participate in the decision-making process itself.

The problem with framing the duty to act in the company's interests in terms of subjective intentions, however, is that in practice determining what the directors' true objectives are will often be beyond the court's capabilities. One situation in which there will be no great difficulty in establishing that the directors have broken their duty is where there is overt evidence of divergent motivation. Thus the mistake of management in *Dodge v Ford Motor Co*[69] was to admit that part of their aim was to benefit the employees. Without that admission the pricing policy in issue could doubtless have been justified as a permissible interpretation of the requirements of long-term profitability. Similarly, establishing liability will be feasible where it is clear that the company's interests have not been addressed by management.[70] These unusual circumstances, and cases of corrupt diversion of corporate assets aside, however, it will in general be very difficult to demonstrate that the directors did not believe that what they were doing would maximize profits, because of the often insuperable problem of distinguishing between means and ends that this entails.

[67] *Howard Smith Ltd v Ampol Petroleum Ltd* [1974] AC 821, at 832, [1974], All ER 1126, at 1131.
[68] On which, see further Ch. 6 below. The practicability of the judicial review of 'business judgment' is considered in more detail in Ch. 4 below.
[69] Above, n. 30.
[70] See, e.g. *Re W & M Roith Ltd* [1967] 1 WLR 432, [1967] 1 All ER 427.

Separating Ends from Means

Chapter 2 noted that managements may adopt non-profit-maximizing policies for two broad reasons. The first is self-interest. They might consider, for instance, that their own welfare is linked to the size of the enterprise independently of whether the return to shareholders is maximized, perhaps because high remuneration, power, or prestige are associated with large scale rather than profitability. The second reason, less plausibly, is that they regard non-shareholder groups as having legitimate claims on the company and believe that these claims should be satisfied, even though a reduction in shareholder wealth is involved.

Policies with a growth motivation, for example, expansion by take-over, will normally give no clue on their face that their purpose is something other than the maximization of profits. Nor is it likely to be possible to infer motive from the outcome or likely outcome of a transaction, since the fact that a project yields less than optimal profits is an inherent risk in all business ventures and except in extreme cases will not reveal the existence of a non-profit goal. Absent actual evidence of motive, therefore, the court will be unable to establish whether expansion was a means to profit maximization or an end in itself.

Conduct within the second category, for example, a donation to charity, will sometimes be sufficiently disconnected from ordinary business practice to make an attack on motive potentially more manageable. But the obscurity of the means/end relationship will again normally prevent divergent expenditure being identified, since a plausible case can usually be made for donations in terms of their contribution to goodwill and hence to long-term profitability. The shareholders enjoy an additional layer of protection with regard to gratuitous payments, in that in order to show that a payment is authorized by the company's memorandum it will usually be necessary to establish that it is reasonably incidental to the company's business purposes, in essence, that it is for the company's benefit, which is an objective question. However, in practice, because of the difficulties associated with assessing objective benefit already mentioned, the test is diluted to one of whether the transaction is *capable* of benefiting the company,[71] thus adding little of substance to the subjective test. In other cases of benefiting non-shareholder interests, for example, installing more effective anti-pollution equipment than is consistent with maximum profits or required by law, or delaying closure of a redundant factory in order to preserve jobs, the conduct, as with growth-motivated behaviour, is an integral part of business activity and so not susceptible to this kind of attack.[72]

[71] See *Hutton v West Cork Railway* (above, n. 29); *Evans v Brunner, Mond & Co* [1921] 1 Ch 359, and see discussion in Ch. 9 below. Where the company has an express object sanctioning gratuitous payments the issue of authorization by the memorandum does not arise: see *Re Horsley & Weight* (above, n. 49).

[72] The validity of expenditure for 'socially responsible' purposes will be considered in more detail in Ch. 9 below.

We might finally note that the court is able to rely as an aid to discovering intention on the proposition that what no reasonable board could have believed to be beneficial to the company, the actual board could not have believed either,[73] or in other words, that where the means adopted could not on any reasonable view lead to the end of benefiting the company, the directors could not have been motivated by a desire to achieve that end. This technique may have some application where there is a manifest disproportion between the scale of expenditure and any benefit that could possibly result to the business. It may thus be of value in controlling outlays for 'socially responsible' purposes, or, conceivably, on a limited range of projects motivated by management self-interest, for example, the acquisition of an over-lavish corporate headquarters. To evoke a judicial response in either situation, however, it is likely that the company's behaviour will need to be glaringly out of line with that of similarly situated enterprises.

Conclusion

To sum up, the duty to act in the interests of the company (i.e. the shareholders) imposes only a weak control on managerial discretion, since any plausible assertion that a course of action is designed to increase the company's financial well-being will be enough to protect it from attack. It follows that the duty cannot be expected to play a major part in controlling managerialist tendencies. Whether this has serious implications for the efficiency of large companies depends on the effectiveness of other forms of control over management, and on the prior question of the intensity of non-profit motivations. The duty to act for the benefit of the company does not exhaust the contribution of legal duties to the regulation of management goals. Chapter 5 looks at the connection between a further duty, the duty to act for a proper purpose, and the commitment to profit maximization. Before that the role of the duty of care in controlling managerial inefficiency will be examined.

---

[73] See *Shuttleworth v Cox Bros & Co (Maidenhead) Ltd* [1927] 2 KB 9 (re constraints on the voting power of the majority in general meeting). This is seemingly not strictly an objective test; the issue is not whether the court considers the behaviour in question to be beneficial to the company, or whether the board had reasonable grounds for the belief that is was, but whether the board *could* have considered their actions to be beneficial, in the light of what can be regarded as believable by a reasonable board. This in not quite the same test as that familiar in administrative law: see, e.g. *Associated Provincial Picture Houses Ltd v Wednesbury Corporation* [1948] 1 KB 223, CA, allowing an exercise of discretion to be attacked where it is objectively unreasonable to a very high degree. Cf *Heron International Ltd v Lord Grade* (above, n. 19) at 266, where the court considered it necessary to ask whether 'a *genuine* belief [of the board] was a belief that could reasonably be held' (emphasis added). This was, however, in the context of the unorthodox issue of whether a duty owed to the shareholders personally had been breached. The *Wednesbury* test was expressly applied in *Byng v London Life Association Ltd* [1990] Ch 170, [1989] 1 All ER by Sir Nicholas Browne-Wilkinson V-C, in connection with the chairman's discretion to adjourn a meeting i.e. not re a decision about the operation of the business, but see also *Re a Company* (above, n. 61).

4

Managerial Efficiency

The previous chapter examined the effectiveness of the duty to act in the interests of the company in holding directors to the goal of profit maximization against the background of the separation of ownership and control. The concern in this chapter is with the impact of weak owner control on management efficiency. The term 'efficiency' is used here to refer to the expenditure of appropriate levels of effort and skill on the part of the company's directors and top managers. Clearly, a company's senior executives may become lethargic where shareholder pressure is lacking, and profitability is likely to be prejudiced where incompetent directors are effectively unremovable. Assuming that these risks are real ones in the large public company, this chapter will survey the law of negligence as it applies to directors, and will consider whether the role of the courts as external monitors of management efficiency could usefully be increased. The contention that the separation of ownership and control does not lead to serious inefficiency, on the ground that market forces cause management self-interest and shareholder welfare to coincide, has already been mentioned. This claim will be considered in more detail later in the chapter, together with the view of some market theorists that the operation of market forces renders liability rules in this area superfluous.

I DIRECTORS AND THE DUTY OF CARE

This section examines the current law relating to the duty of directors to devote adequate attention to the company's affairs and to carry out their functions competently. It will consider whether it would be feasible for the courts to act as monitors of management standards on a scale significantly greater their current (very low) level of involvement. An evaluation of whether or not it would be *desirable* to extend judicial activity in this area will be undertaken in Section III, after the role of market forces in shaping management behaviour has been examined. The courts do not, of course, monitor management on their own initiative, but only when an issue is brought before them by a suitably qualified plaintiff. A consideration of the problem of standing and the practical difficulties faced by would-be litigants will be postponed until other aspects of directors' duties have been examined, and will appear in Chapter 8.

Monitoring Management Effort

Directors are required to satisfy minimum standards of diligence, care, and skill.[1] 'Diligence' refers to the expected level of active engagement in company affairs. It seems quite likely that lack of management diligence, in the form of lethargy or a preference for a 'quiet life', and leading, for example, to failure to adapt to new trading environments or to technological change, is the most serious source of avoidable damage to company profitability. In aggregate, it will certainly be a greater cause of loss than the various forms of self-dealing, discussed in Chapter 7, which have generated a substantial body of case law and are subject to detailed statutory regulation. Historically, the standard of diligence set by the courts has been comically low,[2] as can be seen from the cases concerning failure to supervise fellow directors and managers who turn out to have been defrauding the company.[3] These old cases generally involve directors lacking executive responsibilities, however, and provide little guidance about the position of the modern executive director. Executive directors have a contractual relationship with the company which imposes on them, either expressly or by implication, an obligation to devote such attention to the business as is necessary properly to carry out their functions. This will normally mean that they must work for the company full-time.[4] Comparatively recent authority also indicates that a

[1] For the possibility of a remedy under CA 1985, s 459 for mismanagement falling short of a breach of these duties see *Re Elgindata Ltd* [1991] BCLC 959. Warner J expressed the view at 993 that 'it is open to the court to find that serious mismanagement of a company's business constitutes conduct that is unfairly prejudicial to the interests of the minority shareholders . . . [but] the court will normally be very reluctant to accept that managerial decisions can amount to unfairly prejudicial conduct.' This is especially likely to be so in a company with marketable shares.

[2] See generally M. J. Trebilcock, 'Liability of Company Directors for Negligence', (1969) 32 *MLR* 499.

[3] For example, *Re Denham* (1883) 25 Ch D 752, where a 'country gentleman' was held not liable where he had failed to attend any board meetings in four years and accordingly did not notice that the chairman was falsifying the company's accounts; *Re Cardiff Savings Bank* (*Marquis of Bute's Case*) [1892] 2 Ch 100, where a director attended only one board meeting in 38 years and not surprisingly failed to detect improprieties in the company's lending practices: he was found not to have been negligent. In *Re Brazilian Rubber Plantations and Estates Ltd* [1911] 1 Ch 425, at 437, Neville J expressed the opinion that a director 'was not bound to take any definite part in the conduct of the company's business'. This had not always been the position however: see L. S. Sealy, 'The Director as Trustee', [1967] *CLJ* 83, at 88 and 93. And liability would have been imposed in *Re City Equitable Fire Insurance Company Ltd* [1925] 1 Ch 407, CA, but for the presence of an exculpatory article (see now CA 1985, s 310). In that case the directors had effectively abdicated all responsibility by leaving control of the company's funds for short-term investment entirely in the hands of the chairman, who fraudulently misdirected them.

[4] The *dictum* of Romer J in *Re City Equitable Fire Insurance Company Ltd* (above, n. 3) at 429 to the effect that 'a director is not bound to give continuous attention to the affairs of his company.

higher level of involvement is now required of non-executives than the old cases suggest, in line with changed social expectations of those performing that role.[5] The precise content of the duty of non-executive directors is, however, obscure. While they undoubtedly have a duty of some sort in relation to the detection of management fraud, the details of that obligation have not been articulated. Whether non-executives have any responsibility for company performance in general, arising from a duty to supervise the quality of management decision-making, also awaits further litigation. Where non-executive directors are active participants in culpable decisions there is no reason why they should not be liable, though as will be seen below, they may owe a lower standard of care than executive directors.

Statutory developments as well have set limits to permissible directorial inactivity. The court has the power under section 214 of the Insolvency Act 1986 to impose personal liability on a director for the debts of a company that has gone into liquidation where the director is guilty of 'wrongful trading'. The section makes it dangerous for a director to be unaware of the company's financial position, since liablility may ensue where a director fails to take appropriate action to 'minimize the potential loss to the company's creditors' once it would have been apparent to a properly informed director that the company was heading for liquidation.[6] Failure to act, at least if it amounts to 'gross negligence',[7] may also result in a director being disqualified from office under the Company Directors Disqualification Act, where the company has gone into liquidation.[8]

There is, however, a difference between imposing liability or disqualifying directors where the company has collapsed and it emerges that the directors have patently disregarded their duties, and using the law to promote managerial dynamism. Even accepting that executive directors are now required to give their full-time attention to company affairs, the law appears to have little role to play in ensuring that the board engages in proper long-term planning or responds vigorously to changes in the business environment.[9] If,

His duties are of an intermittent nature to be performed at periodical board meetings . . . ' is not applicable to full-time executive directors.

[5] See *Dorchester Finance Company Ltd v Stebbing* [1989] BCLC 498 (decided in 1977). In this case Foster J held two non-executive directors to have been in breach of duty, *inter alia*, in failing sufficiently to supervise the activities of a third executive director who had made improper loans of the company's funds. No board meetings were ever held and the non-executives did not take adequate steps to inform themselves of what the executive director was doing.

[6] For an application of the section see *Re Produce Marketing Consortium Ltd (No 2)* [1989] BCLC 520.

[7] *Re Lo-Line Electric Motors Ltd* [1988] BCLC 698, at 703, *Re City Investment Centres Ltd* [1992] BCLC 956, and see *Re Sevenoaks Stationers (Retail) Ltd* [1991] BCLC 325, CA, at 330.

[8] CDDA 1986, s 6. An inactive director may also be disqualified after a statutory investigation of the company has taken place: s 8.

[9] And see F. H. Easterbrook and D. R. Fischel, *The Economic Structure of Corporate Law* (1991), at 99: 'it is difficult even to imagine using liability rules as a remedy for poor effort by managers, although lack of gumption is the single largest source of agency costs.'

for example, it were to be suggested that management had paid insufficient attention to the development of the company's product base or marketing or training, establishing that this amounted to negligence would be highly problematical. For one thing, there would be problems in establishing causation: showing that steps that a more energetic management might have taken would have made a difference to the company's position would involve an assessment of complex and often imponderable factors. There would also be related difficulties in quantifying what the company had lost as a result of board passivity. Furthermore, the resolution of both of these issues would require the courts to evaluate the merits of alternative business policies which, as we shall see below, is something that they are most reluctant to do.

One area in which the duty to be diligent might usefully be developed, however, is with regard to the installation and supervision by the board of adequate management systems. The vast majority of decisions within large corporate organizations are not made by the board or even by managers that board members could reasonably be expected personally to supervise. It should, however, be the responsibility of the directors to ensure that systems exist for confirming that decision-makers possess appropriate skills and for providing adequate performance monitoring. It is, furthermore, crucial to the profitability of a complex organization that there be effective mechanisms to facilitate the flow of information both internally and from the outside. Information that enters the company at one point (for example the complaints department) must be transmitted to all personnel whose decisions might be affected by it (for example, the design department), and there must also be systems for the collection of information from outside the organization that might affect future profits, in relation for instance to changes in market conditions or the regulatory framework. It is of particular importance that the company have reliable systems of internal financial control, providing decision-makers with up-to-date and accurate financial information and giving some assurance that the company's assets are secure.[10] The law has some part to play in stimulating directors to take appropriate action in these areas by imposing liablility where loss can be attributed to a failure on the part of the board to ensure that the company is equipped with an adequate organizational structure.[11]

---

[10] There is a statutory obligation in this regard, CA 1985, s 221 imposing on the directors a duty to keep accounting records sufficient to show the company's financial position at any time. As the Committee on the Financial Aspects of Corporate Governance (the Cadbury Committee) *Report* (1992) para 4.31 explains, to meet their responsibilities 'directors need in practice to maintain a system of internal control over the financial management of the company, including procedures designed to minimise the risk of fraud.' The Committee goes on to recommend that the directors should report on the effectiveness of their system of internal financial control and that the auditors should report thereon: para 4.32. On the ingredients of an internal control system, see the Chartered Institute of Management Accountants, *A Framework for Internal Control* (1992).

[11] See further 394 below.

Monitoring the Quality of Decision-Making

We now turn to the judicial supervision of the quality of top management decision making. The cases establish the basic requirement that a director must act in accordance with the standard of the 'ordinary prudent man'.[12] The standard of care and skill owed by directors is often described as a subjective one,[13] but this is misleading. It is true that the standard expected of particular directors may be increased in accordance with their individual attributes, but it is clear that there is also an objective base-line standard, though admittedly a low one. This objective, 'ordinary prudent man' standard may be contrasted with that imposed on persons performing professional services (or other services involving technical expertise), who are required to satisfy the standard of 'the ordinary skilled man exercising and professing to have' the relevant skill.[14] The distinction is explicable on the basis that directorship has not been regarded by the courts as a profession, and hence a director is not expected to satisfy a higher standard, for example, that of the reasonably competent business manager, simply by virtue of holding office.[15] Instead, directors have been treated as being in a position similar to that of trustees or agents,[16] that is, as being persons appointed to perform a diverse range of functions that do not of themselves

[12] See *Overend & Gurney v Gibb* (1872) LR 5 HL 480, HL. A distinction is sometimes drawn by commentators between the duty to exercise care and the duty to exercise skill. See also clause 45(1) of the abortive 1978 Companies Bill. While it is possible to differentiate the core meanings of the respective terms, the overlap is considerable and hence the distinction is of little practical value. It will be ignored in the discussion that follows.

[13] See e.g. J. H. Farrar, N. E. Furey, and B. M. Hannigan, *Farrar's Company Law* (3rd ed., 1991), at 397. In the law of negligence generally the courts are hostile to the concept of subjective duties. See e.g. *Wilsher v Essex Area Health Authority* [1986] 3 All ER 801, CA, at 813, a case concerning medical negligence, where Mustill L J was of the opinion that the 'notion of a duty tailored to the actor, rather than the act which he elects to perform, has no place in the law of tort'.

[14] *Bolam v Friern Hospital Management Committee* [1957] 2 All ER 118. See also Supply of Goods and Services Act 1982, s 13, and generally, A. M. Dugdale and K. M. Stanton, *Professional Negligence* (2nd ed., 1989), ch. 15.

[15] Hence the startling proposition that a director 'may undertake the management of a rubber company in complete ignorance of everything connected with rubber, without incurring responsibility for the mistakes which may result from such ignorance', per Neville J in *Re Brazilian Rubber Plantations and Estates Ltd* (above, n. 3) at 437. It is surely doubtful that the 'ordinary prudent man' would engage in such an enterprise if he were so lacking in the attributes necessary to perform his functions.

[16] The standard of care and skill expected of trustees and agents is similar to that of directors. Trustees owe a duty to exercise the care of 'an ordinary prudent man of business ... in managing his own affairs' (*Speight v Gaunt* [1883] 9 App Cas 1, HL), though as regards investment decisions the duty is 'to take such care as an ordinary prudent man would take if he were minded to make an investment for the benefit of other people for whom he felt morally bound to provide': *Re Whiteley* (1886) 33 Ch D 347, at 355. A gratuitous agent must exercise 'such skill and care as persons ordinarily exercise in their own affairs' (see F. M. B. Reynolds, *Bowstead on Agency* (15th ed., 1985) at 152, art 44(3)). It is arguable that a contractual agent must display a higher standard (see G. H. L. Fridman, *Law of Agency* (6th ed., 1990), at 142-7); this is almost certainly now also the case as regards executive directors: see below.

demand the possession of specific technical skills.[17] This view was no doubt reinforced in the past by the fact that those who became directors were frequently individuals of limited capabilities, good breeding often being a more important ground for selection than business acumen.

The cases do suggest, however, that where a director does possess a relevant expertise he should be judged by the standards of a competent practitioner of it, presumably on the ground that he has expressly or by implication held himself out as being appropriately qualified.[18] This is, for example, stated negatively in Romer J's dictum in *Re City Equitable Fire Insurance Co Ltd* to the effect that a director need not 'exhibit in the performance of his duties a greater degree of skill than may reasonably be expected from a person of his knowledge and experience. A director of a life insurance company, for instance, does not guarantee that he has the skill of an actuary or a physician.'[19] The implication would seem to be that an individual who does possess 'knowledge and experience' in some particular technical area of expertise will be required to satisfy a standard higher than that of merely the 'ordinary man'.

Where it is evident that the directors have 'knowledge and experience' in the area of *business*, on the other hand, they have been held to a standard demanding no more than ordinary prudence.[20] Thus in *Overend & Gurney Co v Gibb*, for example, it made no difference that the directors, who acquired for the

---

[17] In *Norman v Theodore Goddard* [1991] BCLC 1028, at 1030–1, Hoffmann J, without taking argument from counsel for the director, indicated that 'a director performing active duties on behalf of the company need not exhibit a greater degree of skill than may reasonably be expected from *a person undertaking those duties*. A director who undertakes the management of the company's properties is expected to have reasonable skill in property management, but not in offshore tax avoidance' (emphasis added). He went on to hold that IA 1986, s 214(4) (linking the standard of skill to the function performed) contained an accurate statement of the test at common law. While eminently desirable, this appears to be inconsistent with the authorities, unless it is to be regarded as describing the position of a director who has contracted to provide particular services: see below.

[18] Similarly, where a gratuitous agent 'has expressly or impliedly held himself out to his principal as possessing skill adequate to the performance of a particular undertaking [he must exercise] such skill and care as would normally be shown by one possessing that skill': *Bowstead on Agency* (above, n. 16) at 152, art 44 (3). This has not been the position, at least until recently, as regards trustees. In *Re Whiteley* (above, n. 15) at 350–51, for example, Cotton L J refused to accept that a trustee with special skills should be held to a standard higher than that of the man of ordinary prudence. In *Bartlett v Barclays Bank Trust Co Ltd* [1980] Ch 515, at 534, however, Brightman J held that a professional trustee 'holds itself out, and rightly, as capable of providing an expertise which it would be unrealistic to expect and unjust to demand from the ordinary prudent man or woman . . . '.

[19] (Above, n. 3), at 428. See also *Lagunas Nitrate Co v Lagunas Syndicate* [1899] 2 Ch 392, CA, at 435, per Lindley MR: 'if directors act within their powers, if they act with such care as is reasonably to be expected of them, having regard to their knowledge and experience, and if they act honestly for the benefit of the company they represent, they discharge both their equitable as well as their legal duty to the company.'

[20] Cf. the decision of the New Zealand High Court in *National Mutual Life Nominees Ltd v Worn* (1990) 5 NZCLC 66,385, in respect of directors' liability to a third party (though not expressly limited to third-party liability).

company an insolvent business at great expense, were 'men of the world, and accustomed to business, and accustomed to speculation, and [had] a knowledge of business'.[21] The ordinary prudent man standard was applied notwithstanding. This seems to be inconsistent with the proposition that a higher standard applies where the director possesses relevant skills, but is presumably explicable on the basis that the higher standard relates only to distinct forms of *professional* expertise, such as that of the actuary or the physician referred to by Romer J,[22] and not where the experience or expertise the director has acquired is that of a business manager.[23] Business management, as mentioned earlier, is not recognized as a professional skill in its own right.

A further significant feature is that the ordinary prudent man standard has itself been applied in such a way as to leave the director's duty of care with little content.[24] This can be seen at work in the House of Lords decision in *Overend & Gurney Co v Gibb*,[25] just mentioned. The directors in that case

---

[21] (Above, n. 12), at 495.

[22] In *Re Brazilian Rubber Plantations and Estates Ltd* (above, n. 3) at 437, Neville J commented, *obiter*, that' . . . if he is acquainted with the rubber business [a director] must give the company the advantage of his knowledge when transacting the company's business.' This suggests that a higher standard is applicable not only where a director exercises his professional skills on the company's behalf but also where he possesses business-related technical knowledge. In this case the directors, several of whom were experienced businessmen, bought a rubber plantation without inspecting it or obtaining independent verification of its value. The directors were, in the event, judged by the ordinary prudent man standard and found not to have been negligent. The use of the latter standard is explicable, despite the dictum mentioned above, on the basis that the mistake the directors made was not one to which a knowledge of the rubber industry was relevant, rather, it was a matter of 'business common sense'. This suggests the existence of a distinction between business matters involving technical knowledge and those which do not, with a higher standard applying in the former case if the director in question possesses the relevant knowledge. This distinction has not been relied on elsewhere and would be difficult to justify.

[23] This is consistent with upper and professional class attitudes to business in the nineteenth century: see generally M. J. Wiener, *English Culture and the Decline of the Industrial Spirit* (1981).

[24] The courts have generally been reluctant to accept breach of a duty of care as a separate head of liability, regarding it, if they recognized the existence of such a duty at all, as an aspect of the duty to act in good faith. Thus in *Turquand v Marshall* (1869) LR 4 Ch App 376, at 386, where the directors had made a loan to one of their number which proved to be unrecoverable, Lord Hatherley seemed only to be concerned that the directors should not have exceeded their powers, stating that 'however foolish the loan might have been, so long as it was within the powers of the directors, the Court could not interfere' and that the directors could not be liable unless something more, such as fraud, were alleged: mere 'default of judgment' was not enough. (He did, however, subsequently modify this view in *Overend & Gurney v Gibb* (above, n. 11), at 494–5). In *Re Denham & Co* (1883) 25 Ch D 752, at 766, Chitty J regarded only such negligence as was so 'gross and wilful' as to be equivalent to fraud to be a basis for liability. In subsequent decisions it has frequently been insisted that in order to ground liability negligence must be 'gross' (see e.g. *Overend & Gurney v Gibb*, above; *Lagunas Nitrate Company v Lagunas Syndicate* (above, n. 18); *Re National Bank of Wales Ltd* [1899] 2 Ch 629). This requirement was explained by Romer J in *Re City Equitable Fire Insurance Co* (above, n. 3), at 427; see also *Re Brazilian Rubber Plantations and Estates Ltd* (above, n. 3), at 436–37 as referring to the standard of duty owed: it did not involve a comparison of different degrees of negligence perpetrated by directors, but indicated that the standard owed was a low one.

[25] (Above, n. 12).

had decided that the company should acquire a brokerage business for a substantial sum. Before acquisition they became aware that, far from being the prosperous enterprise the business had appeared to be, it was in fact insolvent by reason of having incurred a number of bad debts. This did nothing, however, to deter the directors from completing the purchase. The House of Lords held that for the directors to have been negligent in taking this course they would have had to have been 'cognisant of circumstances of such a character, so plain, so manifest, and so simple of appreciation, that no men with any ordinary degree of prudence, acting on their own behalf' would have entered into the transaction.[26] This suggests that the boundaries of acceptable behaviour lie beyond mere unreasonableness, that the directors would have been liable only if, on no tenable view of the facts, their actions could have benefited the company: in other words, if they had behaved in a way that was perverse. Their conduct could not have been so described because the court believed that despite its insolvency, it was not inconceivable that the business could have been returned to prosperity. Since this possibility existed, the court considered that it would be improper to substitute its own judgement as to whether it was wise to proceed for that of the directors.[27]

This is to acknowledge that the court's role is merely to act as a longstop. Decisions that fall outside the parameters of 'ordinary' unreasonableness may give rise to liability, but those indicating a lesser degree of ineptitude will be categorised as merely imprudent,[28] or as involving an error of judgement,[29] and will accordingly be safe from attack.[30] This has the advantage from the

---

[26] At 487, per Lord Hatherley LC. In the Court of Appeal in the same case Lord Hatherley framed the test in terms of the decision being 'ridiculous or absurd': (1869) LR 4 Ch App 701, at 720.

[27] The company went into liquidation; the 'good management . . . and large amount of capital to start the concern afresh' referred to by Lord Hatherley (at 491) as giving the company a chance of survival thus turned out to be too much to have hoped for.

[28] See *Overend & Gurney* (above, n. 12), at 494-95; see also *Lagunas Nitrate Company v Lagunas Syndicate* (above, n. 19), at 418, per Romer J: 'mere imprudence or want of judgment would not in itself make a director liable.'

[29] See, e.g., *Turquand v Marshall* (above, n. 24), at 386. It is true, of course, that 'an error of judgment may, or may not, be negligent; it depends on the nature of the error': per Lord Fraser, *Whitehouse v Jordan* [1981] 1 All ER 267, HL, at 281. As used in the old company cases, the expression refers to non-negligent errors.

[30] The American Law Institute in *Principles of Corporate Governance: Analysis and Recommendations*, Proposed Final Draft (1992) affords the protection of the business judgment rule (see below) to decisions which are 'rational': see para 4.01 This standard 'is intended to permit a significantly wider range of discretion than the term "reasonable", and to give a director or officer a safe harbor from liability for business judgments that might arguably fall outside the term "reasonable" but are not so removed from the realm of reason when made that liability should be incurred': ibid. at 185. The concept of extreme unreasonableness is also relied on in administrative law as a control on the exercise of powers by public bodies; a decision may be reviewed if it was 'so unreasonable that no reasonable authority could ever have come to it': per Lord Greene MR in *Associated Provincial Picture Houses Ltd v Wednesbury Corp.* [1948] 1 KB 223, CA, at 230. For explicit recourse to the Wednesbury test in other areas of company law, see *Re a Company* [1988] 1 WLR 1068 (re payment of dividend); *Byng v London Life Assurance Association* [1989] 1 All ER 561 (re chairman's discretion to adjourn meeting).

point of view of the courts of largely relieving them of the necessity to enter into the merits of business judgement, a matter to which we shall return below. Where loss has been caused by an act or omission which is of a comparatively mechanical character, rather than involving an exercise of business discretion, it might be noted in contrast that the courts have shown themselves to be more willing to impose liability. Thus, in *Dorchester Finance Company Ltd v Stebbing*,[31] two non-executive directors were held to have been negligent in equipping an executive director with signed blank cheques; he used them to make unrecoverable loans. Similarly in *Re New Mashonaland Exploration Company*[32] Vaughan Williams J commented, *obiter*, that where a company has resolved to lend money on security, to have parted with the money before the security had been created would have been negligent.[33]

Two factors explaining the low standard of competence imposed by the courts have thus emerged: management is not a profession, and the courts wish to avoid second-guessing business judgement. A third feature underlying the courts' tolerant attitude to managerial failure is their belief, at least historically, that mismanagement can, and should be controlled by means of shareholder supervision. It is no doubt true that there is a reduced need for rigorous liability rules where the shareholders are in a position to exercise a real, informed choice about the appointment and removal of directors,[34] and are prepared to engage in active monitoring of management. And where the members genuinely have control over the board it is legitimate to regard them as partly responsible for any losses that might result, and hence to view it as inappropriate for the court to come to their aid. This attitude is evident in *Turquand v Marshall*, for example, where Lord Hatherley stated that 'however ridiculous and absurd [the directors'] conduct may seem, it was the misfortune of the company' that it had chosen them.[35] The same sentiment appears in *Lagunas Nitrate Company v Lagunas Syndicate*,[36] where it is suggested, somewhat eccentrically, that effect might be given to it by allowing the directors to plead the defence of *volenti non fit iniuria*.[37]

---

[31] (Above, n. 5).

[32] [1892] 3 Ch 577, at 586.

[33] The distinction, though not referred to in the cases, resembles the policy/operational distinction found in administrative law: see P. P. Craig, *Administrative Law* (2nd ed., 1989), at 449–58.

[34] Though it should be noted that before CA 1948 it was not uncommon for directors to be unremovable by the shareholders or dismissable only in limited circumstances. As a result of s 184 (now CA 1985, s 303) directors may be removed by ordinary resolution and this power may not be taken away by the articles.

[35] (Above, n. 24), at 386.

[36] (Above, n. 19), at 426.

[37] Technically, for the defence to operate it is necessary for the defendant to establish that the plaintiff had full knowledge of the particular circumstances in which damage might result, and consented to the defendant's immunity from suit. It seems very unlikely that these requirements would often be satisfied in the context of business decision making. It is interesting to note that while the court in *Turquand* in 1869 considered negligence to be an inappropriate head of

The Modern Law

In the absence of modern authority, it is possible only to speculate about how far the above account of the law represents the position today.[38] A useful starting-point is to note that two of the three factors just mentioned as having influenced the law's development have little application in modern conditions. Thus, far from shareholder control justifying judicial non-interference, the looseness of shareholder control over management indicates the need for at least considering an expanded role for the courts. And even without the separation of ownership and control, business complexity and the 'organizational distance' of shareholders from managers make owner control over the quality of management decision making, if not over the quality of managers, a fiction, suggesting a need for alternative mechanisms for supervising managerial competence. Second, it is difficult to believe that the courts would now fail to recognize that management involves distinctive skills. Many business issues manifestly demand knowledge that would not normally be possessed by the lay person, for example, concerning the risks inherent in marketing new products, the techniques for maintaining cash-flow, or the steps that should be taken to guard against currency fluctuations, not to mention technical issues specific to particular industries. The twentieth century has seen the growth of a considerable literature on management as an acquired skill and it has for some time been possible to obtain academic management qualifications.[39] It would, furthermore, be difficult to justify the scale of directors' remuneration if the recipients did not possess comparatively scarce abilities, and it would, if only for that reason, be surprising if directors were themselves to deny the possession of special skills.

Once it is accepted that management involves technical expertise, the court could, without departing from the existing but anomalous principle that the standard of care is linked to the attributes of the director, impose an

liability in the company context, by 1899 in *Lagunas* it could not deny that it existed, hence the need to rely on a defence.

[38] The position is much the same in the Commonwealth as in the UK, even where the duty of care has been put into statutory form in modern times: see J. F. Corkery, *Directors' Powers and Duties* (1987), ch. 8 (Australia); B. L. Welling, *Corporate Law in Canada* (1984), at 328–35. There are however proposals in Australia to introduce an objective duty: see L. S. Sealy, 'Reforming the Law on Directors' Duties', (1991) 12 *Co Lawyer* 175, at 176–7, and similarly in New Zealand: NZ Law Commission Report No 9, *Company Law Reform and Restatement* (1989), para 519, and see also *National Mutual Life Nominees Ltd v Worn* (above, n. 20).

[39] e.g. the MBA. However, a survey conducted by the Institute of Directors reveals that 9 out of 10 directors received no formal preparation for becoming a director and that fewer than a quarter have any professional or management qualifications: *Professional Development of and for the Board* (1990). Following reports by C. Handy, *The Making of Managers* (1987) and J. Constable and R. McCormick, *The Making of British Managers* (1987), the Management Charter Initiative was founded in 1988 with a view to devising a qualification of Chartered Manager. On the rise of the professional manager generally in the twentieth century, see H. D. Perkin, *The Rise of Professional Society: England Since 1880* (1989), at 294–306. See also V. Finch, 'Company Directors: Who Cares about Skill and Care?', (1992) 55 *MLR* 179, at 210.

appropriately higher standard, given that most executive directors of large companies do have considerable business experience.[40] It would, however, be preferable for the standard to be linked to the role being performed, irrespective of the actual talents of the individual performing it, since there is no reason why an under-qualified director should enjoy a partial immunity. This may, in fact, already be the position as far as executive directors are concerned, in that they are employees, and it is usual for the court to imply a term in employment contracts to the effect that employees will carry out their duties with reasonable care and skill.[41] Applied to directors, this would mean that they would be required to exercise such care and skill as is reasonably to be expected of a person occupying the relevant position. A director whose functions demand the possession of some technical ability would accordingly be required to comply with the standard of the reasonably competent practitioner of the expertise in question, whether or not it was actually possessed. A finance director, for example, would be judged by the standard of the reasonable person experienced in financial matters, and not by the standard of the ordinary person. Similarly, a director who is in charge of the company's research and development programme would not be able to resist a negligence action by claiming that he or she lacked experience or qualifications in the area concerned. Further, executive directors in general would presumably be required to display administrative and management skills commensurate with their functions.[42]

Business Judgement, Risk, and the Bounds of Negligence Liability

Even if this approach is adopted, however, it does not follow that it will lead to a marked increase in the role of the courts as monitors of business decisions. As already mentioned, a refusal to enter into the merits of business

---

[40] See *National Mutual Life Nominees Ltd v Worn* (above, n. 20), at 66,406, per Henry J:

The standard of care to be exercised by a director has been said as being to exhibit the degree of skill reasonably to be expected from a person of his knowledge and experience. I would add that the standard is to be assessed by also having regard to the circumstances pertaining to the responsibilities which the directors have undertaken . . . [the directors in the instant case] were all knowledgeable and experienced business people, sufficiently versed in the general ramifications of [the company's] operations.

[41] See *Lister v Romford Ice & Cold Storage Co Ltd* [1957] AC 555, HL. It is interesting to note that directors have been expressly excluded from the scope of section 13 of the Supply of Goods and Services Act 1982 (by S.I. No. 1771 of 1982). The section provides that 'In a contract for the supply of a service where the supplier is acting in the course of a business, there is an implied term that the supplier will carry out the service with reasonable skill and care.' The section would have applied only where the director had a contract for services with the company, rather than a contract of employment, since the latter are expressly excluded generally.

[42] The argument (see e.g. Trebilcock, 'The Liability of Company Directors for Negligence' (above, n. 2), at 509-11) that the standard of skill must necessarily be based on the personal attributes of the director in question, because of the considerable differences in type and size of company and the varying roles that directors are required to perform, has no validity since the appropriate degree of flexibility can be achieved by linking the standard to the objective requirements of the role. This is the approach adopted in IA 1986, s 214, and see *Re Produce*

judgement has been an important feature of the courts' attitude towards directors' negligence,[43] and it is suggested that the basis of this refusal is, to some extent, well founded. The main point is that there is an absence of criteria by which the courts can assess the merits of an exercise of business discretion. This should not be confused with the proposition that because judges lack business experience they are not competent to judge business issues. In other technical areas, despite not personally possessing relevant expertise, judges are fully prepared to determine questions of professional competence. Lack of medical knowledge, for example, does not prevent the courts from deciding whether the use of a particular medical procedure was negligent. There is, however, a difference between making an assessment of conduct in a professional negligence case and evaluating a business decision. It is that in the former situation it will be possible to adduce evidence as to established professional practice with which the defendant's actions can be compared, whereas in business, while it may be clear what steps should be taken before a decision is made,[44] it is not obvious by what criteria the decision itself should be judged. In other words, business decisions are of limited justiciability.

This point can be illustrated by making a comparison between the position of directors and that of trustees.[45] *Bartlett v Barclays Bank Trust Co Ltd*[46] is a good illustration of the latter. In this case Brightman J decided that trustees who held most of the shares in a company were negligent when they failed to prevent the directors of the company from entering into a highly speculative property development project, which turned out to be unsuccessful. Whether or not the directors themselves had been negligent was not in issue, but it is suggested that a finding to that effect would have been more problematical. The primary duty of trustees is to ensure that the trust fund remains intact, since the financial security of the beneficiaries may depend on it.[47] On that

Marketing Consortium Ltd (No 2) (above, n. 6) on the company-specific quality of directors' responsibilities. Where non-specialist directors have participated in a decision which has involved some technical error it will be open to them, in appropriate cases, to plead that they have reasonably relied on specialist directors or on outside advice.

[43] For a consideration of the English position by a French academic lawyer, see A. Tunc, 'The Judge and the Businessman', (1986) 102 *LQR* 549, observing at 555 that 'it is inconceivable that a judge [in a French court] would state that business decisions are the sole province of the board.'

[44] See below.

[45] See e.g. *Overend & Gurney Co v Gibb* (above, n. 12) at 495; *Sheffield and South Yorkshire Permanent Building Society v Aizlewood* (1889) 44 Ch D 412, at 454.

[46] (Above, n. 18).

[47] 'The duty of a trustee is not to take such care only as a prudent man would take if he had only himself to consider; the duty rather is to take such care as an ordinary prudent man would take if he were minded to make an investment for the benefit of other people for whom he felt morally bound to provide': per Lindley L J, *Re Whiteley* (1886) 33 Ch D 347, CA, at 355. A trustee must avoid investments that are 'attended with hazard': per Lord Watson, *Re Whiteley* (1887) 12 App Cas 727, HL, at 733.

basis, entering into a hazardous transaction that results in damage is in itself negligent. Directors, on the other hand, are charged with the responsibility of maximizing profits. To do this it will frequently be necessary for them to take risks. Whether a risk is worth running depends on an estimate of its magnitude in the light of the size of the potential reward. Assuming, on facts such as those in *Bartlett*, that the directors have sufficiently researched a project, it is not evident how a court could determine whether the expected profits justify the risks involved, and this is likely to be the case with respect to much business decision-making. In short, the indeterminacy of the issues before the court means that the judicial evaluation of management decision-making will often be an enterprise of doubtful value.[48]

At least in the eyes of the courts, too close a scrutiny of business decisions may, in addition, be dangerous, since it may inhibit legitimate risk-taking.[49] In *Re Faure Electric Accumulator Company*, for example, Kay J stated that 'to apply to directors the strict rules of the Court of Chancery with respect to ordinary trustees might fetter their action to an extent which would be exceedingly disadvantageous to the companies they represent'.[50] The danger of suppressing enterprise is an issue of which the American courts are also particularly conscious, and it is a key justification for the 'business judgement rule'. The rule, which is an articulate version of the policy of judicial reticence that is implicit in the practice of the English courts,[51] is designed to 'stimulate risk taking, innovation and other creative entrepreneurial activities'.[52] The debate on how the rule should be formulated for the purposes of

---

[48] It may be possible to obtain a remedy under CA 1985, s 459 (conduct unfairly prejudicial to the interests of the members) on the basis of mismanagement falling short of negligence, either in the form of inattention or poor quality decision-making: see *Re Elgindata Ltd* (above, n. 1), at 993–4. However, the court will 'normally be very reluctant to accept that managerial decisions can amount to unfairly prejudicial conduct', ibid., even in a closely held company, i.e. the 'business judgment' dimension will normally be overwhelming. See also *Re Sam Weller & Sons Ltd* [1990] Ch 682, at 694, [1990] BCLC 80, at 89. In a listed company the 'unfairness' element is also likely to be weaker, given the marketability of the petitioner's shares.

[49] It has been argued that directors are more risk-averse than the shareholders would wish them to be (because the former are 'over-invested' in the company) even without the possibility of negligence liability, which is likely to exacerbate the problem: see e.g. J. C. Coffee, 'Litigation and Corporate Governance: An Essay on Steering between Scylla and Charybdis', (1984) 52 *Geo Wash L Rev* 789, at 802–3. See also 65–6 above. An excessive willingness to take risks has not been a quality for which British managers are famous: see Wiener, *English Culture* (above, n. 23), ch. 7.

[50] (1888) 40 Ch D 141, at 151. See also the cases mentioned in n. 45.

[51] On the position in America, one commentator has stated 'the search for cases in which directors of industrial corporations have been held liable in derivative suits for negligence uncomplicated by self-dealing is a search for a very small number of needles in a very large haystack': J. W. Bishop, 'Sitting Ducks and Decoy Ducks: New Trends in the Indemnification of Corporate Directors and Officers', (1968) 77 *Yale L J* 1078, at 1100; see also T. C. Lee, 'Limiting Corporate Directors' Liability: Delaware's Section 102(b)(7) and the Erosion of the Directors' Duty of Care', (1987) 136 *U Pa L Rev* 239.

[52] American Law Institute, *Principles of Corporate Governance:* (above, n. 30), at 176. The rule has been applied in a variable way; the narrow version echoes the English approach, holding

the American Law Institute's Corporate Governance Project has revealed the battle lines of those who favour leaving the disciplining of management to the market and those who see an important role for the courts.[53] As far as this country is concerned, the possibility of inhibiting risk taking is undoubtedly a legitimate factor to be taken into account in determining the content of management duties, but the law can surely afford to develop considerably more rigorous rules before problems of risk suppression are encountered.

Enforcing Adequate Decision-Making Procedures

While, for the reasons just explored, raising the standard of care may have only a limited impact on the courts' willingness to categorize a decision as negligent rather than as a mere 'error of judgement', it may still nevertheless lead to the courts playing a greater role as monitors of business efficiency. This is because a higher standard of care may cause the courts to pay more attention to the adequacy of the informational base on which a decision is made[54] and to how thorough the decision-making process has been.[55] These

that the court should not review a business decision that was made in good faith and free from conflict of interest, so long as it was made with due diligence, the latter requiring, for instance, that the decision be made on the basis of sufficient information. The wider version virtually eliminates the duty of care altogether, with the courts refusing to question a decision at all in the absence of conflict of interest or improper motive: see S. R. Cohn, 'Demise of the Director's Duty of Care: Judicial Avoidance of Standards and Sanctions Through the Business Judgment Rule', (1983) 62 *Texas L Rev* 591. In order to explain the apparent obliteration of the duty of care by the wider interpretation of the business judgment rule, it has been suggested that the duty of care should be seen as laying down a *conduct rule*, which management should at least aspire to comply with, and the business judgment rule as being a *decisional rule*, in accordance with which the court imposes liability: see D. M. Phillips, 'Principles of Corporate Governance: A Critique of Part IV', (1984) 52 *Geo Wash L Rev* 653; J. Hinsey, 'Business Judgment and the American Law Institute's Corporate Governance Project: the Rule, the Doctrine, and the Reality', (1984) 52 *Geo Wash L Rev* 609.

[53] See e.g. the literature referred to in n. 60 below. For a discussion of the evolution, and final version, of the statement of the duty of care favoured by the ALI, see J. Seligman, 'A Sheep in Wolf's Clothing: The American Law Institute Principles of Corporate Governance Project', (1987) 55 *Geo Wash L Rev* 325, at 360–7.

[54] A number of DTI reports following statutory investigations attribute corporate collapse to decisions made on the basis of inadequate information. Commenting on the findings of the inspectors in the investigation of Court Line Ltd (Final Report, 1978), for instance, L. H. Leigh, *The Control of Commercial Fraud* (1982), at 172–3, observes that 'it takes a mind of some buoyancy to venture into Caribbean hotel development in entire ignorance of the costs likely to be incurred, the rate of hotel occupancy to be expected, and the probable availability of staff, and even the possibility of mooring leisure boats at the sites selected for the purpose.' See also DTI, *Report on Rolls Royce Ltd* (1973), at 344, 358–9; DTI, *Report on John Willment Automobiles Ltd* (1973), at 209; DTI, *Report on the Vehicle & General Insurance Co Ltd* (1972), at 347–8.

[55] A number of decisions in the United States appear to have reinvigorated the duty of care along these lines: see *Hanson Trust PLC v ML SCM Acquisition Inc* 781 F. 2d 264 (2d Cir. 1986); *Smith v Van Gorkom* 488 A.2d 858 (Del. 1985); *Francis v United Jersey Bank* 87 N.J. 15, 432 A2d. 814 (1981). They have reportedly led to companies finding it difficult to recruit competent non-executive directors: Lee, 'Limiting Corporate Directors' Liability' (above, n. 51), at 267–77. Partly as a response to this several states have amended their company statutes to protect directors from liability: see Lee, ibid.

are, in fact, matters of which the courts have to some extent been prepared to take notice in the past. Thus in *Overend & Gurney* Lord Hatherley stated that the directors would have been liable if there had been any 'undue neglect of any circumstance or transaction which ought to have been inquired into'.[56] In other words, while the court would not have imposed liability in respect of the decision itself (except if it had been perverse) failure to go through the preliminary steps of obtaining essential information could have grounded liability.[57] Vaughan Williams J seems to have had something similar in mind in *Re New Mashonaland Exploration Company*.[58] In that case he refused to hold that directors had been negligent on the ground that he was satisfied that they had made 'a real exercise of discretion and judgement'.

Knowing the right questions to ask often depends on being familiar with the activity in hand and on general business expertise. Raising the standard of care should, therefore, have the effect of demanding that directors make an appropriately detailed investigation of the facts and engage in a suitably thorough decision-making process: directors who must comply with the standard of reasonable occupants of the relevant office, rather than that of 'ordinary prudent men', need to have a more sophisticated grasp of the factors that should influence their decisions. For example, before embarking on a major project it will usually be appropriate for management to commission a feasibility study or market research, and it will obviously be essential to calculate likely costs and potential returns. Where a project requires technical expertise it may also be necessary for the company to recruit suitably qualified personnel or seek outside advice if the expertise is lacking, both at the outset and during the course of the project. By insisting on compliance with minimum decision-making procedures of this kind the courts can impose a valuable discipline on management without having to confront the difficulties inherent in evaluating the merits of actual decisions. Nor are procedural controls likely to interfere unduly with risk-taking. The fact that the duty of care is enforced at all means that there is a possibility that decisions with bad outcomes will attract liability, and so admittedly to that extent procedural standards might suppress risk. Rather than reducing the level of risk-taking in general, however, a requirement to obtain adequate information seems more likely to improve the chances that directors will more accurately discriminate between legitimate and illegitimate risks.

[56] (Above, note 12), at 495.
[57] In *Lagunas Nitrate Company v Lagunas Nitrate Syndicate* (above, n. 19) the Court of Appeal found that the directors had not been negligent in buying a nitrate works at an inflated price; the directors were held to have had adequate knowledge of the works and a survey had been made.
[58] (Above, n. 33), at 587; see also 582.

Of course, deciding how much information to obtain, given the cost in time and money of acquiring it, in itself demands the exercise of judgement.[59] It has been contended accordingly that managers should be allowed to determine for themselves how thoroughly they need to investigate the background to a transaction, since judicial interference in this process is likely to lead only to wasteful investigations and excessive documentation in order to provide a defence if litigation ensues.[60] The implication of this, however, is that directors should be the sole arbiters of the appropriateness of their working methods; the suggestion that 'rational shareholders would not have it otherwise . . . for their welfare is maximized by decisions that yield the highest profits net of the costs of gathering information and making the decision',[61] adds nothing beyond the empirically unsupported assertion that on balance, if left alone, managements *will* make decisions in the most cost-effective way. Shareholders would be unwise to be so trusting and surely have little to lose from the insistence that directors comply with externally monitored rational decision-making procedures. This, after all, is the position in which every other professional group finds itself.

To conclude, therefore, the enforcement of essentially procedural decision-making standards is within the capacity of the courts and might reasonably be expected to have beneficial effects. With this in mind, a legislative change is desirable to make clear that directors, both executive and non-executive, owe a duty of care and skill with a standard linked to the functions they perform within the company. A set of statutory guidelines, similar to those proposed in Australia, indicating factors to be taken into account in deciding whether a director has met the relevant standard, might also have educative value and be useful in stimulating the development of a more detailed body of jurisprudence. The Australian guidelines direct the court to consider, for example, the steps taken by a director to obtain information and to ensure that those from whom advice is sought are competent, to monitor decisions made by lower-tier management, and to monitor the company's compliance with law.[62] A consideration of additional factors bearing on the merits of an extension of negligence liability along the lines suggested in this section will

---

[59] This may have influenced the decision in *Re Brazilian Rubber Plantations and Estates Ltd* (above, n. 3), where a company bought a rubber plantation on the strength of representations made by the vendor and without making any attempts at verification, but even so the court seems to have been excessively lenient.

[60] See e.g. Phillips, 'Principles of Corporate Governance' (above, n. 52), at 683; B. Manning, 'The Business Judgment Rule and the Director's Duty of Attention: Time for Reality', (1984) 39 *Bus Lawyer* 1477, at 1486; Cohn, 'Demise of the Director's Duty of Care' (above, n. 51), at 596; Easterbrook and Fischel, *The Economic Structure of Corporate Law* (above, n.9), at 107-8.

[61] F. H. Easterbrook and D. R. Fischel, 'The Proper Role of A Target's Management in Responding to a Tender Offer', (1981) 94 *Harv L Rev* 1161, at 1196.

[62] Corporate Reform Bill 1992, cl 232.

be undertaken in Section III, after the role of markets in raising the standard of management performance has been examined.

II THE DISCIPLINE OF THE MARKET

It was suggested in the foregoing discussion that the laxity of the duty of care can be explained partly by reference to the confidence of the courts, at least historically, in the effectiveness of shareholder control. Given the inadequacy of the democratic control mechanisms, it was contended that an appropriate response might be to enhance the courts' monitoring function. More rigorous liability rules are, however, opposed by market theorists, who believe that the operation of markets imposes a discipline which is sufficient to secure an acceptable level of managerial efficiency, without giving rise to the costs that flow from reliance on a liability regime. Some of these possible costs have already been mentioned. They include the damaging effect on the willingness of directors to take risks, wasteful research, excessive documentation of the decision-making process, and also the expense associated with litigation itself. The object of control is not, market theorists emphasize, to eradicate inefficiency, but to 'minimize the sum of the existing inefficiencies and the costs of the solution'.[63] Thus it has been suggested that 'the likely effect of legal regulation on top of that already provided by the markets . . . would be an inefficient and otherwise undesirable distortion of managerial behaviour'.[64] The validity of this statement rests, however, on the assumption that market forces create an optimal set of incentives and deterrents. It should be emphasized at the outset that this *is* an assumption, not an empirically established or necessary truth: what theory dictates should happen in a state of perfect competition may not occur in real, imperfect markets. The validity of the claims made for the efficacy of market forces will, therefore, be assessed on the basis of their inherent plausibility in the context of the complex circumstances in which they operate. We shall now examine in turn the markets likely to affect management behaviour. The analysis is, of course, relevant not only to issues of managerial efficiency as defined in this chapter, but also to the selection of management goals, the subject of Chapters 2 and 3. And it will be called on again in Chapter 9, as revealing the practical scope for profit-sacrificing, 'socially responsible' management behaviour.

---

[63] G. S. Rehnert, 'The Executive Compensation Contract: Creating Incentives to Reduce Agency Costs', (1985) 37 *Stan L Rev* 1147, at 1160.
[64] Phillips, 'Principles of Corporate Governance' (above, n. 52), at 673.

The Product Market

The market which affects management behaviour in the most obvious way is the market for the company's products. An inefficient firm will face higher production costs than rival businesses and may eventually become insolvent as customers buy elsewhere.[65] The product market ought, therefore, to stimulate management efficiency: if managers are to keep their jobs they must strive to make the company as profitable as possible. While this may be true of highly competitive markets, however, 'an imperfectly competitive market will not quickly convert . . . inefficiency into insolvency'.[66] In reality, and notwithstanding increased competition from the growing internationalization of business, optimal performance is unlikely to be a condition of survival for many firms, and, where a company dominates a market which is difficult to enter, a high level of inefficiency may be tolerated indefinitely.

Product market signals can, however, be amplified by linking management remuneration to company performance, and thus while the market may be of only limited effectiveness in so far as it offers threats, it can be made to function better by providing incentives. Linkage can happen informally in that high salaries are easier to justify where the company is profitable, but in many companies the connection between profitability and remuneration is now made explicit, through the use of bonus payments or share options.[67] Such schemes are said to help align the interests of managers with those of shareholders and hence make the former behave more like owners.[68] It is argued, furthermore, that while incentive pay may be of value at all levels in an organization, it is particularly beneficial at the highest level. Thus a principal function of top management is to coordinate and monitor the efforts of those lower down the hierarchy. Managers are not themselves subject to these processes, and so in order to ensure that they carry out their duties efficiently, it is contended that they should be given the incentive of performance-linked pay.[69] Viewed in terms of agency theory, the problem is

---

[65] See R. A. Posner, *Economic Analysis of Law* (3rd ed., 1986), at 383.

[66] M. A. Eisenberg, 'The Structure of Corporation Law', (1989) 89 *Colum L Rev* 1461, at 1489.

[67] In 1986 63 per cent of larger UK companies had some form of incentive scheme, and the average payment in executive schemes was 25 per cent of base salary: the *Financial Times*, 20 January 1987. A more recent survey shows that 81 per cent of 196 companies taken from *The Times* 1,000 have an incentive bonus plan for top executives: Korn/Ferry International, *Boards of Directors Study UK* (1991). Share option schemes operate by giving the beneficiary the right to buy a certain number of shares at some date in the future at the price at the time the option is created, thereby giving an incentive to increase share value: see further 223–4, below.

[68] In theory, in addition to possible incentive effects, pay which is calculated *ex post* rather than *ex ante* involves less risk to the company of over-payment. However, the difficulties in calculating the contribution of management in general, and especially of individual managers, may make this advantage illusory.

[69] A. Alchian and H. Demsetz, 'Production, Information Costs and Economic Organization', (1972) 62 *Am Econ Rev* 777.

essentially one of the low visibility of management effort.[70] Because share-holders cannot tell how hard managers are exerting themselves on their behalf, managers have an incentive to shirk. By linking rewards to what *is* observable, namely company performance, this tendency can be reduced.

The effectiveness of incentive schemes is in practice hard to assess. There are certainly grounds for scepticism. As Herman points out, 'it is possible that the "incentive" effects of different kinds of income may be overrated if the determinants of income are under management control and management can re-arrange them to achieve a predetermined result'.[71] Support for the view that remuneration schemes *are* designed to produce a particular outcome can be derived from the findings of Jensen and Murphy. Their survey of the remuneration of chief executives in the United States reveals that, although on average bonuses represent 50 per cent of salary, such bonuses are awarded in ways that are not highly sensitive to performance.[72] They estimate that, in the 250 largest corporations, a 1,000 dollar increase in corporate value (defined as share price appreciation plus dividends) produces an increase in the salary and bonus of the chief executive over a two year period of less than 10 cents, and share options add only another 58 cents.[73] As one commentator has thus pointed out, 'Although the relationship between compensation and corporate performance is *statistically* significant, it is not *economically* significant'.[74] Jensen and Murphy go on to suggest that for pay to have a genuine incentive effect rewards should be made considerably more sensitive to performance. This means that managers in companies that perform well should be paid very much more than they are now (and the prospects of dismissal for poor performance should be increased). Whether large rises in what are already often massive salaries, even assuming them to be efficacious, would be politically acceptable, however, is doubtful.[75] The incentivie effect of performance-related pay can, furthermore, be over-rated. Herman, for instance, queries whether 'elaborate compensation systems' are

---

[70] See D. A. Hay and D. J. Morris, *Industrial Economics and Organization: Theory and Evidence* (2nd ed., 1991), at 311–17.

[71] E. S. Herman, *Corporate Control, Corporate Power* (1981), at 96. For further consideration of the role of management in determining their own remuneration, see Ch. 7 below.

[72] M. C. Jensen and K. J. Murphy, 'Performance Pay and Top-Management Incentives', (1990) 98 *J Pol Econ* 225, at 262.

[73] M. C. Jensen and K. J. Murphy, 'C.E.O. Incentives — It's Not How Much You Pay, but How', (May-June 1991) *Harv Bus Rev* 138, at 140. See also the similar findings in a British survey: P. Gregg, S. Machin, and S. Szymanski, *The Disappearing Relationship between Directors' Pay and Corporate Performance*, LSE Centre for Economic Performance Working Paper no. 282 (1992).

[74] Eisenberg, 'The Structure of Corporation Law' (above, n. 66), at 1490 (emphasis in original). Jensen and Murphy themselves acknowledge that in 'most large companies, cash compensation for [chief executive officers] is treated more like an entitlement program than as a way to motivate outstanding management performance': 'C.E.O. Incentives' (above, n. 73), at 141.

[75] Jensen and Murphy attribute existing low pay sensitivity to political opposition to 'excessive' management rewards: 'Performance Pay' (above, n. 73), at 254–260.

necessary to motivate 'highly paid executives nurtured to be "achievers" in any case'.[76] Even if there were a strong positive relationship between perform-ance and pay it could therefore be questioned whether increases in pay are actually needed to stimulate improvements in corporate performance. Rather than take the route advocated by Jensen and Murphy, it seems more attractive to respond to the problem of the low visibility of management effort directly, by improving internal monitoring, for example, through board reform.

It should be noted finally that depending on their design, incentive schemes may actually be counter-productive. Where, for instance, remunera-tion is linked to earnings per share, managers have an interest in increasing short-term profits, which may be detrimental to investment and the company's long-term value.[77] Furthermore, accounting-based measures of performance are manipulable and hence do not guarantee an ideal incentive structure. Linking rewards to share-price movements[78] overcomes the latter problem, but whether it will instil a more forward-looking perspective depends on how well stock prices reflect a company's future prospects, a matter on which there is some doubt.[79]

The Market for Managers

Much has been made of the disciplinary power of the market for managerial services. One theorist has gone so far as to claim that 'the viability of the large corporation with diffuse security ownership is . . . explained in terms of a model where primary disciplining of managers comes through managerial labor markets, both within and outside of the firm'.[80] As regards the market within the firm, it is obviously true that managers are frequently competitive by nature and hence will exert themselves in their quest for personal advancement within the organizational hierarchy. It is also likely that they will monitor and criticize the performance of their colleagues to the same

---

[76] Herman, *Corporate Control, Corporate Power* (above, n. 71), at 97. See also D. F. Vagts, 'Challenges to Executive Compensation: for the Markets or the Courts?' (1983) 8 *J Corp Law* 231, at 240: 'the most scientific research — studies of the effect of piece work and similar types of pay — were done with persons at a level of operation where tasks, and presumably motivational links, are much simpler and more direct than in executive offices.'

[77] See Vagts, ibid. at 241–42. See also Jensen and Murphy, 'Performance Pay' (above, n. 72), at 246: 'paying executives on the basis of accounting profits rather than changes in shareholder wealth not only generates incentives to directly manipulate the accounting system but also generates incentives to ignore projects with large net present values in favor of less valuable projects with large immediate accounting profits.' The two most popular indicators of perform-ance in the UK appear to be earnings per share growth and pre-tax profits: Korn/Ferry International, *Board of Directors Study UK* (above, n. 67).

[78] See Rehnert, 'The Executive Compensation Contract' (above, n. 63), at 1168–80.

[79] The relationship between share prices and underlying value is considered below.

[80] E. F. Fama, 'Agency Problems and the Theory of the Firm', (1980) 88 *J Pol Econ* 288, at 295.

end. These are not insights unique to market theory. While such pressures will no doubt improve performance within the company generally, they are, however, likely to be at their least effective in increasing efficiency at the most senior level, since there, by definition, managers have little scope for promotion, and managers lower down the hierarchy have no power to unseat their superiors.[81] With regard to the board itself, its group dynamics are likely to inhibit the instigation of disciplinary action against insiders: it is common for personal relationships between the directors and other senior managers to be such that they will stand together as a team and only consider removing one of their number in situations of obvious incapacity or wrongdoing.[82] The problem may be particularly acute where power is effectively vested in the hands of a dominant chief executive.[83] It is likely, therefore, that the forces of the internal market, such as they are, will often be defeated by management power and board cohesiveness.

The external version of the theory holds that the 'market value' of top managers (which takes account of the remuneration they could command if they moved to a different employer) will increase where they are associated with a successful company, and therefore that directors will do all they can to boost profitability. Since results are dependent on team effort, managers are also given an incentive to ensure that each member of the team pulls his or her weight. While there is again doubtless some validity in this, there is a problem precisely because of the dependence of results on team effort. The team as a whole will have the incentive to be diligent, including being diligent in monitoring each other, but individual managers will have this incentive only if their own contribution is identifiable, and in the nature of

[81] The American literature posits a model wherein managers bring the performances of themselves and rival managers, including superiors, to the attention of outside board members, who act as arbitrators: Fama, ibid. at 293–4; E. F. Fama and M. C. Jensen, 'Separation of Ownership and Control', (1983) 26 *J L and Econ* 301, at 315. Such a model has no application in the UK, and very doubtful relevance in the US, given the dependence of outside directors on insiders for their appointment: see L. L. Dallas, 'Two Models of Corporate Governance: Beyond Berle and Means', (1988) 22 *U Mich J L Ref* 19, at 66.

[82] For a discussion of the group dynamics of the board see anonymous note, 'The Propriety of Judicial Deference to Corporate Boards', (1983) 96 *Harv L Rev* 1894, at 1896–1902. A survey conducted in the UK over a period of six months in 1988 found a surprisingly high level of involuntary departures of chief executives, but the largest proportion was related to take-over, and less than a sixth were associated with financial distress or managerial failure: J. Franks and C. Mayer, 'Capital Markets and Corporate Control: a Study of France, Germany and the UK', (1990) 10 *Economic Policy* 191, at 201–5. Similarly in the US, Jensen and Murphy, 'Performance Pay' (above, n. 72) at 239–40, commenting on the results of a number of studies, note 'only a single case of an outright firing and only 10 cases in which poor performance was cited as one of the reasons for the separation'.

[83] A number of DTI Inspectors' reports reveal cases of chief executives whose behaviour fellow directors have seemingly been incapable of controlling; see R. I. Tricker, *Corporate Governance* (1984), at 21–22. The Cadbury Committee *Report* (above, n. 10), para 4.9, recommends that the offices of chairman and chief executive should not be held by the same person, but that where they are there should be a 'strong, independent element on the board'.

things this will probably not be possible.[84] The prospect of increased future earnings will have no impact furthermore where a manager plans to leave the employment market, as will often be the case with chief executives who may be in their final period of office.[85] It is also important to note that while the external labour market may act as an incentive for directors to be more diligent, it is not obvious that it will improve the position where they lack flair or are simply inept. The solution is to recruit managers who are more talented than themselves, but in so doing they risk losing decision-making power and may ultimately put their own positions in danger.[86] As with the internal market for managerial services, therefore, the external market is likely to have little effect in the face of entrenched management power.[87]

The Capital Market

If a company is run inefficiently it will be penalized in the capital market, that is, its shares will be lowly rated as compared with more profitable companies. This need not be of great concern to management, however, given the capacity of most companies to finance themselves through retained earnings. Some companies never go to the new issues market, and it has been calculated that 'in the past decade, in no single year have ordinary share issues accounted for as much as 10 per cent of the sources of capital funds, and the average has been less than half that amount'.[88] While capital market considerations may accordingly have an effect in some cases it could be a long time before resolutely indolent or constitutionally inept directors regarded the problems of raising money as a reason for modifying their behaviour.

Even when a company does have recourse to the equity market, its depressed share price will affect management only indirectly. Thus, because its shares trade at a low price, the company will need to issue a larger number of them to raise a given amount of capital than would otherwise be the case. The effect of this will be to dilute further the value of the company's exisiting shares. This is a cost, but, as Eisenberg has pointed out, it is a cost that is borne by the company's shareholders rather than its managers.[89] It is true, nevertheless, that a falling share price will be of major concern to manage-

[84] See Hay and Morris, *Industrial Economics and Organization* (above, n. 70), at 307 - 8.

[85] See Eisenberg, 'The Structure of Corporation Law', (above, n. 66), at 1495.

[86] See V. Brudney, 'Corporate Governance, Agency Costs and the Rhetoric of Contract', (1985) 85 *Colum L Rev* 1403, at 1421-22.

[87] Posner's comment, *Economic Analysis of Law*, (above, n. 65) at 383 that managers 'have a strong incentive to manage the firm well or, if they are unable to manage it well themselves, to sell their offices to those who can', hardly seems to meet the point.

[88] A. Peacock and J. Bannock, *Corporate Takeovers and the Public Interest* (1991), at 30–1. See also Hay and Morris, *Industrial Economics* (above, n. 70), at 427.

[89] Eisenberg, 'The Structure of Corporation Law' (above, n. 66), at 1500–5. See also Posner, *Economic Analysis of Law* (above, n. 65), at 383–4, and see further, Ch. 6 below.

ment, because of possible repercussions in the market for corporate control. This is examined next.

The Market for Corporate Control

The market for corporate control has generated an enormous literature.[90] Some theorists regard the discipline it imposes as the only truly effective constraint on managerial discretion, at least in Anglo-Saxon 'market-based' systems,[91] and therefore consider its operation to be crucial to the efficiency of the private-enterprise economy.[92] The market is said to function in the following way. If management is inefficient the company's securities will have a low stock market valuation as compared with those of similar, but well managed, businesses, since the prospects for future dividends and share-price appreciation will be relatively poor. Observers of the stock market will interpret the low share price as a signal that the company's assets are being under-utilized and that an efficient management could employ them more profitably. A bid will therefore be made to gain control of the company and unlock its assets, enabling them to be managed more profitably. In order to persuade the company's existing members to sell their shares, it will be necessary for the bidder to offer a premium over the current stock market price.[93] In effect the bidder thereby divides the profit which is expected to result from improved efficiency between itself and the original shareholders. By this process control passes out of the hands of the inefficient management team to those who are able to utilize the company's assets at a level closer to their true potential.

The effectiveness of the market for control rests on the proposition ('the efficient market hypothesis') that stock markets behave rationally, that is, that shares are priced at a level that reflects a company's prospects under existing management and that prices are not merely the outcome of speculations on the part of market participants about each other's behaviour, causing price and underlying value to become detatched. If the latter were

---

[90] Early explorations of this subject are found in R. Marris, *The Economic Theory of Managerial Capitalism* (1964) and H. G. Manne, 'Mergers and the Market for Corporate Control', (1965) 73 *J Pol Econ* 693. See also Easterbrook and Fischel, 'The Proper Role of a Target's Management' (above, n. 60); J. C. Coffee, 'Regulating the Market for Corporate Control: A Critical Assessment of the Tender Offer's Role in Corporate Governance', (1984) 84 *Colum L Rev* 1145.

[91] For a brief consideration of corporate governance in the contrasting 'bank-based' systems, see 170–1 below.

[92] See e.g. R. J. Gilson, 'A Structural Approach to Corporations: The Case Against Defensive Actions in Tender Offers', (1981) 33 *Stan L Rev* 819, at 841; B. Chiplin and M. Wright, *The Logic of Mergers* (1987).

[93] See L. A. Stout, 'The Unimportance of Being Efficient: an Economic Analysis of Stock Market Pricing and Securities Regulation', (1988) *Mich L Rev* 613, at 687: 'These premiums reflect the different forces that set prices in two different markets: the public markets for trading marginal shares, and the tender offer market for corporate control.'

the case depressed share prices would not be a reliable indicator of badly-managed companies and hence the market for control could not have the efficiency-stimulating effect that is claimed for it.[94] While Jensen contends that 'Although the evidence is not literally 100 percent in support of the efficient market hypothesis, no proposition in any of the sciences is better documented',[95] there is in fact substantial disagreement about whether the market is efficient in the most relevant sense, that is, in reflecting companies' underlying value. If shares are not accurately priced then there is 'considerable scope for take-overs based on speculative and other motives where corporate control changes hands because of differences in information, or of opinion about the accuracy of stock market valuations, between sellers and purchasers of control, rather than because of proposed changes in management objectives or operating efficiency'.[96] We shall return to this issue below.

The main significance claimed for the market for corporate control as an efficiency-inducing device is not so much that companies are actually taken over and inadequate managements displaced, though of course this does happen and is regarded as a valuable effect of the mechanism, but that incumbent managements fear take-over and hence will do all they can to make the company efficient and the share price correspondingly high.[97] Since it is the threat of take-over that is crucial it is not possible to measure the effects of the market for control in any very scientific way, but there is nevertheless an intuitive plausibility in some of the claims made for it. The market suffers from a number of imperfections, however, and it seems likely that these have a significant limiting effect on its disciplinary power. The fact, as one commentator has pointed out, that bidders are prepared to pay substantial premiums over the existing stock-market valuation of a company in order to gain control indicates that despite the presence of the take-over threat, bidders still believe that there is considerable scope for efficiency gains.[98] The discussion that

---

[94] See T. Hadden, *Company Law and Capitalism* (2nd ed., 1977) at 69–75; L. Lowenstein, 'Pruning Deadwood in Hostile Takeovers: A Proposal for Legislation', (1983) 83 *Colum L Rev* 249, at 268–309. In particular, if a company's share price is too high, it is given an artificial layer of protection against take-over. If it is too low, existing management are at risk of being replaced by a less efficient bidder.

[95] M. C. Jensen, 'Takeovers: Their Causes and Consequences', (1988) 2 *J Econ Persp* 21, at 26.

[96] A. Hughes, 'The Impact of Merger: A Survey of Empirical Evidence for the UK', in J. A. Fairburn and J. A. Kay, *Mergers and Merger Policy* (1989), 30, at 33 (refs omitted).

[97] Removal from office after a take-over is common, but not inevitable, and may, in any event, not be too painful after compensation for loss of office has been paid. See further below.

[98] Brudney, 'Corporate Governance' (above, n. 86) at 1425-26, though some hoped-for gains may result not so much from improved managerial efficiency as e.g. from synergy or increased market power. A study of take-overs in the UK in 1967 discovered average premiums of one third of the pre-bid price: H. B. Rose and G. D. Newbould, 'The 1967 Take Over Boom', (Autumn 1967) *Moorgate and Wall Street* 5. In the United States an analyst has calculated that the average premium over the period studied was 49 per cent. For a summary of the American evidence, see Coffee, 'Regulating the Market for Corporate Control' (above, n. 89) at 1162, n. 34; Stout, 'The Unimportance of Being Efficient' (above, n. 93).

follows will examine the imperfections in the market for control and then consider the wider implications of reliance on it as a disciplinary mechanism.

Imperfections in the Market for Control

A major obstacle to the smooth operation of the market is the scale of transaction costs involved in changing control. It has been estimated that the total fees paid to third parties in the take-over process in the UK in 1985 came to £500 million, about 7 per cent of the value of the transactions,[99] and the figure will be much higher in the case of contested bids.[100] Underwriting, professional fees, and advertising cost Argyll nearly £50 million in their unsuccessful offer for Distillers in 1985,[101] for example, and the abortive consortium bid by Hoylake for BAT is reputed to have cost £140 million.[102] Added to these costs (and also the cost of management time), a bidder will have to pay a premium over the current market value of the target's shares of anything up to 50 per cent in order to gain control.[103] Costs of this magnitude and doubts about the ability to recoup them through improvements in efficiency or other gains are likely to be a significant disincentive to attempting a take-over[104] and their scale suggests that they constitute a barrier behind which sub-optimally performing boards can find a substantial measure of protection. Indeed, one commentator has argued that the cost of acquiring control is so great that the disciplinary force of the market is 'likely to be limited to instances of gross managerial failure'.[105] As against this, if raiders are in the habit of overestimating the likely efficiency gains[106] they will pose a threat to potential target managements in a broader range of cases, that is, including those cases in which, as it turns out, a bid is not justified by its cost.

[99] J. A. Kay, *The Role of Mergers*, Institute of Fiscal Studies Working Paper 94 (1986), quoted in J. Franks and R. Harris, 'Shareholder Wealth Effects of UK Take-overs: Implications for Merger Policy', in Fairburn and Kay, *Mergers and Merger Policy* (above, n. 94) 148, at 169–70.

[100] See Peacock and Bannock, *Corporate Takeovers* (above, n. 94), at 13.

[101] CBI, *Investing for Britain's Future: Report of the City/Industry Task Force* (1987, London), para 61.

[102] Peacock and Bannock, *Corporate Takeovers* (above, n. 88), at 13.

[103] See n. 100 above.

[104] Ironically, advisers and lenders appear often to have played a key role in instigating offers. See e.g. J. Plender, in A. Cosh, et al. *Take-overs and Short-termism in the UK*, IPPR Industrial Policy Paper no. 3 (1990), at 36: 'the market in corporate control had been hi-jacked in the second half of the 1980's by the bankers, for the purpose of addressing the problem of declining profitability in their wholesale business.' A possible way of reducing fees etc is to require public disclosure of them: see the *Financial Times* 24 July 1986.

[105] Coffee, 'Regulating the Market' (above, 90) at 1200. One survey indicates that the value of a company's shares can fall approximately 13 per cent below their potential (i.e. their value if the company were efficiently managed) before there is a significant risk of take-over: R. Smiley, 'Tender Offers, Transaction Costs and the Theory of the Firm', (1976) 58 *Rev of Econ and Stats* 22.

[106] That they do this is possibly borne out by the poor post-acquisition results of acquired companies: see 125 below.

A different difficulty with the market for control derives from the particular character of that market as a market. As Fairburn and Kay explain,

'if I produce a poor product, then I will gradually lose market share, and my competitors will gradually gain it. If I run a company badly, however, the market does not gradually transfer its management to someone else; it leaves me with the monopoly of corporate control until, at the consummation of a take-over bid, it transfers it abruptly and completely'.[107]

They go on to note that it is this feature of the market that necessitates detailed regulation to protect the interests of the shareholders, a principal objective of the City Code on Take-overs and Mergers being, for instance, to ensure a fair distribution of the take-over premium among the members. Of greater relevance here, they also observe that it is an 'important reason why the market for corporate control is less efficient and effective than most other markets'.

The point is that individual shareholders, each with a holding insufficient to affect the outcome of the bid, have an incentive to reject the offer to buy their shares in order to be able to 'free ride' on the efforts of the bidder, if successful.[108] The idea is that the bidder must think that the shares in the company are worth more than the bid price, for example, because under the bidder's control the company will be operated more efficiently, otherwise the bid would not be made. By retaining a holding the member will be able to participate in this post-bid increase in value. The result, however, is that because of the free-riding element the bid may fail, and hence a substantial gap may arise between a company's actual and potential earnings without an inefficient management being ousted by a take-over.[109]

A further doubt about the operation of the market for control is created by evidence suggesting that inefficient companies as such are not regarded as favourable targets. A survey conducted in the United States in 1981 revealed that directors considered the feature that made a company most attractive as a take-over target was that it had 'excellent management' and the majority of respondents regarded management inefficiency as something which would

---

[107] Fairburn and Kay, *Mergers and Merger Policy* (above, n. 96), at 19.
[108] See S. J. Grossman and O. D. Hart, 'Takeover Bids, the Free-rider Problem and the Theory of the Corporation', (1980) 11 *Bell J* 42. The problem arises because of the conditionality of bids. Given that the individual shareholder cannot affect the success of the bid, and will be able to sell (and realize the premium) only if the minimum level of acceptances is reached, there is nothing to be gained by accepting, and an incentive to reject.
[109] See Hay and Morris, *Industrial Economics* (above, n. 70), at 512–6, for a rigorous consideration of this issue. The authors discuss a number of ways in which the free-rider problem might be overcome, e.g. by the threat of oppression of minority shareholders post-bid, compulsory acquistion legislation (see CA 1985, Pt XIIIA), and the building of a 'toe-hold' stake, but conclude that none is likely to be entirely successful. See also Easterbrook and Fischel, *The Economic Structure of Corporate Law* (above, n. 9) at 179–80 (two-tier bids as a way of overcoming the problem).

actually put them off.[110] A recent British study, summarizing the evidence on the financial characteristics of acquiring, acquired, and non-acquired companies, concludes that it is difficult to distinguish between them.[111] This is perhaps not surprising, given that bidders are attracted to targets for a variety of reasons that may be unconnected with the potential for improving the target's management. Other motives include diversification, gaining access to new markets and increasing market share, reaping economies of scale and other synergistic gains, and sheer empire-building. If badly managed companies are no more at risk than efficient ones, however, it seems fair to assume that the disciplinary effect of the market for control is significantly diminished. As Buxbaum suggests, 'Since takeovers appear to have no systematic impact on weak management or suboptimal resource use ... takeover threats cannot affect management behaviour except in an inconsistent manner. If doing well is no protection, the incentive to avoid doing badly is weak'.[112] There will, though, always be some incentive for managers to increase share price, since a more expensive company is harder to swallow and satisfied shareholders are less likely to sell.

The Market for Control and Efficiency

What is not in doubt is that there is a highly active market in take-overs in the UK,[113] and therefore not surprisingly managements do commonly take steps to safeguard their positions. Leaving aside for the moment purely defensive moves, not calculated to increase efficiency, responses may, following Eisenberg's terminology, lead to improvements in *operating* efficiency or *resource* efficiency.[114] The former refers to the more efficient management of the company's existing stock of assets, the latter to changes in the combination of assets held by the company with a view to raising profitability. Some improvements in operating efficiency are likely to occur under the pressure of

[110] See Coffee, 'Regulating the Market' (above, n. 90) at 1212. Coffee also points out that take-over activity tends not to be dispersed throughout the corporate sector, but rather has a cyclical character, with a wave of take-overs moving through particular industries, seemingly for reasons specific to the industry concerned. This again suggests that bidders are not purposefully seeking out badly managed companies, and that poor managements have no more to fear than good ones: see ibid. at 1210-11. For a similar view of the position in the UK, see D Kuehn, *Takeovers and the Theory of the Firm* (1975), at 20.
[111] Chiplin and Wright, *The Logic of Mergers* (above, n. 92), at 64-5. From their study of the 42 hostile take-overs that took place between January 1989 and March 1990, T. Jenkinson and C. Mayer, *Takeover Defence Strategies* (1991), at 33, conclude that 'there is little relation between the financial performance of a target before acquisition and with the likelihood of a hostile bid emerging or the outcome of that bid.' For the American position, see Coffee, 'Regulating the Market' (above, n. 90) at 1207; E. S. Herman, 'The Limits of the Market as a Discipline in Corporate Governance' (1984) 9 *Del J Corp L* 530, at 536-37.
[112] R. M. Buxbaum, 'Corporate Legitimacy, Economic Theory and Legal Doctrine', (1984) 45 *Ohio State L J* 516, at 531.
[113] See Cosh et al. *Takeovers and Short-termism* (above, n. 104), at 9.
[114] Eisenberg, 'The Structure of Corporation Law' (above, n. 66), at 1498 n. 175.

the take-over threat, but they depend on managements recognizing current weaknesses and on their having the ability to remedy them. Where managers are of limited competence any increases in efficiency are more likely to result from improved resource efficiency, particularly through disposal of under-performing activities or subsidiaries in order to improve the group's financial profile.[115] A growth in divestment was a prominent feature of the 1980s, with parent companies making disposals both to other groups[116] and to existing managers in the form of management buy-outs. Economic gains may flow from this process through unscrambling previous misconceived acquisitions, for example, or simply from an injection of fresh and more dynamic management. Management buy-outs in particular may lead to increases in efficiency by reducing the layers of administration and enabling key decisions to be made by managers with industry-specific experience. There may also be stronger incentives as a result of management's having a significant equity stake in the company, and the stringent repayment conditions that banks and other institutions attach to the finance they provide to make the buy-out possible.[117] While this restructuring activity is likely to prove beneficial to the economy, the more fundamental problem of operationally inefficient managements may, however, remain relatively immune to the stimulus of the take-over threat.

Other Effects of the Market for Control

As we have seen, market theorists regard the threat of take-over as the main contribution of the market for control to the promotion of efficiency. In evaluating the market as a mechanism for disciplining management, however, it is necessary to take account of its wider impact, both in terms of the results of consummated mergers and of the overall effects of the threat of a change in control on management behaviour. The extent to which the market for control should be relied on as a disciplinary device can be determined only in the light of an approximation of the social costs it may impose. The direct costs of the take-over process, in the form of fees to banks and professional advisers, have already been noted. The level of transaction costs, and the scale of third-party and other effects, invite speculation about whether management changes could be effected in a less costly and disruptive way.

---

[115] See Jensen, 'Takeovers: Their Causes and Consequences' (above, n. 93), at 23 - 39.

[116] Discussed in M. Wright, B. Chiplin, and J. Coyne, 'The Market for Corporate Control: The Divestment Option', in Fairburn and Kay, *Mergers and Merger Policy* (above, n. 96), 116.

[117] For advocacy of the replacement of public shareholders by a 'leveraged buy-out association' as a means of overcoming the problems of the separation of ownership and control, see M. C. Jensen, 'Eclipse of the Public Corporation', (Sept.-Oct. 1989) *Harv Bus Rev* 61. A study of post-buy-out performance indicates that in the first three years buy-outs perform better than the average company in the relevant sector, but that performance then falls below average: Touche Ross Corporate Finance, *The Performance of Management Buy-outs in the Longer Term* (1989).

The Effects of Mergers

The efficiency of the combined enterprise in concluded take-overs as compared with the pre-merger performance of the target and the acquirer is of crucial importance in evaluating the merits of reliance on the market for control as a disciplinary mechanism. The evidence is mixed. Studies based on relative accounting profits reveal that on average mergers have been unprofitable.[118] An alternative approach is to measure share price changes; prices at any given time reflect the market's estimate of future performance and, if it is assumed that this estimate is reliable,[119] then a comparison of 'before and after' figures should provide an accurate guide to the change in earning potential brought about by merger. The evidence not surprisingly shows that there are gains to acquiree shareholders, given the need to pay a premium to persuade them to part with control. The crucial issue is whether this merely represents a transfer in wealth from the acquirer, or whether there is an increase in wealth overall. On this the evidence is conflicting, some studies finding that take-overs were on the whole value-creating, others that target shareholder gains were more than offset by losses to the shareholders of the acquiring companies.[120] Furthermore, even if there are net gains to shareholders it is not clear to what extent these result from increased efficiency, and hence represent net *social* gains, or are the product of what may be socially detrimental increases in market power, or gains made at the expence of other groups, such as employees.[121] In short, the evidence does not permit a concluded view on whether consummated mergers have led to the creation of more or less efficient enterprises.

As just suggested, take-overs may lead to increased market dominance, and

---

[118] See M. A. King, 'Takeover Activity in the United Kingdom', in Fairburn and Kay, *Mergers and Merger Policy* (above, n. 96), 99, at 111. For inadequacies in the accounting profits approach, see ibid. at 22–24.

[119] See 129–31 below. For a criticism of the reliability of share price analyses see E. S. Herman and L. Lowenstein, 'The Efficiency Effects of Hostile Takeovers', in J. C. Coffee, L. Lowenstein, and S. Rose-Ackerman (eds), *Knights, Raiders and Targets: The Impact of the Hostile Takeover* (1988), 211, at 217–18.

[120] See the review of the evidence in J. Franks and R. Harris, 'Shareholder Wealth Effects of UK Take-overs: Implications for Merger Policy', in Fairburn and Kay, *Mergers and Merger Policy* (above, n. 96), 148, at 154–155. They note that the most recent survey, conducted by themselves, (*Shareholder Wealth Effects of Corporate Takeovers: the UK Experience 1955–85*, London Business School and University of North Carolina at Chapel Hill Working Paper) shows that 'acquiree shareholders gained substantially with bid premiums of 22 per cent in the month of the bid. At the same time, acquirer shareholders gained 1 per cent.' For similar findings in the USA see M. C. Jensen and R. Ruback, 'The Market for Corporate Control: the Scientific Evidence', (1983) 11 *J Fin Econ* 5.

[121] In other words the relative efficiency of the new enterprise is not the only consideration in assessing the impact of completed take-overs on the economy, since take-overs also impose 'external' social costs. One of these is transitional unemployment (post-merger efficiency gains are likely in part to result from reduced labour inputs). The social cost of unemployment must therefore be set against the efficiency gains in an overall economic assessment: see M. C. Sawyer, *The Economics of Industries and Firms* (2nd ed., 1985), at 222–23.

hence the consequences of the market for control on competition must also be taken into account in any overall assessment. Chiplin and Wright observe that

'The impact of large acquisitions on the number of independent companies in the UK is quite profound. Of the top 200 companies, ranked by profitability in 1971–72, some 45 ceased to be independent companies by 1984. Between 1982 and 1986, 137 of the top 1,000 quoted companies in the UK in terms of market value in 1982 were acquired or had merged with other companies . . . '.[122]

These figures do not necessarily correlate with increased market power, however, there being evidence to indicate that aggregate concentration and concentration in individual industries have not increased since the mid-1970s.[123] This is explicable, at least in part, by a shift from horizontal to diversifying mergers. But while the latter may not have a material impact on competition, they do nevertheless contribute to an incremental drift of decision-making power to a steadily diminishing number of companies. The significance of this was discussed in Chapter 1, and it might be added here that there is some evidence to suggest that concentration may have an adverse effect on the level of invention and innovation in the economy.[124]

A dimension of increased decision-making concentration which has attracted particular notice concerns the effects on regional diversity and development. A recent report by the Confederation of British Industry observed that take-overs contribute to 'the gradual accretion of financial and management power in London and the South-East and the demise of independent companies based elsewhere that are able to contribute to the local community'.[125] This view is supported by a number of empirical studies of the regional impact of mergers.[126] A common result is an upward shift of decision-making to the new parent company, often located in the south-east. This can have an adverse effect on local suppliers of materials, and in particular of support services, such as insurance, advertising, and legal advice, with consequential damage to the vigour of the regional economy and its attractiveness to inward investment.[127] In terms of the performance

---

[122] Chiplin and Wright, *The Logic of Mergers* (above, n. 92), at 19. Only a minority of these control changes resulted from contested take-overs.

[123] See S. Littlechild, 'Myths and Merger Policy', in Fairburn and Kay, *Mergers and Merger Policy* (above, n. 96), 301, at 303–05.

[124] See Peacock and Bannock, *Corporate Takeovers* (above, n. 88), at 29–30.

[125] CBI, *Investing for Britain's Future* (above, n. 101), para 127.

[126] The results are summarized in Hughes, 'The Impact of Merger' (above, n. 96), at 88–89. And see Peacock and Bannock, *Corporate Takeovers* (above, n. 88), ch. 5 and 86–7.

[127] Regional considerations have in the past influenced the Monopolies and Mergers Commission in its assessment of whether a take-over is in the public interest: see K. George, 'Do We Need a Merger Policy?', in Fairburn and Kay, *Mergers and Merger Policy* (above, n. 96), 281, at 295–96. The maintenance and promotion of a 'balanced distribution of industry and employment in the United Kingdom' is a factor which the Commission is expressly required to consider: Fair

of the economy as a whole it is not entirely clear what the impact of regional disparities is, though it seems plausible that congestion in the southeast and the under-utilization of resources elsewhere represent a net loss to the economy overall.[128] In broader social terms the costs are fairly self-evident.

The regional implications aside, a group that will inevitably be affected by take-over activity is the target company's employees. After a take-over a common way of making an acquired company more profitable is to reduce the size of the workforce or otherwise to change working conditions to lower costs or increase productivity. Similarly, in order to integrate the target's business within the enlarged organization, overlapping or ill-fitting activities may be disposed of or discontinued. New owners may have fewer qualms than long-serving managers about taking action of this kind, which is likely to be damaging to the company's employees and the wider host community.[129] It has been argued that the dismissal of employees following a change in control is a (moral) breach of trust,[130] in that employees have legitimate expectations of continuing employment, arising, for example, from their investment in the company in the form of firm-specific training. Similarly, in the language of implicit contracting, employees accept lower remuneration in exchange for job stability, and this (unenforceable) understanding is breached when employees are laid off following a take-over.[131] The market for control may be seen from this perspective, therefore, as having a negative side-effect in so far as it gives shareholders an opportunity to make unfair gains at the employees' expense.[132] Whether this is a form of unfairness specific to the take-over process, however, or whether control changes merely highlight the more general vulnerability of employees within the corporate framework,[133] is debatable. Issues of fairness aside, the disruption of implicit contracting by an active market in control may contribute to

Trading Act 1973, s 84(1)(d). As noted at 157–8 below, it has been government policy in recent years to make referrals almost exclusively on competition grounds.

[128] See Peacock and Bannock, *Mergers and Merger Policy* (above, n. 88), at 71–2.

[129] Cf. Easterbrook and Fischel, *The Economic Structure of Corporate Law* (above, n. 9), at 181–3, who argue that it is contrary to the interests of an acquiring firm to damage its reputation as an employer by acting in a way that will be perceived as unfair.

[130] A. Schleifer and L. Summers, 'Breach of Trust in Hostile Takeovers', in A. J. Auerbach (ed.), *Corporate Takeovers: Causes and Consequences* (1988) 33.

[131] Ibid. and see J. C. Coffee, 'Liquidity Versus Control: The Institutional Investor as Corporate Monitor', (1991) 91 *Colum L Rev* 1278, at 1333–4 and material cited therein.

[132] For a discussion of ways of protecting employee interests in take-overs, including collective bargaining agreements which are binding on successors and 'tin parachutes', see A. C. Gavis, 'A Framework for Satisfying Corporate Directors' Responsibilities Under State Nonshareholder Constituency Statutes: The Use of Explicit Contracts', (1990) 138 *U of Penn L Rev* 1451.

[133] On which see J. W. Singer, 'The Reliance Interest in Property', (1988) 40 *Stan L Rev* 611, arguing that the company is a common enterprise the legal structure of which should recognize employee interests additional to those founded on narrow contractual rights, particularly in relation to plant closings. On the protection of employee interests generally see chs 11 and 12 below.

an excessively short-term focus on the part of management and employees, with adverse consequences for the economy's long-term growth prospects.[134]

The Effects of the Threat of Take-over

A well-documented response to the threat of take-over is for the company to increase its capitalization by itself becoming a predator or otherwise absorbing additional businesses to enable it to obtain the relative security that comes with increased size.[135] Clearly, if the acquirer is not particularly efficient in the first place, this response will simply result in more assets being controlled by an unimpressive management. Growth and other manœuvres[136] motivated by no logic other than a defensive one are economically damaging by-products of an active market for control, causing a 'huge diversion of managerial effort into devising ways to reduce a vulnerability that did not grow out of managerial inefficiency'.[137]

The side-effect that has caused greatest concern in recent years, however, is that of 'short-termism'. This is a condition in which managements become excessively concerned with short-term profits with a view to keeping share price high and thus avoiding the attention of bidders. In order to boost short-term accounting profits companies may be tempted to cut expenditure on items such as training, research and development, and investment in productive capacity, all of which are essential to a healthy economy, on the basis that they will show a positive return only in the longer term.[138] This tendency is said to be exacerbated by the growth of institutional holdings, the institutions themselves exhibiting a short-termist attitude, conspicuous in the fund managers engaged by them. These, under pressure to increase the returns on their portfolios over very short review periods, turn over their

---

[134] See further 131 below.

[135] P & O, for example, increased its market capitalization from £300 million to £1.6 billion in two years by a policy of merging with other companies in similar and dissimilar industries: see 'Sterling Qualities on the Crest of a Wave', *Sunday Times*, 7 December 1986. See also Chiplin and Wright, *The Logic of Mergers* (above, n. 92) at 49–50. The defensive advantages of size are, however, being eroded. Changes in financing methods, particularly a trend towards paying for acquisitions with borrowed money, and the emergence of consortium bids, have increased predatory purchasing power: see Chiplin and Wright, ibid. at 14–18, 58–61; C. Moir, *The Acquisitive Streak* (1986), at 122–23. Cosh et al. *Takeovers and Short-termism* (above, n. 104) at 10, conclude that while size does not in itself confer immunity, the probability of the largest companies being acquired is still very low.

[136] For examples of defensive tactics, see Ch. 5 below.

[137] Herman and Lowenstein, 'The Efficiency Effects of Hostile Takeovers', in Coffee, et al. *Knights, Raiders, and Targets* (above, n. 119) 211, at 215.

[138] For an expression of this view, see Innovation Advisory Board (DTI), *Innovation: City Attitudes and Practices* (1990), and *Promoting Innovation and Long Termism* (1990). The *Financial Times*, 21 April 1990 comments that a 'striking feature of many of the more significant technological advances and their financing in post-war Britain is how often success has been achieved under the umbrella of private or restricted voting ownership structure — witness Pilkington's float glass process, Reuter's dealing systems or 3i's dominant position in venture capital'.

holdings frequently (known as 'churning'), disposing of a company's shares on the first sign that they are under-performing the market.[139] Similarly, institutions are accused of 'disloyalty' in bid situations, preferring to take the premium rather than await longer-term growth.[140] Since the threat of take-over is the most potent source of management concern with share price, the market for control is seen as profoundly implicated in converting this alleged investor short-termism into management short-termism.[141]

Whether the charge of investor short-termism is valid turns essentially on whether the stock market is efficient in pricing shares. According to corporate finance theory, 'the share price of any company should reflect the present value of the company's stream of future cash flows'.[142] In other words, the *current* price of a company's shares should reflect expected *future* returns. Thus, even though an investment may produce income only in the longer term, if it is financially worthwhile it will have an immediate positive effect on share price, assuming an efficient stock market. As we have mentioned, the efficient market hypothesis holds that the market is efficient, in the sense that share prices are determined in the light of all relevant publicly available information.[143] It follows that there should be no pressure on management from share prices to sacrifice profitable investment opportunities, because, even though these may depress short-term accounting profits, undertaking them will cause a rise, rather than a fall, in share price.[144] Similarly, if prices

[139] For a review of the evidence on this point, see CBI, *Pension Fund Investment Management* (1988) at 25, 28–9, and 59. See also P. D. Jackson, 'Management of UK Equity Portfolios', (May 1987) *Bank of England Quarterly Bulletin* 253.

[140] There is some evidence to the contrary, that institutions show a disposition to be loyal to incumbent managements in the face of a bid: J. B. Bracewell-Milnes, *Are Equity Markets Short Sighted?* (Institute of Directors, 1987), at para 69. For a different view see Cosh et al, *Takeovers and Short-Termism* (above, n. 104), at 15.

[141] Disquiet about these issues on the part of the industrial sector led to the setting up in 1986 of a City/Industry Task Force to look into the position. The ensuing report, *Investing for Britain's Future* (above, n. 101), concluded that managements' fears about short-term attitudes on the part of investors were largely misplaced. Whatever the validity of this view, a survey conducted after the publication of the Report found that 64 per cent of managers believed that institutions did not make a long-term or strategic evaluation of their companies: *Financial Times*, 4 November 1988. This perception, whether valid or not, seems likely to be a causative factor in managerial short-termism

[142] P. Marsh, *Short-termism on Trial* (1990), at 9 (ref omitted). The following attack on the view that institutional behaviour forces management to act in a short-termist way is taken from Marsh, at 8–42.

[143] This is the 'semi-strong' form of the hypothesis; in the 'strong' form a market is said to be efficient where share prices reflect *all* relevant information. The requirements of the strong form are clearly not met, since in the case of any company there will frequently be a considerable amount of price-sensitive information available only to insiders. Increasing the speed with which such information flows to the market is the main argument relied on by those who oppose prohibitions on insider dealing: see, H. G. Manne, 'In Defense of Insider Trading', (1966) 44 *Harv Bus Rev* 133; D. W. Carlton and D. R. Fischel, 'The Regulation of Insider Trading', (1983) 35 *Stan L Rev* 857. See also Chiplin and Wright, *The Logic of Mergers* (above, note 92) at 41–3.

[144] There is evidence of this in J. J. McConnell and C. J. Muscarella, 'Corporate Capital Expenditure Decisions and the Market Value of the Firm', (1985) 14 *J Fin Econ* 399; see also the

accurately reflect long-term prospects, a fund manager required to improve short-term performance can do so only by identifying and buying under-valued shares, and identifying and selling over-valued ones, which in turn depends on a balanced evaluation of both the company's short- and long-term position. There is accordingly no reason why institutional behaviour should induce short-term behaviour in management.

The counter-argument, naturally enough, is that the stock market does not accurately price shares. It has thus been suggested that while there is 'substantial evidence of information arbitrage market efficiency, meaning that prices respond quickly to new information . . . this technical efficiency is very different from the claimed ability of the market to value stocks in accordance with the expected stream of future earnings or dividends'.[145] Part of the explanation for this failure is that not enough information about investment plans is available to the market, and also that market participants lack the technical ability to evaluate what may be highly complex and specialized projects.[146] This aspect of the problem is in principle remedi-able,[147] though no doubt in practice the demands of commercial confidentiality will always to some extent limit information flow.[148] The other cause may, however, be inherent in the stock market system. This is that the evaluation of a company's prospects is ultimately a matter of subjective judgement, and hence what 'economists frequently characterize as quantifiable risks are in reality uncertainties of such large and incalculable proportions as to intimidate investors and send them scurrying to the seemingly safer ground of follow-the-leader'.[149] In this way share prices are determined not by reference to estimations of fundamental value, but by a series of guesses about the behaviour of other market participants; they result from '[s]peculations on the speculations of other speculators who are doing the

material cited in Marsh, *Short-Termism on Trial* (above, n. 42), at 19, nn. 18 and 19. There is, however, also evidence that certain forms of investment which are considered high-risk are not favoured by the market: see D. Goodhart and C. Grant, *Making the City Work*, Fabian Tract no. 528, (1988), at 20-22. George, 'Do We Need a Merger Policy?' (above, n. 127), at 286 presents some evidence that companies which have adopted measures to improve long-term competitiveness may suffer share-price falls through depressed profits and hence be particularly susceptible to take-over.

[145] Herman and Lowenstein, 'The Efficiency Effects' (above, n. 119), at 214. See also Peacock and Bannock, *Corporate Takeovers* (above, n. 88), at 45-9.
[146] See H. T. C. Hu, 'Risk, Time, and Fiduciary Principles in Corporate Investment', (1990) 38 *UCLA L Rev* 227, at 339-41.
[147] See e.g. the proposals for 'innovation reports' in D. A. Walker, 'Some Perspectives for Pension Fund Managers', (1987) 27 *Bank of England Quarterly Bulletin* 247 and IAB, *Promoting Innovation and Long Termism* (above, n. 138), at 2. The Institutional Shareholders' Committee, *Suggested Disclosure of Research and Development Expenditure* (1992) has also made proposals for more expansive disclosure of R and D in the annual accounts than is currently required by SSAP 13, as well as for disclosure through other channels.
[148] And see 173, below.
[149] Herman and Lowenstein, 'The Efficiency Effects' (above, n. 119), at 215.

same thing'.[150] In other words, share prices may be driven by fads and other forms of market irrationality, and particularly by a concentration on tangible short-term earnings figures rather than on relatively imponderable longer-term prospects.[151]

An alternative explanation of short-termism, also attributable to the take-over market, should finally be noted. Thus it has been suggested that

'Short-termism may not be so much a product of the mispricing of assets, . . . but more a reflection of contractual failures in securities markets in part brought on by the takeover process. According to this view, short-termism is a feature of investments in firm-specific assets that have a low resale value outside the firm. Thus, it will be less prevalent in the development of oil fields and property sites, than in R & D and training'.[152]

The point is that the threat of take-over reduces the long-term security of employees and managers. If a change in control occurs employment contracts may be terminated, with the result that employees lose the gains from firm-specific training. Investment in training will therefore be discouraged, and managers are similarly discouraged from causing the company to engage in research and development and other projects the return from which will only be reflected in managers' rewards in the long term. It may thus be observed that there is a 'trade-off between the disciplinary effect of takeovers and their disruptive impact on investment and long-term growth'.[153]

No conclusive view about the contribution of the market for control to management short-termism is possible, at least as yet. To the extent that managers do pursue short-term goals the explanation may be a false perception of capital market short-termism, or it may be unrelated to the operation of the market. Management short-termism may, for example, be a result of one or more of performance-based remuneration systems linked to near-term targets, high management turn-over rates, or reliance on divisionalized goals.[154] That take-overs might be centrally implicated, however, adds to the overall impression that the stimulus to efficiency that the market undoubtedly, though variably, creates, is achieved at a high price, and might be achievable with fewer side-effects by other means.

[150] J. Tobin, 'On the Efficiency of the Financial System', (July 1984) *Lloyds Bank Review* 1, at 7.
[151] See Hu, 'Risk, Time and Fiduciary Principles' (above, n. 146), at 341–42. On 'bubbles' and 'fads' see G. C. Reid, *Efficient Markets and the Rationale of Takeovers*, Hume Occasional Paper no. 22 (1990), at 19–23.
[152] Franks and Mayer, 'Capital Markets and Corporate Control' (above, n. 82), at 194; see also 213–4.
[153] Jenkinson and Mayer, *Takeover Defence Strategies* (above, n. 111), at 24. The 'implicit contracts' literature also argues that since management and employee expectations about continued employment and delayed rewards may be defeated after a hostile take-over, the risk of take-over reduces the incentive to undertake investments for which there is a deferred pay-back: see Coffee, 'Liquidity Versus Control' (above, n. 131), at 1333–4 and material cited therein.
[154] See Marsh, *Short-termism on Trial* (above, n. 142), at 52–63.

Market Discipline: Conclusion

The conclusion to be drawn from the above discussion is that while market forces undoubtedly constrain management behaviour, the disciplinary framework they impose is far from complete. Claims of market optimality rest on standard neo-classical assumptions about economically rational motivation, competitive market conditions, availability of full information, and absence of transaction costs. The failure of these assumptions to hold in practice suggests that it would be unsafe to rely on markets as a substitute for all other forms of control. It does not, of course, follow that, because markets are of only limited effectiveness, legal intervention, in the shape of a more active liability regime or a reformed governance structure, would necessarily lead to an outcome closer to the ideal, since the costs of intervention may exceed the benefits. In the absence of empirical evidence to that effect, however, the argument that intervention is inherently inefficient makes no stronger claim to validity than the original assertion of market competence. With these points in mind the next section will return to the contribution that liability rules can make to increased management efficiency. It should finally be noted that it has also emerged that reliance on markets as a disciplinary device, and in particular on the market for control, is itself far from costless. The negative impact of the market invites the question whether it might be desirable to find a substitute for, and not merely a supplement to, the discipline the latter market provides. This issue is taken up in the next chapter, where some of the rules of company law that support the functioning of the market are examined. A possible substitute, by way of a reformed governance structure, is discussed in Chapter 6.

III THE ROLE OF LIABILITY RULES

Section I concluded that the impact of the duty of care on managerial efficiency, even with a more rigorous content, will inevitably be rather modest, but that the duty nevertheless is capable of playing an important role. A principal aspect of that role is as a deterrent. The threat of personal liability provides directors with an incentive to comply with applicable standards of conduct. This section begins with a group of contrasts concerning the deterrent effects of markets and liability regimes.

First, because markets are imperfect in various ways they will tolerate serious levels of inefficiency. We have seen, for instance, that the magnitude of transaction costs in the market for control may shield all but the most egregious cases of management failure. Liability, on the other hand, at least in principle, can be triggered by less serious, but still costly defaults. Second, a distinguishing characteristic of negligence liability (and indeed of the legal approach in general) is that it attaches to single episodes of management failure. Market sanctions, in contrast, depend on the net outcome of an aggregate of performances. Negligent conduct will thus frequently engender no market response, not simply because the loss that results is too small to register, given market insensitivity, but because its effects are masked by above-average returns from other, successful projects. By focusing on discrete activities liability rules are capable of creating a potentially more pervasive field of deterrence.[155]

A third point of distinction concerns the nature of legal and market sanctions. The severest market penalty for under-performance is loss of office following corporate collapse or, more probably, a change in control. But the availability of generous compensation in the latter case will often mean that this fate holds no great terrors for management, and may even be positively welcomed. Thus directors may receive substantial compensation for premature termination of their employment contracts, or may benefit from a 'golden parachute', that is, a contractual provision authorizing a generous additional severance payment in the event of take-over.[156] The payment of damages for negligence, is, in contrast, entirely without redeeming features.

There is an at least theoretical possibility that a liability regime with teeth would deter not only negligent conduct, but also talented individuals from becoming directors. There seems little likelihood of this occurring in the case of executive directors, at least unless the risk of liability were to increase massively, but a reduction in the supply of more modestly remunerated non-executives is not implausible.[157] Directors may, and frequently do,[158] however,

[155] Cf. Manning, 'The Business Judgment Rule and the Director's Duty of Attention: Time for Reality', (1984) 39 *Bus Lawyer* 1477, at 1494:

the heart of the director's true responsibility is attention to his ongoing multiple functions: a process, a flow of events, a continuum of the company's current history . . . the referent of the automobile driver's legal duty is the isolated event of the accident, not his general performance as a driver. In the case of a director, the proper referent for his legal duty should be the flow of his performance of his directoral functions, not the individual incident' (emphasis omitted).

It is not clear why this should be so. Liability attaches not to poor outcomes as such, but to poor performances, i.e. situations in which directorial conduct has fallen below acceptable standards. It is a legitimate objective of law to minimize these occurrences.

[156] See further 220 below.

[157] See R. Cranston, 'Limiting Directors' Liability: Ratification, Exemption and Indemnification', [1992] *JBL* 197, at 210. The argument that liability will deter directors from taking office has been successfully deployed in some American states, see e.g. Del. Code Ann., tit 8, s 102(b)(7), allowing corporations to limit or eliminate directors' liability in negligence. This measure was a response to the unavailability or prohibitive cost of directors' and officers' indemnity insurance: see R. John, 'Relieving Directors from the Liabilities of Office: the Case for Reform of Section 241, Corporations Law', [1992] *Co & Sec L Jo* 6, at 12–13. J. C. Coffee, 'No Exit?: Opting Out, The Contractual Theory of the Corporation, and the Special Case of Remedies', (1988) 53 *Brooklyn L Rev* 919, at 925–31, argues that *limitation* of liability is justifiable, in that liability continues to have a deterrent effect, and disproportionate liability and the associated reluctance of the courts to impose it are avoided. Limitation clauses are accepted as valid in the ALI's *Principles of Corporate Governance* (above, n. 30): see para 7.19 and 871–900

[158] It has been estimated that directors in 65–70 per cent of the largest 250 companies have cover: see the *Financial Times*, 16 July 1991.

insure against negligence liability and this is likely, at least in part, to offset any reluctance to take office through the fear of having to meet a damages award. But there is a price to pay for this advantage, in that the effect of insurance is a reduction in the deterrence value of liability. As against this, it is argued that insurance companies act as an additional monitoring agency: in fixing premiums insurers will assess the degree of risk and directors thus have an incentive to minimise the chances of liability arising in order to keep premiums as low as possible.[159] This is not persuasive where directors do not pay their own premiums,[160] however, and in any case the difficulties faced by insurers in distinguishing high-risk from low-risk directors (i.e. performing the monitoring function) are considerable, given the low visibility of the management decision-making process and the wide range of functions that a director may be called upon to perform.[161] It is therefore difficult to avoid the conclusion that the effect of insurance is in general to reduce the deterrent effect of liability.

An undoubted limitation of liability rules in promoting managerial efficiency is that while they provide a deterrent, they cannot, unlike the market and market-linked devices, create a more positive motivational environment. They lay down minimum standards, and do not as such provide an incentive, exerting upward pressure to achieve top-quality performance. The educational role of law in increasing efficiency should not, however, be overlooked.[162] It was suggested above that the duty of care is best conceived as imposing essentially procedural standards. By laying down such standards the law is capable of defining what is expected of managers, of giving normative guidance on how they should fulfil their role. In particular we have seen how the law can structure the decision-making process by insisting that decisions are made on the basis of a proper appreciation of the facts and by persons who are appropriately qualified. Although the law imposes only base-line standards, therefore, it can nevertheless create conditions which increase the chances of high-quality performances being achieved.

Finally, an objection to relying on the law to regulate decision-making quality, additional to those considered earlier, should be noted. It has been stated that one of the justifications for the American business judgement rule is that it limits 'judicial intrusiveness with respect to private-sector

---

[159] See Finch, 'Company Directors: Who Cares About Skill and Care?' (above, note 39), at 211–3; John, 'Relieving Directors from the Liabilities of Office' (above, n. 157), at 29.

[160] It is now possible for companies to pay for directors' indemnity insurance as a result of CA 1989, s 137(1), amending CA 1985, s 310.

[161] Finch, 'Company Directors' (above, n. 39), at 211–13.

[162] See J. C. Coffee, 'Litigation and Corporate Governance: An Essay on Steering Between Scylla and Charybdis', (1984) 52 *Geo Wash L Rev* 789, at 796, who refers to the law's 'educational and socializing effect'. These effects are not, he suggests, dependent on high levels of enforcement.

decisionmaking'.[163] This suggests a contrast between the public realm of the legal system and the private realm of business, with a presumption against interference by the former in the latter. Even where the company is viewed as a purely private phenomenon, however, there is no justification for regarding the quality of management decision making as a matter that is 'private' in relation to the shareholders.[164] From this perspective, in imposing negligence liability the court can be seen merely as upholding private rights, and that is hardly an 'intrusion'.

But in any case if, as was argued in Chapter 1, companies should be viewed as social enterprises, that is, they should be understood as vehicles for the promotion of the general good, then a requirement that managers should comply with publicly articulated decision-making standards, and that mechanisms should exist visibly to test compliance with them, should be regarded as something that is desirable in itself. Quite distinct from the implications for increased efficiency, where managers are seen as holding positions of power for the purpose of furthering the public interest it is appropriate that there should be public participation in the formulation of appropriate performance standards and that those who have culpably fallen below them should be held to account in a public forum. The underlying principle of responsibility that is entailed is scarcely capable of expression in the language of markets.

Problems of Enforcement

A final note on the enforcement of the duty of care is called for. If liability rules are to perform any of the functions mentioned there must be at least some prospect of their being enforced. The scarcity of modern director's negligence cases suggests that the likelihood of liability actually being imposed is currently minimal.[165] Part of the explanation lies in restrictive rules of

---

[163] ALI *Principles of Corporate Governance* (above, n. 30), at 176.

[164] But it has been argued further that the existence of a liability regime is contrary to the interests of shareholders in any event on the ground that the costs of enforcement will on balance exceed the compensation received: see, e.g., Philips, 'Principles of Corporate Governance' (above, n. 52), at 701–702. Shareholders are good risk-bearers on account of their ability to diversify their holdings, and given the costs of litigation, the likelihood of failure in many cases, and the inability of directors' to meet damages awards, the net effect might be to make shareholders as a whole worse off. To the extent that this is true it certainly means that the argument for compensating shareholders (via damages paid to the company) is weaker, say, than that in support of compensating clients who have suffered as a result of the negligent performance of a professional service. Compensation is not, however, the whole story, or even a part of it (the ALI Corporate Governance Project, for instance, has abandoned the compensation rationale: *Principles of Corporate Governance:* (above, n. 30) para 7.19 and 874–7). The point is that the disciplinary and educative effects of liability rules are likely to make shareholders, and the community as a whole, better off.

[165] Discussions between the author and brokers specializing in director's liability insurance suggest that claims against directors which do not reach the courts are also rare.

standing, which appear to deprive minority shareholders of the right to bring an action in respect of negligence.[166] This means that realistically it is only a new board, after a boardroom coup or a take-over, or the liquidator, who will be in a position to act. The unclear and undeveloped state of the law, which makes litigation more than usually unpredictable, is no doubt also a major negative influence. Even without the element of uncertainty, however, potential plaintiffs may be reluctant to inflict on the company the disruption that an action against a director can involve, or expose it to the unfavourable publicity that might result from airing its difficulties in public. The problem of the damage that may result from litigation is undoubtedly a real one, and argues against giving shareholders unrestricted standing to sue, which might otherwise be regarded as a plausible means of increasing the chances of enforcement. Chapter 8 will discuss where the balance should lie between ensuring that the rules are effective on the one hand, and avoiding unproductive litigation on the other. In the meantime it is sufficient to note that the position in which the rules are barely enforced at all is far from satisfactory.

---

[166] See Ch. 8 below. Many shareholders do not in any case have the incentive to bring an action, since even if it is successful the effect on the member personally is likely to be minimal, the damages being payable to the company and hence benefiting the members generally. The position may be different with a large institutional sharcholder, which may look beyond the outcome of a particular action and be interested in strengthening the liability framework in which managements operate.

5

Reinforcing—and Challenging—the Legal Model

This chapter examines the contribution made by a further legal duty, the duty to act for a proper purpose, to the control of managerial discretion and the promotion of management efficiency. The duty to act for a proper purpose is not concerned on its surface with profit maximization, but has an important, indirect role in securing compliance with that objective in two ways. First, it helps protect the democratic shareholder controls from being subverted by management. Second, by safeguarding the shareholders' financial interests in a take-over situation it prevents management from insulating the company from the impact of the market for corporate control. These two effects will be considered in Sections I and II respectively. Chapter 4 noted that the operation of the market for control may have socially and economically damaging consequences. In a number of jurisdictions with active markets in control these consequences have prompted a limited reassessment of the legal model and the introduction of measures to dampen market activity. These developments are considered in Section III.

I PROTECTING THE GOVERNANCE STRUCTURE

As we have mentioned, and as we shall discuss in more detail below, the law provides a set of democratic shareholder controls over the board. The intended framework of shareholder decision-making and management accountability would, however, be undermined if the board were free to alter the composition of the majority in order to neutralize shareholder power. The most obvious form of manipulation is for the directors to allot additional shares to themselves or their supporters in order to guarantee a majority of votes.[1] Given the

---

[1] The creation of statutory pre-emption rights by the Companies Act 1980 (see now CA 1985, ss 89–96) has made this more difficult, but by no means impossible: pre-emption rights do not apply to issues for a non-cash consideration (s 89(4)), or to shares to be held under an employee share scheme (s 89(5)), and the rights may also be disapplied by special resolution (s 95). On the other hand, see *Pennell v Venida Investments Ltd* (unreported, 1974, but see S. J. Burridge, 'Wrongful Rights Issues', (1981) 44 *MLR* 40), where Templeman J held that a share issue was

importance of shareholder control within the legal model, it is not surprising that the courts have invalidated this and similar tactics.[2] Thus in one case where the directors created a majority sufficient to enable them to change the articles,[3] and in another where they issued shares in order to defeat a member's attempt to be elected to the board,[4] they were held to have exercised their powers for an 'improper purpose' and hence in breach of fiduciary duty.

The most serious threat to owner control arises where the directors use their powers to entrench themselves in office. The ability to remove the directors, and the threat of being able to do so, are the principal means provided by company law for ensuring that the board acts in conformity with shareholder interests. Attempts at entrenchment have come before the courts mainly, but not exclusively,[5] in the context of management defences against take-over bids. In *Hogg v Cramphorn Ltd*,[6] for example, after a bid had been made for the company the directors created a trust for the benefit of employees and issued to it sufficient shares to ensure that the directors could always rely on more than 50 per cent of the votes. In holding the issue voidable Buckley J explained that the court would not 'permit directors to exercise powers, which have been delegated to them by the company in circumstances which put the directors in a fiduciary position when exercising those powers, in such a way as to interfere with the exercise by the majority of its constitutional rights.'[7] Similarly the board is not entitled to interfere to enable a particular bidder to gain control. In *Howard Smith Ltd v Ampol Petroleum Ltd*,[8] where the board, despite the opposition of the pre-existing majority, issued shares to a bidder with a view to bringing about a change in control, Lord Wilberforce held that it was 'unconstitutional for directors to use their fiduciary powers over the shares in the company purely for the purpose of destroying an existing majority, or creating a new majority which did not previously exist. To do so is to interfere with that element of the company's constitution which is separate from and set against their powers.' The emphasis on constitutionality makes clear the role of the proper purpose duty in upholding the allocation of decision-making power made by the Companies Act and the articles. Given this objective, it follows that a plea by

improper as being an attempt on the part of the majority to extend their control, notwithstanding the minority's pre-emption rights. At the time of issuing the shares, the majority knew that the minority would not be able to afford to take up their rights.

[2] Exercises of other powers for the purpose of affecting control have fallen within the prohibition: see, e.g. *Galloway v Hallé Concerts Society* [1915] 2 Ch 233 (calls on selected shareholders only).

[3] *Punt v Symons & Co Ltd* [1903] 2 Ch 506.

[4] *Piercy v S Mills & Co Ltd* [1920] 1 Ch 77.

[5] See e.g. *Piercy v Mills & Co Ltd* (above, n. 4).

[6] [1967] Ch 254, [1966] 3 All ER 420. See also *Bamford v Bamford* [1970] 1 Ch 212, CA, [1969] 1 All ER 969.

[7] Ibid. at 268.

[8] [1974] AC 821, PC, [1974] 1 All ER 1126.

the directors that they have acted only in accordance with what they considered to be the company's interests will necessarily be misconceived:[9] whether a particular resolution should be passed or the board replaced are matters to be determined by the appropriate majority of members. The board may not reconstruct the majority in order to secure its favoured outcome. The directors may give advice to the members and use company funds to put their view across,[10] but they may not exercise their powers in order to guarantee the result of their choice.

The use of management power in order to interfere with shareholder control is, then, the 'improper purpose' against which the proper purpose duty is directed. It should be viewed as an essential supplement to the duty to act in good faith for the benefit of the company, since the latter, subjective duty is incapable of preventing the directors from overriding the shareholders' decision-making rights and imposing their own views in respect of those issues which the company's constitution sets aside for shareholder determination.[11]

This being the rationale of the duty there is clearly no inconsistency, at least at a theoretical level, in holding that exercises of power that have the purpose of affecting control should be ratifiable in general meeting.[12] The

[9] See e.g. *Lee Panavision Ltd v Lee Lighting Ltd* [1992] BCLC 22, CA. It is suggested that directors of an ordinary commercial company can derive little assistance from *Gaiman v National Association for Mental Health* [1971] Ch 317, [1970] 2 All ER 362. It was held in this case that the board were entitled to expel (under an expulsion power in the articles) Scientologists whom, it was feared, were attempting to gain control. This is explicable on the grounds that the association existed for specific non-commercial purposes which the Scientologists were pledged to undermine.

[10] So long as their intention is to benefit the members and not merely to preserve themselves in office or seek some other personal advantage: see *Peel v N W Rly Co* [1907] 1 Ch 5, CA.

[11] A number of writers have suggested that the proper purpose cases should be explained by reference to the construction of the company's articles: see e.g. D. D. Prentice. 'Expulsion of Members from a Company', (1970) 33 *MLR* 700; B. V. Slutsky, 'Canadian Rejection of the Hogg v Cramphorn "Improper Purposes" Principle' (1974) 37 *MLR* 457; B. L. Welling, *Corporate Law in Canada* (1984) at 350–1: 'there is no "proper purposes" doctrine. The scope of any particular power is to be determined by interpreting the wording of the grant of power.' Lord Wilberforce's observation in *Howard Smith* (at 1133) that a use of power may be attacked on the ground that 'it was not exercised for the purpose for which it was granted' suggests that a question of construction might be involved, but in none of the cases is there anything to indicate from the wording of the relevant articles that the directors were not entitled to issue shares for any purpose. Given that a construction analysis must therefore treat purpose restrictions as implied into the articles it is not clear that such an analysis adds anything, though it does raise questions about whether the incidence of the duty can be modified by the drafting of the articles, on which see *Whitehouse v Carlton Hotel Pty Ltd* (1986) 162 CLR 285, Aust HC, at 292. In *Lee Panavision Ltd v Lee Lighting Ltd* (above, n. 9), an agreement vesting management powers in relation to the company in a second company was held unconstitutional without reference to the articles. The judgment refers to the agreement as being 'beyond the directors' powers' (at 31, per Dillon L J), but it should be noted that in *Howard Smith* [1974] AC 821, at 834, [1974] 1 All ER 1126, at 1133 Lord Wilberforce makes plain that a lack of authority is not involved.

[12] See *Hogg v Cramphorn* (above, n. 6), at 265, where Buckley J commented that where the majority had approved an issue he did not think that 'any member could have complained . . . for in those circumstances, the criticism that the directors were, by the issue of the shares,

objective of preserving the decision-making rights of the majority is satisfied
if the directors' acts are valid only where authorized or confirmed by the
shareholders.[13] In practice, however, because of the low level of participation
in general meetings, obtaining shareholder consent may often be little more
than a formality. There is likely to be more substance to the procedure where
there is an outstanding bid for the company, since in that situation the
shareholders' attention will be more clearly focused, but even here the
directors are still in an advantageous position, as 'They retain control of the
proxy machinery, they can choose the date of the meeting to their tactical
advantage and they can use their continuing relationship and prestige with
the shareholders to muster support.'[14] Furthermore, the result of the directors'
intervention is likely to be not only to defend the company against the
current attack, but also to strengthen the position of the existing management
on a continuing basis. For these reasons the effect of the availability of
consent may in practice be to undermine the functions of the proper purpose
rule.

II PROTECTING THE SHAREHOLDERS' FINANCIAL INTERESTS

As far as the shareholders are concerned a more significant effect of the
proper purpose duty in practical terms is that it prevents the directors from
frustrating a take-over bid and thus depriving the members of an opportunity

attempting to deprive the majority of their constitutional rights would have ceased to have any
force'; see also *Bamford v Bamford* (above, n. 6). Cf. *Winthrop Investments Ltd v Winns Ltd* [1975] 2
NSWLR 666, at 700-2, where Mahoney J A left open whether a resolution would be effective
when passed by members having the same purpose as management—that of defeating a bid.
This should make no difference, since as far as the members are concerned, defeating a bid is an
entirely permissible objective. See also *Rights and Issues Investment Trust Ltd v Stylo Shoes Ltd* [1965]
Ch 250, [1964] 3 All ER 628, where, on increasing the company's share capital, a resolution
was also passed to enhance the voting rights attached to a special class of 'management shares'
sufficiently to restore the previous control position; the resolution was held to be valid. This is
consistent with principle, given that the control issue was determined by the shareholders and
not the board. The underlying rationale does dictate, however, that a manipulation of voting
rights by management to convert a simple majority into a special majority (in order to facilitate,
for example, a change in the articles) should not be ratifiable by *ordinary* resolution, since this
would involve an overriding of the corporate constitution.

[13] It is not entirely clear whether the duty not to exercise a power for an improper purpose is
owed to each member individually or whether it is owed exclusively to the company. In *Re a
Company (No 005136 of 1986)* [1987] BCLC 82, Hoffman J decided the former. It is difficult,
however, to reconcile this view with the ratifiability of the breach (if members have rights they
cannot be taken away by majority vote). The better view is that the duty is owed to the
company, but enforceable by a minority shareholder through a derivative action. There is no
Foss v Harbottle obstacle, despite ratifiability, since otherwise there would be a 'constitutional
impasse': see C. Baxter, 'The True Spirit of Foss v Harbottle', (1987) 38 *NILQ* 6, at 34 (judicial
intervention is necessary to prevent the impugned shares being voted in any decision in general
meeting about whether to attack their validity).

[14] L. Rabinowitz, *Weinberg and Blank on Take-overs and Mergers* (5th ed., 1989), at para 3-817.

to sell their shares at an advantageous price.[15] The duty to act in the interests of the company is unable adequately to protect this interest of the shareholders because defensive action can often plausibly be justified in terms of shareholder benefit, that is, on the ground that the bid is under-priced.[16] Defensive measures adopted avowedly for that reason could not be invalidated on the ground that the directors were failing to act for the benefit of the company, except in the unlikely event that it could be shown that they did not honestly believe that defeating the bid was in the company's (i.e. the shareholders') interests. There is clearly a significant risk in this context that the directors will act contrary to the interests of the shareholders, since in determining whether or not a bid should succeed the directors are confronted with a severe positional conflict of interest,[17] given that the normal consequence of a change in control is that the incumbent board is removed from office. It is in overcoming the limitations of the subjective duty to act in the interests of the company in controlling such conflicts, therefore, that the proper purpose duty plays an important role. By invalidating take-over defences regardless of motive, it ensures that the members are able to make their own evaluation of the merits of a bid without management interference.[18] This in turn means that the members can prevent the outcome

---

[15] In order to obtain control by means of a take-over the offeror will generally have to pay a substantial premium over pre-bid stock market prices, hence the opportunity for shareholder gain: see 121 above. A principal objective of the non-statutory City Code on Take-overs and Mergers, in the interests of fairness, is to ensure that all members have the opportunity to share rateably in this premium and that it is not offered merely to a sufficient number of favoured shareholders to enable the bidder to obtain control. This is achieved by requiring a mandatory bid where there is a change in control, this being deemed to occur where a member's holding is increased beyond 30 per cent: Rule 9 of the Code, discussed in J. H. Farrar, N. E. Furey, B. M. Hannigan, *Farrar's Company Law* (3rd ed., 1991), at 635–8.

[16] The duty to act in the interests of the company excludes consideration of non-shareholder interests (subject to the effect of CA 1985, s 309), as noted earlier. In *Hogg v Cramphorn* it was held to be irrelevant that the directors firmly believed that 'to keep the management of the company's affairs in the hands of the existing board would be more advantageous to the shareholders, *the company's staff and its customers*' than if the company were taken over (above, n. 6, at 266; emphasis added). See also L. C. B. Gower, 'Corporate Control: The Battle for the Berkeley', (1955) 68 *Harv L Rev* 1176. On whether the position is now different because of the statutory duty to take into account the interests of employees, see 154 below.

[17] To use M. A. Eisenberg's phrase again, see "The Structure of Corporation Law', (1989) 89 *Colum L Rev* 1461, at 1472–4.

[18] The directors are not, however, precluded from taking all forms of action to defeat a bid. They are entitled, and indeed required by the City Code (see General Principle 4 and Rule 25(1)) to advise the shareholders on the merits of a bid, and may make a recommendation as to acceptance or otherwise. In so doing, the directors must comply with a duty owed directly to the shareholders to be honest and not to mislead: *Gething v Kilner* [1972] 1 WLR 337, [1972] 1 All ER 1166. They also owe a duty of care to the members (and in certain circumstances to the bidder: *Morgan Crucible Co plc v Hill Samuel & Co Ltd* [1991] 1 All ER 148, CA). Attempts by management to persuade the members not to sell, which in practice are unlikely to be impartial, do not conflict with the principles discussed in the text, since they do not deprive the members of the opportunity of deciding for themselves whether to accept an offer. They may also have the effect of causing the offeror to increase its offer, or of attracting a rival bidder, to the advantage of the members.

from being determined other than in accordance with considerations of shareholder wealth.[19]

The proper purpose duty protects the shareholders' interests, not only by preventing management from defeating a bid, but also by invalidating action which is designed to deter a bid from being launched, by making it more difficult for an offeror to obtain a majority or otherwise making the company a less attractive target. It should be noted too that the manipulation of voting control is not by any means the only way of protecting a company from a predator. Other possible defensive tactics include making the company less appealing to a potential or actual bidder by disposing of prized assets ('crown jewels'), or granting an option enabling a third party to acquire such assets in the event of a bid; dissipating cash reserves, or accumulating debt;[20] and entering into joint-venture agreements or other long-term commitments which tie up the company's resources and thereby make it difficult for a would-be acquirer to dismember the business.[21] All of these measures may fall within the proper purpose rule's prohibition.

In this country defensive tactics are unlikely to be employed once a bid has actually been launched or the board of the offeree company has reason to believe that an offer is imminent,[22] since the self-regulatory City Code on

[19] Though it has been argued that allowing the board to block an under-priced bid facilitates the holding of an 'auction', and prevents shareholders, who must necessarily act individually, from effectively being forced to sell at what they know to be a low price for fear of a majority accepting and their being left as a vulnerable minority: see L. A. Bebchuk, 'The Case for Facilitating Tender Offers', (1982) 95 *Harv L Rev* 1028, and n. 41, below. On the merits of management-sponsored 'auctions' of control, see O. Hann, 'Takeover Rules in the European Community: An Economic Analysis of Proposed Takeover Guidelines and Already Issued Disclosure Rules', (1990) 10 *Int Rev Law and Econ* 131, at 137-42, and the material cited therein. See also F. H. Easterbrook and D. R. Fischel, *The Economic Structure of Corporate Law* (1991), ch 7. On the permissibility in the US of frustrating action in order to encourage an auction, see *Unocal Corp v Mesa Petroleum Co* 493 A. 2d 946 (Del 1985) and *Revlon, Inc v MacAndrews & Forbes Holdings* 506 A. 2d 173 (Del 1986). On the extent to which a British board is free to recommend acceptance of a second bid having given an undertaking to a first bidder to make a recommendation to the shareholders, see *Rackham v Peek Foods Ltd* [1990] BCLC 895; *John Crowther Group plc v Carpets International plc* [1990] BCLC 460; *Dawson International plc v Coats Paton plc* [1991] BCC 276, Ct Sess.

[20] There are many other defensive tactics: see Rabinowitz, *Weinberg and Blank on Take-overs and Mergers* (above, n. 4), paras 3-283-3-333; B. Chiplin and M. Wright, *The Logic of Mergers* (1987) at 47-50; T. Steel, 'Defensive Tactics in Company Takeovers', (1986) 4 *C and SLJ* 30. For a review of the tactics relied on by target companies in the UK in 1981-2, see Y. F. Danziger, 'Remedial Defensive Tactics Against Take-overs', (1983) 4 *Co Law* 3. For case studies of the defences used in the 42 hostile bids that occurred between January 1989 and March 1990 see T. Jenkinson and C. Mayer, *Takeover Defence Strategies* (1991).

[21] See *Darvall v North Sydney Brick & Tile Company Ltd* (1988) 6 ACLC 154. For a different example of tying up assets as part of an anti-bid strategy, see the material on the Savoy Hotel affair in n. 46 below.

[22] This is not so, e.g., in Australia, where stock-exchange rules permit *pari passu* offers to existing members even after a bid has been launched: see D. A. De Mott, 'Comparative Dimensions of Takeover Regulation', in J. C. Coffee, L. Lowenstein, and S. Rose-Ackerman (eds), *Knights, Raiders, and Targets* (1988), 398, at 417. See e.g. *Pine Vale Investments Ltd v*

Take-overs and Mergers proscribes action, in the absence of shareholder consent, which could 'effectively result in any bona fide offer being frustrated or in the shareholders being denied an opportunity to decide on its merits'.[23] This rule has the same objective as the proper purpose duty, safeguarding the members' right to determine for themselves where their interests lie in a take-over situation, and is structurally similar to it. Both allow defensive measures only with the approval of the shareholders, and both focus on the effects of management action, ignoring questions of good faith.[24] The City Code is narrower, however, in so far as it confines its prohibitions to the situation where an offer has been made or is imminent. This means that defensive measures adopted, without shareholder consent,[25] where no identifiable bid is about to be mounted are challengeable only in the courts. For reasons considered next, however, the chances of such a challenge being successful are in practice somewhat limited.

Substantial Purposes

In *Howard Smith v Ampol*[26] Lord Wilberforce, relying on earlier Commonwealth decisions,[27] held that a course of action which had the effect of frustrating a bid would amount to a breach of duty only where that was its substantial purpose. An issue of shares, for instance, might be valid even though the result was to prevent a bidder from gaining control, if the directors' substantial purpose in making it was not to bring about that result but to raise capital, or it was motivated by similar 'considerations of

McDonnell & Far East Ltd (1983) 8 ACLR 199, at 208, where a rights issue frustrated a partial bid by invalidating the financial assumptions on which it had been made.

[23] The Panel on Takeovers and Mergers, *The City Code on Takeovers and Mergers* General Principle 7, and Rule 21.

[24] The City Code is, however, more absolute in its application (though the Panel has a dispensing power), ignoring questions of 'substantial purpose' discussed in the next paragraph. Rule 21 gives examples of actions which the board may not take during the course of an offer or if an offer is believed to be imminent. These include acquiring or disposing of assets of a material amount and entering into contracts other than in the course of business. The latter includes amending the terms of directors' service contracts, thus preventing them from equipping themselves with 'golden parachutes' which have the effect of raising the cost of the bid (see further 220 below). The Panel has held that frustrating action includes litigation commenced by the company to hinder the bid: see Panel statement on *Minorco plc/Consolidated Goldfields plc* May 9, 1989, discussed by G. K. Morse, 'General Principle 7, The Law and Directors' Duties—The Consolidated Goldfields Affair', [1989] *JBL* 427.

[25] See the doubts expressed at 140 above about the reality of shareholder consent to measures which strengthen management control.

[26] [1974] AC 821, at 835–6, [1974] 1 All ER 1126, at 1134–5.

[27] *Harlowe's Nominees Pty Ltd v Woodside (Lakes Entrance) Oil Co No Liability* (1968) 121 CLR 483, Aust HC and *Teck Corporation v Millar* (1973) 33 DLR 288, BC Sup Ct. See also *Whitehouse v Carlton Hotel Pty Ltd* (above, n. 11), at 294, indicating that the test is whether the improper purpose is causative of the exercise of the power.

management, within the proper sphere of the directors'.[28] It is easy to see practical advantages in this distinction as a means of avoiding management paralysis where there is no current or anticipated bid. Any company is a potential bid target and it would be contrary to the interests of the members for the board to be prevented from taking action to improve the profitability of the business simply because it might have the side-effect, or be motivated by the secondary purpose (these in practice being virtually indistinguishable), of providing some protection against a possible but undefined risk of take-over. An asset disposal, group restructuring, or the creation of a cross-shareholding or employee share scheme, for example, may well have a sound commercial justification, while at the same time reducing the take-over threat. Nor can it be the case that a member building a stake in a company with a view to bidding at some future date has the right to insist that management takes no action that might make it more difficult for that member eventually to obtain control.

These considerations suggest, therefore, that it would be undesirable to invalidate management action in the absence of an actual or expected bid simply because it had the effect of strengthening the control position of the existing board, without first looking at its underlying purpose. This flexibility is likely to be achieved, however, at the price of making measures which *are* primarily defensive much more difficult to overturn. It will be recalled that the strength of the proper purpose rule lies in the fact that it enables the court to set aside actions that have the effect of interfering with the bid process without the need to enquire into questions of intention. The 'substantial purpose' qualification does not detract from this where it is clear that the main purpose of management is to protect their control position (i.e. the court can ignore the directors' protestations that in so doing they acted in good faith). But the result of the qualification is to introduce questions of subjective intention at the earlier stage of deciding whether or not management actions were taken primarily for the purpose of affecting control. Since it will usually be easy to justify measures with control consequences in commercial terms in the absence of a concrete bid, it is unlikely that it will often be demonstrated that the proper purpose duty has been breached in that situation. As a result boards have a considerable freedom in practice to entrench their position without the need to seek shareholder consent.

While there is a degree of inevitability about the use of the distinction drawn by Lord Wilberforce where there is no bid on the horizon (though it is not expressly limited to that situation), reliance on it is much harder to justify where an offer is outstanding or it appears likely that an offer will be made in the near future.[29] This issue is unlikely to come before the courts in

---

[28] Per Lord Wilberforce in *Howard Smith*, [1974] AC 821, at 837, [1974] 1 All ER 1126, at 1135.

[29] See also J. R. Birds, 'Proper Purposes as a Head of Fiduciary Duty', (1974) 37 *MLR* 580.

the UK because of the City Code's prohibition on actions that have a frustrating *effect* where a bid is imminent, but there are a number of Commonwealth cases where the point has arisen. In *Winthrop Investments Ltd v Winns*,[30] for example, the directors of a company which owned a chain of retail stores resolved to buy a number of additional stores, the purchase price being paid partly in cash and partly in shares and debentures. It was accepted by the court that entering into the transaction would have the effect of deterring a bid which the directors feared would be launched from an indentifiable source, and that the directors were well aware of this. It was held, nevertheless, that since their 'main or fundamental or basic'[31] object in entering into the transaction was to improve the financial position of the company, their actions could not be impeached. The result of using the substantial purpose distinction in this way is in large measure to undermine the proper purpose rule. To permit action which has a frustrating effect on the ground that it is primarily motivated by an ordinary commercial purpose reintroduces in a different guise questions of 'company benefit' that the proper purpose rule is designed to exclude. Allowing this justification in the face of an actual or identifiable bid is inconsistent with the policy that supports the rule, which holds that in a bid situation the shareholders should have a right to decide for themselves what their best interests are and not to have this decision pre-empted by management.

Whatever the merits of the substantial purpose distinction in principle, the process of drawing it in practice is far from straightforward. Taking *Winthrop Investments* as an illustration, given the problems of proof and the inevitable mixture of motives both within and among individual directors, it is difficult to be confident that the court successfully isolated the board's predominant motivation in this or in other similar cases.[32] Sealy's view that 'the learned language only serves to conceal the reality: the courts are in truth making naked value judgments'[33] is surely correct. Indeed, the way in which the substantial purpose distinction has been employed seems to reflect more a dissatisfaction with the proper purpose rule itself, and the consequent disarming

---

[30] (1979) 4 ACLR 1.

[31] At 13.

[32] See also *Harlowe's Nominees Pty Ltd v Woodside (Lakes Entrance) Oil Co NL* (above, n. 27); *Pine Vale Investments Ltd v McDonnell & Far East Ltd* (above, n. 22). *Teck Corporation Ltd v Millar* (above, n. 27). In *Teck* (for the facts see below) the court applied the substantial purpose distinction in such a way as to cause it to collapse altogether. It was held that the directors' purpose was not to defeat Teck's attempt to take control, but rather to obtain the best agreement they could for the development of the mine. Since, however, destroying Teck's majority was a prerequisite of the mine being developed in collaboration with Canex, the court's reasoning is equivalent to the proposition that the directors may adopt the direct purpose of frustrating a bid so long as they are motivated by commercial considerations: this is precisely what the proper purpose rule prohibits. (The court then went on to refuse to follow *Hogg v Cramphorn* (above, n. 6) in any case: see below.)

[33] L. S. Sealy, '"Bona Fides" and "Proper Purposes" in Corporate Decisions', (1989) 15 *Mon U L Rev* 265, at 276.

of management in the face of a hostile bid, than the application of any coherent principle. Instances will be examined below in which the courts, rather than evading the rule by invoking the distinction, have taken the bolder course of rejecting the rule altogether.

Proper Purposes and the Market for Corporate Control

The foregoing discussion emphasized the role of 'proper purposes' in protecting from management interference the shareholders' interest in realizing their investment on favourable terms. The connection between the priority given by the legal model to the shareholders' financial benefit in the takeover context and the social interest in corporate efficiency is the market for corporate control.[34] By enabling shareholders to sell control, it is argued, resources are transferred to those who can most efficiently manage them, as indicated by their willingness to pay a price for control that is in excess of the company's pre-bid market value. Efficiency gains may result, *inter alia*, from the replacement of under-performing management teams or breaking up agglomerations of assets which are currently employed at less than their full potential. Furthermore the pervasive threat of take-over, characteristic of a buoyant market for control, is said to impose a vital discipline on managements which might otherwise be effectively entrenched. As considered in Chapter 4 the market can thus be viewed as a form of external control over management that serves as a substitute for the lack of internal control which is the result of shareholder dispersal. Clearly, the proper purpose rule plays an important part in this process of external control by limiting the ability of the directors to take their company off the market. It protects the right of the members to sell control, thus making possible hostile bids on which the market's disciplinary power depends.

It is argued with equal conviction that an active market in control, far from being beneficial, is damaging to the economy overall. This charge was considered in some detail in Chapter 4, and can be summarized as follows. First, there is no guarantee that acquirers will operate the business more efficiently than incumbent managements; the former may be pursuing a strategy of growth rather than maximizing value and, further, the replacement management team may lack industry-specific experience. Second, at a more general level, the existence of an active market for control imposes pressure on managements to keep up share price in order to avoid the attention of predators. The result is likely to be the disease of short-termism, with sufferers tending to avoid expenditure on measures necessary for long-term success, such as investment and training, in order to keep profit figures high. Third, there are also adverse 'external' effects, notably on employees

---

[34] For a more detailed discussion, see 119–31 above.

and on regional balance, as well as a reduction in competition (to the extent that the effect of merger is to increase concentration).

The arguments for and against the market for control have already been evaluated. Our purpose here is to consider the role of fiduciary duties in allowing the market to function. The belief that at least an 'over-active' market is damaging to the economy has begun to influence the design of management duties in a number of jurisdictions in which take-overs are a frequent occurrence. These developments will be examined in Section III, which will also consider whether it would be appropriate for English law to respond in a similar way.

Structural and Cultural Prerequisites of a Market in Control

Before that it is important to note that appropriate fiduciary or other regulatory constraints on the powers of management are only one of the ingredients necessary for a market in control, the existence of which depends on a much broader set of background rules and practices. In order to put the discussion of the role of fiduciary duties in its proper context a brief digression to consider these other factors is warranted.

An important prerequisite of hostile bids is the public availability of financial information on potential targets. Without this a bidder will be unable to assess whether an acquisition is likely to be profitable. The absence of reliable financial data in some European countries is cited as one of the reasons for very low levels of hostile take-over activity,[35] and similarly explains the rarity of take-overs in this country prior to the introduction of the 1948 Companies Act disclosure requirements.[36] Some other aspects of the regulatory fabric that are preconditions for a functioning market in control can also be highlighted by comparing the position in the UK, where the controls are highly conducive to take-over activity, with the situation in other parts of Europe.[37] Thus British companies legislation requires that there be public access to the share register and disclosure of the beneficial ownership of voting shares where a person holds more than 3 per cent of the company's share capital,[38] thereby enabling a potential bidder to discover

[35] There have e.g. been only three hostile take-overs in Germany since the war: Jenkinson and Mayer, *Takeover Defence Strategies* (above, n. 22), at 17, and see generally, the study prepared by Coopers & Lybrand for the DTI, *Barriers to Takeovers in the European Community* (1989), at 1–4.

[36] See L. Hannah, 'Takeover Bids in Britain before 1950: an Exercise in Business Pre-history', (1974) 16 *Business History* 65.

[37] See Coopers & Lybrand, *Barriers to Takeovers* (above, n. 35); DTI, *Barriers to Takeovers in the European Community: A Consultative Document* (1990); A. J. Boyle, 'Barriers to Contested Takeovers in the European Community', (1991) 12 *Co Lawyer* 163. It has been suggested that taxation policy and accounting and disclosure requirements also create a climate favourable to take-overs in this country: see A. Peacock and G. Bannock, *Corporate Takeovers and the Public Interest* (1991), at 34–6; J. Carty, 'Accounting for Takeovers', in A. Cosh et al. *Takeovers and Short-termism in the UK*, IPPR Industrial Policy Paper no. 3 (1990), 21.

[38] CA 1985, Pt VI, as amended by CA 1989, s 134.

the pattern of ownership of shares (permitting a judgement about the possible success of a bid to be made) and facilitating communication with offerees. These processes are hindered substantially in those countries in which unregistered bearer shares are common, and/or where registration details do not have to be made public. Another feature promoting take-over activity in the UK is the comparative ease with which the board can be removed, that is, by ordinary resolution, a requirement that cannot be varied by the company's constitution.[39] In contrast in Germany, for example, where public companies have a two-tier board structure, members of the management board may be appointed for a period of up to five years and may only be removed prior to the end of that period in limited circumstances. Furthermore, a new majority shareholder may be unable to obtain control of the shareholder seats on the supervisory board, which appoints the management board, since a 75 per cent vote is often necessary to remove the directors elected by shareholders, and the employee representatives, which in companies with over 2,000 employees constitute half the membership of the supervisory board, cannot be removed by the shareholders at all.[40] These factors will have a tendency to inhibit take-overs by limiting the ability of a bidder to take effective managerial control.[41]

In addition to these general regulatory factors, the marketability of companies is also affected by the tolerance of the regulatory system or of investors to the adoption of structural defences. These take the form of share structures which give voting power to 'inside' shareholders disproportionate to their percentage holdings, with the effect that a bidder who obtains a majority of the shares may fail to take voting control. Measures include issuing non-voting shares or shares with enhanced voting rights, and limiting the voting rights of a member to a fixed percentage regardless of the total shares held. These and other arrangements with a similar effect are common in a number of European countries.[42] In Britain there are no legal barriers[43]

---

[39] CA 1985, s 303.   [40] See below, Ch. 12.

[41] Provisions regulating the take-over process itself also have an impact on the incidence of contested bids. In the EEC only the UK (the City Code) and Ireland have a well developed set of regulations, but the proposed *Thirteenth Directive on Takeover and other General Bids*, *OJ*, Vol 32, C64, 14/4/1989, 8, will lay down standards for member states, *inter alia*, limiting the scope for frustrating action and requiring equal treatment of target shareholders. The latter, by e.g. excluding partial bids (which are also prohibited by the City Code without the consent of the Panel), may reduce the number of take-overs by increasing their cost. For an analysis of the likely effects of the directive on the market for control, see Hann, 'Takeover Rules in the European Community' (above, n. 19) and for a discussion of the merits of partial take-overs (which may have a tendency to coerce shareholders who would prefer to reject the offer) see I. Ramsay, 'Balancing Law and Economics: The Case of Partial Takeovers', [1992] *JBL* 396. Similarly merger regulation (i.e. regulation primarily concerned with the competitive effects of business combinations) also inhibits the free operation of the market for control.

[42] See DTI *Consultative Document* (above, n. 37), at 8–10.

[43] Except that where a company's shares are already divided into separate classes and the directors wish to enhance the voting rights of a particular class the statutory provisions for the variation of class rights must be complied with: see CA 1985, s 125, and generally, Rabiowitz, *Weinberg and Blank on Takeovers and Mergers* (above, n. 14), at paras 3-798–3-805. The merits of

to issuing voteless shares or shares with weighted votes (either in regard to all matters[44] or specifically in relation to a change in control),[45] but Stock Exchange discouragement and market pressure from institutional investors mean that they are now increasingly rare.[46]

Of perhaps even greater importance than the precise framework of rules and the scope for constitutional creativity are the distribution of control and also 'cultural' factors. It is estimated that in France, for example, over half of the largest 200 companies are subject to family control;[47] in Germany the banks have a position of dominance arising from the voting power attached to their own holdings and bearer shares held on deposit; and in France, Italy, and the Netherlands (and in Japan, where take-overs are a rarity also) companies frequently hold stakes in each other for mutual protection. Such factors make it difficult for an outsider to break in and obtain a controlling interest and hence to a greater or lesser extent inhibit market activity. In contrast shareholdings in Britain are widely dispersed and shareholder ties to existing management are much less common.

The 'cultural' differences are summarized by the Coopers and Lybrand report on barriers to take-over in the EEC, prepared for the DTI, in this way:

To someone steeped in the UK culture, of management being accountable primarily to shareholders and being judged essentially in value terms (shareholder value), [take-over] defences appear unethical and designed to maintain the interests of the existing management group. However, in the absence of that cultural background, opinion in these countries can tend to regard the possibility of 'predators' seizing control of companies, without regard to the interest of the companies, as in itself being quite unethical.[48]

What underlies the latter attitude is in part a different system of corporate governance. In Germany in particular, influential banker-shareholders perform an active supervisory function that is largely lacking in this country,[49] and which makes take-overs much less important as a disciplinary

---

voteless shares were considered by the Jenkins Committee, which recommended against their prohibition: *Report of the Company Law Committee* (Cmnd. 1749, 1962), paras 123–36.

[44] See *Rights and Issues Investment Trust Ltd v Stylo Shoes Ltd* (above, n. 12).

[45] See *Bushell v Faith* [1970] AC 1099, HL, [1970] 1 All ER 53.

[46] Weighted voting structures are not, however, unknown. After the battle for the control of the Savoy Hotel Ltd (see n. 21 above), its capital was reorganized in such a way as to give the holders of less than 3 per cent of the equity the ability to outvote the rest: see Rabinowitz, *Weinberg and Blank* (above, n. 14), at para 3-798. The granting of a 'golden share' in privatized companies to the government, conferring special rights, including the right to block a take-over, should also be noted: see C. Graham and T. Prosser, *Privatizing Public Enterprises* (1991), at 141–51. It has been estimated that when the privatization programme is complete, companies protected in this way will constitute over one third of the FT-Actuaries All-Share Index: see Peacock and Bannock, *Corporate Takeovers* (above, n. 37), at 91.

[47] See Coopers & Lybrand, *Barriers to Takeovers* (above, n. 37), at 22.

[48] Ibid. para 2.33.

[49] See 170–1 below.

mechanism. The system of control depends on stable, long-term investor and creditor relationships with the company, which an active take-over market is liable to disrupt. Furthermore groups other than shareholders, notably the employees, are regarded as having a stake in the business that is not reducible to their interest as contractual claimants. The interests of the shareholders accordingly are not afforded an overriding significance but are just one of an number of interests that the enterprise is meant to serve. This 'partnership' perspective is incompatible with viewing the company as a commodity to be bought or sold as the shareholders alone may choose. As the Coopers and Lybrand Report makes plain, such attitudes are alien to the financial community in this country, again creating appropriate conditions for an active market in control.

Notwithstanding these differences in modes of governance and the way in which the enterprise is conceived it is the ostensible policy of the European Commission,[50] strongly supported by the British government,[51] to reduce barriers to take-over in the Community with a view to creating a 'level playing-field' and stimulating the market for control. The Commission has stated that it 'does not wish to encourage takeover bids as ends in themselves. Its standpoint is rather that takeover bids may generally be viewed in a positive light in so far as they encourage the selection by market forces of the most competitive companies and the restructuring of European companies which is indispensable to meet international competition.'[52] Some of the factors that limit the marketability of companies most crucially, however, such as low levels of stock-market capitalization[53] and closely held shareholdings, are not susceptible to regulatory 'correction'. Further, the commitment of member states, and the Commission itself,[54] to stimulating the market for control is questionable, given local cultural and philosophical variables. Whether a free market in corporate ownership is likely to bring net advantages to European industry is in any case disputable.[55] Certainly there is little in the comparative performance of British industry to indicate that emulation of our stock market-based corporate economy would be beneficial.

---

[50] See generally *CES* (90) 901 final. The Commission proposes to reduce barriers by amendments to the proposed Fifth Company Law Directive (*OJ* 7/4 of 11. 1. 91), to the already-implemented Second Directive (*OJ* 8/5 of 12. 1. 91), and by the introduction of the Thirteenth Directive (above, n. 41, and see amendments *OJ* C240/7 of 26 . 9. 90).

[51] See DTI, *Consultative Document* (above, n. 37), introduction; A. Burnside, 'Overcoming Barriers to European M & A', (1992) 13 *Co Law* 19.

[52] See *Com* (90) 629 final, at 2. The encouragement of mergers to create European companies of equal strength to giant enterprises from outside the Community is an explicit goal of Community policy. For a discussion see H. Ramsay, *1992 — The Year of the Multinational? Corporate Behaviour, Industrial Restructuring and Labour in the Single Market*, Warwick Papers in Industrial Relations no. 35 (1990).

[53] See Coopers & Lybrand for DTI, *Barriers to Takeovers* (above, n. 35), at 14–15.

[54] See Burnside, 'Overcoming Barriers' (above, n. 51), at 23.

[55] See Ch. 4 above.

In Germany, for example, there is evidence that the system of bank monitoring is highly effective in limiting agency costs, and the problem of short-termism there appears to be non-existent,[56] suggesting that an activated market in control is unlikely to bring net benefits. The developments discussed in the next section reveal a certain irony in the pro-market position.

III CHALLENGING THE LEGAL MODEL: THE REDEFINITION OF MANAGEMENT DUTIES

In contrast to the direction of the proposals just mentioned, in a number of jurisdictions which have well-developed markets in control the movement has been towards suppressing the level of activity. Thus a concern in the United States with the negative effects of the take-over market, particularly on local employment levels[57] and on long-term investment, has prompted many states to pass anti-take-over legislation,[58] to the point that intervention has 'largely succeeded in eclipsing the hostile takeover as a mechanism of corporate accountability'.[59] Techniques adopted include increased disclosure requirements imposed on bidders, shareholder approval by a pre-existing 'supermajority' for changes in control, and requirements for board consent to any form of post-acquisition business combination between the company and the acquirer of a set percentage of its shares. With regard to fiduciary duty amendments, which are the primary concern in this chapter, these have redefined the corporate constituency, involving an explicit departure from the traditional legal model by deviating from the 'shareholder primacy, shareholder wealth maximization standard that is the bedrock of corporate law'.[60] Massachusetts, for example, has provided that

In determining what he reasonably believes to be in the best interests of the corporation, a director may consider the interests of the corporation's employees,

---

[56] J. C. Coffee, 'Liquidity versus Control: The Institutional Investor as Corporate Monitor', (1991) 91 *Colum L Rev* 1277, at 1304. Coffee goes on to suggest, however, that the system of bank monitoring may already be breaking down owing to the growth of the international capital market: see 1287, 1305–6, 1312.

[57] See T. L. Hazen, 'Corporate Directors' Accountability: The Race to the Bottom—the Second Lap', (1987) 66 *N C L Rev* 171, at 176–7; A. C. Gavis, 'A Framework for Satisfying Corporate Directors' Responsibilities under State Nonshareholder Constituency Statutes: The Use of Explicit Contracts', (1990) 138 *U Pa L Rev* 1451, at 1461 (the benefits of take-overs are enjoyed generally, but the costs fall within the target's home state).

[58] See J. C. Coates, 'State Takeover Statutes and Corporate Theory: The Revival of an Old Debate', (1989) 64 *NYULR* 806, at 846–50; D. Millon, 'Redefining Corporate Law', (1991) 24 *Ind L Rev* 223, at 241 n. 76, 240–6; Easterbrook and Fischel, *The Economic Structure of Corporate Law* (above, n. 19), ch. 8.

[59] Coffee, 'Liquidity versus Control', (above, n. 56) at 1279. See also J. N. Gordon, 'Corporations, Markets, and Courts', (1991) 91 *Colum Law Rev* 1931, at 1931–3.

[60] Gordon, ibid. at 1977.

suppliers, creditors and customers, the economy of the state, region and nation, community and societal considerations, and the long-term and short-term interests of the corporation and its stockholders, including the possibility that these interests may be best served by the continued independence of the corporation.[61]

The purpose of these provisions is to authorize defensive action either in anticipation of a bid or where a bid has actually been launched.[62] The right to take such action has also been recognized by some state courts at common law. Thus in Delaware the courts have determined that boards may take account of the impact of a bid 'on "constituencies" other than shareholders (i.e. creditors, customers, employees, and perhaps even the community generally)' except where the sale of the company is inevitable.[63] The Supreme Court of Delaware has since gone further, in *Paramount Communications Inc v Time Inc*,[64] holding in effect that the erection of take-over defences is simply a matter falling within unreviewable good faith business judgement.[65]

An early example of a similar attempt to restrict the operation of the take-over market in a Commonwealth jurisdiction can be found in the Canadian case of *Teck Corporation v Millar*, where Berger J held that in the face of a hostile bid 'the directors ought to be allowed to consider who is seeking control and why. If they believe that there will be substantial damage to the company's interests if the company is taken over, then the exercise of their powers to defeat those seeking a majority will not necessarily be categorised as improper.'[66] The facts were that the target company, Afton, owned a property which it wished to develop as a copper mine, but to do this it needed the technical and financial assistance of a larger enterprise. Teck, a resource conglomerate, was keen to give this assistance, but the directors were of the opinion that another mining group, Canex, would be more suitable because of its greater experience and high-quality personnel. Teck therefore began to buy Afton shares in the market and in due course obtained a majority. Before Teck could replace them, however, the directors of Afton entered into an agreement with Canex. This involved issuing shares to Canex and would result in Teck being reduced to a minority position. In holding the directors' conduct to be lawful, Berger J was of the opinion that 'in defining the fiduciary duties of directors, the law ought to take into account the fact that the corporation provides the legal framework for the

---

[61] Mass Gen Laws Ann ch. 156B, para 65.

[62] For some examples of the forms of defensive action that might be taken, see J. P. Lowry '"Poison Pills" in US Corporations—A Re-examination', [1992] *J B L* 337.

[63] *Unocal Corporation v Mesa Petroleum Co* (above, n. 19) at 955. See also *Revlon, Inc v MacAndrews Forbes Holdings Inc* (above, n. 19).

[64] 571 A 2d 1140 (Del 1989).

[65] Gordon, 'Corporations, Markets, and Courts' (above, n. 56), at 1941–8.

[66] Above, n. 27, at 315. It may be noted that a high proportion of Canadian companies are in fact under family control, limiting the scope for hostile take-over activity: see Coffee, 'Liquidity Versus Control' (above, n. 56), at 1306–9.

development of resources in the private sector of the Canadian economy.'[67] With this in mind, he rejected the 'classical theory . . . that the directors' duty is to the company [and that the] company's shareholders are the company',[68] and replaced it with a theory to the effect that the directors are entitled to act in accordance with a broader range of interests, including those not only of the shareholders but also of the company's employees and of the community. On a definition of 'the company' expanded in this way it follows that the board should be permitted to take defensive action to prevent an inferior management team from gaining control of the company's assets. The broadened constituency allows the directors to weigh the impact of a take-over on the various interests and if necessary to override the members' 'right' to sell at a premium, or, as in *Teck*, the right of a majority to take control. The proper purpose rule, which has the effect of preserving these rights, clearly has no place in a model of the company in which the shareholders' interests are no longer the exclusive concern. Berger J accordingly refused to follow the English cases.

The only sign of judicial approval for defensive tactics in this country appears in an *obiter dictum* of Sir Robert Megarry V-C in the unreported decision of *Cayne v Global Natural Resources PLC*.[69] His lordship suggested that if a company were to attempt to gain control of another in order to run it down and thereby reduce the competition it offered to the company's own business, the directors of the target would be justified in creating voting power to preserve themselves in office, since in such circumstances their 'object is not to retain control as such, but to prevent [their company] from being reduced to impotence and beggary, and the only means available to the directors for achieving this purpose is to retain control. This is quite different from directors seeking to retain control because they think they are better directors than their rivals would be.' Unlike the reasoning in *Teck*, this *dictum* does not involve a rejection of the proper purpose rule, but rather the recognition of a limited exception to it. Thus an exercise of power with the objective of defeating a take-over may be legitimate, even though bringing

---

[67] At 314. He goes on to quote Jackson J in *State Tax Commission v Aldrich* (1942) 316 US 174, at 192, to the effect that

the corporation has become almost the unit of organization of our ecomimic life. Whether for good or ill, the stubborn fact is that in our present system the corporation carries on the bulk of production and transportation, is the chief employer of both labor and capital, pays a large part of our taxes, and is an economic institution of such magnitude and importance that there is no present substitute for it except the State itself.

[68] At 313. See also *Pine Vale* (above, n. 22), at 211, where the interests of the company and those of the majority are distinguished, and the former preferred.

[69] 1987. Upheld by the Court of Appeal without discussing this issue: [1984] 1 All ER 225. See also the Scottish decision of *Dawson International plc v Coats Paton plc* [1989] BCLC 233, Ct Sess; this did not concern take-over defences, but the validity of an undertaking given to a bidder to recommend an offer and not co-operate with rival bidders. *Dicta* appear to suggest that the court would have been sympathetic to defensive measures in certain circumstances.

about that result is its substantial purpose, depending on how the board's motive should be classified. The mere retention of 'better directors' cannot constitute a valid motive, but the avoidance of 'impotence and beggary' will. It is suggested, however, that this reasoning is inconsistent with the underlying rationale of the proper purpóse rule. The objective of the rule is to protect the shareholders' right to decide whether or not to sell, and the degree of potential damage to the business if they do sell is not the issue.[70] It can only become the issue where a break with the exclusivity of shareholder interests is made.

Section 309 of the Companies Act 1985 appears to present the court with the opportunity to make such a break. Since the section requires the directors to take account of the interests of employees as well as those of the shareholders in performing their functions, it might be thought that this would permit a circumvention of the proper purpose rule by an application of reasoning similar to that in *Teck*. Such an outcome seems unlikely,[71] however, in the light of the points made in the discussion of the section in Chapter 3 above. The courts will almost certainly require a clearer mandate before permitting management to interfere in so fundamental an aspect of the British corporate system as the take-over mechanism.[72]

It may finally be noted that in none of the developments overseas where fiduciary duties have been amended does it seem to be of much practical

---

[70] It has been commented with reference to this point that

it is apparently permissible to issue shares for the purpose of retaining control if the reason why one wishes to retain control is to secure the welfare of the company by excluding opponents who might otherwise destroy it but it is not permissible to issue shares for the purpose of retaining control if it is merely because the directors think that they are better directors than their rivals would be. It is submitted that this is a distinction without a difference. The approach seems to be that, if one merely thinks that one is a better director than someone else, one may not endeavour to retain control by issuing shares, but if that one can foresee a particular deleterious act which might be done by one's rival (or, perhaps, a particular advantageous act that one might do oneself which one's rival would not do) then the purpose becomes legitimate.

D. M. J. Bennett, 'The Ascertainment of Purpose when Bona Fides are in Issue—Some Logical Problems', (1989) 12 *Sydney L R* 5, at 13.

[71] Cf. *Dawson International v Coats Paton* (above, n. 69), in which the proper purpose cases do not appear to have been cited.

[72] It seems unlikely that the courts would be influenced by the economic arguments for or against the market for control. Referring to the disciplinary effects of the market (as a factor relevant to whether a duty of care should be imposed on accountants in respect of company financial statements), Hoffmann J recently observed that '[s]uch speculative thoughts, while occasionally entertained by judges, tend to be left unarticulated and with good reason: the courts are ill-equipped to evaluate them in any convincing fashion. If the wider economic effects of a decision are contrary to the public interest, the legislature must correct it': *Morgan Crucible Co plc v Hill Samuel Bank Ltd* (above, n. 18), at 335. On the position in the US, it has been commented that '[t]he inadequate development of a theory of mergers undoubtedly contributes to judicial uneasiness over extensive meddling in takeovers': R. Romano, 'Metapolitics and Corporate Law Reform', (1984) 36 *Stan L Rev* 923, at 978. The British position is not so much that economic theory gives equivocal guidance, as that it is not an appropriate factor for the courts to take into account.

significance precisely which additional constituencies the directors have been allowed to consider in a bid situation. After all, the interests of any of these groups are not assured of protection, since the changes permit, but do not require, boards to take account of them.[73] Nor are the developments aspects of a conspicuously broader concern with the welfare of non-shareholder interests, which can, of course, be prejudicially affected by the actions of current as well as predatory managements,[74] and by new managements after an agreed merger, the latter being more common that contested changes in control.[75] The fiduciary duty amendments are thus more realistically seen as inspired by a wish to create a theoretical framework tolerant of defensive action in general rather than a desire to protect the welfare of specific groups.[76] As already mentioned, uncoupling the exclusive connection between directors' duties and shareholder interests provides a conceptual basis for the permissibility of protective measures. One explanation for the developments allowing these measures is that they reflect a belief that an active market may damage overall efficiency. Their effect is not, of course, only to limit the number of consummated bids, but also to reduce the impact on existing managements of the threat of take-over. By enabling the board 'to throw some sand' into the take-over mechanism,[77] short-termist pressures on management, if such there be, will be reduced, and the destruction of what may be well-managed independent businesses in circumstances in which the net wealth-creating effects are dubious can be prevented.

As distinct from a purely economic objective in slowing down the market in control, Gordon has identified a different motive, exemplified in the judgment of the Supreme Court of Delaware in *Paramount Communications, Inc v Time Inc.*[78] This is to prevent an unbridled market in corporate control from threatening 'fundamental social values such as loyalty, continuity, and community . . . [T]he *Paramount* decision responds to the historical moment in which, for reasons wise or unwise, people want to ensure that the human

---

[73] See e.g. Coates, 'State Takeover Statutes' (above, n. 58) at 855. Gavis, 'A Framework' (above, n. 57) considers ways in which employee interests may be protected in the take-over situation which are less dependent on management discretion, e.g. by collective bargaining agreements which are binding on successors and 'tin parachutes'.

[74] In all but two of the non-shareholder constituency statutes passed in the US, however, management is permitted to take account of non-shareholder interests in all situations, not merely where there is a hostile bid: Gavis, ibid. at 1463.

[75] Hostile bids constituted about a quarter of total bids for quoted companies in the UK in the 1970s and eighties: Jenkinson and Mayer, *Takeover Defence Strategies* (above, n. 20), at 15–16.

[76] Gordon, 'Corporations, Markets, and Courts' (above, n. 59), at 1977, comments that most of the non-shareholder constituency statutes 'seem more managerialist than constituency-oriented, since the balancing of interests is left to non-reviewable management discretion'.

[77] J. Tobin, quoted in Cosh et al. *Takeovers and Short-termism* (above, n. 37), at 19.

[78] Above, n. 64. See also Millon, 'Theories of the Corporation', [1990] *Duke L J* 201 at 251–61, detecting in that case a general public interest justification for departing from the principle of shareholder primacy.

hand, rather than the invisible hand of the market, authors their fate.'[79] It is impossible to do justice to the richness of Gordon's argument in summary form, but its essence is as follows. Drawing on the work of Karl Polanyi,[80] Gordon contends that in the absence of appropriate state regulation the market for control (like other markets) will become 'self-regulating'. In self-regulating markets 'land, labor, and money become commodities, and market forces directly shape people's lives. Thus a self-regulating market system will eventually disrupt the "human and natural substance of society", particularly, employment and residence patterns and the web of social relationships that follow from those patterns.'[81] The market for control is particularly implicated in this process of disruption because of the scope and rapidity of the changes it engenders.[82] This explanation of the justification for limiting the operation of the market Gordon distinguishes from an economic explanation,[83] in that the justification holds that, even if hostile take-overs make a net contribution to the efficiency of the economy overall, their incidence should be reduced in order to protect 'non-economic' community values. This, it may be noted, is a particular example in connection with the market for control of the more general question raised at the end of Chapter 1, namely, whether companies should be designed to contribute to the maximization of social wealth or whether we should be prepared to accept less wealth overall (in the sense of tradable goods and services) in favour of safeguarding more community-orientated values. This issue, and its implications for company law, will be addressed in Chapter 9 and beyond.

The Merits of Departing from the Proper Purpose Rule

The previous two paragraphs described an economic and a social justification for curbing the operation of the market for corporate control. Whatever their merits, there is an obvious problem in allowing managements in Anglo-American stock market-based economies to protect their companies from hostile bids. Given the problems with shareholder supervision and replacement of management in British companies, as matters stand a successful take-over may frequently offer the only realistic prospect of changing an unsatisfactory board and in the absence of other forms of oversight the threat of take-over undoubtedly provides a crucial discipline. Weakening the market for control is thus liable to have serious consequences for corporate efficiency:

[79] Gordon, 'Corporations, Markets, and Courts' (above, n. 59), at 1933. For a similar theme in relation to plant closings generally see J. W. Singer, 'The Reliance Interest in Property', (1988) 40 *Stan L Rev* 611.
[80] K. Polanyi, *The Great Transformation* (1944).
[81] Gordon, ibid. at 1972–3, citations omitted.
[82] Ibid. at 1972.
[83] Ibid. esp. 1986–8.

a situation in which the board could be removed only with its own consent might seem a high price to pay to avoid the negative impact of the market. In *Teck* Berger J was mindful of the risk that, in the absence of the proper purpose rule, managers might be free to defend their jobs regardless of the interests of the company, and so went on to hold that for protective measures to be valid, the directors must believe that if the bid went ahead it would cause substantial damage to the business, and also that they must have reasonable grounds for their belief.[84] This elaboration and objectification of the duty to act for the benefit of the company make it easier to exclude measures inspired by a blatantly self-interested motive, but the inevitably limited nature of any investigation by the court into the merits of rival claims to control means that judicial monitoring will fall far short of guaranteeing that the directors will not use their powers to defeat a bidder who would have installed a more effective management team.

A possible alternative solution is the supervision of bids by a specialist regulatory body. There could then be vetting, not of the appropriateness of a take-over in those cases in which the target happens to have employed defensive tactics (which should be prohibited), but in all cases where a company of a specified size or economic significance faces a change in control. The existence of a veto power over mergers adjudged to be contrary to the public interest would enable the brake to be applied to the take-over process, at the same time rendering unnecessary the undesirable expansion of the discretionary powers of the directors or the adoption of constitutional devices to hinder control transfers. Such a regulatory mechanism already exists, of course, in the form of review by the Monopolies and Mergers Commission. Under the Fair Trading Act 1973 the Commission is charged with evaluating mergers in accordance with general public interest criteria, not just with their impact on competition.[85] And indeed, in a number of references the Commission has specifically addressed issues such as the quality of the rival management teams and the regional impact of a change in control in making its recommendations.[86] In 1984, however, the then Secretary of State for Trade and Industry announced that bids and agreed mergers would be referred 'primarily on competition grounds',[87] reflecting the government's confidence that safeguarding the other components of the

---

[84] Above, n. 27, at 315–16. Similar safeguards are built into some of the American developments: see e.g. *Unocal Corp v Mesa Petroleum Co* (above, n. 19), at 954–5, but see now *Paramount Communications Inc v Time Inc* (above, n. 64).

[85] S 84; a non-exhaustive range of public interest considerations are listed. The European Commission now has jurisdiction to scrutinize cross-border mergers of the requisite size on competition grounds: EEC Council Regulation 4064/89, OJ 1989 L.395/1.

[86] See J. Fairburn, 'The Evaluation of Merger Policy in Britain', in J. A. Fairburn and J. A. Kay (eds), *Mergers and Merger Policy* (1989), 193, at 214–16.

[87] 'The Tebbit guidelines': see ibid. at 204.

public interest could safely be left to market forces.[88] Since then references to
the Commission inspired by non-competition issues have been rare.[89]

Increased reliance on the Monopolies Commission or a similar body might
certainly be of value (especially if the onus were shifted to the bidder to show
that a change in control would be in the public interest),[90] but some doubt
the ability of a regulatory authority to make the necessary strategic decisions[91]
and it is in any case unlikely to be a complete solution to the problems
created by the market for control. Use of a regulatory agency makes it
possible to prevent control from changing hands where adverse consequences
are anticipated, but, while the negative pressures associated with the threat
of take-over may be reduced, they are unlikely to be eliminated given the
unpredictability of the referral process. Rather than relying on the market
for control as a source of management discipline but seeking to limit its
adverse effects through regulation, a more comprehensive answer may lie in
the reform of corporate governance. While the conditions for the creation of
a system of German-style bank monitoring do not exist (and the
concentration of power that this would entail might in any case be politically
unacceptable) it does not seem too far-fetched to suppose that effective
arrangements for internal supervision of management could be devised. A
reformed governance structure might thus allow the problems of the separation of ownership and control to be ameliorated without the need to rely on
external 'supervision' via the market for control. The issue of governance
reform is taken up in the next chapter.

[88] See also DTI, *Mergers Policy. A Department of Trade and Industry Paper on the Policy and
Procedures of Merger Control* (1988), para 2.8:
> Government should not normally intervene in the market's decisions about the use to which
> assets should be put, since private decision-makers will usually seek (and usually be best
> placed to achieve) the most profitable employment for their assets, and in competitive
> markets this will generally lead to the most efficient use of those assets, for the benefit both of
> their owners and the economy as a whole.

[89] Where a proposed merger is referred on competition grounds the Commission is, however,
free to consider its impact on other heads of public interest. A number of reports produced after
the Tebbit guidelines have considered the management efficiency issue: see C. Bradley,
'Corporate Control: Markets and Rules', (1990) 53 *MLR* 170, at 185. For a discussion of the
unlikelihood that the Commission will now conclude that a change in control is contrary to the
public interest on non-competition grounds, however, see J. Swift, 'Merger Policy: Certainty or
Lottery?' in Fairburn and Kay, *Mergers and Merger Policy* (above, n. 86) 264, at 271–80.

[90] See J. Plender, 'Some Policy Options', in Cosh et al. *Takeovers and Short-termism* (above, n.
37) 33, at 41.

[91] See ibid.: 'past attempts to address regional and social problems through competition
policy have tended to create market distortions and provide only a temporary reprieve for
uneconomic jobs.'

6

Corporate Governance: Shareholder Democracy and the Monitoring Board

This chapter discusses shareholder democracy as a mode of corporate governance. The term 'corporate governance' is used here as it has been used so far throughout the book, somewhat prescriptively, to refer to the processes of supervision and control (of 'governing') intended to ensure that the company's management acts in accordance with the interests of the shareholders.[1] Governance is thus distinguishable from executive decision making, the former being the process by which managers are held accountable for their performance of the latter function. The 'governance structure' is the set of rules and institutions, of statutory, common law, or elective origin, by which the processes of supervision and control are established. The central feature of the current governance structure is the vesting of executive powers in the board, and of control rights, most importantly the power to remove the directors but also the right to decide certain other issues, in the general body of shareholders. It is made up also of crucial ancillary rules relating to such matters as disclosure of financial information and audit, and the holding and conduct of shareholder meetings. Liability rules, restricting managerial discretion and imposing standards of fair dealing and competence, and the rules determining who has standing to enforce those rules are also part of the overall structure of control.

The chapter is organized as follows. Section I will examine the areas of company decision-making that are usually assigned to the shareholders, and will consider whether corporate efficiency could be increased by expanding the range of issues over which the members have the final say. The effectiveness of shareholder democracy as a means of controlling management is

---

[1] For a more expansive definition, see R. I. Tricker, *Corporate Governance: Practices, Procedures and Powers in British Companies and their Boards of Directors* (1984), at 6: 'the governance role is not concerned with the running of the business of the company, per se, but with giving overall direction to the enterprise, with overseeing and controlling the executive actions of management and with satisfying legitimate expectations of accountability and regulation by interests beyond the corporate boundaries.' See also A. Demb and F.-F. Neubauer, *The Corporate Board: Confronting the Paradoxes* (1992), at 2–3, 14–17, and 187, and Committee on the Financial Aspects of Corporate Governance (the Cadbury Committee), *Report* (1992), para 2.5. Means by which other interest groups might be given a role in governance are discussed in Ch. 11 below.

clearly dependent on active shareholder participation. With this in mind Section II will look at the current level of involvement of institutional investors in the affairs of their portfolio companies, and whether, as is hoped for in some quarters, the institutions are likely to assume a more sustained governance responsibility as the ownership of companies becomes increasingly concentrated in their hands. Section III takes up the argument, first outlined in Chapter 2, that the separation of ownership and control is a non-issue, and that the fact that shareholders might fail to play an active supervisory role through internal governance mechanisms is unimportant. This is the perspective adopted by the nexus of contracts model of the company, the central elements of which will be discussed with particular reference to the adequacy of current governance arrangements. The final section, which will be based on the assumption that the exising controls over management *are* too lax, will consider ways in which governance might be improved, principally by board reform.

I CONTROL THROUGH SHAREHOLDER DEMOCRACY

The Role of Information

The availability of accurate and up-to-date information on company perform-ance is of fundamental importance. In the absence of reliable accounting data effective shareholder supervision of management is impossible, as is the accurate pricing of shares which is crucial to market modes of control. The sudden collapse in recent years of a number of well-known companies which, according to their duly audited accounts, were thriving,[2] has focused atten-tion on the considerable scope for the distorted presentation of financial information. The Committee on the Financial Aspects of Corporate Govern-ance ('The Cadbury Committee'), a body set up by the Financial Reporting Council, the London Stock Exchange, and the accountancy profession partly in response to these incidents, notes that a 'basic weakness in the current system of financial reporting is the possibility of different accounting treat-ments being applied to essentially the same facts, with the consequence that different results or financial positions could be reported each apparently complying with the overriding requirement to show a true and fair view'.[3] For example, companies have been able to inflate reported profits by reducing the apparent level of debt through techniques such as off-balance-sheet financing, and to improve earnings figures by classifying costs as 'extraordinary items' and thus presenting them 'below the line'. Such practices may not only conceal questionable solvency but also make it more

---

[2] E.g. Polly Peck, British and Commonwealth, Parkfield, and Coloroll.
[3] The Cadbury Committee (above, n. 1), para 4.47.

difficult to assess the quality of the board's stewardship and the company's prospects in general.[4] A further issue of concern is auditor independence. Although the auditors' primary responsibility is to report to the members, and the auditors are formally appointed by the members,[5] in practice the audit firm is selected by the board, and the members have no role in determining the audit brief.[6] The doubts which these arrangements cast on the rigour with which the audit function is performed are increased by the practice of audit firms also providing to their company clients non-audit services, such as management consultancy and staff recruitment. A desire to retain this lucrative business may deter auditors from adopting too challenging a stance towards management's preferred accounting treatment of the company's financial position.[7]

The form and content of company accounts and the adequacy of auditing procedures is a specialist topic which will not be considered here.[8] It should, however, be noted that in 1990 a new body, the Accounting Standards Board, was established, with statutory authority to lay down and amend accounting standards.[9] Changes introduced in the Companies Act 1989 now require companies to state in their accounts whether applicable accounting standards have been followed and to give reasons for any material departures

---

[4] Distorted accounting figures also have an impact in a wide variety of other areas, e.g. in relation to covenants in debt instruments and management performance pay. For other examples see P. F. Pope and A. G. Puxty, 'What is Equity: New Financial Instruments in the Interstices between the Law, Accounting and Economics', (1991) 54 *MLR* 889, at 889-90.

[5] CA 1985, ss 235 and 385, respectively.

[6] The existence of an 'independent' audit committee of the board is likely to be of some benefit here: see below. Audit committees do not offer a complete solution to the problem of audit independence. See, e.g. Auditing Practices Board, *The Future Development of Auditing: A Paper to Promote Public Debate* (1992), para 4.4: 'because their members are non-executive directors bound by the concept of unitary board responsibility, audit committees may themselves, albeit unwittingly, be subject to conflicts of interest in matters relating to the audit equivalent to those currently held to jeopardize auditors' independence.' The Board canvasses as possible alternatives the giving to auditors of security of tenure through fixed-term appointments (para 4.5) and the appointment of a shareholder representative body to liaise with the auditors (paras 4.10-14).

[7] The obligation to disclose non-audit fees in a note to the company's accounts, imposed by the Companies Act 1989 (Disclosure of Remuneration for Non-Audit Work) Regulations 1991, SI 1991/2128 seems unlikely to make much difference, likewise the Cadbury Committee's proposed extension of the disclosure requirement to enable 'the relative significance of the company's audit and non-audit fees to the audit firm to be assessed': *Report* (above, n. 1), para 5.11. The committee did not favour prohibiting auditors from providing other services to audit clients. Another issue of topical concern is the adequacy of the liability regime to secure auditor competence, in the wake of the decision of the House of Lords in *Caparo Industries PLC v Dickman* [1990] 2 AC 605, [1990] 1 All ER 568. For that and subsequent litigation see L. C. B. Gower, *Principles of Modern Company Law* (5th ed., 1992), at 490-500.

[8] See generally J. H. Farrar, N. E. Furey, and B. M. Hannigan, *Farrar's Company Law* (3rd ed., 1991), ch. 28.

[9] CA 1985, s 256(1), and Accounting Standards (Prescribed Body) Regulations 1990 SI 1990/1667. For a discussion of the background to the changes introduced by CA 1989, see N. E. Furey, *The Companies Act 1989: A Practitioner's Guide* (1990), at 6-8.

therefrom.[10] The Board has set about a systematic revision of current accounting standards with a view to reducing the directors' discretion to present financial information in a way that is unduly favourable to the company and to increasing generally the fidelity of disclosure.[11] In the event of accounts failing to comply with the requirements of the Act another new body, the Financial Reporting Review Panel,[12] may now apply to the court for an order requiring the directors to prepare revised accounts, with the court having a discretion to order the directors to bear the cost of the proceedings and of the revision.[13] For the future, the accountancy profession has begun a wide-ranging review of the content of financial reports and the scope of the audit function. The Accounting Standards Board has, for example, recommended that the financial statements be accompanied by interpretation and discussion by management of the enterprise's business, the risks to which it is exposed, and the structure of its financing.[14] The Auditing Practices Board has similarly advocated a departure from an exclusively backward-looking approach to the auditor's role, which might include an obligation to report on risks to which the business is subject, and more generally that the function of the audit report should be seen not merely 'as adding credibility to a company's financial statements, but rather as a check and balance on the proper conduct of enterprises in the public interest'.[15]

It should be borne in mind that the information that companies are statutorily obliged to provide in the annual report is by no means the only source of information about management's stewardship of the business. Listed companies must make interim reports,[16] and they make announcements publicly through the press and by way of briefings to members of the investment community.[17] Whether the totality of this information is adequate for effective shareholder supervision depends on how the shareholders' supervisory role is conceived. It is quite clear that the information needed to provide a historical record of the board's stewardship of the business, to enable the shareholders to make decisions about the management of their investment portfolios, and to facilitate intervention by the shareholders in

[10] CA 1985, sch 4, para 36A.
[11] See Financial Reporting Council, *The State of Financial Reporting* (1991), especially 14–23.
[12] For its role, see ibid. at 12–3 and 24–5.
[13] CA 1985, s 245B.
[14] Accounting Standards Board, *Operating and Financial Review* Discussion Paper (1992, London), para 2 *et seq*.
[15] Auditing Practices Board, *The Future Development of Auditing: A Paper to Promote Public Debate* (1992, London), paras 3.13–3.16 and 3.20, respectively.
[16] The company must report on the group's activities and profit or loss during the first six months of each financial year: see the International Stock Exchange, *Admission of Securities to Listing* (1992 revision; the 'Yellow Book'), s 5, ch. 2, para 23. The Cadbury Committee has proposed that the interim report be reviewed by the auditors (as distinct from being audited): para 4.56.
[17] See 168 below. Shareholder access to information for the purposes of litigation is considered in Ch 8 below.

the conduct of the business, respectively, will differ widely in its required timeliness, scope, and detail. The proper role of shareholder supervision and other forms of governance will be considered throughout the rest of this chapter.

The Powers of the General Meeting

In addition to the power to dismiss the directors, the powers of the general meeting currently include the right to alter the company's constitution, the right to authorize an increase or a reduction in its capital and the issuing of new shares, and the purchase or redemption of the company's shares, the right to resolve that the company be wound up, and the right to sanction the payment of dividends.[18] Shareholders also have a role in confirming transactions in which the directors have a conflicting interest. This aspect of shareholder governance is examined in Chapter 7. So far, suggestions that the members be given a statutory right to veto decisions more intimately connected with matters of operational management have been resisted. Among the proposals are those of the Jenkins Committee, which recommended that shareholder consent be required for the disposal of the whole or part of the company's assets.[19] Hadden has gone further, suggesting that there is 'no reason why the approval of shareholders should not be required for all major disposals or acquisitions, whether by take-over or the purchase of assets, for major investment programmes and for ventures into entirely new spheres of activity'.[20] While such proposals have not been given statutory effect, the rules of the Stock Exchange do, however, require the consent of the general meeting to be given for the acquisition or disposal of assets where their value exceeds 25 per cent of the value of the company's existing assets or where one of a number of similar tests is satisfied.[21] Shareholder consent is therefore required, *inter alia*, for the acquisition of another company where the stipulated value criteria are met. It should however be noted that the effect of the current criteria is such that any of the largest 20 listed companies can acquire any company outside the top 100 without the need for shareholder approval.[22] Very considerable expansion is thus possible without consulting the members.

[18] The latter depends on the articles rather than the Companies Act; see e.g. CA 1985, Table A, art 102.
[19] The Committee itself rejected the suggestion that there be a requirement for shareholder consent before a fundamental change in the nature of the company's activities: *Report of the Company Law Committee* (Cmnd. 1749, 1962), at 41, paras 117 and 118.
[20] See T. Hadden, 'Company Law', in P. Archer and A. Martin (eds), *More Law Reform Now* (1983) 21, at 31.
[21] The International Stock Exchange, *Admission of Securities to Listing* (above, n. 16) s 6, ch. 1. These are known as Super Class 1 transactions.
[22] See A. Peacock and G. Bannock, *Corporate Takeovers and the Public Interest* (1991), at 109.

The shareholders' right to remove the directors is clearly central to any system of shareholder governance, and is also crucial to the disciplining of management through the market for corporate control. The prospect of dismissal, resulting from the action of either the current shareholders or their transferees after a take-over, is fundamental to containing managerial slackness and the pursuit of divergent goals. The selection of the other issues that must be determined by the shareholders reflects a collective view about the decision-making rights that are appropriate to the shareholders as owners. From an ownership perspective the shareholders should, in addition to the right to replace the individuals who perform the management function on their behalf, have at least the right to amend the framework within which the business is carried on, to determine its capitalization, and to bring the business association to an end.

These matters constitute statutory exceptions to the provision invariably adopted in the company's articles to the effect that the directors shall have exclusive powers of management.[23] There is an obvious efficiency justification for limiting shareholder involvement in this way, given the damage to effective management and future planning that might result from allowing interference in executive decision-making by a possibly ill-informed and shifting majority of members. There would seem to be advantages, however, in subtracting from the scope of management discretion those classes of decision in which there is a particular risk that non-profit-maximizing motives would prevail if the directors were left with the final say. As the discussion in Chapter 2 suggested, the relevant decisions are primarily those concerned with the expansion of the enterprise and diversification, on the assumption that shareholder and management interests with regard to these issues are imperfectly aligned.

Against the gains that may flow from reducing management discretion by insisting on shareholder consent in these areas must be weighed increased administration costs, and also possible losses resulting from delay and error.[24] As to the last of these, the risk that the shareholders might make inferior decisions to the directors can easily be exaggerated. As Eisenberg suggests, it is apparent with respect to at least some of the decisions that entail a hightened possibility of conflict of interest that investment, rather than

[23] See e.g. CA 1985, Table A, art 70.
[24] See also B. D. Baysinger and H. N. Butler, 'The Role of Corporate Law in the Theory of the Firm', (1985) 28 *J L and Econ* 179, at 181–2:
Increases in the legal rights of shareholders potentially opposed to managerial prerogatives reduce the ability of managers to exercise delegated authority. At some point, increases in the constraints will reduce shareholders' wealth by stifling innovation and increasing the likelihood of opportunistic behavior by individual shareholders. The provisions of stricter corporation law, for example, allow maverick shareholders to block mergers, acquisitions, changes in the articles of incorporation and by-laws, or other major organic changes that would increase shareholders' wealth.

purely business, skills are required. He goes on to note that 'the skills involved in formulating a decision to merge with Corporation B or to liquidate Corporation B are similar to the skills involved in formulating a decision to invest in Corporation B, and are quite different from the skills needed to formulate an advertising campaign, conduct employee relations, or make steel'.[25] Shareholders, particularly professional investors such as the institutions, are likely to possess the former skills themselves, and hence it is plausible to assume that decisions, for example, about the acquisition or disposal of major assets or businesses, could be made by the members without prejudicing the efficiency gains that flow from management specialization. The matters appropriate to shareholder decision making might conceivably extend, on the same rationale, to the 'major investment programmes . . . and ventures into entirely new spheres of activity' suggested by Hadden.[26]

It seems possible then that corporate performance could be improved by expanding the range of issues for which shareholder consent is required, thereby limiting the ability of management to pursue non-profit-maximizing goals. A procedural approach of this kind would certainly seem to have greater potential than control by judicial review: as was evident in Chapter 3, it is not possible to design legal duties with the required degree of sophistication to exclude the pursuit of divergent objectives, and effective policing is problematical. But we will not consider with greater exactness which decisions, if any, should be made subject to shareholder consent because there is an underlying problem which, if unresolved, makes any extension of shareholder democracy largely futile: shareholder passivity. It should be recalled that the ability of managers to pursue non-profit-maximizing goals on a significant scale is premised on weak ownership control, attributable to the lack of incentives to exercise control where a large number of members each owns a very small percentage of the shares. If this incentive problem reflects a fundamental truth about shareholding in large public companies, then extending shareholder consent requirements will serve little purpose. Mass abstentions, proxies, and voting with management as a low-cost 'rule of thumb' make consent procedures largely a formality. It was the view of the Jenkins Committee that 'to say that it is useless to provide investors with further safeguards . . . which, if provided, they will not use is a counsel of despair. Legislation can only proceed on the footing that new powers meeting real needs will, if created, be used.'[27] Sealy's observation

---

[25] M. A. Eisenberg, *The Structure of the Corporation: A Legal Analysis* (1976), at 15. For a favourable view of institutional investor decision-making competence, see B. S. Black, 'Agents Watching Agents: The Promise of Institutional Investor Voice', (1992) 39 *UCLA L Rev* 811, at 852–5.

[26] (Above, n. 20.)

[27] *Report of the Company Law Committee* (above, n. 19), at 39, para 107.

that the 'idea that shareholder democracy is a practicable concept, or that it is a good solution to any problem, has been shown time and again to be fallacious'[28] seems rather more realistic.

The growth of institutional shareholdings is cited by some as offering a prospect that shareholder control might again become a functioning reality. If it does, institutions are likely to seek to influence company behaviour not only by exercising their voting rights with respect to particular topics,[29] but also by engaging in more informal and wide ranging supervision of management. We shall now assess the reasons for thinking that these changes might come about.

II INSTITUTIONAL CONTROL

In 1969 financial institutions (pension funds, insurance companies, unit trusts, and investment trusts) held around 34 per cent of UK equities.[30] It has been estimated that by 1985 their combined holdings had grown to 66 per cent of the total, with the pension funds alone owning 29 per cent of all shares.[31] There is little to indicate that the proportion of equities held by the institutions will not continue to rise. Recent privatization issues have led to an increase in the total number of individual shareholders, but they have done nothing to increase the proportion of shares held by the personal sector, which continues to decline, standing at the end of 1988 at around one quarter.[32] Control over institutional holdings is in fact more concentrated than the total number of investing institutions would appear to suggest, given that day-to-day management of pension funds is often delegated to one or more of the relatively small number of investment houses.[33] It has been calculated, for instance, that in 1984 approximately a third of all UK

---

[28] L. S. Sealy, *Company Law and Commercial Reality* (1984), at 60.

[29] Current use of voting rights by institutions appears to be slight. In a recent CBI survey it was discovered that more than half of the pension funds questioned never or only rarely voted: CBI, *Pension Fund Investment Management* (1988), at 64–6.

[30] A. Cosh et al. 'Institutional Investment, Mergers and the Market for Corporate Control', (1989) 7 *Int J Industrial Econ* 73, at 77.

[31] *Investors' Chronicle*, June 1986. Much of the growth of institutional ownership, at the expense of direct, individual, ownership, can be explained by reference to the favourable tax treatment of the former. Pension contributions by employer and employee are deductible for tax purposes, for example, and pension funds themselves are not subject to taxation. Government policy on provision for retirement has been of central importance in the growth not only of pension funds, but also of insurance companies, which provide insurance-linked pension schemes. See generally J. Coakley and L. Harris, *The City of Capital* (1983), at 91–4; L. Hannah, *Inventing Retirement* (1986).

[32] Peacock and Bannock, *Corporate Takeovers and the Public Interest* (above, n. 22), at 30. As many as a quarter of the adult population may now own shares, a large proportion of them in privatized utilities: see the *Financial Times*, 19 February 1990.

[33] For a consideration of the scope of the discretion of external investment managers employed by pension funds, see CBI, *Pension Fund Investment Management* (above, n. 29), at 54.

pension fund assets were managed by 15 fund managers, mainly merchant banks.[34] Banks also control a significant proportion of investment and unit trust assets, and insurance companies, as well as managing their own funds, offer investment management services to other institutions.[35] This concentration in the management of holdings creates an obvious potential for intervention in the affairs of portfolio companies.

Apart from institutional dominance of the stock market leading to an increased concentration of holdings, of particular importance from a corporate governance point of view is the proportion of a given company's equity that is held by a single institution. While institutions and fund managers spread their holdings in order to minimize risk and hence rarely hold more than 5 per cent of the shares of an individual company, and usually much less,[36] an institution's stake will nevertheless frequently be so large as to have a significant adverse effect on share price if disposed of in the market. The result is that institutions in many cases are locked into their portfolio companies and therefore have an incentive to play an active supervisory role, rather than merely selling, if they become dissatisfied with company performance (though in practice they may simply wait to be released by a bidder). The absolute value of an institution's holdings may also suggest that the costs of intervention are justified by the expected return, even if this does allow other investors a 'free ride' on the institution's efforts.[37]

Given the policy of diversification an individual institution's stake in a company will not in most cases be of sufficient size to enable it acting alone to impose changes on management, but intervention does become possible through collaboration with other institutions. The relatively small number of institutions that would need to cooperate in order to put themselves into a control position and their mutual accessibility make joint action enormously more feasible than in the case of individual investors.[38] Furthermore, knowledge that portfolio companies are under-performing or of other ir-regularities is necessarily collected by institutions in the ordinary course of investment management.[39] As large-scale professional investors they are able

---

[34] T. Schuller, *Age, Capital and Democracy* (1986), at 95–6. See also R. Minns, *Pension Funds and British Capitalism: The Ownership and Control of Shareholdings* (1980), ch. 1.

[35] Coakley and Harris, *The City of Capital* (above, n. 31), at 110.

[36] See Minns, *Pension Funds and British Capitalism* (above, n. 34), ch. 2.

[37] Cf. A. Cosh et al., *Takeovers and Short-termism in the UK*, IPPR Industrial Policy Paper no. 3 (1990), at 33–4, where it is suggested that since they operate in a competitive market for fund management services, institutions are reluctant to put themselves into a position where competitors will benefit from their efforts in reorganizing portfolio companies.

[38] For American data on the proportions of institutional ownership in particular companies and the numbers of institutions that make up these proportions, see A. F. Conrad, 'Beyond Managerialism: Investor Capitalism?', (1988) 22 *U Mich J L Ref* 117, at 131–5.

[39] There is nevertheless a widely-held belief among industrialists that institutions have an inadequate understanding of the businesses in which they invest. The City/Industry Task Force set up in 1987 made a series of recommendations on how the flow of information to institutions could be improved: see CBI *Investing for Britain's Future* (1987), ch. 2.

to devote considerable resources to specialized performance analysis. They also have access to information additional to that provided by published accounting and technical data,[40] through special briefings or a seat on the board[41] (again, attributes of the size of their holdings). Institutions are in consequence in a position to identify cases in which active supervision would be beneficial, and might be expected to have some insight into the changes in management policy or personnel that may be required.

It would thus appear that institutions have both greater incentives to intervene in management than the individual shareholder, and that intervention by them is much more practicable. These factors have prompted one commentator to announce the birth of a new form of capitalism. According to this view, while the growth of corporate size and the consequent dispersal of shares led to a transformation from owner to managerial capitalism, the compacting of individual wealth within institutions makes possible a transition to 'investor' capitalism: 'the holdings of these institutions are now so large that a manageable number of funds could feasibly join hands to supervise managers in a new system of control.'[42] Should this come about, the problems associated with the separation of ownership and control would clearly diminish.[43]

The Practical Experience

The experience so far, however, does not lend much support to this thesis. Institutional intervention in corporate affairs in this country has been of two main types. The first has involved collective action through representative bodies to influence the behaviour of portfolio companies in general by laying down standards with which they are expected to comply. The investment protection committees ('IPC's') of the National Association of Pension Funds

[40] The possibility of criminal liability under the Company Securities (Insider Dealing) Act 1985, for transmitting or dealing on the basis of unpublished price sensitive information, however, is likely to inhibit the free flow of information: see further below.

[41] Using data from 1970, P. Stanworth and A. Giddens, 'The Modern Corporate Economy: Interlocking Directorships in Britain 1956–1970', (1975) 23 *Sociological Review* 5, report that 67 directors in the top 50 British industrial companies were representatives of banks, and 94 of 'City' firms. But see Lord Alexander, 'Investor Relations—Does the British System Work?' in National Association of Pension Funds, *Creative Tension?* (1990) 1, at 8: 'there are very few cases, if any, where directors are appointed to respresent specific investment funds, such as say a life insurance company or a pension fund.'

[42] Conrad, 'Beyond Managerialism' (above, n. 38), at 119.

[43] For an assessment of the likely effects of institutional monitoring should it occur on a significant scale, see J. C. Coffee, 'Liquidity Versus Control: The Institutional Investor as Corporate Monitor', (1991) 91 *Colum L Rev* 1278, at 1328–36. While accepting that institutions could make an important contribution to corporate efficiency, Coffee suggests, at 1334, that the 'power of institutional investors presents many of the same issues as did the hostile takeover', since 'pools of investors could form and reform.' For the impact of increased institutional control on social responsibility issues see 375–7 below.

and the Association of British Insurers have, for instance, drawn up guidelines concerning such matters as management share incentive schemes[44] and the disapplication of pre-emption rights.[45] The other form of intervention, at the individual company level, has usually involved informal collaboration between institutions to exert pressure on boards to persuade them to make policy changes or replace top management. The more conspicuous examples include the restructuring of Vickers, Debenhams,[46] Turner and Newall, and the Rank Organization[47] at the behest of some of their institutional shareholders. It is difficult to assess the full extent of this kind of activity because in most cases influence is exercised privately. This is in part to avoid damaging the relationship with company managements and thereby inhibiting the flow of information (or, in the case of banks and insurance companies, to avoid losing business),[48] and also because publicizing a company's problems is likely to undermine the confidence of lenders, suppliers, and customers, and so impede a resolution of the company's difficulties. Nevertheless, such evidence as there is[49] suggests that while institutional involvement at the individual company level is not uncommon, it is sporadic and largely

[44] The IPC's were active in the 1970s in combating incentive schemes which they regarded as excessively generous to management and leading to an unacceptable dilution of their interests: see L. Midgley, *Companies and their Shareholders—The Uneasy Relationship* (1975), at 79–80. The rules were revised in 1987 after an ambitious scheme was proposed by Burtons PLC (see 225 below).

[45] To avoid the risk of dilution the institutions have insisted on restrictions on the percentage of newly issued shares that do not have first to be offered to existing members, and on the discounts on market price at which such shares can be offered. Managements have been keen to disapply increasing percentages of pre-emption rights in order to take advantage of cheaper methods of issuing equity, but the institutions have jealously guarded what they consider to be an important prerogative of ownership. The NAPF and ABI guidelines were amended in 1987 after a number of controversial attempts to exceed the limits on disapplication of pre-emption rights were withdrawn after institutional opposition. See further 79–80 above.

[46] See S. Nyman and A. Silbertson, 'The Ownership and Control of Industry', (1978) 30 *Oxford Economic Papers* 74, at 94–6.

[47] See Coakley and Harris, *The City of Capital* (above, n. 31), at 116; Schuller, *Age, Capital and Democracy* (above, n. 31), at 99–100; R. Minns, *Pension Funds and British Capitalism* (1980), at 103–7. For more recent institutional activity in disposing of unsatisfactory chief executives see the *Financial Times*, 11 June 1991. For examples of institutional activism in the US see Coffee, 'Liquidity Versus Control' (above, n. 43), at 1288, 1293.

[48] Coffee, 'Liquidity Versus Control' (above, n. 43), at 1321–2.

[49] It has been reported that in 1988 more than 52 per cent of large companies had decisions influenced by institutional shareholders: Korn/Ferry International, *Board of Directors Study UK* (1989). The CBI, *Pension Fund Investment Management* (above, n. 29), at 20; 64–6, notes that one in eight of the pension funds surveyed were aware that their managers had participated in at least one instance of 'ginger group' activity in the previous five years, intended to stimulate a portfolio company's management. Midgley, *Companies and their Shareholders* (above, n. 44) reports that an insurance company investment manager had told him that his company had intervened in companies 25 times over a period of 18 months. See also Committee to Review the Functioning of Financial Institutions (Cmnd. 7939, 1980), *Report and Appendices* (the Wilson Committee), at 252–3; J. Plender, 'The Limits to Institutional Power', the *Financial Times*, 22 May 1990.

confined to the most obvious cases of mismanagement or blatant misuse of position.[50]

The Prospects

There is not much to indicate, therefore, that the re-concentration of shareholdings in the hands of the institutions is leading to a new era of shareholder activism. Indeed, it has been suggested by R. E. Artus, a leading investment manager, that

> any conceivable increase in [institutional] activity will not amount to a major new element of accountability in our system matching that of the bank-based economies, since share ownership unaccompanied by the additional involvement in providing finance and other services will never provide the depth of knowledge and committment that arises with the combination of banking and proprietary interests.[51]

The contrast between the incentives towards, and the feasibility of, intervention in the 'bank-based' economies and in our own stock-market-based economy are worth emphasizing. The most celebrated examples of the former are Germany and Japan. The systems in the two countries are quite different from each other, but share the feature that in both banks play a close and continuous monitoring, and where necessary, interventionist role. In Germany the banks' position as major shareholders in their own right is strengthened substantially by their ability to exercise the voting rights attached to bearer shares held by them on behalf of customers.[52] Debt finance is a more important source of funding in Germany than equity,[53] which means that the position of the banks as providers of loan capital gives them influence additional to that attributable to ownership, and also a significantly increased incentive to exercise active supervision. Thus, as well

---

[50] As to the latter, see e.g. the successful blocking of a record compensation payment to the former managing director of Associated Communications Corporation, and institutional disquiet over the favourable terms on which housing was made available to Marks and Spencers' directors, referred to in Schuller, *Age, Capital and Democracy* (above, n. 34), at 99.

[51] R. E. Artus (Group Chief Investment Manager of Prudential Corporation plc) in *Creative Tension?* (above, n. 41), at 14. One suggestion for producing the necessary 'commitment' is for institutions to increase substantially their individual holdings in a company, say to 25 per cent: see M. J. Roe, 'A Political Theory of American Corporate Finance', (1991) 91 *Colum L Rev* 10. Since this is contrary to the institutions' policy of managing risk by holding a diversified portfolio it is unlikely to occur without external pressure.

[52] See generally F. Vogl, *German Business After the Economic Miracle* (1973), ch. 2; E. J. Horn, *Management of Industrial Change in Germany* (1982), at 40–2; J. Charkham, *Corporate Governance and the Market for Control of Companies*, Bank of England Panel Paper (1989) at 5–9; Coffee, 'Liquidity Versus Control' (above, n. 43), at 1302–6. It has been estimated that taking into account proxy votes, the banks represented over 25 per cent of the votes in 41 of the largest companies in Germany, and over 50 per cent in 30 companies: Horn (above), at 41.

[53] See DTI, *Barriers to Takeovers in the European Community: A Study by Coopers & Lybrand for the DTI* (1989), vol 1, at 14-15. As well as providing debt finance, the banks act as 'broker, investment analyst, dealer and much else besides': Horn, *Management of Industrial Change in Germany* (above, n. 52), at 40.

as having an interest in rising share values, the banks are keen to protect and expand their profitable lending relationship. By virtue of their representation on the supervisory board the banks enjoy a formal channel for intervention, though the significance of this in practice may be limited. Such is the influence of the three main banks (Deutsche Bank, Dresdner Bank, and Commerzbank), that one commentator has noted that they 'are often regarded as a super-supervisory board of the supervisory boards of industrial concerns'.[54] In Japan many large companies are members of a *keiretsu*—an informal group of companies made up of a number of independent industrial and trading companies and centred on a bank.[55] The constituent parts hold shares in each other and are also involved in long-term reciprocal trading relationships. Thus,

Mitsubishi Bank, for example, is both a major lender to Mitsubishi Electric and a purchaser of its electronic equipment. Mitsubishi Steel simultaneously sells steel to Mitsubishi Heavy Industries and buys the latter's equipment and construction services. Mutual trade credit agreements also accompany these commercial trading arrangements.[56]

Banks play a coordinating role within these networks, and mutual interdependence encourages the performance by them, and by other group members, of a close monitoring and supportive function.[57] It can thus be seen, in short, that the key feature that causes the banks to exercise an active 'ownership' role in Germany and in Japan is their stable, long-term interest in the companies in which they invest, which is reinforced by the multifaceted character of the relationships between the parties.

In contrast, the financial institutions in this country have a much more limited relationship with their portfolio companies and indeed can be seen as investing 'in the market' rather than in the underlying companies on a long-term basis.[58] As one writer has commented:

Despite the size of their holdings in industry, the institutions still look upon them primarily as investments, to be bought or sold according to investment criteria; the

[54] Horn, ibid. at 40.
[55] See generally Coffee, 'Liquidity Versus Control' (above, n. 43), at 1294–1302.
[56] W. C. Kester, *Japanese Takeovers: The Global Contest for Corporate Control* (1991), at 58–9.
[57] Kester, ibid. at 59–60, underlines the interdependence of keiretsu members, as follows:
a typical corporate stakeholder is likely to possess a rather complex 'blend' of claims against other group companies in which it has invested—a combination of equity, credit, and trading contracts. The stakeholder may well accept subnormal rates of return on one component of its blend, such as equity, provided it is able to compensate with supranormal returns on another part, such as the trading relationship.
For doubts about the effectiveness of Japanese monitoring, see Coffee, 'Liquidity Versus Control' (above, n. 43), at 1299–1301.
[58] This is not to say that institutions are necessarily 'short-termist', that is, place undue weight on companies' short-term performance and under-value investment because of its depressive effect on short-term profits, thus imposing pressure on managements to be short-termist too. If, as the 'efficient market hypothesis' holds, share prices reflect all the information

financial institutions have their own businesses to run (of providing insurance cover, etc) and neither wish nor need to be involved in managing the businesses in which they invest.[59]

Contrary to the arguments considered above indicating a likely increase in institutional participation in governance, there are a number of factors which suggest that the economics of modern portfolio investment actually militate against shareholder intervention on a significant scale. An important consideration seems to be that institutions, responsive to the requirements of diversification and liquidity, hold shares in too many companies to make monitoring at more than a superficial level a practical possibility.[60] It has been suggested that the situation is exacerbated by an agency problem arising at the level of the relationship between the investing institution and the fund manager. Thus, Coffee argues that 'money managers are rationally apathetic because the expected gains from most ... governance issues are small, deferred, and received by investors, while the costs are potentially large, immediate, and borne by money mangers.'[61] The problem is likely to be especially acute with regard to external managers who are under competitive pressure to keep down the cost of their services,[62] and who may no longer be retained by the institution by the time any intervention in a portfolio company has borne fruit.[63] A further point is that institutions would seem to stand to gain less from intervention in the companies in which they invest than traditional owners, particularly where funds are passively managed through indexing.[64] Gilson and Kraakman argue that many of the factors that might lead to a rise in the value of one company in a portfolio

that is available about a company's future prospects, investment should have a favourable effect on share price. Even though institutions may not take a long-term position in particular companies, this would not, therefore, signify that the future was being 'sold short'. But for doubts about this analysis see 128-31 above.

[59] S. J. Prais, *The Evolution of Giant Firms in Britain* (1976), at 114. See also J. Charkham, 'Are Shares Just Commodities', in *Creative Tension?* (above, n. 41), 34.

[60] See R. J. Gilson and R. Kraakman, 'Reinventing the Outside Director: An Agenda for Institutional Investors', (1991) 43 *Stan L Rev* 863, at 865-7.

[61] Coffee, 'Liquidity Versus Control' (above, n. 43), at 1328. Cf. Black, 'Agents Watching Agents' (above, n. 25), at 876-82.

[62] See ibid. at 1326-7, 1352. See also Alistair Blair (ex corporate finance director, Fidelity Investments), the *Financial Times*, 27 May 1992, cataloguing the problems that will be faced by a fund manager in 'taking on' a company management, including lack of time, lack of support from the manager's employer and the client institution, and an inadequate budget to meet the professional fees that opposition will entail. He concludes that 'at every stage there is only one rational course of action for the fund manager: sell the stock.'

[63] Coffee, 'Liquidity Versus Control' (above, n. 43), at 1324-5. For ways of ameliorating these agency problems, see ibid. at 1336-68. For a consideration of the possibility that fund managers suffer from conflicts of interest that may cause them to side with managements at the expense of fund beneficiaries, see B. S. Black, 'Shareholder Passivity Reexamined', (1990) 89 *Mich L Rev* 520, at 595-608.

[64] i.e. holding a weighted portfolio of all shares in a given index, e.g. the FT 100.

(for instance, an increase in market share) will result in a fall in the value of another, and hence 'from the portfolio holder's point of view, this improvement merely transfers money from one pocket to another in the same pair of pants.'[65] These considerations appear to suggest, reinforcing the view of Artus, that the institutions are unlikely to become actively involved in the supervision of individual companies much above the current level of occasional crisis management.

Even if institutions *wanted* to be more activist, the nature of their relationship with portfolio companies creates obstacles to the free flow of information, and hence stands in the way of detailed, continuous monitoring of the kind found in the bank-based economies. As active traders in the shares of the companies in which they invest fund managers will be reluctant to receive unpublished price sensitive information for fear of their capacity to deal being curtailed in view of possible liability for insider dealing.[66] Furthermore, as the report of the City/Industry Task Force points out, 'companies face a dilemma in their choice of channels of communication.'[67] On the one hand Stock Exchange rules restrict the freedom to disclose information only to a limited group,[68] and on the other general publication is both expensive and, with regard to much of the material relevant to the monitoring role, commercially inexpedient. It is not clear that this dilemma is capable of being solved in a such way as would permit the release to the institutions of the detailed and timely information that is necessary for effective supervision, assuming in the first place that companies were disposed to release it.[69] But even if information sufficient for monitoring purposes could be obtained, institutions would still in many cases face considerable problems in mounting a successful campaign against a management with which they were dissatisfied. As compared with the board, dissident investors suffer from a number of tactical disadvantages, including the need to form and keep together a shareholder coalition with sufficient votes to threaten management's position. With the benefit of much more detailed knowledge than the outsiders of the company's affairs and future plans, the directors are in a strong position to rebut outside criticism and may also enjoy the loyalty of many of the small shareholders, as well as 'friendly' institutions. Against the prospect of a

---

[65] Gilson and Kraakman, 'Reinventing the Outside Director' (above, n. 60), at 866.

[66] Company Securities (Insider Dealing) Act 1985, s 1.

[67] *Investing for Britain's Future: Report of the CBI/City Industry Task Force* (1987), at 33.

[68] See the International Stock Exchange, *Admission of Securities to Listing* (above, n. 16), s 5, ch 2, 1.1: 'Information should not be divulged outside the company and its advisers in such a way as to place in a privileged dealing position any person or class or category of persons.'

[69] Clearly, the proposal of the CBI/City Task Force, *Investing for Britain's Future* (above, n. 67), at 33-5, that there be increased voluntary disclosure in the annual report on such matters as long-term strategy and expenditure on research and development would not adequately fill the information gap.

lengthy and damaging public dispute, activist shareholders may decide that the chances of success are too low to justify the costs involved.

Institutional Involvement at the 'Macro' Level

Gilson and Kraakman argue that although there may be no prospect of a significant increase in institutional involvement at the micro level, there are incentives for institutions to improve the corporate governance *system*.[70] The best way, they suggest, for the holder of a widely diversified portfolio to increase its return is to improve the performance of all the companies in the portfolio—effectively, of the economy as a whole—by ensuring that corporate governance arrangements are conducive to maximum efficiency. This insight, they contend, provides a normative model of how institutions in a market-based corporate system should behave towards companies in which they invest. In advocating intervention at the macro level the model recognizes that it is not feasible for shareholders who invest 'in the market' to engage in active supervision of individual companies in the manner of traditional owners, but it also notes the limitations of markets as constrainers of management behaviour.[71] It thus suggests a third means by which shareholders might exercise control, between, in Hirschman's terminology, 'voice' (participation in the organization's decision-making mechanisms to improve performance) on the one hand, and 'exit' (selling shares when dissatisfied with performance) on the other.[72] In so doing, it may be noted, it also indicates a re-legitimating basis for shareholder ownership and the rights associated therewith.

The particular governance reform that Gilson and Kraakman propose is the appointment of a minority of genuinely independent directors to corporate boards.[73] The essence of the idea is that the effects of the separation

---

[70] See also Black, 'Shareholder Passivity Reexamined' (above, n. 63), at 524. There is an increasing number of institutional initiatives at the macro level. E.g. in addition to the guidelines noted at 169 above, in 1988 the Institutional Shareholders Committee was revived. Its membership includes the representative bodies of the various institutions, and was first set up in 1972 to encourage more systematic intervention in poorly managed companies: see the *Financial Times*, 10 August 1990. It has produced a statement of best practice on *The Role and Duties of Directors* (1991).

[71] Gilson and Kraakman, 'Reinventing the Outside Director' (above, n. 60), at 870–1, and see 113–32 above.

[72] A. O. Hirschman, *Exit, Voice and Loyalty, Responses to Decline in Firms, Organizations, and States* (1970).

[73] See also 'Redirecting Directors', *The Economist*, 17 November 1990, 19. As Gilson and Kraakman, 'Reinventing the Outside Director' (above, n. 60), at 871–2 point out, board reform is clearly superior to the creation of shareholder advisory or representation committees. These might have some advantage in facilitating a concentration of shareholder voting power. Committee members could, e.g., be appointed proxies for other members. As compared with independent directors, however, committee members would have less information, and being outside the decision-making structure, fewer opportunities to influence policy. For proposals concerning shareholder committees, see Hadden, 'Company Law' (above, n. 17), at 32, and the

of ownership and control can be overcome by inserting a block of expert and well-informed monitors into the organization at the highest level. How independent directors might be expected to perform this monitoring function, and the differences between the proposed arrangement and the current practice of appointing non-executive directors, will be examined in some detail in Section IV. The discussion here will be confined to a consideration of the role of the institutions, as envisaged by Gilson and Kraakman, in bringing the new governance arrangement into existence and in securing its effectiveness.

The suggestion is that institutions[74] might form an agency or 'clearinghouse' which would recruit suitable independent directors and nominate them for appointment to particular companies. (The institutions would routinely use their voting power to ensure election of the nominees.) The directors would be full-time, and would serve on the boards of around six companies each. The individuals appointed would possess considerable relevant expertise: examples suggested are 'a 50-year-old professor of finance at a graduate school of business, or a partner at either a Big Six public accounting firm or a major management consulting firm'.[75] The appointees would be well, though not extravagantly, remunerated for their services. One of the main virtues claimed for this scheme is that it provides 'an analytically satisfying answer to the question of who will monitor the monitors'.[76] This task is to be performed by the appointing agency on behalf of the institutions. The solution to the monitoring problem is thus said to lie in making the directors ultimately dependent for their positions on the shareholders. If institutional shareholders are dissatisfied with the performance of directors they can refuse to re-elect them to any of the boards on which they serve.[77]

sources referred to by Midgley, *Companies and Their Shareholders* (above, n. 41), at 103. There is a history of informal shareholder committees in the form of 'ginger groups' which have occasionally had some success in forcing changes of policy by threats to vote directors out of office or to reject management resolutions, and more particularly, as a result of the ensuing publicity. Such groups have, however, generally depended on the initiative and determination of strong-willed personalities reacting to specific perceived abuses, and are rarely able to sustain an adequate level of shareholder support on a continuing basis. See generally Midgley (above) at 60–72; A Rubner, *The Ensnared Shareholder* (1965) ch. 7; B. A. K. Rider, 'Burmah Oil Loses Claim against Bank of England', (1981) 2 *Co Law* 220 (Burmah Oil Shareholders Action Group).

[74] They suggest (above, n. 60) at 887–8, that 'one or more of the industry groups and consulting organizations that now promote the collective interests of institutional investors might initiate such a clearinghouse' (in the UK, e.g. the NAPF or the ABI). While some institutions would free-ride on its services by refusing to contribute, this need not prevent a clearinghouse being created so long as those who do contribute enjoy net benefits.

[75] Ibid. at 885.

[76] Ibid. at 873–4. The effectiveness of director-monitors is problematical from the standard market-theorist position because the directors, as non-residuaries, are considered to lack adequate incentives to monitor efficiently: see e.g. A. A. Alchian and H. Demsetz, 'Production, Information Costs and Economic Organization', (1972) 62 *Am Econ Rev* 777, at 782; F. H. Easterbrook and D. R. Fischel, 'Corporate Control Transactions', (1982) 91 *Yale L J* 698, at 701.

[77] See Gilson and Kraakman, 'Reinventing the Outside Director' (above, n. 60), at 886.

It can be seen, therefore, that the scheme is tied to institutional investors in two ways. First, the institutions have the role of setting up the scheme, and second, they provide a solution to the second-order monitoring problem. It is not clear, however, that the shareholders are as central to the viability of the scheme as Gilson and Kraakman suggest. Thus, while the scheme is presented as an agenda for the institutions, the appointment of independent directors could, self-evidently, be made mandatory and the nominating agency set up, though not necessarily operated, by the state. The directors might then be elected to office by the members in the way proposed, though even here there are other possibilities. Further, the 'monitoring of the monitors' problem is solved not so much through the dependence of the directors on the shareholders as by their dependence on the appointing agency, which, rather than the shareholders, performs the second-order monitoring function. The main operative factors encouraging good-quality performance on the part of the directors are likely to be the prospect of damage to their reputation (particularly in view of the high profile of the appointees), and loss of income, in the event of dismissal. It is the appointing body that would effectively make decisions about dismissals, and the factors that encourage good performance will apply whether or not the agency is founded and financed by shareholders.

The possibility of there being an effective mechanism for maintaining efficiency that is not tied exclusively to the shareholders is an important one. Its implications will become clearer later in the book, when the merits of companies focusing on a wider range of interests than those of the members are considered.

Conclusion

This survey of the role of institutional investors in corporate governance suggests that direct institutional intervention consequent on an increasing re-concentration of ownership is unlikely to have a major impact in overcoming the problems of the separation of ownership and control. While institutions may lack incentives to take action individually, there is, however, a stronger rationale for collective action at the 'macro' level, a potential example of which has been considered. Whether or not the institutions actually take the initiative in reforming company boards, there are obvious attractions in seeking to improve management accountability in this way. The appointment of 'supervisory' directors, either to a separate supervisory board or to the exisiting management board, is the solution favoured by the European Commission to overcome the consequences of shareholder dispersal.[78] Such a

---

[78] See also the advocacy of a monitoring role for non-executive directors by the Cadbury Committee *Report*, (above, n. 1), para 4.5.

reform is likely to be of value in controlling divergent motivation and as a means of combating managerial inefficiency, and also as part of the mechanism for regulating management self-dealing (see Chapter 7). Section IV will consider in greater detail the EEC proposals and the issue of board reform more generally, but before that the anti-interventionist position supported by the nexus of contracts theory of the company needs to be examined.

III THE NEXUS OF CONTRACTS MODEL OF THE COMPANY

The discussion in this and earlier chapters has been based on the premise that weak ownership control leaves managers with a discretion to pursue non-profit goals and otherwise to act in ways that are at variance with the shareholders' interests. As we have seen, the theory of management power assumes a breakdown of the ownership model: dispersal of holdings creates a partial control vacuum. This gives rise to the problem of how to reimpose on management a commitment to profit maximization, some of the possible solutions to which have been considered.

Supporters of the nexus of contracts model reject this analytical framework and its accompanying policy agenda. They contend that current governance arrangements are an efficient means of controlling managerial discretion, notwithstanding limited shareholder participation, and argue accordingly that externally imposed reforms are unnecessary and liable to be counter-productive. Their position does not in general rely on empirical evidence to rebut managerialist claims, but rather on a re-conceptualization of the company and a series of assumptions about the efficacy of private ordering. It begins with an attack on the validity of the ownership model, in particular its characterization of the relationship between corporate participants and the assumptions it makes about appropriate modes of management discipline. Thus the ownership model depicts owner control as central to the viability of the corporate form. It is by the shareholders behaving as owners, that is, by their actively supervising management, that compliance with the profit maximization goal is maintained. The idea that there is a disciplinary gap in the modern company is premised on the failure of the shareholders to perform this control function. But if we stop viewing the shareholders as owners, it is argued, we need no longer regard a lack of supervisory effort on their part as in itself indicating an organizational breakdown. With the ownership misconception out of the way, we can begin to see how, through a process of interaction between self-interested individuals, efficient forms of control do, and have, evolved.

The Alternative Model

This is the function of the nexus of contracts model. The model redefines the company as 'the nexus of a set of contracting relationships among individuals',[79] or as one commentator has put it, as 'a marketplace where various constituencies contract for their own protection'.[80] The company as an entity capable of being owned thus disappears from the picture—it is merely a device to facilitate contracting between individuals—and rather than being the company's owners, the shareholders are reclassified as one of the parties (the others include management, employees, suppliers, and customers) who enter into contracts through the medium of the company in order to coordinate production for their mutual benefit. While the members own their capital contributions, we are cautioned that 'ownership of capital should not be confused with ownership of the firm. Each factor [of production] in a firm is owned by somebody. The firm is just the set of contracts covering the way inputs are joined to create outputs and the way receipts from outputs are shared among inputs.'[81]

The 'tenacious notion that a firm is owned by its security holders'[82] having thus been dispelled, it becomes clear that there is no a priori reason why the shareholders should exercise control over company decision-making. Indeed, *'no reason exists* why investors, who provide the firm with capital in anticipation of receiving a certain rate of return generated by the firm's assets, should have any input into the firm's decisionmaking processes.'[83] Nor, it is argued, do the shareholders wish to be involved, or stand to benefit from involvement. They are 'rationally ignorant' of managerial practices, choosing to diversify risk by spreading their holdings

---

[79] M. C. Jensen and M. Meckling, 'Theory of the Firm: Managerial Behavior, Agency Costs and Ownership Structure', (1976) 3 *J Financial Economics* 305, at 311.

[80] L. L. Dallas, 'Two Models of Corporate Governance: Beyond Berle and Means', (1988) 22 *U Mich J L Ref* 19, at 23.

[81] E. F. Fama, 'Agency Problems and the Theory of the Firm', (1980) 88 *Jo Pol Econ* 288, at 290. On this, the neoclassical version of the contract model, no distinct firm entity remains. The model is thus at variance with Coase's definition of the firm as a discrete organization, with authority relations replacing the price mechanism where the costs of contracting are too great, and with relative costs determining the firm's boundaries: see R. H. Coase, 'The Nature of the Firm', (1937) ns 4 *Economica* 386. The institutional variant of the contract model, on the other hand, retains the notions of hierarchy and differentiation: see O. E. Williamson, 'The Modern Corporation: Origins, Evolution, Attributes', (1981) 19 *J Econ Lit* 1537, at 1537–46; O. E. Williamson, *Economic Institutions of Capitalism: Firms, Markets, Relational Contracting* (1985), at 294–7. For a summary of the development of the contract model see W. Bratton, 'The "Nexus of Contracts" Corporation: A Critical Appraisal', (1989) 74 *Cornell L R* 407, at 415–23; R. I. McEwin, 'Public Versus Shareholder Control of Directors', [1992] *Company and Sec L J* 182, 184–7.

[82] Fama, ibid. at 290.

[83] D. R. Fischel, 'The Corporate Governance Movement', (1982) 35 *Vand L Rev* 1259, at 1276 (emphasis added).

rather than engaging in time-consuming and non-cost-effective monitoring,[84] and disposing of their shares where they are dissatisfied with management performance rather than incurring the costs of attempting to effect changes in policy or personnel.[85] In short, 'the arguments of those who advocate the need for a change in corporate governance are based on a failure to understand the economics of the corporate form.'[86]

The next step is to explain these 'economics' and to show why the process of contracting should lead to arrangements which optimally align management behaviour with shareholder interests. The consequences of the divergence between manager and shareholder interests are referred to by contract theorists as 'agency costs'.[87] These are the sum of the loss to the shareholders resulting from management decisions (or non-decisions) which diverge from their interests and the cost of the controls employed to limit divergences, for example, the cost of monitoring.[88] It is argued that the contractual terms settled on by shareholders and managers will minimize the incidence of agency costs. That they cannot be eliminated altogether is accepted. Either managers will consume perquisites, shirk, and pursue deviant goals, or the costs of limiting such behaviour must be incurred. In reality, since the controls will be imperfect, costs of both kinds must be borne. The objective is to minimize their sum. The nexus of contracts theory presents the parties as choosing the most effective, least-cost combination of available managerial controls. These might include monitoring (by shareholders, 'independent' directors, or auditors), liability rules, management compensation contracts, and internal hierarchy. In addition, the corporate contract 'also specifices the extent to which the parties rely on the competitive pressures from the capital, product, and managerial labor markets'.[89]

Free contracting between the parties leads to the adoption of efficient governance controls for the following reasons. First, it is claimed that where

---

[84] See H. N. Butler, 'The Contractual Theory of the Corporation', (1989) 11 *Geo Mason U L Rev* 99, at 107–8.

[85] Fischel, 'The Corporate Governance Movement' (above, n. 83), at 1276–8.

[86] Ibid. at 1260.

[87] For objections to the approximation of the relationship between managers and shareholders to one of agency (on the ground that the agency relationship connotes a level of control by the principal over the agent that is lacking in this case) see R. C. Clark, 'Agency Costs versus Fiduciary Duties', in J. W. Pratt and R. J. Zeckhauser (eds), *Principals and Agents: The Structure of Business* (1985) 55, at 56 - 9; V. Brudney, 'Corporate Governance, Agency Costs, and the Rhetoric of Contract', (1985) 85 *Colum L Rev* 1403, at 1427–30; Dallas, 'Two Models of Corporate Governance' (above, n. 80), at 34–6.

[88] Jensen and Meckling, 'Theory of the Firm', (above, n. 79), at 308–10.

[89] H. N. Butler and L. E. Ribstein, 'Opting Out of Fiduciary Duties: A Response to the Anti-Contractarians', (1990) 65 *Wash L Rev* 1, at 7. Presumably, the 'specification' is by way of 'implicit contracts'; see ibid. at 7 and 45. For criticism of reliance on implicit contracting in company law, see M. A. Eisenberg, 'The Structure of Corporation Law', (1989) 89 *Colum L Rev* 1461, at 1487–8.

the original owner/manager of a business sells shares to the public, that owner will bear the whole of the agency costs, or at least will bear them to the extent that they are anticipated by the equity market. Thus, as Jensen and Meckling explain, 'Prospective minority shareholders will realize that the owner-manager's interests will diverge somewhat from theirs, hence the price which they will pay for shares will reflect the monitoring costs and the effect of the divergence between the manager's interest and theirs.'[90] This being so, the owner has an incentive to offer assurances to prospective investors, by way of the provision of an appropriate governance mechanism, that agency costs will be kept to a minimum. In that way the owner maximizes the sale price of the shares about to be issued. Second, having gone public, during the life of the company it continues to be in the interests of managers to incorporate into the governance controls terms that ensure that the shareholders' interests are properly protected. Easterbrook and Fischel tell us that the 'history of corporations has been that firms failing to adapt their governance structures are ground under by competition'.[91] A disciplinary effect is attributed particularly to the capital market, with those firms relying on comparatively weak controls over management facing an increased cost of capital. That is, investors will pay less for the securities of companies whose managers fail to give adequate structural assurances that the value of the firm will be maximized.[92] The competition for the control of resources thus gives rise to an evolutionary process, a process of natural selection: 'Over tens of years and thousands of firms . . . the firms and managers that make the choices investors prefer will prosper relative to others.'[93]

Given the existence of this evolutionary process and the accompanying competitive pressure to emulate successful structures, it is concluded that at any particular time the bulk of companies will have adopted the set of governance arrangements (allowing for the different circumstances of individual firms) that are generally recognized as most likely to minimize agency costs. This being so, we can be confident that current governance practices, notwithstanding limited shareholder participation in 'internal'

---

[90] Jensen and Meckling, 'Theory of the Firm', (above, n. 79), at 313. See also F. H. Easterbrook and D. R. Fischel, 'The Corporate Contract', (1989) 89 *Colum L Rev* 1416, at 1418–22, 1430, reproduced with amendments in F. H. Easterbrook and D. R. Fischel, *The Economic Structure of Corporate Law* (1991), ch. 1.

[91] Ibid. at 1427.

[92] Ibid. at 1426–34.

[93] Ibid. at 1421. See also C. S. Axworthy, 'Corporate Directors—Who Needs Them?', (1988) 51 *MLR* 273, at 281:

unless there are legislative constraints placed upon the corporate forms available, the form of organization 'chosen' will be the one which most efficiently controls the agency costs, arising consequent upon the need to hire people to carry out functions required for the performance of the organization's stated objectives . . . Corporations will establish a system of checks and balances in an attempt to ensure that the most efficacious decisions are reached by the corporation.

modes of control, are efficient. The point is not, it should be stressed, that shareholder supervision via the governance mechanism is itself an effective means of control over management. Rather it is because there are other sources of discipline, particularly discipline stemming from various markets, that there is no need for governance reform. If existing arrangements did not adequately protect their interests, shareholders would demand, and it would be in the interests of managers to supply, superior control mechanisms. This descriptive conclusion is then relied on to support an important normative conclusion: given the optimality of the existing governance structure, the imposition of governance reforms by non-market means can only lead to a less efficient outcome. Strengthened controls might conceivably reduce still further divergences from profit maximization, but only at a price that exceeds the benefit. If a particular reform were cost-justified market pressures would already have led to its adoption. Accordingly, there is no case for regulatory interference in the governance process.

Is the Model Persuasive?

A major line of criticism of the contract model questions its descriptive accuracy. Thus, Eisenberg offers the following alternative account of the company's make-up:

A corporation is a profit-seeking enterprise of persons and assets organized by rules. Most of these rules are determined by the unilateral action of corporate organs or officials. Some of these rules are determined by market forces. Some are determined by contract or other forms of agreement. Some are determined by law'.[94]

Contract, in other words, accounts for only a very limited proportion of the totality of the rules of company law. To take Eisenberg's last point first, as far as English companies are concerned it is the case that a substantial proportion of the rules that make up the corporate governance structure are 'determined by law'. The rules concerning the removal of directors by the shareholders, the disclosure of financial or other types of information and its verification, the raising and maintenance of capital, and many of the rules relating to the holding of general meetings, for example, are imposed by statute and are mandatory. One approach taken by contract theorists to statutory and common law rules is to assimilate them into the contractual model by arguing that they represent standard terms provided 'off the shelf' as a way of reducing transaction costs. Ideally, they are the terms that the parties would themselves have adopted if they could have explicitly considered the matter at no cost.[95] Fiduciary duties, for example, provide on

[94] Eisenberg, 'The Structure of Corporation Law' (above, n. 89), at 1461.
[95] See e.g. F. H. Easterbrook and D. R. Fischel, 'The Proper Role of a Target's Management in Responding to a Tender Offer', (1981) 94 *Harv L Rev* 1161, at 1182.

this view a ready-made (if sometimes uncertain) solution to a host of possible contingencies that would otherwise have to be anticipated and bargained over in advance.[96] Whatever the aptness of this reasoning in general,[97] it is, however, inappropriate as far as mandatory rules are concerned. As just noted, the statutory rules defining the governance structure are mandatory, and there are in English law restrictions on the freedom of the corporators to amend the fiduciary controls. These rules will apply even where the parties would not have selected them had they been left with the choice, and hence in such cases they are clearly non-volitional.

In response contract theorists have indicated that the contract analysis should in relevant respects be regarded as a normative rather than a positive analysis.[98] That is, they contend that the rules of company law *ought* to be treated as contracts; it is not necessarily the case that all of them *are* contracts. This aspect of the contract debate has had a practical impact in the United States,[99] where the possibility of allowing companies to opt out of federal and state corporation laws is a live issue, with contract theorists arguing that a regime of contractual freedom is more efficient than one involving mandatory rules (essentially on the basis that the parties are better informed about, and better able to provide for, the different circumstances of individual companies than are regulatory authorities).[100] The 'opt out' controversy is, however, currently of limited significance in this country as

[96] See Fischel, 'The Corporate Governance Movement' (above, n. 83), at 1265: 'optimal fiduciary duties should approximate the bargain that investors and managers would reach if transactions costs were zero.'

[97] See 203–5 below.

[98] See F. S. McChesney, 'Economics, Law and Science in the Corporate Field: A Critique of Eisenberg' (1989) 89 *Colum L Rev* 1530, at 1537–8; Butler and Ribstein, 'Opting Out of Fiduciary Duties' (above, n. 86), at 12. Cf. Easterbrook and Fischel, 'The Corporate Contract' (above, n. 87), at 1428: 'Even terms that are invariant . . . are contractual to the extent that they produce offsetting voluntary arrangements'. See also ibid. at 1433, and see Easterbrook and Fischel, *The Economic Structure of Corporate Law* (above, n. 90), at 15.

[99] See L. A. Bebchuk, 'The Debate on Contractual Freedom in Corporate Law', (1989) 89 *Colum L Rev* 1395, at 1397–8. An example is the legislative change in Delaware to permit companies to make charter amendments eliminating the directors' duty of care: Del Code Ann tit 8, § 102(b)(7) (Supp 1988).

[100] Butler and Ribstein, 'Opting Out of Fiduciary Duties' (above, n. 89); McEwin, 'Public Versus Shareholder Control of Directors' (above, n. 78). Acceptance of the contract model does not, however, necessarily involve a commitment to opting out: see Bebchuk, ibid. at 1408–9. For an intermediate position see J. C. Coffee, 'No Exit? Opting Out, the Contractual Theory of the Corporation, and the Special Case of Remedies', (1988) 53 *Brooklyn L Rev* 919, esp. at 950–3, 970–4 (opt-out provisions may be unfair to shareholders and allocatively inefficient, but it is false to assume that existing company law rules are optimal; opt out should be permitted, therefore, but with the burden of proof on the company to establish that the change is not contrary to public policy). Some contract theorists also accept that there is a need for some mandatory rules, i.e. in accordance with conventional market principles, to avoid inefficiencies resulting from externalities and inadequate information: see Easterbrook and Fischel, 'The Corporate Contract' (above, n. 90), at 1436–42 (sanctioning regulation to prevent the adoption of take-over defences and requiring mandatory financial disclosure).

far as public companies are concerned and will not be considered further here.[101] Of greater relevance is whether, in so far as the model provides a positive account in terms of contract of those rules that *are* determined voluntarily, the analysis is sufficiently convincing to support the conclusions about the optimality of existing arrangements and the dangers of regulatory intervention.

The Articles as a Contract

As distinct from the mandatory elements of the corporate structure just mentioned it is true that there are also major features which are not laid down by statute but which are instead reserved for determination by the corporators. Thus issues as important as the division of decision-making authority between the directors and the shareholders, and the structure of the board, are left to private ordering to be set out in the company's articles. The articles, as the Companies Act prescribes,[102] have the effect of a contract between the company and its members, one consequence of which is that provisions in the articles, or at least some of them,[103] can be enforced by a member in a contract action. It is open to the corporators to provide in this contract whatever safeguards for shareholders additional to those laid down by the Companies Act that they might desire. They might, for instance, require more detailed information to be disclosed by management, or a broader range of issues to be submitted for shareholder approval than the Act specifies. In some companies a variation along these lines of the standard terms offered by the Companies Act and Table A can realistically be expected. Thus a small group of individuals intending to form a private company are likely to negotiate the terms that are to govern their relationship, and the provisions duly incorporated in the articles will often reflect the interests and concerns of the different participants. In such cases, as well as having the legal status of a contract, the articles' *content* can also be meaningfully described as having been determined by a contractual process. This is much less true, however, where the large public company is concerned. Here there is no active negotiation between the 'corporators'; rather, the provisions in the articles are selected by management and the shareholders' role is limited to deciding whether or not to invest at the issue price. Investors who buy shares in the market *a fortiori* buy a package of rights, the contents of which are non-negotiable.

---

[101] For a consideration of the limited ability of companies to modify fiduciary duties, see 210–14 below. In the case of *private* companies certain regulatory requirements (e.g. the obligation to hold an annual general meeting and to lay accounts before a general meeting) may by unanimous shareholder resolution be disapplied: see CA 1985, s 379A.

[102] CA 1985, s 14.

[103] See K. W. Wedderburn, 'Shareholders' Rights and the Rule in *Foss v Harbottle*', [1957] *CLJ* 194, at 209–15; R. J. Smith, 'Minority Shareholders and Corporate Irregularities', (1978) 41 *MLR* 147.

The inferences about outcomes that it may be appropriate to draw in the case of contracting in the 'richer' sense (as in the case of a private company) are likely to be misleading if made with respect to these public company 'contracts'. Brudney explains that, on conventional assumptions, 'If the contract (under which the stockholder is said to offer his investment in exchange for managerial services) is "knowingly" and "freely" made by the parties . . . its performance makes each of the parties better off and creates a larger pie for society.'[104] On the basis of certain assumptions, the process of contracting is likely, in other words, to produce efficient governance terms. But Brudney goes on to observe that the cognitive and volitional requirements necessary for Pareto-efficient exchange are absent in the public company context.[105] Shareholders are mainly ignorant of a company's actual or proposed governance arrangements and the practical scope of managerial discretion, and '[s]cattered stockholders cannot, and do not, negotiate'[106] either with owners who go public, or with management, about the nature of the controls that should be imposed. If this is so, then we should hardly be surprised if the governance arrangements that are offered are less than ideal from the shareholders', and society's, point of view.

In the main, however, contract theorists do not appear to rely on the claims that this reasoning seeks to rebut. Easterbrook and Fischel, for example, fully accept that many governance provisions are in effect laid down by management. The factor that is said to justify treating them as contractual, notwithstanding, is that they are priced: 'all the terms in corporate governance are contractual in the sense that they are fully priced in transactions among the interested parties.'[107] Governance provisions are contracts, in other words, because they result from interactions between management and shareholders in the capital market. Accordingly, the generation of efficient governance provisions is not seen to depend on bilateral negotiation between parties with symmetrical information and bargaining power, but, as mentioned earlier, on the exposure of terms, admittedly selected by management, to the evaluative and sanctioning processes that the price mechanism constitutes.

Contract Terms and Markets

But is the cumulative effect of buy/sell decisions sufficient to induce managers to adopt governance arrangements that minimize agency costs, given their own conflicting interest in retaining a discretion to pursue

[104] Brudney, 'Corporate Governance' (above, n. 87), at 1404 (footnote omitted).
[105] Ibid. at 1404–20.
[106] Ibid. at 1412. See also Clark, 'Agency Costs versus Fiduciary Duties' (above, note 84), at 60: 'the core notion of contract, and the most relevant for theorizing about the optimality of commercial relationships, is that the rights and duties between the two parties are specified and fixed by their own voluntary and actual agreement.'
[107] Easterbrook and Fischel, 'The Corporate Contract' (above, n. 90), at 1430.

divergent goals? Certainly it does not seen unreasonable to expect a different outcome to emerge from a situation in which terms laid down by management are merely '"reviewed" by interactions with other self-interested actors',[108] from the one that would result from bargaining under ideal conditions. The first problem is that capital-market encounters between managers and shareholders are likely in practice to be rare. Only a small proportion of funds overall is raised in the form of new equity, with internal funding being a much more important source.[109] If a company does not need to go to the market for funds then it is insulated from direct capital-market pressure. Second, where a company does raise new equity, the market's ability to price a given governance structure, let alone its individual elements, is suspect. As Brudney again explains, 'a purchase or sale [of shares] embodies a lump choice, one in which the many components of firm success—or expected success—are combined in the single bundle to be bought or sold. The choice to buy or sell thus represents a complex mixture of satisfactions and dissatisfactions with components of the bundle.'[110] The result is that variations in governance arrangements as between companies may simply fail to generate differential prices,[111] thereby frustrating selection by the market of efficient terms.

But there is a further problem, even assuming the salience of the capital market and the correct pricing of governance provisions. This concerns the adequacy of the means by which the price of the company's equity is translated into pressure on managers to adopt provisions attractive to investors. Brudney explains that

pricing efficiency . . . is not to be confused with pressure on management to operate efficiently or to maximize shareholder wealth in any given firm. At best, the market price correctly reflects the existence of managerial discretion and the concomitant potential for diversion of assets and for operating inefficiency. The 'efficiency' of the stock market does not of its own force drive management to compete in limiting its rewards or its power to divert assets, or even to be more efficient managers.[112]

Reliance on the efficient market hypothesis, even if valid,[113] is not in itself sufficient, in other words, to make convincing the claim that the operation of the capital market will induce managers to adopt efficient governance terms.

Thus it is clear in principle how the owners of a company about to go

[108] Ibid. at 1418.
[109] See D. A. Hay and D. J. Morris, *Industrial Economics and Organization: Theory and Evidence* (2nd ed., 1991), at 427, and 118 above.
[110] Brudney, 'Corporate Governance' (above, n. 87), at 1424.
[111] See Eisenberg, 'The Structure of Corporation Law' (above, n. 89), at 1502: 'There is strong evidence that many significant changes in a corporation's constitutive rules do not have a statistically significant effect on the price of the corporation's stock.' Easterbrook and Fischel, however, argue strongly to the contrary: see *The Economic Structure of Corporate Law* (above, n. 90), esp. at 20.
[112] Brudney, 'Corporate Governance' (above, n. 87), at 1425, ref omitted.
[113] See 119-20, 129-30 above.

public are affected by a low market valuation, but what impact does share price have on managers in the more usual case of the company that is already listed? One possibility, as Easterbrook and Fischel suggest, is that companies that face a higher than average cost of capital will ultimately collapse, that is to say, they will fail in their product markets because they must pay more for capital than their competitors. However, as Eisenberg explains,[114] this result is implausible since a company which wishes to raise £X by issuing equity, but whose shares command a reduced price, simply has to issue more shares than would a company also wishing to raise £X but which had a more satisfactory governance structure. It is true that this will have a depressive effect on the value of the company's existing shares, but the resulting wealth loss will be experienced by the holders of those shares and not by the company itself, and hence there will be no adverse product market consequences. The other possibility, as this implies, is that managers face pressure to adopt appealing governance provisions because of possible effects in the market for corporate control. If a new issue drives down the price of existing shares the company will face an increased risk of take-over, and this is something that its directors will wish to avoid, given that their jobs may be endangered. How realistic this risk is will depend, however, on the likely size of the fall in share price. As Chapter 4 described, the level of slack in the market for control suggests that in order to provoke a bid a company's share price will need to fall by a significantly greater amount than might plausibly be expected to result simply from offering sub-optimal governance provisions.

It may be noted that the company's product market and the market for control might also impose pressure on managers to adopt efficient governance arrangements directly, that is, without the intermediation of the capital market (though a description of the processes involved in terms of contract becomes increasingly difficult). A company with inadequate controls over management might in theory be forced out of business on account of having to charge higher prices than better regulated competitors. Rather than tying their hands with more restrictive governance provisions, however, a more predictable response to this risk is simply for management to curtail the self-interested behaviour that creates it.

Similarly with regard to the market for control, the company's share price might fall on account of its failure to give sufficiently convincing assurances to investors (by way of an appropriate governance structure) about how management discretion will be used, whether or not the company seeks new capital. It is important to recall, however, that what is in issue here is the effectiveness of the market in stimulating constitutional innovation in the event of exisiting governance arrangements proving inadequate. If companies

---

[114] Eisenberg, 'The Structure of Corporation Law' (above, n. 89), at 1500–05.

were free to dispense with the mandatory provisions that protect shareholder interests, for instance, the obligation to produce audited accounts or the right of the members to remove the directors from office, a company making such changes could certainly be expected to provoke a significant adverse market response. What is much less certain is that market pressure is sufficiently intense to make companies seek out *additional* forms of protection for shareholders. On the contrary, it seems more likely, as Dallas suggests, that in imperfectly competitive markets governance structures become 'traditionalized',[115] that is, companies exhibit a tendency to adopt the same basic structure and the structure selected remains largely unchanged because managers have inadequate incentives to out-bid each other with stricter governance provisions. It is true that if a company were to impose more rigorous controls (for example, the appointment of a board genuinely independent of management) this might lead to an increase in the value of the company's shares if such a change were perceived to be in the shareholders' interests. The positive impact on managers' own positions is likely to be too limited, however, to justify the loss of discretion that would be involved, thus removing the impetus for change. And even if some companies were to innovate, there would for the same reason be only weak incentives for others to follow suit, at least until reformed structures became the norm rather than the exception. This picture of self-interested passivity in the face of limited market pressure seems to offer an explanation for the absence of evolutionary change during the period in which active shareholder involvement in governance became severely restricted, consequent on the dispersal of holdings, that is at least as convincing as the view that the prevailing arrangements were, and are, the best obtainable.[116] It cannot be argued on the basis of this conclusion that any particular governance reforms would necessarily improve corporate performance, but it does provide a reason for keeping an open mind about the efficacy of existing arrangements.

It is important finally to emphasize the distinction between the role of markets in limiting management discretion, and their role, and hence that of 'contract', in shaping corporate governance structures. It is undeniable that markets are of considerable importance in aligning management goals with shareholder interests. To the extent that the operation of markets is effective

---

[115] Dallas, 'Two Models of Corporate Governance' (above, n. 80), at 46. It should be emphasized that what is in issue here is the controls over management discretion. Enterprises exhibit a very wide variety of *organizational* structures.

[116] Dallas, ibid. at 46–7 attacks the use of 'natural selection' arguments to justify current governance structures on the ground that they are largely 'outcome determinative'. That is, existing structures that have been around for awhile are presumed to be efficient by definition. These existing structures are then compared to see if cost and incentive arguments can be made to justify their special features. The problem is that virtually any institution can be justified if enough subjective and objective cost, benefit, and incentive factors are taken into account, because there is no way to weigh any of these variables.

in controlling the pursuit by managers of divergent objectives and limiting shirking and incompetence, the significance of shareholder passivity is reduced and the case for governance reform diminished or even undermined. It was, however, suggested in Chapter 4 that markets are far from being a complete solution to problems of management discretion and effectiveness. If this is so, and if there are governance reforms that are capable of improving the position, then for reasons that have just been mentioned the operation of markets alone cannot be relied on to generate them.[117] This conclusion thus leaves little ground for confidence in the contract theorists' claim that the process of contracting (as defined) will, if left free from outside interference, inevitably lead to the 'natural selection' of the most efficient governance provisions.

The significance of the contract model

The nexus of contracts model does not provide a definitive or objectively valid explanation of what a company is. No model could. Nor similarly is it conclusive about what approach to the company and company law the theorist or the reformer ought to adopt. Rather, from the various different ways in which the relationships between corporate participants might plausibly be characterized, the model abstracts and commends one particular type of characterization. As such, as Bratton has suggested, it 'embodies less an ontological breakthrough than a shift of perspective'.[118] In fact the model adopts several perspectives, since it functions in a number of different dimensions, modelling the relationships involved for a variety of purposes. At least three overlapping contract models or theories can be distinguished.

The first theory is an explanation of the company's origins in terms of contract, as opposed to 'concession'. Its function is to establish the company as 'private' and hence capable of being defended against state interference. As Chapter 1 considered at some length, however, even if the existence of companies can be satisfactorily explained in contractual terms, this says little about the propriety of intervention by the state, be its object to strengthen the protection of shareholders against management or to alter the company's behaviour to the advantage of third parties or society more generally. More substantial theorizing is required to justify the proposition that the state may not intervene to ensure that the position of power that results from the private aggregation of capital is exercised on terms that are acceptable to society.

[117] Cf. Butler and Ribstein, 'Opting Out of Fiduciary Duties' (above, n. 89), at 45: 'Even if markets cannot perfectly constrain acts of managers, that does not mean that they cannot discipline the development of agency contracts, the terms of which are readily observable and reflected in market price.' The writers fail to explain, however, how pricing efficiency can be expected adequately to discipline these 'contracts'.

[118] Bratton, 'The Nexus of Contracts Corporation' (above, n. 81), at 410.

The second contract model describes, and also prescribes, judicial and legislative practice in company law. As a piece of description, it reports the attitude typically adopted by the courts to the relationship between corporate participants: they are contracting parties. Similarly, prescriptively, from the premise that a company is a series of contracts, it holds that the role of the judge is to enforce the relevant contracts, and, where a contract is silent on a particular issue, to supply the term that the parties would themselves have selected had they thought about it. The model incorporates a similar statement of management objectives to that set out in Chapter 3 above, namely that it is the duty of the board to maximize the value of the firm, but it involves a different approach to determining the content of liability rules, with the contract model generally entailing a lower level of protection for shareholders than that flowing from the fiduciary standard characteristic of the traditional legal model.[119] The contract model, furthermore, views all such rules as default rules that may be overriden by contrary agreement. Since it is the fiduciary standard that prevails in English company law, and given the mandatory character of the bulk of common-law and statutory provisions, the contract model in this second dimension is better understood as a purely normative device. Whether the model's normative message should be heeded depends on the extent to which the third model should be regarded as persuasive.

The third model explains how in a regime of free contracting optimal governance controls will evolve. Contract theorists claim that such controls have indeed emerged, arguing that concerns about efficiency stemming from the so-called 'separation of ownership and control' should be laid to rest, together with the ownership model of the company and its counterpart, the managerial model, which together constitute the analytical foundation of those concerns. Given that management discretion is suitably constrained by a web of institutional and market mechanisms, it follows that regulatory intervention to improve corporate governance is unwarranted. Brudney also sees in this nexus-of-contracts version of contract theory a carrying forward of the ideological objectives of traditional contract theory into the era of the modern large company with dispersed shareholdings. The object of traditional theory was, by offering a 'private' explanation of corporate existence, to disconnect the enterprise from dependence for its power on state authority, and therefore from 'subjection to state regulation of that power in the interest of consumers, employees, suppliers and the public'. The nexus-of-contracts model provides a similar legitimating basis for management power *within* the company and a corresponding justification for non-intervention in the investor-management relationship.[120]

[119] See 203–5 below.
[120] Brudney, 'Corporate Governance' (above, n. 87), at 1409–10.

The contract model in this third guise is undoubtedly illuminating for some purposes. The standard investor with a small proportionate holding seems closer to being a contractual provider of capital on the conditions set out in the articles or in the issue document, in a way similar to a debenture holder, than an owner of the business with the rights and behavioural consequences that this implies.[121] Further, apart from the trivial point that the relationship between the shareholder and the company is technically founded in contract, certain aspects of the relationship have also the contractual characteristic that they are priced. For example, shares carrying differential rights, such as to voting or dividends, are valued differently, in accordance with their rights, by the market. What is much more question-able, however, is the extent to which variations between governance structures are reflected in share prices, and the extent to which the market mechanisms that are supposed to make managements responsive to those prices are effective. If the doubts expressed on these points above are warranted then it would seem that the contract model's explanation of the derivation of governance provisions is seriously misleading, exaggerating the role of the shareholders in generating them and correspondingly de-emphasiz-ing the scope for managerial discretion in that process. Clark's view that reliance on the contract model leads to 'facile optimism about the optimality of existing institutions and rules'[122] seems hard to resist.

By way of conclusion it is appropriate to quote again Eisenberg's descrip-tion of the company as 'a profit-seeking enterprise of persons and assets organized by rules'.[123] We have suggested that the formulation of such of these rules as relate to corporate governance cannot safely be 'left to the market' since market pressures are likely to be inadequate to offset the interest of managers in holding on to their discretion. The controls that result are accordingly liable to be excessively lax. If existing controls are too lax, what should the response be? The earlier discussion of institutional activism cautioned against too optimistic a forecast of future shareholder involvement in governance responsibilities, and hence regulatory intervention designed to improve governance, based on the ownership model and notions of shareholder control, appear to hold only limited promise. Nevertheless, control through internal supervision, which is the concept on which the ownership model relies—control through 'voice', rather than 'exit'[124]—still seems central to effective governance and in that connection Section IV now turns to a way of facilitating voice, through board reform.

---

[121] See J. Hicks, 'Limited Liability: the Pros and Cons', in A. Orhnial (ed.), *Limited Liability and the Corporation* (1982), 11, at 12.

[122] Clark, 'Agency Costs Versus Fiduciary Duties' (above, n. 87), at 65.

[123] See note 94 above.

[124] See Hirschman, *Exit, Voice and Loyalty* (above, n. 72).

IV BOARD REFORM

It has been argued that the confidence of contract theorists in the effectiveness of markets is exaggerated, both as a direct source of discipline and in contributing to the evolution of an efficient system of corporate governance. It also appears that a resurgence in shareholder monitoring consequent on the re-concentration of ownership in the hands of the institutions is unlikely to come about on a very significant scale. The need for a reassessment of the corporate governance structure is therefore apparent. What seems to be required is a substitute provider of the monitoring function that the owner-ship model attributes to the shareholders, but which they are unable or unwilling to perform. The most promising source of this monitoring may be the board, and hence the solution appears to lie in board reform. As the European Commission has pointed out in a discussion paper in connection with the draft Fifth Company Law Directive,

legislators in many Member States have attempted to solve the problem of supervision . . . by introducing into the company's structure a new element: a body distinct from either the general meeting or the managing board or council which has as its function the supervision and control on behalf of the shareholders of those managing the company.[125]

It was noted in Chapter 2 that in theory one of the most important functions of British boards currently is the supervision of management, but as the board is invariably dominated by executive directors, that is, the most powerful representatives of the supervised group, it is clear that the monitor-ing and executive functions, which need to be kept distinct, have become fused.

One of the objects of the Fifth Directive, which has yet to be finalized, is to mandate a separation of these two functions. The Directive has attracted great controversy, mainly because of the proposals for employee participation that it contains, but also with respect to its suggested reform of board structure, to which the British government in particular (and large sections of British industry) has been opposed. Leaving aside the employee representa-tion aspects,[126] the draft provides two alternative models.[127] Under the first companies have a supervisory board and a separate management board.

[125] 'Employee Participation and the Company Structure in the European Community', (1975) *Bull/Supp* 8/75, at 18. Public companies in Germany and the Netherlands are required to have two-tier boards and French law offers the option of a two-tier structure, but it is infrequently adopted.

[126] See Ch. 12 below.

[127] For the latest version of the Directive, see the amended proposal attached to DTI, *Amended Proposal for a Fifth Directive on the Harmonisation of Company Law in the European Community: A Consultative Document* (1990). This proposed draft has not yet achieved the status of an actual draft, the most recent complete version of the draft being that adopted in 1983: see *OJ*, C 240, 9.9.1983, 2.

Under the second there is a single board, but it is made up of a majority of 'supervisory' directors, with executive directors constituting the remainder. In either case the supervisory directors are appointed by the members. Under the two-tier system the executive directors are appointed by the supervisory directors, or, where the company's constitution permits, by the members directly. With a single-tier board all directors are appointed by the shareholders, with the executive directors being designated by the board from among its members (or by the shareholders). Corresponding provisions exist for removal of either group.[128] As might be imagined, it is not proposed that the supervisory directors should be involved in day-to-day management. In the case of the two-tier model they are to receive reports on the company's finances and progress on a three-monthly basis, and have full rights to information and may institute an investigation into any aspect of the company's affairs. Where the company has a single-tier board the precise division of responsibilities between the two types of director is a matter to be determined by the board itself, but the performance of supervisory functions is facilitated by the requirement that a board meeting be held at least quarterly to discuss the company's progress, and by giving all board members the right to insist that a particular matter be considered by the board and also rights to information. Whether these proposals would result in public companies having a genuinely independent majority of directors would depend on the procedures by which supervisory directors were selected (as distinct from appointed) on which the Directive is silent. There is an obvious risk that without additional mechanisms for the selection of directors they will frequently be nominees of the executives, as is the current position. We shall return to this issue below.

Non-executive Directors under the Existing Law

Before discussing the merits of these proposals it will be useful to review the current practice relating to the appointment of non-executive directors. The use of non-executives might, perhaps, be taken as an example of market-induced, evolutionary governance reform. Non-executive directors are in general not involved in the actual running of the business, and so an obvious advantage is their ability to assess the company's performance, and that of management, from a more neutral standpoint. They are now common in large companies[129] and their appointment has been encouraged by the Bank

---

[128] It should be noted that this latest proposal for the unitary structure represents a substantial shift from earlier drafts in which the executive directors were to be appointed, and removable by, the non-executive element. Existing UK practice is thus now accommodated save as to the requirement that there be a majority of non-executives.

[129] Over 95 per cent of the top 200 companies now have at least one non-executive director: ICAEW, *Report of the Study Group on the Changing Role of the Non-Executive Director* (1991), s 8.

of England, the Confederation of British Industry, and the Stock Exchange, who, among others, have given their support to PRO NED, an organization formed to advertise the merits of non-executive appointments. In 1987 PRO NED published a voluntary code of practice which indicates that companies with a turnover of £50 million or more or whose employees exceed 1000 should appoint at least three independent non-executives, who should comprise about a third of the board.[130] The code provides that one of their principal functions is to ensure the 'continuing effectiveness of the Executive Directors and management'. A similar code put forward by the Institute of Directors requires them to 'monitor executive performance against agreed objectives'.[131]

The position has now become somewhat more formal following the recommendations in 1992 of the Cadbury Committee. The Committee proposes that all listed companies should appoint audit committees consisting exclusively of non-executive directors, and remuneration committees with a membership mainly or wholly of non-executives.[132] The functions of audit committees, which are already common among large companies in this country and particularly so in the United States,[133] include liaison with the company's outside auditors, consideration of the scope of the audit, and review of the adequacy of the company's financial control systems.[134] The purpose of remuneration committees, which are also a regular feature of the existing large-company landscape, is to 'recommend to the board the remuneration of the executive directors in all its forms',[135] with a view to bringing a degree of impartiality to the determination of management rewards.[136] As to the board itself, the Committee recommends rather vaguely that 'the calibre and number of non-executive directors on a board should be such that their views will carry significant weight in the board's decisions,' but provides more definitely that there should be at least three non-executives.[137] Where the chairman is also the chief executive (which is discouraged),[138] there should be a 'strong and independent element,'[139] on the board,

---

[130] PRO NED *Code of Practice on Non-Executive Directors* (1987).
[131] Institute of Directors, *A Code of Practice for the Non-Executive Director* (1982).
[132] Cadbury Committee, *Report* (above, n. 1), paras 4.33–8 and 4.42.
[133] Ibid. at para 4.33.
[134] Audit committees are not generally regarded as having any responsibility to review executive decisions or monitor the effectiveness of management: see Coopers and Lybrand, *Audit Committees: The Next Steps* (1988); ICAEW, *Report of the Study Group on the Changing Role of the Non-Executive Director* (above, n. 129), s 9.
[135] Ibid. Cadbury Committee, *Report* (above, n. 1), para 4.42.
[136] On the role and effectiveness of remuneration committees, see further 218–26 below.
[137] Cadbury Committee, *Report* (above, n. 1), para 4.11.
[138] See also Institutional Shareholders' Committee, *The Role and Duties of Directors* (1991), at 2.
[139] Cadbury Committee, *Report* (above, n. 1), para 4.9 and see also para 4.5.

but what this entails is not more specifically delineated. It is also provided that the non-executive element on the board should be entitled to seek outside professional advice at the company's expense.[140] Compliance with these recommendations remains optional, save that it is proposed to amend the Stock Exchange listing obligations to require companies to state in their annual report and accounts that they have satisfied them (together with the other recommendations in the Cadbury Committee's 'Code of Best Practice'), or otherwise to identify and explain areas of non-compliance. The statement of compliance is to be subject to review by the company's auditors as regards those matters which are capable of objective verification. It is envisaged by the Committee that where companies fail to comply they will be exposed to shareholder pressure either through the market or in the form of direct persuasion.

While the Cadbury proposals seem likely to have a positive effect it is in the nature of voluntary arrangements of this kind that those whose behaviour is most in need of reform are the least likely to comply. But in any case, it is suggested that without a more radical transformation of the position of non-executive directors, they are likely to be of only limited effectiveness in performing a control function[141] (this is not to deny their value, for example, in providing special expertise or advice to the board). Under the Companies Act non-executive directors do not enjoy any special legal status or powers. Since they are usually in a minority, without the cooperation of management they are effectively impotent: they do not have a power base from which to insist on explanations or to impose appropriate remedies.[142] Of even greater importance, they may lack the will to do these things, since appointees will frequently have economic or social ties with management, and are therefore unlikely to be particularly demanding or prepared to take decisions which are contrary to the wishes or interests of their sponsors. A recent study has shown that three-quarters of non-executives are independent of the company in the sense of not being former executives or advisers of it,[143] but since they are board nominees it seems unlikely that many of them will be disposed to rock the boat, at least where the issue is managerial ineffectualness as opposed to impropriety. Sir John Harvey-Jones, former chairman of ICI, has said that on hearing of a possible candidate 'the very first thing you do is talk to a

[140] Ibid. para 4.18.

[141] Note the comment of E. S. Herman, *Corporate Control, Corporate Power* (1981), at 283, that: 'if there is pressure to do something, but one doesn't think anything *ought* to be done, there is nothing much better than an appeal to business to spruce up its independent directors, voluntarily' (emphasis in original).

[142] For a discussion of the practical difficulties faced by non-executive directors in monitoring management, see Demb and Neubauer, *The Corporate Board* (above, n.1), at 116–23.

[143] *Financial Times*, 12 May 1988.

mutual friend' and it is important to ask whether the potential non-executive is 'the sort of person you could get on with'.[144] This does not sound like the kind of relationship in which the non-executive is expected to be overly assertive. The Cadbury Committee recommendations for a more formal selection process[145] may help here, but while appointment is still in the hands of the executive directors a significant improvement in non-executive independence cannot be expected. An additional factor is that, since the majority of non-executive directors are also, and primarily, executive directors of other companies, they are liable to have a community of interest with the directors it is their function to supervise. It has thus been suggested that 'most outside directors share management's ideological disposition toward the single issue most central to their monitoring responsibilities: how intensely outside directors *should* monitor management.'[146] Not surprisingly, studies show that non-executives are likely to be involved in action which is prejudicial to the interests of management, for example, dismissing the chief executive, only when the company's affairs have reached crisis point.[147]

The Monitoring Board

If non-executive directors are to be effective monitors a number of preconditions need to be met. The first is that they must be genuinely independent of management. This means at the least that they must not be appointed by the executive directors, nor should they be nominated by the executives and elected by the shareholders, given the predictable outcome of such a

[144] *Financial Times*, 24 June 1988.
[145] Cadbury Committee, *Report* (above, n. 1), paras 4.15 and 4.30. See also para 4.12, recommending that a majority of non-executives should be 'independent of management and free from any business or other relationship which could materially interfere with the exercise of their independent judgement'.
[146] Gilson and Kraakman, 'Reinventing the Outside Director' (above, n. 60), at 875 (emphasis in original). The Cadbury Committee recommendation (above, n. 1), para 4.9, that 'the majority of non-executives on a board [i.e. not necessarily a majority of the board as a whole] should be independent and free of any business or financial connection with the company apart from their fees, or their shareholding', does not allay these wider doubts about non-executive independence. Nor does the suggestion (para 4.24) that candidates be proposed by a nomination committee consisting of a majority of non-executives, not least because it is still the board itself that decides on appointments.
[147] Thus, in America where non-executives are often in the majority, one commentator has observed that 'boards of directors of most companies do not do an effective job in evaluating, appraising, and measuring the company president until the financial and other results are so dismal that some remedial action is forced upon the board': M. L. Mace, *Directors: Myth and Reality* (1971), at 41. See also M. L. Mace, 'Directors: Myth and Reality—Ten Years Later', (1979) 32 *Rutgers Law Rev* 293. A British study produces a similar picture: see R. E. Pahl and J. T. Winkler, 'The Economic Elite—Theory and Practice', in P. Stanworth and A. Giddens (eds), *Elite and Power in British Society* (1974) 103. For a more up-to-date statement of the American position, however, see J. C. Coffee, 'Regulating the Market for Corporate Control: A Critical Assessment of the Tender Offer's Role in Corporate Governance', (1984) 84 *Colum L Rev* 1445, at 1202.

procedure against a background of shareholder passivity. Gilson and Kraak-man's suggestion, discussed in Section II, that a specialist nominating agency be set up, is helpful in this respect.[148] What their proposals entail is essentially the creation of a new profession of expert monitoring director. They may be over-optimistic about the supply of '50-year-old professors of finance at graduate business schools' or partners at 'either a Big Six public accounting firm or a major management consulting firm'[149] able to fulfil this role, but there is no reason why a shortage of suitably qualified candidates need be a problem in the longer term. Their suggestion that the directors serve on the boards of about six companies, but that independent directorship be their full-time occupation, is also an attractive one, since it should ensure that the appointees have enough time to devote to each company's affairs properly to fulfil their role. Gilson and Kraakman point to the additional advantage that this would avoid their becoming financially dependent on any particular company, which might otherwise jeopardize their independence, though in fact the risk of this could be excluded altogether by making the directors employees of the nominating agency rather than the companies concerned. Direct employment by the nominating agency would reinforce Gilson and Kraakman's further point that the desire to remain on the books of the agency would provide the directors with an incentive to be effective monitors. The performance of the independent directors themselves could then in turn be monitored by the nominating body.[150] These outline proposals seem therefore together capable of fulfilling the further preconditions of effective monitoring, that the directors possess relevant expertise, that they are able to devote adequate time to their functions, and that they are themselves subject to effective supervision.

The final issue is the relationship between the monitoring directors and executive management. The EEC Fifth Directive proposals envisage the monitoring directors as having powers of appointment and removal with regard to the executive directors[151] where the two-tier structure is adopted, and it is suggested that this should also be the position in relation to unitary boards. The Gilson and Kraakman scheme, on the other hand, involves the monitoring directors being in a minority position on the board and hence as lacking these powers. They argue that a minority (25 per cent) of monitoring

---

[148] See Gilson and Kraakman, 'Reinventing the Outside Director' (above, n. 60). The writers envisage such an agency being set up by, and run on behalf of, institutional investors, but as mentioned above, there is no necessity for the proposal to be made dependent on the willingness of institutions to take the initiative.

[149] Ibid. at 885.

[150] Ibid. at 890–1.

[151] If the option were adopted whereby powers of appointment and removal are retained in the general meeting (DTI, *Amended Proposal for a Fifth Directive*, (above, note 127) art 3(1)(B)) presumably in practice they would normally be exercised on the recommendation of the supervisory directors.

directors would be able to exert a positive influence on the company through cooperation with management.[152] This may well be true, but an arrangement in which the monitors are able to remove the executive directors seems more likely to create an appropriate relationship of accountability. Whether the monitoring directors are better situated on a separate supervisory board or within a unitary board is not of fundamental importance, so long as the role of the monitors is clearly demarcated and they have the appropriate powers. With a unitary structure, the two elements are in any case in practice likely to function separately. There may, however, be some symbolic value in the clarity of the differentiation of roles that the two-tier structure achieves.

Some commentators suggest that internal monitoring is likely to have only a limited impact on corporate efficiency and therefore that reforms of this kind are misplaced.[153] Apart from pointing out the costs resulting from increased bureaucracy, they insist that the distinction between executive decision-making and monitoring is more apparent than real. Accurate evaluation of managerial performance demands that the monitors have business and technical skills at least as great as those possessed by the managers themselves. As this is unlikely to be the case, and also because of their remoteness from the practicalities of the business, the probable outcome is that the monitors will simply rubber-stamp management decisions. If, on the other hand, the monitors are a team of experts who 'know better' than executive management, the question arises as to why they are not running the business in the first place!

These criticisms miss the point. The primary object of internal monitoring is to prevent senior managers from being the sole arbiters of their own destiny. If they are genuinely accountable to some other body, which can demote them or remove them from office, they are provided with a strong incentive to perform as well as they can.[154] According to this model monitors are not, as the criticism suggests, required to act as a parallel management. Rather, their role is to set targets for management and to compare their company's performance with that of competitors.[155] It is not suggested that this process is a straightforward one. Since companies can perform badly for

---

[152] Ibid. at 888–90.

[153] See, e.g. V. Brudney, 'The Independent Director—Heavenly City or Potemkin Village?', (1982) 95 *Harv L Rev* 597, at 632–5; Fischel, 'The Corporate Governance Movement' (above, n. 83), at 1280–5, discussing various proposals in the United States for a formalized monitoring role for independent directors. For a discussion of the effectiveness of German supervisory boards, see D Vagts, 'Reforming the 'Modern' Corporation: Perspectives from the German', (1966) 80 *Harv L Rev* 23, at 52–3.

[154] There is evidence that the obligation to make formal reports to a higher authority is in itself a spur to efficiency: see Mace, *Directors: Myth and Reality* (above, note 147), at 393–4.

[155] And see Gilson and Kraakman, 'Reinventing the Outside Director' (above, n. 60), at 890, who suggest that the nominating agency could 'at relatively little cost, supply directors with routine outside information, such as comparative rankings of corporate performance or reports of respected securities analysts'.

reasons other than the pursuit of divergent goals or managerial weakness the monitors would have to be able to distinguish between extraneous factors, such as a downturn in the market, and management failure.[156] Nevertheless, this is precisely what advocates of the market for corporate control claim that potential bidders do with great accuracy, and it seems certain that internal monitors will be in a better position than outsiders to perform the task. Thus for one thing, information can be collected and processed within the company more quickly than by outside analysts, enabling immediate action to be taken to rectify sources of inefficiency. Second, as insiders, and free of the constraints of confidentiality, monitoring directors are likely to have access to more detailed information than the stock market and will accordingly have a better understanding of the company's prospects and the context of its published results. With these factors in mind it has been suggested that 'a truly independent board would not tolerate suboptimal performance by management resulting in a share discount large enough to elicit a takeover at any historically prevailing premium level.'[157] In other words, a company which had effective mechanisms for internal monitoring would detect and rectify management failure before the consequences became serious enough to attract the attention of a predator. A further advantage of internal supervision is that by a process of selective hiring and firing it is possible to build up a proficient management team. This is something that can be achieved only by the fact, and not the mere threat, of take-over, and not necessarily even then. The appointment of genuinely independent monitoring directors seems therefore to offer the possibility of reinstating an effective system of control over management. Much would depend in practice on the availability of appropriately qualified and suitably motivated monitors, but there is no need to confine the search to the pool of existing executive directors.

Conclusion

The contrast between reliance on the market for control (taking this to be the most effective market form of management discipline) and on internal monitoring exemplifies key differences between the use of 'exit' and 'voice' as

---

[156] And as Eisenberg, *The Structure of the Corporation* (above, n. 25), at 165, points out, monitors would also need to concern themselves with policy, since 'objectives must be set, explicitly or implicitly, against which to measure management's results, and the selection of objectives will partly depend on the directors' broad notions of policy and will interact with the question of what business policies are suitable for the particular firm.' But as he goes on to explain, 'the selection of an objective is distinguishable not only in theory but also pretty largely in practice from the determination of how an objective will be met: it is one thing, for example, to demand a certain return on capital; it is another to decide upon the strategy and tactics which promise to yield that return.'

[157] Coffee, 'Regulating the Market for Corporate Control' (above, n. 147), at 1203.

methods of disciplining management.[158] Where adequate structures for the exercise of voice are available, the advantages in terms of immediacy and flexibility of response are apparent. By way of conclusion it may be noted that the flexibility that voice allows is not confined to the choice of means of achieving the single end of profitability. It provides in addition a mechanism for securing efficiency within a more complex goal structure. The market for control operates (in ideal terms) by eliminating discretion. Managers, in order to survive, must maximize profits. Internal monitoring, on the other hand, can be employed to make the company efficient, in the sense that managerial goal pursuit and various manifestations of slack or incompetence are controlled or removed, yet without at the same time demanding adherence to a goal of strict profit maximization. Efficiency can therefore be combined with an approach, say to employees or the environment, which is not dictated by rigid profit and loss criteria, but which allows a trade-off to take place between protecting the interests of affected groups and profitability.[159] In practice the market, for reasons that have been discussed, also permits such choices to be made, but within a limiting and hostile framework. The idea that trade-offs of this kind are desirable has so far been excluded by our assumption that a policy of profit maximization within the law best serves the public good. The merits of that assumption are reconsidered in Chapter 10.

---

[158] See Hirschman, *Exit, Voice and Loyalty* (above, n. 72).
[159] See J. N. Gordon, 'Corporations, Markets, and Courts', (1991) 91 *Colum L Rev* 1931, esp. at 1984.

7

Management Self-Dealing

Outright dishonesty is presumably rare in the upper echelons of corporate management,[1] though recent revelations of spectacular corruption, for example, following the collapse of the Bank of Credit and Commerce International and of the Maxwell empire, show that it is by no means unknown. The concern of the present chapter is not with such cases, however, but with what are generally more modest and subtle means of transferring wealth to managers, by way of 'self-dealing'. This term will be used to refer to transactions involving the company in which a director has a conflicting interest, and to the diversion by directors to themselves or affiliates of 'corporate opportunities'.[2] Judicial attempts to control abuse in these areas have thrown up a number of conceptual puzzles that affect the legal control of management conduct more widely, and accordingly it is important to clarify the issues involved. The reason self-dealing presents special problems for company law is that much of it is harmless, and may even be beneficial, to the company. But in all cases of self-dealing there is a risk that the directors will give way to 'that businessman's standard of morality which easily blinds the possessor of it to the distinction between right and wrong where the interests of the possessor are affected',[3] and it is this that gives rise to the need for regulation.

The aim in this chapter is to show that the current governance structure, involving no independent element between management and the dispersed and largely passive body of shareholders, creates considerable difficulties for the effective regulation of self-dealing. The point is not that self-dealing is a *result* of the separation of ownership and control, though no doubt the possibilities for abuse increase with size and organizational complexity. The risk of wealth being improperly transferred through self-dealing is in fact

---

[1] For the suggestion that the structure of large-scale corporate enterprise is likely to militate against fraud, see M. Moran, 'Investor Protection and the Culture of Capitalism', in L. Hancher and M. Moran (eds), *Capitalism, Culture and Regulation* (1989) 49, esp. at 69.

[2] A further category is the receipt by a director of a bribe, commission or other inducement to show favour to a third party. The legal response in this situation is similar to that discussed in the text: the director is accountable to the company without proof that his or her judgement was swayed: see e.g. *Boston Deep Sea Fishing & Ice Co Ltd v Ansell* (1888) 39 Ch D 339, CA.

[3] Per Danckwerts J, *Fine Industrial Commodities Limited v Powling* (1954) 71 RPC 253, at 257.

inherent in any situation in which one person has control over assets belonging to another, to be actively managed for the benefit of that other. This is reflected in the development of strict rules to prevent exploitation of position in a wide variety of relationships, paradigmatically that between trustee and beneficiary. The point is rather that the separation of ownership and control has given rise to a second-order problem, that is, a problem about the operation of the mechanisms that the law has provided for the regulation of self-dealing. As will emerge, the relevant principles were formulated on the basis of assumptions about active shareholder involvement, with the result that they apply uneasily in the context of the management-controlled company. A major aspect of the problem concerns enforcement. The inadequacy of the arrangements for the enforcement of directors' duties in relation to self-dealing and more generally will mainly be considered in the next chapter. This will round off the examination of the contribution of judicial supervision to the control of management conduct and performance undertaken in this chapter and in Chapters 3 to 5.

The control of improper managerial self-enrichment is relevant to the concerns of this book for two reasons, both rooted in the idea that companies should be seen as social enterprises.[4] In whatever way the public interest that companies should be required to serve is conceived, unauthorized transfers of wealth to management and the effectiveness of the techniques for controlling abuse of position become matters of legitimate public concern, and do not merely raise issues of private fairness, where the justification for the corporate system is expressed in public-interest terms. The public interest is affected, first, because the diversion to managers of corporate assets (or what should be regarded as corporate assets) is liable to be inefficient, in a number of ways. At the most general level the efficiency of a market system is premised on the idea of mutually beneficial exchange; unbalanced, non-consensual transfers represent a misallocation of resources.[5] Further, the ability to extract funds from the company may encourage managerial slackness, with

---

[4] See Ch. 1, above. For judicial recognition (in Canada) of the public role of management, and the corresponding need for strict standards of conduct, see *Canadian Aero Service Ltd v O'Malley* (1974) 40 DLR (3d) 371, at 384, per Laskin J: the application of strict fiduciary principles 'is a necessary supplement, in the public interest, of statutory regulation and accountability which themselves are, at one and the same time, an acknowledgment of the importance of the corporation in the life of the community and of the need to compel obedience by it and by its promoters, directors and managers to norms of exemplary behaviour'. See also Lord Wedderburn, 'The Social Responsibility of Companies', (1985) 15 *Melbourne U L Rev* 4, at 24: '[fiduciary duty] is imposed in private law, but with a *public* function. It is a vehicle of a social purpose' (emphasis in original). See also the same author's 'The Legal Development of Corporate Responsibility: For whom will Corporate Managers be Trustees?' in K. J. Hopt and G. Teubner (eds), *Corporate Governance and Directors' Liabilities* (1985), 3, at 24–25, and 'Trust, Corporation and the Worker', (1985) 23 *Osgoode Hall L J* 203, at 221. And see C. D. Stone, 'Corporate Vices and Corporate Virtues: Do Public/Private Distinctions Matter?', (1982) *U Pa L Rev* 1441, at 1449 and 1480.

[5] See R. C. Clark, 'Agency Costs versus Fiduciary Duties', in J. W. Pratt and R. J. Zeckhauser, *Principles and Agents: The Structure of Business* (1985) 55, at 77–8.

the possibility of obtaining illicit wealth transfers from the shareholders offering a more attractive alternative to maximizing the overall return.[6] Finally the perception of unfairness undermines investor confidence, and if widespread would seriously diminish the capacity of the corporate system to raise capital, and ultimately to survive.[7]

Second, aside from questions of efficiency, the public interest is affected by improper self-enrichment in the sense that such behaviour constitutes a violation of public standards of fair dealing. The imposition of fiduciary duties in order to control unconscionable conduct within private relationships, over and above the protections expressly bargained for, has long been regarded as a legitimate function of the state.[8] The justification for intervention has, however, an additional dimension where the relevant relationships, while private in intent, are seen as existing for public purposes and sustained on that basis. Thus from the social-enterprise perspective, financial impropriety on the part of managers, and inadequate methods of accountability and control, are no more to be tolerated in the corporate sphere than they are within the organs of government. Given this concern with the vindication of standards of fair dealing in the public realm, furthermore, it ought rarely be an acceptable answer that sums diverted are insignificant in comparison with gross assets, turnover, or profits. While it is important to be aware of the direct and indirect costs that the controls may impose, they should not be evaluated merely on the basis of a crude comparison between cost on the one hand and the damage to the company that is avoided on the other.[9] The maintenance of public standards of fairness should be seen rather as being something of value in its own right.

That the risk that managers will enrich themselves at the company's expense requires some form of legal response is accepted even by market theorists, who, as we have seen, are normally averse to regulatory solutions.[10] Slack in the various market mechanisms allows managers to divert substantial

[6] See E. M. Dodd, 'Is Effective Enforcement of the Fiduciary Duties of Corporate Managers Practicable?', (1935) 2 *U Chi L Rev* 194, at 197: 'It is often more profitable for the directors and managers of these [management-controlled] enterprises to seek gains at the expense of the security holders or some class of security holders, rather than to seek loyally to obtain the maximum amount of profits for them.'. He notes that making profits for others is not an inspiring motivation, and that the lauding of self-interest inherent in the capitalist ethic may encourage illicit private gain.

[7] Alfred Marshall believed that companies were only viable because of the growth of commercial morality: if 'the leading officers of great public companies . . . showed an eagerness to avail themselves of opportunities for wrong-doing at all approaching that of which we read in the commercial history of earlier civilization, their wrong uses of the trusts imposed on them would have been on so great a scale as to prevent the development of this democratic form of business': A. Marshall, *Principles of Economics* (1890), at 253, discussed in M. A. King, *Public Policy and the Corporation* (1977), at 16.

[8] See the articles by Wedderburn in n. 4 above.

[9] This is not, of course, the view of market theorists; see, e.g. F. H. Easterbrook and D. R. Fischel, 'The Corporate Contract', (1989) 89 *Colum L Rev* 1416, at 1424.

[10] See e.g. R. A. Posner, *The Economic Analysis of Law* (3rd ed., 1986), at 383–4; R. J. Gilson,

sums without triggering a significant market reaction. It has been observed with respect to the market for corporate control, for instance, that because of the need to expend large premiums and fees 'a takeover bid will almost never be economically justified if the bidder's only strategy is to end unfair self-dealing by incumbent managers'.[11] Other market-related factors that link managers' income to shareholder welfare, such as management shareholdings and performance-linked remuneration, are similarly stultified by the simple fact that the direct gains from self-dealing will exceed the indirect losses borne by the managers, given that the latter are necessarily shared with the members as a whole. And the company is particularly vulnerable to the 'one-shot' or 'last period' raid, where wrong-doing managers sufficiently enrich themselves to be able to withdraw from active business life.[12]

While accepting the need for regulation, proponents of the contract model of the company[13] nevertheless attempt to assimilate the controls within a framework based on management/shareholder contracting rather than state imposition. They thus contend that the fiduciary duties enforced by the courts to control self-dealing either do, or should, reflect the arrangements the parties would themselves have decided upon as fully informed, rational wealth-maximizers in the absence of transaction costs.[14] The role of the courts is accordingly simply to provide and enforce low-cost standard form terms. Content is given to the hypothetical bargain by arguing that the parties would agree to the rule that in any situation of conflict of interest between managers and shareholders the former should act in such a way as will maximize their joint wealth, independently of how the gains from the particular transaction are distributed in practice. Managers should, for instance, be entitled to divert a corporate opportunity to a company with which they are associated if this would enable it to be exploited more profitably, because in that way a 'larger pie' is created, from which the shareholders will also benefit, one way or another.[15]

'A Structural Approach to Corporations: The Case Against Defensive Tactics in Tender Offers', (1981) 33 *Stan L Rev* 819, at 839–41; F. H. Easterbrook and D. R. Fischel, 'Corporate Control Transactions', (1982) 91 *Yale L J* 698, at 701; D. M. Phillips, 'Principles of Corporate Governance: A Critique of Part IV', (1984) 52 *Geo Wash L Rev* 653, at 692–98.

[11] M. A. Eisenberg, 'The Structure of Corporation Law', (1989) 89 *Colum L Rev* 1461, at 1498.

[12] See F. H. Easterbrook and D. R. Fischel, *The Economic Structure of Corporate Law* (1991), at 92 and 103.

[13] See Ch. 6 above.

[14] See Posner, *Economic Analysis of Law* (above, n. 10), at 369–72; Easterbrook and Fischel, 'Corporate Control Transactions' (above, n. 10), at 702. It has been suggested that writers who adopt this position as description of judicial practice, rather than prescription, are 'traveling light as legal theorists' and that 'the rhetorical and ideological appeal of contract law should be distinguished from its analytic aptness in various legal contexts': D. A. DeMott, 'Beyond Metaphor: An Analysis of Fiduciary Obligation', [1988] *Duke L J* 879, at 889. One normative consequence of the contractual analysis is that fiduciary duties should be open to modification by the parties. This is not the position adopted in general by English company law: see CA 1985, s 310, but see also 210–11, below.

[15] See Easterbrook and Fischel, 'Corporate Control Transactions' (above, n. 10), at 733–5,

But this is precisely not the stance traditionally embodied in fiduciary duties. As far as self-dealing is concerned the law treats directors as being in a position similar to that of trustees. In the modern, management-controlled company this is particularly apposite, given the practical inability of the shareholders to exercise a meaningful choice in the selection of the directors or effectively to supervise them. Despite the commercial context, the shareholders are in a position not unlike that of the beneficiaries the fiduciary controls were originally devised to protect, namely those who through infancy or other incapacity are unable to protect themselves. As the next two sections will consider, the law does not allow the fiduciary to make *any* profit without the specific consent of the beneficiary, even though this rule may on occasion mean that joint wealth is not maximized[16] and that the beneficiary loses an opportunity to share in a 'larger pie'. The strictness of this rule reflects the difficulties of determining when self-dealing is wealth increasing overall, or just constitutes a transfer of wealth from shareholders to managers, and the absence of mechanisms to ensure that the members obtain a share of any wealth increases that might result from self-dealing, rather than their accruing entirely to management. As is typically the case the law is concerned with the distribution of gains and losses and not just with increases in wealth in the aggregate. It is suggested, furthermore, that it is not merely the particular characterization of the content of the hypothetical bargain that is inapposite, both as a description of the judicial stance in practice and as a policy factor that should shape the regulatory response, but the entire contractual approach. As one commentator has pointed out, if the hypothetical bargaining situation is intended to reveal the terms the particular parties would have agreed to *ex ante* the outcome is indeterminate, but if, as appears to be the case, it is 'truly hypothetical', then the bargain metaphor adds nothing of substance.[17] In the latter situation, the contract analogy allows

discussed further below, 231. The authors also argue that even where an episode of self-dealing that is wealth maximizing overall involves a loss to the shareholders, it is still nevertheless in the latter's interests that such transactions be permissible because diversified shareholders will on balance gain from the larger pie that results, by occasionally being on the winning as well as the losing side: 'Corporate Control Transactions' (above, n. 10), at 703–15. However, as J. N. Gordon, 'The Mandatory Structure of Corporate Law', (1989) 89 *Colum L Rev* 1549, at 1595 points out, this only works if the shareholders are diversified in respect of the risk in question, and in 'these cases, the risk relates to management's opportunism in running the corporation's affairs. A party is diversified with respect to that risk only if her portfolio contains the right amount of the *managers'* outcomes, and of course only a few shareholders can possibly be managers' (emphasis in original; footnote omitted).

[16] It does not necessarily follow that the rule is inefficient, given the likely effects on investor confidence of a more liberal rule: see Clark, 'Agency Costs Versus Fiduciary Duties' (above, n. 5). See also V Brudney, 'Corporate Governance, Agency Costs, and the Rhetoric of Contract', (1985) 85 *Colum L Rev* 1403, at 1439 n. 91: the 'question is whether the problematic saving of costs or lost transactions caused by prophylactic rules would be offset by problematic increases in the price investors charge for capital if they are adequately informed about the risk of diversion under nonprophylactic rules'.

[17] DeMott, 'Beyond Metaphor' (above, n. 14), at 889–90. On the indeterminacy of the

the theorist to impose his or her own favoured rule, and as such its status seems to be merely that of a rhetorical device to legitimate less rigorous controls over management discretion than those currently in force.[18]

With these issues in mind, the legal controls on self-dealing will now be examined. Section I will look at transactions with the company in which a director has an interest, and Section II at directors' service contracts, which are a sub-category of self-interested transactions, but raise special problems of their own. Section III will consider the exploitation by managers of corporate opportunities.

I SELF-INTERESTED TRANSACTIONS

English company law regulates self-dealing by means of what will be referred to as the 'fiduciary principle'. It dictates that 'a person in a fiduciary position . . . is not, unless otherwise expressly provided, entitled to make a profit; he is not allowed to put himself in a position where his duty and interest conflict'.[19] It is suggested that the 'profit' and 'conflict' components of the principle are operationally equivalent.[20] A slightly more precise formulation, but having

contractual analysis, see also Clark, ibid. at 68–71; Brudney, ibid. at 1415–6 n. 31. H. N. Butler and L. E. Ribstein, 'Opting Out of Fiduciary Duties: A Response to the Anti-Contractarians', (1990) 65 *Wash L Rev* 1, at 17, hold that it is 'a mistake to identify the hypothetical bargain approach with the contract theory of the corporation', but they do not explain how the content of contract terms is to be determined where they are not explicit.

[18] And in particular to legitimate opting out of fiduciary standards, see Butler and Ribstein, ibid. and see further 231 below.

[19] *Bray v Ford* [1896] AC 44, HL, at 51, per Lord Herschell. See also *New Zealand Netherlands Society 'Oranje' Incorporated v Kuys* [1973] 1 WLR 1126, PC, at 1129, per Lord Wilberforce: a director has a duty 'not to profit from a position of trust, or, as it is sometimes relevant to put it, not to allow a conflict to arise between duty and interest'.

[20] Some writers maintain there are separate rules concerning conflicts and profits: see, e.g. J. R. Birds, 'Excluding the Duties of Directors', (1988) 8 *Co Lawyer* 31, at 32, and the separate treatment of these rules in J. H. Farrar, N. E. Furey, and B. M. Hannigan, *Farrar's Company Law* (3rd ed., 1991), ch. 26. See also P. D. Finn, *Fiduciary Obligations* (1977), para 464. It is also contended, to different effect, that one rule is basic and the other a derivative of it, with the scope of the latter being determined by the former: see J. H. McLean, 'The Theoretical Basis of the Trustee's Duty of Loyalty', (1969) 7 *Alberta L Rev* 218. It can, e.g., be argued that the avoidance of conflict of interest is the rationale for not allowing the retention of profits, and therefore that since the profit rule need be no wider than its rationale requires, where there is no possibility of conflict a director should be allowed to keep a profit. On this see Lord Upjohn's dissenting speech in *Boardman v Phipps* [1967] 2 AC 46, at 124, making liability depend on proof of a 'real sensible possibility of conflict'. This is not, however, the orthodox position, which treats the fact of profit as the badge of conflict: see further below. The two rules are also different if the 'profit rule' is expressed as a rule that fiduciaries may not make a profit *out of* their office; such a rule would not apply in some situations in which there was a clear conflict of interest. Further, if the profit rule governed the conflict rule then no liability would in those cases ensue: see e.g. *Re Lewis* (1910) 103 LT 495. That the profit rule does not require the profit to be made out of the office, but merely that it be made in circumstances that could conceivably cast doubt on the loyal performance of duty, is, however, evident from cases such as *Industrial Development Consultants Ltd v Cooley* [1972] 1 WLR 443, [1972] 2 All ER 162 (discussed below).

the same effect, is that a director may not retain an unauthorized profit[21] made in connection with the performance of his or her duties.[22] The purpose of the principle is to protect the managerial decision-making process from being distorted by self-interest, and hence to prevent the company from being damaged.[23] Clearly, where a director has a personal interest[24] in a contract with the company there is a risk that that interest will be served at the expense of the company. The principle operates (disregarding for the moment its modification by the articles) by holding that all such transactions, in the absence of shareholder consent, are voidable by the company regardless of their terms, that is, whether or not they can be shown to be damaging.[25] The principle is as strict as it is in order to overcome the consequences of an informational asymmetry between management and shareholders: by dispensing with the need for detection and proof of loss the protection it provides is substantially increased.

The Fiduciary Principle in Theory

The Invalidation of Self-Interested Transactions

That self-interested transactions are voidable in themselves brings considerable advantages in terms of the overall effectiveness of the controls. These advantages become apparent when a comparison is made with the position under a possible alternative rule requiring proof that a self-interested trans-

[21] In this context 'profit' means simply a transfer of value; a profit is made for these purposes even though, for example, a director sells an item to the company for less than he or she paid for it or below its market value.

[22] How this 'connection' is defined determines the scope of the prohibition on directors making private use of business opportunities: see below.

[23] See *Bray v Ford* (above, n. 19), at 51, per Lord Herschell: the principle is not 'founded upon principles of morality. I regard it rather as based on the consideration that, human nature being what it is, there is a danger, in such circumstances, of the person holding a fiduciary position being swayed by interest rather than duty, and thus prejudicing those whom he was bound to protect.'

[24] The fiduciary principle applies equally to transactions in which a director has a direct or indirect financial interest, and to transactions which give rise to a conflict of duty and duty, as where the director is also a director of the other party to the contract: see *Transvaal Lands Co Ltd v New Belgium (Transvaal) Land and Development Co Ltd* [1914] 2 Ch 488, CA. And see 503, per Swinfen Eady L J: 'the validity or invalidity of a transaction cannot depend on the extent of the adverse interest of the fiduciary agent any more than how far in any particular case the terms of a contract have been the best obtainable for the interests of the cestui que trust.' For more recent guidance on what constitutes an interest for present purposes see *Cowan de Groot Properties Ltd v Eagle Trust plc* [1991] BCLC 1045.

[25] See *Movitex v Bulfield Ltd* [1988] BCLC 104, at 120, per Vinelott J: 'The true principle is that if a director places himself in a position in which his duty to the company conflicts with his personal interest or his duty to another, the court will intervene to set aside the transaction without inquiring whether there was any breach of the director's duty to the company.' A contrast is being drawn here between the director's *disability* from entering into transactions with the company without more, and the *duty* to act in its interests, breach of which supposes damage. See also *Tito v Waddell (no 2)* [1977] Ch 106, at 248–49; [1977] 3 All ER 129, at 247–48.

action is prejudicial to the company. Under such a rule there is a risk not only that meritorious actions will fail, but also that the uncertainties of proving loss[26] and the associated costs of litigation will deter meritorious actions from being brought. But there is a more fundamental problem. A rule demanding proof of damage creates a need to monitor all self-interested transactions in order to discover whether the company has been prejudiced in the first place and thus whether redress should be sought. The monitoring process is likely to require not only a consideration of factors which lie within the directors' exclusive knowledge, but also a re-opening and an evaluation of issues which involve business judgement and which are difficult to second guess.[27] In the case of a purchase of assets by the company from a director or associate, for instance, it would be necessary to assess not only whether the price and other terms were fair, but whether the company needed the assets in question, and whether an alternative product from a different source would have better suited its requirements. Because of these monitoring problems many cases of abuse would escape detection, and the low probability of detection would in itself encourage abuse.

---

[26] The dangers of requiring proof of harm have long been recognized by the courts. In *Ex parte James* (1803) 8 Ves Jun 337, at 345, Lord Eldon explained that the rule that a fiduciary may not buy from the beneficiary 'rests upon this; that the purchase is not permitted in any case, however honest the circumstances, the general interests of justice requiring it to be destroyed in every instance; *as no court is equal to the examination and ascertainment of the truth in much the greater number of cases*'. The same idea is expressed, somewhat hyperbolically, in the well-known *dictum* of James L J in *Parker v McKenna* (1874) 10 Ch App 96, at 124–25:

> it appears to me very important that we should concur in laying down again and again the general principle that in this court no agent in the course of his agency, in the matter of his agency, can be allowed to make a profit without the knowledge of his principal; that rule is an inflexible rule, and must be applied inexorably by this court, which is not entitled in my judgement, to receive evidence, or suggestion, or argument, as to whether the principal did or did not suffer injury in fact, by reason of the dealing with the agent; *for the safety of mankind requires that no agent shall be able to put his principal to the danger of such an enquiry as that* [emphasis added in both cases].

In many US jurisdictions self-interested transactions are permitted, subject, *inter alia*, to satisfying a fairness standard. It has been commented that applying such a standard 'amounts to a formidable task . . . since it implies that the courts either make own business judgements on the price-value relationship of the contract at stake or develop operational criteria for unfairness on the basis of the circumstances under which the contract is concluded'; the result in either event is a high level of unpredictability: see K. J. Hopt, 'Self-Dealing and Use of Corporate Opportunity and Information: Regulating Directors' Conflicts of Interest', in Hopt and Teubner, *Corporate Governance and Directors' Liabilities* (above, n. 3) 285, at 289. Cf. n. 95 below. The position could be significantly eased by reversing the evidential burden, that is, by requiring directors to establish that a transaction is fair, though Hopt, ibid. comments that while 'this requirement restricts self-dealing considerably, it tends to turn the legal question into a factual one and very often makes the court's decision completely unpredictable'. Further, unlike the fiduciary principle, it does not dispose of the need for a process of continuous scrutiny of self-interested transactions: see below.

[27] See *Regal (Hastings) v Gulliver* [1942] 1 All ER 378, at 392; [1967] 2 AC 134n, at 154; W. Bishop and D. D. Prentice, 'Some Legal and Economic Aspects of Fiduciary Remuneration', (1983) 46 *MLR* 289, at 303; V. Brudney and R. C. Clark, 'A New Look at Corporate Opportunities', (1981) 94 *Harv L Rev* 998, at 1021-22.

Management Self-Dealing

In contrast the fiduciary principle, by invalidating transactions regardless of damage to the company, has broad prophylactic and deterrent[28] effects. But in addition it makes the whole costly appraisal process unnecessary. Under a regime in which self-interested transactions are permissible so long as they are fair, it is incumbent on the shareholders to monitor and evaluate, or to employ experts to monitor and evaluate, all instances of them. And because they are permissible they are likely to be common. Where self-interested transactions are voidable *per se*, on the other hand, the costs of monitoring are substantially reduced, since the task is merely to identify that a transaction has taken place. Improper transactions are no doubt often easy to conceal, but at least all monitoring then entails is the discovery of plain facts.

Shareholder Consent

It is important to note the structure of the fiduciary principle: transactions are: (i) voidable, without more (ii) in the absence of shareholder consent. That a consent procedure is available is advantageous to the company, since entering into a transaction with a director or with a company associated with a director may occasionally be beneficial to it. Thus the cost of having to seek out a suitable outside contracting party is avoided, as is the need to assess reliability and credit-worthiness, since the company will either already have the relevant information or, where the transaction is with a person connected with a director, it will flow more freely than it would from a third party at arm's length.[29] Similar benefits may accrue during the course of a

---

[28] See Brudney, 'Corporate Governance' (above, n. 16), at 1407–8 n. 15. The strictness of the principle increases the deterrent effect, but that effect may still be comparatively weak. If deterrence depends on the prospect of liability multiplied by the magnitude of the sanction, then given that the probability is substantially less than 100 per cent, the liability ought to be proportionately greater than the expected gain. Since the remedy is voidability this is not, of course, the result. Clark, 'Agency Costs Versus Fiduciary Duties' (above, n. 5), at 78–9, explains the moral opprobrium associated with breach of fiduciary duty as an attempt to increase the weight of the overall sanction. An alternative is to impose penal damages or even criminal penalties for fiduciary violations, the latter being an approach adopted in Australia: see Corporations Law 1990, s 232.

[29] See Brudney and Clark, 'A New Look at Corporate Opportunities' (above, n. 27), at 1028 n 102. D. M. Phillips, 'Managerial Misuse of Property: The Synthesising Thread in Corporate Doctrine', (1979) 32 *Rutgers L Rev* 184, at 191, suggests that in addition to the direct saving by the company it may also benefit as a result of the reduced costs of the other party: e.g. where the company and a bank have a common director, the bank saves the cost of searching out the borrower and assessing the risk of lending, and may pass these savings on to the company in the form of a lower interest rate. Phillips maintains that in the same way that firm organization is often more efficient than external contracting, on account of the comparative ease of internal information flow, the company can likewise realise efficiencies through the flow of information to and from an interested party, which situation he likens to the existence of a 'quasi-firm' for the limited purpose of the trading relationship. For an account of the considerable advantages enjoyed by Japanese companies resulting from linkages with suppliers and customers see W. C. Kester, *Japanese Takeovers: The Global Contest for Corporate Control* (1991), at 60–7.

relationship, for example, permitting more informal and flexible adjustment of contract terms.

It might appear at first sight that in view of the difficulties faced by those outside the management team in obtaining the full facts and making a proper assessment of them, the ability to give consent might undermine the benefits of the fiduciary principle, producing similar results overall to those to be expected under a rule that holds merely that the directors must not damage the company. There are, however, important differences. First, making the validity of self-dealing conditional on consent should result in a lower volume of self-interested contracts being entered into than where transactions are permissible so long as they are fair. The need to obtain consent is likely to deter directors from entering into transactions that are liable to be refused consent, thus reducing the scale of the self-dealing problem. Second, there will be different outcomes in that wide band of transactions in which it is unclear whether the company's interests have been properly served or not, or where the detriment to the company is evident but marginal. Under a regime in which damage must be proved, doubtful and marginal cases of abuse will be resolved in favour of management, since efforts to obtain a remedy are likely to be more trouble than they are worth. With an authorization procedure, all that is necessary where there are doubts is the withholding of consent, and that is achieved without cost.

As so far discussed, the fiduciary principle can be seen as offering a low-cost, procedural solution to the problem of management conflicts of interest. Where directors enter into contracts with the company there is a risk that they will serve their own interests at the company's expense. On the other hand, many such transactions will be unobjectionable, and some will be beneficial to the company. By making all transactions voidable in the absence of shareholder consent, the fiduciary principle obliges directors to seek consent, and thus allows conflicts of interest to be resolved through a process of independent internal scrutiny. The role of the court in this arrangement is a limited and comparatively straightforward one: it underpins the internal procedural controls by providing a remedy where a transaction has already taken place, and consent has been refused or has not been sought. The uncertainties attached to the judicial evaluation of business issues and the increased costs associated therewith are thus avoided. The mechanism, in other words, is in theory largely self-sustaining.

This account is, however, very much in ideal terms; as will now be seen, the practice is very different. First, the fiduciary principle does not apply as described because invariably it is substantially modified by the articles, but then partially reimposed by statute. Second, the consent procedure as conceived of by the courts is not, contrary to the suggestion above, necessarily an independent one. Third, and more fundamentally, the general meeting is not a competent body to give consent. And finally, the shareholders are incapable of providing the effective enforcement of the fiduciary principle on which the whole edifice depends.

The Fiduciary Principle in Practice

Ousting the Fiduciary Principle

It is virtually a universal practice to oust the fiduciary principle as it applies to transactions in which directors have an interest by the adoption of a suitable article. The need to obtain shareholder consent is unattractive to management, involving as it does delay, publicity, and the possibility of rejection. Companies as a result invariably adopt the provision in Table A,[30] or a variant of it, which prevents transactions being impeached simply because of the presence of a conflicting interest on the part of a director and substitutes an obligation merely to disclose the interest to the board. The validity of ouster clauses has been a matter of extended academic debate,[31] and there is certainly an incongruity between the forthright insistence on the part of the courts that the fiduciary principle is essential for the protection of the company on the one hand, and the ease with which its restrictions can be evaded on the other. The controversey is focused on the question of the compatibility of ouster clauses with section 310 of the Companies Act, which renders void provisions exempting directors from liability for 'breach of duty or breach of trust'.[32] In the only decision in which the validity of ouster clauses has so far been examined, it was held that they escaped nullification by section 310, on the basis of what was essentially a linguistic argument.[33] Thus in *Movitex Ltd v Bulfield*[34] Vinelott J, following the reasoning of Megarry V-C in *Tito v Waddell (No 2)*,[35] held that the fiduciary principle does not involve a duty, but rather a disability. This being so, clauses which prevent it from operating do not fall within the scope of the section, since its wording does not embrace provisions affecting the incidence of disabilities, but only the application of duties. This analysis is apposite, and may be

---

[30] See CA 1985, Table A, arts 85 and 86.

[31] See e.g. C. D. Baker, 'Disclosure of Directors' Interests in Contracts', [1975] *JBL* 181; J. R. Birds, 'The Permissible Scope of Articles Excluding the Duties of Company Directors', (1976) 39 *MLR* 394; J. E. Parkinson, 'The Modification of Directors' Duties', [1981] *JBL* 335; R. Gregory, 'The Scope of the Companies Act 1948, Section 205', (1982) 98 *LQR* 413.

[32] Prior to CA 1929 and the introduction of what is now s 310, it was open to companies to adopt articles excluding directors' liability for all breaches of duty except those involving fraud: see *Re City Equitable Fire Insurance Co Ltd* [1925] 407, CA. The equivalent of s 310 was included in the 1929 Act on the recommendation of the Greene Committee (Cmnd. 2657 of 1926), paras 46 and 47 in the light of this decision.

[33] An alternative one is that ouster clauses do not exclude liability for *breach* of duty, but instead take the duty away: see Parkinson, 'The Modification of Directors' Duties' (above, n. 31).

[34] (Above, n. 25), at 116–120.

[35] [1977] Ch 106, at 248–49; [1977] 3 All ER 129, at 247–48.

sufficient to dispose of the technical section 310 point, but an explanation of why disabilities should be waivable when duties are not is clearly called for.

The most obvious candidate is an analogy with the shareholders' ability to authorize self-interested transactions in general meeting: there is something inherently waivable about the fiduciary principle, and a blanket waiver in the articles is not qualitatively different from waiver by resolution in respect of a specific transaction. The analogy is, however, almost entirely false. When the members authorize a specific transaction they do not waive the fiduciary principle but rather act within the protective framework that it lays down. The role of shareholder consent within this scheme, as noted above, should be viewed as a vetting procedure to ensure that self-interested transactions are fair to the company. A provision in the articles, in contrast, simply deprives the company of the benefit of the vetting mechanism. Consent here is thus merely consent to a standard form exclusion clause. Consent to a provision in the articles, furthermore, for reasons considered in Chapter 6, is at least in a public company usually consent in only a severely impoverished form. There is accordingly no basis for viewing ouster clauses as proceeding from a rational calculation on the part of shareholders that such costs as the fiduciary principle might impose (loss of beneficial self-interested transactions and the costs of obtaining consent) outweigh the putative benefits. Rather, their inclusion in the articles simply represents an exercise, and effects a strengthening, of managerial autonomy.

In *Boulting v Association of Cinematographic, Television and Allied Technicians*[36] Upjohn L J explained that the

reason why the law permits the [fiduciary principle] to be relaxed is obvious. It is frequently very much better in the interests of the company, the beneficiaries or the client, as the case may be, that they should be advised by someone on some transaction, although he may be interested on the other side of the fence.

But as we have seen, in the corporate context the possibilities are not restricted either to the complete prohibition of self-interested transactions on the one hand, or to a virtually unregulated freedom to enter into them on the other. Furthermore, the reasoning fails to recognise that without some process of independent scrutiny there is no assurance that the potential benefits of such dealings will flow to the company rather than to the interested party.[37] In view of these considerations it is not surprising that the scope of operation of clauses ousting the fiduciary principle is now limited by statute.

---

[36] [1963] 2 QB 606, CA, at 637.
[37] See V. Brudney, 'The Independent Director — Heavenly City or Potemkin Village?', (1982) 95 *Harv L Rev* 597, at 624–25.

Statutory Restoration of the Fiduciary Principle

As already mentioned, ouster clauses do not protect self-interested transactions from all scrutiny, in that they generally substitute a duty to disclose the nature of a material interest to the board. There is also a statutory disclosure obligation reinforced by a criminal penalty in respect of contracts that come before the board.[38] While disclosure to the board gives some protection against an individual rogue director, it is, however, of little value where the directors as a whole are corrupt, or the interested director enjoys a position of ascendancy over them, or they simply lack vigilance: as Gower points out, 'it hardly seems over-cynical to suggest that disclosure to one's cronies is a less effective constraint on self-seeking than disclosure to those for whom one is a fiduciary.[39] The courts have traditionally shared this view, as evidenced by their refusal, in the absence of an ouster clause, to regard a self-interested contract as valid simply on the ground that the interested director has not taken part in the vote.[40] The unsatisfactory nature of the protection afforded by board scrutiny has also been recognised by Parliament. Thus there is now, for instance, subject to a number of minor exceptions, a total prohibition of loans to directors and persons connected with them, putting an end to the ability of directors to extract money from the company on very favourable terms without the risks attached to actually having to steal it.[41]

Of more general scope is section 320 of the Companies Act 1985, which overrides ouster clauses in the articles and imposes a statutory version of the fiduciary principle in the case of 'substantial property transactions'.[42] These

[38] C A 1985, s 317. Breach of s 317 seemingly has no effect on the validity of the transaction: *Guinness plc v Saunders*, [1990] 2 AC 663, HL, [1990] BCLC 402, but see L. C. B. Gower, *Principles of Modern Company Law* (5th ed., 1992), at 562–4 and at 567—8 for defects in the section. Table A also prohibits an interested director from voting on the relevant transaction, or being counted in the quorum (arts 94 and 95), but it seems that the articles could provide otherwise: see *Boulting v ACTAT* (above, n. 36), at 636. Details of transactions in which directors have an interest have to be given in the accounts: C A 1985, s 232 and sch 6. This at least means that the fact that such transactions have taken place is discoverable, assuming compliance.

[39] L. C. B. Gower, *Principles of Modern Company Law* (4th ed., 1979), at 587. The position may be compared with that in France, where in addition to the consent of the board, there must be an auditor's report to the general assembly on a proposed contract, and then the approval of that body: see Hopt, 'Self-Dealing' (above, note 26), at 290.

[40] The more commonly-stated explanation is that the company is entitled to the disinterested advice of all its directors and hence a director should not be able to escape his responsibilities by not taking part in the company's decision-making: see *Imperial Mercantile Credit Association Ltd v Coleman* (1871) LR 6 Ch App 558, at 567–68; *Movitex Ltd v Bulfield* (above, n. 25), at 118. See also L. S. Sealy, 'The Director as Trustee', [1967] *CLJ* 83, at 96.

[41] See CA 1985, ss 330–344. The loan provisions were strengthened in the 1980 Act to cover loans made to relatives of directors and companies in which the director has an interest, and to include transactions having a similar effect to loans, referred to in the Act as 'quasi-loans' and 'credit transactions'. The provisions applicable to private companies are less strict. The 1980 Act amendments followed malpractice involving loans discovered in DTI investigations: see *The Conduct of Company Directors* (Cmnd. 7037, 1977), at 2–4.

[42] CA 1985, ss 320–322. The Stock Exchange *Admission of Securities to Listing* (1992 revision)

are transfers of assets to or from the company involving a director or person connected with him[43] where the consideration provided by the company exceeds £100,000 in value.[44] In the absence of shareholder consent such transactions are voidable, the interested director must account for any profit made, and that director and any other director who authorized the arrangement is liable to indemnify the company for any loss suffered.[45] That the section does not involve a complete restoration of the fiduciary principle is, however, clear. Apart from the value of the transaction needed for the section to bite, the definition of 'non-cash assets'[46] does not include the important category of management services, and so shareholder consent is not required in respect of directors' remuneration, either in the sense of payment for the performance of regular management duties, or reward for 'special services'. Whether or not Guinness, for instance, received good value for the £5.2 million it paid to one of its directors for services rendered in connection with the Distillers take-over,[47] the ability of directors to pay each

also requires shareholder consent to transfers of assets between a company and a director or associate which are not in the ordinary course of business, and to other 'Class 4' transactions: see s 6, ch. 1, paras 1 and 7.

[43] Connected persons are defined in s 346. They include various relatives and companies in which a director has a significant shareholding. Another company in which a director holds office is not included. Disclosure to the members in this situation would no doubt be particularly inconvenient, given that transactions with the other company might be frequent and of a confidential nature, e.g. where a director is on the board as nominee of the company's bank. Arguably, greater faith can be placed in the board in controlling this problem than where direct financial interests are involved, because of a reduced risk of mutual back-scratching.

[44] Or 10 per cent of the company's asset value. The figure was originally £50,000, but increased by SI 1990 No 1393.

[45] The existence of a duty to account (see s 322(3) and (4)) is an improvement over the position at common law, where it has been held that (except where he originally buys the property on behalf of the company) a vendor/director cannot be required to disgorge if the members affirm or the right of rescission is otherwise lost: *Re Cape Breton* (1885) 26 Ch 221, CA; *Burland v Earle* [1902] AC 83, PC. Fry L J in *Re Cape Breton*, at 812, sought to justify this position on the basis that the profit in that case resulted 'not from the original contract, but from the affirmation of the contract by the principal' (i.e. the shareholders), which is accordingly bound. However, affirmation of the contract does not necessarily evince a willingness to allow the vendor to retain the profit; loss of the right to recover the profit only follows if, as a matter of law, that is the effect of affirmation, which is the point at issue. Cotton L J held that requiring disgorgement of the vendor's profit would be for the court to make a new contract between the parties. He did, however, qualify this by stating, at 805, that 'we have not to decide that in no case could a fiduciary . . . be made answerable for the difference between the price paid by the company and the market value of an article which had some definite market value', suggesting that the problem is a practical one of quantification, rather than a principled objection to allowing recovery. Bowen L J's strong dissent in which he refuses to be put off by this difficulty is much to be preferred. See also *North-West Transportation Co Ltd v Beatty* (1887) 12 App Cas 589, PC, at 600–01.

[46] This expression is defined in s 739 and includes, for instance, the creation or transfer of a lease. This limits the freedom of the company to lease property to a director at a low rent, though could presumably be evaded by allowing directors the use of a property without giving them an interest in it of the necessary value, e.g through a series of short lets.

[47] See *Guinness plc v Saunders* (above, n. 38). On the facts the payment was held to be void.

other large sums without the need for shareholder approval illustrates the potential for serious abuse.[48]

Problems with Shareholder Consent

Section 320 has revived the importance of shareholder consent as part of the mechanism for controlling self-dealing. There are, however, a number of problems associated with the use of the general meeting as the consent-giving body. The first problem, in fairness, is a characteristic of all consent procedures and does not flow specifically from allocating the consent function to the members. Thus authorization does not dissolve conflicts of interest, and hence, although a particular self-interested transaction may not be seriously unfair to the company and accordingly will obtain approval, it may still be less favourable than one agreed at arm's length. Vinelott J has suggested that the giving of shareholder consent is analagous to the situation where a trustee enters into a transaction with a fully informed beneficiary; here the fiduciary principle does not apply, since the trustee is not dealing with himself, but is making an agreement with an independent party in the normal way. Similarly, 'to the extent that the company in general meeting gives its informed consent to the transaction there is no breach, the conflict of duty and interest is avoided'.[49] There is, however, an important difference between a contract between a trustee and a beneficiary and a transaction authorized by the general meeting. In the former case the agreement is *negotiated* and hence there is no particular reason why its terms should deviate from the market standard, whereas in the latter the terms are still fixed by the interested directors, and as one commentator has suggested, even 'if it be assumed that the deal is fair, that is not what the shareholders are entitled to. They are entitled to have someone negotiate the best deal obtainable'.[50] In other words, even with the vetting procedure of shareholder consent there is no guarantee that transactions in which management are interested will be entered into on terms equivalent to those that would be agreed between parties at arm's length. It follows that, although the flexibility introduced by allowing the shareholders to authorize contracts with directors means that potential cost savings are not lost to the company, the requirement of shareholder consent cannot exclude a residual risk that the directors will exploit their position.

---

[48] Nor does the section apply where the company enters into a succession of separate transactions each involving a consideration of less than £100,000. It has no application, either, to transactions with senior employees below board level, on the theory that the company's interests are sufficiently protected in such circumstances by the board. This no doubt underrates the influence on the outcome of board decisions wielded by senior executives and the potential for collusion.

[49] *Movitex Ltd v Bulfield* (above, n. 25), at 118.

[50] H. Marsh, 'Are Directors Trustees? Conflict of Interest and Corporate Morality', [1966] *Business Lawyer* 35, at 49. See also Brudney, 'Corporate Governance' (above, n. 16), at 1437.

The next problem is that, although the giving or withholding of consent has so far been regarded as a vetting procedure, there are in fact two quite separate conceptions of shareholder authorization. The 'vetting model' regards the shareholders' role as being to determine whether the transaction is fair to the company. This being so, emphasis is placed on the independence of the participating shareholders, that is, the outcome should not be determined by shareholders with an interest conflicting with the company's financial well-being. The second model is the 'policy model'. From its perspective the general meeting is viewed as making the policy decision about whether to enter into the transaction that would normally be made by the directors, but which the latter are disqualified from making on account of their conflicting interests. In this model there is no reason why the interested directors, as shareholders, should not be allowed to vote, since they have as much right as any other member to participate in determining questions of company policy.

It is this second model, and not the vetting model, that the courts have adopted. So in *North-West Transportation Co Ltd v Beatty*[51] it was held that a resolution to confirm the purchase of a ship from a director was valid, even though it was passed only on the strength of the votes of the vendor. Whether or not consent should be given involved 'a pure question of policy, as to which it might be expected that there would be differences of opinion, and upon which the voice of the majority ought to prevail'.[52] In other words, the general meeting was not being asked to scrutinize the fairness of the transaction (there was in fact no evidence that it was unfair),[53] but instead simply to decide on a 'free vote' what the company should do. The majority having confirmed the transaction, it could only then be attacked if it could be shown to be damaging to the company, the court acknowledging that 'it may be quite right that . . . the opposing minority should

[51] (Above, n. 45). The court below, the Supreme Court of Canada, in a forthright endorsement of the vetting model had held that 'if the acts or transactions of an interested director were to be confirmed by the shareholders, it should be by an exercise of the impartial, independent, and intelligent judgement of disinterested shareholders': *ibid* at 599. The constitution of the company in *North West Transportation* gave the shareholders an original power to enter into contracts, though nothing in the Privy Council's decision appears to turn on this: see generally, G. R. Sullivan, 'Restating the Scope of the Derivative Action', (1985) 44 *CLJ* 236, at 249.

[52] *Ibid*, at 601, per Sir Richard Baggallay.

[53] It seems to have been accepted by all parties that the purchase was in itself unobjectionable, or even positively beneficial: the court declared, at 596, that

It is proved by uncontradicted evidence, and is indeed now substantially admitted, that at the date of the purchase the acquisition of another steamer . . . was essential to the efficient conduct of the company's business; that [the steamer purchased] was well adapted for that purpose; that it was not within the power of the company to acquire any other steamer equally well adapted for its business; and that the price agreed to be paid for the steamer was not excessive or unreasonable.

In these circumstances the only dispute remaining between the factions could have been over policy, and in this particular context the court was presented with an obvious dilemma: should it allow the minority to prevail over the majority on a matter of pure business judgement?

be able . . . to challenge the transaction, and to shew that it is an improper one'.[54]

But the result of counting the votes of the interested directors is to render the consent process useless in those cases in which the directors are able to affect the outcome. It becomes a pointless formality, inevitably producing the same result as the original board decision. Instead of the directors being required to satisfy an independent body within the company that the transaction is fair, the onus is thrown back onto an objecting shareholder to demonstrate to the court that it is unfair, the problems associated with which the fiduciary principle is expressly designed to avoid.[55] The objective of equipping the company with an internal procedure for the management of conflicts of interest is thus undermined, and the protection against improper self-dealing substantially weakened. In the modern, large, public company the directors' personal shareholdings are likely to be too small to have much effect on a confirmatory resolution,[56] but through the use of proxy votes and support from shareholders with whom they are connected, and against the background of low participation, the capacity of management to tilt the balance of voting in their own favour should not be underestimated.

While adoption of the policy model appears to result from conceptual muddle, it is unlikely that the courts would in any event be capable of constructing out of the shareholders at large a truly impartial vetting body. In order to achieve this it would be necessary to exclude the votes not only of interested directors, but also of any other shareholders whose motivation was suspect. In *Smith v Croft (No 3)*[57] Knox J took on this task, in the different context of a decision by the shareholders about whether it was appropriate for a derivative action to be brought against the directors, but there the number of shareholders was small and their affiliations clear. In a company with a mass of shareholders of undisclosed orientation, purging the consent-giving body of tainted participants will prove much more difficult.[58] But

---

[54] Ibid. at 600–1. The judge goes on to say that the minority would in such circumstances be freed from the objection that the action could be brought only by the company itself, i.e. the 'fraud on the minority exception' to the rule in *Foss v Harbottle* would apply (see Ch 8, below). In *Prudential Assurance Co Ltd v Newman Industries Ltd (No 2)*[1981] Ch 257, at 309, [1980] 2 All ER 841, at 864, referring to this *dictum*, Vinelott J stated that 'prima facie the transaction would have been an improper one if no steps had been taken to ensure that the price was within the range of what could be reasonably considered a fair price and that the transaction was in other respects within the range of what could be considered a commercial transaction.'

[55] Though it is true that under present arrangements this will be the case where 'wrongdoers' have control, even if the formality of seeking shareholder consent is not followed, since minority shareholders do not have standing to enforce the fiduciary principle: see Ch. 8 below.

[56] And the Stock Exchange may require a director to abstain from voting: see *Admission of Securities to Listing* (above, no. 42), s 6, ch 1, para 7.2

[57] [1987] BCLC 355; see further Ch. 8 below.

[58] See also Lord Wedderburn, 'Derivative Actions and Foss v Harbottle', (1981) 44 *MLR* 202, at 208, considering the difficulties of the similar proposal made by Vinelott J in *Prudential Assurance Ltd v Newman Industries (No 2)* (above, n. 54). Cf. The Stock Exchange *Admission of*

badly motivated shareholders are not the only problem. Many shareholders vote with management out of habit or a sense of loyalty which even the existence of articulated opposition may not overcome; others lack the competence to vet transactions and for most the investment of time and effort needed to obtain information and evaluate directors' dealings will not be justified by the potential return.[59] When the delay and expense involved in summoning a general meeting are also taken into account, it becomes clear that the shareholders are comprehensively ill-suited to performing the vetting function.

Enforcement of the Fiduciary Principle

The operation of the fiduciary principle is also ultimately dependent on the shareholders for its enforcement. Clearly the principle will function effectively only if there is an agency, independent of management, that is able to take action in appropriate cases to enforce it. Without ready enforceability its prophylactic effects are lost. We shall see in Chapter 8 that the members are able to enforce the fiduciary principle only by majority decision,[60] and probably have to remove the existing board to do so. The same factors that render the general meeting unsuitable as a consent-giving body ensure also, however, that it will rarely be able to give meaningful consideration to the merits of an action. Ironically minority shareholders, who of all plaintiffs will find proving that the company has been damaged most difficult, given their problems over access to the facts, do not have standing to enforce the principle, but must establish a 'fraud on the minority'. But even if minority shareholders had standing, there must be doubts about the adequacy of their incentives to take action. These issues are considered in Chapter 8. All in all, it seems again that the effective control of self-dealing is prejudiced by reason of the outmoded governance structure in which the fiduciary principle is embedded.

Securities to Listing section 6, ch 1, para 7.2, wherein the Council reserves the right to require a Class 4 party interested in the transaction to abstain from voting. The provision in the draft Fifth Directive that shareholders should not vote on a resolution to approve a contract with the company in which they have an interest has been dropped from the latest proposals: see DTI, *Amended Proposal for a Fifth Directive on the Harmonisation of Company Law in the European Community: A Consultative Document* (1990), art 34. There are other situations in which votes are excluded, see e.g. CA 1985, s 164(5) (purchase by company of its own shares, resolution invalid if passed with aid of selling shareholders' votes) and *Bamford v Bamford* [1970] Ch 212, CA (holders of shares issued for an improper purpose may not vote the contested shares in a ratificatory resolution), but in these cases the exclusion relates to particular shares rather than shareholders, and there are no problems of indentification.

[59] These problems would be lessened by the requirement that an independent auditor's report on a transaction be given to the shareholders prior to any vote. This is one of the functions of the *commissaires aux comptes* in France: see A. Tunc, 'The French Commissaires aux Comptes', [1984] *JBL* 279, at 282; Hopt, 'Self-Dealing' (above, n. 26), at 290.

[60] There are long-stop possibilities of enforcement by a replacement management (e.g. after take-over) and by the liquidator. Existing management may, of course, in principle bring an action against one or more of their number.

II DIRECTORS' TERMS OF EMPLOYMENT AND REMUNERATION

Directors' service contracts form a category of self-interested transactions that pose special problems. Since they must be paid for their services, some form of contractual arrangement between directors and the company is inevitable, but the difficulties of valuing management services make it particularly important that directors should not be involved in fixing their own employment terms. The practice nevertheless is invariably to oust the fiduciary principle by a provision in the articles, leaving the board with a wide discretion over the level of remuneration, pension arrangements, the circumstances in which the contract may be terminated, and so on.[61] The contrast between the courts' traditional horror of unregulated conflicts of interest,[62] and the ease with which the judicially provided mode of regulation is evaded, is thus particularly stark in this context. It is true that many large companies now appoint a remuneration committee, made up of non-executive directors, to settle the executive directors' terms of service,[63] but as noted in Chapter 6, non-executives are appointees of senior management and hence cannot be relied on to make an objective assessment of what a particular director merits. Furthermore, non-executive directors are frequently executive directors of other companies, or at least established members of the business community. Even though direct reciprocity in determining rewards may be rare, non-executives have thus a community of interest in the general level of management remuneration with the executives whose pay they set, which will do nothing to curb generous instincts. Accordingly, while the use of remuneration committees may reduce the number of cases where payments are very conspicuously out of line, they are by no means a substitute for arm's-length negotiation. Indeed there is empirical support to this effect. A recent survey on the impact of remuneration committees notes that a chief executive whose remuneration committee includes non-executive directors who are particularly well paid by their own companies is likely to be paid more in turn. The authors conclude that merely setting up a remuneration committee is no answer to controlling top executive pay and that 'these committees seem to do little more than legitimize generous pay awards'.[64]

---

[61] See e.g. Table A, art 84. The fact that the particular director whose contract is being agreed cannot vote (see e.g. Table A, art 94) is largely irrelevant, given the collective interest of the board in favourable terms of employment. The directors may also be awarded fees which are voted by the company in general meeting (see e.g. Table A, art 82). These are paid for holding office as director, rather than in relation to executive employment, and usually involve comparatively small amounts.

[62] See n. 28 above.

[63] And see the Committee on the Financial Aspects of Corporate Governance (the Cadbury Committee), *Report* (1992) para 4.34, recommending that the boards of all listed companies appoint remuneration committees.

[64] B. Main and J. Johnston, 'Deciding on Top Pay by Committee', [1992] July *Personnel Management* 32, at 35.

Statutory Controls

The only statutory limitation of substance on the directors' discretion is section 319 of the Companies Act 1985, which prohibits companies from entering into service contracts with directors for a term of more than five years without shareholder consent. This provision was introduced in the 1980 Act after disquiet about directors entering into long-term contracts with a view either to making their dismissal prohibitively expensive for the company, and thus entrenching themselves in office, or alternatively, highly lucrative. Of course, compensation for premature termination even where a contract has less than five years to run may still amount to a very substantial sum.[65]

The other restrictions are aimed at regulating *ex gratia* payments to directors on cessation of office.[66] Shareholder approval must be obtained for amounts to which a director has no contractual entitlement,[67] though anomalously this does not extend to pensions in respect of past services.[68] Quantifying a director's entitlement to damages is not an exact science, particularly where there is some form of bonus scheme, the value of which has to be capitalized, and bearing in mind the impact of taxation and the possibility of mitigation, and hence it is appropriate that contractual settlements should also require shareholder consent.[69] The Act is also defective in

[65] With this in mind, the Cadbury Committee, ibid. para 4.41 recommends that service contracts should not exceed three years and that s 319 be amended to that effect.

[66] CA 1985, s 312 relates to payments made by the company; s 313 to payments, from whatever source, in relation to loss of office in connection with the sale of the whole or part of the undertaking; s 314 to payments made in connection with a change in control, consent in this case to be given by the offeree shareholders. Payments which cannot be justified as being intended to bring some benefit to the company may, independently of these sections, be challengeable on the ground that they exceed the powers contained in the memorandum or constitute a breach of fiduciary duty: see *Hutton v West Cork Railway Co* (1883) 23 Ch D 654, CA; *Gibson's Executor v Gibson* 1980 SLT 2.

[67] CA 1985, s 316(3) provides that no consent need be obtained for *bona fide* damages for breach of contract. There is an argument to the effect that shareholder consent to contractual compensation must be obtained by reason of CA 1985, s 320, on the ground that paying it constitutes a 'substantial property transaction' by virtue of s 739. This provides that a reference to the transfer of a non-cash asset includes 'the discharge of any person's liability'. The argument is that s 320 thus applies to the discharge of the company's liability to the director. This suggestion was rejected in the unreported decision of *Gooding v Cater* 13 May 1989, Ch, on the ground that 'any person' does not include the company and that there is nothing to indicate that s 320 is intended to restrict the application of s 316(3).

[68] S 316(3). L. C. B. Gower, *Review of Investor Protection Report: Part 1* (Cmnd. 9125, 1984), para 9.33, contrasting the position with CA 1985, s 320, points out that 'a *sale* for more than [£100,000] of a company house to a retiring director requires approval in general meeting; but, at present, a *gift* of a far larger sum as a superannuation gratuity does not' (emphasis in original).

[69] See Gower, ibid. The recommendation of the Jenkins Committee that the amount of contractual compensation payable be disclosed to the shareholders when their consent to an *ex gratia* payment is being sought, to enable them to assess the fairness of the terms overall, has not been implemented: see *Report of the Company Law Committee* (Cmnd. 1749, 1962), para 93. Gower, ibid. has also suggested that on a resolution to approve compensation payments, the directors

that it does not require consent for payments to former, as opposed to present, directors, and applies only to compensation for the loss of the office of director as distinct from some particular executive office, such as managing director.[70] Furthermore, the consent requirement relates only to payments with respect to cessation of office in the company making the payment and not some other group company. It is clearly desirable that these loopholes be closed, though the whole approach appears to place greater faith in the astringent powers of shareholder consent than is warranted in practice.

It may be noted finally that because consent is needed only in relation to non-covenanted payments, it follows that the company must comply with the terms of such 'golden parachutes' as the directors may have chosen to equip themselves. These are contractual provisions that entitle a director to a large severance payment on certain contingencies, most commonly a change in control, if the director is dismissed[71] or exercises an option to resign. In *Taupo Totara Timber Co v Rowe* a director's service contract included a term which allowed him to resign and claim five times his gross annual salary if the company were taken over.[72] This occurred, and since the ensuing payment was a contractual entitlement the Privy Council held that it was unnecessary to obtain shareholder consent under the equivalent of section 312. It should be noted that there is, however, a prior issue of the validity of terms of this kind. On the facts[73] it was held that 'reasonable and honest' directors might consider that contracts of the type in question would encourage valuable employees to stay, and would therefore be in the interests of the company.[74] But presumably a court might decide that particular arrangements were sufficiently extravagant to make a finding that they could possibly be beneficial to the company untenable.

concerned, connected persons, and, where relevant, the take-over bidder, should not be allowed to vote.

[70] See *Taupo Totara Timber Co Ltd v Rowe* [1978] AC 537, [1977] 3 All ER 123, PC, applying the equivalent New Zealand provision. There is clearly no merit in the distinction, since what is crucial is the ability to exploit the position of being a director, and not the capacity in respect of which the payment is made. The recommendation of the Jenkins Committee (above, n. 69), para 93, that s 312 be amended in the same way has not been implemented; see also Gower, ibid.

[71] Though the term may be void at common law as constituting a penalty: see *Dunlop Pneumatice Tyre Co Ltd v New Garage and Motor Co Ltd* [1915] AC 79. Golden parachutes are seemingly not as yet common among directors of large UK companies: see the *Financial Times*, 17 May 1987.

[72] (Above, n.70) Cf. *Buckhorn, Inc v Ropak Corp* 656 F Supp 209, 233-35 (SD Ohio), *aff'd by summary ord*, 815 F 2d 76 (6th Cir 1987) (golden parachute enforceable only where related to termination of office, not merely change in control).

[73] In particular, the option was contained in the contracts of employees in addition to directors and it had been company policy for some years to confer this benefit. Where a contract of this kind is entered into with a view to frustrating a take-over it may be held invalid as being motivated by an 'improper purpose' and it may breach Rule 21 of the City Code on Take-overs and Mergers (see generally Ch. 5, above).

[74] For an argument in support of golden parachutes see C. Knoeber, 'Golden Parachutes, Shark Repellants and Hostile Tender Offers', (1986) 76 *Am Econ Rev* 155 (the possibility of

The Level of Remuneration

While, therefore, there are some restrictions on the payments that can be made on termination of directors' service contracts, aside from the limits on duration the terms of the contracts themselves are largely unregulated.[75] Most notably, the directors are left free to set the level of their own remuneration, though there are provisions for disclosure, of a rather inadequate kind.[76] The issue of directors' rewards is one of great sensitivity, and attracts regular press comment and public discussion. Whether individual directors, or directors in general, are paid too much raises broad questions of economic and political judgement which will not be entered into here. But it follows from the social-enterprise concept of the company adopted in this book that there is a legitimate public interest in the level of directors' remuneration, and as a minimum this dictates a concern with the adequacy of the procedures by which pay is determined. That these procedures should be seen to be fair is important for reasons of general social equity, but there are also more concrete considerations. Pleas from the board for pay restraint on the part of employees generally are less likely to be effective when perceived as hypocritical, with consequential adverse effects for the company concerned and the economy as a whole.[77] And more generally, employees are liable to be more positively motivated where the rules and practices of the organization for which they work command their respect.

The Problems of Setting and Monitoring the Level of Remuneration

As far as the legal model of the company is concerned, only the shareholders are residuary claimants: all the directors are entitled to is the 'market rate' for the services they provide.[78] The concept of the market rate for

termination on take-over is a disincentive to acquiring firm-specific skills, the effects of which are countered by golden parachutes). They may, on the other hand, be viewed as 'rewards for failure', as where the company is taken over as a result of the failure of management sufficiently to increase 'shareholder value': see 'Bosses' Pay', *The Economist*, 1 February 1992, 21, at 24.

[75] CA 1985, s 311 also prohibits the payment of tax-free remuneration to directors.

[76] The aggregate amount of all compensation paid to directors, the remuneration of the chairman, and of any director paid more than the chairman and the number of directors falling within specified bands of remuneration, must be disclosed in the accounts: CA 1985, s 231; sch 6, part I. No details, e.g. of what proportion of pay is performance-linked, or how performance is measured, need be disclosed, but see further 225 below. A small minority of companies make some additional voluntary disclosures along these lines: see the *Financial Times*, 28 July 1992. Directors' service contracts must also be available for inspection by the members: C A 1985, s 318; see also the Stock Exchange *Admission of Securities to Listing*, s 5, ch. 2, para 42.

[77] It is interesting to note in this respect that between 1981 and 1990 the pay of 'top managers' increased by an average of 351.5 per cent, which was more than three times the percentage increase in average earnings (106.8 per cent). The retail price index during the period rose by 68.6 per cent. See the *Financial Times*, 29 June 1991.

[78] It has been noted that the contractual model of the company introduces an ambiguity concerning management entitlements: see Brudney, 'Corporate Governance' (above, n. 16), at 1435–6, and for an example of the ambiguity, see R. K. Winter, *Government and the Corporation*

managerial services is, however, problematical, in two different ways. First, managers are not standard 'commodities' with a price revealed by the interplay of market forces, but are highly differentiated in terms of skills and relevant experience.[79] Determining what a particular director should be paid is thus largely dependent on a subjective judgement of the value of the director's services to the company. But since they work in teams, isolating the contribution of an individual director with any precision is likely to be impossible. Further, the extent to which the company's success is attributable to management generally, as opposed, for instance, to the skills of the workforce, favourable market conditions, or lack of competition, is also somewhat indeterminate. Because of these uncertainties—in essence, because of the absence of an objective yardstick—monitoring the fairness of management rewards is extremely difficult, which is precisely why the task of setting them in the first place should be not left to the directors themselves.

The problem runs deeper, however, than the simple risk that the directors will award themselves more than the going rate, in the same way that they might, for instance, cause the company to pay more than market value for a piece of land acquired from one of their number. In a normal market, market price is determined by the interaction of buyers and sellers who are at arm's length. In a market in which the sellers are systematically able to determine how much the buyers are willing to pay it seems likely that the market price itself will be higher than it would be in one in which the buyers were disinterested. In other words, allowing the directors to set their own remuneration involves not only the episodic risk that they will pay more than the market rate in a given case (in so far as this is calculable), but more fundamentally, it also means that what the market rate is distorted upwards by reason of the defective institutional setting in which the market operates.[80]

(1978), at 27. If the allocation of rights between managers and shareholders depends on the contract they make, there is no reason *a priori* why, for instance, managers should not be viewed as hiring capital, rather than the other way around, and with the managers thus entitled to the residual income and the shareholders to a fixed return. The contract model might accordingly be used to legitimate increased management income.

[79] See D. Helm, 'Mergers, Take-overs, and the Enforcement of Profit Maximisation', in J. A. Fairburn and J. A. Kay, *Mergers and Merger Policy* (1989) 133, at 144–45: the managerial labour market 'is heterogeneous, and to a varying extent is often informationally inadequate, relatively thin, and characterised by considerable immobility due to housing market imperfections, educational considerations for children, two-job requirements, and so on. Managerial jobs often require specialist firm-specific skills and have non-negotiable entry costs.'

[80] Since over-payment, even on a substantial scale, is likely to constitute a relatively small percentage of the turn-over of a major company, the product and capital markets and the market for control are unlikely to be an effective constraint on this aberrant tendency. See D. Vagts, 'Challenges to Executive Compensation: For the Markets or the Courts?', (1983) 8 *J Corp Law* 231, at 238–240; cf. Winter, *Government and the Corporation* (above, n. 78) at 33: 'because corporate management's discretion in determining its own share of the corporate return is directly related to the market for management control and stock price [the incentives created by such discretion] benefit shareholders'.

The importance of this is that setting salary levels by reference to directors' rates of pay generally only compounds the distortion. The validity of the market rate as a standard by which remuneration can be independently monitored is similarly compromised.

These problems are not diminished where directors' rewards are linked to some measure of company performance. Chapter 4 noted that incentive pay might have a positive effect on profitability (the details need not be repeated here), but how much of an incentive directors need in order to persuade them to expend maximum effort is clearly problematical. Where the scale of incentive payments, and, perhaps more importantly, the factors that trigger them, are determined by management, there is an obvious risk that performance-related schemes will be used simply as a device to legitimate higher rewards: in other words, they will mask a transfer in wealth from shareholders rather than produce an increase in wealth overall. An example concerns the 'strike price' at which share options may be exercised. Share option schemes allow directors to subscribe for shares at some date in the future at a predetermined price. The incentive effect is clearly much greater if that price is significantly higher than market price at the scheme's commencement, yet it is commonly the practice to set it at the latter date.[81] Another questionable arrangement is to link rewards to growth in earnings per share, which is again a feature of many remuneration packages. This measure is open to manipulation by management and may bear only a limited relationship to the underlying performance of the business.[82] Some support for the view that performance-related schemes are at least partly cosmetic is contained in the findings of Jensen and Murphy, considered earlier. They note that although bonuses accounted for about 50 per cent of the salaries of the chief executives studied in their survey, there was little year-to-year variation in their overall rewards.[83] This lack of sensitivity to company performance suggests that the schemes were not designed to be an incentivie so much as to provide a stable, high-level return. Similarly in this country the authors of a recent survey conclude that an investigation of changes in directors' remuneration in almost 300 large quoted companies

---

[81] Referring to the position in the United States, *The Economist* notes (above, n. 74), at 22, that

> In most option schemes, the strike price is the market price of the shares on the day of the grant, which normally has a life of ten years. In other words, the boss can buy the shares at that day's price at any time in the next ten years. This is generous indeed. Standard & Poor's index of 500 leading shares has risen by 225% in the past decade. Any firm whose shares do not rise at all over ten years is headed for the dustheap, or already there. The few companies which do set a higher strike price never set it high enough even to require shareholder gains equal to the return on risk-free Treasury bonds.

[82] See 116 above.

[83] M. C. Jensen and K. J. Murphy, 'Performance Pay and Top-Management Incentives', (1990) 98 *J Pol Econ* 225, at 251, and see above 114-16.

failed to reveal any important relationship between directors' rewards and the performance of their companies.[84]

Against this background, it is evident that judicial monitoring of remuneration can take place only in a most rudimentary way.[85] It is in theory open to the court to categorize excessive remuneration as unlawful on a variety of grounds. Thus the sum paid might be so large that it cannot be regarded as a genuine exercise of the company's remuneration power, and therefore that it constitutes an unauthorized gift.[86] Alternatively, it might indicate that the board has failed to act in good faith for the benefit of the company. Or relief might be available under section 459 of the Companies Act 1985, on the ground that the remuneration fixed by the directors amounts to conduct which is unfairly prejudicial to the interests of the members.[87] Whatever the ground of attack, however, the court will be faced with the difficulty in each case of establishing a standard against which the amount paid can be compared. In so doing it will be able to obtain some assistance from the information on average salary levels for directors in companies of different sizes that is now published on a regular basis by management consultants and others. But since considerable variation around the average is entirely proper, to reflect differences in what the management task entails or in the abilities of individual managers, and, as noted, these factors are difficult to evaluate, the court is unlikely to be in a position to interfere unless remuneration is very seriously out of step with the comparative data.[88] And the need

[84] P. Gregg, S. Machin, and S. Szymanski, *The Disappearing Relationship between Directors' Pay and Corporate Performance* LSE Centre for Economic Performance Working Paper no. 282 (1992), at 9.

[85] For a survey of the position in the United States where questions of remuneration have more frequently come before the courts, see Vagts, 'Challenges to Executive Compensation' (above, n. 80), at 252–268.

[86] See *Re Halt Garage* [1982] 3 All ER 1016; the court's decision here that the director had been over-paid was easier to reach than will normally be the case: she had performed no services during the relevant period, which enabled the excess to be categorized as reflecting her ownership stake rather than being payment for services. Cf. *Smith v Croft (No 3)* [1987] BCLC 355, at 378–379, and 382.

[87] In *Re Carrington Viyella PLC* (1983) 1 BCC 98,951 Vinelott J held that a petition could not be presented under what is now section 459 where the conduct complained of affected all the members, as opposed to only some of them. He therefore rejected the petition in that case involving a complaint about the terms of a director's service contract. Cf. *Re Cumana Ltd* [1986] BCLC 435. This obstacle has been removed by the Companies Act 1989 which amends section 459 to provide that a petition may be presented in respect of conduct which is prejudicial to the interests of the members generally. See also *Re Jermyn Street Turkish Baths Ltd* [1970] 1 WLR 1194; reversed, [1971] 1 WLR 1042. Excessive remuneration might also constitute a transaction at an undervalue for the purposes of IA 1986, s 238, and be a factor in determining whether a director should be disqualified: see *Re Keypak Homecare Ltd* [1990] BCLC 440, at 444.

[88] See *Smith v Croft* (1986) 1 WLR 580, [1986] BCLC 207 and *Smith v Croft (No 3)* [1987] BCLC 355. In considering the appropriateness of the level of remuneration the court in each case had regard to the figures for pay of other employees in the relevant industry (films) in forming the opinion that the amounts in question were not excessive. In the first case Walton J observed, at 219, that the salaries which persons operating successfully in [the film] world enjoy are so manifestly out of line with that which ordinary mortals, condemned to the mere pittance which falls to

to rely on such data underlines the inherent limitations in the capacity of external monitoring to overcome the conflict of interest problem. The court may be able to intervene in individual cases of conspicuous non-comparability, but it is unable to influence the prevailing average rates which, it has been suggested, are likely to be distorted owing to management participation in the level-setting procedure.[89]

Nor would a restoration of the traditional fiduciary response offer much greater promise. In default of permissive articles, directors' remuneration would have to be authorized by the shareholders in general meeting, since directors' service contracts would otherwise be voidable. The practicalities of the matter would, however, confine the shareholders' role to approving or rejecting proposals put to them by management. A reactive function of this kind might in theory be effective in controlling the inherent tendency towards inflation of salary levels, but in practice the picture of general shareholder inactivity suggests that the members would be likely to rubber-stamp management proposals except in cases of gross overreaching[90] or where manifestly excessive salaries were awarded to the sitting management of a company in apparent decline. More limited[91] proposals to strengthen disclosure requirements should be assessed with this in mind. The Cadbury Committee has, for example, recommended that separate figures be given for salary and performance-related elements paid to the chairman and highest-paid UK director, and that the criteria on which performance is measured should be explained.[92] While it is inexcusable that this information should not be publicly revealed, what effect its disclosure is likely to have will depend on the willingness of major shareholders to exert pressure on

those who reach the top of their profession in almost any other field enjoy, that even fashionable silks feel a twinge of envy from time to time. Judged by that scale ... coupled with the fact that one of the company's leading executives ... has already left the company to go to higher paid employment in basically the same field, I think the directors are entitled to say that they stand astonished at their own moderation, as Lord Clive once said.

[89] See A. F. Conrad, 'Beyond Managerialism: Investor Capitalism?', (1988) 22 *U Mich J L Ref* 177, at 166: 'when levels of compensation are reviewed in derivative suits, judges can only compare compensation in the case before them with compensation in other enterprises that are subject to the same biases'.

[90] There are occasional press reports of shareholder rebellion in the face of over-generous remuneration, e.g. in 1987 pressure from institutional shareholders forced the board of Burtons to modify a planned share option scheme. The scheme as originally proposed could in theory have led to the chairman, Sir Ralph Halpern, being granted options worth £8 million. Under revised arrangements a ceiling of £2.5 million was imposed on the value of options that could be granted to any participant. See the *Financial Times* 21 July 1987 on this affair and institutional guidelines subsequently drawn up. Shareholder consent is necessary where an incentive scheme involves share options, by virtue of Stock Exchange rules: see *Admission of Securities to Listing* (above, n. 42), s 6, ch. 1, para 7.2.

[91] The Cadbury Committee rejected suggestions that remuneration should be voted in general meeting on the ground that this would be unworkable: *Report* (above, n. 63), para 4.43.

[92] Ibid., para 4.40. See also Institutional Shareholders' Committee, *The Role and Duties of Directors — A Statement of Best Practice* (1991), at 4–5.

managements where they consider pay to be excessive or calculated in accordance with inappropriate criteria.

The installation of a body of genuinely independent directors, as considered in Chapter 6, seems to offer a better prospect of taking effective control over management terms of service. Unlike the general meeting, independent directors can actually negotiate terms with management and do not merely have to accept or reject terms decided elsewhere. This substantially improves the chances that the outcome will reflect a proper balance of interests. And because it is the function of independent directors to monitor the performance of management, this should make it possible for them to obtain a clearer idea of the contribution of individual directors, allowing their remuneration to be adjusted accordingly. In contrast with existing non-executive directors, independent directors would not be appointees of inside management, and hence are likely to be more astute in defending the company's interests. Further, should a distinct profession of independent directors evolve,[93] the current community of interest between supervisor and supervisee in the general level of management remuneration might be dissipated. Indeed, the ability of the independents to obtain 'value for money' in management services might come to be regarded as one of the indicators of the quality of the independent directors' own performance.[94]

Independent directors are likely to be of value not only in settling the terms of management service contracts, but also in resolving conflict of interest problems more generally (and also, of course, in detecting and deterring outright fraud). We have noted the advantages of the fiduciary approach of allowing self-interested transactions only with the consent of an independent body, but also how the shareholders are ill-suited to perform the consent-giving role. With a small group of supervisory directors the problems of lack of information, expertise, and independence are largely overcome, and the cost and delay of summoning a general meeting are avoided. Independent directors might also perform a similar role in relation to corporate opportunities, though as the next section will show, the need for an authorization procedure is less pressing there.

III CORPORATE OPPORTUNITIES

Where a director makes use of a commercial opportunity that might conceivably have been exploited by the company there is a risk that any profit the director makes will be at the company's expense. Determining whether or not the company has in fact been damaged is fraught with the same kind of

---

[93] See 175 above.
[94] See R. J. Gilson and R. Kraakman, 'Reinventing the Outside Director: An Agenda for Institutional Investors', (1991) 43 *Stan L Rev* 863, at 891.

difficulties that arise in connection with self-interested transactions. Thus, whether the director's gain implies a loss to the company depends on whether the company would have taken the opportunity itself but for the director's action, which in turn depends on a number of complex factors, such as the compatibility of the new venture with the company's existing activities, the likely rate of return, the availability of funds, or the willingness of other parties involved to deal with the company. In order to avoid the problems of having to assess these issues the fiduciary principle is applied in respect of corporate opportunities in a similar way to that already considered: it requires disgorgement of profits without proof of damage,[95] but (it is suggested) allows profits to be retained in certain circumstances with shareholder consent.

The Application of the Fiduciary Principle

In parallel with the court's refusal to assess the terms of self-interested transactions, evidence that the company would not, or could not, itself have exploited an opportunity that has been taken by a director personally is excluded by the fiduciary principle. The directors must account to the company for any profit they have made from a relevant opportunity, without the plaintiff having to show that it has in any way suffered a loss. The leading case is *Regal (Hastings) Ltd v Gulliver*.[96] The facts, somewhat simplified, are that the company formed a subsidiary for the purpose of acquiring the leases of two cinemas. In the course of the transaction the directors concluded that the company did not have the resources to capitalize the subsidiary to the necessary extent, and decided that they themselves should take up the outstanding shares. In due course all the shares in Regal, the parent company, were sold, and the directors also disposed of their own shares in the subsidiary, thereby making a profit. The directors were held liable to account to Regal for the proceeds.[97] Clearly, in any situation in which directors reject an opportunity on the company's behalf and then

---

[95] L. S. Sealy argues for a more finely tuned approach, on the basis that 'there is no evidentiary problem for the modern court': *Company Law and Commercial Reality* (1984), at 38–40. See also *Holder v Holder* [1968] Ch 353, CA, at 398 and 402. Although the difficulties faced by the court in distinguishing objectionable from harmless transactions may be over-stated in the old cases (see note 28 above), the more substantial objections that a more flexible rule increases monitoring costs and reduces deterrence remain.

[96] (above, n. 27).

[97] The result was that the purchasers of Regal unmeritoriously obtained a windfall. This is, however, simply a consequence of separate corporate entity and is liable to occur whenever a company which has changed control brings an action in respect of prior defaults. It should also be noted that directors are permitted to make profits in similar circumstances to those in *Regal* where the company has adopted an appropriate article: see e.g. Table A, art 85(b). Similar considerations arise to those discussed above with regard to articles ousting the fiduciary principle as it applies to self-interested transactions.

make use of it themselves, there is a risk that the decision to reject will not have been made in the company's best interests. It is easy to see the sort of difficulties that would have faced the plaintiff in *Regal* if liability had depended on showing that the directors' profit was made at the company's expense. It would have been necessary to assess, for example, the likelihood of the company being able to obtain a loan to acquire all the shares, or the possibility of the transaction being structured in some other way that would have allowed the company to make the whole profit. By rendering the resolution of such issues unnecessary, the effect of the fiduciary principle is significantly to reduce the problems of monitoring and enforcement, thereby establishing an effective prophylactic regime.[98]

Although it is not necessary to demonstrate that the company has suffered a loss, it is necessary to show that it has a legitimate interest in the opportunity, in other words, that the opportunity is a *corporate* one. An approach to determining whether or not an opportunity is 'corporate', consistent with the rationale of the fiduciary principle, is to consider whether the directors had obligations to perform in respect of it. Where they do, they should not be allowed to take the opportunity for themselves, since in such circumstances there is a risk that the profit they make will be at the expense of the company. It is that risk that brings the fiduciary principle into play.

There was no doubt in *Regal* that the opportunity was corporate, since the directors' ability to acquire the shares arose 'by reason and in the course of' their fiduciary position.[99] But as Laskin J commented with regard to this formula in *Canadian Aero Service v O'Malley*:[100] 'the particular facts may determine the shape of the principle of decision without setting fixed limits to it.' Thus in *Industrial Development Consultants Ltd v Cooley*[101] it was held that a director is not entitled to retain a profit made on a contract for which the company has been negotiating, even though the other party refuses to deal with the company and, in particular, the contract is offered to the director, not by reason of his position, but because of his personal attributes. In this situation the profit is not made 'by reason . . . of' the fiduciary position, but that is not the central issue. The point is that the director has a duty to attempt to obtain the contract for the company, and doubt is cast on the loyalty with which that duty is performed where he takes it in his own name. Similarly a director should be precluded from entering into a contract which the company has rejected and which is subsequently offered by the other

---

[98] Where the utilization of an opportunity depends on the company entering into a contract with a third party, evidence that the third party would not have been prepared to deal with the company is similarly excluded: see *Industrial Development Consultants Ltd v Cooley* (above, n. 20). Roskill J was prepared to hold that there was a 10 per cent chance of the company being awarded the contract, but this is not material to the decision.

[99] Per Lord Russell, [1967] 2 AC 134 n, at 143, [1942] 1 All ER 378, at 385.

[100] (1973) 40 DLR (3d) 371, at 390.

[101] (Above, n. 20).

party to the directors personally, since participating in the prior decision about whether or not to accept the contract on the company's behalf obviously falls within the scope of their responsibilities.[102] It should make no difference in either of these situations that the directors obtain the profit only after they have resigned,[103] since the relevant factor is the existence of a duty in respect of the opportunity during their period of office. It also follows, however, that a director should be free to take up what may be considered a 'fresh' opportunity after resignation even though it comes from a source with which the director has previously dealt on the company's behalf.[104]

It is clear that the fact that the company does not have independent knowledge of a potential business venture will not in itself prevent it being classified as a corporate opportunity. At least where a director becomes aware of an opportunity by virtue of his or her office, there is a duty to evaluate it on the company's behalf, and performance of that duty would be compromised if directors were free to take up rejected opportunities personally. It is suggested however that it should also make no difference that a director learns of an opportunity in a private capacity, though this has not yet been established by an English court. As Bishop and Prentice explain, the directors are 'the eyes and ears of the company with an overriding responsibility to channel economic opportunities to the company and the legal rules should reinforce this obligation and not attenuate it'.[105] And in an age of conglomerates, no activity from which an adequate rate of return might be

---

[102] Cf. *Peso Silver Mines Ltd v Cropper* (1966) 58 DLR (2d) 1. In this case decided by the Supreme Court of Canada several directors profited personally from a mining claim which had been first offered to the company. The court held that it had been rejected by the company in good faith and that therefore the directors were free to take it themselves. This is a departure from the principles in *Regal*, since it is the presence or otherwise of good faith on the part of the directors that *Regal* specifically holds to be irrelevant: see D. D. Prentice, 'Regal (Hastings) Ltd v Gulliver — The Canadian Experience', (1967) 30 *MLR* 450.

[103] *IDC v Cooley* (above, n. 98); *Canadian Aero Service Ltd v O'Malley* (above, n. 4).

[104] See *Island Export Finance Ltd v Umunna* [1986] BCLC 460. The opportunity could be regarded here as 'fresh' in that the company was not actively pursuing it when the director resigned, and hence he had no duties to perform in respect of it. It could be objected that the director while in office had a duty continuously to review the prospect of obtaining business from the relevant customer, and that the director's subsequent contract raises questions about the loyalty with which that duty was performed. But the same could be said of a contract with a customer with which the company had not previously dealt. Clearly, there is a need to compromise between protecting the interests of the company and not rendering ex-directors economically impotent. The judge's finding that the defendant's resignation was not influenced by a desire to obtain the contract personally seems sufficient to settle doubts about whether there was any realistic conflict of interest, and in the absence of such a conflict it is appropriate that the issue should be settled in accordance with the law relating to the use of confidential information. In this case knowledge of the existence of a particular market was held to be too wide to give rise to obligations of confidentiality.

[105] Bishop and Prentice, 'Some Legal and Economic Aspects of Fiduciary Remuneration' (above, n. 27), at 303. If this 'overriding responsibility' were to be recognized the current uncertainty about the permissibility of directors competing with their companies would be clarified, in favour of non-competition: see generally M. Christie, 'The Director's Fiduciary Duty Not to Compete', (1992) 55 *MLR* 506.

expected should be regarded as falling outside the company's potential line of business and hence beyond the scope of the directors' 'channelling' duty.[106] The effect of defining directors' responsibilities in these broad terms, and assuming the application of the fiduciary principle without any reduction in its rigour,[107] is that all opportunities, whether exploitable by the company or not, become corporate ones, and it follows that directors must account for the proceeds of any (unauthorized) outside business activity.

The Fairness and Efficiency of the Controls

It might appear that controls as wide-ranging as this excessively restrict the freedom of managers to use their entrepreneurial skills for their own advantage. The force of this criticism depends, however, on how the commitments of directors to the company should be conceived. It is suggested that while they cannot be expected to give attention to the affairs of the business every waking hour, public companies should be entitled to assume that full-time executives will not be distracted by active involvement in searching for and executing private profit-making ventures.[108] A broad corporate opportunity doctrine should not accordingly be regarded as unfairly restricting management freedom of action, since managers should not be viewed as legitimately possessing the freedoms that are curtailed by it. Furthermore, given the difficulties of monitoring management effort referred to in Chapter 4, the exclusion of activities that compete for management time can be regarded as playing a positive role in promoting managerial diligence.

Nor in general[109] are there advantages to the company in allowing directors to take corporate opportunities for themselves such as to warrant a more

---

[106] See Brudney and Clark, 'A New Look at Corporate Opportunities' (above, n. 27) at 1025: 'In economic theory, and in practice as evidenced by the growth of conglomerates, the modern publicly held corporation should accept any opportunity that it expects will produce a risk-adjusted rate of return at least matching that of its current operations' (emphasis and references omitted). They suggest that since all opportunities are of potential interest to a company, the 'expectation' and 'line of business' tests adopted in some American jurisdictions are too narrow.

[107] It would, in contrast, be perfectly possible to have a duty to pass on information about potentially exploitable opportunities without reinforcing it with the fiduciary principle, the latter having the effect of prohibiting a director from profiting from any opportunity, even though it is clear that the company would have no interest in it.

[108] See Brudney and Clark, 'A New Look at Corporate Opportunities' (above, n. 27), at 1028–1032, who also suggest at 1002–4 that a less restrictive approach should be applied in close companies, *inter alia* because in such companies there may be no expectation that executives will work full-time and terms of service can meaningfully be agreed by the parties, and more generally the shareholders are able to exercise a real choice in the selection of directors and are better able to monitor them. Note also that suppression of outside business involvement on the part of members of the management board of public companies is an explicit objective of German company law. As Hopt, 'Self-Dealing' (above, n. 26), at 301, comments, 'The underlying regulatory idea is to preserve the full working capacity of the managing directors to the corporation.'

[109] But see n. 116 below.

flexible approach. Easterbrook and Fischel, however, argue otherwise.[110] Thus, if a director can exploit an opportunity more profitably than the company he should be entitled to take it (with the consent of fellow directors), because 'the increase in the value of the opportunity creates the possibility of a mutually beneficial transaction between manager and firm: the manager takes the venture, and the firm reduces the manager's other compensation.' In effect, the company recognizes that the director will serve the company part-time, for lower remuneration. While salaries are not 'typically' reduced at the time the opportunity is utilized, the director may be paid less in future, or might be awarded lower remuneration from the outset where the appointment is on terms that permit the making of private profits.[111] But this reasoning is subject to a number of rather obvious objections. First, the size of the director's salary sets a ceiling on the extent to which the company can benefit from management use of an opportunity, whereas its value to the company, even if the company could exploit it less profitably than the manager, may easily exceed this figure. Second, the assumption that managers will take opportunities for themselves only when they can exploit them more efficiently than the company rests on a view of the ability of markets to align management and shareholder interests that is for familiar reasons seriously exaggerated. Slack in the relevant markets will mean that managers will be able to take opportunities not only to create 'a bigger pie, which [they] may slice in favor of both investors and themselves',[112] but also to take the whole of rather smaller pies for their exclusive consumption. Third, the same market defects make the occurrence of realistic salary adjustments highly implausible, nor is it obvious that the company's interest in having an effective management team could be properly safeguarded where directors are free to make casual transitions from full- to part-time employment.

A final objection to the strict rule on corporate opportunities supported above is that the non-selectivity of the fiduciary prohibition means that potentially profitable ventures will remain unexploited, and therefore that the protection of the company is achieved at a social cost that might outweigh the social benefits.[113] This is unlikely to be true, however, since most opportunities which merit realization will in the alternative be taken up by a third party. Brudney and Clark point out that the majority of

[110] See Easterbrook and Fischel, 'Corporate Control Transactions' (above, n. 10) at 733–35; criticized by Clark, 'Agency Costs Versus Fiduciary Duties' (above, n. 5), at 70–1.

[111] See also P. K. Chew, 'Competing Interests in the Corporate Opportunity Doctrine', (1989) 67 *N C L Rev* 435, at 499–501, to the effect that directors should explicitly contract with the company about the terms on which they may make use of opportunities. It is, however, difficult to envisage how compliance with the terms of such an agreement could be successfully monitored.

[112] Easterbrook and Fischel, 'Corporate Control Transactions' (above, n. 10), at 735.

[113] See Chew, 'Competing Interests' (above, n. 111).

opportunities are not internally generated 'trade secrets', but ventures available to the world at large, and that the former can in any case be sold.[114] There may be some waste involved in third-party exploitation arising from duplicated effort in obtaining information about an opportunity and exploring its viability, but any such costs are probably more than offset by the social advantages that flow from reduced monitoring costs and the removal of the temptation for directors to dissipate their energies on private business ventures.

The Application of the Rules to Non-executive Directors

The strict rules advocated for executive directors are inappropriate for non-executives, though the courts have yet to draw a distinction. Looked at from the company's point of view, it does not depend on non-executives for the funnelling of business, and does not usually need them to attend to its affairs full-time. Similarly, from the directors' side, they are not paid a full-time salary and hence have a legitimate entitlement to engage in other business activities, including being executives of other companies. A suitable response, recognizing non-executives' limited functions and the company's limited entitlements, is to prevent them from taking personally opportunities that arise within the company or which the company is actively seeking, or passing on information about them to another employer, but to impose no duties as regards opportunities that occur exogenously.

This arrangement would necessitate an attentuation of the obligations owed by an executive director to his or her company where that director also holds non-executive office in another company, namely a subtraction of the duty to transmit information obtained in the latter capacity. Unless officers are to be prohibited from holding more than one position, which would clearly be undesirable, a compromise along these lines is unavoidable.[115]

Shareholder Consent

Shareholder consent to the taking of corporate opportunities by directors or associates seems unobjectionable in principle, that is, if it could somehow be ascertained that an independent and fully-informed majority was satisfied that the company's interests were not harmed by the taking. And although, as already noted, in general the company will not benefit from allowing directors to make use of opportunities, there may be rare instances in which the directors' personal participation is necessary to enable the company to

---

[114] Brudney and Clark, 'A New Look at Corporate Opportunities' (above, n. 27), at 1028–29.
[115] For a more detailed consideration of these issues, see ibid. at 1042–1045. The position where a director holds more than one part-time *executive* appointment gives rise to greater difficulty, which as Brudney and Clark suggest (ibid. at 1045) does not yield to a generalized solution.

benefit,[116] suggesting the need for a consent procedure. However, for the reasons discussed in connection with the suitability of the shareholders as a body for vetting transactions between directors and the company, there is a danger that in practice shareholder authorization would lead to the diversion of some opportunities which the company itself could profitably have exploited.[117] Authorization by fellow board members would for obvious reasons afford even less protection.[118] In view of the conclusion that the strict application of the fiduciary principle generally involves neither unfairness to directors nor damage to the wider economy, it would seem preferable not to permit the giving of consent at all in public companies.

Whether the members can as the law stands authorize the private taking of corporate opportunities is controversial. The argument that they cannot is usually supported by reference to *Cook v Deeks*.[119] In that case three out of the company's four directors entered into a railway constuction contract in the name of a separate company they had created for the purpose. The first company had successfully completed a number of similar contracts for the same employer and it is fairly clear that it would have been successful in obtaining the contract in dispute but for the directors' intervention. Using their votes in general meeting, the directors purported to ratify their actions, but the resolution was held to be invalid. That authorization/ratification with regard to corporate opportunities is in some circumstances effective, on the other hand, derives from *dicta* of Lords Russell and Wright in *Regal (Hastings) Ltd v Gulliver* to the effect that the directors in that case could have protected themselves by obtaining the prior or subsequent approval of the general meeting.[120] It is suggested that these *dicta* are correct from a doctrinal point of view, and also that they are reconcilable with *Cook v Deeks*. The relevant analogy is not with *Cook*, but with *North-West Transportation Co Ltd v Beatty*.[121]

Where a director is interested in a contract with the company the contract

---

[116] As conceivably e.g. in *Regal v Gulliver* (above, n. 27). See also *Boardman v Phipps* (above, n. 20).

[117] See Brudney and Clark, 'A New Look at Corporate Opportunities' (above, n. 27), at 1032–36.

[118] The advice of the Privy Council in *Queensland Mines Ltd v Hudson* (1978) 52 ALJR 399 indicates that permission may be given by the board for a director to take a corporate opportunity. If correct, this would expose the company to a severe risk of improper diversion. It is, however, inconsistent with the well-established proposition that only the shareholders can release the directors from their fiduciary duties. No support is given by *New Zealand Netherlands Society 'Oranje' Incorporated v Kuys* (above, n. 19), where it is clear that authorization was given by the members. The result in *Queensland Mines* is justifiable on its particular facts, in that all the sharcholders were represented on the board.

[119] [1916] AC 554, PC.

[120] [1967] 2 AC 134n, at 150, 157 respectively, [1942] 1 All ER 378, at 388–9, 393–4. Viscount Sankey also implied that ratification was possible at 139, 382, and Lords Macmillan and Porter concurred with the speech of Lord Russell.

[121] (Above, n. 45.)

is voidable not because its terms are necessarily substantively unfair, but on account of the defective procedure whereby the company is bound: the company should not be represented by directors who have a conflicting interest. Similarly, the directors in *Regal* were required to account for their profit not because in taking the shares personally they had necessarily harmed the company (the decision assumes that they had acted in good faith), but because it is procedurally irregular for directors to make a decision about whether the company is able to exploit a corporate opportunity where they will profit personally from a negative finding.[122] We have seen that in the case of self-interested transactions the procedural defect is 'corrected' by allowing the general meeting to confirm or disaffirm the contract. It is suggested that the explanation of the *dicta* of Lords Russell and Wright in *Regal* is that their lordships considered that by substituting the general meeting as the decision-making body the procedural defect that afflicted the company in that case could have been resolved in the same way.[123] After all, there was no evidence that in taking the shares personally the directors had deprived the company of a profit that it could have made itself, and they may actually have benefited the company by allowing the venture to proceed.[124] In such circumstances it is not surprising that the

---

[122] The position is more complex if liability is imposed in corporate opportunity cases on the ground that opportunities or information about them constitute corporate property, and not merely on the basis of conflict of interest: see e.g. the speeches of Lords Hodson and Guest in *Boardman v Phipps* (above, n. 20) but see also Lord Upjohn, *contra*. If the directors have made a profit from the use of company property then the profit belongs to the company, and ratification would be invalid as constituting a gift of corporate assets. The classifying of opportunities or information as property is, however, of doubtful vaildity (though appropriate in 'trade secrets' cases), unnecessary for the imposition of liability, and obscures the policy factors that justify liability: see G. Jones, 'Unjust Enrichment and the Fiduciary's Duty of Loyalty', (1968) 84 *LQR* 472; S. M. Beck, 'The Saga of Peso Silver Mines: Corporate Opportunity Reconsidered', (1971) 49 *Can Bar Rev* 80, at 117. A similar problem might be thought to arise if, whether or not the 'information as property' analysis is used, the proper remedy is the imposition of a constructive trust, rather than the personal remedy of account (in *Phipps* the former, the latter in *Regal*). Whatever the merits of constructive trusteeship in a particular case (on which see Jones ibid. at 498), it would, however, be undesirable to allow the form of the remedy to determine the effectiveness of ratification, and thus the prior issue of liability. It would be anomalous, furthermore, if antecedent authorization were permissible, but not subsequent ratification, as would follow from making the remedy determinative of the outcome.

[123] In *Prudential Assurance Co Ltd v Newman Industries Ltd (No 2)* [1981] Ch 257, at 308, [1980] 2 All ER 841, at 862–863, Vinelott J suggests that the *Regal dicta* contemplate that ratification would not have been valid if effected only through the use of the directors' own votes. The analogy with the ratification of self-interested transactions drawn above, however, suggests that the existence of an independent majority is not necessary. Lord Wedderburn, 'Derivative Actions and Foss v Harbottle', [1981] *MLR* 202, at 210–211, argues that Vinelott J's reading of the *dicta* is a false one. Cf. Sullivan, 'Restating the Scope of the Derivative Action' (above, n. 57), at 248.

[124] In the Court of Appeal, Lord Greene had commented that 'as a matter of business . . . there was only one way left of raising the money, and that was putting it up themselves . . . That being so, the only way in which [the directors] could secure [the] benefit for the company was

court should have considered that sanctioning the directors' conduct should have been permissible.

In contrast, the directors' conduct in *Cook v Deeks* was substantively, and not merely procedurally, objectionable. With regard to the railway contract, they 'deliberately designed to exclude, and used their influence and position to exclude, the company whose interest it was their first duty to protect'.[125] In other words, their object was manifestly to make a profit at the company's expense, in which aim they succeeded. Conduct of this kind ought not to be, and was held not to be, capable of being regularized through shareholder consent, at least where the majority is made up of the wrongdoers.[126] It will be recalled that the court accepted in *North-West Transportation* that if a minority were able to show that the terms of a contract in which a director was interested were prejudicial to the company ratification would likewise be ineffective. Similarly, it may be supposed that minority shareholders in *Regal* would have been permitted to attack the ratificatory resolution, if the matter had gone that far, if they could have demonstrated that the directors in taking the shares had acted contrary to the interests of the company (i.e. of the shareholders *qua* shareholders).[127] In the absence of evidence in *Regal* to that effect, however, the *dicta* indicating the availability of ratification are perfectly comprehensible.

If it is true that the members may permit the private taking of corporate opportunities unless it can be shown by a dissenting shareholder that the directors have failed to act in the company's interests, then the controls are likely to be much less effective in practice than the strict formulation of the fiduciary principle would appear to suggest. Given the malleability and other shortcomings of the general meeting as a consent-giving forum in a company with widely held shares, it would seem that directors minded to divert opportunities which the company could profitably have exploited will not find it unduly difficult to obtain consent, even where they do not themselves command a majority of the votes. In these circumstances, and bearing in mind the absence of compelling reasons for allowing directors to take corporate opportunities in the first place, it is preferable that shareholder authorization should not be possible at all in public companies. The controls on the exploitation of corporate opportunities are also weakened by the practical and technical obstacles to enforcement. These have been mentioned

by putting up the money themselves': unreported, quoted in the speech of Viscount Sankey, [1942] 2 AC 134 n, at 137, [1942] 1 All ER 378, at 381.

[125] (Above, n. 119) at 562.

[126] See further, Ch. 8 below.

[127] Assuming that the 'wrongdoer control' requirement for bringing a derivative action was satisfied: see Ch. 8, below. As Beck, 'The Saga of Peso Silver Mines' (above, n. 122) at 117, points out, the court is put into the position of 'judging directors' *bona fides* at the ratification stage, a judgement they have refused to make, and have protested they are incapable of making at the initial stage of deciding if there has been a breach of duty'.

already in relation to self-interested transactions and will be considered in more detail in the next chapter.

IV CONCLUSION

It has been suggested that for the proper management of directors' conflicts of interest there needs to be a body that is able to give consent in appropriate cases to self-interested transactions and to determine directors' terms of service, and also to enforce the fiduciary principle. The body currently charged with these functions (to only a very limited extent in relation to terms of service) is the general meeting. In companies with widely held shares the general meeting is, however, scarcely capable of performing these functions, with the result that the strictness of the fiduciary controls is undermined. The practical effect of this is unclear, though certainly with regard to remuneration the level and rate of increase of directors' pay is now widely perceived to be a serious problem. Only the insertion of a genuinely independent element into the governance structure seems likely to offer a satisfactory solution to this problem in particular, and to be able to provide a suitable mechanism to administer the fiduciary controls in general.

8

The Enforcement of Directors' Duties

Earlier chapters have examined the role of legal duties in obliging directors to act in the interests of the shareholders, and hence, on the basis of the provisional assumptions made in Chapter 1, in the interests of society as a whole. We have seen that legal standards have a part to play, though sometimes subject to severe limitations: in controlling management goals, by setting bounds to directors' discretion; in improving efficiency, by insisting on adequate decision-making procedures; and in regulating conflicts of interest (as well as in providing a remedy for the grosser kinds of fraud), by prohibiting transactions, in the absence of shareholder consent, where there is a heightened risk of self-interested behaviour. For any of these functions to be fulfilled effectively, however, there must be a realistic prospect of enforcement, and it is with this issue that the present chapter is concerned. The main aim is to highlight the obstacles to enforcement that are created by the continuing dominance of the principle of majority rule, and more fundamentally, the limitations of a system of enforcement that is largely dependent on shareholder action.

I ENFORCEMENT BY THE COMPANY

A right to commence proceedings in respect of wrongs done to the company is vested in the directors, as an aspect of the board's general management powers. Directors involved in wrongdoing are unlikely, for obvious reasons, to bring actions against themselves, and board dynamics may create a reluctance to sue even where those in breach of duty are in a minority position. Directors become vulnerable if there is a major change in the composition of the board, typically following take-over, though litigation against former directors is not a conspicuous feature of the post-take-over experience. Another possibility arises if the company goes into liquidation. It is, however, the function of the liquidator to collect in as much of the corporate estate as possible for the benefit of the creditors rather than to pursue errant directors for its own sake. The liquidator will therefore be assiduous in retrieving assets wrongfully transferred to directors or third parties, but other actions, notably in respect of negligence, where the outcome is speculative and the defendants may in any case be unable to meet the liability imposed, are unlikely to prove cost-effective.

An alternative to private enforcement is the commencement of civil proceedings by the Department of Trade and Industry in the company's name and on its behalf, following a statutory inspection of its books or an inspector's report.[1] This power is rarely used, which may be accounted for in part by the shortage of staff at the DTI, which has restricted the Department's ability both to collect information about malpractice and to take action where relevant information has come to light.[2] More fundamentally, the Department appears to have a limited perception of its role, no doubt bolstered in recent years by the Government's anti-interventionist philosophy. The Department has, for instance, lately expressed the view that it is not its function to duplicate the company's own system of controls.[3] That the DTI has the power to instigate civil proceedings is nevertheless an acknowledge-ment that there is a public interest in the honest and efficient operation of business that may not be adequately served by the involvement of public agencies in criminal prosecutions, winding-up proceedings, and disqualifica-tion of directors alone. The extent of the need for the public enforcement of management duties obviously depends on the efficacy of private enforcement. At least in the absence of a fundamental reform of the mechanisms of private enforcement, a more active policy of state involvement would seem to be desirable. As will be seen further below, there are motivational and technical problems that deter the bringing of private proceedings, notwithstanding that an action might self-evidently be beneficial to the company. It is also arguable, however, that even if private enforcement could always be relied on in cases in which the company stood to benefit, a yet higher level of enforcement would be in the public interest. This is because deterrence, and the creation and refinement of standards of conduct and performance, have the quality of 'public goods' which private enforcers, pursuing only private gain, are liable to under-produce. The existence of a 'positive externalities'

[1] CA 1985, s 438. For examples, see *Selangor United Rubber Estates Ltd v Cradock (No 1)* [1967] 1 WLR 1168, [1967] 2 All ER 1225; *Karak Rubber Co Ltd v Burden* [1971] 1 WLR 1748, [1971] 3 All ER 1118. The Secretary of State may also petition for an order on grounds of unfair prejudice to all or some of the members: CA 1985, ss 460 and 461, or for winding up under IA 1986, s 124A.

[2] See D. Chaiken, 'The Companies Act 1981 (3)', (1982) 3 *Co Lawyer* 115; V. Finch, 'Company Directors: Who Cares about Care and Skill?', (1992) 55 *MLR* 179, at 195 - 7.

[3] See Department of Trade and Industry, *Company Investigations: Government's Response to the Third Report of the House of Commons Trade and Industry Committee: 1989-90 Session* Cm. 1149 August 1990, at 3. The DTI explained to the Ombudsman some years previously that 'they have never operated a policy of active intervention in company matters, that it was not their job to set themselves up as an extension of the welfare state, and that they have no general duty to intervene against directors as champions of shareholders': see D. Foulkes, 'The Supervision of Companies — The Parliamentary Commissioner's Reports', [1974] *JBL* 23, at 26.

problem may therefore indicate a gap that would exist even if the private enforcement regime were not institutionally defective, and which state enforcement, through the DTI or a separate companies commission, might be able to fill. In any event, these factors suggest a rationale for a much more systematic policy of state intervention than is currently practised.

In the absence of enforcement by any of the above means and in the ordinary course of things, the proper functioning of the legal controls under current governance arrangements depends on the shareholders. Shareholder demands for action might have majority support or be voiced by only a minority. The rights of the latter to sue will be considered later. Whether there is a right vested in the general meeting to commence proceedings, as well as in the board, has long been uncertain.[4] In *Breckland Group Holdings Ltd v London and Suffolk Properties Ltd*, the most recent case in which the issue has arisen, Harman J held that the shareholders had no such right,[5] including, which is the point at issue here, when the action is against a member of the board. This would certainly seem to follow if the matter is treated, as it was in *Breckland*, as depending simply on the construction of the articles. The company in *Breckland*, as is commonly the case, had adopted article 80 of the 1948 version of Table A,[6] which vests exclusive management powers in the board, and it was held that these powers included the power to litigate. It is of course by no means certain that the directors will resolve to take action against a fellow board member even though the merits indicate that they should. The effect of the *Breckland* analysis is therefore that if the shareholders want an action to be brought they will have to remove the board and replace it with a more amenable one if the existing directors are unwilling to sue, rather than simply resolve that proceedings be commenced. This may be of limited practical significance in a company with widely held shares, given the difficulty of attracting majority support for action against the board anyway, but making the removal of the board a precondition for litigation will certainly not make that task any easier. Whatever the practical consequences, it is conceptually inelegant that the duties designed to control management should be enforceable only by management itself; the right to enforce the apparatus of control is surely distinguishable from the power to make decisions about the operation of the business and as such should not be regarded as a matter falling within the exclusive discretion of the board. It may be noted that when all the directors, or so many of them that the board

[4] See Lord Wedderburn, 'Control of Corporate Litigation', (1976) 39 *MLR* 327.

[5] [1989] BCLC 100; noted by Lord Wedderburn, 'Control of Corporate Actions', (1989) 52 MLR 401. Harman J held that the finding in *Marshall's Value Gear Co Ltd v Manning Wardle & Co Ltd* [1909] 1 Ch 267, which holds otherwise, could not stand with subsequent authority.

[6] Though it has been argued in the past that art 80 allows shareholder intervention in general by ordinary resolution: see e.g. G. D. Goldberg, 'Article 80 of Table A of the Companies Act 1948', (1970) 33 *MLR* 177. Its replacement in the 1985 version of Table A, art 70, makes clear that the general meeting may give instructions to the board only by special resolution.

would be inquorate, are the potential defendants, then notwithstanding *Breckland* the general meeting may be entitled to authorize proceedings. In this situation, depending on the articles, the board may be disqualified from acting, with the result that authority becomes vested in the general meeting in accordance with ordinary principles.[7]

Regardless of the technical position, as just suggested, it is extremely rare for a public company to sue its directors or ex-directors at the behest of the general meeting. The explanation is that the dispersal of shareholdings that is the cause of the separation of ownership and control is a phenomenon that inhibits shareholder involvement, not only in the democratic controls but also in the enforcement of the duty-based controls. Quite simply, the cost of active engagement borne by any given shareholder will normally far outweigh the benefits. If the litigation is successful the members as a whole may gain, but the increase in value of the activists' shares is unlikely to justify their efforts.[8] The task facing activist shareholders will usually be formidable. The existence of a breach of duty, and the desirability of litigation, will seldom be patent, and so it will be necessary first for individual shareholders to be alerted to, and then to investigate and evaluate possible breaches. Having decided that litigation is desirable, they must persuade and organize or collaborate with other members in order to generate the necessary majority support. But this is likely to prove impossible to obtain. With considerable informational advantages, and by virtue of traditional shareholder loyalty to the incumbent board and a desire on the part of the members to avoid costly disruption, together with their control over the proxy mechanism, the directors will in all but the most exceptional cases be able to protect themselves from attack.

---

[7] See *Foster v Foster* [1916] 1 Ch 532; L. S. Sealy, *Cases and Materials in Company Law* (4th ed., 1992), at 462. The 1985 Act version of Table A, art 94, provides that a director shall not vote on 'any resolution concerning a matter in which he has ... an interest', as distinct from the 1948 version, art 84, which stipulates that a director shall not vote in respect of 'any contract or arrangement in which he is interested'. The latter, applicable in *Breckland*, may explain why Harman J considered that the director against whom the proceedings would have been brought was entitled to vote on the issue as a member of the board, *ibid.* at 103. Special factors also applied in *Breckland* in that a shareholders' agreement provided expressly that litigation should be under the exclusive control of the board, and that an action should not be commenced without the consent of a director representing each of the two shareholder factions in the company.

[8] More so, for instance, than in replacing an under-performing board, which promises increased future returns on the shareholder's investment, and in cases where no take-over bid is likely may be privately cost-justified. There will rarely be a positive return on litigation, on the other hand. Even where the claim is of significant size and the defendants are able to meet it, there is no guarantee that an award will be translated into an increase in share price; indeed, the resulting disruption and damage to the company's reputation may depress share values even in a successful action.

II ENFORCEMENT BY MINORITY SHAREHOLDERS

In view of the difficulties involved in obtaining majority support for litigation and the limited prospect that actions will be brought in the company's name by other means, the effectiveness of the system of duty-based controls would seem to depend largely on enforcement by minority shareholders. There are, however, three important reasons why minority shareholder litigation is unlikely to lead to an adequate level of enforcement, namely that shareholders lack sufficient incentives to initiate proceedings, they have very limited access to information that might reveal a cause of action, and they must first wade through '140 years' accumulation of procedural codswallop'[9] in order to establish that they have standing to sue. These factors will now be examined in turn.

Incentives

As to the first of these, the would-be minority plaintiff will be spared the problems of assembling majority support that have just been discussed, but will still have to expend considerable effort in investigating the board's conduct and in pursuing any subsequent action. The availability of an order that the company should indemnify the plaintiff in respect of costs, thus spreading the expense of litigation among its potential beneficiaries, will go some way to reducing the plaintiff's financial exposure, though the direct legal costs are likely to be only a fraction of the total costs of involvement.[10] The prospect of these costs being recouped from any increase in the value of the plaintiff's shares following a successful action is remote. While the availability of an order for costs therefore reduces one of the reasons for not acting, it does not provide a positive inducement to litigate. The position may be contrasted with that in the United States, where 'the concept of the plaintiff's attorney as an entrepreneur who performs the socially useful function of deterring undesirable conduct'[11] has long been accepted. Under this system the nominal shareholder plaintiff may have an insignificant stake in the corporation and hence in the outcome of the litigation, and indeed may be selected by the attorney to enable the attorney to prosecute the action only after the latter has discovered the relevant misconduct. What creates the incentive for the attorney to do this is the size of the fee payable if the action is successful, which may take the form of a 'bounty' running

---

[9] L. S. Sealy, '*Foss v Harbottle*: A Marathon Where Nobody Wins', (1981) 40 *CLJ* 29, at 31.

[10] See *Wallersteiner v Moir (No 2)* [1975] QB 373, CA, [1975] 1 All ER 849; but see also *Smith v Croft* [1986] 1 WLR 580, [1986] BCLC 207, restricting the grounds on which an order will be made.

[11] J. C. Coffee, 'Understanding the Plaintiff's Attorney: The Implications of Economic Theory for Private Enforcement of Law through Class Actions', (1986) 86 *Colum L Rev* 669, at 678.

historically at 20–30 per cent of the amount recovered.[12] This arrangement has the advantage that it should in principle encourage the attorney 'to invest in search costs and seek out violations of the law that are profitable to him to challenge, rather than wait passively for an aggrieved client to arrive at his door'.[13] While no shareholder may thus have the incentive to incur these costs or initiate proceedings, their lawyers have. This system is open to abuse, notably the bringing of 'strike suits' (unmeritorious actions brought for their nuisance or settlement value) and collusive settlements between the defendants and the plaintiff's attorney whereby reduced recovery to the company is negotiated in exchange for a high fee to the attorney (itself payable by the corporation).[14] American practice is mentioned here not because it would necessarily be desirable to emulate it, but in order to account for the much higher level of derivative litigation in that country. Merely indemnifying the plaintiff against costs, or lowering the procedural hurdles faced by a minority shareholder, are not in themselves likely to lead to a very significant increase in derivative litigation in the UK.

A reason the level of minority litigation might conceivably rise is the growing concentration of holdings in the hands of institutional investors.[15] Apart from the greater likelihood of a direct return from their efforts, investors with sizeable stakes in a large number of companies may see some advantage in attempting to increase the deterrent effect of the legal controls in general by seeking occasionally to hold wrong-doing or inept directors to account. It is unfortunate in this connection that the Court of Appeal in *Prudential Assurance Co Ltd v Newman Industries Ltd (No 2)* should have sought to discourage such initiatives. Their lordships refused to give approval 'to the public spirit of the plaintiffs [Prudential, who held 3 per cent of the shares] who, it was said, are pioneering a method of controlling companies in the public interest without involving regulation by a statutory body. In our view the voluntary regulation of companies is a matter for the City. The compulsory regulation of companies is a matter for Parliament'.[16] However, the Prudential was not, of course, attempting to regulate the company in the sense of trying to impose some novel set of restrictions on its management; the aim was merely to enforce the company's existing rights at common law. That the Prudential might have been motivated by a desire to serve the public interest as well as its own interests by making the rules of company

[12] Ibid. at 678 n. 26.
[13] Ibid. at 679.
[14] See ibid. 701–20; American Law Institute, *Principles of Corporate Governance: Analysis and Recommendations* Proposed Final Draft (1992), 589 *et seq.*
[15] On the possibility of increased institutional involvement in the affairs of companies generally, see Ch. 6 above.
[16] [1982] Ch 204, CA, at 224, [1982] 1 All ER 354, at 367–8. These remarks are perhaps explicable in the context of the specific litigation, where even the direct costs far exceeded the damage inflicted on the company by the wrongdoing.

law into a functioning mechanism of control rather than just a set of elective behavioural standards hardly seems a basis for condemnation.[17]

Access to Information

The aspiring minority litigant, as an 'outsider', faces considerable problems in gaining access to the facts that will form the basis of any potential action. Only slender assistance is likely to be provided by the principal medium of communication between the company and its members, the annual report. The aggregate figures in the profit and loss account may reveal poor overall performance, but nothing, for instance, about the particular ventures or transactions that have contributed to that performance, and indeed losses resulting from negligent operations may be masked by success in other areas of the business. A possible source of relevant information is the directors' report, in which the directors are obliged to make a statement containing a fair review of the development of the business of the company and its subsidiary undertakings during the financial year and its position at the end of it.[18] According to the Financial Reporting Council the directors have a duty in their report 'to give a clear and informative account of substantial matters that have gone badly as well as those that have been a success . . . [there must be] a clear, frank statement when things go wrong, on what happened, why, and what the cost to shareholders has been'.[19] Such confessions are not, however, a notable feature of annual reports and, assuming that it is the obligation of the directors to comment in this way, the mechanism to compel them to do so does not currently exist.[20] It is true that the auditors are required to state in their report whether the information provided by the directors is consistent with that in the annual accounts,[21] but clearly there will often be no inconsistency where the directors fail to comment at all on a particular matter, and also a statement in the directors' report, while in itself misleading, need not actually be inconsistent with the accounts.

[17] And see the comments in G. R. Sullivan, 'Restating the Scope of the Derivative Action', (1981) 44 *CLJ* 236, at 237–8:
Judicial intervention in the affairs of public companies remains firmly within the realm of private law. The role of the court is limited to affording a practical remedy to a wronged plaintiff. There is no receptiveness to the principle, emerging in public law, that the vindication of legality is an interest in its own right. Unlike their counterparts in the United States and Canada, the judges of the Court of Appeal disclaim any analogy between directors of public companies and public officials [references omitted].
[18] CA 1985, s 234(1).
[19] Financial Reporting Council, *The State of Financial Reporting: A Review* (1991), para 12.9.
[20] The proposal for a more detailed commentary by the board, *inter alia* on the company's operating results, to accompany its financial statements is at the moment that this be on a voluntary basis: see Accounting Standards Board, *Operating and Financial Review* Discussion Paper (1992).
[21] CA 1985, s 235(3).

Turning to the functions of the auditors generally, it is their responsibility to report to the members whether the accounts prepared by the directors present a true and fair view of the company's affairs. In so doing it is not a central part of their obligations to detect or prevent fraud or other breaches of duty,[22] though the relevant professional standard (auditing guideline) provides that it is the auditor's responsibility to 'plan, perform and evaluate his audit work so as to have a reasonable expectation of detecting material misstatements in the financial statements, whether they are caused by fraud, other irregularities or errors',[23] and if the auditor does discover fraud he must 'probe it to the bottom'.[24] The auditing guideline provides that if there are irregularities of such materiality that the financial statements no longer give a true and fair view (which assumes that the directors were not prepared to alter them after the irregularities were drawn to their attention, for example, because they were themselves implicated) then it is the duty of the auditor to qualify the audit opinion. If, however, the amounts at stake are not material in the context of the accounts overall, and this may be so even though considerable sums are involved, no qualification is required, and indeed there is probably no duty on the auditors to take steps to detect irregularities that are insufficiently material to invalidate the financial statements in the first place. Instances of substantial malpractice may therefore fail to be drawn to the members' attention.[25] It is also currently no part of the duty of the auditors to investigate management efficiency or to comment on the wisdom or otherwise of business decisions made by the board.[26] All in all, the audit function cannot be regarded as a particularly fruitful source of information about managerial misconduct.

Assuming that the shareholders have become aware of possible irregularities or instances of incompetence, perhaps anecdotally or through press speculation or as a result of 'whistle-blowing', they will then face the task of obtaining more detailed information to enable them to evaluate the merits of

---

[22] It is however the responsibility of the auditors, 'so far as they are reasonably able to do so', to include in their report details of loans and other transactions involving directors which the latter have failed to disclose in the accounts: CA 1985, s 237(1) and (2), and sch 6. Some of these transactions may be unlawful.

[23] Auditing Practices Committee, *The Auditor's Responsibility in Relation to Fraud, Other Irregularities and Errors* (1990), para 9.

[24] *Re Kingston Cotton Mill Co (No 2)* [1896] Ch 279, CA, at 288–9. See generally D. Gwilliam, 'The Auditor's Responsibility for the Detection of Fraud', (1987) 3 *P.N* 5.

[25] The auditors may, if sufficiently concerned about management conduct, resign, in which event they must provide the company with a report of the circumstances connected with their resignation, which must then be circulated to the members: CA 1985, s 394. The auditors have a discretion (within the bounds of their duty of confidentiality), but not a duty (except in relation to companies in the financial services industry, see e.g. Financial Services Act 1986, s 109), to report misconduct to the relevant regulatory authorities.

[26] There has been a tentative proposal that the scope of the audit be extended to include 'aspects of propriety and efficiency': Auditing Practices Board, *The Future Development of Auditing: A Paper to Promote Public Debate* (1992), para 3.8.

litigation and to begin to put together a case. The members do not have a general right to information about the company's affairs in addition to that which must be statutorily disclosed, and the opportunity to question directors at the annual general meeting is likely to be of no assistance in this regard. The most appropriate course of action will usually be to attempt to persuade the Secretary of State for Trade and Industry to exercise his or her powers to appoint inspectors to investigate the company's affairs.[27] If the request is granted, the material contained in the ensuing inspectors' report will be invaluable in directing the minority plaintiff to sources of evidence.[28] The process of investigation is slow, however, and far more applications for an inspection are rejected than are approved.[29] It has been suggested futhermore that the power to appoint inspectors will not be used where no more than incompetence or carelessness is alleged.[30] The shareholder faces the dilemma in any event of trying to convince the DTI that an investigation is warranted, but without access to the facts that it is the purpose of the investigation to reveal. The DTI is much more willing to order a lower-key inspection of the company's documents by its own staff, which is quicker and cheaper.[31] The information discovered is, however, confidential and hence of no assistance to a would-be shareholder plaintiff,[32] though if sufficiently damning evidence is uncovered this may lead on to a full-scale inspection.

The Right of Minority Shareholders to Sue

Assuming that the shareholder has collected sufficient information to be confident that it is worth pressing ahead, the technical obstacles erected by the rule in *Foss v Harbottle*[33] must next be surmounted. At least in principle, there are good reasons for not giving standing to every shareholder to complain of every breach of duty to the company. The shareholder may be obsessive, or pursuing a vendetta against the board, or harassing management for its own commercial advantage. Even where an action is well-founded, the remedy that is ultimately awarded may not justify the expense of litigation

---

[27] Under CA 1985, s 431 or 432. See generally L. C. B. Gower, *Principles of Modern Company Law* (5th ed., 1992), ch. 25.

[28] CA 1985, s 441 provides that an inspector's report is admissible as evidence of the opinion of the inspectors in relation to any matter contained in the report, though as Gower, *Principles of Modern Company Law*, ibid. at 685, points out, this is likely to be of little value in itself. Note that pursuant to s 432(2A) inspectors may be appointed on terms that their report is not for publication.

[29] For the statistics, see J. H. Farrar, N. E. Furey, and B. M. Hannigan, *Farrar's Company Law* (3rd ed., 1991), at 518–9.

[30] See A. J. Boyle, 'Draft Fifth Directive: Implications for Directors' Duties, Board Structure and Employee Participation', (1992) 13 *Co Law* 6, at 7.

[31] CA 1985, ss 447.

[32] CA 1985, s 449. Information may be passed to regulatory authorities.

[33] (1843) 2 Hare 461.

and the other costs to the company in terms of the lost management time and adverse publicity that might be involved.[34] There is, then, a need for a filtering mechanism of some sort, but not one, as is currently the case, that manages to be highly restrictive and at the same time extremely ponderous. The danger of disruptive litigation can, furthermore, be exaggerated. Actions brought specifically for their nuisance value in the hope that the company will buy off the plaintiff are not, for instance, a feature of the British corporate landscape as they are in the United States, for reasons mentioned above.

The rule in *Foss v Harbottle* holds that in respect of a wrong done to the company, only the company may sue. The rule reflects the formal position that directors' duties are owed to the company itself and hence that it is the company, as the victim of the breach, that is the proper plaintiff,[35] and the substantive principle that the right to decide whether or not to bring proceedings should lie with the majority. There is, however, an exception to the rule,[36] to the effect that a minority shareholder may sue where there is 'wrongdoer control' (though, as we shall see, this may not be sufficient) and the breach complained of is unratifiable. Without this exception, directors with a majority of the votes (or enough votes to tilt the balance in their favour),[37] would be able to breach their duties with impunity. Owing to the wrongdoers' position of dominance the company's own machinery for considering and instigating litigation is paralysed, and so the courts, as a 'mere matter of procedure in order to give a remedy for a wrong which would otherwise escape redress',[38] allow a minority shareholder to enforce the company's rights by what is now known, following the American usage, as a derivative action. The more obvious expedient of liberating the company's own procedures from the malign influence of the wrongdoers, thereby facilitating a conventional action in the company's name, has never been adopted.[39] This would be inconsistent with the idea that voting rights

[34] The avoidance of litigation which is likely to be prejudicial to the company forms at least part of the justification for the rule in *Foss v Harbottle*: see K. W. Wedderburn, 'Shareholders' Rights and the Rule in *Foss v Harbottle*', [1957] *CLJ* 194, at 195.

[35] A principle which is 'fundamental to any rational system of jurisprudence': see *Prudential v Newman* [1982] Ch 204, at 21, [1982] 1 All ER 354, at 357.

[36] For the other 'exceptions', which are not relevant for present purposes, see *Farrar's Company Law* (above, n. 29), at 445–9. On the difficult issue of the extent of the ability of a shareholder to enforce the company's constitution by way of a personal action, see Wedderburn, 'Control of Corporate Actions' (above, n. 5), at 407–8 and the material cited therein. See also Gower, *Principles of Modern Company Law* (above, n. 27), at 660–1.

[37] See *Attwool v Merryweather* (1876) LR 5 Eq 464n.

[38] *Burland v Earle* [1902] AC 83, PC, at 93.

[39] See *Mason v Harris* (1879) 11 Ch 97, at 109, CA, per James L J:

It has been suggested that the Court has some means of directing a meeting to be called in which the corrupt shareholders shall not be able to vote. If the Court had any such power that mode of proceeding might furnish the best remedy in cases of this nature, but I cannot see how any directions for holding such a meeting could be given.

are rights of property that the members may exercise self-interestedly,[40] and in any case the 'wrongdoers' would not at the date of the resolution have been shown to be such.

The requirement that the breach be unratifiable is a further reflection of the principle of majority rule. If the majority are content to ratify, and hence to 'forgive' the wrongdoers, the minority should not be allowed to reopen the breach. The resolution is therefore binding on the company, and a minority cannot have 'a larger right to relief than the company itself would have if it were plaintiff'.[41] In determining whether a minority shareholder has standing, the question is not, however, merely whether a breach has actually been ratified, but whether it is *ratifiable*. The exception thus applies only to certain classes of breach; the remainder are placed beyond the reach of the minority plaintiff. The rationale for denying standing to a minority in respect of a breach that is ratifiable, even though it has not been ratified, depends on the assumption that, as the majority have chosen not to sue, they must be content that no remedy should be sought. If this assumption is well founded, the majority will ratify the breach if a minority is allowed to bring an action, thereby rendering the proceedings pointless. This assumption about the conduct of the majority would seem to be a realistic one, given that the minority has standing in any event only where there is wrongdoer control and the votes of the wrongdoers are counted in any ratificatory resolution, though, as will be seen below, it becomes less realistic on a liberal interpretation of what 'wrongdoer control' entails. That concept will now be examined.

Wrongdoer Control

The concept of wrongdoer control evolved in the context of the traditional company with a relatively small number of shareholders. Where the shareholders are active and reasonably well-informed the requirement serves its purpose fairly well and the test of wrongdoer control is more or less self-applying. If the defendant directors and their affiliates command a majority of the votes meritorious actions will inevitably be suppressed. If, on the other hand, there is a majority unconnected with the defendants the shareholders can be relied on to act in their own interests and to bring an action in an appropriate case. Where no remedy is sought it can be assumed with some justification that to do so would on balance be disadvantageous, and there is no reason to allow a minority shareholder taking a contrary view to override the wishes of the majority. It follows that there is a rationale for minority standing only in the former case, where the wrongdoers control a majority of

---

[40] See e.g. *Carruth v Imperial Chemical Industries Ltd* [1937] AC 707, HL at 765: 'the shareholder's vote is a right of property, and prima facie may be exercised by a shareholder as he thinks fit in his own interest', per Lord Maugham.

[41] Per Lord Davey, *Burland v Earle* (above, n. 38), at 93.

[45] [1982] ch 204, at 222, [1982] 1 All ER 354, at 366.

the votes. But in the modern public company with a large number of dispersed, passive shareholders, the justification supporting the wrongdoer control exception, that wrongs that deserve to be litigated will otherwise escape redress, applies in a broad range of situations in which the wrongdoers do not command a majority of the votes or anything like it. No action may be forthcoming, notwithstanding that it would be in the interests of the shareholders in general to sue, not because the directors are able to stifle it either through the use of their own voting power or with the assistance of shareholders who are in any way ill-motivated, but simply because of the inadequacy of the incentives to take collective action.

That a test based on strict voting control is unsuitable in the context of the modern public company was recognized by Vinelott J in *Prudential v Newman Industries*,[42] in which he held that there was 'no good reason why the court should not have regard to any other circumstances which show that the majority cannot be relied on to determine in a disinterested way whether it is truly in the interests of the company that proceedings should be brought'. Factors tending to undermine the integrity of majority decision-making, in his lordship's view, included the ability of the board to determine the success of a resolution in general meeting through the use of proxy votes, particularly against a background of low attendance, and the board's control over information, which might enable it to ensure that 'the question whether proceedings should be brought . . . would [not] be fairly put to the shareholders or even that a full investigation would be made into all the circumstances'.[43] In short, the wrongdoer control requirement would be satisfied 'wherever the persons against whom the action is sought to be brought on behalf of the company are shown to be able "by any means of manipulation of their position in the company" to ensure that the action is not brought by the company', with 'means of manipulation' not to be defined 'too narrowly'.[44]

As pointed out on appeal, however, the court is likely to be in a position to know whether the general meeting is incapacitated from reaching a proper decision only after a fairly full investigation of the merits of the claim: for instance, what are the damaging facts, if any, that the board has concealed from the members? The more realistic the assessment of the company's decision-making capacity, therefore, the lengthier and more complex, and ultimately futile, the preliminary proceedings become. The Court of Appeal's suggestion in *Prudential* that in trying the preliminary issue it might be appropriate for the judge 'to grant a sufficient adjournment to enable a meeting of shareholders to be convened by the board, so that he can reach a conclusion in the light of the conduct of, and proceedings at, that meeting'[45]

[42] [1981] Ch 257, at 324, [1980] 2 All ER 841, at 875.
[43] Ibid. at 327 and 877 respectively.
[44] Ibid. at 325 and 875 respectively. The test was suggested by counsel.
[45] [1982] Ch 204, at 222, [1982] 1 All ER 354, at 366.

seems not to take the matter much further. If the majority vote in favour of an action then the position is (relatively)[46] clear, but if a resolution to sue is rejected the judge still has to determine the decision-making competence of the majority before holding that a minority action should be disallowed. With a relatively crude test there is a risk that a minority will be denied standing in respect of actions that deserve to be litigated,[47] whereas with a more searching enquiry, including an assessment of the adequacy of the shareholders' knowledge of the circumstances and effects of the breach, much of the expense, disruption, and reputational damage that might be expected to flow from a substantive action will be inflicted at the preliminary stage. Restricting the standing of a minority shareholder to situations in which there is wrongdoer control, however defined, is therefore problematical in the large public company. It runs the risk on the one hand of rendering minority actions barely conceivable, and on the other of requiring a detailed, self-defeating enquiry into the merits of the claim at the preliminary, 'filtering' stage. It is difficult to see how this dilemma can be resolved so long as issues of standing are determined in the shadow of the wrongdoer control requirement. In any case, as suggested above, wrongdoer control, even on a wide definition, is too restrictive a concept as far as the large public company is concerned, if the aim is to allow a derivative action in all cases in which the company itself is incapacitated from acting. In order to fulfil that aim a test of standing that takes full account of the realities of shareholder passivity is required (see page 257).

Just because a company is subject to wrongdoer control, even when strictly defined, it does not of course follow that any action that a minority might choose to bring will be meritorious. The plaintiff might be ill-motivated or have a false impression of the chances of success. If such actions are to be excluded, therefore, an additional filter is required. Further, a plaintiff could evade the rule in *Foss v Harbottle* by falsely alleging that an unratifiable wrong had been committed, unless there is some procedure to substantiate that claim before allowing the action to continue. With these issues in mind the Court of Appeal in *Prudential* held that, as well as wrongdoer control, it

---

[46] Presumably, it will still not be possible for the action to proceed in the company's name without the board's cooperation: see above.

[47] This would seem to be the case with the test employed (in a slightly different context: see below) by Knox J in *Smith v Croft (No 3)* [1987] BCLC, 355, at 404, to the effect that 'votes should be disregarded if, but only if, the court is satisfied either that the vote or its equivalent is actually cast with a view to supporting the defendants rather than securing benefit to the company, or that the situation of the person whose vote is considered is such that there is a substantial risk of that happening.' The Court of Appeal in *Prudential* [1982] Ch 257, at 321; [1982] 1 All ER 354, at 364, did not go beyond observing that 'control' was capable of embracing 'a broad spectrum extending from an overall absolute majority of votes at one end to a majority of votes at the other end made up of those likely to be cast by the delinquent himself plus those voting with him as a result of influence or apathy',

was necessary for the plaintiff to establish a *prima facie* case that the company was entitled to the relief claimed and that the action fell within the proper boundaries of the exception to the rule.[48] In principle, some form of pre-trial judicial scrutiny of minority actions seems an attractive way of protecting the company from the eccentric or *mala fide* plaintiff. There is an obvious tension, however, between on the one hand ensuring that the process is sufficiently rigorous to be effective but on the other avoiding such a level of scrutiny that it becomes a wasteful duplication of the substantive action. The process advocated by the Court of Appeal virtually guarantees that the proceedings will be at the latter end of the scale. The effect of the court's insistence that allegations in the statement of claim should not be assumed to be true (as on the trial of a preliminary point of law) is evident from *Smith v Croft (No 3)*, where Knox J engaged in a lengthy and detailed consideration of the plaintiff's case. Under such a procedure not only is the company spared little of the damage that preliminary proceedings are supposed to avoid, but also the plaintiff is put into a particularly difficult position. As Sealy points out, being typically not 'at the centre of corporate activity' the plaintiff is 'singularly disadvantaged if the law insists that he follows the orderly sequence of pleading which requires a case to be clearly formulated from the start, and which does not allow discovery until the issues are well defined'.[49] Knox J's suggestion that the onus should instead be placed on the defendants to show that the claim is effectively unarguable, rather than on the plaintiff to establish that the action is likely to succeed,[50] is certainly much to be preferred.

A possible alternative to judicial filtering is to press into service the company's own decision-making resources in order to determine whether a derivative action should be allowed to proceed. This has the advantage of allowing attention to be paid not only to the chances of success of the action but also the commercial merits of bringing it. This was the approach adopted by Knox J in *Smith v Croft (No 3)*,[51] though as just noted a detailed

---

[48] [1982] 1 All ER 354, at 366.

[49] L. S. Sealy, 'Problems of Standing, Pleading and Proof in Corporate Litigation', in B. Pettet (ed.), *Company Law in Change* (1987) 1, at 12. The Court of Appeal's ruling on this point has not been followed in Australia, where in *Hurley v BGH Nominees Pty Ltd* (1982) 6 ACLR 791, at 794, it was observed that

in many cases, a hearing to determine whether there was a prima facie case would be almost as long as a full trial and a good deal less satisfactory. In such cases the only reasonable course may be to determine the issue of standing, if raised as a preliminary issue, on the assumption that the allegations in the statement of claim are correct. Even on that basis it may be desirable in certain cases to distinguish sharply between the issue whether the allegations in the statement of claim, if true, disclose legal liability to the company and the issue whether the plaintiff has standing to enforce any liability which might be disclosed.

On the latter point, see also *Smith v Croft (No 3)* [1987] BCLC 355, at 407.

[50] Ibid. at 407.

[51] Ibid. See also *Taylor v National Union of Mineworkers (Derbyshire Area)* [1985] BCLC 237.

process of external filtering was applied as well. His lordship held that the purpose of summoning a shareholders' meeting, as advised by the Court of Appeal in *Prudential*, was not to determine whether the defendants had control, but to ensure that 'a realistic assessment of the practical desirability of the action going forward should be made and should be made by the organ that had the power and the ability to take decisions on behalf of the company'.[52] To this end, the court proceeded to 'refine' the general meeting, constructing out of it a body able to decide on the merits of litigation uncorrupted by self-interest.[53] In the instant case the defendant directors held around 62 per cent of the votes and the plaintiffs 14 per cent. A third, institutional shareholder, with around 20 per cent, was opposed to the action. The court held that it should have regard to the wishes of the majority within the minority of 'independent' shareholders, and the plaintiff's right to sue was accordingly denied. Whatever the merits of this approach in relation to companies with a small number of shareholders,[54] it is difficult to see that it could provide any assistance in determining whether minority litigation should be allowed to proceed in the standard public company with widely dispersed shares. The independent shareholders are consulted only after it has been established that the company is subject to wrongdoer control (the issue is whether the minority plaintiff should be allowed to proceed, not whether the *company* should sue). Such a finding is likely to be made in a company with a large number of shareholders (where the wrongdoers will rarely have *de jure* control over a majority of the votes) only if a liberal interpretation of the requirement is employed, and the finding is likely to signify that in general the shareholders are insufficiently informed to make a rational decision about the merits of litigation. In such circumstances seeking to identify 'independent' (well-informed?) shareholders and allowing them to determine the issue, apart from posing considerable practical difficulties, would be a distinctly arbitrary exercise.

A more manageable procedure is that followed in the United States of allowing the fate of a minority action to be determined by a special litigation

---

[52] [1987] BCLC 355, at 402. It is not at all clear that this is what the Court of Appeal had in mind. Knox J observes that in *Prudential* 'the question of control pure and simple hardly admitted of any doubt', the defendants having no significant shareholding. But if the Court of Appeal was contemplating a broader test of control than voting control, e.g. if they accepted Vinelott J's view that the question was whether the majority could be relied on to determine in a disinterested way whether an action would be in the company's interests, 'the conduct of, and proceedings at' a general meeting would cast some light on whether the test was satisfied.

[53] In having regard only to the votes of the independent shareholders the court is not disenfranchising the alleged wrongdoers contrary to *Mason v Harris* (above, n. 30). The shareholders are not deciding whether the company should sue, but enabling the court to determine whether it is appropriate to allow an action in derivative form.

[54] For a critical view see A. J. Boyle, 'The Judicial Review of the Special Litigation Committee: The Implications for the English Derivative Action after Smith v Croft', (1990) 11 *Co Law* 3.

committee of the board. The practice that has evolved over the last 15 years or so, and which is confirmed by the American Law Institute's *Corporate Governance Project*,[55] in essence involves the court ordering an action to be discontinued where an independent committee of the board reports that prosecution of the action will be contrary to the company's interests. There are, however, judicial safeguards (not present in the *Smith v Croft* version),[56] in that the court must be satisfied that the committee's determination is based on detailed findings, and there are limits to the ability of the committee to forestall derivative suits in respect of fraud or improper self-dealing, even though the company is unlikely to benefit from the litigation, in recognition of the importance of the deterrent effect of the derivative action in such cases. The litigation committee procedure is of obvious value in a jurisdiction in which minority shareholders have a broader right of standing than in the UK and where under the impetus of the costs system there is a substantial risk that derivative actions will be brought from doubtful motives.[57] There would, however, only conceivably be a case for importing it into this country if the other hurdles facing the minority litigant were removed and unwarranted shareholder suits somehow became a serious problem. But it should be noted in any event that a British company that has an 'independent' board need not go to the trouble of setting up a litigation committee, since if the wrongdoers do not constitute a majority of the board a minority plaintiff will not satisfy the first requirement of a derivative action, that the company be subject to wrongdoer control.[58]

Ratifiable Wrongs

The remaining restriction is that a minority shareholder is allowed to sue, subject to the exception discussed in a moment, only where the wrong complained of is unratifiable. The term 'ratification' in company law bears a number of different meanings, the process serving different purposes. One usage refers to the normal agency phenomenon of curing a defect in the authority of an officer and thus binding the company in a transaction with a third party that would otherwise be void. Ratification in this sense is not relevant to present concerns. In Chapter 5 a second meaning was noted, namely the regularization of a use of directors' powers exercised for an improper purpose. The availability of ratification here is unobjectionable in principle. It is consistent with the interest that the proper purpose duty is

---

[55] See above, n. 14, at 685–796.

[56] See Boyle, 'The Judicial Review of the Special Litigation Committee' (above, n. 54).

[57] See above, 241–2. It has, however, been observed that the credibility of litigation committees is called into question by the uniformity with which they determine that derivative actions are not in the corporation's interests: see D. A. De Mott, 'Shareholder Litigation in Australia and the United States', (1987) 11 *Sydney L Rev* 259, at 275–9.

[58] See *Prudential v Newman Industries* [1982] Ch 204, at 221, [1982] 1 All ER 354, at 365–6; D. D. Prentice, 'Shareholder Actions: The Rule in Foss v Harbottle', (1988) 104 *LQR* 341, at 345.

designed to protect, that is, the shareholders' decision-making rights, since ratification in effect constitutes an exercise of those rights, though a positive vote may in practice be a poor reflection of member preferences, given the realities of shareholder voting.[59] A third sense of 'ratification', considered in the previous chapter, is the confirmation of transactions otherwise impeachable, in accordance with the fiduciary principle, on grounds of conflict of interest. In this case the ability to ratify is also in theory advantageous to the company, since a particular self-interested transaction may well be beneficial to it, but in practice, because interested shareholders are allowed to vote and by virtue of the unsuitability of a large number of shareholders as a consent-giving body, ratification fails to operate as an effective vetting procedure. The latter point was also made in relation to corporate opportunities.

The availability of ratification with regard to breaches of the proper purpose duty has in fact not been treated as a bar to minority actions, for the sensible reason that if it were the duty could be breached with impunity: the specific object of the behaviour that constitutes the breach is usually to manipulate majority voting power.[60] The fact that breaches of the fiduciary principle are ratifiable, on the other hand, currently excludes the possibility of a derivative action even though ratification has not taken place, forcing the would-be litigant either to accept the position or to undertake the difficult task of establishing that there has been a 'fraud on the minority' (see below).

The fourth meaning of 'ratification' is for the company to give up its right to a remedy[61] in respect of damage inflicted on it as a result of a breach of duty.[62] In so far as releasing the directors from liability in such circumstances is capable of benefiting the company at all, the advantage may perhaps lie in giving directors whose services the company wishes to retain the security of knowing that they will not be sued at some time in the future: release from liability can be seen as part of the terms on which the directors agree to continue to serve.[63] However, the court has generally regarded the shareholders in voting for or against ratification not as deciding whether releasing the

---

[59] See 139–40 above.

[60] It has been suggested that an allotment of shares for an improper purpose constitutes an infringement of the shareholders' individual rights: see *Re a Company (No 005136 of 1986)* [1987] BCLC 82, at 84–5. If this is so the rule in *Foss v Harbottle* ought not to be applicable in any case and relief should be available by way of a personal action. This view is difficult to reconcile, however, with the fact that such an allotment is ratifiable; this ought not to be so if the personal rights of the shareholders are involved, since it is not open to the members acting by majority to waive a duty owed to members individually.

[61] As Vinelott J points out in *Taylor v N U M* (above, n. 51), at 255, a binding release, as opposed to a decision not to institute proceedings, requires consideration. See also R. J. C. Partridge, 'Ratification and the Release of Directors from Personal Liability', (1987) 46 *CLJ* 122.

[62] Where the company ratifies a transaction caught by the fiduciary principle it also gives up a remedy, but the availability of the remedy here is not premised on damage to the company.

[63] See e.g. *Smith v Croft* [1986] BCLC 207, at 223.

directors from liability is in the interests of the company, but simply as making an unfettered decision about what they want the company to do.[64] It follows that in reaching a decision they are entitled to act in accordance with their own interests.[65] A consequence of this is that a resolution to absolve the directors may be perfectly valid even though it is passed on the strength of the directors' own votes and is of benefit to no one other than the directors concerned.

Not surprisingly, the law has recognized that it is necessary to impose some limits on the freedom of the shareholders to waive liability: the directors would otherwise be able to plunder the company's assets at will where they commanded a majority of the votes. Indeed, without some restrictions on the ability of the majority to act in their own interests but contrary to the interests of the company, the viability of the corporate form would be threatened, since it would be too risky to invest in a company in which the directors had, or might obtain, voting control. The cases hold therefore that ratification will not be effective in respect of certain types of breach, namely those that involve a 'fraud on the minority'. To constitute a fraud in the relevant sense no deceit or dishonesty need necessarily be present;[66] what is required is a breach which is damaging to the company and hence prejudicial to the interests of the minority. The mere existence of damage is not sufficient, however, since the principle operates only where there has been an enrichment of the majority at the minority's expense, as where the majority have 'directly or indirectly [appropriated] to themselves money, property or advantages which belong to the company, or in which the other shareholders are entitled to participate'.[67]

It is not possible then to ratify breaches involving the misappropriation of company assets or analogous breaches, but the ratification of negligence is permissible, regardless of the extent of the loss, because the element of differential treatment of majority and minority will normally be lacking. Moreover, since breach of the duty of care is classified as a ratifiable breach it also follows that a minority plaintiff will not fall within the *Foss v Harbottle* exception, even though ratification has not actually taken place. Thus in *Pavlides v Jensen* a minority shareholder was denied standing to sue in respect

[64] The following discussion assumes a model of the company in which only the shareholders' interests count. The whole topic of ratifiability will need to be reassessed if the courts adopt a multi-constituency model embracing creditor and employee interests: see e.g. *Fulham Football Club Ltd v Cabra Estates plc* [1992] BCC 863 and 85 above.

[65] See e.g. *Burland v Earle* (above, n. 38), at 94: 'a shareholder is not debarred from voting or using his voting power to carry a resolution by the circumstance of his having a particular interest in the subject-matter of the vote.'

[66] See e.g. *Cook v Deeks* [1916] 1 AC 554, PC; *Alexander v Automatic Telephone Co* [1900] 2 Ch 56, CA.

[67] *Burland v Earle* (above, n. 38), at 93. See also *Atwool v Merryweather* (above, n. 37); *Menier v Hooper's Telegraph Works Ltd* (1874) 9 Ch App 350; *Cook v Deeks* (above, n. 66), and *Daniels v Daniels* [1978] Ch 406, [1978] 2 All 89, and the cases cited therein.

of an allegedly negligent sale of a corporate asset at an excessively low price, there being no 'allegation of fraud on the part of the directors or appropriation of assets of the company by the majority shareholders'.[68] A limited exception to the ratifiability of negligence was, however, recognised in *Daniels v Daniels*,[69] where company property was again sold at less than its full value, but this time to one of the controlling directors. While as pleaded the directors' conduct involved only negligence, the transfer of value from minority to majority enabled Templeman J to hold that it fell within the fraud on the minority principle. In buying the property too cheaply the majority had benefited at the minority's expense.

That the fraud on the minority principle does not extend to cases of 'ordinary' negligence probably reflects a reluctance to curtail the right of the shareholders, seen as a property right, to vote in their own interests, and hence the right of the majority to prevail,[70] beyond the point necessary to prevent the self-interested diversion of corporate assets which would otherwise render investment in companies too hazardous. This minimalist conception of what the protection of shareholder interests demands is surely now seriously inadequate. It is no more acceptable for negligent directors to protect themselves from suit with the use of their own voting power than it is for them to condone wilful expropriation. From the wider perspective of this book it is not just the interests of the shareholders that are at stake but also the effectiveness of any attempt to regulate managerial efficiency by means of the duty of care.

There is, however, a 'revisionist' account of ratification which, contrary to the 'orthodox' one given here, casts doubt on the validity of self-interested absolution. In *Prudential Assurance Co Ltd v Newman Industries Ltd (No 2)* Vinelott J expressed the view that 'fraud' lies not in the character of the act or transaction giving rise to the cause of action, but in the use of voting power by interested shareholders to prevent a remedy from being obtained.[71] It might thus be said to be 'a fraud on the minority that those against whom the claim would be brought are in a position to procure ... that the company's claim, however strong it may appear to be, will not be enforced'.[72] The judge was obliged to concede that the authorities hold that self-interested ratification of negligence is permissible, but on his redefinition of the fraud on the minority principle this is exposed as an anomaly. In *Estmanco (Kilner House) Ltd v GLC*,[73] admittedly on facts unrelated to the ratification of

[68] [1956] 1 Ch 565, at 576, per Danckwerts J. See also *Turquand v Marshall* (1869) LR 4 Ch App 376, at 386; *Multinational Gas and Petrochemical Co v Multinational Gas and Petrochemical Services Ltd* [1983] Ch 258, CA, at 289, [1983] 2 All ER 563, at 586.
[69] (Above, n. 67).
[70] For an extreme statement of this idea, see *Pender v Lushington* (1877) 6 Ch D 70, at 75–6.
[71] [1981] 1 Ch 257, at 307, [1980] 2 All ER 841, at 862.
[72] Ibid, at 316 and 869 respectively.
[73] [1982] 1 WLR 2, [1982] 1 All ER 437.

negligence, Sir Robert Megarry V-C held on similar lines that it was an abuse of majority voting power to surrender a cause of action where this had the effect of discriminating between different groups of shareholders. As distinct from the traditional concept of fraud on the minority, the discriminatory treatment between groups of shareholders that brings the principle into play lies not in the breach of duty itself, but in the release of the right to redress. There is also a body of academic opinion to the effect that it is not the character of the wrong that explains the inability to ratify, but the impropriety of the wrongdoers using their voting power to exonerate themselves and leave the minority without a remedy.[74] It would follow on this view that negligence should not be ratifiable by the use of wrongdoer votes, but also that any wrong should be capable of ratification if an independent majority is in favour.

Whether or not these positions offer a better account of the authorities than the 'orthodox' view,[75] it is suggested that they do not provide a practicable or indeed an appropriate test for determining when a breach should be ratifiable in a public company. As noted earlier, in companies other than those with a very small number of shareholders, applying any meaningful test of independence will be problematical. But the issue is not merely one of independence. Shareholders who are independent in the sense of not having an interest that conflicts with that of the members generally might nevertheless vote with the directors out of habit or because they are unwilling to expend the effort needed to become sufficiently informed about the issues. Decisions by public company general meetings cannot therefore be regarded as a reliable means of determining whether the company should forego its rights, even where a majority of the shareholders are uninvolved in the irregularity concerned. It is suggested that significant progress in removing the obstacles that block minority suits in meritorious cases, enforcing the duty of care or other aspects of the directors' fiduciary responsibilities, will only be made by detaching questions of standing and liability from the principle of majority, including 'purified' majority rule. Plaintiffs should not, therefore, be denied standing merely because a breach is ratifiable, and there need to be limits on the ability to ratify that take account of the reality of voting in companies with widely dispersed shares.

---

[74] See Sullivan, 'Restating the Scope of the Derivative Action' (above, n. 17); C. Baxter, 'The True Spirit of Foss v Harbottle', (1987) 38 *NILQ* 6.

[75] For a statement of the 'orthodox' position, see Wedderburn, 'Shareholders' Rights and the Rule in *Foss v Harbottle*' (above, n. 34), at 96: 'Fraud lies rather in the nature of the transaction than in the motives of the majority.' And see Lord Wedderburn, 'Derivative Actions and Foss v Harbottle', (1981) 44 *MLR* 202.

The Way Forward

Two ways of escaping from this tangle of complex and restrictive authorities present themselves. The first demands legislative change, in the shape of implementing the proposals in the draft Fifth Directive, which may yet be some years from finalization. The second relates to the use of the remedies already available under sections 459–461 of the Companies Act 1985.

The latest draft of the Directive provides that a member or members holding shares of a nominal value of 10 per cent of issued capital, or such lower percentage as national legislation may provide, may require proceedings to be brought on behalf of the company.[76] This would allow a minority shareholder to bring an action regardless of 'wrongdoer control' and the ratifiability of the breach, and free of the other limitations attached to the derivative action. A successful ratification would continue to be a bar to recovery, but the Directive goes on to provide that the shareholders may not 'renounce the right to initiate company proceedings' in the face of dissent from members holding 10 per cent or more of the shares, or such lower figure as a member state's legislation might provide.[77] In other words, shareholders holding the requisite proportion of the shares would be able to block a ratificatory resolution.[78] It would seem desirable in each case to set a figure rather lower than 10 per cent, since the forces of inertia may prevent that target from being reached in deserving cases. A figure of 5 per cent (as in the previous draft) would in the typical public company allow an action to be brought or ratification to be blocked if perhaps two or three institutions were to collaborate. This is a somewhat crude way of proceeding but it has the virtue of being straightforward, and it would be likely to exclude eccentric or otherwise ill-conceived actions without at the same time being unduly limiting.

[76] See DTI Consultative Document, *Amended Proposal for a Fifth Directive on the Harmonisation of Company Law in the EEC* (1990), art 16. This is the position in Germany: see A. J. Boyle, 'The Private Law Enforcement of Directors' Duties', in K. J. Hopt and G. Teubner (eds), *Corporate Governance and Directors' Liabilities* (1985) 261, at 279–80.

[77] See DTI Consultative Document (above, n. 76), art 18(2). An alternative approach is that adopted in Canada, where it is provided by statute that ratification is not in itself a bar to actionability, but simply a factor that the court should take into account in deciding whether to impose liability: Canada Business Corporations Act, s 239. This seems to introduce an undesirable element of uncertainty, though it has been suggested that the upshot is that in fact few companies now rely on ratification as a basis for absolution: see B. R. Cheffins and J. M. Dine, 'Shareholders' Remedies: Lessons from Canada', (1992) 13 *Co Law* 89, at 94 n. 59. The rule in *Foss v Harbottle* has been abolished in Canada; the minority plaintiff will be allowed standing subject to demonstrating that reasonable notice has been given to the directors, the complainant is acting in good faith, and it appears to be in the interests of the company that the action be brought: see ibid. at 93–5.

[78] It would be desirable to extend this provision to resolutions giving prior authorization to transactions caught by the fiduciary principle, and also to approval under CA 1985, s 320. Presumably the directive is not intended to apply to breaches of the proper purpose duty, since this would enable a bidder with a sufficient stake to attack defensive measures that enjoy majority support.

It may be, however, that the dead hand of *Foss v Harbottle* can already be evaded through recourse to the statutory provisions on unfair prejudice. It is undoubtedly the case that behaviour that constitutes a breach of directors' duties can found a petition; a shareholder is not confined to seeking a remedy by way of a derivative action in order to complain of unfairly prejudicial conduct that is also a breach of duty.[79] Furthermore, the amendment of section 459 by the Companies Act 1989,[80] so that it now refers to unfair prejudice to the members generally and not just to 'some part' of the members, removes any possibility of arguing that an unlawful act or omission that has the effect of damaging the interests of *all* the members does not fall within the section. It is, therefore, open to a shareholder to seek an order under section 461 in favour of the company, in effect to enforce the company's rights. It seems, however, that the existence of a breach of duty will not be a sufficient ground for relief, in other words, that unlawful conduct will not necessarily of itself be indicative of unfairness. In *Re Charnley Davies Ltd* (*No 2*) Millett J held that while misconduct may be relied on as evidence of unfair prejudice, it was not the essential factor on which the petitioner's cause of action depends.[81] Some element of unfairness additional to breach of duty needs to be shown. If this element connects with the common predicament of the minority shareholder locked into a private company, who needs the court's assistance to escape, in the form of an order requiring the majority to buy the minority's shares, then section 461 will have little application in the public company as an alternative to the derivative action. Successful applications under section 459 for breach of duty would be confined to situations such as where the majority habitually treat the company's property as their own or a constitutionally inept board is sustained in office by a majority family shareholding.[82] As against this restrictive view, however, it would not be an unnatural use of language to describe, without more, the interests of a shareholder as being unfairly prejudiced where the breach complained of involves a diversion of corporate assets (the issue in *Charnley Davies* was negligence).[83] It would surely be perverse to argue that there is no unfairness in such a case because an action for damages or a restitutionary remedy commenced by writ will provide sufficient relief, if in practice those remedies are virtually unobtainable. Even in a case of negligence, while the breach of duty itself may not suggest unfairness, the necessary element of unfair prejudice may at least in some cases lie in the

---

[79] See e.g. *Re a Company* (*no 005287 of 1985*) [1986] 1 WLR 281, [1986] BCLC 68.
[80] CA 1989, s 145 and sch 19, para 11.
[81] [1990] BCLC 760, at 783.
[82] See *Re Elgindata Ltd* [1991] BCLC 959, at 994.
[83] The petition, under IA 1986, s 27, sought compensation payable to the company from an administrator alleged to have been negligent.

failure of the company itself to seek a remedy, particularly since here relief by way of a derivative action is not available at all.[84]

The role of sections 459–61 as an alternative to the derivative action is therefore as yet unclear. It would perhaps be unwise to be too optimistic. The recent cases on the derivative action show the courts ever more willing to erect new procedural obstacles, presumably in the belief that enforcement of the company's rights is a matter to be determined through the company's 'democratic' channels and that where a minority shareholder seeks to bypass these channels damage to the company is likely to result. If this is so there is sufficient latitude in the concept of 'unfairness' to give the court the scope to adopt a correspondingly restrictive attitude to the statutory remedy.

Conclusion

The implementation of the Fifth Directive proposals or a liberal approach to sections 459–61 would considerably enhance the ability of minority shareholders to enforce management duties. The underlying problem of the lack of an incentive to bring proceedings would however remain. Even if a shareholder is indemnified as to costs, this does not provide a positive inducement to take action.[85] One way of compensating for under-enforcement by shareholders was noted above: proceedings taken by a public agency. A genuinely independent supervisory board, considered in earlier chapters, offers another possibility. It could be a function of an independent board, not as with the American litigation committee to reject shareholder actions, but rather to bring actions against members of the management board on its own motion. With an obligation to monitor management and with unlimited access to the company's records, the independent directors would be in a much stronger position than minority shareholders so to do. Under such an arrangement minority actions could then be regarded merely as a fail-safe, available (not necessarily unrestrictedly) where the independent board has declined to act, or in relation to misconduct on the part of the independent directors themselves.

---

[84] It was the intention of the Jenkins Committee that relief should be available on a similar basis in proposing the reform of s 459's predecessor, CA 1948, s 210: see *Report of the Company Law Committee* (1962, Cmnd. 1749), para 206.

[85] A *Wallersteiner* order appears not to be available in relation to s 459 proceedings: see *Re a Company (No 005136 of 1986)* (above, n. 60). But as argued by D. D. Prentice, 'The Theory of the Firm: Minority Shareholder Oppression: Sections 459–461 of the Companies Act 1985', (1988) 8 *OJLS* 55, at 65–7, there is no good reason why an order should not be made where the shareholder is enforcing the company's rights.

9

Social Responsibility within the Current Legal Fabric

The discussion so far has proceeded mainly on the supposition that it is in the social interest for companies to maximize their profits, and that the rules of company law should be designed with that end in view. The justifying assumption, considered in Chapter 1, was that profit-maximizing behaviour on the part of individual companies leads to the maximization of society's wealth overall. Chapter 1 also noted that the right to pursue profits cannot be an unqualified one. This was both for reasons consistent with the wealth-maximization rationale (for example, extracting the maximum profit may impose costs on others, with the result that resources are used sub-optimally), and also for reasons of non-market social policy (certain forms of behaviour, whatever the efficiency implications, are deemed socially desirable or unacceptable). By assuming the capacity of external legal controls to steer company behaviour in socially approved directions, we were, however, able to arrive at a provisional 'ideal' rule for corporate conduct: companies should strive to maximize their profits, within the law.

It is the possible deficiencies of the 'ideal rule' that lead us into the topic of corporate social responsibility. In the sense that is relevant here, 'corporate social responsibility' means 'incurring uncompensable costs for socially desirable but not legally mandated action'.[1] It refers, that is, to behaviour that

---

[1] V. Brudney, 'The Independent Director—Heavenly City or Potemkin Village?', (1982) 95 *Harv L Rev* 597, at 605. See also E. S. Herman, *Corporate Control, Corporate Power* (1981), at 255–7; D. L. Engel, 'An Approach to Corporate Social Responsibility', (1979) 32 *Stan L Rev* 1. There are innumerable other definitions; for a list of some of them see G. A. Steiner and J. F. Steiner, *Business, Government and Society: A Management Perspective* (3rd ed., 1980), ch. 13; and see also Lord Wedderburn, 'Trust, Corporation and the Worker', (1985) 23 *Osgoode Hall L J* 203, at 226–8; N. C. Smith, *Morality and the Market: Consumer Pressure for Corporate Accountability* (1990), at 53–69. The relationship between corporate social responsibility and the wider subject of business ethics is explained by K. E. Goodpaster, 'The Concept of Corporate Responsibility', (1983) 2 *J Business Ethics* 1, at 2–3; see also F. P. McHugh, *Keyguide to Information Sources in Business Ethics* (1988), ch. 1; R. E. Freeman (ed.), *Business Ethics: The State of the Art* (1991), at 3–7; N. Barry, *The Morality of Business Enterprise* (1991), at 9–10 and ch. 2. Corporate social responsibility is a topic within business ethics, and hence narrower than it, in that it is concerned with the behaviour of corporate organizations rather than of business actors in general. Social responsibility relates not to the personal moral dilemmas of executives (e.g. whether to break a promise or engage in bribery) but to 'choices made *for and in the name of* the corporation': Goodpaster

involves voluntarily sacrificing profits, either by incurring additional costs in the course of the company's production processes, or by making transfers to non-shareholder groups out of the surplus thereby generated, in the belief that such behaviour will have consequences superior to those flowing from a policy of pure profit maximization. Clearly there are important implications for the legal regulation of companies if society would be served better by such behaviour than by companies seeking to maximize their profits within the law. It would seem to follow that, as well as using external modes of control to constrain particular types of conduct that are privately profitable but socially damaging or otherwise objectionable, the law should also be employed to modify corporate objectives to allow third-party interests to be given precedence over maximum profits in appropriate cases. In doing this, a relaxation of the obligation of management to operate the business in the interests of the shareholders would be required, and it would also be desirable to the extent that it is practicable to design mechanisms that would ensure that the various components that make up 'the public interest' were properly weighted in the decision-making process.

Social responsibility in the sense just mentioned will be referred to below as 'profit-sacrificing social responsibility' in order to distinguish it from a less specialized usage of the term. This describes behaviour as socially responsible where it reflects an increased sensitivity to the impact of the company's activities on third parties, or a corporate concern with social issues more generally, without any necessary implication that a divergence from the profit goal is involved.[2] Social responsibility in this sense may have a neutral effect on profits, or may even lead to an increase in profitability in the long run. It may, for example, have a beneficial effect on the company's reputation with customers and potential employees, thus improving sales and recruitment, or lead to direct cost savings, as where the company adopts energy conservation or waste recycling measures. The terms 'social involvement' and 'social policy' will also be used to describe corporate interventions in the social sphere in this wider sense. Social responsibility of this kind has not given rise to the theoretical controversies to which profit-sacrificing responsibility is subject, though this is not to say that identifying the conduct within the long-term profit constraint that is also the most appropriate from society's point of view is free of theoretical or practical difficulties. Nor does social responsibility in this looser sense have radical implications for company

(above, emphasis in original). Goodpaster also suggests that the issues that arise in relation to corporate responsibility are of narrower scope than those encompassed by business ethics , 'since they presuppose to a great extent the fundamental legitimacy of capitalism'. This view of the subject seems unduly restrictive, however, since it is possible to approach social responsibility from a critical position, seeing it as being concerned not only with the meaning, and methods of institutionalizing, responsibility, but also with its limits. See also n. 155 below.

[2] For a discussion of responsibility in 'profit-undifferentiable' situations, see C. D. Stone, 'Public Interest Representation: Economic and Social Policy Inside the Enterprise', in K. J. Hopt and G. Teubner (eds), *Corporate Governance and Directors' Liabilities* (1985) 122, at 137–40.

law, since it does not challenge the assumptions on which the legal model is based. Reforms will be noted later that might have the effect of increasing corporate responsiveness to social needs without damaging, and possibly even enhancing, profitability.[3]

An assessment of the merits of departing from the profit maximization within the law formula, and an exploration of the controversies just mentioned, will be undertaken later in the book. The purpose of the present chapter is to clarify what the concept of corporate social responsibility entails (not to decide what conduct *is* socially responsible),[4] to examine the extent to which company law is currently a barrier to profit-sacrificing behaviour, and to consider whether profit-sacrificing responsibility is actually practised within the existing legal fabric. The layout of the chapter will accordingly be as follows. Section I contains some preliminary observations about social responsibility and the separation of ownership and control, an issue with which it has been connected for over 60 years. Section II sets out a formal analysis of possible modes of corporate social involvement. With the help of that analysis Section III will examine the current legal position, involving a more focused consideration of some of the issues touched on in Chapter 3. The framework set out in Section II will also form the basis for an (inevitably incomplete) account in Section IV of current forms of corporate activity in the social sphere, with the issue particularly in mind of whether companies at the present time depart from the profit goal to any significant extent. A discussion (in Chapter 11) of ways in which the law might be reformed to permit or induce profit-sacrificing responsibility awaits the evaluation of the merits of social responsibility in Chapter 10.

I SOCIAL RESPONSIBILITY AND THE MODERN PUBLIC COMPANY

According to a view now no longer popular, profit-sacrificing social responsibility over a sustained period is impossible, on the ground that it is incompatible with the company's long-term survival. The view rests on the assumption that product markets are highly competitive, which as noted earlier, in the modern large-company economy is frequently not the case.[5] Companies enjoying a degree of market power are able to pass part of the cost of social expenditure on to customers without losing all their business (the rest of the cost is borne by the shareholders).[6] Their ability to do this is

---

[3] See Ch. 11 below.
[4] On which see 344–5 below.
[5] See further the discussion in J. L. Mashaw, 'The Economic Context of Corporate Social Responsibility', in Hopt and Teubner, *Corporate Governance and Directors' Liabilities* (above, n. 2), 55 at 58–60; Engel, 'An Approach to Corporate Social Responsibility', (above, n. 1), at 25–6.
[6] This is demonstrated in R. A. Posner, *Economic Analysis of Law* (3rd ed., 1986), at 393–7. A

not, however, unlimited,[7] and while competitive pressures do not make social responsibility impossible, they do provide disincentives against engaging in it. Baumol and Blackman for example point out that the 'business executive who chooses voluntarily to spend until it hurts on the environment, on training the handicapped, or on support of higher education is likely to find that he is vulnerable to undercutting by firms without a social conscience that, by avoiding such outlays, can supply outputs more cheaply'.[8]

The notion that management-controlled companies might nevertheless use their relative freedom from product market pressure for social ends came to prominence in 1932 with the publication of Berle and Means' *The Modern Corporation and Private Property*, though business philanthropy and 'humane' management have a much longer history.[9] In Berle and Means' view the separation of ownership and control and conditions of limited competition had opened up the possibility that the managements 'of the great corporations [might] develop into a purely neutral technocracy, balancing a variety of claims by various groups in the community and assigning to each a portion of the income stream on the basis of public policy rather than private cupidity'.[10] As noted in Chapter 2, however, Berle and Means exaggerated the extent to which management had escaped shareholder control: they underestimated the continuing force of ownership interests and their writings predated the recognition of the importance of market constraints arising outside the product market, particularly those imposed by the market for corporate control. Although these factors will in many cases still leave management with considerable discretion, they undoubtedly set narrower limits on the potential space for responsible action than Berle and Means supposed.[11]

At least as important as Berle and Means' underestimation of the significance of external influences is their implausible interpretation of management

company may also be able to pass the cost of responsibility on to employees, where it enjoys power in the labour market: see Mashaw, ibid. at 62.

[7] Where trading conditions are competitive the scope for social expenditure will also be curtailed, even where it is not unambiguously profit-sacrificing. As C. Kaysen points out, 'The Social Significance of the Modern Corporation', (1957) 47 *Am Econ Rev* 311, at 314: 'only the ability to earn a substantial surplus over costs makes possible a variety of expenditures whose benefits are broad, uncertain, and distant.'

[8] W. J. Baumol and S. A. B. Blackman, 'Social Policy: Pricing Devices to Aid the Invisible Hand', in Baumol and Blackman, *Perfect Markets and Easy Virtue: Business Ethics and the Invisible Hand* (1991) 46, at 53.

[9] See R. I. Johns, *Company Community Involvement In the UK: An Independent Study* (1991), ch. 2; Business in the Community, *Guidelines on Corporate Responsibility: IV A History of Corporate Responsibility* (1990); Herman, *Corporate Control, Corporate Power* (above, n. 1), at 251–5. And see n. 19 below.

[10] *The Modern Corporation and Private Property* (1932, rev. ed. 1967), at 312–3.

[11] See Chs 2 and 4, above. Manne suggests that the limit to management discretion is set by the costs that would have to be incurred by a non-altruistic bidder in order to remove the board: see H. G. Manne and H. C. Wallich, *The Modern Corporation and Social Responsibility* (1972), at 15–20.

motivation, amounting to 'an expression of an ideological position rather than to serious analysis'.[12] Thus, even if management had attained a position of autonomy, it is not unduly cynical to suppose that they would use their freedom more in their own interests than in support of an ethic of social responsibility.[13] Berle and Means anticipated the working out of a 'convincing system of community obligations'[14] to replace the duty to act only in the interests of the shareholders, but it seems clear that that system would in the main have to be imposed on managers from the outside: it has not evolved, and it would appear unlikely to, in the course of unaided management practice.[15]

Such evidence as there is does not support the view that management-controlled companies incur higher social policy expenditure than those under ownership control.[16] In fact, as Herman has suggested, there are good reasons for thinking that management-controlled companies are likely to be less, rather than more, responsible, at least in certain respects. Thus, large multi-location enterprises have limited, if any, regional or national loyalties, leading, in matters such as plant closures, to a 'structural bias toward *irresponsibility*'.[17] Further, the widely observed phenomenon of the subordination of individual ethical values to profit-orientated goals in large bureaucracies is liable to undercut the development of an organizational culture sympathetic to responsible action.[18] And in contrast owner-controlled companies, in the event of the owners being disposed towards expenditure

[12] Herman, *Corporate Control, Corporate Power* (above, n. 1), at 258.

[13] Ibid. 257–60.

[14] Berle and Means, *The Modern Corporation and Private Property* (above, n. 10), at 312.

[15] This is the position adopted by Berle himself in 'For Whom Corporate Managers *Are* Trustees: A Note', (1932) 45 *Harv L Rev* 1365. See also J. L. Weiner, 'The Berle-Dodd Dialogue on the Concept of the Corporation', (1964) 64 *Colum L R* 1458. And see C. Kaysen, 'The Corporation: How Much Power? What Scope?', in E. S. Mason (ed.), *The Corporation in Modern Society* (1959) 85, at 104, doubting the possibility of the development of 'professional' standards to control management discretion in the social field. For an expression of confidence in managerialism (meaning here the balancing by managers of the interests of affected groups and support for the expansion of management discretion to permit this) see A. A. Berle, *The 20th Century Capitalist Revolution* (1954) at 109–15, 164–88. Cf. E. S. Mason, 'The Apologetics of "Managerialism"', (1958) 31 *J Bus* 1, and see also M. A. Eisenberg, *The Structure of the Corporation* (1976), at 24–9.

[16] Herman, *Corporate Control, Corporate Power* (above, n. 1), at 260–4, presents some impressionistic evidence of the absence of a greater tendency towards responsibility in managerially controlled companies. N. J. Mitchell, *The Generous Corporation: A Political Analysis of Economic Power* (1989), at 40, in a study of the 200 largest US corporations on which Berle and Means' findings were based, has concluded that there was 'no significant relationship between type of control and the presence or absence of social policy'. For a UK study, see B. Shenfield, *Company Boards: Their Responsibilities to Shareholders, Employees, and the Community* (1971), at 114, who finds no correlation between size of directors' shareholdings (as an indicator of the degree of ownership control) and company charitable giving.

[17] Herman, ibid. at 216 (emphasis moved).

[18] See e.g. R. A. Dahl, *A Prelude to Economic Democracy* (1985), at 98: 'Complexity and giantism have created such a distance between our actions and their consequences that our capacity for moral action has been dangerously impoverished.'

for socially responsible purposes, are unencumbered by the investor-related constraints that inhibit similar inclinations in companies under management control. It may be noted in this context that what are perhaps the best-known examples of business philanthropy in this country, the various 'model' communities established by nineteenth-century industrialists and the provision by them of related welfare benefits, were not the product of management-controlled enterprises but were the creations of dominant individual owners,[19] often inspired by nonconformist religious beliefs (though even here motives were rarely unambiguously charitable),[20] and with strong local loyalties. Without prejudging the issue of the extent, if any, to which modern public companies engage in profit-sacrificing social responsibility, it is clear at least that the organizational and motivational factors which permitted and encouraged nineteenth-century business philanthropy are unlikely to be reproduced in the modern, large company context.[21]

We might finally note certain weaknesses in the argument that the separation of ownership and control provides a reason why companies *should* depart from the conventional goal of maximizing profits for the benefit of

---

[19] See e.g. J. F. C. Harrison, *Robert Owen and the Owenites in Britain and America* (1969) (New Lanark); J. Reynolds, *The Great Paternalist* (1983) (Sir Titus Salt and Saltaire); C. Wilson, *The History of Unilever* vol. 1 (1954), ch. 10 (William, later Lord, Lever and Port Sunlight); I. O. Williams, *The Firm of Cadbury, 1831–1931* (1931) (George Cadbury and Bourneville); and see generally I. C. Bradley, *Enlightened Entrepreneurs* (1986), and R. Fitzgerald, *British Labour Management and Industrial Welfare 1846–1939* (1988), at 125. The businesses of Owen and Salt were unincorporated; Port Sunlight was begun in 1888, two years before Lever Brothers was incorporated, though development continued for many years after, and other employee benefits not associated with the village were provided by the company. For much of this period, however, the company was dominated by Lever family interests. Bourneville was built by George Cadbury, not the company, though the latter subsequently provided financial assistance.

[20] Against the background of the appalling living and working conditions endured by industrial workers, improved domestic standards and the provision of educational and recreational facilities would undoubtedly, and were expected to, lead to higher productivity. Nor should the paternalistic character of these interventions be overlooked. The benefits were often provided on terms which involved major intrusions into employees' personal affairs. A contemporary witness observed, for instance, that 'no man of independent turn of mind can breathe for long the atmosphere of Port Sunlight.' The flavour of Lever's attitude is revealed in the following explanation of his preference for company-provided benefits over direct profit-sharing: 'I told them [the workers]: "£8 is an amount which is soon spent, and it will not do you much good if you send it down your throats in the form of bottles of whisky, bags of sweets, or fat geese for Christmas. On the other hand, if you leave this money with me, I shall use it to provide for you everything which makes life pleasant — viz nice houses, comfortable homes, and healthy recreation"' : Wilson, ibid. at 146–7. Problems of employer dominance and interference were also evident on a larger scale in the 'company towns' in the USA. The most famous was Pullman, Illinois: for a description, see M. Heald, *The Social Responsibilities of Business: Company and Community 1900–1960* (1970), at 7–9, and for a political analysis M. Walzer, *Spheres of Justice* (1983), at 295–8, and 300–3.

[21] See further, H. J. Perkin, *The Rise of Professional Society: England Since 1880* (1989), at 302–5, and for an example of a company which was actively involved in community affairs under family control ceasing to be so as a subsidiary of a foreign multinational, see B. Harvey, S. Smith, and B. Wilkinson, *Managers and Corporate Social Policy: Private Solutions to Public Problems?* (1984), ch. 5.

shareholders, in favour of serving 'third-party' or social interests. Berle and Means' case relies on the view that the shareholders' role has become functionally attenuated: as mere 'passive' property-owners, no longer involved in the running of the enterprise, the shareholders play little part in causing the company to fulfil the profit maximization objective.[22] This being so, they have 'surrendered the right that the corporation should be operated in their sole interest'.[23] As noted earlier, however, while the shareholders are generally passive in relation to the exercise of their governance powers, they are active as sellers of shares. Their right to the residual income does therefore have a functional significance, given the operation of the market for control.[24] But even if the shareholders did not have a role in providing management with an incentive to maximize profits, this in itself would say little about the desirability of companies ceasing to behave strictly in accordance with the dictates of profit and the market. The proper response to the inadequacy of current methods of inducing the directors to maximize profits might be to seek alternative modes of control over management, not to abandon the goal of profits and its supporting theory of social wealth maximization. What is needed before rejecting the profit goal, therefore, is an explanation of why profit maximization within the law might fail adequately to serve the social interest. If it does so fail it also follows, it might be noted, that corporate objectives should be changed, whether or not there has been a separation of ownership and control. The possible deficiencies of the profit maximization within the law formula, and the possible advantages of profit-sacrificing responsibility, are the subject of the next chapter.

II A TYPOLOGY OF CORPORATE SOCIAL RESPONSIBILITY

This section will set out a particular way of categorizing social responsibility. At this stage the analysis will be purely formal, in that it will not describe actual behaviour and some of the distinctions drawn may in practice be difficult to apply with precision. The categories may furthermore in reality partially overlap. The purpose of classifying responsibility in this way is to create a framework that should make the task of interpreting business attitudes to the social role of companies and the actual practice of social responsibility more manageable. Equally, it will provide a context for a consideration of the legal rules which regulate corporate social involvement and enable us to discriminate between different forms of responsibility for the purposes of evaluation.

[22] Berle and Means, *The Modern Corporation* (above, n. 10), book IV, chs 1 and 2.
[23] Ibid. at 312.
[24] See further the debate between Manne and Berle: H. G. Manne, 'The "Higher" Criticism of the Modern Corporation', (1962) 62 *Colum L Rev* 399; A. A. Berle, 'Modern Functions of the Corporate System', (1962) 62 *Colum L Rev* 433.

What kinds of behaviour are envisaged when it is said that a company acts or should act in a socially responsible way? An appropriate starting point is to distinguish between what might be termed 'relational responsibility' and 'social activism',[25] ignoring for the moment the profit implications of either kind of behaviour. The first category refers to attempts to promote the welfare of groups such as employees, customers, or neighbours, who are affected by the conduct of the company's mainstream business activities. It involves limiting the damaging impact of the company's processes or products ('self-regulation'), or treating more 'fairly' the groups with which the company comes into contact as a necessary part of carrying on its business. 'Social activism', on the other hand, refers to conduct which is putatively beneficial to society or particular interest groups, but which falls outside the scope of the company's ordinary commercial operations (though the conduct may nevertheless be commercially beneficial to it). Examples include charitable donations, arts sponsorship, and certain forms of involvement in education or inner-city regeneration. The distinction is an important one because the two types of behaviour involve different perceptions of the function of social responsibility and the role of business in the life of the community. The practice of relational responsibility involves an attempt to achieve a improved accommodation of the various interests affected by corporate activity, but does not envisage a wider social role for the company. Social activism, in contrast, constitutes an effort by companies to address social issues that arise independently of the way the company conducts is business and thus represents an extension of corporate activity into essentially non-commercial spheres. To draw this distinction is neither to applaud nor condemn the phenomena described, but merely to point out that different evaluative criteria may apply.

Relational Responsibility

Taking relational responsibility first, there is an important distinction to be drawn within this category between responsibility which involves a shift in corporate goals and responsibility which, more modestly, requires the recognition of a constraint on the pursuit of existing goals. This distinction calls for some elaboration. By a 'goal' is meant the ultimate objective for which an organization exists. A 'constraint', on the other hand, is something which limits or structures the means which may be adopted in fulfilling that objective; it may block certain courses of action or restrict the space within which the organization is free to act in achieving its objectives. The existence

[25] For a distinction along similar lines, see J. Simon, C. Powers and J. Gunnemann, *The Ethical Investor: Universities and Corporate Responsibility* (1972), at 27, and S. Beck, 'Corporate Power and Public Policy', in I. Bernier and A. Lajoie (eds), *Consumer Protection, Environmental Law and Corporate Power* (1985), 181, at 204–5.

of constraints may make pursuit of a goal more difficult, but unlike goals they are not ends to be maximized, but rather reflect interests that must be respected only to a finite degree.

A demand for social responsibility might, then, involve a demand that a company change its goals, for instance, that the business be run so as to maximize the welfare of employees or of customers, and no longer with a view to maximizing shareholder wealth. Or the company might adopt multiple goals, with the role of management being to balance the interests of the various affected groups at its discretion. The conception of social responsibility invoked might, in contrast, require only that the company recognize additional or more rigorous constraints in the course of pursuing the traditional profit-maximization (or at least, profit-making) objective.[26] A company might be regarded as socially responsible on this view where managers accept, for example, an obligation to provide safe working conditions and to pay 'fair' wages, but without there being any suggestion that directors do or should see their role as being to arbitrate between employees and shareholders in the manner of Berle and Means' 'neutral technocracy', as though these groups, or others, had equal claims on the company's resources.

Constraint-Based Responsibility

'Responsibility' involving a shift in goals should now be sufficiently clear, but constraint-based responsibility requires further discussion. Constraints on corporate action are of different origins. In addition to practical constraints, such as a lack of capital or a shortage of skilled employees, companies are most obviously bound by legal constraints.[27] For example, in seeking to maximize its profits a company is not permitted to discharge unlimited noxious gases into the atmosphere, bribe government officials, or sell dangerously defective products. If a claim of responsibility is to mean more than a mere commitment to compliance with law, however, it must refer to the acceptance of some form of additional, self-imposed constraints. Our final distinction within the category of relational responsibility is thus between two kinds of self-imposed constraint. These are 'prudential constraints' and 'other-regarding constraints'.

Prudential constraints are reflected in rules and practices that require a

---

[26] Profit maximization is for convenience referred to here and below as the conventional management goal, though it should be borne in mind that as a description of management conduct this will often be an over-simplification, since divergence from the pursuit of profit may take place for self-interested reasons: see Ch. 2, above.

[27] A company might not view legal constraints as involving absolute prohibitions, but might treat them instead as prudential constraints (see below), to be complied with only to the extent required for long-term profitability. It has been argued, furthermore, that it is in the public interest that companies should adopt this approach: see below 330–3. For the time being, legal constraints will be regarded as imposing more or less absolute obligations.

sacrifice of profits in the short term, but which have a long-term profit pay-off for the company. It may be profitable in the short term to produce shoddy goods, for example, or to provide poor working conditions for employees, or to use production processes that are injurious to the environment, either at home or overseas, where legislative controls may be less stringent. If, however, the facts become widely known, then at least in some cases the loss to the company as a consequence of reputational damage might exceed the immediate financial returns. The purpose of prudential constraints is to prevent long-term profitability from being put at risk by attempts of this kind to make gains in the short term.

Although not legally mandated, prudential constraints are 'self-imposed' in only a limited sense. They constitute an economically rational response to the preferences of the parties with whom the company interacts in various markets or of public opinion more generally, and to that extent should be viewed as being externally induced rather than wholly voluntary. A company with a good environmental record, for example, is likely to find it easier to sell its products or to recruit high-quality employees, and accordingly has an incentive to practise, or at least to claim, environmentally sound policies. Market pressure is functioning here as a mechanism of social control, supplementary to legal regulation, by giving effect to the preferences of market participants with regard to company behaviour, both as it affects themselves and sometimes also third parties. Social responsibility as manifested by the adoption of prudential constraints can thus be described as achieving an accommodation of corporate and social interests within the bounds of self-interested behaviour, which is superior to that likely to result from cruder, less reflective means of attempting to maximize profits. While the non-voluntary aspect of prudential constraints has been stressed, it should however be noted also that precisely which constraints should be adopted for a profit-maximizing outcome is far from self-evident; selecting them involves interpretation and judgement and hence involves an exercise of management discretion rather than an automatic response to unambiguous market signals.

Although the company and affected groups both benefit from companies being socially responsible in the way just described, the adoption of constraints to the extent necessary to maximize profits in the long term is, for reasons that will be considered later, still compatible with substantial and possibly unacceptable damage to third-party interests.[28] This therefore leaves room for the second type of self-imposed constraints. *Other-regarding* constraints are directly focused on protecting the interests of parties likely to be affected by the company's activities. They are adopted not with the ultimate aim of protecting profitability, but for the sake of the relevant

---

[28] See 288 and Ch. 10 below.

interests themselves. They are thus a response to a supposed moral imperative that conflicts with profit maximization, not merely a self-interested response to the moral preferences of others.[29] Examples include compliance with higher health and safety standards than the local law or maintenance of the company's reputation demand, or a refusal to make employees redundant where maximization of shareholder wealth would so dictate. Other-regarding constraints may also reflect more abstract ethical concerns. Thus a company may subscribe to the principle that it should not trade in a country which is guilty of oppressing a section of its population on racial or religious grounds, or that it should not deal in certain commodities, such as tobacco, animal products, or armaments. Other-regarding constraints have so far been expressed in negative terms, but a constraint may also reflect a positive obligation, for example, to treat customers fairly, or to provide working conditions that allow employees to enhance their skills rather than reducing opportunities for personal development and self-expression. Notwithstanding their positive character, these obligations can be viewed as constraints in that they are conditions that a company might set itself as a prerequisite of pursuing profits.[30] To sum up, the function of other-regarding constraints is to safeguard the interests of outsiders (including employees), not those of the company. As such, their acceptance reflects an acknowledgement of some form of moral obligation on the company's part, compliance with which may be profit-reducing.

The extent to which in practice a given company's acceptance of other-regarding constraints will involve a departure from profit maximization depends on two factors. First, naturally enough, it depends on the particular constraints that the company decides to respect. A company might, for example, accept a moral obligation with regard to employee safety, but not one in relation to the environment. The second factor is the weight that the company attributes to the constraint adopted. For instance, a company may view making employees redundant as something to be avoided (because it recognizes a moral obligation to them), but only if this can be arranged without excessive cost to itself.[31] In other words, the moral obligation that

---

[29] See J. Ladd, 'Morality and the Ideal of Rationality in Formal Organizations', (1970) 54 *The Monist* 489, at 499; K. E. Goodpaster, 'Ethical Imperatives and Corporate Leadership', in R. E. Freeman (ed.), *Business Ethics: The State of the Art* (1991) 89, at 95–9.

[30] Distinguishing between the adoption of an other-regarding constraint and a shift in goals may prove difficult in practice, e.g. with regard to product quality, attention to consumer interests might in principle indicate that consumer satisfaction was a corporate goal (and profitability merely a survival condition or concurrent goal), or alternatively that the supplier accepts a moral obligation to treat customers 'fairly', but has a single goal of benefiting shareholders. The distinction turns on the arcane issue of the content of 'fairness', with action in the interests of customers which goes beyond fairness indicating espousal of a non-profit goal.

[31] This is not the same thing as a prudential constraint, and in principle may result in different behaviour. The purpose of a prudential constraint with regard to redundancy is to protect the company's interests (e.g. to avoid damaging employee morale). An other-regarding

underlies the constraint may not be regarded by the company as an absolute one. The effect of the constraint here may be to stimulate the company into seeking alternative courses of action so as to avoid the need for redundancy, or to decrease the numbers of employees involved, or into taking steps to ameliorate the consequences of lay-offs. It does not, however, entail a prohibition on discharging employees no matter how serious the implications for the company may be. Other-regarding constraints are accordingly not necessarily impervious to cost considerations, but unlike prudential constraints they entail costs that may not be recouped, even in the long term.

Social Activism

A parallel set of distinctions to those found within relational responsibility also exists within the social activism category and can be dealt with more briefly. Thus a company might, in theory, adopt as a *goal* the amelioration of a social problem that exists independently of the way it conducts its business, for example, youth unemployment, urban decay, or Third-World poverty. Alternatively, while it adheres to a single goal of profit maximization, it may accept that companies must comply with certain finite social *obligations* as an adjunct to carrying on business. The language of obligations is here more appropriate than that of constraints, but a similar contrast between other-regarding and prudential considerations applies. Thus management may subscribe to the view that donations or other forms of social activism are an authentic moral duty that companies must discharge irrespective of whether they also serve the corporate self-interest. Companies may, on the other hand, make donations to charity or become involved in community activities in response to the perceived demands of social convention, anticipating that failure to give or to participate will have adverse effects on the company's image. More positively, and unrelated to any idea of obligation, company involvement may be regarded by management as a form of advertising, with an intended, if somewhat uncertain, pay-back, or it may similarly be viewed as an investment in the community, by contributing to the preservation of the company's markets or the development of the skills of potential employees.

III THE SCOPE FOR SOCIAL POLICY WITHIN THE LEGAL MODEL

With the above distinctions in mind, this section will consider the extent to which social involvement is permitted by the rules that set boundaries to

---

constraint in contrast would countenance some loss to the company in the long term, albeit not of an unlimited amount.

management discretion. The important issue of the extent of managers' awareness of the relevant rules and the degree to which their behaviour is affected by them will not be discussed, since there is insufficient evidence relating to these questions to make such a discussion worthwhile.[32] Rather, the object is to examine the content of the legal controls and the extent to which they are capable of being enforced in accordance with their terms. This will provide some indication of the practical scope for socially responsible action within the existing legal framework. An idea of the extent of the space for social responsibility is a prerequisite for judging whether changes in the law would be needed should an increased level of responsibility be considered desirable.

As discussed in Chapter 3, the directors' duty to act in the interests of the shareholders entails an obligation to maximize profits. Chapter 3 also considered the impact of the statutory duty to have regard to the interests of the employees, noting that it is as yet unclear whether this gives the directors a discretion to depart from long-term profit maximization if they believe that the protection of employee interests so requires. For present purposes it will be assumed that the statutory duty does not have that effect. A duty to maximize profits clearly rules out social responsibility of the goal-shifting type which need not be considered further. It is, however, worth examining in a little more detail the extent to which the duty to maximize profits excludes more limited forms of social responsibility. Most of the cases in which the courts have considered the propriety of company involvement in social issues have concerned social activism, specifically donations for charitable and similar purposes, and there is also some authority on political donations. We will, therefore, examine the restrictions on activism first, before going on to discuss the legal propriety of companies allowing their behaviour to be controlled by self-imposed constraints.

Social Activism

As might be anticipated, the rhetoric of the judgments indicates that corporate generosity is acceptable only so long as a net benefit to the company can be expected. In the well-known words of Bowen L J, there is 'a kind of charitable dealing which is for the interest of those who practise it, and to that extent and in that garb (I admit not a very philanthropic garb) charity may sit at the board, but for no other purpose.'[33] More technically,

---

[32] There is some limited evidence in M. Fogarty and I. Christie, *Companies and Communities: Promoting Business Involvement in the Community* (1990), at xvi–xvii, suggesting that the legal controls are not regarded as a significant obstacle to corporate giving for charitable and social purposes.

[33] *Hutton v West Cork Railway Co* (1883) 23 Ch 654, CA, at 673. Similarly, ibid. the 'law does not say that there are to be no cakes and ale, but there are to be no cakes and ale except such as are required for the benefit of the company'.

charitable donations and other forms of giving, as with ordinary commercial expenditure, must be authorized by the company's memorandum and be consistent with the directors' fiduciary duties. With respect to the first of these requirements, unless the company has an object specifically sanctioning relevant non-commercial activities,[34] it is necessary to establish that a gift is reasonably incidental or conducive to carrying on the company's business.[35] This is an objective test, but in order to satisfy it it is not essential to prove that the company will receive a net benefit as a result of making a particular gift. What must be shown in effect is that the donation is *capable* of benefiting the company.[36] This lower hurdle is inevitable in view of the courts' reluctance to reopen issues of business judgement, and especially so given that it is virtually impossible to quantify the expected return to the company on most forms of 'social investment'. The second, fiduciary control demands that the directors *believe* that the costs incurred are in the interests of the company, that is, that they are compatible with the (long-term) interests of the shareholders.

These requirements can be seen at work in *Evans v Brunner, Mond and Co Ltd*.[37] The shareholders passed a resolution[38] authorizing the directors to make donations up to a total sum of £100,000 'to such universities, or other scientific institutions in the United Kingdom as they may select for the furtherance of scientific education and research'. The company was involved in the manufacture of chemicals, and the directors hoped that, by making appropriate donations, the company might in due course benefit from an enlarged pool of trained personnel from which to draw staff. The resolution was challenged by a shareholder who contended that it was the community

---

[34] See 278–9 below.

[35] As a result of amendments to CA 1985 by CA 1989, s 108, a company's memorandum no longer limits its capacity. A company may, however, still be restrained by a shareholder from entering into a transaction which is not authorized by its objects clause (CA 1985, s 35(2)), and directors who cause the company to enter into such transactions will be liable for any loss that results (CA 1985, s35(3)). Further, the objects clause is still relevant to the authority of the company's agents to bind it, and hence a third party will be affected where the directors have exceeded the powers conferred on them by the company's constitution unless that party is in 'good faith' (CA 1985, s 35A). For a party not to be in good faith it seems that it must know that the transaction is not in the interests of the company; mere knowledge that the directors are exceeding their powers is not sufficient (s35A(2)(b)).

[36] Benefit to the company has not in the past been regarded as the sole test, since in order to be reasonably incidental a transaction must previously also have had a thematic connection with the company's stated objects. For a strict application of this requirement, see, e.g. *Tomkinson v South-Eastern Railway Co* (1887) 35 Ch D 675. Kay J held that a donation of £1,000 by a railway company towards the construction of the Imperial Institute was *ultra vires*. While the donation might have contributed to an increase in travel on the company's lines, and hence have been beneficial to the company, it had no connection with the business of running railways. See also *Attorney-General v Mersey Railway Co Ltd* [1907] AC 415, HL. If applied today this reasoning would undermine most corporate giving.

[37] [1921] 1 Ch 359.

[38] In modern companies, donations are generally made without reference to the shareholders. See n. 42 below.

at large that would be the true beneficiary, and that 'the company, as part of the community, may derive some distant, remote and more or less insignificant benefit but a benefit out of all proportion to the cost.'[39] The court held that the resolution was valid. It accepted the view of the directors, there being no evidence to the contrary, that the advantages to the company were likely to be substantial, and not 'too speculative or too remote'. The resolution was accordingly *intra vires*. It is evident that this result turned on what could have been little more than a judicial guess. The court was not in a position to make an accurate assessment of the likely return to the company in the long term, though no doubt in principle a company might make a donation that was so large, with the benefit so intangible, that a court would not find it difficult to make a negative finding. On the particular facts, the further, subjective issue of the directors' good faith did not arise, with the court noting simply that when the time came to make a specific donation it would be 'for [the directors] to decide after full consideration whether any particular application of the monies' would be to the company's advantage. It is suggested that there are three situations in which the directors' good faith in making such a decision might realistically be challengeable, namely: (i) in the unlikely event of there being evidence (for example, an earlier admission) that they were not acting with a view to increasing long-run profits, but rather were motivated by a desire to benefit the recipient;[40] (ii) if an improper motive could be inferred from the existence of a personal involvement with the recipient; or (iii) the directors' behaviour was so unreasonable as to indicate that they could not have believed that their actions would on balance be beneficial to the company.[41]

It follows from this discussion of the objective and subjective controls that in practice corporate gifts (and social activism more generally) will normally be valid so long as it can plausibly be argued that the company will ultimately derive *some* benefit from its involvement. The third requirement mentioned in the previous paragraph is available to set an outer boundary to corporate generosity, limiting social-policy expenditure (from which no obvious tangible benefits can be expected) to amounts which are not wildly in excess of the current level of giving by similarly situated companies, though there are no examples in the authorities. Establishing a benefit of some kind will not usually be difficult. As has been mentioned and will be noted in more detail in the next section, it is not unreasonable to expect public-relations advantages from the company being perceived to be 'socially aware' and willing to commit its resources for social purposes,[42] and more

---

[39] (Above, n. 37), at 365.

[40] See e.g. *Dodge v Ford* 204 Mich 459, 170 N.W. 668 (1919), discussed at 81 above.

[41] See *Shuttleworth v Cox Bros & Co (Maidenhead) Ltd* [1927] 2 KB 9, CA, and see 92–6 above.

[42] The Jenkins Committee, *Company Law Committee Report* (Cmnd. 1749, 1962), para 52 was of

specific benefits may ensue from involvement, for instance, in education (as was found to be the case in *Evans*) and other community projects.

Political Donations

Corporate donations to political parties and related bodies would be better described as 'political activism' than 'social activism', but similar issues arise as far as the legal propriety of company giving is concerned. In the case of political donations, identifying a (legally acceptable) benefit to the company may be more difficult than where the involvement is with some social cause. The public relations argument is problematical, since the advantages of being associated in the public mind with a political party are dubious. If the party is elected and implements policies favourable to the company the company will clearly be benefited, but any connection between the benefit and the donation would surely be extremely speculative and remote. Possible benefits to the company by way of quid pro quo would be tainted with corruption and so could not be relied upon in support of a gift. Notwithstanding these points it seems likely that the issue of whether or not the company was actually benefited would in practice be lost within the courts' customary deference to management opinion, and in the case of the fiduciary control, the subjective nature of the test.

Too much significance should not be attributed to a first-instance decision,[43] but it is interesting to note a comparatively recent novel ground of attack on a political donation that may compensate for the insensitivity of the usual legal techniques. In *Simmonds v Heffer*[44] the company, the League Against Cruel Sports Ltd, an organization formed to oppose cruelty to animals, had made two donations to the Labour Party. One was to the party's election campaign fund generally, the other to help finance publicity for the party's manifesto commitment to make certain sports illegal. The latter was held to be valid as furthering the League's object of opposing cruelty. The gift to the Labour Party generally, however, was held to be *ultra vires* on the ground that it contravened an 'implicit prohibition' (inferred from the objects clause) on spending money for purposes 'alien' to the

the opinion that image considerations provided a legal justification for corporate gifts: 'the practice ... of making donations to general charities of no direct interest to the company's business has never been challenged in the Courts in this country [since *Evans v Brunner, Mond*] and we venture to think that this practice, which is regarded by businessmen as necessary to create or preserve goodwill for their companies, would, on that ground, be acceptable today.' The closest authority is *Taunton v Royal Insurance Co* (1864) 2 Hem & M 135, where it was held permissible for an insurance company to pay out on uninsured risks on the ground that this would enhance its reputation for fair dealing, but cf. n. 36 above.

[43] Though there is also House of Lords' support for the proposition that companies may not make political donations in *Amalgamated Society of Railway Servants v Osborne* [1910] AC 87, HL. See generally K. D. Ewing, 'Company Political Donations and the Ultra Vires Rule', (1984) 47 *MLR* 57.

[44] [1983] BCLC 298.

company's stated objects. In other words, since the Labour Party had a host of policies on matters totally unrelated to opposing cruelty to animals, a general donation to its election campaign, notwithstanding that it might have the effect of increasing the likelihood of the Labour Party being able to implement those policies, was inconsistent with the League's objects clause, given the implicit prohibition. If this reasoning is applicable to gifts made by ordinary commercial companies, and there is no obvious point of distinction,[45] it would appear that most of the donations currently made by British companies are unlawful, since in general contributions are not tied to some specific purpose closely related to the objects of the donor.[46] The fact that the recipient party would implement some policies (for instance, with respect to the management of the economy) which the directors might genuinely consider favourable to the company is irrelevant, given that it would undoubtedly pursue others which would have no impact on the company's affairs one way or the other.[47]

It could be argued that the reasoning in *Simmonds v Heffer* should be rejected on the ground (subject to the reservations expressed above) that if a donation is likely to bring net benefits to the company, the fact that the money might also assist in the implementation of other policies which have no bearing on the company's affairs is no of moment. It is suggested that the decision can, however, be justified on the basis that the 'implicit prohibition' is likely in any given case to reflect a plausible view of the wishes of the members, and hence is consistent with the underlying principles of the legal model. Political donations are a matter of some sensitivity, and while a gift might be in the interests of the business, and hence also in the financial interests of the shareholder (in the case of a company formed for an ordinary commercial purpose), it is reasonable to suppose that the members would not wish to advance their material well-being at the price of giving money to a party whose policies in general they do not support.[48] We shall see in the

---

[45] A possibility is that making donations might be beneficial to a trading company's image, but political contributions are not usually widely publicized and are in any case likely to alienate at least as many people as they attract.

[46] Few companies have as a substantive object the making of political donations, which would presumably avoid the problem of the implicit prohibition: see 278–9 below.

[47] The facts of *Simmonds v Heffer* are particularly strong in that since the Labour Party was at the time the only party pledged to introduce anti-blood sports legislation, assisting the party in being elected would have been the most effective way of seeing the League's objects fulfilled.

[48] Note in this connection the US Supreme Court decision in *First National Bank of Boston v Bellotti* 435 US 765 (1978), quoted in K. D. Ewing, *The Funding of Political Parties in Britain* (1987), at 44:

Although it is arguable that corporations make such expenditures because their managers believe that it is in the corporations' economic interest to do so, there is no basis whatsoever for concluding that these views are expressive of the heterogeneous beliefs of their shareholders whose convictions on many political issues are undoubtedly shaped by considerations other than a desire to endorse any electoral or ideological cause which would tend to increase the value of a particular corporate investment.

A way of avoiding this problem is to require companies who wish to make donations to establish

next section that virtually all corporate donations are to the Conservative Party, and it is reasonable to expect that many shareholders are Conservative supporters. But whether or not a majority of the members are in fact admirers of the Conservative Party and hence approve of a donation is irrelevant. The issue is whether the objects clause sanctions donations to any party which are not tied to specific purposes relevant to the company. A legal challenge to a donation by an ordinary commercial company to a political party bringing these issues to the fore would be of obvious theoretical interest,[49] and, given the reliance of the Conservatives on corporate financial support, of considerable practical importance to the question of party funding in general.[50]

Constraint-Based Responsibility

Responsibility that takes the form of voluntary self-regulation, that is, of taking steps to avoid damage to non-shareholder interests such as those of employees and consumers, or of minimizing adverse environmental impacts, or of engaging in other forms of ethically motivated behaviour, such as withdrawal from South Africa, has not been the subject of express judicial consideration.[51] If the implications of the duty to maximize shareholder

---

a political fund, with the agreement of the members, from which payments would be made. Members who objected to donations would be paid proportionately higher dividends. These are analagous to the provisions which operate with respect to trade unions (see the Trade Union Acts 1913 and 1984). Bills introduced into Parliament to change the law along these lines have failed: see Ewing (above), at 45–8. An amendment to the Companies Bill 1989 was successfully introduced in the House of Lords, contrary to the Government's wishes, simply requiring shareholder consent to political donations, but was subsequently lost through a procedural irregularity. A small minority of companies voluntarily seek shareholder consent: see (1987) 76 *Labour Research* no. 1, 13.

[49] It would be open to a minority shareholder to challenge the validity of a donation in a personal action: see e.g. *Taylor v NUM* [1985] BCLC 237. An attempt to recover a donation would create greater difficulty, on both substantive (see CA 1985, ss 35 and 35A) and procedural grounds (see *Taylor v NUM*).

[50] The Constitutional Reform Centre, *Company Donations to Political Parties: A Suggested Code of Practice* (1985), at 10, estimate that over 55 per cent of Conservative central party funds come from corporate donations. See also Ewing, *The Funding of Political Parties in Britain* (above, n. 48), at 38–40.

[51] The position of other fiduciaries has, however, come before the courts. See e.g. *Cowan v Scargill* [1984] 2 All ER 750, at 761, per Sir Robert Megarry V-C:

Trustees may even have to act dishonourably (though not illegally) if the interests of their beneficiaries require it. Thus where trustees for sale had struck a bargain for the sale of trust property but had not bound themselves by a legally enforceable contract, they were held to be under a duty to consider and explore a better offer they received, and not to carry through the bargain to which they felt in honour bound: see *Buttle v Saunders* [1950] 2 All ER 193.

Similarly, an Official Receiver 'must do his best by his creditors and contributories. He is in a fiduciary capacity and cannot make moral gestures, nor can the court authorise him to do so': *Re Wyvern Developments Ltd* [1974] 2 All ER 535, at 544, per Templeman J. There is no reason to think that in principle the position of directors is any different, though the importance of

wealth are followed to the full, companies are entitled to incur expenditure
or sacrifice revenue for these purposes only to the extent dictated by considerations of long-term profit. Companies may, in other words, be guided by
prudential, but by not other-regarding constraints. The difficulties involved
in applying legal controls to restrict expenditure to that which is profit-
justified are, however, considerable. As we have seen, the disconnectedness of
charitable donations and similar forms of activism from the company's
mainstream business at least in principle provides some manageable ground
of attack. Policies for the avoidance of damage to non-shareholder interests,
in contrast, are an integral part of the management function. The adoption
of constraints *to some degree* is frequently essential to profitability. In order to
substantiate a charge that management had shown 'excessive responsibility'
it would be necessary to make a detailed examination of the way the
company operates and to demonstrate that, had some alternative policy been
followed, it would have produced higher long-term returns.[52] As discussed in
Chapters 3 and 4, however, the comparative analysis of business decisions is
precisely the kind of process in which the courts, largely for good reasons, are
not prepared to become involved. Unless, therefore, the directors admit that
they have acted against the shareholders' interests in, for instance, installing
anti-pollution controls in excess of those required by law or delaying closure
of a sub-optimally profitable plant,[53] or unless the incompatibility of their
conduct with long-term profitability is manifest, such behaviour will not be
open to effective legal challenge. Thus it may be concluded that the law in
practice leaves directors with considerable flexibility in safeguarding non-
shareholder interests, should they so choose, and is unable in general to
discriminate between measures dictated by considerations of long-term profitability or regulatory requirements on the one hand, or by an altruistic
concern for those affected by the company's activities on the other.

Substantive Non-commercial Objects

It is should be noted that the discussion so far has been premised on the
assumption that the company has conventional commercial objects. However,
in *Re Horsley & Weight Ltd*[54] Buckley L J explained that the

objects of a company do not need to be commercial; they can be charitable or
philanthropic; indeed, they can be whatever the original incorporators wish, provided

reputation, and the ongoing nature of the enterprise, cause the conduct that best serves the
interests of the beneficiary to be less clear-cut. Because of this, for the reasons explained in the
text, the fiduciary constraints are in practice difficult to apply.

[52] For another discussion of the issues raised here, see M. A. Chirelstein, 'Corporate Law
Reform', in J. W. McKie (ed.), *Social Responsibility and the Business Predicament* (1974) 52.

[53] Subject to the correct interpretation of CA 1985, s 309, it is possible that the latter is in any
case permissible even though shareholder interests may be harmed: see Ch. 3 above.

[54] [1982] Ch 442, CA, [1982] 3 All ER 1045.

that they are legal. Nor is there any reason why a company should not part with its funds gratuitously or for non-commercial reasons if to do so is within its declared objects.[55]

Most companies do not have 'charitable or philanthropic' *objects*, and so expenditure for these purposes will be permissible, as we have seen, only where it falls within an express or implied power. If, however, a company does have a non-commercial object[56] there can never be a problem of social expenditure of the kind provided for being unauthorized by its memorandum, and in such a case limits on the scope of the directors' powers are similary avoided. The effect of non-commercial objects on directors' duties, on the other hand, is less clear. One possibility is that the presence of a non-commercial object converts the company into a multi-goal organization whose function is to make profits for shareholders but also to carry out the stated charitable or public purposes. If this is so then, as long as the directors give proper consideration to the shareholders' interests and are not affected by a personal conflicting interest, a decision, to take an extreme example, to devote the bulk of the company's profits to charity would not constitute a breach of duty.[57] It seems more likely, however, that the court would not regard what looks like a technical drafting point, designed to avoid challenges to the company's capacity to make gifts broadly in line with shareholder interests, as having brought about a fundamental change in the character of what would otherwise be an essentially commercial company, and hence the directors' overriding duty to maximize shareholder wealth might well remain, notwithstanding the presence of non-commercial objects in the company's memorandum.[58]

Conclusion

It is clear from the above discussion that the legal model will in practice accommodate a measure of profit-sacrificing responsibility notwithstanding the duty of management to maximize profits, given that the strict enforcement of that duty is not feasible. It is likely as a result, to anticipate the discussion in the next section, that the law will rarely present an obstacle to the limited

---

[55] Ibid. at 1052.

[56] Hanson PLC, for instance, one of Britain's largest companies, has as an object 'to support and subscribe to any body of persons or trust established for the advancement of education or carrying on any educational establishment'.

[57] Though relief under CA 1985, s 459 (conduct unfairly prejudicial to the interests of members) might well be available.

[58] In *Re Horsley & Weight* itself, in which a gratuitous pension had been arranged for a retired director, it was unnecessary to consider this issue since the directors who awarded the pension owned all the shares. Different considerations may in any event apply in a small closely-held company, in which a non-commercial object might be a genuine reflection of the parties' intention that the company should pursue philanthropic as well as commercial purposes.

social-policy objectives that companies currently espouse, and that in fact there is room for companies to take their activities considerably further before the legal controls begin to pose a serious threat.

In the United States, in the context of social activism, the courts have accepted explicitly (as distinct from acquiescing in the technical limitations of law application) that companies should play a distinctively social role. Thus, in *A P Smith Manufacturing Co v Barlow*,[59] in upholding the validity of a gift to Princeton University, the court paid lip-service to the likelihood of benefit to the company, but placed particular emphasis as a justification for the gift on the value of corporate altruism to society as a whole.[60] Noting the drift of wealth into corporate hands, and legislative encouragement of,[61] and public support for,[62] company donations, the court applauded the company's 'long-visioned . . . action in recognizing and voluntarily discharging its high obligations as a constituent of our modern society'.[63] There are as yet no indications that the courts in this country consider that companies have the relevant 'high obligations', or even more modestly that they are prepared expressly to uphold profit-sacrificing responsibility designed to limit the more obvious social costs of corporate activity or to comply with widely accepted ethical standards.[64] An acceptance of activism or constraint-based responsibility that is not premised on a return to the company at least in the long term

---

[59] 39 ALR 2d 1179 (1953), at 1187.

[60] In language suggestive of the concession theory of the company (see Ch. 1 above), the court argued, at 1187, that 'just as the conditions prevailing when corporations were originally created required that they serve public as well as private interests, modern conditions require that corporations acknowledge and discharge social as well as private responsibilities as members of the communities in which they operate.' The social vision of the court in *Smith* clearly embraces the private performance of functions which from other perspectives are regarded as falling within the public sphere: thus 'free and vigorous non-governmental institutions of learning are vital to our democracy and the system of free enterprise': at 1192.

[61] Many states had by then adopted statutes permitting donations within certain limits (and have since been joined by others); there are also tax incentives to corporate giving: see Engel, 'An Approach to Corporate Social Responsibility', (above, n. 1), at 14–8.

[62] The court noted, for instance, the remarks favourable to social responsiblity in Berle and Means, *The Modern Corporation and Private Property* (above, n. 10) and E. M. Dodd, 'For Whom are Corporate Managers Trustees?', (1932) *Harv L Rev* 1145.

[63] (Above, note 59), at 1192. The ALI Corporate Governance project proposals appear to go beyond the existing law in recognizing that the company 'may devote a reasonable amount of resources to public welfare, humanitarian, educational, and philanthropic purposes' regardless of corporate profit or shareholder gain, though given the largely fictitious character of the latter requirement in practice this is unlikely to make much difference. See American Law Institute, *Principles of Corporate Governance: Analysis and Recommendations* Proposed Final Draft (1992), para 2.01 and accompanying commentary. For proposals on constraint-based responsibility, see ibid. For a critical discussion see S. R. Munzer, *A Theory of Property* (1990), at 362–8.

[64] Cf *DPP v P & O European Ferries (Dover) Ltd* (1991) 93 Cr App R 72, at 83, per Turner J: Since the nineteenth century there has been a huge increase in the numbers and activities of corporations whether nationalised, municipal or commercial, whose activities enter the private lives of all or most of 'men and subjects' in a diversity of ways. A clear case can be made for imputing to such corporations social duties *including* the duty not to offend all relevant parts of the criminal law [emphasis added].

would require a transformation of the legal model from one founded on shareholder-wealth maximization to one that explicity reflected public-welfare functions. Whether it is desirable that companies should become actors in the non-business realm or should in other respects make social-policy decisions is the subject of the next chapter.

IV SOCIAL RESPONSIBILITY IN PRACTICE

This section will examine social responsibility in practice using the distinctions drawn in Section II as a set of organizing principles. The aim is to give some substance to the theoretical issues and to provide an outline account of current experience rather than to present a comprehensive survey. Much of the analysis will, of necessity, be impressionistic and speculative. As Manne has pointed out: 'The most difficult problem in talking about corporate social responsibility relates to the practical problem of classification of conduct.'[65] With regard to the central issue of the extent to which companies depart from the profit goal there is, as we shall see, simply insufficient evidence on which to base any very definite conclusions. Behaviour falling within the relational responsibility and social activism categories will be examined in turn.

Relational Responsibility

The first difficulty encountered in attempting to study relational responsibility is in identifying the relevant behaviour. To mention just two areas, employee safety and environmental protection, no comprehensive information is available on whether company expenditure exceeds that required by law.[66] Even if the relevant data existed, determining whether any additional expenditure represented a departure from long-term profit maximization in any particular case would be highly problematical. The issues which managers must resolve do not yield unique profit-maximizing solutions, and hence there are no objective standards with which management behaviour can be compared in order to discover whether or not there has been a divergence

---

[65] Manne, in Manne and Wallich, *The Modern Corporation and Social Responsibility* (above, n. 11), at 8.

[66] In a survey conducted by the CBI, *Waking up to a Better Environment* (1990), at 20–1 (based on 2,500 questionnaires sent to companies operating in the UK, 250 of which were returned), fewer than half the respondents who had recently undertaken, or were about to undertake, major capital investment on environment-related matters were able to identify the costs involved. Seventy per cent were unable to estimate the continuing costs to their business of environmental protection measures (largely because of the problem of distinguishing between environmental protection expenditure and expenditure on more efficient processes). In other words, a substantial proportion of companies do not even themselves know what pollution abatement costs, let alone whether they spend more than the law requires.

from the profit goal. If, for instance, it appeared that a company had spent more on pollution control than the law required, the explanation might be the acceptance of a moral responsibility towards the environment on the company's part. But there might be a self-interested explanation, such as that the expenditure was incurred to safeguard the company's public image, or to increase the likelihood of obtaining planning permission for future expansion. Or the company might have anticipated that the regulatory regime would be tightened and that installing suitable equipment now would be cheaper than modifying or replacing it later. The answer may be that management was motivated by a mixture of these factors. In short, the company's behaviour in combating pollution, providing employees with leisure facilities or avoiding employment discrimination, or treating customers[67] and suppliers fairly, may be part of a perfectly conventional profit-maximizing strategy, or it might involve the conscious sacrifice of profits, but neither motive can readily be deduced from the observable facts.[68]

In the absence of direct evidence about the significance of socially responsible motives in practice, it is necessary to rely on more subjective indicators. There is a need for caution here, since management assertions of responsibility may be unreliable. As will be seen below, the term 'responsibility' is used by management in a variety of senses, but often without explanation or precision. Further, claiming (in addition to, or instead of, practising) social responsibility may be part of the company's public-relations efforts, and thus a profit-maximizing strategy in its own right.[69] With these reservations in mind, the light shed on the practice of relational responsibility, first by statements of company policy in corporate codes of conduct, and then by the results of surveys of managers' attitudes to their role, will now be examined.

[67] In relation to consumer protection, see R. Cranston, *Regulating Business: Law and Consumer Agencies* (1979), at 139–40, concluding that: 'Some businesses adopt a deliberate policy of ensuring that their practices conform with—indeed are in advance of—legal requirements. This may derive from self-interest or it may be that a sense of social responsibility acts as a brake on economically determined interests.'

[68] Some work has been done going beyond the observable facts: see e.g. R. Gray, *The Greening of Accountancy: The Profession After Pearce* (1990), at 43: 'research ... suggests that, in the end, in a conflict between profit and environmental enhancement/protection, profit usually wins' (reference omitted). And see the historical studies of the degree of cooperativeness of particular companies with government, and other aspects of social policy practised by them, in J. S. Boswell, *Business Policies in the Making: Three Steel Companies Compared* (1983) (steel industry prior to the Second World War); J. S. Boswell and B. R. Johns, 'Patriots or Profiteers? British Businessmen and the First World War', (1982) 11 *J European Economic History* 2; J. S. Boswell, 'The Informal Social Control of Business in Britain, 1880–1939', (1983) 57 *Business History Review* 2; and generally, J. Boswell, *Community and the Economy: The Theory of Public Co-operation* (1990), at 61–5.

[69] As Manne in Manne and Wallich, *The Modern Corporation and Social Responsibility* (above, n. 11), at 11–12, comments it is possible that 'businessmen still behave precisely as the utility maximizers classical economic theory described. But today's maximizing behavior includes advocating the non-maximization of profits.'

Codes of Conduct

Some impression of what managers consider a company's social responsibilities to be can be gained from an examination of corporate 'codes of conduct' or 'statements of business principles'. Before looking at the codes of individual companies, it may be useful to take note of the report of the CBI, *The Responsibilities of the British Public Company*[70] (the Watkinson Committee report), published in 1973. While now rather dated, it still casts some light on what business leaders consider best practice to be in the area of corporate responsibility. In the committee's view, companies have 'moral obligations that go beyond the pursuit of profit and the specific requirements of legislation'. Boards should recognize obligations 'arising from the company's relationships with creditors, suppliers, customers, employees and society at large; and in so doing to strike a balance between the interests of the aforementioned groups and the interests of the proprietors of the company'.[71] This could be summarised as a duty to 'behave like a good citizen in business'.[72] There was, on the other hand, no duty of 'general benevolence at the shareholders' expense'; rather:

the obligations that are to be recognised are limited to those that arise in the pursuit of the company's main objects. The company remains an association formed for the purposes specified in the Memorandum and no others. Any company which regards its word as its bond, which gives a fair deal and is a good neighbour has gone most of the way.[73]

The responsible company does not, in other words, have an obligation to use its resources and expertise to help solve the problems of society at large, nor is it authorized to make 'an incursion into fields of social welfare unconnected with the company's business such as are the province of central and local government'.[74] A company's responsibilities are more circumscribed, compris-

---

[70] The report was produced in a climate of general questioning about the role of the public company. The (Conservative) Government White Paper published earlier in the same year, *Company Law Reform* (Cmnd. 5391, 1973), had marked a departure from an agenda dominated by the relationship between the company and its shareholders and creditors. While applauding the virtues of the private enterprise system, it acknowledged a need for change and accepted that 'ownership involves responsibilities as well as rights' and that companies 'have a manifest obligation towards all those with whom they have dealings': ibid. at 5. Some of the background to the White Paper is discussed in D. Imberg and P. MacMahon, 'Company Law Reform', (1973) 1 no. 2 *Social Audit* 3; see also Shenfield, *Company Boards* (above, n. 16), at 11–14, where it is suggested that an increased concern with corporate behaviour and regulation can be attributed to disenchantment in the Labour Party with nationalization, giving 'fresh impetus to the search for other ways of effecting public control over private industry and of securing a more powerful representation of interests other than those of the shareholders in company policies'. In this context the report of the Watkinson Committee can be seen as an attempt to put the corporate house in order with a view to deflecting more radical reform.

[71] Ibid. paras 22 and 23.

[72] Ibid. para 61.

[73] Ibid. para 24.

[74] Ibid.

ing an obligation to act fairly towards the parties with whom it deals and to strive to limit the negative impact of its activities on third parties and the physical environment. In terms of the typology of social responsibility adopted above, it is clear, therefore, that the report favours some forms of relational responsibility but is largely opposed to social activism. As to the latter, we will see later that attitudes may have changed in the intervening years. Not surprsingly, within the field of relational responsibility the report endorses profit-making for the benefit of shareholders as the company's exclusive goal, and respect for the various interests to which it refers are treated as constraints. The language used (the reference to 'moral obligations') suggests a commitment to at least some other-regarding constraints, but the discussion is at too high a level of generality to reveal their precise content or the extent to which they should be expected to withstand the countervailing pressures of profit.

We turn now from the views of representatives of industry in general to those of individual companies. Company codes are doubtless sometimes intended more as a public relations exercise than as a serious means of changing the organization's behaviour,[75] and their language is usually vague, probably in part because of the risk of more specific guidelines creating a hostage to fortune. They are nevertheless of some value in indicating the parameters of corporate social concern, and the fact of their existence at least evidences an awareness of questions of social impact and ethical behaviour. Although there are earlier examples, companies began to adopt formal codes in significant numbers in the 1970s. As well as, or instead of, formal codes, many companies publish statements about how they see their responsibilities in annual reports, company newsletters, and miscellaneous material distributed to employees or more widely. A survey published by the British Institute of Management in 1976 reveals that about half of the large company respondents had codes of one sort or another.[76] In 1988 a survey conducted by Schlegelmilch and Houston, using a different sample, put the figure at 42 per cent.[77] The most recent survey, that of the Institute of

[75] Seriousness of purpose may be indicated by e.g. the setting of measurable targets (for emissions, accidents, etc.), appointment of senior management with specific responsibility for compliance, auditing performance, and ensuring that compliance is reflected in pay and promotion structures. For some evidence of practice re these matters in the environmental area see B. Burke and T. Hill, *Ethics, Environment and the Company* (1990), at 8–13, and generally D. Clutterbuck and D. Snow, *Working with the Community: A Guide to Corporate Social Responsibility* (1990), at 169–70.
[76] J. E. Melrose-Woodman and I. Kverndal, *Towards Social Responsibility*, British Institute of Management, Management Survey Report no. 28 (1976), ch. 3. Part of the sample was made up of companies known to have codes and hence the result may over-state the use of codes at the time.
[77] B. B. Schlegelmilch and J. E. Houston, *Company Codes of Ethics in Large UK Companies: An Empirical Investigation of Use, Content and Attitudes* (1988). The results are derived from 98 responses from the largest 200 UK companies.

Business Ethics carried out in 1991, found that 71 per cent of respondents had a code, though this represented only 28 per cent of the total sample.[78] The content of codes varies. Most contain a general statement of the company's objectives, with many adopting the 'good citizen in business' formula advocated by the CBI in the Watkinson report. They then commonly go on to express the company's policy towards the various groups likely to be affected by its operations; relationships with employees (e.g. health and safety, equal opportunities) are the most popular topics, and the interests of consumers, suppliers, shareholders, and the wider community, are also frequently covered.[79] In recent years statements on policy towards the environment have become increasingly common. A study published in 1990 by the Institute of Business Ethics on management attitudes towards the environment reports that 50 per cent of large company respondents had written statements on environmental policy.[80]

Turning to what the codes reveal about management attitudes (this account does not purport to be in any way a comprehensive survey of the contents of codes) there is, as might be expected, given the legal, market, and expectational contexts in which companies operate, little that indicates a restructuring of corporate goals.[81] With respect to employee remuneration, for instance, the undertaking is usually only to attempt to pay no less than the market rate.[82] Some companies have policies on job security, claiming

[78] S. Webley, *Business Ethics and Company Codes*, Institute of Business Ethics (1992), at 22. The results are based on a questionnaire sent to the 400 largest companies operating in the UK. The figures are an increase on the 55 per cent and 18 per cent, respectively, obtained in an earlier survey: S. Webley, *Company Philosophies and Codes of Business Ethics* (1988), at 4.

[79] See Melrose-Woodman and Kverndal, *Towards Social Responsibility* (above, n. 76), at 25 *et seq.*; Schlegelmilch and Houston, *Company Codes of Ethics* (above, n. 77), at 16–20. For further examples of codes, see Clutterbuck and Snow, *Working with the Community* (above, n. 75), at 169–93.

[80] Burke and Hill, *Ethics, Environment and the Company* (above, n. 75), at 6. This was based on 82 responses from a sample of 500 of The Times 1000 companies. See also the statistics in CBI, *Waking up to a Better Environment* (above, n. 66), ch. 5; and examples of company statements on environmental policy in J. Elkington, *The Environmental Audit: A Green Filter for Company Policies, Plants, Processes and Products* (1990), ch. 6 and in P. Kirkman and C. Hope, *Environmental Disclosure in UK Company Annual Reports* (1992), at 15–19.

[81] See e.g. *The Responsibilities of Unilever* (1981), at 5: 'There can be no dispute that in order to safeguard the continuity of Unilever, our first objective and, indeed, responsibility, is to be profitable.' See also the statements of general principle taken from a number of codes in Melrose-Woodman and Kverndal, *Towards Social Responsibility* (above, n. 76), at 11. And note the model code set out ibid. at 58: 'the Company's overall objective is to maximize its revenue surplus in the long term subject to [complying with various environmental standards and safeguarding the interests of employees, consumers, and the community].' Cf. the more recent Institute of Business Ethics survey, *Business Ethics and Company Codes* (above, note 78), at 6, commenting that 'hardly any companies state that they exist to maximize profits and dividend returns . . . Frequently the investment returns they seek are described as being "fair", "acceptable" or "satisfactory".'

[82] See e.g. Lloyds Bank, *Corporate Philosophy* (1982): the bank aims to 'provide remuneration and other benefits, including retirement pensions, which compare favourably with similar organizations'.

that they will explore all reasonable alternatives to compulsory redundancy, such as redeployment or a freeze on new appointments, but unsurprisingly there are few guarantees of continuity of employment.[83]

To the extent that codes can be regarded as laying down constraints, determining whether prudential or other-regarding constraints are envisaged is not possible in any definitive way. A long-term profit-maximizing rationale can normally be suggested for the policy statements that codes contain, though of course this does not of itself demonstrate that constraints are adopted or applied only to the extent that profitability requires. An obvious interpretation of benign employment policies is, nevertheless, that they are designed to attract good quality employees and to increase motivation. Statements of responsibility towards customers are frequently more detailed than those relating to employment,[84] but again they have public-relations value and, if complied with, will attract repeat custom by generating a reputation for fair dealing. With respect to the environment companies do occasionally state that their policy is to exceed legislative requirements,[85] but for reasons already mentioned, this cannot automatically be equated with profit-sacrificing behaviour.

By way of summary there is, then, nothing in the content of company codes to suggest that there has been a shift away from the profit goal: the attitude to responsibility that is expressed is of the constraint variety. Within that category the vague language of policy statements makes it difficult to discern whether the constraints mentioned are intended to be of the other-regarding as opposed to the purely prudential kind, though it is fair to say that there is little positive indication of a willingness to accept reduced profits in the long term in the event that countervailing moral or social considerations might so dictate.[86]

Surveys of Management Attitudes

Survey evidence is of value in providing less formalized indications of what managers consider the role of companies to be in the social sphere.[87] In a

[83] See e.g. the statement by the chairman of United Biscuits quoted in Melrose-Woodman and Kverndal, *Towards Social Responsibility* (above, n. 76), at 26. On corporate job protection generally see J. J. Richardson, *The Development of Corporate Responsibility in the UK* (1983), and CBI, *Company Responses to Unemployment, A Report by the Social Affairs Directorate* (1981).

[84] See e.g. the British Gas publication, *Commitment to Our Customers* (undated), which sets out in detail such matters as how quickly the company will respond to requests for the installation of equipment and to make repairs, for how long spare parts for old equipment will be available and so on.

[85] See e.g. the Boots Company plc, *Social Responsibilities*, quoted in Webley, *Business Ethics and Company Codes* (above, n. 78), at 17: 'In the Company's manufacturing operation its policy in regard to effluent disposal, gaseous emission and noise emission in not only to observe statutory controls and regulations, but to set even higher standards where appropriate.'

[86] A declaration to that effect would of course be unwise given the directors' legal responsibility to maximize profits: see 271-81 above.

[87] For a review (by a British author) of some of the American literature on 'management'

survey carried out among chief executives after publication of the CBI's *The Responsibilities of the British Public Company* in 1973 it was found that over 90 per cent agreed with the report's view that companies had obligations which went beyond the pursuit of profits.[88] A clearer idea of what this might mean in practical terms, however, can be obtained from the more detailed research conducted by Fidler a few years later. On the basis of extensive interviews with business leaders from a selection of *The Times* list of the 1000 largest companies Fidler concluded that for them 'the "soulful corporation", to use Berle's phrase, has already arrived. But "soulfulness", social responsibility or socially desirable ends, are seen as being compatible with, and to be pursued, via the very traditional route of making profits.'[89] He goes on to note that an ethos has evolved 'that presents other goals (growth, serving the interests of customers or of employees) as only short-term alternatives to the long-term pursuit of profit; and, indeed, these may be seen as the means to long-term profitability.'[90] This would seem to suggest that, while there is a willingness on the part of managers to respond to the interests of affected groups, the response involved does not, and is not perceived to require, a departure from a conventional long-run profit goal.[91]

Fidler also reports that managements frequently described their role as one of balancing the various interests connected with the company. In an earlier study Shenfield similarly observed that boards commonly claimed that their decision processes involved 'a balancing of interests in which the board takes into account the interests of the various groups'.[92] The idea that directors balance interests is, however, quite consistent with the conclusion

creeds' and social responsibility, see N. C. Smith, *Morality and the Market: Consumer Pressure for Corporate Accountability* (1990), at 64–9.

[88] S. Webley, *Corporate Social Responsibility* (1975).

[89] J. Fidler, *The British Business Elite: Its Attitudes to Class, Status and Power* (1981), at 117–18. The phrase 'the soulful corporation' was actually coined by C. Kaysen in 'The Social Significance of the Modern Corporation', (above, n. 7), at 314.

[90] Fidler, ibid. See also R. E. Pahl and J. T. Winkler, 'The Economic Elite: Theory and Practice', in P. Stanworth and A. Giddens (eds), *Elites and Power in British Society* (1974), at 118–19: 'Evidence of a social responsibility ethic which we encountered was very limited and conventionally defined — a corporate philanthropy budget, conformity with government social legislation, and a grudging responsiveness to some of the more obvious social protest movements (e.g. pollution control and office development).' See also A. Demb and F.-F. Neubauer, *The Corporate Board: Confronting the Paradoxes* (1992), at 43–5.

[91] See also J. Humble and M. A. Johnson, *Corporate Social Responsibility: the Attitudes of European Business Leaders* (1978), at 16–8, where it is stated that of the companies that had carried out an 'audit' of their social responsibilities, three-quarters had said that their most important motivation was to look at ways to protect long-term profitability.

[92] Shenfield, *Company Boards* (above, n. 16), at 12. This finding is also consistent with the 'stakeholder' approach to the various interests affected by company decision making, popular in management literature, and criticized for its indeterminacy in J. W. Kuhn and D. W. Shriver, *Beyond Success: Corporations and their Critics in the 1990s* (1991), at 75–8. See also Smith, *Morality and the Market* (above, n. 88), at 54–6 and 344 n. 113 below. See also Demb and Neubauer, *The Corporate Board* (above, n. 90), at 43–5.

that the management conception of social responsibility does not involve a sacrifice of profits in the long run. It is true that 'balancing' can have a distributive connotation: a balance can be struck between various interests by favouring some at the expense of others (for example, customers at the expense of shareholders). Understood in this way, an ethos of balancing interests is compatible with a profit-sacrificing conception of responsibility, involving a shift in goals or the adoption of other-regarding constraints. In practice, however, as Fidler makes plain, these are not the conceptions that typically feature in managers' thinking. Rather, their attitude is that 'the directorate only arbitrates [between the conflicting interests] in the short term: for in the long term the interests of all concerned with the company coincide.'[93] The belief that the relevant interests coincide is based on the assumption that they all ultimately depend on the company's profitability. This point of view holds that without profits there would, for instance, be no job security, or funds to support research into product improvements or finance environmental protection measures. In accordance with this reasoning the company will be in the best position to serve the interests of affected groups, therefore, if it maximizes its profits. It seems to follow that 'balancing' should not be understood in a distributive sense, as involving a sacrifice of profits, but instead as implying the satisfaction of affected interests only to the extent necessary to achieve maximum long-term profitability.

The idea that policies favouring the interests of affected groups and those serving long-run profit maximization always coincide is manifestly false. From the point of view of avoiding environmental damage, for instance, it is preferable that a company whose processes or products pollute the atmosphere should go out of business, rather than that it should finance methods of reducing adverse environmental impacts from the proceeds of its polluting activities. And while a certain level of profitability is necessary in order to secure enterprise survival and renewal and hence employment stability, the interests of employees are not necessarily best served by running the business in such a way as to maximize the return to the shareholders. What is more open to debate is the different issue of whether a policy of long-run profit maximization creates the conditions that enable a more satisfactory overall compromise between the various, partially conflicting, interests to be reached. This was the assumption provisionally adopted in Chapter 1 and which will be evaluated in Chapter 10.

The results of a survey recently conducted by the CBI on management attitudes towards the more specific issue of the relationship between business and the environment may finally be noted.[94] Over 85 per cent of respondent

        [93] Fidler, *British Busines Elite* (above, n. 89), at 120.
        [94] CBI, *Waking Up to a Better Environment* (above, n. 66). See also Kirkham and Hope, *Environmental Disclosure* (above, n. 81), at 2–3, summarizing the results of a number of other surveys:

companies considered concern for the environment to be a very important or significant matter for business. Over 60 per cent reported that 'corporate social responsibility' was an important factor in shaping the company's environmental policies, a figure which was only marginally lower than that for UK legislation as a stated influence. 'Corporate social responsibility' is not defined, however, and there is no indication of whether a sense of responsibility translates into environmental protection measures which exceed those legally required. As used here, 'responsibility' might simply be a motive for complying with legal standards, for example where they are difficult to enforce.[95] Nor can much be inferred from the survey's conclusion that in general 'low priority [is] accorded to environmental responsibility as a valuable contribution to corporate image',[96] particularly as nearly 40 per cent of companies regarded public perception of their environmental impact as a major problem. It may simply indicate that companies consider that publicizing environmental expenditure is unwise because it tends to draw unwelcome attention to their environmental performance more generally. The finding is thus consistent with the possibility that companies invest in pollution control techniques for public-relations reasons, that is, in order to reduce the risk of their commercial interests being damaged through acquiring a poor environmental record.

The conclusion to be drawn from this discussion would seem to be that the form of relational responsibility for which managements predominantly voice support is the adoption of prudential, but not other-regarding, constraints. In reaching this conclusion, it is not intended to suggest that management decisions are reached by the application of an amoral long-term profit-maximizing calculus, to the exclusion of social or ethical considerations. Other-regarding and prudential constraints are to a degree coextensive, and in the area of overlap, at least in some companies with respect to some matters (for example, health and safety), the motivation may be as much moral as self-

Environmental issues were still given a relatively low profile on most corporate agendas during the late 1980s and early 1990s. Although some industries are more environmentally sensitive than others, there appeared to be a huge disparity between different companies' attitudes towards environmental issues; whilst some were adopting a positive stance and introducing environmental initiatives, policies and reporting, others, it would seem, were doing very little indeed.

[95] Uncertainty as to the meaning of 'corporate social responsibility' is also created by the reference in the report to 'conscience' as a distinct factor motivating environmental protection measures (20 per cent of respondents claimed to have been influenced by it). This suggests that behaviour in the 'responsibility' category is not necessarily to be equated with the adoption of measures in excess of those required by law. And see M. Jacobs, *The Green Economy: Environment, Sustainable Development and the Politics of the Future* (1991), at 40: 'Evidence that firms have become environmentally conscious either "voluntarily" (as a result of changes in corporate values), or because market forces have encouraged them, is in fact rather thin. The vast majority of new environmental activities have been explicitly developed as a result of statutory regulation of markets or of political pressure from environmentalists.'

[96] Ibid. at 17.

interested. Motivation is tested, however, where protecting the interests of affected parties conflicts with long-term profitability; it seems from the literature that the conflict is likely to be resolved in favour of the latter.

Social Activism

'Social activism' connotes company action to alleviate social problems that exist independently of the way the company conducts its business, and also corporate support for community activities which are similarly unrelated to the company's ordinary commercial operations. Social activism is often easier to identify than relational responsibility, because in many cases, charitable giving and arts sponsorship, for instance, it is visibly disconnected from the company's mainstream commercial activities. But this is not always the case. For example, a policy of employing members of disadvantaged groups is an aspect of an ordinary business function—acquiring staff— although its object may be to address a social problem. It should also be noted that in describing a company as engaging in social activism it is not intended to suggest that the behaviour necessarily involves a departure from long-run profit maximization. As with constraint-based responsibility, the motivation may be entirely conventional, and whether or not social-policy objectives are being pursued in a particular case at the expense of profits will frequently have no clear answer. In what follows corporate social involvement in a number of different fields will be examined with the issue of motivation particularly in mind.

Charitable Giving and Community Support

The type of social activism about which the most concrete evidence is available is traditional charitable giving, in part because of the obligation to disclose donations in the company's accounts.[97] The amounts given by the top 200, and more recently, 400 donors are published annually by the Charities Aid Foundation (CAF). Total cash donations in 1991/2 by the 213 companies responding to the CAF survey amounted to nearly £85 million.[98] Twenty-three companies gave over a million pounds each, and twelve over two million. The median cash donation was £152,000. A more comprehensive survey conducted by the Directory of Social Change has estimated total corporate charitable donations for 1988 at £170 million.[99] These figures, while obviously revealing expenditure of very significant amounts, seem less impressive when placed alongside the estimated total charitable donations by households in 1989/90 of between £3.4 and £5 billion.[100]

[97] C A 1985, s 235, and Sch 7, Part 1.
[98] Charities Aid Foundation, *Charity Trends* (15th ed., 1992, Tonbridge), at 54–6.
[99] Directory of Social Change, *Company Giving News*, November, 1989.
[100] Though it has been pointed out that corporate donations constitute a more significant

The practice of making donations of some sort appears to be virtually universal among very large companies. The recipients are diverse, with education, medical and health organizations, and community projects the most popular destinations for cash donations. Civil rights organizations were the least favoured destination for corporate support, receiving only 0.08 per cent of total cash donations.[101] Since 1986 corporate giving has been encouraged by the Per Cent Club, an offshoot of Business in the Community, a private sector organization formed to promote social activism, particularly in the areas of unemployment and community development. The Per Cent Club now has over 300 large company members, each pledged to give at least half of 1 per cent of pre-tax UK profits to community causes.[102] Corporate charitable donations also benefit from a favourable tax regime, which has been extended in recent years to cover one-off gifts as well as covenanted donations.[103]

In 1988 the CAF began to compile statistics on the wider involvement of companies in community affairs, going beyond traditional cash donations to charities (only the latter need to be disclosed in the accounts).[104] An attempt is now made to put a money value on staff secondment[105] and gifts in kind, and to quantify financial support in such areas as arts sponsorship and participation in enterprise agencies and training schemes for the young.[106] When the value of assistance of this kind from the CAF respondents is added to cash donations the total figure for corporate support for 1991/2 rises to £206.6 million.[107] As to the trend in giving, while noting that total corporate contributions from a matched sample of companies has increased over the last three years, the CAF point out that when inflation is taken into account there is actually a decrease over the period, with a fall of 1.5 per cent between 1990/1 and 1991/2.[108] This is perhaps not surprising in a period

proportion of charities' voluntary income (i.e. that not coming from investments, trading, government grants, etc.), and thus provide scope for development and flexibility of response: Fogarty and Christie, *Companies and Communities* (above, n. 33), at 3–4.

[101] See CAF, *Charity Trends* (above, n. 98), at 55–6.

[102] 'The member companies 'see private sector involvement in the community as an integral part of corporate life, which can improve both business itself and the relationship between the business sector and the community as a whole': the Per Cent Club, *Annual Report 1989*.

[103] Finance Act 1986, s 29; Finance Act 1990, s 26. See generally D. Morris, 'Corporate Support for Charity', [1990] *JBL* 495.

[104] See also Directory of Social Change, *Company Giving News* (above, n. 99).

[105] Research suggests that secondment may well have advantages for the company, as well as the recipient, e.g. in easing out pre-retirement staff: see Centre for Employment Initiatives, *Seconds Out* (1988), and H. Metcalf, R. Pearson and R. Martin, *Stimulating Jobs: The Charitable Role of Companies*, Institute of Manpower Studies Report no. 166 (1989), at 43–7.

[106] One of the criteria for choosing these categories was that activities should be counted only where the benefit to society would be greater than that to the company (which would exclude e.g. sponsorship of spectator sports). This does not mean, however, that the expenditures registered would not have been at least partially commercially motivated.

[107] CAF, *Charity Trends* (above, n. 98), at 54–6.

[108] Ibid. at 55.

of recession and falling profitability. To put the figures in perspective, total corporate support amounted to an average of 0.64 per cent of pre-tax profits in 1989/90, the latest year for which figures are available.[109] Some of the main areas of corporate involvement will now be examined together with the possible reasons for it.

Education

There is a long tradition of companies making donations for educational purposes, particularly grants to universities. As Shenfield points out, it is easier 'to justify educational expenditure as likely to yield a direct if unquantifiable benefit to companies as well as serving the public interest. It is less likely to provoke an adverse reaction from shareholders than patronising the arts or giving to denominational religious causes.'[110] Funding research in institutions of higher education may bring specific benefits in the form of information that can be commercially applied, and more generally, raising the company's profile among high-quality potential employees is of obvious value. In recent years companies have also begun to increase their links with schools.[111] Initiatives have included 'compacts'—partnerships between a company and a local school, involving a guarantee of employment to pupils who meet certain educational and personal targets, pupil and teacher placements in industry, the appointment of school governors from business,[112] and (rather limited) support for city technology colleges.[113] This increased level of activity seems in part to be a reaction to demographic changes which are predicted to lead to a shortage of new recruits during the present decade.[114] A concern with an apparent lack of skills on the part of school-leavers, together with active government encouragement of business involvement in education,[115] also appear to be important factors.

---

[109] CAF, *Charity Trends* (13th ed., 1990), at 9.

[110] B. Shenfield, *Company Giving* (1969), at 490.

[111] The provision of educational materials by companies is longstanding. For concern that these materials might constitute or contain undesirable advertising, see National Consumer Council, *Business Sponsorship of Teaching Material: Classroom Commercials* (1986). See also Shenfield, *Company Boards* (above, note 16), at 123–4, for a discussion of the Industrial Fund for the Advancement of Scientific Education in Schools, a collaborative venture between a number of companies to support science teaching in independent schools.

[112] See Fogarty and Christie, *Companies and Communities* (above, n. 33), at 51–4.

[113] i.e. schools independent of local authority control, where an emphasis is placed on science and technology. The original intention was that the bulk of the initial capital would come from business, though company support for this government initiative has been lukewarm, at least in part because of the political controversey that it has generated: see the *Financial Times*, 17 October 1989.

[114] See Fogarty and Christie, *Companies and Communities* (above, n. 33), at 13.

[115] e.g. The Foundation for Education Business Partnerships was launched in 1989, with joint government and business funding. See also National Consumer Council, *Business Sponsorship of Teaching Materials* (above, n. 111), at 20–1.

Involvement in the Local Community

Business involvement in the regeneration of inner cities and other economically depressed regions began in the late 1970s and grew steadily throughout the 1980s. Unemployment levels remained (and continue to be) high in these areas, following the recession in the early 1980s, and the longer-standing decline of 'traditional' manufacturing industries. The most easily observed corporate response has been participation in various job-creation schemes, especially support for local enterprise agencies.[116] By the end of 1988 these numbered nearly 400. They are mostly jointly financed by local and central government as well as companies. Their main functions are to provide advice and facilities in connection with business formation and development.[117] A survey conducted by the Institute of Manpower Studies (IMS)[118] in 1987 estimates that nearly half the companies involved gave £100,000 or more, with 19 companies donating over a million pounds each. Company support consists not only of cash contributions but also secondment of staff and provision of various benefits in kind. The motives for company involvement are not wholly clear. The IMS survey reports that 95 per cent of respondents considered that they benefited from support for job creation. More detailed case study evidence, however, suggests that a majority of companies regarded benefit to the company as incidental, and not as a factor which would influence either the extent or type of involvement. Forty per cent of companies, on the other hand, were influenced by the possibility of commercial benefits, and for a quarter of the respondents this influence was strong.[119] The advantages mentioned included improvements in staff morale (after the company had made employees redundant or where it was anticipated that it might), making the company more attractive to potential recruits, improving the company's image in general, increased custom through stimulating the local economy, and keeping suppliers in business. Similarly, Christie et al. in a survey of corporate participation in community projects note that long-term revival of economic activity in depressed areas was often cited by companies as a motive: 'helping communities and investing in the local economy would eventually bring new custom and business

---

[116] For a discussion of these and other efforts in stimulating employment, see Richardson, *The Development of Corporate Responsibility in the UK* (above, n. 84) and CBI, *Company Responses to Unemployment* (above, n. 83). For case studies of various types of corporate community involvement in a number of English towns and cities, see Fogarty and Christie, *Companies and Communitites* (above, n. 33), chs 3–5, and I. Christie, M. Carley and M. Fogarty, with R. Legard, *Profitable Partnerships: A Report on Business Investment in the Community* (1991), chs 6–9.

[117] See generally, Metcalf, Pearson and Martin, *Stimulating Jobs: The Charitable Role of Companies* (above, n. 105).

[118] Ibid. at 42–3. The results are based on a 46 per cent response rate to a survey sample of 401 companies believed to be supporting job creation. The initial survey was followed up by case studies involving 25 companies.

[119] Though the report notes that 'most companies do not attempt to assess benefits in any way': ibid. at 67.

294   *Responsibility and the Current Legal Fabric*

opportunities as overall prosperity spread.'[120] Preserving a stable social environment in which to conduct business also seems likely to be an important factor. In his study of business initiatives to combat unemployment Richardson mentions the severe jolt to management attitudes caused by the inner-city riots in the early 1980s. He suggests that Marks and Spencer's community expenditure, for instance, can be seen as a 'sensible long term investment in its marketplace. If urban disorders became a regular fact of life, many of its 260 stores would not survive.'[121]

Arts Sponsorship

Corporate support for the arts has risen considerably during the 1980s. As the Director of the Association for Business Sponsorship of the Arts (ABSA), an independent private-sector body established in 1976 to promote and coordinate arts sponsorship, has commented, 'Inflation has eroded the financial base of many of our arts companies. Business sponsorship has become critical to many in the arts as a result of government funding having decreased in real terms. Sponsorship used to be seen as the icing on the cake, now it is the butter, flour and raisins.'[122] ABSA has calculated that for 1990/91 total corporate support for the arts was just over £57 million.[123] Some appreciation of the significance of private sector involvement can be gained by comparing this figure with the £175 million allocation of central funds to the Arts Council for the same period.[124] As ever, the precise motives for sponsorship are difficult to establish. It is, however, possible to identify not inconsiderable benefits flowing to companies from an involvement with the arts. Apart from general image considerations, arts sponsorship is a way of reaching members of high-income groups and hence has great value as a targeted advertising medium. It also offers opportunities for entertaining business contacts and providing staff perks. It is interesting to note in this connection that for the purposes of the government's Business Sponsorship Incentive Scheme sponsorship is regarded as a form of promotional expenditure.[125]

[120] Christie et al., *Profitable Partnerships* (above, n. 116), at 23.
[121] Richardson, *The Development of Corporate Responsibility in the UK* (above, note 83), at 5, quoting *The Economist* 20 February 1982. See also Fogarty and Christie, *Companies and Communities* (above, n. 33), at 34–5.
[122] ABSA, *Annual Report 1989*, at 12.
[123] ABSA, *An Overall Total for Business Sponsorship of the Arts During 1990/91* (1991). The figures do not include donations for which no commercial return is sought. Individual sponsorships are listed in the ABSA annual reports.
[124] For a fuller comparison, central goverment allocations to museums and galleries should also be taken into account: see ABSA (above, n. 123), at 11, and local-authority support for the arts, museums and galleries: see K. Manton, 'Funding the Arts in Seven Western Countries' in CAF, *Charity Trends* (above, n. 109) 108, at 115.
[125] Under this scheme the government matches new or increased sponsorship in varying proportions, up to a limit of £25,000. The Office of Arts and Libraries defines arts sponsorship as 'the payment of money by a business to an arts organization for the purpose of promoting the

Corporate Political Donations

Donations by companies to political parties and associated bodies raise rather different issues from the forms of social activism so far discussed. They do not involve direct attempts at ameliorating social problems, though presumably some of the managements who sanction donations believe that financial support for a particular political party will be indirectly socially beneficial, in enabling that party's policies to be carried out. Whatever the social implications of corporate political donations, they are clearly an example of corporate activity outside the normal commercial sphere. Companies are statutorily required to disclose donations for 'political purposes' in excess of £200 in the directors' report.[126] Annual reports published in 1983–4 reveal that around 15 per cent of *The Times* 1000 largest companies made donations to the Conservative Party, and when donations to right-wing research bodies and 'conduit' organizations such as British United Industrialists, which channel funds to the Conservative Party, are included the figure rises to about 25 per cent.[127] Donations to other parties are negligible, though there was some corporate support for the SDP during the brief period of its existence as a national party.[128] Research conducted by the Labour Party indicates that the Conservative Party and related organizations received £3.5 million from companies in 1988, with 49 companies giving more than £25,000 each. The largest single donation was £95,100.[129] Motives for giving are no more clear-cut than with other types of donation. No doubt many directors believe that the Conservatives, as 'the party of free enterprise', will create a climate in which companies will prosper. In one sense making payments can therefore be seen as profit-led behaviour, though in fact, since it is improbable that any individual donation will affect the

---

business name, its products or services. Sponsorship is part of a business's general promotional expenditure. It can encompass a sense of corporate or social responsibility': *Business Sponsorship Incentive Scheme: Application for an Award*, at 1. From the scheme's inception in October 1984 up till the middle of 1990, over £22 million had been raised from industry, which amount has been supplemented by over £10 million in government funds: *Office of Arts and Libraries*, press release, 23 May 1990.

[126] CA 1985, s 235 and sch 7 part 1. Donations for political purposes are defined in para. 5(2) of the schedule as donations to a political party or to a person whose activities to the company's knowledge 'can reasonably be regarded as likely to affect public support' for a political party. It has been suggested that this definition does not catch donations made to 'conduit' organizations which then pass them on to a political party: see Constitutional Reform Centre, *Company Donations to Political Parties* (above, n. 52), at 7–8. Were the matter ever tested, however, it is doubtful that the courts would accept this evasion of the disclosure requirements, and it can in any case be argued that passing on donations is an 'activity' which is likely to affect public support for the recipient party. It is, nevertheless, clear that not all donations to conduit organizations are disclosed. The Labour Research Department has, for instance, calculated that of the 35 leading companies that made donations to British United Industrialists in 1986–7, 11 were not declared: (1988) 77, no. 7, *Labour Research* 7.

[127] Constitutional Reform Centre, ibid. at 10.

[128] See W. Grant, *Business and Politics in Britain* (1985), at 185–6.

[129] See the *Financial Times*, 22 September 1989.

party's election prospects, they are unlikely to be cost-effective from the donor's point of view. Reputational benefits will presumably not accrue to a company from political, as distinct from charitable, gifts, since they are likely to alienate at least as many people as they attract, and such benefits are probably not generally expected, given the lengths to which some companies go to conceal donations.[130] Corrupt motives should perhaps not be excluded, namely where there is some hoped-for pay-off, either for the company, by way of a government contract or a change in government policy, or for individual directors, in the form of an 'honour'.[131] Possibly a more important motive, however, is straightforward personal support for the Conservatives on the part of directors, with the company used simply as a vehicle for their 'generosity'.

Activism as a Departure from Profit Maximization?

The next few pages will speculate in more general terms about the extent to which these various forms of social activism entail a divergence from profit maximization. In its *Guidelines on Corporate Responsibility*, Business in the Community comments that although corporate responsibility 'is often motivated by personal concern, it is not "altruism" or "good works". On the contrary, it is often called "enlightened self-interest" because it has well documented benefits for business.'[132] It would, nevertheless, be difficult to argue that all the forms of involvement that are currently practised would satisfy normal financial criteria. As Kaysen noted some years ago:

the uncertainty attached to some benefits (say those of being a high wage employer), the difficulty of translating into cash terms others (such as maintaining good community relations), the remoteness in time of still others (such as supporting liberal arts education) indicate that profit maximization must be given a very elastic interpretation indeed to cover all these activities.'[133]

It does seem quite likely that some company involvement in the social sphere stretches beyond what is required by or is consistent with long-term profits. In a survey conducted by Fogarty and Christie the reason most consistently expressed by senior managers for company giving and involvement in community projects was 'social responsibility—need to put something back into the community'.[134] Second was 'personal views of the chairman or

[130] See e.g. the *Independent* 16 January and 22 September 1989.
[131] Discussed in Ewing, *The Funding of Political Parties in Britain* (above, n. 48), at 36-7. See also the *Financial Times* 29 December, 1990.
[132] Business in the Community, *Guidelines on Corporate Responsibility* (1990), at 3. For a consideration of the meaning of the concept of 'enlightened self-interest', see Smith, *Morality and the Market* (above, n. 1), at 66.
[133] Kaysen, 'The Social Significance of the Modern Corporation' (above, n. 7), at 313.
[134] Fogarty and Christie, *Companies and Communities* (above, n. 32), at 11-12. The survey was based on responses to a questionnaire sent to a sample from EXTEL data of 300 medium-sized companies, employing 500 to 2,999.

chief executive', followed by 'influence from employees' and 'enlightened self-interest—promoting the company's image'. The authors note an ambiguity in the responses, however. For example, an electronics company, while claiming that its community programme was 'driven' by social responsibility, 'then illustrated how its programme varies from establishment to establishment according to its need to establish its status as an employer and the impact a community support programme would be expected to have for this purpose in communities of different kinds'.[135] A study by Shenfield in the early 1970s similarly found an attitude of philanthropic concern to be widespread among directors in large companies, with the reasons for charitable giving including a special interest on the part of the chairman or managing director or positive approval by the board for the concept of business responsibility, but again motives overlapped, long-term business interests and the need to respond to public expectations about donations also being significant factors.[136] A more recent survey by Clutterbuck and Snow found that corporate social involvement was more emphatically a response to image-building and marketing needs.[137] They note that the dominance of self-interest over community well-being is indicated by the fact that only 24 per cent of companies claimed to have made decisions on social responsibility grounds that were counter to their direct commercial interests.

Whatever the precise significance of the profit motive it is clear that the level of social activism increased significantly in the 1980s and has largely been sustained since. The last decade has also been marked by a growth in bodies whose aim is to promote social activism, such as Business in the Community, the Per Cent Club, and the Action Resource Centre.[138] There has evidently been a change in attitude since the expression by the CBI of its opposition to social activism in 1973 in *The Responsibilities of the British Public Company*, noted earlier. One possible explanation is simply that business has become more aware in the intervening years of the public-relations benefits of community involvement, and as more companies undertake social expenditure competitors may feel under pressure to join in.

---

[135] Ibid. at 12.

[136] Shenfield, *Company Boards* (above, n. 16), at 118–20; see also generally Christie et al., *Profitable Partnerships* (above, n. 121), ch. 2.

[137] Clutterbuck and Snow, *Working with the Community* (above, n. 75), at 169–77. The results are derived from the responses to questionnaires sent to 800 companies known to have an interest in social responsiblity programmes, almost all of the respondents being large or medium-sized. See also Metcalf, Pearson and Martin, *Stimulating Jobs* (above, n. 105), at 21–5. And see the study of the community programme of Pedigree Petfoods (a subsidiary of Mars Inc) in Harvey et al., *Managers and Corporate Social Policy* (above, n. 21), ch. 6 generally and at 135–49. For a clear example of the self-interested approach to social activism, see the speech by Nigel Whittaker, Corporate Affairs Director of Kingfisher plc, at the CBI Marketing Forum event, 'Corporate Conscience Goes to Work', reported in (1992) 1 *Business Ethics: A European Review* 29, at 38–40.

[138] See Fogarty and Christie, *Companies and Communities* (above, n. 32), chs 2 and 6.

Government policy may also have been an important influence.[139] The Conservative administration that came to office in 1979 has had a marked ideological preference for private sector solutions to economic and social ills. This preference has been demonstrated in the economic sphere in a policy of privatization and a creed of non-interventionism. It has also had a social dimension, with, for example, the transfer of state welfare functions to private charities.[140] With regard specifically to the social role of companies, the government has promoted charitable giving through tax changes and has provided incentives for private sponsorship of the arts. Encouragement of business funding and involvement in education of a more active kind, for example, the appointment of company executives as school governors, has been conspicuous too. Other government initiatives, notably regarding inner-city redevelopment and unemployment, have presupposed substantial cooperation from private industry. This is also the case with regard to the administration of employment training, which since 1989 has been the responsibility of local Training and Enterprise Councils. The boards of these bodies, which receive the bulk of their funding from the state, are required to draw two-thirds of their members from chief executives of local companies. The government can thus be seen in each of these areas to have promoted a conception of business responsibility that embraces the performance by private-sector bodies of what have hitherto been regarded as public-sector functions, and increased levels of activism may be partly explicable as a response to the climate thereby created. That said, there would seem to be limits to the willingness of industry to comply with government intentions, particularly where the likely returns to the company are remote or non-existent, as evidenced in the lack of support for city technology colleges. Fogarty and Christie comment similarly in connection with their survey of business attitudes to corporate involvement that '[t]hough grants for health and education do in fact make up a large part of company giving, we were told repeatedly that companies resent being expected to "pick up the tab" for basic provision which they see as properly the responsibility of government: the same point was sometimes made about personal social services and the arts.'[141]

It may be that in involving themselves in social affairs companies are also following a wider agenda of their own. A standard explanation for the

---

[139] See Fogarty and Christie, *Companies and Communities* (above, n. 32), at 61–5.

[140] The accompanying philosophy denies the existence, or downgrades the importance, of welfare *rights*, and instead emphasizes the dispensation of benefits on a discretionary basis, by charities or the state (e.g. the Social Fund). Voluntary corporate responses to social problems fit easily into such a scheme, and indeed are seen to be preferable to state solutions: see further, D. S. King, 'Voluntary and State Provision of Welfare as Part of the Public-Private Continuum: Modelling the Shifting Involvements in Britain and the US', in A. Ware (ed.), *Charities and Government* (1989), 29.

[141] Fogarty and Christie, *Companies and Communities* (above, n. 32), at 6–7 and 61.

adoption of voluntary constraints is that they are an attempt to avoid compulsory regulation. Companies have, for instance, an obvious collective interest in reducing pollution levels in order to remove the pressure for more stringent restrictions, and a preference for self-regulation generally rather than (more rigorous) external control is characteristic of most industries and professions.[142] A desire to forestall state involvement may explain not only the adoption of constraints to limit harm caused by the company's commercial operations, but also certain forms of social activism. Thus, with respect to the stimulation of employment, for example, the CBI has noted that

companies fear that if they make no attempt to find solutions to community problems, the government may increasingly take on the responsibility itself. This might prove costly to employers both in terms of new obligations and greater intervention in the labour market. Many companies prefer to be one step ahead of government legislation or intervention, to anticipate social pressure themselves and hence to be able to develop their own policies in response to them.[143]

Social activism, like self-regulation, may thus have a defensive aspect.

The Institute of Directors' *A New Agenda for Business* takes up the CBI's theme, but advocates a programme that is rather more ambitious, declaring that 'It is now time for business leaders to work out how to achieve a larger aim, going beyond the success of their own companies. This aim is the creation of a genuine "enterprise culture" [requiring business to use] its financial and managerial strength to *help solve public problems*.'[144] The expressed purpose is to create an 'enterprise culture' that is 'sufficiently stable and enduring to make a return to collectivism and corporatism virtually impossible' and which will have the effect that 'attitudes and public policy cannot revert to the pattern which prevailed up to the end of the seventies.' More particularly, the objective is to create 'a low tax, relatively unregulated, reskilled economic environment'.[145] The role of social activism in securing

[142] The adoption of self-regulatory codes of practice applying across an industry as a whole is an attempt to promote consistency of action among its members. Cranston, *Regulating Business: Law and Consumer Agencies* (above, n. 67), at 136, notes the tightening of the voluntary controls over advertising following government intimations that legislation would be introduced if they were not improved. For a consideration of the limited effectiveness of self-regulatory codes, see P. Medawar, *The Social Audit Consumer Handbook: A Guide to the Social Responsibilities of Business to the Consumer* (1978), at 12–15.
[143] CBI, *Company Responses to Unemployment* (above, n. 83), at 7. Richardson, *The Development of Corporate Responsibility in the UK* (above, n. 83), at 14, notes contemporary calls for legislation to compel employers to provide training places. See also the quote from the chairman of IBM, ibid. at 10: 'if [business] leaves society's problems to others to solve it may find the outcome takes little account of the needs of business.'
[144] Institute of Directors, *A New Agenda for Business* (1987), at 1 and 6; emphasis in original. The IOD is associated with the radical 'free market' wing of British politics: see Grant, *Business and Politics in Britain* (above, n. 128), at 127–31.
[145] Institute of Directors, ibid. at 1, 5, and 4, respectively.

that environment would seem to be to increase the standing of business in public esteem. Social-policy expenditure is thus the price that is paid for improving the image of business in general and for creating a climate which is unsympathetic to government interference: where companies engage in social policy state intervention can be portrayed as prejudicing their ability not only to satisfy economic needs through their ordinary productive activities, but also their ability to satisfy wider social goals. It follows that social activism has a political purpose: the aim is to generate a belief that business competence should not be prejudiced by state interference in the business realm. What is not clear, of course, is the extent to which this objective is shared by company managements and is an operative explanation of corporate social policy, as distinct from being a piece of advocacy from a business interest group with a distinctive ideological position.

The idea that the practice of social responsibility does have a political purpose is found in the thesis put forward by Mitchell, though with a different emphasis.[146] Drawing on American experience over the last 60 years, he contends that 'corporate social policy is the result of an ideology of business power that emphasizes social responsibility and is a response to threats to corporate legitimacy.'[147] Problems of legitimacy arise because of the general perception that companies are powerful, and he sees assurances that corporate power will be used responsibly as an attempt to deflect challenges to it. He notes that the 'old business ideology' which pictured power as diffused in the market rather than wielded by individual corporate actors ceased to be credible over the period studied, and in any case was 'based on an economic theory that was too abstract and whose policy consequences were too brutal to engender continued acceptance'.[148] In order to prevent doubts about corporate legitimacy being translated into demands for increased regulation,[149] endangering profitability or even survival, companies adopted a social responsibility ethic: by reassuring the public about corporate virtues legitimacy would be re-established or reinforced.[150]

---

[146] Mitchell, *The Generous Corporation* (above, n. 16). For a more wide-ranging account of corporate social activity in the United States, see Heald, *The Social Responsibilities of Business* (above, n. 20).

[147] Mitchell, ibid. at 53.

[148] Ibid. at 107.

[149] There is also evidence of activism being motivated by '[r]esistance to government intervention into previously private precincts of charity, education, the arts and other voluntary activities': see Heald, *The Social Responsibilities of Business* (above, note 20), at 272.

[150] See also the earlier comment of Dodd: 'Desire to retain their present powers . . . encourages [management] to adopt and disseminate the view that they are guardians of all the interests which the corporation affects': 'For Whom are Corporate Managers Trustees?' (above, n. 62), at 1157. In support of his thesis Mitchell relies, *inter alia*, on the correlation between social involvement and size (not profits, therefore suggesting a link with power), and with the unpopularity of the industry: *The Generous Corporation*, at 147–53. Responsibility does not of course reduce corporate power (and that of management in particular); as Kaysen remarks, 'No direct responsibility, made effective by formal and functioning machinery of control, exists. No

This analysis leads to an important conclusion about the likely limits to corporate social involvement. If the purpose of social policy is 'to establish the legitimacy of the profit-seeking corporation, to promote public "quiescence" rather than solve society's problems',[151] that is, to build legitimacy rather than to address social issues for their own sake, then the beneficial effects are likely to fall short of the promise. The commitment is not to 'solving society's problems' as such, but to demonstrating a concern with society's problems for business ends and only to the extent that securing those ends requires.

It should be noted that Mitchell characterizes social policy as essentially an individual company response, whereby a company attempts to be perceived as a 'good company' rather than a 'bad company', and hence makes itself relatively safe from regulatory attention. He contends in a related opinion that social-policy efforts are likely to be worthwhile only within a context of broad support for capitalist institutions,[152] and ascribes lower levels of corporate social involvement in Britain and Europe to the supposition that social policy is likely to be ineffective where criticism is preponderantly directed at the capitalist system rather than at the behaviour of particular firms.[153] It is suggested, however, that whatever the company-specific advantages of being thought of as a 'good company' may be,[154] Mitchell underestimates the significance of the collective business interest in being perceived to be responsible. As well as industry-wide advantages in avoiding regulatory intervention with respect to particular issues, such as pollution or product safety, the business community as a whole has an interest in maintaining public confidence in the private enterprise system. Thus, while the political climate in this country is not currently hostile to business, maintaining an image of responsibility is nevertheless of continuing

matter how responsible managers strive to be, they remain in the fundamental sense irresponsible oligarchs in the context of the modern corporate system': 'The Social Social Significance of the Modern Corporation' (above, n. 7), at 316. Nor is this power diminished by appeals to 'professionalism': see Heald, *The Social Responsibilities of Business* (above, n. 20), at 285. On the 'myth' of managerial expertise see A. MacIntyre, *After Virtue: a Study in Moral Theory* (2nd ed., 1985), esp. at 74–8.

[151] Mitchell, *The Generous Corporation* (above, n. 16), at 59.

[152] An acceptance of the legitimacy of big business appears to be a feature of much US pressure group activity directed at companies. See Kuhn and Shriver, *Beyond Success: Corporations and Their Critics in the 1990s* (above, n. 92), at 74: 'The willingness of constituencies to act on their own and to use available, non-governmental, market means suggests that their disagreements with business managers are narrowly based. They disagree, not over fundamentals, but over solutions to problems in particular circumstances.'

[153] For an alternative explanation see Harvey et al., *Managers and Corporate Social Policy* (above, n. 21), at 19–22, who contrast the general acceptance of the welfare state by British managers, with a desire to keep the state at bay on the part of American business, with a much higher level of activism of the part of American companies being the result.

[154] There are obvious advantages in the anti-trust context: see Mitchell, *The Generous Corporation* (above, n. 16), at 90–91, 95, and 100–1.

importance to companies in keeping reform proposals off the political agenda and in marshalling public support against them when they do emerge.[155]

By way of conclusion it should be borne in mind that wherever the precise balance lies between self-interested motivation (whether narrowly or widely defined) and a concern with community welfare for its own sake, for even the most generous companies the total budget for social involvement (i.e. including that from which a pay-back is expected) averages just over a half of 1 per cent of pre-tax profits. While this still means that the figures are significant in absolute terms, it is hard to resist the conclusion that for many companies community involvement is a rather peripheral activity.[156] Expenditure is, for example, much lower than in the United States, where the corresponding proportion is 2–2.5 per cent.[157] Companies appear, furthermore, to make little attempt to calculate the return to themselves from their expenditure,[158] nor, in many cases, to monitor the effects of their involvement or to adopt a pro-active, systematic approach to their community programmes.[159] It seems fair to conclude that most large companies accept that social expenditure up to some conventional figure is now an expected facet of business practice. The size of the budget that a particular company adopts would then appear to depend on a mix of altruistic commitment on the part of management to support for particular social causes; variable degrees of responsiveness to a perceived obligation on companies to contribute to social welfare (with possible reputational damage if they do not); positive promotion of the

---

[155] e.g. the success of campaigns to defend business interests (such as that against the proposals of the Bullock Committee for employee directors in 1977, see Ch. 12 below) is likely to be greater where the public perception of companies is favourable. Social responsibility is only one facet of the efforts to create pro-business attitudes: for a discussion, see R. Miliband, *The State in Capitalist Society* (1969), at 211–18. H. J. Glasbeek views the 'corporate social responsibility movement' (i.e. advocates of responsibility and sometimes of legal reforms to promote it) as also being ideologically motivated, and suggests that the movement's agenda is 'the continued legitimation of capitalist liberal democracy': 'The Corporate Social Responsibility Movement— The Latest in Maginot Lines to Save Capitalism', (1988) 11 *Dalhousie L J* 363, at 368. It is true that the writers to whom he refers are generally supporters of the private-enterprise system and as such their efforts to reform it can be seen as demonstrating also a desire to preserve it. It is, however, possible to support reforms the purpose of which is to increase responsibility without being committed to the virtues of capitalism, on the basis that responsible, is preferable to irresponsible, capitalism. Whether Glasbeek's pessimistic prognosis for the effectiveness of proposed reforms is justified will be considered in the next chapter.

[156] To put social expenditure in perspective, it may be noted that the advertising budget for Unilever companies worldwide in 1989 (with admittedly a particularly large advertising budget) was £1.1bn: see R. Adams, J. Carruthers, and S. Hamil, *Changing Corporate Values: A Guide to Social and Environmental Policy and Practice in Britain's Top Companies* (1991), at 506.

[157] Fogarty and Christie, *Companies and Communities* (above, n. 32), at 121. The CAF, *Charity Trends* (above, n. 109) at 7, refers to the deep-seated problem for charities that there is not the same 'established tradition of widespread corporate philanthropy' in this country as in others.

[158] See Metcalf, Pearson and Martin, *Stimulating Jobs* (above, n. 105), at 67, who report that companies made very little effort to assess the benefit to themselves from participation in job-creation schemes, partly because of the intrinsic difficulty of so doing, but also because the expenditure involved was too small in proportionate terms to warrant investigation of its effects.

[159] See Fogarty and Chrisitie, *Companies and Communities* (above, n. 32), at 17–22.

company's image; a desire to obtain a variety of more tangible benefits associated with particular forms of involvement; and the defence of the collective interests of business. It is consistent with this conclusion that companies do engage in some profit-sacrificing behaviour, but the divergence is likely to be minor and rarely unambiguous.

10

An Evaluation of Profit-Sacrificing Social Responsibility

The previous chapter noted that the legal model of the company is hostile to profit-sacrificing social responsibility but that imperfections in the techniques of legal control mean that managements are able, should they so desire, to make quite substantial departures from the profit goal without fear of judicial intervention. We also saw that companies probably sometimes do sacrifice profits in favour of social interests, though almost certainly within narrow bounds. The purpose of this chapter is to consider whether the public interest would be better served if companies were sometimes to engage in profit-sacrificing social responsibility rather than rigidly adhering to the formula of profit maximization within the law. If it would, there are important implications for the legal model, since it would seem to be desirable to reform the controls regulating management power in order to permit or mandate increased corporate responsiveness to the interests of non-shareholder groups. A search for other measures to ensure that proper weight is given to these interests in company decision-making might also be required.

That companies should sometimes forgo profits in order to reduce the harmful impact of their activities, to treat beneficently groups with whom they deal, or to bring their resources to bear in helping to solve social problems, has a certain intuitive appeal. To see whether this appeal can withstand more sustained analysis, in what follows the main objections to profit-sacrificing social responsibility will be examined. At the risk of distorting the views of individual writers, the criticisms will for convenience be grouped in three categories. The criticisms will thus be referred to as the 'efficiency argument', the 'deference argument', and the 'shareholders' money argument'.

While the criticisms either expressly or by implication include an attack on forms of responsibility that involve a shift in corporate goals, an assessment of the merits of a change in goals will be deferred until Chapter 12. It is realistic to imagine that companies will adopt goals in addition to or instead of the goal of making profits only if there is a fundamental transformation of their decision-making structures and the market context in which they operate.[1] Assuming the continuance of recognizably capitalist institutions, the debate about social responsibility should be seen therefore as a comparatively limited one. It is a debate about whether and to what extent companies in pursuing profits should take account of the impact of their activities on third parties or should comply with moral or social obligations to promote community welfare, rather than about whether profit-seeking should be accompanied or replaced by an open-ended commitment to the furtherance of non-shareholder interests. The justification for the more radical programme of attempting to bring about a shift in business goals will be considered in Chapter 12, which will examine in particular various ways of 'democratizing' the company as a means of effecting a change in goals in the interests of employees. The three groups of criticisms as they relate to the more modest forms of responsibility will now be set out.

I THE THREE CRITICISMS

The *efficiency argument* is simply the corollary of the wealth-maximization justification of corporate enterprise: if social wealth is maximized by the single-minded pursuit of profits, then social responsibility must by definition be inefficient. The view that social responsibility is inefficient is a widely expressed objection to it, exemplified in Friedman's famous and ironic slogan that 'the social responsibility of business is to increase its profits.[2] The suggestion that it is socially responsible to do other than maximize profits within the 'rules of the game'[3] shows 'a fundamental misconception of the character and nature of a free economy'.[4] A central virtue of this 'free economy' is said to lie in its ability to allocate resources with optimal efficiency, a property which depends on the existence of a market in which

---

[1] On the distinction between a change in goals and other forms of responsibility, see 261–71 above. It is accepted that in practice respect for constraints and positive obligations on the one hand and a change in goals on the other are likely to merge into each other.

[2] M. Friedman, 'The Social Responsibility of Business is to Increase its Profits', in T. Beauchamp and N. Bowie (eds), *Ethical Theory and Business* (1988; first published 1970). For a consideration of Friedman's views and of other arguments against (and for) responsibility see N. C. Smith, *Morality and the Market: Consumer Pressure for Corporate Accountability* (1990), at 60–4, 69–76.

[3] The 'rules of the game' are embodied in law and 'ethical custom': Friedman, ibid. The content of the latter is not elaborated, though the relevant ethical principles which apply in addition to those incorporated within the law are presumably intended to be very narrowly drawn, since otherwise they contradict Friedman's basic position. Cf. F. A. Hayek, 'The Corporation in a Democratic Society: In Whose Interest Ought it and Will it be Run?', in H. I. Ansoff (ed.), *Business Strategy* (1969), at 226: 'certain generally accepted rules of decency and, perhaps, even charitableness should probably be regarded as no less binding on corporations than the strict rules of law.'

[4] M. Friedman, *Capitalism and Freedom* (1962), at 133.

utility-maximizing agents make exchanges in response to 'correct' market signals. Acceptance of a social-responsibility ethic involving a disregard for these signals would result, it is argued, in the sub-optimal use of resources and would cause the signals themselves to become blurred and distorted. Thus Rostow insists that if a company were to charge less for its products than the maximum price the market will bear, or pay its employees above the rate necessary to retain their services, this conduct would 'sabotage the market mechanism and systematically distort the allocation of resources'.[5] Further, pricing structures which are not chosen to maximize profits will result, he suggests, in capital 'being attracted to areas which would have claimed less if the market mechanism had been more accurate in measuring the comparative intensity of consumers' desires for different products'.[6] Similarly Hayek insists that, where a plant becomes unprofitable, management should unhesitatingly obey the market and close it down, irrespective of the hardship that might be caused to employees. Even though the plant could be kept going out of the profits of the rest of the enterprise, artificially prolonging its life can only lead to inflated production costs and cause resources to be locked into activities in which they do not yield their full potential return,[7] with a net loss to society as a whole being the inevitable result.

A separate charge is that corporate involvement in social affairs may damage efficiency by distracting management effort from the company's legitimate business activities.[8] While managers are devising affirmative action programmes or attempting to revive the inner city, the business itself may be floundering. It has been argued finally that expenditure for social purposes may lead to a dangerous breakdown in investor confidence.[9] If companies serve social interests at the expense of shareholder gain, equity investment will become comparatively unattractive. An increase in the cost of capital is likely to ensue, bringing with it a reduction in business activity and a corresponding decrease in social welfare.

Proponents of the *deference argument* contend from a number of perspectives that it is inappropriate for issues of social policy to be decided by companies.

[5] E. V. Rostow, 'To Whom and for What Ends is Corporate Management Responsible?', in E. S. Mason (ed.), *The Corporation in Modern Society* (1959) 64. Also Friedman, *Capitalism and Freedom*, (above, n. 4), at 134–135.

[6] Rostow, ibid. at 65.

[7] F. A. Hayek, *Law, Legislation and Liberty* Vol 3 (complete ed., 1982), at 81–82.

[8] See T. Levitt, 'The Dangers of Social Responsibility', in H. D. Marshall (ed.), *Business and Government: The Problem of Power* (1970), at 35–36; Friedman, 'The Social Responsibility of Business is to Increase its Profits' (above, n. 2).

[9] See e.g. C. D. Stone, 'Public Interest Representation: Economic and Social Policy Inside the Enterprise', in K. J. Hopt and G. Teubner (eds), *Corporate Governance and Directors' Liabilities* (1985) 122. at 123; F. H. Easterbrook and D. R. Fischel, 'The Corporate Contract', (1989) 89 *Colum L Rev* 1416, at 1447, reproduced with amendments in F. H. Easterbrook and D. R. Fischel, *The Economic Structure of Corporate Law* (1991), at 37.

The argument points to the public character of social responsibility issues and contends that it is inappropriate for them to be resolved in a private forum: in matters of social policy companies should defer to the cumulative effect of individual preferences expressed through the market and to collective judgements expressed through the political process. If obeying the market produces undesirable results, it is the role of the state and not of companies to correct defects in the behavioural signals. One common strand denies the competence of business managers to deliberate on social matters. Business leaders are chosen for their technical skills, ultimately in making money, and have no special insight into broader questions of community welfare or conflicting social values.[10] As Posner enquires, 'how are managers to decide what is a politically or ethically correct stance?'[11] A second strand questions the legitimacy of such issues being resolved by individuals selected by private, non-representative, and publicly unaccountable groups. Rostow points out that companies 'are not accepted in public opinion as institutions through which society makes its educational policy, its foreign policy, or its political policy',[12] and Friedman asks whether it is tolerable that the 'public functions of taxation, expenditure, and control be exercised by the people who happen at the moment to be in charge of particular enterprises, chosen for these posts by strictly private groups'.[13] Social policy is a matter for the democratically elected legislature and organs accountable thereto. Engel incorporates the latter proposition in a comprehensive normative political theory modelling the relationship between the company and the state, arguing that 'public corporations should pursue only goals whose pursuit by corporations is supported by broad public consensus.' That consensus, manifested in the outcome of the legislative process, authorizes only a policy of profit maximization within the law.[14]

[10] See e.g. Friedman, *Capitalism and Freedom* (above, n. 4), at 133-134; Hayek, 'The Corporation in a Democratic Society' (above, n. 3), at 231. See also H. G. Manne, in H. G. Manne and H. C. Wallich, *The Modern Corporation and Social Responsibility* (1972), at 30-1. Manne indicates that this incompetence does not necessarily result from a lack of expertise, but is a consequence of the fact that 'we have no definition of a social welfare function that is universally acceptable. This strongly suggests that any effort to maximize public good by private effort or otherwise is doomed to failure.'

[11] R. A. Posner, *Economic Analysis of Law* (3rd ed., 1986), at 396.

[12] Rostow, 'To Whom and for What Ends is Corporate Management Responsible?' (above, n. 5), at 68. And see V Brudney, 'The Independent Director — Heavenly City or Potemkin Village?', (1982) 95 *Harv L Rev* 597, at 641: 'Whether it is desirable to permit aggregations of capital to be untrammeled players in the political arena or in social or economic affairs not directly connected with profitmaking, is a question that our society has not yet answered in the affirmative.'

[13] Friedman, *Capitalism and Freedom* (above, n. 4), at 133-4. See also W. J. Baumol and S. A. B. Blackman, 'Social Policy: Pricing Devices to Aid the Invisible Hand', in Baumol and Blackman, *Perfect Markets and Easy Virtue* (1991), 46.

[14] D. L. Engel, 'An Approach to Corporate Social Responsibility', (1979) 32 *Stan L Rev* 1, at 34; see further below 331-3. See also T. M. Jones and L. D. Goldberg, 'Governing the Large Corporation: More Arguments for Public Directors', (1982) 7 *Academy of Management Rev* 603.

A related point is that in making social-policy decisions companies arrogate to themselves social power. Thus Hayek insists that if companies are allowed to act as arbiters of social policy they will become 'centers of uncontrollable power'; from being institutions 'serving the expressed needs of individuals' they will be transformed into institutions determining which ends the efforts of individuals should serve.[15] For those who are conscious that companies in pursuing the conventional profit goal already possess substantial economic and social power,[16] corporate social involvement can nevertheless be seen an extension of that power. Wedderburn, for example, notes that 'All corporate decisions to buy church bells or create jobs, noble though they both may be, are dispositions of social power and raise the issue of social accountability'.[17]

Finally, in the 'free market' anti-responsibility literature the above objections are underscored by a fear that social involvement by business will lead ultimately to a take-over of the running of companies by the state. Friedman warns that 'Few trends could so throughly undermine the very foundations of our free society as the acceptance by corporate officials of a social responsibility other than to make as much money for their stockholders as possible ... [it is a] fundamentally subversive doctrine'.[18] It would lead to business managers being chosen by the 'public techniques of election and appointment', but long before that, he foretells, their decision-making powers are likely to have been confiscated.[19] Hayek similarly considers it 'a logical consequence' of the conception that management should aim to promote the general welfare that 'the appointed representatives of the public interest should control the management'.[20] These latter points can be disposed of briefly here. While state participation is a possible consequence of an assumption by companies of public-welfare functions, it is not a necessary one. Indeed Chapter 9 discussed the possibility that one purpose of corporate social involvement is to discourage or displace government intervention in what companies consider to be the proper sphere of business. Furthermore, whether state involvement in the internal management of companies is the evil that Friedman, Hayek, and those of like mind regard it is in large part a matter of political conviction, though it is certainly not self-evident

---

[15] Hayek, 'The Corporation in a Democratic Society' (above n. 3), at 231.
[16] See Ch. 1 above.
[17] Lord Wedderburn, "Trust, Corporation and the Worker', (1985) 23 *Osgoode Hall L J* 203, at 229 (emphasis omitted). See also J. Melrose-Woodman and I. Kverndal, *Towards Social Responsibility: Company Codes of Ethics and Practice*, British Institute of Management, Management Survey Report no. 28 (1976), at 9.
[18] Friedman, *Capitalism and Freedom* (above, n. 4), at 133. This view is endorsed by Hayek, 'The Corporation in a Democratic Society' (above, n. 3), at 238–239. Furthermore, in recognizing a social policy-making function with outcomes that may contradict the verdict of the market, the practice of profit-sacrificing social responsibility constitutes 'pure unadulterated socialism': M Friedman, *An Economist's Protest* (1972), at 177.
[19] Friedman, *Capitalism and Freedom* (above, n. 4), at 134.
[20] Hayek, 'The Corporation in a Democratic Society' (above, n. 3), at 231.

that the involvement of the state would undermine 'the very foundations of our free society', at least unless freedom and the existence of capitalist institutions in their current form are to be equated.

The *shareholders' money argument* speaks for itself. It suggests that any policy other than profit maximization involves a non-consensual transfer of wealth from the members and that this is morally improper.[21] Whether the shareholders are viewed as the company's owners or as parties to a nexus of contracts, their legal status as residuary claimants, the argument runs, has a moral foundation. It is accordingly an infringement of the shareholders' moral as well as their legal rights for the company to increase its expenses in order to safeguard the interests of non-shareholder groups or to use the corporate surplus to finance social programmes.

The validity of the three arguments will now be examined. Section II will evaluate the adoption of other-regarding constraints in the light of them, and Section III, similarly, the practice of social activism. During the course of the discussion the positive case for social responsibility will emerge. Section IV will consider, as a precursor to the next chapter, how the concept of social responsibility should be understood if progress is to be made in establishing a legal framework conducive to improved standards of corporate behaviour.

II THE ADOPTION OF OTHER-REGARDING CONSTRAINTS

The Efficiency Argument

As noted in Chapter 1, the equation of private profit-maximizing behaviour with social wealth-maximizing effects presupposes that the market is fully competitive and assumes the absence of other forms of market failure. Advocates of the efficiency argument generally accept the existence of 'real-world' market imperfections, but argue that these are adequately resolved through the use of external regulatory techniques: the adoption of constraints over and above those required by law is liable to be counter-productive.[22] From this perspective the validity of the efficiency argument turns on the capacity of legal controls to produce desired social outcomes, in this case to correct market failure and hence realign profit maximization with the maximization of social wealth. Whether external controls are capable of adjusting company behaviour to the full extent and in all the respects that are deemed to be socially desirable will be discussed below as part of the

---

[21] See e.g. D. R. Fischel, 'The Corporate Governance Movement', (1982) 35 *Vand L Rev* 1259, at 1273; Easterbrook and Fischel, 'The Corporate Contract' (above, note 9), at 1446–8; N. Barry, *The Morality of Business Enterprise* (1991), ch. 2.

[22] See e.g Easterbrook and Fischel, ibid. at 1447–8.

consideration of the deference argument. Here the inefficiencies to which market failure gives rise and the possibility of ameliorating them by voluntary action will be examined.

Uncompetitive Market Structure

An obvious respect in which the corporate economy departs from the perfect competition model is that the markets for many goods and services are oligopolistic in character. Firms that enjoy some element of monopoly power maximize profits at a lower output and higher price than those operating in the notional world of perfect competition. This being so, it is not self-evident that where a firm forbears to charge the full profit-maximizing price, to quote Rostow's example, this will be less efficient overall than if it had taken advantage of its market power. Forbearance may actually improve efficiency by bringing the company's prices and output closer to the levels that would prevail in more competitive conditions.[23] A similar point can be made in relation to a company's decision not to exploit its dominant position as a purchaser, for example, of raw materials or labour. Whether or not self-restraint will be beneficial in any particular case is difficult to establish, however, by virtue of the intractable 'problem of second best'. This is the problem that where there are monopolistic elements in any sector of the economy, or any of the other requirements for perfect competition are not met (for example, there are barriers to entry or a lack of information about market conditions), then because of the effect on the structure of relative prices it cannot be stated on a priori grounds that mimicking the way a firm would behave in a perfectly competitive market will produce results that are 'second-best' to the ideal ones. Rather, determining what will lead to the best available outcome in the circumstances depends on a complex analysis of the particular facts of each case.[24]

The uncertainty that results once the artificial assumptions of perfect competition are dropped is of wider importance in evaluating the efficiency argument because it means, not only that it becomes unclear what pricing policy is most conducive to social wealth maximization, but also that it becomes difficult to assess the efficiency effects of socially responsible practices of other kinds, such as improving product quality or delaying plant closures. It is at least plausible, however, that if the signals provided by the market are systematically distorted as a result of weak competition and other forms of market failure, then following those signals will not always lead to the

---

[23] See M. Bronfenbrenner, 'The Consumer', in J. W. McKie (ed.), *Social Responsibility and the Business Predicament* (1974), ch. 7; D. Helm, 'Mergers, Take-overs, and the Enforcement of Profit Maximization', in J. A. Fairburn and J. Kay (eds), *Mergers and Merger Policy* (1989) 133, at 146–7.
[24] See F. M. Scherer, *Industrial Market Structure and Economic Performance* (2nd ed., 1980), at 24–29. The problem is of particular importance in framing competition policy.

most efficient available outcomes. Once this is acknowledged the local and tangible benefits of social responsibility begin to look more attractive than the speculative and abstract social gains flowing from a rule of strict profit maximization. This is not to say that the market in practice fails to operate as an effective coordinating mechanism and that companies could or should ignore its signals, but only that limited departures from profit maximization may not in reality have the consequences predicted by the theoretical model.

Externalities

A second source of disjunction between profit-maximizing behaviour and allocative efficiency is the problem of externalities. In the absence of legal restrictions, producers are sometimes able to inflict part of the costs of their activities, known to economists as 'external costs' or 'negative externalities', on third parties.[25] For example, where a company disposes of waste products by discharging them into a nearby river, disposal may be free as far as the company is concerned, but it is not without cost from the point of view of the third parties who are thereby affected. All those who use the river for other purposes, such as for industrial processes that require clean water or for recreation, will suffer as a result of the deterioration in water quality. In other cases the consequences of environmental degradation will be much more widespread, as where by contributing to the greenhouse effect gaseous emissions bring about changes in world climate. Apart from moral objections to the destruction of the natural environment and questions of fairness as between those who cause damage and those who suffer from it,[26] where producers can externalize costs there is also an efficiency issue, since they will make decisions that involve a misallocation of resources. This is because, as external costs are not borne by the firm, the firm will fail to reflect them in the prices it charges for its products. Output in consequence will be higher than it would be if price matched the social cost of production (the sum of internal and external costs), with the result that the resources devoted to the activity in question are in excess of the socially efficient level.

If producers could be made to pay their 'victims' the full cost of the damage created by their operations the inefficiency would disappear: goods would no longer be produced beyond the point at which they made a positive contribution to aggregate welfare.[27] Companies would, furthermore,

---

[25] See R. G. Lipsey, *An Introduction to Positive Economics* (7th ed., 1989), at 400–2, 424–5; G. Richardson, A. Ogus, and P. Burrows, *Policing Pollution: A Study of Regulation and Enforcement* (1982), at 7–10; M. Jacobs, *The Green Economy: Environment, Sustainable Development and the Politics of the Future* (1991), at 27–34.

[26] See Richardson et al. ibid. at 9–10.

[27] The requirements of allocative efficiency would be served equally if those affected by pollution paid the firm not to pollute, i.e. compensated it for lost production, up to the point at which they valued a pollution-free atmosphere more than the alternative uses of their money: see R. H. Coase, 'The Problem of Social Cost', (1960) 3 *J Economics* 1, discussed in F. H.

have an incentive to install pollution control devices to the extent that this would be cheaper than making compensation payments, again increasing efficiency overall. A compensation system will, however, rarely be a practicable solution to the externality problem. With regard to atmospheric pollution, for example, since the air is unowned its use as a medium for the disposal of waste products cannot be charged for.[28] The alternative of imposing liability in tort for damage inflicted is likely to be feasible for only a limited range of small-scale interdependencies: poor air quality in general is the cumulative effect of discharges from many sources, making attribution of liability impossible, and the costs of pollution are borne by whole populations and even future generations and cannot realistically be recouped in damages actions. The main solution to environmental externalities in practice is government intervention to make companies limit the harmful effects of the processes they employ. Intervention can take a variety of forms, including conventional regulation, such as imposing retrictions on permissible discharges and requirements to use approved production methods and pollution-control techniques, and other devices such as pollution taxes and tradable pollution permits designed to give companies an incentive to reduce damaging environmental effects.[29] If, to anticipate the discussion below, the regulatory regime at any given time fails to require all costs to be internalized, as seems virtually inevitable,[30] then an appropriate level of voluntary 'environmental responsibility', such as changing production methods, using less polluting raw materials, or spending more on the abatement of emissions than the law requires, ought to increase rather to than reduce efficiency overall notwithstanding that these actions might make a negative contribu-

Stephen, *The Economics of Law* (1988), ch. 3 and see also the criticisms in J. W. Singer, 'The Reliance Interest in Property', (1988) 40 *Stan L Rev* 611, at 726–7. This solution is not available either, however, *inter alia*, because of the 'free-rider' problem: since the air is available to all without restriction, the benefits of clean air can be enjoyed without paying, and so no one would be willing to pay: see Jacobs, *The Green Economy* (above, n. 25), at 29–34.

[28] It is sometimes argued that a solution to the problem of externalities is the extension of private property rights. See however Richardson et al, *Policing Pollution* (above, n. 25), at 11: 'The outcome of previous studies of the possible resolution of interdependencies through free market bargains is the conviction that the market cannot be expected to generate socially efficient outcomes in any but the small-scale interdependencies between neighbours' (ref omitted).

[29] On the respective merits of the techniques, see Jacobs, *The Green Economy* (above, n. 25), chs 11 and 12. As Jacobs points out, at 151, the view that pollution taxes are 'right-wing' because they are a 'free-market' solution and regulation is 'left-wing' is 'nonsense', since both taxes and regulations 'operate within markets; they are both state interventions designed to influence the behaviour of otherwise autonomous firms and consumers. Neither has anything to do with the 'free market': on the contrary, if such a thing existed both would be seen as its enemy.'

[30] Cf. Hayek, 'The Corporation in a Democratic Society' (above, n. 3), at 229, who is confident that the 'special difficulties' resulting from externalities can be remedied by the 'gradual improvement of the law'. And see Baumol and Blackman, 'Social Policy: Pricing Devices to Aid the Invisible Hand' (above, n. 13), expressing confidence in the superiority of 'changing the rules of the game' over corporate voluntarism.

tion to profits.[31] It should be recalled that the issue here is not whether companies do or can successfully be encouraged to make such expenditures, but rather whether the adoption of other-regarding constraints is inimical to efficiency in principle.

External diseconomies have been discussed in relation to production but external effects are not confined to the production process. The goods that result and their packaging may themselves be environmentally damaging, either in use or after disposal. And concern about the environment involves not only questions of pollution, but extends to problems of resource depletion, which can also be analysed in externality terms.[32] Nor do externalities occur only in relation to the environment: they can be of a more broadly social character. The construction of a factory on open land surrounding a town, for example, will reduce the amenity of those who previously used the land for recreation or just liked to look at it or derived a sense of well-being from its existence. The costs that these deprivations represent will not in the ordinary course of things form part of the developer's calculations in assessing the profitability of the project. Similarly, plant closures can have catastrophic effects on the economy of local communities, setting in motion a spiral of decline as unemployment rises, dependent service industries collapse, and the crime rate and other problems associated with poverty and demoralization increase. These are costs borne by society but which need not figure in private profit-maximizing calculations.[33] They suggest again that a willingness to forgo profits can in certain circumstances be wealth increasing overall.

Allocative inefficiency arises also from the existence of *positive* or benefit externalities. These result in too little of an activity taking place because all the benefits flowing from it cannot be captured by the actor: the optimal level of the activity in question is not privately profitable.[34] An important example is the training of employees (others include research and attention to the aesthetic quality of the company's premises). Thus, because at some point in the future an employee may move to a different firm, an employer has little incentive to provide training beyond the minimum necessary for the satisfactory performance of the employee's current tasks.[35] The employer, in

---

[31] A. Etzioni, *The Moral Dimension: Toward a New Economics* (1988), at 34, sees an efficiency-increasing role for responsibility, suggesting that 'Morality is a major way externalities are "introduced" into one's deliberations and decision-making . . . Indeed, morality is a much more widely used and less costly and less coercive mechanism for attending to the commons than government inducements or public "incentives" provided via the market.'

[32] See Jacobs, *The Green Economy* (above, n. 25), at 29–31.

[33] See Singer, 'The Reliance Interest in Property' (above, n. 27), at 712–20.

[34] See generally, R. Musgrave, 'On Social Goods and Social Bads', in R. Marris (ed.), *The Corporate Society* (1974) 251.

[35] The poor record of British industry in providing training is evidence of this phenomenon: see Department of Employment, *Training in Britain: A Study of Funding, Activity and Attitudes* (1989). For example, in 1987 one in three economically active adults claimed not to have received any job-related training or education in the previous three years: *Main Report*, ch. 2.

other words, will recognize a risk that any additional investment in training may not be fully recouped, and hence will be unwilling to undertake it. If, however, companies in general were to provide a higher level of training, those with a need for employees with the relevant skills at some time in the future, and society as a whole, would benefit from the existence of a better qualified workforce. Shortfalls in training can obviously be ameliorated by state subsidy or state provision of training. Equally, additional expenditure on training by employers beyond the level that is privately profitable is capable of making a positive contribution to social welfare.

Lack of Information and the Problem of Trust

A third problem with the operation of markets is that in practice, as distinct from in the economist's model, parties often enter into transactions without the benefit of full information about the characteristics of the goods or services being traded, or about the availability of superior products or more favourable terms. Lack of information has adverse implications for overall efficiency because it leads to sub-optimal exchanges: a better allocation of resources would be achieved if the parties had full access to the facts. Arrow has commented that because knowledge is often incomplete 'the price system is no insurance of efficiency in all respects ... Some alternative system of determining quality and providing assurance for buyers is needed'.[36] One possibility, he suggests, is 'a sense of social responsibility on the part of the seller'. This might take the form of voluntary disclosure of information, reflecting a concern with the well-being of the purchaser rather than simply a desire to obtain the best possible bargain consistent with the requirements of the law of contract and statutory controls. The effect of a business voluntarily disclosing information may be to cause customers to deal with a different supplier, one better able to satisfy their needs, or it may lead to a variation in the terms on which the parties contract. The resulting transactions will be more efficient than the ones that would have been entered into had the first supplier exploited customer ignorance. A similar point can be made where the company is a buyer of goods or services (including labour) and has more accurate information than the seller about the commodity's value, that is, knows that the commodity can command a higher price in an alternative use. In such circumstances openness may again result in a more efficient allocation of resources. Finally, voluntary disclosure can lead to a significant increase in efficiency by reducing transaction costs, that is, the cost of obtaining information and negotiating detailed contractual provisions to protect the parties' respective interests.

[36] K. J. Arrow, 'Gifts and Exchanges', in E. S. Phelps, *Altruism, Morality and Economic Theory* (1975) 13, at 22. One method of providing assurance is through statutory controls. As with legal intervention to cure externalities, however, the protection offered may be less than complete: see further below.

What has been said about truthfulness in dealings is likely to be applicable to ethical behaviour more generally. A relationship with a customer, employee, or supplier which is intended to endure demands a measure of mutual trust. Trust is likely to break down where one party exploits the ignorance, miscalculation, or weak bargaining position of the other, attempts to palm off substandard goods, or generally cuts corners. In an environment in which such behaviour is common, parties must inevitably incur substantial transaction costs in drafting and policing terms designed to safeguard their interests, and may even be deterred from dealing at all, with the result that there is a reduced level of business activity overall.[37] Indeed, the successful operation of markets may depend on the existence of a set of underlying moral values that are insufficiently produced by the market mechanism itself.[38] Since adherence to these values involves positive externalities (the benefits from contributing to an atmosphere of trust are not fully captured by the agent), they are likely to be generated only where market participants are on occasion willing to respect the interests of others at their own expense.[39] In that it increases the supply of the 'public good' of trust, therefore, compliance with ethical standards contributes to the efficient functioning of the economy. This is not to say that self-interested market behaviour should be replaced by a self-denying concern for the welfare of others; taken too far, altruism would undermine the assumptions on which a system of mutually advantageous exchange depends. The point is merely that the maximization of social wealth does not demand the merciless pursuit of self-interest, but rather requires a degree of mutual support and forbearance.

[37] See Arrow, ibid. at 24; R. N. McKean, 'Collective Choice', in McKie (ed.), *Social Responsibility and the Business Predicament* (above, n. 23), at 121-122. For an analytically rigorous consideration of the role of trust in commercial relationships see M. Casson, *The Economics of Business Culture: Game Theory, Transaction Costs, and Economic Performance* (1991).

[38] See F. Hirsch, *Social Limits to Growth* (1977), at 80-81; 117 - 118; J. W. Kuhn and D. W. Shriver, *Beyond Success* (1991), at 9-14; W. C. Kester, *Japanese Takeovers: The Global Contest for Corporate Control* (1991), at 60 - 7 (long-term trading relationships between companies in Japan resting on trust and implicit contracting); E. H. Lorenz, 'Neither Friends Nor Strangers: Informal Networks of Subcontracting in French Industry', in D. Gambetta (ed.), *Trust: Making and Breaking of Cooperative Relations* (1989) 194 (role of trust and co-operation in French engineering industry).

[39] Appropriate standards of fair dealing can to an extent be reinforced by law. The contrast between the English law of contract, with its traditional emphasis on arm's length dealings and the principle of *caveat emptor*, and the principles of good faith and contractual justice enshrined in German law, is instructive. Para 242 of the German Civil Code (Bürgerliches Gesetzbuch/BGB), for example, gives 'legal force to broad ethical values': N. Horn, K. Kötz, and H. G. Leser, *German Private and Commercial Law: An Introduction* (1982), at 137. Cf. *Interfoto Picture Library Ltd v Stiletto Visual Programmes Ltd* [1989] QB 433, CA, [1988] 1 All ER 348, at 325-3, per Bingham L J; *Walford v Miles* [1992] 1 All ER 453, HL, at 460, per Lord Ackner.

The Costs of Responsibility and the Effect on Investor Confidence

The remaining ingredients of the efficiency argument against the adoption of other-regarding constraints are first, that responsibility is inefficient because the process of formulating and self-applying constraints is one that itself imposes costs on the organization, and second, that these costs, and especially the profits forgone as a result of companies practising responsibility, will damage investor confidence. The first of these points has only limited application to responsibility of the constraint type. Managing the relationship between the company and the various affected parties is not a distraction or digression from 'legitimate' business activity, but an integral part of it. Undertaking an environmental audit, for example, is now recognized by many managements as bringing advantages to the company itself in terms of avoiding prosecution and bad publicity and reducing avoidable waste. It is true that a commitment to other-regarding, as distinct from prudential, constraints may involve some additional management effort in terms of assessing the impact of company behaviour and designing and enforcing appropriate standards. These reformed decision-making processes may also impose additional costs on the company because decisions are delayed. Whether incurring any of these extra costs means that the outcome overall is less efficient, however, clearly depends on whether the responsible behaviour that is engendered is itself more efficient than 'non-responsible behaviour'. It is, in other words, ultimately a matter of degree, but it seems certain that there will be cases in which the additional private costs associated with a more responsive decision-making process will be more than compensated by the gains made in increased efficiency in aggregate.

The investor confidence objection is more difficult to assess. It is possible in theory that companies might incur so much expense in safeguarding the interests of third parties that the attractiveness of holding equities as against other forms of investment would be reduced, with a consequent damaging effect on the flow of funds into industry. There is little reason to believe, however, that current or realistically imaginable levels of social expenditure are liable to have this result. There is in fact some evidence on the attitude of shareholders to expenditure for social-policy purposes, in relation to social activism in the form of corporate charitable donations.[40] This indicates that institutional investors are prepared to tolerate donations at a significantly higher level than is currently experienced. With regard to the adoption of constraints, institutional investors with a typical broad spread of investments might rationally conclude that behaviour which is beneficial to the economy overall is in their interests, even though it might involve a sacrifice

---

[40] Allied Research International, *The Views of Shareholders on Donations by Companies to Charity*, report to the Charities Aid Foundation (1985); and see M. Fogarty and I. Christie, *Companies and Communities* (1990), at 15–16.

of profits on the part of individual portfolio companies. In any event, any tendencies towards 'excessive responsibility' are likely to be held in check by governance and market pressures.

Conclusion

To summarize, the consideration of the efficiency argument above has suggested that some forms of socially responsible behaviour are capable of correcting for market failure and as such, contrary to the efficiency argument, will tend to promote rather than diminish allocative efficiency. It is possible of course that companies might show 'excessive responsibility' (viewed purely in efficiency terms), that is, their conduct might go beyond what is required for a socially efficient outcome. A company motivated by a concern for the impact of its decisons on affected groups might at least in theory protect the interests of such groups to an extent that is not socially optimal in aggregative terms. That this possibility exists does not, however, establish a conclusive case on efficiency grounds against *all* instances of social responsibility. In a similar way, the other aspects of the efficiency argument may be valid depending on the types and level of responsibility practised, but they are not convincing objections to profit-sacrificing responsibility as such. It should be stressed in conclusion that even to the extent that the efficiency argument is valid, it does not necessarily follow that profit-sacrificing behaviour is undesirable, since we might be prepared to tolerate a reduction in efficiency in order to protect individual interests and ethical or social values that conflict with it. Efficiency is not, in other words, the only issue at stake.

The Deference Argument

The central claim of the deference argument as it relates to other-regarding constraints is that decisions to forgo profits in favour of third party interests involve issues of social policy and that such issues should not be addressed by companies, but rather by bodies that are democratically accountable. Thus, in so far as the pursuit of maximum profits may lead to inefficient results owing to market failure, the appropriate response is for the state to amend the regulatory framework within which companies operate, not for companies to impose on themselves controls of their own design. Similarly, social-policy objectives distinct from that of wealth maximization, such as protecting employees from redundancy, safeguarding the environment (for its own sake), securing non-exploitative treatment of Third-World trading partners, or preserving the vitality of city centres by curtailing out-of-town shopping developments, are matters to be determined democratically after public debate, not privately by company managements.

The Argument

Before assessing the deference argument a number of points need to be clarified. It should be noted first of all that the argument derives its force from the fact that large companies possess power. There is nothing intrinsic to the policy issues that the argument reserves for the democratic process to suggest that they should be determined solely by public bodies. It is not inherently objectionable to exceed regulatory requirements, for example, for a small manufacturing business to spend more on environmental protection than the law demands. Private individuals and associations, as well as governments, are free to make their own decisions about the value of an unpolluted environment, or, for instance, about the ethics of trading with oppressive regimes or dealing in tobacco products. The point is rather that because of the scale of their activities, and particularly because they typically possess a degree of market power, large companies make decisions that have significant public effects. Thus, by virtue of their market position, large businesses are often able to pass part of the costs of social responsibility on to their customers.[41] It follows that management-ordained environmental improvements, for example, are achieved by raising prices and reducing output, and therefore that a trade-off is involved between increased material prosperity brought by high output at low prices on the one hand, and the maintenance of environmental quality on the other. It is here that the deference argument comes into play, in contending that the balance between these conflicting social aspirations should be struck by democratically account-able, and not by private and largely self-appointed bodies. Similar issues arise in relation to the other constraints that companies might impose on themselves, for example, with regard to employee safety and rewards, job preservation, trading standards, and product quality. These matters involve questions of resource allocation and social priority, and entail value choices that can legitimately be made, the argument holds, only in a public forum. Likewise, if there is a demand for tobacco or out-of-town retail complexes, or a profit to be made from carrying on business in states that violate their citizens' human rights,[42] companies should obey the signals of the market and leave countervailing ethical and social considerations to the relevant political authorities.

Second, it should be emphasized, as the previous paragraph implies but the deference argument frequently overlooks, that social policy-making of a certain kind by companies is inescapable. Decisions about whether to close factories or to invest in new plants and where to locate them, about research

---

[41] See Posner, *Economic Analysis of Law* (above, n. 11), at 395–6.

[42] The celebrated withdrawal of Barclays from South Africa in 1986 is more easily attributable to consumer and political pressure than to preponderantly ethical considerations, and hence is an example of behaviour influenced by prudential as opposed to other-regarding constraints. For a discussion, see Smith, *Morality and the Market* (above, n. 2), at 234–241.

and development programmes, about employment conditions, and the broad range of other issues that companies must confront inevitably have important social consequences. There is no unique, market-determined solution to these questions; rather, companies make choices, and the choices they make are liable to have widely differing effects. What the deference argument contends on its most coherent interpretation is that this managerial discretion should always be exercised in accordance with the same general criterion, that is, profit maximization within the law. Underlying the argument is the assumption that by adopting this criterion companies submit to the maximum degree of social control. Market signals cannot fully determine company behaviour, but if companies pursue profits that is the best way of ensuring that they are responsive to the public's preferences. Control by the market is supplemented by control through the political process, brought to bear where market signals alone fail to produce the socially desired result. The deference argument portrays profit-sacrificing social responsibility as involving a disregard for these processes of social control, holding that 'it is for public representatives, accountable to the general electorate, to decide when and how to override the market signals, and not for the managers of private firms, whose training, expertise, and accountability is nonpolitical'.[43] By departing from profit maximization within the law companies therefore expand their discretion, and this is objectionable.

Finally, a variant of the deference argument should be noted. The version of the argument just described relies on a preference based in political theory that company behaviour should be shaped exclusively by market pressures supplemented by state-imposed constraints. A second version contends that not only is it desirable from the viewpoint of political theory that company behaviour should be determined in this way, but that there is actually a popular consensus to that effect, and that this consensus should be respected.[44] That the consensus disapproves of companies adopting additional constraints of their own choosing is said to be evident from the ability of the legislature to alter company behaviour in whatever ways it wishes by the imposition of appropriate sanctions. Its failure to apply sanctions in all other cases should be taken as an endorsement of the pursuit by companies of maximum profits in those cases.[45] The second version of the argument against social responsibil-

---

[43] C. D. Stone, 'Corporate Social Responsibility: What it Might Mean, If it Were Really to Matter', (1986) 71 *Iowa L Rev* 557, at 566. Stone does not espouse this view himself.

[44] See Engel, 'An Approach to Corporate Social Responsibility' (above, n. 14), esp. at 2–5, 34–6. Engel's argument is actually not that companies should maximize profits 'within the law', that is, that the law should be regarded as imposing an absolute prohibition on certain forms of behaviour. Rather, it is that companies should always maximize profits, regarding legal penalties as the price of infringing behaviour. If the behaviour is still profitable taking into account the price (the discounted penalty) then society has ordained that the conduct should take place. See further 331–3 below.

[45] Engel makes the assumption, ibid. at 2, that

the measures coming out of the legislative process either accurately reflect the political will of

ity does not merely rest therefore on a political preference that 'public' issues be determined in a democratic forum, but also on the claim that by making social policy companies commit a breach of their political mandate.[46]

The Merits of the Argument

Having made these points of clarification, whether the deference argument offers a convincing case against the adoption of other-regarding constraints can now be assessed. The argument holds that company behaviour should be controlled exclusively by markets and the political process, but an obvious reply is that these mechanisms themselves suffer from serious defects and therefore that superior results could be achieved if companies were free to correct for market failure and regulatory shortcomings. Before considering whether the existence of these defects has the effect of undermining the deference argument, it will be useful to summarize the main problems.

As to market defects, the dulling of producer responsiveness to consumer tastes found in imperfectly competitive markets and the unwelcome spillover effects associated with the externalization of costs have already been noted and need not be examined again here. It is, however, worth giving brief consideration to the deficiencies in the claim that is sometimes made, that markets are an effective way of ensuring that companies respect the social and ethical preferences of customers and other market participants, as well as satisfying more immediate demands for goods and services. The likelihood that companies sometimes do impose constraints on themselves in excess of those set by law was noted in the previous chapter. An important reason for this behaviour is no doubt to avoid reputational damage, since this may be converted into damage to profitability through the operation of the market for the company's products, the market for employees, or the capital market.[47] If social and ethical preferences could be fully transmitted through markets then there would arguably be no need for companies to depart from the profit maximization objective, since complying with those preferences would be a precondition of maximimum profitability. Social expectations would thus be satisfied by companies adopting prudential constraints; any 'responsibility' additional to that dictated by long-term profit considerations would seemingly be unwarranted (and the need for regulatory intervention also considerably reduced).

the relevant constituencies — on the basis of facts known — or may be taken to reflect that will because of a widely shared acceptance of legitimacy . . . even legislative inaction should be taken to reflect political consensus — a consensus that nothing should be done about a particular matter.

[46] Of course, as Engel must accept, see ibid. at 33–4, the argument against responsibility based on political consensus is inapplicable where the legislature endorses voluntary profit-sacrificing behaviour by altering the corporate constitution and control mechanisms in order to encourage such behaviour.

[47] i.e. through the activities of 'ethical investors': see 376–7, Ch. 11 below.

There are, however, several reasons why markets may fail to align company behaviour with social preferences in the way that this reasoning suggests.[48] The discussion here will concentrate on the product market; employment and capital-market pressure for responsible action will be considered in Chapter 11, in connection with methods for enhancing market control in general. First, and rather obviously, many people who are affected by a company's activities have no market relationship with it, for example, householders next to a heavy engineering plant or the as yet unborn who will in due course be injured by the pollution the company creates. Such persons have no opportunity to influence company policy through their market behaviour.[49] There is a second problem of inadequate information. Consumers will often be unaware, for example, of the comparative environmental consequences of the production, use, and disposal of rival products. Or many of the company's customers, even if they care, may be ignorant of the company's exploitative treatment of Third-World employees or of its exports of dangerous products banned in the home country. In each of these cases the market penalty for behaviour that meets with social disapproval will be slight, because in the absence of information customers will fail to 'vote' to change the behaviour in question by buying elsewhere.

A third factor is that attempts to alter company policies by way of the market often suffer from 'collective action' problems. Purchasing behaviour is most likely to influence how companies operate where what is disapproved of is a feature of the goods or services being sold and thus affects customers directly. If I believe that a certain product is dangerous or contains additives harmful to health I will buy a substitute. There is much less incentive to do this, however, where what I want to do is to change company policy on some issue that is not reflected in the product itself. I may, for example, disapprove of the company's equal-opportunities record or of its involvement in the arms trade, but in order to register that disapproval by buying a substitute product I may incur added expense. Since I know that my own individual purchase decision will have a minimal impact on the company concerned, it will not be worth incurring the additional cost unless others are also prepared to do so, and as I have no assurance that they will I may well decide to buy the cheaper product notwithstanding my objections to the company's policies.[50] The outcome is that the impact of 'ethical purchase behaviour' on corporate conduct is substantially reduced because only a minority of

[48] See also Stone, *Where The Law Ends: The Social Control of Corporate Behaviour* (1975), ch. 10.
[49] The former might in theory band together and pay the company not to pollute, but this will rarely be feasible (or desirable): see n. 27 above.
[50] This problem can to an extent be overcome by coordinated action in the form of an organized boycott. These are likely to be successful, however, only in relation to very specific campaign issues and it may be difficult to sustain the momentum on a continuing basis: see generally Smith, *Morality and The Market* (above, n. 2); Kuhn and Shriver, *Beyond Success* (above, n. 38), ch. 2.

consumers with strong convictions are prepared to engage in it, at least where buying substitute goods from non-offending producers (assuming that they exist) involves a significant private cost.

The same problem of collective action lies behind what Hirsch refers to as the 'tyranny of small decisions'. He explains for example that

purchase of books at discount stores eventually removes the local bookshop. Yet bookbuyers can never exercise a choice between cheaper books with no bookshop and dearer books with one. The choice they are offered is between books at cut price and books at full price; naturally, they take the former.[51]

Book discounting will, in other words, drive some bookshops out of business, and while book-buyers might prefer that this should not happen, the logic of individual market behaviour means that they are unable prevent it. The collective action problem therefore implies a form of market failure: the market fails fully to reflect consumer choices. That consumers do in fact have policy preferences that the market mechanism cannot adequately communicate is illustrated by Jacobs, who notes that

There is ample evidence to show people's valuations in the political arena are different from their market ones—that is, that their behaviour as *citizens* is different from their behaviour as *consumers*. For example, in opinion polls (which are proxies for democratic choice) substantial majorities of people say that they wish to protect the environment, and are willing to pay higher taxes and prices to do so. But as consumers they continue to buy goods and services which cause serious environmental degradation.[52]

The appropriate response to the failure of the market as a communication medium, as the last quotation implies, will usually be the imposition of mandatory controls. If, however, there are also doubts about the effectiveness in some circumstances of regulatory intervention, is there not also room for voluntary action?

A final problem, more fundamental than and underscoring the preceding ones, is that market-determined outcomes are a function of the prevailing distribution of wealth and hence coincide in only a limited way with the demands of social welfare maximization.[53] Even in perfectly functioning markets companies may, in other words, because of wealth and income inequality, be 'directed' to allocate the resources under their control to uses that are not fully reflective of 'true' social preferences. One consequence is the disproportionate production of luxury goods at the expense of those satisfying more basic needs. But where outcomes are determined by the ability to pay, distributive questions affect not only what is produced, but

---

[51] Hirsch, *Social Limits to Growth* (above, n. 38), at 40.

[52] Jacobs, *The Green Economy* (above, n. 25), at 215 (emphasis in original). People do not, of course, always tell the truth in opinion polls.

[53] See 49 above.

also all the other issues connected with production. As Jacobs explains, 'if beef consumption in the North causes rainforest destruction in the South, the valuations of the forest dwellers are likely to go unnoticed, since they do not have the income to compete with the valuations of richer consumers'.[54] Even if social preference could be adequately transmitted through markets, therefore, accepting the outcome as 'optimal' involves an ethical judgement that is controversial and which accordingly requires independent support.[55]

Turning now to defects in the techniques of political control, there is a host of reasons why interventions to supplement or override market processes may prove incapable of producing outcomes much closer to the ideal. One reason of course is that what counts as 'ideal' is a matter for subjective evaluation, and one may simply consider that the behavioural standards set down by law and the regulatory process and the values they reflect are inadequate or inappropriate. There is also a likelihood that the rules will sometimes be constructed on the basis of defective factual premises, as where, for example, the difficulty of evaluating third party effects causes environmental controls to be set at too permissive a level.[56] There may in addition be more systematic flaws in the processes of democratic decision-making, resulting in the protection of sectional interests at the expense of impartial consideration of the general welfare. Thus the rules that emerge may reflect the self-interested reactions of the politicians and officials responsible for them to pressure from cohesive minority groups (as suggested by Public Choice theorists),[57] or (from a Marxist perspective) the rules may be designed to bolster the interests of the dominant class.[58] Distortions in the regulatory framework may in particular result from the involvement of companies themselves in the rule-making process. Businesses may be able to resist the imposition of standards or dilute their content through the lobbying or manipulation of government,[59] or by way of a more general steering of

[54] Jacobs, *The Green Economy* (above, n. 25), at 68.
[55] See ibid. at xvi.
[56] See ibid. ch. 6.
[57] See generally, 'Symposium on the Theory of Public Choice', (1988) 74 *Va L Rev* 167, and from a different perspective, see Hayek, *Law, Legislation and Liberty* vol. 3 (above, n. 7), ch. 16.
[58] See also the discussion in McKean, 'Collective Choice' (above, n. 37), at 113-9, and J. L. Mashaw, 'The Economic Context of Social Responsibility', in Hopt and Teubner, *Corporate Governance and Directors' Liabilities* (above, n. 9) 55, at 67-8.
[59] For a particularly graphic account of manipulation in the US see M. Dowie, 'Pinto Madness', in S. L. Hills (ed.) *Corporate Violence: Injury and Death for Profit* (1987) 13 (motor industry resistance to car safety legislation). See also 19-21 above. Corporate interference in the application of regulation is well documented, e.g in relation to the 'capture' of regulatory agencies by those whom they regulate: see Richardson et al. *Policing Pollution* (above, n. 25), at 63-4 and references therein. See also L. Hancher and M. Moran, 'Organizing Regulatory Space', in Hancher and Moran (eds), *Capitalism, Culture and Regulation* (1989) 272, at 275-6 and refs. Baumol and Blackman, *Perfect Markets and Easy Virtue* (above, n. 13), at 50, 57-62, suggest that business best gives expression to a sense of social responsibility by cooperating with government in designing the most effective external controls, but comment that little such

public opinion designed to reduce the demand for regulation or its stringency.[60]

Whatever the validity of these points about market and regulatory failure individually, it seems undeniable that the set of external constraints that companies face at any particular time will be far from perfect (however judged) and therefore that at least in theory the outcomes dictated by the market, as modified by regulatory intervention, could be improved through corporate voluntarism. In response, however, a proponent of the deference argument might contend that there is little reason to suppose that voluntarism would *on balance* lead to superior outcomes, but more particularly that the invocation of market and regulatory failure misses the point. Thus the principal claim of the deference argument is one about the legitimacy of the processes by which controversial issues of social policy are resolved, rather than one about the quality of the output of those processes: whatever their defects, the market and political decision-making at least enjoy a (qualified) legitimacy that is denied to the social and ethical judgements of company managements.

It is suggested that while there is some validity in these points, the deference argument, or at least strong forms of it, should be rejected. First, rather mundanely, behaviour that involves merely a more complete fulfilment of the public purposes expressed in existing regulation (respecting the 'spirit' and not just the 'letter') hardly constitutes a usurpation of the public policy-making function, and in fact seems likely more fully to satisfy social expectations than literal obedience to law, but no more. For that reason, limited additional expenditure on anti-pollution or health and safety measures, for example, is surely unobjectionable. The second reason for rejecting the deference argument is more complex. The argument implies that the techniques of regulation are such that the state has the capacity to alter company behaviour in any way that appears appropriate, even though regulatory interventions may in practice be based on false premises or otherwise distorted. If, however (as will be seen in a moment), external controls are in certain circumstances incapable of adequately reflecting social preferences,[61] then it would seem to be desirable to allow companies a

cooperation has in fact been forthcoming. See also E. S. Herman, *Corporate Control, Corporate Power* (1981), at 172–84, 263–4.

[60] Special problems arise in connection with the standard of regulation applicable in some overseas, particularly developing, countries, e.g. a health and safety regime that would be considered wholly inadequate at home may be imposed by local law simply through tradition or in order keep down production costs so as to attract inward investment. For a consideration of the conflicting issues at stake and the approach that multinationals should adopt in relation to them, see generally T. Donaldson, *The Ethics of International Business* (1989).

[61] That this is so was the view of the government expressed in the White Paper, *Company Law Reform* (Cmnd. 5391, 1973), at para. 56, which is worth quoting at length:

'The law sets limits to the pursuit of profit — be they limits on acts affecting the public generally, such as fraudulent dealing, exploiting monopolies or polluting the atmosphere, or discretion to digress from the requirements of profit maximization within the law, since the alternative is to hold that in those areas that fall outside the scope of the state's regulatory capacity the profit-maximizing outcome is always to be preferred, regardless of the consequences. This is surely too a high price to pay for maintaining the public monopoly over the social policy-making function. The fact that there might be limits to the ability of the state to 'nudge corporate behaviour in the direction society prefers'[62] also casts doubt on the 'political mandate' version of the deference argument mentioned above. If, through the inadequacies of the regulatory process, society's preferences can be only imperfectly reflected in law, then it does not follow that, to the extent that the legislature is silent, companies should be regarded as mandated to maximize profits. Whether society wants companies to maximize profits or to behave in some other way in areas that are beyond the reach of the law is surely indeterminate. The alternative inference that the consensus is that companies should compensate for the limited competence of regulation by a voluntary assumption of social responsibility is at least as plausible as the profit maximization inference.[63]

One reason why the framework of legal controls may at any given time be deficient is what Stone refers to as the 'time-lag problem'.[64] Frequently there is a considerable delay in the adverse consequences of products, manufacturing processes, sales techniques, and so on gaining public recognition. It has also been suggested that there is an ideological factor that reduces the likelihood of government intervention in the early stages of a problem's emergence. As Weiss notes, particularly with regard to market transactions, 'government operates largely by exception; it relies on market forces to

domestic matters such as the amount of redundancy payments and the keeping of books of account. These are in the main specifically indentifiable duties or proscriptions; and it is for society, through the general body of law, to alter those limits for all companies if it is thought right that they should be altered. [There is another] kind of responsibility, a more general and moral kind, [which] is much more difficult to specify and define in terms that can assist any board to decide in any particular situation just where that responsibility leads them, or that can be translated into law.'

[62] Engel, 'An Approach to Corporate Social Responsibility' (above, n. 14), at 34.

[63] There are some areas of law where the legislative history makes it quite clear that the intention is to stimulate higher standards of conduct than those laid down by statute: e.g. it has been said of the Health and Safety at Work Act 1974 that 'Instead of simply punishing employers or workers who did not observe external rules, its aim was to encourage improved safety standards by stimulating the development of mechanisms for the self-regulation of safety with minimum statutory requirements': S. Dawson et al. *Safety at Work: The Limits of Self-Regulation* (1988), at xv, referring to the Robens Report, *Safety and Health at Work, Report of the Committee* (Cmnd 5034, 1972). And as Engel, 'An Approach to Corporate Social Responsibility', at 32–3 acknowledges, the formulation of social policy by companies might be given much broader statutory approval, as where corporate governance arrangements are reformed, e.g. to require constituency representation.

[64] Stone, *Where the Law Ends* (above, n. 48), ch. 11. See also E. J. Weiss, 'Social Regulation of Business Activity: Reforming the Corporate Governance System to Resolve an Institutional Impasse', (1981) 28 *UCLA L Rev* 343, at 379–81.

achieve most societal objectives and intervenes in the marketplace only after affected persons have demonstrated that a serious social problem exists'.[65] Apart from delay in acknowledging that corporate behaviour does have damaging effects, it may take a considerable time for appropriate standards to be agreed and the implementation machinery set up. A company at the 'front line', in contrast, will frequently be aware of potential or actual hazards well before they come to the attention of outside bodies.[66] Company insiders will normally be the first to receive complaints about dangerous products or environmental damage, for example, or to know that there is an increasing incidence of accidents or illness among employees. And once companies have become aware of problems they are in a position to take appropriate action to eliminate or reduce sources of harm well before external controls can be put in place. It is not being argued that companies necessarily will take the relevant action, but that it would be socially advantageous if they did.

Second, while the law is capable in due course of curtailing activities once their potential for harm has become clear, its ability to play a more positive role in shaping company behaviour is usually limited. Stone suggests, for example, that 'law seems most appropriate where it is used to enforce acceptable minimums, rather than to force from each person what he is fully capable of.' Thus one might feel that companies are not 'aspiring to develop enough new products, not investing enough in research and development, "sitting on" (not developing or licensing) their patents. These problems of corporate inaction or omission seem somehow harder for the law to "get at" than acts of commission—problems connected with corporate action that is substandard or does harm'.[67] The law has little role to play in inducing companies to perform at this higher, 'aspirational' level, largely because the behaviour that is required cannot be expressed in sufficiently precise terms. There is, for example, a social interest in car manufacturers conducting research into improved safety features, but the corporate interest in selling large volumes of cars at low prices tends to conflict with that interest, with the result that too little research in certain areas is undertaken. Society might consequently wish to amend the behaviour of car makers to ensure that they manifest a greater concern with product safety. Since, however, the particular safety features that should be discovered, the form that the research should take, or the scale on which it should be conducted, could not

---

[65] Weiss, ibid. at 379–80 (footnote omitted).

[66] For this reason, Engel regards voluntary disclosure to state authorities of known sources of damage, together with limited forbearance from interference with the rule-making process, as exceptions to his general condemnation of corporate social responsibility: see Engel, 'An Approach to Corporate Social Responsibility' (above, n. 14), at 70–85. See also W. J. Baumol, 'Business Responsibility and Economic Behaviour', in Phelps, *Altruism, Morality, and Economic Theory* (above, n. 36), 46.

[67] Stone, *Where the Law Ends* (above, n. 48), at 101.

in the nature of things be specified with any precision, it would be impossible to impose external controls with any enforceable content.

The time-lag problem and the inability of the state to set 'aspirational' standards suggest the existence of areas in which social preferences about corporate conduct might be better fulfilled by companies adopting other-regarding constraints than by their adhering to a policy of strict profit maximization within the law. A further, and important, situation in which this would seem to be so is where society might prefer a non-profit-maximizing outcome but the circumstances are too context-specific for a solution readily to be imposed by means of external controls. It may, for instance, be thought desirable in an area of high unemployment to keep open a factory, even though divestment would increase the company's profits, or to delay closure, or to limit redundancies by expanding into new product lines at the site. Whether any of these courses of action should be adopted rather than closing the factory demands an assessment of the practical consequences of each alternative and a balancing of the interests of the groups involved. A resolution of these issues clearly cannot be achieved by means of general rules, and so allowing company decision-makers a discretion to take account of non-profit considerations may be an appropriate alternative.[68] It is not of course the only alternative. Public authorities might choose, for example, to offer a subsidy to a struggling plant or to intervene more directly, but the difficulties faced by outside bodies in collecting the relevant information and in making the necessary evaluations suggest at least a supplementary role for decentralized, company-level discretion in solving such problems of interest adjustment. Society can also influence closure decisions by increasing the cost of closure by requiring the company to make redundancy payments, but again there may still be room for a more flexible, localized response.

The limitations of regulatory techniques are an important feature of Teubner's writings on corporate social responsibility, which draw on the work of the sociologist Luhmann on systems theory in similarly justifying a company-centred approach to the control of enterprise behaviour.[69] From a systems theory perspective, society is seen as composed of functionally differentiated systems, for example, the religious, educational, and economic systems. Their functional autonomy and distinctive internal logic mean that

[68] This is arguably the effect of CA 1985, s 309, but see the discussion at 82–6 above.
[69] See G. Teubner, 'Corporate Fiduciary Duties and Their Beneficiaries: A Functional Approach to the Legal Institutionalization of Corporate Responsibility', in Hopt and Teubner, *Corporate Governance and Directors' Liabilities* (above, n. 9) 149; 'After Legal Instrumentalism? Strategic Models of Post-Regulatory Law', (1984) 12 *Int J Sociology of Law* 375, at 391–5; 'Substantive and Reflexive Elements in Modern Law', (1983) 17 *Law and Society Review* 239, at 272–3. See also H. Steinmann, 'The Enterprise as a Political System', in Hopt and Teubner (above, note 9) 401, at 415–7; K. J. Hopt, 'New Ways in Corporate Governance: European Experiments with Labor Representation on Corporate Boards', (1984) 82 *Mich L R* 1338, at 1358–9.

individual systems are excessively 'self-referential', that is, they operate without due regard for their effects on other systems. The economic system thus 'works selectively via the language of monetary action and is not able adequately to re-translate its environmental consequences into its own language'.[70] Successful integration cannot be achieved by the centralized steering mechanisms at the disposal of the state, particularly substantive rules, because of limitations in these devices of the kinds that have been noted above. A similar analysis to the foregoing applies at the level of sub-systems (enterprises), which are 'inclined towards sub-optimal and dysfunctional behaviour'[71] by virtue of the narrow focus of their internal profit-maximizing rationality, which traditional legal controls fail adequately to correct. More specifically, there is a problem of balancing the 'function' of the enterprise (maximizing the yield from the production process to guarantee the satisfaction of future social needs), with its 'performance' (the relationship of the enterprise with other societal interests). The suggested solution is a procedural rather than a substantive one, invoking a reflexive rather than an instrumental model of law.[72] It requires that 'restrictions . . . be built into the reflexion structure of every functional subsystem, insofar as they do not result directly from ongoing relations with its environment'.[73] In other words, there is a need for a form of decentralized control,[74] located at the level of the enterprise itself, the aim of which is to make companies reflect on and be responsive to outside interests, in effect, to prevent them from operating as closed systems. This is to be achieved through mechanisms that will increase the sensitivity of companies to the social problems they create. Systems theory thus envisages a clear role for profit-sacrificing social responsibility as 'a compensatory institution which builds social side-purposes into economic actions'.[75]

With or without the systems-theory perspective, the discussion in the preceding paragraph points to a mode of controlling company behaviour that lies between substantive regulation on the one hand and reliance on managerial voluntarism on the other. Rather than seeking to protect affected interests exclusively through the imposition of minimum standards, prohibitions, positive duties, or other techniques of substantive regulation, the interests of the relevant groups might be safeguarded by enabling them to

---

[70] Teubner, 'After Legal Instrumentalism', ibid. at 392.

[71] H. Steinmann, 'The Enterprise as a Political System', in Hopt and Teubner (above, n. 9) 401, at 415. See further 390 below.

[72] See T. Daintith, 'Legal Research and Legal Values', (1989) 52 *MLR* 352, at 358 - 60.

[73] N. Luhmann, *Funktion der Religion* (1977), quoted in Teubner, 'Substantive and Reflexive Elements in Modern Law' (above, n. 69), at 272.

[74] Thereby, according to Teubner, achieving integration of economic and non-economic interests without losing the efficiency advantages of a high degree of enterprise autonomy: 'Corporate Fiduciary Duties' (above, n. 69), at 161–2.

[75] Teubner, 'After Legal Instrumentalism?' (above, n. 69), at 392.

influence company behaviour directly, perhaps by strengthening their ability to put pressure on the company or by giving their representatives a voice in enterprise decision-making. In this way the limitations of substantive regulation might be overcome, with results that might be regarded as legitimate, to a degree that the outcome of a purely voluntary managerial response might not, in virtue of the participation of affected groups in shaping company policy. Further, as the strengthening of the position of third parties or the granting to them of rights of representation would flow from statute, the results could also be viewed as deriving a generalized legitimacy from the involvement of the legislature in creating the new set of power relations from which the results emerge. Whether or not it is desirable to attempt to bring about a change in the relationship between the company and affected interests in this way is of course a matter for political judgement.

Conclusion

It has been suggested that the deference argument does not provide a convincing reason for condemning profit-sacrificing responsibility. On the contrary, a positive case for it has been made out, as a means of compensating for the limited capacity of conventional external regulation. Two overlapping but rather different models of responsibility have been implied. These will form the basis of a discussion in the next chapter of ways of institutionalizing social responsibility. For the moment it is sufficient to make some concluding remarks about the relationship between social responsibility and the core of truth that the deference argument contains, that we should be concerned about an expansion of managerial discretion.

The first model sees responsibility as an essentially voluntary response, for it requires managers to assess the impact of their policies on third parties and to exercise moral judgement in deciding whether adjustments should be made. Were managements to adopt an agenda that differed radically from that set by market and state or to adopt some esoteric moral code the implementation of this model would rightly give cause for concern. As it is, however, the incentive structure of managers is such that a relaxation of the existing legal restrictions on their discretion, coupled with measures to encourage a more other-regarding attitude, would seem likely at best to lead to marginal changes in corporate behaviour in the direction of a superior accommodation of third-party interests. The second model views responsibility as the product of reformed decision-making processes, where the object of reform is not merely to encourage managers to take third-party interests into account, but rather to induce an organizational response through interest group empowerment. As such it seems capable of producing more substantial changes in company behaviour. While some expansion of managerial discretion is involved, these changes are not the result of a potentially arbitrary voluntary response, but the product of increased social pressure. As such, for reasons that have been suggested, objections on deference grounds are here more difficult to sustain. That said, implementation of the model seems likely to encounter practical difficulties, and a number of additional theoretical objections would also need to be faced. There may, for example, be problems over deciding who is to represent affected groups and in determining modes of accountability, which, if not resolved, might cause questions of legitimacy to reappear. And whether methods for allowing third parties an input into decision-making can be devised that would in practice lead to an acceptable balancing of all the interests concerned, as opposed to producing a rather more arbitrary outcome reflecting the differing power positions of affected groups, is unclear, but there are grounds for scepticism in relation to some of the proposals. These issues will be addressed in Chapter 11.

Compliance with Law: a Digression

Before leaving the deference argument it will be convenient to deal here with the suggestion that in certain circumstances compliance with law should be regarded as a species of voluntarism, and therefore susceptible to deference objections. Whether or not it is desirable that companies should do more than the law requires, the proposition that they should do no less was central to the hypothesis that they should seek to 'maximize profits within the law' and has so far been treated as uncontroversial. This is not so, however, since there is a view that the 'optimal level of violations of law ... is not zero',[76] and paradoxically, that strict compliance with law, that is, acting as though there were an absolute moral or political obligation to comply with whatever standards the law lays down, can represent an 'arrogation of legislative power'.[77] The essence of these claims is that the criminal law (and relevant civil law prescriptions) should be treated as setting prices for specified conduct, rather than as imposing absolute prohibitions, and so if after taking the price into account it seems that the conduct (or non-conduct) will still be profitable, then the company should proceed with it. The social judgement is that companies should break the law if they can pay the price and still make a profit; compliance in those circumstances contradicts the behavioural signals that the relevant law contains.

The crude version of this position assumes that criminal sanctions reflect the social cost of infringing behaviour, and therefore that if unlawful conduct is still profitable bearing in mind the likely penalty, then it must be in the social interest for the company to engage in it, because by so doing a net increase in social wealth will result. This being so, companies should adopt a policy of profitable breach. This argument will not be given further consideration here, since it is clear that wealth maximization is not the only goal that

---

[76] Fischel, 'The Corporate Governance Movement' (above, n. 21), at 1271.

[77] Stone, 'Public Interest Representation' (above, n. 9), at 141. Stone regards this reasoning as a *reductio ad absurdum* of the anti-CSR position, ibid. at 142.

the law is intended to serve. Laws relating to environmental protection, workplace safety, discrimination in employment, corrupt payments, and so on, as well as having an efficiency objective, reflect a concern with individual rights and distributive[78] and other non-consequentialist values that cannot be subsumed within a wealth maximization goal. The proposition that companies should break the law where so doing will result in a net increase in social wealth, far from coinciding with social judgements about appropriate corporate conduct, enjoins them to override the purposes that legal rules may have been specifically designed to serve.

The more sophisticated argument put forward by Engel does however warrant brief examination.[79] Engel introduces a refinement with a view to overcoming the objection to the argument so far described, namely that it overlooks the fact that regulation serves purposes that are distinct from wealth maximization. He makes the point that company behaviour should be governed by social consensus, and holds that this consensus is embodied in the law. He accepts that the consensus is not necessarily committed to the maximization of social wealth as society's only goal. On the contrary, it might require 'corporate mechanisms to redistribute wealth, or perhaps even to accomplish goals that are in some sense "noneconomic"'.[80] He therefore acknowledges that regulation may serve purposes additional to the correction of wealth-reducing instances of market failure. The law fulfils its objectives by attaching penalties to disfavoured conduct, thereby inducing companies to behave in ways that conform to whatever range of goals society wishes to promote. The legislature is understood as doing this, however, by modifying 'the profit consequences of any given corporate action, so as to nudge corporate behavior in the direction society prefers'.[81] The law does not, in other words, ever seek to divert companies from the course of profit maximization, but rather it operates by changing the kinds of behaviour that will actually be profit-maximizing. It follows that total compliance with the express content of legal norms is not demanded. Rather, the signal contained in those norms must be interpreted in the remedial context. The size of the penalty attached to breach, and also the likelihood of enforcement (a function of the budget society is prepared to set aside for this purpose), must be taken into account, because these indicate *how much* the conduct in question is disapproved: only when legal norms are read in the light of these limiting factors are they a 'reliable indicator of legislative will'.[82] The signal

---

[78] e.g. environmental regulation has a distributive significance since the effects of pollution tend to fall more heavily on low-income groups who have fewer choices than the wealthy about where to live: see E. J. Mishan, *The Costs of Economic Growth* (1967), at 105; Musgrave, 'On Social Goods and Bads' (above, n. 34), at 288.

[79] Engel, 'An Approach to Corporate Social Responsibility' (above, n. 14).

[80] Ibid. at 35. See also 28.

[81] Ibid. at 34.

[82] Ibid. at 2.

given by the law is thus not to abstain from disfavoured conduct in all circumstances, but only where, in view of the discounted penalty,[83] that conduct is no longer profit-maximizing from the individual company's point of view. 'Compliance' above this level Engel portrays as a species of voluntarism. Since it involves behaviour over and above that required by law properly understood, voluntary compliance is not socially mandated and hence is politically objectionable in the same way as is voluntarism in the more conventional sense, that is, exceeding the express requirements of legal norms.

Can it be right that 'voluntary' compliance with law amounts to a usurpation of legislative authority? The basis of Engel's argument is that discounted penalties should be read as the price of unlawful behaviour, but the idea that the law should be understood in this way is only an assumption, and in fact one that has a very doubtful foundation. Thus it is not at all clear that the notion of pricing is meaningful in relation to many social or ethical values, and therefore that where society attaches a financial penalty, for example, to corrupt or discriminatory practices, that the penalty (duly discounted) reflects how much the relevant practices are disfavoured. Second, even where the law might be taken to have an efficiency objective, the assumption that penalties are in fact set at a level that represents the social cost of disobedience is, to say the least, questionable. Whatever the rational support for the view that they should,[84] and assuming that social costs are calculable with any degree of accuracy,[85] it simply does not correspond with experience.[86] Rather than inferring from this that legislation is directed towards achieving an economically sub-optimal result, it is more plausible to assume that the degree of compliance required is simply not limited to that

[83] Penalties are set at levels above 'the external social costs of the conduct at issue, because of the possibility of nondetection or nonprosecution': ibid. at 41 (emphasis and references omitted).

[84] See Mashaw, 'The Economic Context of Corporate Social Responsibility' (above, n. 58), at 64–65:

In some sense it may be inconsistent for society to provide a structure of legal rules and institutions that limits both sanctions and implementation resources and at the same time to affirm the notion that no criminal or tortious conduct is socially approved. Yet this is surely what society does. If economic analysis cannot explain the apparent contradiction, then that fact merely demonstrates a limitation in economic analysis, not the non-existence of a domain of moral action beyond existing structures of legal incentives.

[85] On the difficulties of calculating the social costs of pollution, see Mishan, *The Costs of Economic Growth* (above, n. 78), at 83–4; D. Pearce, A. Markandya and E. B. Barbier, *Blueprint for a Green Economy* (1989), ch. 3; Richardson et al. *Policing Pollution* (above, n. 25), at 49–53. In any particular case the fine that is actually imposed must be decided by a court, a body not well-equipped to make accurate assessments of social cost except in the most straightforward circumstances. The cost to society in terms of reduced respect for the law as a whole where companies are perceived to flaunt mandatory rules appears incapable of meaningful quantification; cf. Engel, 'An Approach to Corporate Social Responsibility' (above, n. 14), at 47–48.

[86] To take one example, the *Digest of Environmental and Water Statistics* (1990) reveals that the average fine in respect of water pollution in the 327 cases prosecuted, out of 266,926 reported incidents, was £560. This can hardly be an accurate measure of the total damage inflicted.

suggested by the value of discounted penalties.[87] Finally, as Chapter 11 will consider, there is currently a major debate about how levels of corporate compliance with law might be increased. The debate recognizes the inadequacy of fines as an enforcement mechanism in many cases; its underlying text is about how to make compliance non-optional, and not about setting appropriate prices, carrying with it the implication that profitable non-compliance is somehow considered desirable.

It is suggested therefore that 'voluntary' compliance should not be regarded as objectionable on deference grounds, as argued by Engel. This is not to say that total compliance is always desirable or is necessarily a correct interpretation of the 'legislative will', as, for example, where *guaranteeing* obedience to environmental or health and safety regulations would require massive expenditure on the supervision of employees and the installation of fail-safe devices.[88] But surely even here companies are not invited to comply or not, depending purely on the outcome of a calculation of the cost to the company of alternative courses of action, and certainly businesses do not usurp public power where they decide to obey the law, notwithstanding that so doing is not privately profitable.

The Shareholders' Money Argument

We turn now to the third and final objection to profit-sacrificing social responsibility. Where a company adopts other-regarding constraints its costs will rise. In the absence of a perfectly competitive market (in which social responsibility would in any case be incompatible with survival) the company will be able to pass on a proportion of the increased costs to its customers, but the consequent drop in sales will also mean that there is a reduction in profits.[89] To that extent, therefore, the third parties who are protected by the constraints that have been adopted benefit at the shareholders' expense. It is of course open to shareholders not to invest in companies which are in the habit of incurring social policy expenditure, or to disinvest where they

[87] Further, a policy of limited prosecution need not express a desire for a corresponding level of compliance, but may reflect an enforcement policy based on education or persuasion, or a simple lack of resources. And as has been argued by Mashaw, 'The Economic Context of Social Responsibility' (above, n. 58), at 66, 'anywhere self-application is more efficient than modifying the expected value of sanctions, there is a straightforward efficiency argument for seeking to increase voluntary compliance', i.e. because there are theoretical and practical limits to the level to which fines can be raised (see 356–7 below), increasing compliance will require an increase in enforcement costs — voluntary compliance can involve lower costs overall.

[88] Of course, regulatory provisions often do not in any case impose strict standards, but are sensitive to cost considerations, e.g. the duty imposed by the Environmental Protection Act 1990 to use the 'best available technology not entailing excessive cost', or the duty under the Health and Safety at Work Act 1974, to ensure the health etc. of employees so far as 'reasonably practicable'. Similarly, cost factors are relevant to the imposition of civil liability in negligence.

[89] See Posner, *Economic Analysis of Law* (above, n. 11), at 395–6; Mashaw, 'The Economic Context of Corporate Social Responsibility' (above, n. 58), at 61–2.

acquire that habit, but investors are still exposed to the possibility of unanticipated expenditures, or expenditures of an unanticipated amount. Should the use of the 'shareholders' money' in this way be regarded as morally objectionable?

Easterbrook and Fischel, leading theorists of 'anti-responsibility',[90] argue that the propriety of social policy expenditure from a shareholders' money perspective depends entirely on the terms on which investment in the company is solicited. Where the venture 'is designed in the ordinary fashion—employees and debt investors holding rights to fixed payoffs and equity investors holding a residual claim to profits, which the other participants promise to maximize', the shareholders have a 'legitimate complaint' if the 'binding promise' to maximize profits is broken.[91] If, on the other hand, it is clear that profit-seeking is to be tempered by social considerations, then investors who buy shares on that basis implicitly consent to the company's social-policy expenditure and also acquire their shares at a price that reflects the expectation of a reduced rate of return. Social policy in such cases is accordingly unobjectionable. As a description of the approach of company law to determining the corporate purposes that the courts should enforce this analysis is broadly correct. The ends that a company is intended to serve are set out in its objects clause and these may be whatever lawful purposes the corporators choose.[92] The assumption, however, that the ends for which companies exist and the values they should respect in pursuing those ends *ought* to be viewed as a purely private matter between managements and shareholders (and other contracting parties) is more open to dispute.

Chapter 1 argued that the shareholders' right to have the company managed in their interests could not be justified in terms of antecedent moral rights, but was justifiable only to the extent that that arrangement was conducive to the public good. From this 'social-enterprise' perspective, how companies should behave is not merely a matter for private agreement therefore, but should be determined in accordance with a theory of how the public interest is best served. If, as seems likely, the public interest is better served where companies in some circumstances act to safeguard the interests of third parties even though this involves sacrificing profits, then it is appropriate that the shareholders' rights should be regarded as correspondingly diminished. Thus some forms of voluntary action constitute an internalization of costs that would otherwise be imposed on third parties. There is little to commend the view that shareholders should receive rewards

[90] i.e. they do not advocate that companies should act irresponsibly, but hold that they act in accordance with society's interests where they seek to maximize profits.

[91] Easterbrook and Fischel, 'The Corporate Contract' (above, n. 21), at 1446. See also Fischel, 'The Corporate Governance Movement' (above, n. 21), at 1273.

[92] See 278–9 above.

that do not fully reflect the social cost of the activities from which they are derived. Similarly, investors should not be regarded as entitled to the proceeds of conduct that conflicts with generally accepted non-consequential-ist social or moral values. It follows that social responsibility is not morally objectionable *per se* even if it does contradict the assumptions on which the shareholders' investment has been made. None of this is to say that the financial interests of the shareholders are of no account, not least because the provision of an adequate supply of capital is crucial to the proper functioning of the economy. Its providers are a group whose interests accordingly merit protection. The point is that there is no need to regard the shareholders as having a moral right to the largest possible profits.

If the rules of company law were to be changed in order to permit or encourage profit-sacrificing social responsibility then all investment would of necessity be made on that basis and Easterbrook and Fischel's objection could no longer apply. What might then be objectionable would be the interference with contractual freedom that such a change in the law implies. The social-enterprise perspective licenses this 'interference', however, on the ground that the state is entitled to lay down the terms on which companies operate in order to ensure that the public interest is adequately served. The mandatory provisions of the Companies Act already constitute a substantial curtailment of 'freedom of contract', principally in the interests of sharehold-ers and creditors. Where it is accepted that the legitimacy of companies depends on their compliance with social objectives, and that in order to satisfy those objectives a departure from profit maximization within the law is required, then intervention on behalf of other groups is to the appropriate extent also permissible.

Conclusion

The idea that it might be in the social interest for companies to adopt other-regarding constraints has survived the efficiency, deference, and shareholders' money arguments. Given market failure and the limited capacity of law, some forms of profit-sacrificing behaviour are likely to increase overall efficiency rather than undermine it.[93] The notion that it is politically unaccept-able for companies to adopt more rigorous controls than those imposed by law to regulate their relationships with affected parties, while indicating a need for caution, does not warrant a prohibition on all forms of profit-sacrificing conduct. The implementation of social policy need not, finally, be regarded as involving an inequitable infringement of the rights of the shareholders.

[93] It is not, of course, the case that *no* constraints that might be adopted would damage efficiency; they might nevertheless be thought desirable on overriding non-efficiency grounds.

In considering the three clusters of anti-responsibility arguments the outline of a positive case for social responsibility also emerged. In essence, the voluntary adoption of constraints is capable of producing a better integration of corporate enterprise into its social and physical environment than could be achieved by reliance on external controls alone. And with less emphasis on voluntariness, an opening up to outside influence of corporate decision-making procedures can be regarded as an additional, less specific, means of fulfilling the objectives of more traditional forms of regulation. The techniques that might be adopted to induce responsible behaviour are considered in Chapter 11. In the meantime, it should be stressed that the role for social responsibility that is envisaged here is as a supplement to external legal controls and not as a substitute for them.[94] Thus, as far as purely voluntary self-regulation is concerned, the prospects seem undeniably limited. While they may exaggerate the obligatoriness of market pressures, there is a substantial core of truth in Baumol and Blackman's observation that

the same competitive process which prevents laziness or incompetence also precludes voluntarism on any significant scale. The business executive who chooses voluntarily to spend until it hurts on the environment, on training the handicapped, or on support of higher education is likely to find that he is vulnerable to undercutting by firms without a social conscience that, by avoiding such outlays, can supply outputs more cheaply'.[95]

In view of the market penalties for voluntary self-regulation, very significant changes in behaviour are likely to result only where all companies face the same restrictions, and that requires compulsion. Measures to increase the sensitivity of companies to interest group pressure seem to have better prospects of success, but the unpredictability of outcomes means that here too a programme for increasing corporate social responsibility should be seen

---

[94] See Brudney, 'The Independent Director' (above, n. 12), at 653–6. This is not to deny that there is a disputed territory in which external legal controls are feasible but possibly counter-productive: see e.g. Stone, 'Public Interest Representation' (above, n. 9), at 136–7, who suggests that in some circumstances voluntary responsibility is preferable to regulation, in order to overcome the 'bright line' effect of law — by laying down a precise standard of impermissible conduct 'we may tempt actors to press their conduct to the outer bounds of what they can get away with.' See also Stone, *Where The Law Ends* (above, n. 48), at 100–1; 103–10.

[95] Baumol and Blackman, *Perfect Markets and Easy Virtue* (above, n. 13), at 53. The fact, as T. C. Schelling, 'Command and Control', in McKie (ed.), *Social Responsibility and the Business Predicament* (above, n. 23) 79, at 90, points out, that 'there is often no source of reliable guidance, no acknowledged source of policy, no easy choice between the responsible and the selfish', is another reason why good intentions are liable to be translated into only very limited behaviour changes. And see similarly McKean, 'Economics of Trust, Altruism, and Corporate Responsibility' (above, n. 23), at 38. Lack of clarity about standards also prevents the evolution of customary norms supported by group pressure. Companies have, e.g. a collective interest in reducing pollution in order to avoid increases in the regulatory burden, but customary norms must be 'relatively clear-cut, so that violations can be detected and punished by social pressure'. Otherwise collective action will be undermined by free-riding: See R. N. McKean, 'Collective Choice', in McKie, *Social Responsibility* (above, n. 23) 109, at 110–112.

as an additional regulatory strategy and not a substitute for conventional regulatory techniques.

III SOCIAL ACTIVISM

The main themes having already been set out, the objections to social activism (corporate action with regard to social problems or issues that arise independently of the company's own business) can be dealt with more briefly. The three arguments will again be considered in turn.

The Efficiency Argument

The effect of expenditure for social activist purposes where there is no long-term profit justification is to redistribute wealth from the shareholders to the various recipients, for example, charities and their beneficiaries, arts companies and their publics, the inhabitants of inner cities, and those involved in education and training. Efficiency in the sense of allocative efficiency is not an appropriate standard by which to judge these redistributive consequences, since the concept is concerned with the assessment of different allocations of resources given a particular distribution of wealth, with an allocation being regarded as efficient where no reallocation could make anyone better off without making someone else worse off. Rather, in the context of corporate social activism, the issues are whether companies are suitable agents for carrying out a redistributive policy (assuming that redistribution is justifiable at all), and whether it is morally acceptable for managements to redistribute at shareholders' expense. These questions will be considered under the heads of the deference and shareholders' money arguments respectively.

Social activism does, however, have some efficiency implications, in terms of the 'out of pocket' expenses of engaging in social policy, including the cost of management time and losses that might flow where managers are distracted from the company's mainstream business, and also the possible contraction of business activity resulting from a reduced supply of capital, consequent on a fall in investor confidence. In view of its scale, and given that much current corporate social policy seems to have a long-term profit justification,[96] there are probably at present no more than trivial efficiency implications. Were companies to take on an increased burden, for example, in education or inner-city programmes, the administration costs, particularly in terms of management time, could, however, be considerable. As to investor confidence, it was noted earlier that there is evidence that

---

[96] See Ch. 9 above.

shareholders do not consider corporate charitable donations at existing levels to be excessive,[97] though there are no doubt limits beyond which social policy expenditure might so reduce the return on equity as to have adverse capital market effects.

The Deference Argument

The deference argument is an argument about power. As it applies to social activism, the charge is that engagement in social policy increases corporate power because it involves an extension of company influence into areas unconnected with mainstream business activity. As one writer has put it, the use of company funds for social activist purposes connotes an extension of power from the economic realm 'to social, educational, cultural, and political areas, which would give [managers] the ability to control other people's lives and the direction of social development. This is a task for the people themselves, operating through institutions formally and substantially account-able to the people.'[98] The argument is thus that 'unrelated' social issues should be left to public agencies, charitable or voluntary bodies, and individual effort, and should not be addressed by companies which already exert a pervasive influence over our lives.

More specifically, corporate involvement in the social realm[99] might cause concern on two accounts. First, even where support is given for wholly disinterested reasons, company managements are not obviously well qualified to play a part in decision-making in areas that lie outside the boundaries of ordinary business activity, nor is it apparent by what right they should assume such a role. Baumol and Blackman, for example, ask why the business executive should be entrusted with the power to set priorities for all of society among 'the competing claims of hospitals, educational institutions, arts organizations, and environmental causes'.[100] There are thus problems of competence and legitmacy. Second, while the return to the company will often be uncertain, it is argued that for much of the time activism will be underscored by a desire to promote the corporate interest, be it for instance by way of improving the company's image,[101] preserving its markets, or securing the availability of an appropriately educated workforce. Where companies are pursuing their own agenda there is a danger that their involvement will lead to a distortion in decision-making in the areas

---

[97] See above, n. 94.

[98] M. D. Reagan, *The Managed Economy* (1963), at 148.

[99] It is not intended by the use of this term to suggest that companies do not exercise decision-making power with major social effects when also making decisions on mainstream business issues: see 9–19 above.

[100] Baumol and Blackman, *Perfect Markets and Easy Virtue* (above, n. 13), at 51–2.

[101] Or even outright advertising: see National Consumer Council, *Classroom Commercials: Business Sponsorship of Teaching Material* (1986).

concerned in favour of commercial interests. Levitt expresses these concerns clearly, if perhaps over-emphatically, in the following terms:

at bottom [the company's] outlook will always remain narrowly materialistic. What we have, then, is the frightening spectacle of a powerful economic functional group whose future and perception are shaped in a tight materialistic context of money and things but which imposes its narrow ideas about a broad spectrum of unrelated noneconomic subjects on the mass of man and society . . . If the corporation believes its long-run profitability to be strengthened by these peripheral involvements—if it believes that they are not charity but self-interest—then that much the worse. For, if this is so, it puts much more apparent justification and impulse behind activities which are essentially bad for man, bad for society, and ultimately bad for the corporation itself'.[102]

Whether or not these criticisms are valid, it is clear that the attack on social activism on deference grounds ought, although the point is often overlooked, to be regarded as applicable to cases in which the company is motivated by long-term profit considerations as well as those in which a sacrifice of profits is involved. If the extension of corporate influence into non-business spheres is objectionable then this is so whether or not, or sometimes especially because, the intervention has a commercial justification. The counter-argument, that profit-led interventions are legitimate as constituting a response to public preferences expressed through the market, has validity only in very qualified terms. Expenditure designed to improve the company's image will presumably be successful only if customers approve of it, but such approval cannot be construed as entailing popular consent to any increase in corporate influence that might result. Similarly, a company may consider, for example, that the provision of assistance to local schools will in due course improve the productivity of its employees and hence the company's profits, but this is hardly evidence of support for a policy of corporate educational involvement.

That the exercise of influence by companies outside their mainstream business activities might be undesirable has been noted, but we need to be more specific about how this influence might be brought to bear and the respects in which it may be damaging before the charge can be properly evaluated. One obvious way in which activism may represent an extension of corporate power is that by offering financial assistance or other forms of support companies might gain the ability to exert a measure of control over the recipients or would-be recipients of their largesse. In the case of education, for example, companies might use this control to influence course content and teaching methods, in particular with a view to securing a supply of employees with skills that match the needs of business, and possibly at the expense of programmes aimed at a more rounded development of the

---

[102] T. Levitt, 'The Dangers of Social Responsibility' (above, n.8), at 27–8.

individual student. Clearly there is no reason why business representatives should not participate in the debate about educational issues to the same extent as any other group, but it may be thought to be undesirable that they should have the ability to bypass that debate by virtue of the leverage obtained through the provision of financial support. Concern has similarly been expressed about the relationship between pharmaceutical companies and medical charities,[103] and the risk that large-company support will alter the objectives of community industry in the direction of conventional profit-maximizing capitalism.[104]

A second way in which activism might have a socially damaging effect is that even without active interference the corporate presence may cause distortions within the fields of activity supported. If, for instance, companies offer funding for scientific research only in relation to topics that will ultimately bring them commercial benefits, this may alter the balance of research undertaken both within particular institutions, and also at a regional or national level, skewing research activity in accordance with corporate funding priorities. Similarly in the area of arts sponsorship it seems quite likely that companies will tend to concentrate support on prestige productions, well-known artists, and ventures that are thought to be 'safe', and will avoid the experimental and controversial, since they may consider that only the former will have positive 'image' effects. While it may be true that selective patronage does not in general make it any more difficult for disfavoured research or artistic projects to proceed, there would seem to be a risk of it diverting endeavour into directions more likely to attract corporate support.[105] These concerns become that much greater if commercial patronage or sponsorship is seen as an opportunity to cut public funding.

Finally sponsorship and other forms of corporate involvement, particularly in education and the arts, may have a more subtly damaging effect by undermining the perceived autonomy of what are essentially non-commercial activities. The result may be to reduce confidence, justifiably or not, in the integrity of those involved and in their output. More generally, company involvement may contribute to the uncomfortable feeling that all forms of communication and cultural activity are increasingly being colonized by large-scale corporate interests.[106]

Against these negative aspects of social activism must be weighed the undoubted benefits. Although social activism may carry some risks — and they are somewhat speculative — it might be argued that it is churlish to insist

---

[103] See e.g. A. Ware, 'Introduction, the Changing Relations between Charities and the State', in A. Ware (ed.), *Charities and Government* (1989), at 21–2.

[104] See e.g. R. I. Johns, *Company Community Involvement in the UK: An Independent Study* (1991), at 14, 42–4.

[105] An important factor here is the availability of funding from public sources: for the figures on corporate and public arts funding see 294 above.

[106] See generally H. I. Schiller, *Culture Inc: The Corporate Takeover of Public Expression* (1989).

that companies should not behave in ways that are manifestly advantageous to needy groups or which promote community interests in a direct and effective way simply because by so doing they may acquire an additional increment of social power. If social activism increases corporate power then that is a price worth paying.

A way of assessing these conflicting views is to ask whether companies possess any comparative advantages in dealing with social issues such as to offset the fears associated with the growth in their power. When the merits of adopting other-regarding constraints were considered earlier, it was suggested that social responsibility was able to make a contribution to social welfare or to protecting the interests of affected groups that it might not be possible to achieve by other means. To the extent that this is the case, it was contended that there is a justification for allowing companies a policy-making function, even though such a function might entail some increase in their social decision-making power. Are there equivalent comparative advantages in relation to social activism?

Are, then, companies capable of improving social welfare through donations of money or material resources (other forms of activism will be considered below) in a way that cannot be achieved at least as well by other means? It is difficult to see that they are. Taking arts sponsorship as an example, company managements possess no unique insights in deciding how best to allocate arts subsidy. Indeed, in comparison with public bodies established for that purpose they are likely to have a lower level of expertise and are largely unaccountable for the decisions they make. Even though this may be conceded, it might be argued nevertheless that company involvement can be justified on grounds of pluralism — it is desirable that there be a variety of autonomous providers, potentially applying different standards. This argument can be deployed not only in relation to arts subsidy, but to all forms of corporate support, particularly in areas in which government might be considered to be too dominant, such as university funding. The argument for pluralism is an argument about power, however, and it hardly seems an appropriate response to worries about power to wish to increase the range of areas of life in which corporate values are brought to bear. It is suggested that the demands of pluralism are better satisfied by addressing the problems of over-centralization in public decision-making, for example, through the re-empowerment of local democracy, than by expanding corporate influence. There is of course also room for individual initiatives and for the activities of charities and private foundations to offset over-dependence on public funding.

The most obvious benefit from activism is simply that it increases the financial support available for social projects beyond that provided by individuals and from public funds. Corporate support does not, however, come out of thin air. It is appropriate to distinguish here between activism with an expected profit pay-off and more 'altruistic' forms, acknowledging that in practice the categories merge into each other. Corporate expenditure of the latter kind is ultimately paid for by the shareholders. It can be regarded as involving a form of private taxation, and now that a large percentage of the population has an interest in shares, either directly or, more commonly, indirectly as members of pension schemes, it is evident that it is not levied only on the very wealthy. There is surely little to be said for a form of taxation that is arbitrary in its application (being linked purely to the form in which wealth is held and regardless of the individual 'taxpayer's' financial position) and where the spending of the proceeds lacks public accountability. Social activism of this kind may, therefore, increase the supply of funding, but only by an assumption of powers that are better exercised under democratic control. If we want to increase collective support, the relevant decisions should be made and enforced through public channels. Where, on the other hand, corporate social involvement will ultimately bring a return to the company, the taxation analogy is less appropriate. It can be regarded as a source of 'extra' funding, rather than funding obtained at the expense of the shareholders, in that while furthering some social purpose it also serves the company's commercial ends. Here the issue must be left as a matter of political judgement: given that companies have no inherent advantages as funding bodies, do the beneficial consequences of their support outweigh the concerns about multi-faceted corporate power?[107]

The discussion so far has placed an emphasis on activism that takes the form of cash donations. There is, however, another form of activism for which a justification may more readily be found. The distinction is brought out by Simon, Powers, and Gunnemann in describing three types of corporate social policy, namely:

(1) self-regulation in the avoidance of social injury . . . [and] on the other end of the spectrum, (2) the championing of political and moral causes unrelated to the corporation's business activities, perhaps including gifts of charity. Somewhere in the continuum between these poles (but sharing some aspects of each) lies (3) affirmative action extending beyond self-regulation but falling short of the championing of causes—for example, cooperation with governments in training the hard-core unemployed, or the use of corporate resources (including manpower and facilities) in response to certain needs or social problems in the corporation's home community.[108]

The first of these categories approximates to constraint-based responsibility, and the second and third to social activism, though with the third, as Simon et al. point out, having something in common with constraint-based responsibility as well. What distinguishes the second category from the third

---

[107] See Engel, 'Corporate Social Responsibility' (above, n. 14), at 23 n. 66.
[108] J. Simon, C. Powers and J. Gunnemann, *The Ethical Investor: Universities and Corporate Responsibility* (1972), at 27. For practical examples of business involvement falling within the third category see I. Christie et al. *Profitable Partnerships: A Report on Business Involvement in the Community* (1991).

is the existence of a possible comparative advantage enjoyed by companies as regards behaviour falling within the latter category. It does seem to be true in relation to some issues, as the Institute of Directors points out, that 'the special ability of business to turn ideas into reality and to make things happen quickly is uniquely valuable and it is extremely difficult to bring that ability to bear from other sources'.[109] The 'special ability' may result, for instance, from the company's position as a major employer. If significant progress is to be made in reducing unemployment among members of disadvantaged groups[110] then the collaboration of business is essential. And this will often be so regardless of the precise profit implications. Similarly local purchasing policies or investment decisions, for example, to move part of the company's administrative functions to a depressed area, may have beneficial social effects that cannot readily be achieved by other means. Projects involving collaboration with public agencies furthermore, such as those with local authorities in inner-city redevelopment, seem particularly attractive, given that the latter are, at least in principle, able to perform a coordinating and supervisory role, thus providing a degree of public account-ability. The provision of management expertise to voluntary and community groups through staff secondment, while giving rise to similar worries to those connected with cash donations, may also be desirable on balance, given the absence of alternative sources of help.

The Shareholders' Money Argument

We turn finally in this review of the merits of social activism to a consideration of the shareholders' money argument, which will also serve as a conclusion to this section. The argument applies where activism is not intended to bring a benefit to the company, even in the long term. When discussing the applica-tion of the shareholders' money argument to the adoption of other-regarding constraints it was suggested that the prejudice to shareholders that might result was in principle capable of being justified by reference to the public interest. It has, however, been argued that, except with regard to Simon's third category of responsibility, the public-interest justification for social activism is weak, or even that social activism might on balance be damaging to the public interest. Accordingly, again with that exception, and as preshadowed in the disscussion of the deference argument, there is no obvious moral basis on which to justify activism where this has the effect of contradict-ing the assumptions on which investment in the company was attracted.

---

[109] Institute of Directors, *A New Agenda for Business* (1987), at 8.

[110] Equal opportunities policies in recruitment are also an example of constraint-based responsibility. The issue here concerns taking positive steps to address a social problem that exists independently of the way the company runs its business — unemployment among members of minority groups.

Given the force of the deference argument and the persuasivenss of the shareholders' money argument, social activism that involves the forgoing of profits seems supportable only where it falls within Simon's third category. It is suggested in consequence that it is desirable to leave intact the existing company-law prohibition on social expenditure which is not designed to benefit the business.[111] There is on the other hand a case for third-category behaviour, and this is so even though a sacrifice of profits may be involved. The legal controls do not distinguish between the second and third categories (it is hard to see how a workable distinction could be drawn), but this is unlikely to present problems in practice, given the limited effectiveness of the rules: in most cases there will be a sufficient possibility of commercial benefit to satisfy them. Whether restrictions should be extended to activism in the second category where there is an expected profit pay-off demands a less impressionistic assessment of the conflicting issues that have been touched on here. Perhaps the best way forward is a selective approach, involving a containment of the corporate presence in areas of particular sensitivity. For example, in a number of jurisdictions corporate donations to political parties and related bodies have been restricted or prohibited.[112] More generally, the adoption of policies designed to increase corporate participation seems ill-advised.

IV CONCLUSION: SOCIAL RESPONSIBILITY AS A PROCESS CONCEPT

Section II concluded that not only did responsibility in the sense of building in additional constraints or self-regulation survive the various arguments against it, but that there was a positive case for it, as a means of supplementing external regulation. In Chapter 11 ways in which companies might be made to act with greater responsibility will be considered. In the meantime it will have been noted that Section II said very little about what the specific objectives of self-regulation should be, that is, about which interests companies should protect and to what extent, about the particular 'responsibilities' that companies might be thought to owe. These issues are the subject matter of theories of substantive corporate social responsibility, a field which draws on a broad range of more general ethical positions.[113] The

---

[111] See 272–5 above.

[112] e.g. in the US and Quebec, respectively. On this and for a consideration of the merits of corporate support for political causes, see K. D. Ewing, *The Funding of Political Parties in Britain* (1987), ch. 8.

[113] Theories advanced include 'stakeholder' theories, see e.g. W. M. Evan and R. E. Freeman, 'A Stakeholder Theory of the Modern Corporation: Kantian Capitalism', in T. L. Beauchamp and N. E. Bowie (eds), *Ethical Theory and Business* (3rd ed., 1988) 97. As T. Donaldson, *The Ethics of International Business* (1989), at 44–7 points out, such discussions generally lack a sufficiently explicit underlying moral theory; one consequence is that they fail to give determinate guidance on how the various affected interests should be traded off. See also Kuhn and Shriver,

further elaboration of ethical theory in relation to business decisions, and the acceptance by managers of some substantive ethical outlook, are likely to be important if company behaviour is to change significantly. However, it is possible to introduce reforms designed to create the conditions for more responsible behaviour without first having to resolve controversial substantive issues of ethical principle and social policy. The task of describing and evaluating theories of substantive responsibility need not therefore be undertaken here. In establishing a legal framework for responsible behaviour the controversial substantive issues can be avoided by approaching social responsibility as a 'process concept', that is, as a concept concerned with the characteristics of the corporate decision-making process and not with particular outcomes. Social responsibility as a process concept thus takes responsibility to be an attribute of decision-making processes rather than as involving compliance with a set of specific standards for guiding conduct.[114]

The 'process' to which the concept refers can be understood in two different ways, corresponding to the two models of responsibility outlined earlier. The first relies on an analogy with the decision-making processes employed by an individual committed to acting in a morally acceptable way. On the basis of this analogy, the reform strategy is to 'moralize' the company's decision-making procedures so that its approach resembles that of the responsible individual. The essence of responsibility understood in this way is that in reaching a decision the interests of affected parties are recognized and given an appropriate weight. To describe a person or organization as responsible is thus a form of moral commendation, but of an abstract and qualified kind. It is abstract because taking account of the interests of others complies with the requirements of morality in only a generic sense; it is consistent with the characteristic 'moral point of view' but does not connote the application of moral principles belonging to any

Beyond Success (above, n. 38), at 75–6, on the willingness of managements to accept stakeholder theories precisely because of their indeterminacy and 287–8, above. For Donaldson's own social contract theory of responsibility, see ibid. chs 4 and 5, and his *Corporations and Morality* (1982), ch. 3. A consequentialist substantive theory of responsibility is put forward by Weiss, 'Social Regulation of Business Activity' (above, n. 64), at 422–6. His concept of 'altruistic capitalism' requires companies to correct for market failure, demanding that 'management operates the business: (1) as if the firm were a pure competitor concerned with long-term profitability; (2) as if the firm paid all the external costs and captured all the external benefits of its operations; (3) as if the firm's customers and competitors shared all relevant information that the firm possessed; and (4) as if the firm were liable for all acts of its employees and agents'. For a further contribution to the debate, see Simon, Powers, and Gunnemann, *The Ethical Investor* (above, n. 108), ch. 2 (companies, in common with all social actors, owe a duty not to injure others and to correct any injury they cause). In the environmental field, the concept of 'sustainability' offers substantive guidance on good practice: see Jacobs, *The Green Economy* (above, n. 23), ch 7.

[114] The following account is based on K. E. Goodpaster, 'The Concept of Corporate Responsibility', (1983) *Journal of Business Ethics* 1. See also T. M. Jones and L. D. Goldberg, 'Governing the Large Corporation: More Arguments for Public Directors', (1982) 7 *Academy of Management Review* 603.

specific value system. Approval is therefore also qualified, in that a recognition of responsibility does not necessarily entail approval of the reasoning by which the interests of self and others are mediated in any particular case. An actor may be described as having decided responsibly without there being any implication that the outcome in the relevant situation is, by reference to some substantive moral standard, the best that could be achieved.[115] In seeking to moralize the company the objective is thus necessarily a limited one. The aim is not to institutionalize any specific moral code, nor to produce any particular morally approved outcomes. What is envisaged instead is that by factoring an awareness of third-party interests into the decision-making process, and requiring decision makers to reflect on the consequences of corporate actions, a better balancing of company and external interests is likely to result.

An alternative and more ambitious 'process' is to make the company more responsive to the interests of affected groups by increasing the ability of those groups to shape corporate conduct. This might be achieved by strengthening their ability to impose pressure on the company from the outside or by giving them some constitutional status within the organization. Here the outcome may or may not be influenced by moral reasoning, but in either event the above qualifications about the result of the process apply. The results may not be the 'best' obtainable, but they should be 'better' than those to be expected from a more close-textured body.

The first of these approaches, relying on managerial voluntarism, seems likely to produce only modest changes in company behaviour, since even with moralized decision-making processes a significant reorientation of management attitudes is implausible without some external stimulus, as the next chapter will consider. The second strategy, on the other hand, by increasing the power of interest groups to shape company conduct, seems capable of producing a more radical redirection of corporate conduct. Here too, however, there is room for doubt about the magnitude of the likely effects. Careful attention will need to be paid furthermore to the way in which the model is made operational if outcomes reflecting unequal power positions are to be avoided.

---

[115] Cf. Jones and Goldberg ibid. who seem prepared to suspend substantive evaluation of outcomes altogether, e.g. at 610, 'process-altering responses are valuable for their own sake, without regard to their assumed impact on outcomes, simply because corporate social responsibility itself is best viewed as a process.'

11

Strengthening the Constraints

The previous chapter suggested that it would be beneficial if companies were sometimes to allow their decisions to be influenced by non-profit criteria. The 'profit maximization within the law' formula, which had been provisionally adopted in Chapter 1 as the principle of corporate action most likely to further the public interest, was rejected in its full rigour, largely because of limitations in the methods by which society is able to exercise control over business enterprise. In particular the impossibility of communicating through external legal controls all the circumstances in which it is desirable that profit-seeking should be constrained in the interests of non-shareholder groups was noted. Later this chapter will examine a number of legal reforms by which companies might be induced to give greater weight in their decision-making processes to these interests and to other social considerations than is mandated by the profit maximization rule. Before exploring that new territory we need to step back to consider the difficulties encountered in obliging complex organizations even to comply with conventional external controls. Thus, aside from the issue of whether companies can be made to do more than the law requires, there are also important questions about how best to make companies amenable to existing legal prescriptions.

The last few years have seen a number of disasters connected with large-scale commercial operations. Among the most serious are the explosion at the chemical plant in Bhopal in 1984, the capsize of the ferry *Herald of Free Enterprise* in 1987, the 'Piper Alpha' oil-rig explosion in 1988, and the fire at King's Cross underground station in 1989. No less tragic are the deaths of employees that occur in British industry on a daily basis: in 1988/89 there were 590 deaths at work and in 1989/90, 426.[1] In the latter year there were also over 21,000 'non-fatal major injuries', and 160,000 employees suffered serious injuries. It is estimated that in addition around 10,000 workers die from industrial diseases each year.[2] Many of these occurrences are not unavoidable 'accidents' but result from culpable neglect on the part of management. Commenting on a study of the 739 deaths in the construction

---

[1] *Health and Safety Executive Annual Reports* 1988/89, 1989/90.
[2] Ibid.; see generally D. Bergman, *Deaths at Work: Accidents or Corporate Crime* (1991).

industry between 1981 and 1985, the Director-General of the Health and Safety Executive has for instance observed that in '70% of cases, positive action by management could have saved lives'.[3] Aside from health and safety issues newspaper reports frequently attest to corporate recalcitrance across the range of commercial activity, including cases of pollution, the sale of impure foods and other dangerous products, and the use of improper trading practices. Nor are these failings limited to small enterprises on the margins of profitability. In relation to offences against consumers, for example, Cranston concludes that 'national data available on the prosecution of certain national businesses suggests that size and profitability are not especially important in business wrongdoing'.[4] He goes on to note that there are major businesses 'where a commitment to commercial success takes precedence over obeying the law. These businesses find it worth while to continue with trade practices which cause offences, and treat a degree of wrongdoing as incidental to continuing with their marketing and promotional activities'.[5]

The pervasive presence of large companies, the high incidence of corporate wrongdoing, and the scale of the possible consequences, raise important questions about how the law should be crafted to cope with the harm-creating potential of business. As Stone puts it, in view of the dominant influence of large companies in our lives, 'the success of the law as a social instrument—deterring, rehabilitating, securing effective compensation for victims, educating citizens between right and wrong—turns on its capacity to deal with the corporation as a basic unit of communal activity.'[6] There is a wide range of techniques by which society might seek to control company behaviour. They include taxation and subsidies, licensing and planning controls, the law of tort, the 'ordinary' criminal law, and 'regulatory' laws backed by criminal sanctions. An evaluation of the effectiveness of these and other forms of control and their relative merits is beyond the scope of this study. There are, however, a number of problems that arise at the interface between external controls and the corporate organization that ought to be examined. With regard to the enforcement of the criminal law three issues in particular will be considered: (i) whether in order to maximize the prevention of offences liability should be imposed on individuals or the enterprise or both; (ii) what sanctions should be employed; and (iii), overlapping with (i) and (ii), whether the law should intervene in internal decision-making processes or merely aim to activate the company's own responses by posing

---

[3] Health and Safety Executive, *Blackspot Construction* (1988), at 4. See also HSE, *Agricultural Blackspot* (1986), at 12 (in 62 per cent of deaths in agriculture 'responsibility rested with management'); HSE, *Deadly Maintenance* (1985), at 8 ('management were primarily responsible' for 54 per cent of deaths in a variety of industries).

[4] R. Cranston, *Regulating Business: Law and Consumer Agencies* (1979), at 139.

[5] Ibid. at 140.

[6] C. D. Stone, 'The Place of Enterprise Liability in the Control of Corporate Conduct', (1980) 90 *Yale L J* 1 (reference omitted).

an adequately punitive threat. Section I will now outline the current principles of criminal liability as they apply to companies and their agents, before going on to explore these issues. The section will conclude with a brief consideration of a separate but related topic, namely whether shareholders, and in particular parent companies, should continue to enjoy immunity in relation to tort victims, given the tendency of limited-liability status to undermine the objective of controlling risk that tort liability is intended to serve.

I ENFORCING EXTERNAL CONTROLS

Corporate Criminal Liability

There are a number of ways in which a company can be held liable for crime.[7] Thus a company may breach a duty imposed by statute on the entity itself, for example, as an occupier of premises or as the operator of an industrial process. An illustration is *Alphacell Ltd v Woodward*[8] where the company was held responsible for causing polluted water to enter a river. A company may also be vicariously liable for crimes committed by employees, but only within the same narrow limits that govern the vicarious liability of natural persons. There are two ways in which vicarious criminal liability may arise.[9] One is where statute casts a duty on the company as owner or licensee of premises and the company delegates the management of the premises to an employee, who then commits the offence. The other is where, in order to prevent the purpose of a statute from being defeated, the courts have interpreted its words to apply to the employer where the relevant acts have in fact been performed by an employee, as where the owner of a business is made liable for selling goods where the transaction is actually entered into by an assistant.[10]

The forms of liability considered so far relate only to offences that do not require proof of criminal intent. Where *mens rea* is involved the company can be convicted only if it possesses itself the necessary guilty mind. Treating an

[7] For a more detailed consideration, see Law Commission, *Working Paper no. 44: Codification of the Criminal Law—Criminal Liability of Corporations* (1972, London), at 2–10; Law Commission, *A Criminal Code for England and Wales*, Law Commission no. 177 (1989), at 213–17; L. H. Leigh, *The Criminal Liability of Corporations in English Law* (1969); A. Ashworth, *Principles of Criminal Law* (1991), at 81–8; J. C. Smith and B. Hogan, *Criminal Law* (7th ed., 1992), 178–85; Glanville Williams, *Criminal Law: The General Part* (2nd ed., 1961), ch. 2.

[8] [1972] AC 824, HL, [1972] 2 All ER 475, HL. See also *Birmingham and Gloucester Rly Co* (1842) 3 QB 223; *Great North of England Rly Co* (1846) 9 QB 315.

[9] See Ashworth, *Principles of Criminal Law* (above, n. 7), at 83–4.

[10] See e.g. *Coppen v Moore (No 2)* [1898] 2 QB 306. The governing statute ocassionally provides a defence to the company where the offence was due to an act of another person and the company exercised due diligence to prevent the offence being committed. See e.g. Trade Descriptions Act 1968, s 24, applied in *Tesco Supermarkets Ltd v Nattrass* [1972] AC 153.

artificial entity as having a mind, guilty or otherwise, is problematical, but is achieved for the purposes of the criminal law by means of the doctrine of identification, that is, by deeming the minds of certain senior officers to be the mind of the company itself. As laid down by the House of Lords in *Tesco Supermarkets Ltd v Nattrass* these officers are those who 'represent the directing mind and will of the company and control what it does'.[11] The board of directors or a managing director undoubtedly fall within this definition, but it is not entirely clear to what extent a single director or lower-level managers will be identified with the company. The essence of the tests set out in *Tesco v Nattrass* is that an employee will be treated as (part of) the 'brains' of the company, as opposed merely to being its 'hands',[12] only where some function of the board has been delegated to him or her such as to confer a discretion to make policy on behalf of the company in a particular area without recourse to superior authority.[13] This would seem to rule out identifying with the company even very senior managers, except where the directors have effectively put those managers into their own place with respect to the running of the business or some aspect of it.[14]

The narrowness of the range of officers whose actions and intent will be treated as the actions and intent of the company means that corporate liability for *mens rea* offences will be a rarity in complex organizations. The directors' involvement in, and knowledge about, operational matters in a large company will generally be slight, whereas managers or lower-level employees, against whom it might be possible to establish a case will fall outside the scope of the identification doctrine. The difficulties are well illustrated in *P & O European Ferries (Dover) Ltd*,[15] the prosecution for

---

[11] Ibid. at 171, per Lord Reid.
[12] See *Bolton (Engineering) Co Ltd v Grahman & Sons Ltd* [1957] 1 QB 159, CA, per Denning LJ.
[13] See e.g. Lord Reid in *Tesco v Nattrass* at 171:
Normally the board of directors, the managing director and perhaps other superior officers of a company carry out the functions of management and speak and act as the company. Their subordinates do not. They carry out orders from above and it can make no difference that they are given some measure of discretion. But the board of directors may delegate some part of their functions of management giving to their delegate full discretion to act independently of instructions from them. I see no difficulty in holding that they have thereby put such a delegate in their place so that within the scope of the delegation he can act as the company.
[14] As e.g. in *Bolton (Engineering) Co Ltd v Grahman & Sons Ltd* (above, n. 12), approved in *Tesco v Nattrass* (above, n. 10), where the board met only once a year and left the running of the business to managers. The tests laid down in *Tesco* appear to be narrower than those employed in earlier decisions: see *DPP v Kent and Sussex Contractors Ltd* [1944] KB 551, [1944] 1 All ER 119 (where a transport manager was identified with the company); *Moore v I Bresler Ltd* [1944] 2 All ER 515 (company secretary and branch sales manager). For a further narrowing of the identification doctrine by the Supreme Court of Canada, see *Canadian Dredge & Dock Co Ltd v The Queen* (1985) 19 DLR (4th) 314, at 335, per Esty J: 'The identification doctrine only operates where the Crown demonstrates that the action taken by the directing mind (a) was within the field of operation assigned to him; (b) was not totally in fraud of the corporation; and (c) was by design or result partly for the benefit of the company.' See also Law Commission, *A Criminal Code for England and Wales* (above, n. 7), at 215.
[15] (1991) 93 Cr App R 72.

manslaughter of the owners of the *Herald of Free Enterprise*, which capsized shortly after leaving Zeebrugge because its bow doors had not been properly closed. For a company to be convicted of manslaughter it is necessary to establish *inter alia* (i) that an officer who could be regarded as the 'controlling mind' of the company was responsible for an act or omission that had led to death, and (ii) that in addition to committing the *actus reus* of the offence, that officer also had the relevant *mens rea*, that is, that an ordinary prudent person in the same position as the officer would have realized that there was an obvious and serious risk of injury. On the facts, notwithstanding that '[a]ll concerned in management, from the members of the Board of Directors down to the junior superintendents, were guilty of fault',[16] these requirements were not satisfied and the prosecution failed. It was not clear which, if any, of the directors was responsible for safety and hence it could not be shown that a failure on the part of an individual sufficiently senior to be identified with the company had *caused* the disaster. Similarly it was held not to be obvious to the board, distant from the day-to-day management of the company's affairs, that the mode of operation of its ferries created a serious risk of injury.

In addition to the restrictedness of the range of individuals that the law is prepared to treat as representing the company itself, a further difficulty in the way of imposing corporate liability should be emphasized. This is that the complete *actus reus* and *mens rea* of the relevant offence must be attributable to a single officer. In preliminary proceedings arising out of the Zeebrugge disaster the Divisional Court rejected the argument that the company's guilt could be established by aggregating the acts and mental state of a number of individuals identifiable with the company, thereby showing that the company itself was responsible, even though there was no officer who had personally committed all the ingredients of the offence.[17] The rejection of aggregation makes plain that the identification doctrine actually constitutes a form of vicarious liability, even though it is normally described as involving direct corporate liability.[18] Fault is assumed to lie not in the organization itself, but in specific representatives, responsibility for whose offences is then *imputed* to the company. We shall see below that a number of writers have argued that organizations can meaningfully be regarded as blameworthy in themselves and that without such recognition the ability to hold companies criminally accountable is dangerously restricted.

[16] This was the finding of the official enquiry into the disaster: Department of Transport, *The Merchant Shipping Act 1894, mv Herald of Free Enterprise*, Report of Court No 8074 (the Sheen Report), (1987), para 14.1.

[17] *R v H M Coroner for East Kent, ex p Spooner* (1989) 88 Cr App R 10, at 16–17. See also Law Commission *Working Paper no. 44* (above, n. 7), at 27, 31–2.

[18] See B. Fisse and J. Braithwaite, 'The Allocation of Responsibility for Corporate Crime: Individualism, Collectivism and Accountability', (1988) 11 *Sydney L Rev* 468, at 504–5.

Individual Liability

Whether or not the company is prosecuted as well, it is of course possible to convict directors and employees personally who have committed offences in the course of their employment. For example, as just noted, a conviction of the company for manslaughter assumes that there is a particular individual who is guilty too. In addition to officers being liable as principals, they may also be convicted as accessories to offences committed by the company, that is, for 'aiding, abetting, counselling or procuring' the commission of an offence.[19] Accessorial liability is extended beyond these grounds under a number of modern 'regulatory' statutes, section 37(1) of the Health and Safety at Work Act 1974 being typical, providing that:

Where an offence under any of the relevant statutory provisions committed by a body corporate is proved to have been committed with the consent or connivance of, or to have been attributable to any neglect on the part of any director, manager, secretary or other similar officer of the body corporate or a person who was purporting to act in any such capacity, he as well as the body corporate shall be guilty of that offence and shall be liable to be proceeded against and punished accordingly.[20]

'Consent or connivance' are wider than 'aiding and abetting' since the latter involve active assistance or encouragement, and the attribution of liability on the basis of neglect in failing to prevent the offence has no counterpart in general accessorial liability.[21] Unlike the general offences, however, the persons who can be convicted under these special statutory provisions are limited to a narrow range of senior officers.[22]

Improving the Control Framework

How should the criminal law be designed to maximize compliance with the social policies it reflects? Of key importance is the target of liability: should it primarily be individuals ('agent liability') or the company ('enterprise liability')? One school, premised on the belief that only individuals act and form intentions, holds that appropriately framed rules taking as their target directors and employees exclusively are capable of securing the necessary level of deterrence.[23] The rival view points to the advantages enjoyed by the

[19] Accessories and Abettors Act 1861, s 8 as amended by the Criminal Law Act 1977 (indictable offences), and Magistrates' Courts Act 1980, s 44 (summary offences).

[20] See also e.g. Trade Descriptions Act 1968, s 20; Fair Trading Act 1973, s 132; Consumer Protection Act 1987, s 40(2); Consumer Credit Act 1974, s 169; Environmental Protection Act 1990, s 157(1).

[21] See Smith and Hogan, *Criminal Law* (above, n. 7), at 185.

[22] 'Manager' in this context appears to mean one who manages the affairs of the company in the *Tesco v Nattrass* sense: see *Registrar of Restrictive Trading Agreements v W H Smith Ltd* [1969] 1 WLR 1460, *R v Boal* [1992] BCLC 872, CA.

[23] The assumptions on which this individualist perspective rests (that only individuals are 'real', that individual liability is necessary and sufficient for deterrence, and that punishment of

enterprise in disciplining its employees over those possessed by the state in imposing liability from 'the outside', and hence argues that enterprise liability, giving the company the incentive to activate its own disciplinary mechanisms, is a more efficient form of control.[24] A third view insists that the two forms of liability are complementary and that both are essential if external controls are sufficiently to mesh with companies' internal decision-making procedures.[25]

Agent Liability

It seems fairly plain that a regime of agent liability alone would be incapable of reaching all forms of business wrongdoing.[26] It will frequently be unclear precisely who, if anyone, should be held individually responsible for a particular default. Failure to correct unsafe working practices, for example, may result from a lack of clarity about whose job it is to monitor safety matters, diffusion of information within the organization about hazards and previous accidents, or a breakdown in the system of command, as opposed to an act or omission of a particular individual that can be shown to be culpable. Even where a conviction is feasible in principle, liability may be evaded since 'organisations have a well-developed capacity for obscuring internal accountability if confronted by outsiders. Regulatory agencies, prosecutors and courts find it difficult or even impossible to unravel lines of accountability after the event because of the incentives personnel have to protect each other with a cover-up.'[27]

Further, while the threat of agent liability can be expected to have some deterrent effect on individuals who might otherwise commit offences it may nevertheless fail to generate an appropriate institutional response.[28] This is

artificial entities is inappropriate from a retributive point of view) are critically evaluated in Fisse and Braithwaite, 'The Allocation of Responsibility' (above, n. 18). For an evaluation of some of the objections to *enterprise* liability, see Leigh, *The Criminal Liability of Corporations* (above, n. 7), ch. 9.

[24] See R. A. Posner, 'An Economic Theory of the Criminal Law', (1985) 85 *Colum L Rev* 1193, at 1227–9; Law Reform Commission (Canada), Working Paper No. 16, *Criminal Responsibility for Group Action* (1976).

[25] Stone, 'The Place of Enterprise Liability in the Control of Corporate Conduct' (above, n. 6); J. C. Coffee, 'No Soul to Damn: No Body to Kick: An Unscandalized Enquiry into the Problem of Corporate Punishment', (1981) 79 *Mich Law Rev* 386; R. Kraakman, 'The Economic Functions of Corporate Liability', in K. J. Hopt and G. Teubner (eds), *Corporate Governance and Directors' Liabilities* (1985) 178.

[26] See Fisse and Braithwaite, 'The Allocation of Responsibility' (above, n. 18), at 494–9; Stone, 'The Place of Enterprise Liability' (above, n.), at 28–33.

[27] Fisse and Braithwaite, ibid. at 495 (reference omitted).

[28] And see Council of Europe, *Liability of Enterprises for Offences*, Recommendation no. R (88) 18 (1990), at 10: an

offence may be the result of separate decisions, acts and omissions by different persons, albeit corresponding to a general ethos, generated by management, in the enterprise. In such cases, it may well be impossible to hold any one person liable, and even if this is possible, true

important where breaches result not so much from deliberate acts of wrongdoing, but are rather the consequence of system failures, such as poor methods
of work or facilities or inadequate supervision. Where prosecution of
individual employees is possible in such cases the likely targets may be
regarded by the organization as expendable; it may view their fate as a less
costly way of dealing with the demands of regulation than correcting the
underlying conditions that lead to .violations. It seems plausible that the
more highly placed the potential victim of liability the greater will be the
organizational response, but as mentioned earlier, tracing liability back to
senior managers is likely in many cases to prove impossible. Agent liability
may even reduce the corporate response to the risk of malpractice by giving
senior managers an incentive to distance themselves from operational matters
and to avoid supervising lower-level management in case attaching
responsibility to those at the top should become a realistic possibility. The
multi-divisional structure[29] in particular lends itself to this form of risk
shifting, since it permits 'the central headquarters to insulate itself from
responsibility for operational decisions while simultaneously pressuring for
quick solutions to often intractable problems'.[30] Structural arrangements
may thus encourage divisional managers to economize on precautions necessary to avoid violations in order to be able to meet tight financial targets
imposed from the centre, while at the same time those at the centre are
immune to any risk of prosecution thereby created.

Enterprise Liability

The assumption relied on by those who advocate a regime based primarily,
or exclusively, on enterprise liability is that the threat to profitability that a
criminal penalty (usually a fine) represents provides the organization with
an incentive to discipline its employees and otherwise to adopt structures
that minimize the risk of a penalty being imposed. Thus the company has
easier access to information and can discipline employees at lower cost than
outside enforcement bodies.[31] Because the enterprise as a whole bears the cost
of violations a damaging division between those who carry the risk of
prosecution and those who are in a position to implement policies to
maximize compliance is avoided. The response to the threat to profits does
not of course occur spontaneously, but is mediated through the behaviour of
senior managers, who are regarded as having the same incentives to protect
profits by avoiding criminal sanctions as they have to avoid any other risk to

---

responsibility may be more diffused. A sanction imposed on an individual person may, in such
cases, be neither deterrent enough to prevent the enterprise from committing further offences,
nor induce the management or members of the enterprise to reorganize its supervisory
structure.

[29] See 68–9 above.
[30] Coffee, 'No Soul to Damn' (above, n. 25), at 398 (reference omitted).
[31] See Fisse and Braithwaite, 'The Allocation of Responsibility' (above, n. 18), at 494–6.

profitability, such as a challenge to the company's competitive position or the discovery of operating inefficiencies.[32]

One reason why this model may be over-optimistic is that culpable acts and omissions, notwithstanding the probable penalty, might remain profitable. Practices proscribed by consumer law may, for instance, still make a net contribution to profits even after prosecution, or the cost of avoiding violations, for example, installing devices to guard against the emission of toxic wastes, might exceed the likely fine. The obvious response to this objection, that penalties should be increased to ensure that non-compliance is always unprofitable, will be considered shortly. A second problem with the model is that the assumptions it makes about managerial motivation may be unwarranted.[33] Apart from the possibility that managers may simply fail to respond rationally to the threat to profits, a fine borne by the company may in some circumstances have a minimal impact on their own positions and hence on their behaviour. The fine may simply be too small to have a significant follow-through effect on managers personally, and slackness in the institutional and market mechanisms that align management and enterprise interests may enable them safely to ignore the adverse profit consequences.[34] These mechanisms might in some situations even create perverse incentives for managers to engage in conduct that carries an above-average risk of corporate liability, for example, where performance-linked remuneration has a short time focus and liability is likely to accrue only in the longer term (as where adverse side-effects of the company's products, suspected by management, will become apparent only in later years).[35] Similarly pressure in the market for corporate control may encourage an emphasis on short-term profits and a disregard for longer-term liability risks.

Apart from the perverse incentive issue these problems may be remediable by increasing the level of penalties. Fines imposed on companies have historically been low,[36] but could they not be raised to a level that ensured

---

[32] J. Braithwaite and G. Geis, 'On Theory and Action for Corporate Crime Control', (1982) 28 *Crime and Delinquency* 292, at 301–2, suggest that 'deterrence is doubtful with traditional crime, but may well be strong with corporate crime', *inter alia* because 'corporate crimes are almost never crimes of passion; they are not spontaneous or emotional, but calculated risks taken by rational actors. As such, they should be more amenable to control by policies based on the utilitarian assumptions of the deterrence doctrine.'

[33] See Stone, 'The Place of Enterprise Liability' (above, n. 6), at 15–16, 21–4.

[34] See Ch. 4 above.

[35] See C. D. Stone, 'Corporate Social Responsibility: What it Might Mean, if it Were Really to Matter', (1986) 71 *Iowa L Rev* 557, at 562.

[36] See Bergman, *Deaths at Work* (above, n. 2), at 35: the average fine levied on companies in 1988-90 after deaths at work was £1,940. And see G. Richardson, A. Ogus, and P. Burrows, *Policing Pollution: A Study of Regulation and Enforcement* (1982), at 60–2. In addition to low penalties, the rate of prosecutions of companies and officers for 'regulatory' (and other) offences is very low: see Bergman, ibid. at 34–9; Richardson et al., ibid. at 62–7. This is seemingly because regulatory agencies prefer to pursue a strategy of negotiated compliance rather than deterrence, reserving prosecution for especially blatant offences.

that at least non-compliance was unprofitable? It may be noted that according to the economic theory of deterrence,[37] in order to be effective as a deterrent a penalty must be of a value that not merely deprives the company of its gains or equals the costs of compliance, but will often need to be fixed at a considerably higher sum. This is because an economically rational actor will discount the likely penalty in accordance with the prospects of detection and conviction, and hence in order to cancel out these effects the penalty must be set at a level in excess of the expected benefit from non-compliance. Since many offences likely to be committed by companies are of low visibility, such as exceeding discharge consents or breach of health and safety requirements not resulting in injury, the discount factor is likely to be particularly high.[38]

That penalties may need to be very large is a problem because raising them to the appropriate level may hit against formal or informal sentencing constraints.[39] There is first a formal limit to the size of the penalty that can be imposed bounded by the company's available resources, given limited-liability status.[40] In a large enterprise these resources may be huge, but this need not be so with respect to the particular company within the group that is guilty of the offence.[41] Informal limits are in part derived from a reluctance to visit punishment on those who have no personal responsiblity for the misconduct in question. Fines may harm shareholders by reducing share values (though it might be supposed that those who take the benefits should also bear the burdens),[42] they may be regarded as an ordinary business cost

---

[37] See R. A. Posner, *The Economic Analysis of Law* (3rd ed., 1986), at 205–12.

[38] The deterrent effect of adverse publicity resulting from conviction should however also be added into the equation. Companies which spend considerable sums on advertising and other image-building activities are presumably sensitive to publicity over e.g. prosecution for selling adulterated foods. Fisse and Braithwaite, 'The Allocation of Responsibility' (above, n. 18), at 490, suggest that companies value a good reputation for its own sake, independently of the financial consequences of bad publicity: 'Individuals who take on positions of power within . . . organizations, even if they as individuals do not personally feel any deterrent effects of shaming directed at their organization, may find that they confront role expectations to protect and enhance the repute of the organization.'

[39] Notwithstanding that the courts are now directed to take account of an offender's means in determining the level of a fine: see Criminal Justice Act 1991, s 19.

[40] See Coffee, 'No Soul to Damn' (above, n. 25), at 389–93.

[41] The separate legal identity of companies in a group ensures that e.g. a parent company cannot be held liable for offences committed by its subsidiary. It is however possible that a parent company might be liable in its own right in a situation in which the subsidiary is primarily liable, where the parent (i.e. someone who constitutes the parent's controlling mind: see above) has aided and abetted the commission of an offence by the subsidiary.

[42] As Fisse and Braithwaite (above, n. 18), at 508, point out,
not to punish an enterprise at fault would be to allow corporations to accumulate and distribute to associates a pool of resources which does not reflect the social cost of production. Justice as fairness requires, as a minimum, that the cost of corporate offences be internalised by the enterprise. Where an offence has been committed through the fault of an enterprise, punishment may prevent the cost of that offence from being externalised and thereby imposed on other innocent parties.
See also Law Commission, *Working Paper no. 44* (above, n. 7), at 32–3.

and passed on to customers, or lead to plant closures or even the collapse of the entire company, with obvious consequences for employees[43] and dependent communities. There are also finally constraints on the possible size of fines, stemming from the competing aims and values of penal policy. Thus it has been suggested that the norms of retribution and equal treatment 'support a relationship of rough proportionality between the harm inflicted by offenses and the severity of sanctions; and both oppose the distortions in the penalty structure that result from punishing less harmful delicts more severely that easily-detected egregious offenses'.[44] These factors taken together suggest that in practice financial penalties are unlikely to be raised consistently to the levels that are necessary to achieve effective deterrence.

Fines are not the only conceivable form of punishment for corporate offenders, however, and the availability of a wider range of penalties might enable the difficulties associated with them to be sidestepped. One possibility is the 'equity fine', the imposition of which would require a company to issue shares to a public body which would then dispose of them on the market.[45] By diluting the value of the company's existing shares this would have a direct effect on senior managers, since it would reduce the value of their holdings in the company and any share options they might enjoy, and by releasing a block of equity onto the market would increase the risk of takeover. On the other hand, because the fine would not be levied on the company's resources, spill-over effects on employees and customers would be avoided. The cost would, of course, be borne by the existing shareholders, but it has been suggested that this would have the beneficial effect of making the investing public more sensitive to corporate crime, contributing to 'a more cautious top management that would install greater internal auditing controls to restrain lower echelon managers'.[46] A different approach involves direct intervention by 'interjecting the court or its agents into the corporation's decision-making processes in an attempt to remedy dysfunctions that seem causally related to the criminal behaviour'.[47] Possible vehicles for such intervention include corporate probation, punitive injunctions, and the judicial appointment of directors or other officers.[48] Through these techniques

---

[43] Glanville Williams, *Textbook of Criminal Law* (2nd ed., 1983), at 975 n. 2, refers to an unreported decision in which the judge 'fined the company £375,000 and intimated that it would have been higher but for the risk of causing unemployment'.

[44] Kraakman, 'The Economic Functions of Corporate Liability' (above, n. 25), at 194.

[45] See Coffee, 'No Soul to Damn' (above, n. 25), at 413–24 and the discussion in D. J. Meister, 'Criminal Liability for Corporations that Kill', (1990) 64 *Tulane L Rev* 919, at 934–9.

[46] Coffee, ibid. at 419.

[47] Coffee, ibid. at 448.

[48] See Coffee, ibid. at 448–57; Fisse and Braithwaite, 'The Allocation of Responsibility' (above, n. 18), at 499–502; B. Fisse, 'Recent Developments in Corporate Criminal Law and Corporate Liability to Monetary Penalties', (1990) 13 *U of NSW L J* 1, at 9–11; C. D. Stone, *Where the Law Ends: The Social Control of Corporate Behaviour* (1975), chs 16 and 17.

the court might require the company to investigate breaches of duty and discipline those responsible, or establish procedures to prevent recurrences. As well as avoiding spill-over effects, direct intervention in decision-making processes, rather than trusting to uncertain management responses in the face of threats to profits or share values, guarantees that some form of corrective action is taken.

These ideas, which have been set out in only the briefest outline,[49] seem promising, but there is an issue prior to that of sanctions that must be resolved if enterprise liability is to become a fully effective mode of social control. This is that the narrow basis on which companies may currently be held liable for offences requiring proof of intent must be extended.[50] Ashworth has commented that '[t]he history of legal developments in [corporate criminal liability] suggests a somewhat slow progress towards integrating corporations into a legal framework constructed for individuals, with few gestures towards the differences between corporations and individual human beings.'[51] What is required is a movement away from this individualist perspective and a recognition that, rather than involving a search for blameworthy individuals, liability should be premised on the existence of defective decision-making processes. Without such a reorientation the likelihood will persist that '[c]ollective responsibility [will be] lost in the crevices between the responsibilities of individuals.'[52] This was precisely the case in the *Herald of Free Enterprise* manslaughter prosecution already mentioned. It was unclear whether any particular director had responsibility for safety matters overall; company standing orders concerning safety on board ship were also inadequate but apparently no one had been allocated the task of ensuring that they were properly formulated.[53] That there had been previous 'open door' incidents was known to some masters employed by the company, and there had even been suggestions that indicator lights be fitted on the bridge, but in the absence of a system to collate and respond to this information nothing had been done. With the law as it stands, requiring

---

[49] See also the suggested sanctions in Council of Europe, *Liability of Enterprises for Offences* (above, n. 28), at 6–8, 14–16, including compensation of victims, suspension of certain business activities, and the appointment of a caretaker management.

[50] As Ashworth, *Principles of Criminal Law* (above, n. 7), at 86, points out, an 'alternative strategy would be to rely even more on new offences of strict liability to punish corporate harm-doing, but this might not be a sufficient response to some of the [recent] disasters . . . , or to other harm-doing on a broad scale'. See also B. Fisse, 'The Attribution of Criminal Liability to Corporations: A Statutory Model', (1991) 13 *Sydney L Rev* 277, at 278–9 (strict liability objectionable in principle and likely to be ineffective as regards serious offences).

[51] Ibid. at 84.

[52] S. Field and N. Jörg, 'Corporate Liability and Manslaughter: Should we be Going Dutch?', [1991] *Crim L R* 156, at 162. See also A. Foerschler, 'Corporate Criminal Intent: Toward a Better Understanding of Corporate Misconduct', (1990) 78 *Cal L Rev* 1287.

[53] See the *Sheen Report* (above, n. 16), at 15. See also *Investigation into the King's Cross Underground Fire* (1988) (the Fennell Report), finding that inadequate allocation of responsibility for passenger safety was also a major factor in that disaster.

proof that a person of sufficient seniority committed the *actus reus* of the offence and had the necessary *mens rea*, the very absence of appropriate procedures guarantees that the company will be acquitted.

A possible reform, contrary to the position adopted in *R v H M Coroner for East Kent, ex p Spooner*,[54] is to permit aggregation.[55] This would make it possible to add together the acts and intent of several individuals involved in an offence which could then be imputed to the company. This would, however, be only a very limited solution in complex organizations so long as identification remained the basis of liability. In the Zeebrugge disaster the conduct and state of knowledge of those who constituted the 'controlling mind', even when added together, would not have been sufficient to found liability. And routinely in large enterprises responsibility for such matters as product design, environmental protection, and employee and public safety is devolved to lower-tier managers, with the result that those with whom the company can be identified will be insufficiently implicated in any likely offence.

Rather than increase the coverage of the identification doctrine it seems preferable to abandon the individualistic assumptions on which it rests and instead to premise liability on the responsibility of the company itself. It is sometimes argued that holding an organization, as opposed to individual human beings, responsible for wrongdoing is methodologically incoherent. As Fisse and Braithwaite explain, however, when people blame corporations they are quite rationally 'condemning the fact that the organization either implemented a policy of non-compliance or failed to exercise its collective capacity to avoid the offence for which blame attaches'.[56] Unless liability can be imposed where the company has neglected to bring this 'collective capacity' to bear, the principal objective of enterprise liability, of inducing management to install suitable decision-making and monitoring structures, will remain unfulfilled. The recommendations of the Council of Europe offer an attractive avenue of reform in this regard. The proposal is that a company should be liable 'whether a natural person who committed the acts or omissions constituting the offence can be identified or not', but also that the company should be exonerated 'where its management is not implicated in the offence and has taken all the necessary steps to prevent its commission'.[57] In an offence such as manslaughter liability under these provisions

---

[54] (Above, note 17.)

[55] See C. Wells, 'Manslaughter and Corporate Crime' (1989), 139 *NLJ* 931.

[56] Fisse and Braithwaite, 'The Allocation of Responsibility' (above, n. 18), at 482, and also n. 73 below.

[57] The Council of Europe, *Liability of Enterprises for Offences* (above, n. 28), at 6–7. It is proposed that whether or not the company is held liable, individuals implicated in an offence should remain personally liable. See also the discussion of corporate liability in Dutch law in Field and Jörg, 'Corporate Liability and Manslaughter' (above, n. 51), at 163–71. Liability may be imposed on the company where employees' acts are 'accepted' by the company

would still depend on fault, but this might lie for example in the fact that a breakdown in the channels of communication had resulted in a culpable failure to respond to known (by one part of the organization) risks of harm-causing acts or omissions. At the same time, the availability of a defence where management has taken appropriate action will prevent the company from being held liable for the wayward acts of individual employees beyond the company's control.

Fisse and Braithwaite address the basis of enterprise liability in proposing reforms that involve a more comprehensive strategy for reducing the risks to which society is exposed by corporate activity. Their suggestions are responsive to the objection that although prosecuting the company will frequently be more convenient than proceeding against individuals, and indeed sometimes the enterprise will be the only practicable target, manage-ments may fail to take the disciplinary action against employees implicated in wrongdoing that is a central premise of the theory of enterprise liability.[58] This failure to press home the consequences of culpable conduct is seen furthermore as tending to undermine individual responsibility.[59] In order to rebuild accountability Fisse and Braithwaite recommend that enforcement be structured in such a way as to 'activate and monitor the private justice systems of corporate defendants'.[60] What they propose is that, where the *actus reus* of an offence is shown to have been committed by or on behalf of a company, the court should be able to require management to investigate who was responsible within the organization and to take appropriate disciplinary action and steps to compensate victims and prevent recurrences. Only if the corporate response is deficient would it then be necessary for the court to impose a sanction (on the company or top managers). This proposal is seen as having the additional advantage of dispensing with the problem of establishing within complex organizations that harm-causing conduct was accompanied at the time of commission by the necessary element of fault.

(including where the company has failed to monitor risky behaviour), and where the company has the 'power' to determine employee behaviour (e.g. whether the company could in practice have prevented harm-creating acts). Fisse, 'The Attribution of Criminal Liability to Corpora-tions' (above, n. 50), proposes that companies should be vicariously liable for the external elements of an offence, but that liability in relation to the mental element should depend on 'organizational blameworthiness', as reflected e.g. in a policy of non-compliance or lack of due diligence (not necessarily on the part of an identifiable individual).

[58] Fisse and Braithwaite, 'The Allocation of Responsibility' (above, n. 18), at 472: 'companies have strong incentives not to undertake extensive disciplinary action. In particular, a disciplinary programme may be disruptive, embarrassing for those exercising managerial control, encourag-ing for whistle-blowers, or hazardous in the event of civil litigation against the company or its officers' (references omitted).

[59] On individual responsibility within organizations see J. Ladd, 'Morality and the Ideal of Rationality in Formal Organizations', (1970) 54 *The Monist* 488, and T. C. Schelling, 'Command and Control', in J. W. McKie (ed.), *Social Responsibility and the Business Predicament* (1974) 79, at 107: the large organization is a 'solvent within which personal morality becomes unstuck'.

[60] Fisse and Braithwaite, 'The Allocation of Responsibility' (above, n. 18), at 510.

Fault ('reactive corporate fault') would instead inhere in an inadequate remedial and disciplinary response to the harm-creating conduct of which complaint is made.

A number of reservations may be expressed about these proposals. One is that, notwithstanding court supervision of internal policing, there seems a risk of lop-sided enforcement, with top management enjoying a relative immunity from company-imposed discipline.[61] Nor is the range of sanctions available to the company, the most severe being dismissal,[62] commensurate with the gravity of the offences with which individual employees may be associated. There clearly remains a need for judicially imposed agent liability in relation to serious offences, both to provide an adequate deterrent and in order to express public condemnation.[63] The competence of the court, furthermore, to assess the suitability of measures adopted by the company to prevent subsequent harm or to supervise compliance with them on a continuing basis is questionable.

Whatever the detailed character of the arrangements that are best suited to increasing the effectiveness of external controls over company behaviour, it seems clear in broad outline that there is a need for a regime that makes use of both agent and enterprise liability, that unless the basis of enterprise liability is extended considerably much corporate misconduct will continue to lie beyond the reach of the legal process, and that in regard to enterprise liability an approach that does not rely exclusively on enterprise self-regulation in the face of financial penalties is required. Some alternative, 'interventionist', judicial remedies have been touched on. A different (complementary) approach is for society to intervene in companies' organizational structures without waiting for an offence to be committed, by, for example, insisting on the appointment of high-level executives with specific responsibilities, such as safety or environmental matters. Structural interventions of this kind may be of value in promoting extra-legal responsibility as well as in increasing compliance and so, to avoid repetition, consideration of them will be postponed until page 368 below.

---

[61] See Stone, 'The Place of Enterprise Liability' (above, n. 6), at 30: 'we may suspect the integrity of the enterprise's internal sanctioning process, which is, after all, largely in the hands of high-level managers who have their own welfare to protect. The managers may tend either to find a scapegoat or to accord light treatment to a true culprit in exchange for his not implicating them.'

[62] In an appropriate case the company may also be entitled to an indemnity from an employee, as where the company has incurred a civil liability to a third-party victim.

[63] In such cases the law has a 'retributive, even denunciatory role to play, one that requires the ceremonial trappings of public prosecution for symbolic and educative purposes': Stone, 'The Place of Enterprise Liability' (above, n. 6) at 30.

Limited Liability and Tort

The final purpose of this section is to question the immunity of shareholders from the obligation to meet the liability of the company to tort victims where the company's assets are insufficient, in consequence of the shareholders' limited-liability status. An increasing number of writers have questioned the merits of limited liability for tort,[64] which in effect allows those involved in corporate enterprise to override society's judgements expressed in tort rules about the proper containment of risk and the circumstances in which third parties injured as a result of commercial activity should be compensated.

One effect of limited liability is to reduce the incentives to take care. Because shareholders do not bear the cost of damage tortiously inflicted on third parties (in excess of their investment in the company), they lack sufficient incentives to ensure that the company takes adequate precautions to prevent accidents. Further, as limited liability permits the externalization of costs, the full risk associated with the business will not be reflected in the investor's required rate of return.[65] Limited liability thus 'encourages excessive entry and aggregate overinvestment in unusually hazardous industries'.[66] The adverse effect of limited liability on third parties is frequently justified as the price regrettably to be paid for the benefits society obtains from corporate activity: it is a social subsidy to encourage capital formation. But as Stone points out, it is an odd subsidy 'that dilutes the disincentives for the flouting of public policy, and that singles out the injured as contributors rather than finding support from the community at large'.[67] Whether moving to an unlimited liability regime with respect to tort claims would in practice be likely to discourage investment has yet to be conclusively determined. Hansmann and Kraakman suggest, however, that there is no reason to suppose that a rule of pro rata (as opposed to joint[68]) unlimited liability would increase the cost of equity beyond the level that represents the desirable internalization of risks currently borne by third parties, though they accept that there is insufficient empirical evidence to reveal whether steps that might be taken to evade liability under such a regime (such as

---

[64] See e.g. P. Halpern, M. Trebilcock, and S. Turnbull, 'An Economic Analysis of Limited Liability in Corporation Law', (1980) 30 *U Toronto L J* 117; P. I. Blumberg, *The Law of Corporate Groups: Substantive Law* (1987), at 681–92; H. Hansmann and R. Kraakman, 'Toward Unlimited Shareholder Liability for Corporate Torts', (1991) 100 *Yale L J* 1879; D. W. Leebron, 'Limited Liability, Tort Victims, and Creditors', (1991) 91 *Colum L Rev* 1565.

[65] See Leebron, ibid. at 1585.

[66] Hansmann and Kraakman, 'Toward Unlimited Shareholder Liability' (above, n. 64), at 1883.

[67] Stone, 'The Place of Enterprise Liability' (above, n. 6), at 69. See also the consideration of the subsidy argument in Leebron, 'Limited Liability' (above, n. 64), at 1585–7.

[68] Hansmann and Kraakman, 'Toward Unlimited Shareholder Liability' (above, note 64), at 1903. See also Leebron, 'Limited Liability' (above, n. 64), at 1578–84 (joint liability would create a need for substantially increased shareholder monitoring and change the role of shareholders).

selling risky businesses to highly leveraged individuals) would create significant inefficiencies. They conclude nevertheless that the onus is now on supporters of limited liability to justify their position.

The abolition of limited liability in relation to tort claims might, then, be expected to restore the incentives to take care that tort rules otherwise create. In the case of companies with publicly traded shares the members do not have direct control over management policy, but the threat of shareholder liability is nevertheless likely to have an effect on the way the company behaves, in two ways. First, it gives shareholders an incentive to put pressure on management to ensure that systems exist within the company to allow for the proper supervision of activities that carry a significant risk of liability. Second, where the shareholders are potentially liable for tort losses that exceed the company's ability to pay, the possibility of this liability occurring ought to be reflected in the price of the company's shares. Although the information that reaches the market about the risks associated with the company's business, its safety procedures, and safety record, for example, may be imperfect, these factors ought nevertheless to have an impact on share price and ought therefore to influence management conduct in the same way as any other factors that affect share price, such as poor profit performance.[69]

Of more pressing interest is the effect of unlimited liability within group structures, where hazardous activities may be assigned to subsidiaries specifically with the intention of protecting the parent company's assets from liability risks, that is, as a way of evading damages claims. Were the parent to be responsible for an insolvent subsidiary's tort liabilities the effect would be not only that tort victims would be less likely to go uncompensated, but also that the parent's management would have the incentive to ensure that adequate precautions against damage were taken in the first place. And as distinct from the situation as between a public company and its shareholders, in this case the management of the parent has the ability to control directly the behaviour of the subsidiary. The immunity of parent companies in the existing law with respect to unmet tort claims against subsidiaries is an aspect of the wider immunity of shareholders for corporate debts that results from the courts' general refusal to disregard separate corporate personality, finding early expression in *Salomon v Salomon & Co Ltd*.[70] The Court of Appeal has recently reaffirmed that use of separate incorporation for the express purpose of ensuring that future liability will fall on another member of the group rather than on the parent (and hence of ensuring in some cases that liability will ultimately go unsatisfied) is not a ground for ignoring the separate legal identity of the subsidiary. Using the group structure in this

---

[69] See Hansmann and Kraakman, 'Toward Unlimited Shareholder Liability' (above, n. 64), at 1907.

[70] [1897] AC 22, HL.

way is 'inherent in our corporate law'.[71] In view of the issues discussed above, there is much to be said for reforming our corporate law to remove this particular feature, which may best be achieved by abolishing the limited liability status of all shareholders in respect of tort claims.[72]

II INCREASING CORPORATE RESPONSIBILITY: TWO MODELS

The remainder of this chapter returns to the theme introduced in Chapter 10: the public interest demands something more than profit maximization within the law. Two models of corporate responsibility were outlined, each viewing responsibility as a characteristic of decision-making processes rather than as involving compliance with a particular set of substantive behavioural norms. It is now time to look at these models in more detail and to examine the steps that need to be taken to put them into practice.

The first model views an organization as behaving responsibly where its decision processes resemble those of a morally responsible individual.[73] Goodpaster identifies two values that underlie individual moral responsibility: rationality and respect. 'Rationality' involves choosing means that are most likely to achieve desired ends. 'Respect' entails 'consideration of the perspectives of other persons in the pursuit of one's rational projects and purposes

---

[71] *Adams v Cape Industries plc* [1990] BCLC 479, CA, at 520, per Slade L J. For the situations in which the court will 'lift the veil', see L. C. B. Gower, *Principles of Modern Company Law* (5th ed., 1992), ch. 6; J. H. Farrar, N. E. Furey, and B. M. Hannigan, *Farrar's Company Law* (3rd ed., 1991), at 73–81. For a survey of the French and German law and EC proposals on parent company liability, see K. Hofstetter, 'Parent Responsibility for Subsidiary Corporations: Evaluating European Trends', (1990) 39 *Int and Comp L Q* 576.

[72] There would be considerable practical difficulties attached to a regime which removed immunity from parent companies but not shareholders generally, e.g. companies would organize their affairs in such a way as to fall outside any definition of the parent/subsidiary relationship: see Hansmann and Kraakman, 'Toward Unlimited Shareholder Liability' (above, n. 64), at 1931–2. The arguments in support of unlimited liability apply generally in any event. The cases of liability for torts and for contractual debts are distinguishable: see Leebron, 'Limited Liability' (above, n. 64), at 1584 (limited liability as against debt holders does not involve the externalization of costs and hence is not socially inefficient since lenders demand a return that reflects the level of risk).

[73] There is an extensive literature on whether organizations should be regarded as moral persons or as capable of possessing moral qualities: see e.g. the material cited in Fisse and Braithwaite, 'The Allocation of Responsibility' (above, n. 18), at 482 n 63. See also the efforts of contract theorists to deny the applicability of moral standards to corporate behaviour by deconstructing the company into its constituent contracts, e.g. M. C. Jensen and M. Meckling, 'The Theory of the Firm: Managerial Behavior, Agency Costs and Ownership Structure', (1976) 3 *J Fin Econ* 305, at 311: 'the "behavior" of a firm is like the behavior of a market', and while we seldom 'fall into the trap of characterizing the wheat market or stock market as an individual [we often] make this error by thinking about organizations as if they were persons with motivations and intentions'. Whatever the moral status of the corporation, however, the issue is whether its decision-making processes comply with appropriate moral standards, a notion which is non-problematical from a meta-ethical point of view: see K. E. Goodpaster, 'The Concept of Corporate Responsibility', (1983) 2 *J Bus Ethics* 1, at 15.

... It implies a self-imposed constraint on rationality born of a realization that the worth of our projects and purposes resides in the same humanity shared by those who are likely to be affected by them.'[74] Individuals can, therefore, be described as behaving responsibly where their actions are determined rationally, but with due regard to the consequences for others.[75] As noted in the previous chapter, in holding behaviour to be responsible in this sense the commendation is a qualified one, in that the precise way in which the individual's own interests and the interests of others have been balanced may be open to criticism in the light of substantive moral principles.

Stone has suggested that the responsible individual employs a three-stage decision-making process, and that that process, if replicated within business organizations, might serve as 'an institutional analogue to the role that responsibility plays in the human being'.[76] The first stage is that of perception. The perceptions of the responsible person are 'stamped with moral categories',[77] that is, since the interests of others are regarded as important, it is necessary to obtain information about the consequences for others of realizing one's plans. If harm is likely to result, then it is necessary to move to the second stage, which involves the use of moral reasoning. The second stage requires that one's own interests and the conflicting interests of others be evaluated by reference to some moral index. The result (which will depend on the particular moral principles used, which are themselves likely to be far from self-applying) may indicate that one's project should not proceed, or that it should be modified to avoid or limit its harmful impact. The third stage, which is relatively straightforward in the case of an individual (but much less so where an organization is concerned) is that of implementation. Having identified the possible effects of one's activities on others and having made appropriate adjustments to limit any negative consequences, it is necessary to ensure that one's actions will bring about the desired results.

The second model does not regard the conditions for social responsibility as met where outcomes are left merely to enlightened management discretion, but rather views socially responsible behaviour as being the product of decision-making processes that are open to influence by the parties affected by corporate activity. This influence may be exerted from the 'outside', as

[74] Goodpaster, ibid. at 7. And see generally K. E. Goodpaster, 'Ethical Imperatives and Corporate Leadership', in R. E. Freeman (ed.), *Business Ethics: the State of the Art* (1991), 89.

[75] Responsibility in this sense is thus distinguished from responsibility in a causal and a rule-following sense: see Goodpaster, 'The Concept of Corporate Responsibility' (above, n. 73), at 4–5.

[76] Stone, *Where the Law Ends* (above, n. 48), at 120. See also Goodpaster, 'The Concept of Corporate Responsibility', ibid.; J. S. Coleman, 'Responsibility in Corporate Action: A Sociologist's View', in Hopt and Teubner, *Corporate Governance and Directors' Liabilities* (above, n. 25), 69.

[77] Stone, *Where the Law Ends* (above, n. 48), at 114.

where the company and affected interests are in a bargaining relationship of some kind or the latter have other means of subjecting the company to pressure, or from the 'inside', as where representatives of affected groups enjoy rights to participate in enterprise decision-making. Implementation of the second model thus involves seeking to empower third parties in order to increase their ability to shape company policy rather than, as with the first model, attempting to invoke a voluntary response by ensuring that managerial decision-making complies with procedural standards that incorporate an appropriately other-regarding attitude.[78]

It will be convenient in the discussion that follows to employ the three-stage analysis of responsibility set out above as the organizing principle for an examination of various reform possibilities, with the variations in approach dictated by the differing demands of the two models being identified where appropriate. The intention is not to produce a comprehensive catalogue of reform proposals, but to survey the main techniques by which more responsible action might be induced. It may be noted that, while a distinction has been drawn between the two models for analytical purposes, in practice any strategy to increase corporate responsibility is unlikely to be founded on one of the models exclusively. A programme of reform based primarily on the first model may accordingly seek to increase outside pressure on managers in order to stimulate the making of moral choices that reflect a heightened concern for those affected by company policy. Similarly, a strategy more centrally focused on strengthening the bargaining position or decision-making rights of affected interests is likely to be more successful where managers are already receptive to those interests and hence may draw on aspects of the first as well as the second model. The objective of the second model can be viewed as providing a means of shaping management discretion from the outside, and this will work better if managers are positively disposed to third-party interests. The models should be seen therefore as in varying degrees complementary.

III IMPLEMENTING THE MODELS

Improving the Inward Flow of Information

Unless the company collects information about the effects of its business operations on third parties, and that information is made available to relevant decision-makers within the company, responsible behaviour is hardly likely to result. Gray points out that

---

[78] See e.g. G. Teubner, 'Corporate Fiduciary Duties and Their Beneficiaries: A Functional Approach to the Legal Institutionalization of Corporate Responsibility', in Hopt and Teubner, *Corporate Governance and Directors' Liabilities* (above, note 25), at 165: 'reflexion cannot be voluntary, but needs to be stimulated by powerful external forces. Personal voluntaristic 'responsibility' is not the central question.'

there is a lot of circumstantial evidence that actors will make some attempt to incorporate new information into their actions and, [e.g.] with the case of environmental information, this can be expected to have the effect both of making actors more environmentally aware and having a direct (if perhaps small) influence on decisions taken.[79]

One means of increasing corporate responsibility is thus to expand companies' 'information nets'.[80]

The law can influence the information that companies are required to gather in a number of ways. The first is through substantive legal regulation. In order to be in a position to comply with environmental standards, for instance, a company must monitor the outflow of waste material resulting from its manufacturing processes. Information collected in this way may have a significance for company behaviour that extends beyond mere compliance. Second, companies are required to assemble and report stipulated classes of information in order to obtain authorizations from regulatory authorities. Thus, in order to obtain planning permission for projects such as the construction of oil refineries and chemical works, a company must prepare an environmental impact assessment setting out the likely effects on humans, flora and fauna, and other aspects of the environment.[81] Similarly, applications under the Environmental Protection Act 1990 to operate a polluting process must be accompanied by detailed information about the effects of the process.[82] Third, requirements to disclose information generally (i.e. not merely as a condition of authorization) are liable to increase the company's awareness of the effects of its activities.[83] A duty to disclose accident statistics, for example, self-evidently necessitates that the data first be collected. Finally, an obligation to obtain and analyse information might be imposed specifically for the purpose of broadening the cognitive base on which company decisions are made. Duties of this kind are not unknown currently. A wide-ranging duty has recently been imposed on employers to make a formal assessment of risks of injury to employees and others arising from the conduct of their undertaking. This includes estimating the extent of the risks involved, taking into account precautions that are already in place, and making a record of the findings of the assessment and identifying any

[79] R. Gray, *The Greening of Accountancy: The Profession after Pearce* (1990), at 78.

[80] Stone, *Where the Law Ends* (above, n. 48), ch. 18. For ways of improving the distribution of information within the company see 368 below.

[81] Town & Country Planning (Assessment of Environmental Effects) Regulations 1988, implementing EC Directive 85/337, initially opposed by the UK government. Whether these provisions adequately implement the directive is the subject of continuing dispute: see P. Sands and D. Alexander, 'Assessing the Impact', (1991) 141 *NLJ* 1487.

[82] EPA 1990, sch 1, and Environmental Protection (Applications, Appeals and Registers) Regulations 1991.

[83] Disclosure, as well as widening the company's informational base, is also a technique for improving social performance in its own right: see below.

group of employees particularly exposed to danger.[84] There is at present no obligation on companies to conduct an 'environmental audit' other than in the limited sense already mentioned, though versions of these are now commonly carried out on a voluntary basis and could be put onto a mandatory footing.[85] Other suggestions that have been made include that companies should obtain information about the safety of their products in use,[86] and that where it is proposed to close a plant the company prepare a 'community impact statement', requiring it *inter alia* to quantify the cost of closure to the local community and to consider methods to mitigate these costs.[87]

It is important not only that information about the effects of corporate activities on third parties should be collected, but also that it should reach the relevant decision-makers within the company. Information about dangerous defects in the company's products, for instance, is unlikely to lead to the curing of the defects if it does not move beyond the complaints department. Since the circumstances of individual companies vary greatly it is not feasible for the law to stipulate appropriate mechanisms for the internal circulation of information, but legal intervention can play a useful part in ensuring that top management decisions are made on an adequate informational base and in providing management with an incentive to improve the flow of information within the organization generally. This might be achieved by mandating the appointment of directors with specific responsibilities, for example, for safety or the environment, and requiring those directors to be familiar with specified classes of information, such as accident statistics and reports of the circumstances in which injuries have occurred or of known sources of danger.[88] One result of obligations of this kind should be to increase compliance with substantive law, since directors who are required to possess certain sorts of information will find it more difficult to defend themselves from prosecution on the basis of ignorance, and this in turn will give directors a personalized incentive to ensure that proper compliance procedures exist throughout the company. And of more direct relevance here, the resulting improvement in the flow of information within the organization may conceivably also lead to a response to issues of third party-welfare that is more generous than that required by substantive regulation.

---

[84] Management of Health and Safety at Work Regulations 1992.

[85] Not surprisingly, companies and business-interest groups favour voluntary procedures: see e.g. International Chamber of Commerce, *Environmental Guidelines for World Industry* (1990). The proposed EC Eco-Audit will operate on a voluntary basis: see COM (92) 93 Final; OJ No C 104/5, April 24, 1992.

[86] Stone, *Where the Law Ends* (above, n. 48), at 203-4. See also the discussion of internal reporting of female and minority hiring at 203.

[87] R. Nader, M. Green, and G. Seligman, *Taming the Giant Corporation* (1976), at 120. The suggestion is that the assessment be made public.

[88] See generally Stone, *Where the Law Ends* (above, n. 48), at 141-51, and ch. 18.

Increasing the amount and quality of information that companies are required to consider about their social and physical operating environments and about the effects of their policies might, then, in itself lead to improved standards of behaviour, simply because harm-causing conduct was previously the product of ignorance or lack of understanding.[89] Whether or not to respond to the information made available to the company remains at the option of management, however, save where a failure to respond is likely to be met with legal sanctions. We consider next, therefore, how managements, their awareness of third-party interests having been raised, might be encouraged or obliged to attach more weight to those interests in formulating company policy.

Building in Constraints

Under this general heading a range of methods by which companies might be made to accommodate the interests of affected groups will be considered: how managers might be made to resolve issues by reference to a 'moral vocabulary'[90] or how a 'contradiction to economic rationality' might be built into corporate decision-making processes.[91] Four strategies will be examined in turn: (a) the extension of fiduciary duties to cover the interests of affected parties in addition to those of shareholders; (b) increased disclosure requirements; (c) mandatory consultation; and (d) expanded board representation.

Extending the Scope of Fiduciary Duties

In terms of the analogy with the responsible individual, the purpose of extending fiduciary duties so that they include the interests of certain non-shareholder groups is to construct within the company a suitably other-regarding attitude.[92] It is suggested, however, that fiduciary duty amendments offer no realistic possibility in themselves of altering company behaviour against the will of management. As Sealy explains, duties owed to beneficiaries with potentially inconsistent interests are for all practical purposes unenforceable, because the disputes that are liable to result where the interests of one group are advanced at the expense of another do not give rise to justiciable issues.[93]

[89] See e.g. W. J. Baumol and S. A. B. Blackman, *Perfect Markets and Easy Virtue: Business Ethics and the Invisible Hand* (1991), at 62, discussing voluntary emissions reductions by the Monsanto Company in the US following the introduction of mandatory environmental disclosure rules.

[90] Stone, *Where the Law Ends* (above, n. 48), at 114.

[91] Teubner, 'Corporate Fiduciary Duties' (above, n. 78), at 161.

[92] See e.g. CBI, *The Responsibilities of the British Public Company* (1973), paras 22–4. See also the proposals of G. Goyder in *The Responsible Company* (1961), ch. 13, and G. Goyder *The Just Enterprise* (1987), chs 8 and 10.

[93] L. S. Sealy, 'Directors' "Wider" Responsibilities—Problems Conceptual, Practical, and Procedural', (1987) 13 *Mon U L Rev* 164, at 175. D. F. Vagts, 'Reforming The "Modern" Corporation: Perspectives from the German', (1966) 80 *Harv L Rev* 23, at 46–7, referring to a

Multi-constituency duties might in theory take either an objective or a subjective form. Objective duties would require the courts to consider whether *in their view* the directors' behaviour sufficiently respects the interests of the relevant groups. Disputes about when profit-seeking should be constrained in favour of other interests and to what extent, and about when 'third-party' interests should be traded off against each other (e.g. should the company close an ecologically unsound factory at the expense of jobs?) are not however amenable to resolution by reference to general standards.[94] If they were, the issues could be made the subject of external regulation and the need for an internal response would be substantially reduced. The elusiveness of appropriate general standards is, after all, at the heart of the case for profit-sacrificing social responsibility. In default of such standards the courts would be required to engage in an *ad hoc* evaluation of the way in which management had chosen to balance the relevant interests, but as Wedderburn has pointed out, requiring the courts to administer corporate policy 'by choosing between the different versions of the "reasonable balance" of interests in practice [is] something English judges certainly would not do, and are not equipped to do'.[95] A test of fairness would take the matter no further, since 'fairness' is merely a particular way of characterizing the issues at stake and offers no additional determinate guidance.[96]

A subjective duty would require the court to adjudicate on whether the directors had approached the task of balancing the relevant interests in 'good faith', that is, on whether the directors believed that their decision was an appropriate one, bearing in mind its effects on the groups concerned. But as considered in Chapter 3, even with a duty to act merely in the interests of a single constituency of shareholders, going behind the directors' assertion that they have acted in the interests of the beneficiary is rarely possible, save in

form of multi-beneficiary duty previously a part of German company law, comments that 'the evidence ... points strongly to the conclusion that this is not the sort of concept that gradually acquires shape and substance through case-by-case adjudication but rather one that continues to shift around uneasily.'

[94] See M. A. Chirelstein, who speaks of the impossibility of reflecting a 'complex social purpose in a set of standards precise enough to be includable in a business corporation statute, intellig.ble to lawyers and enforceable by the courts': 'Corporate Law Reform', in McKie, *Social Responsibility and the Business Predicament* (above, note 59) 41, at 76. Nor are the problems likely to be surmounted by a 'code of conduct' enforced by some form of quasi-judicial body applying criteria for determining 'whether in any particular case' management have had sufficient regard to the interests of 'customers, of employees and of the general public': see the musings in the White Paper, *Company Law Reform* (Cmnd. 5391, 1973), para 57. Not surprisingly, the CBI was opposed to the enforcement mechanism, but did suggest some hopelessly indeterminate 'principles of corporate conduct', e.g. a company 'should pay proper regard to the environmental and social consequences of its business activities': *The Responsibility of the British Public Company* (above, n. 92), paras 12 and 13, appendix 1.

[95] Lord Wedderburn, 'The Legal Development of Corporate Responsibility', in Hopt and Teubner, *Corporate Governance and Directors' Liabilities* (above, n. 25) 3, at 15.

[96] Sealy, 'Directors' "Wider" Responsibilities' (above, n. 93), at 175.

cases of gross abuse of position. Multiple constituencies present additional difficulties in that they offer virtually unlimited scope for arguing that an apparent slighting of the interests of one group is essential in order to safeguard the interests of the others. Demonstrating that the directors did not believe that a board decision represented the best available compromise would as a result almost always prove to be impossible.[97] It follows, as noted in the discussion of the duty to have regard to the interests of employees in Chapter 3 on a more limited scale, multi-beneficiary duties, despite their mandatory language, are liable to collapse into mere permissions.

It may be concluded from this discussion that an extension of fiduciary duties, whether they took an objective or subjective form, would not lead in practice to significant pressure being exerted on managers to depart from their preferred course of action. This is not to say, however, that extending fiduciary duties is pointless. Rather, broadening directors' discretion to permit them to depart from the requirements of profit maximization would be a necessary adjustment to create an appropriate legal setting for the changes in management behaviour that are the intended consequence of other methods of inducing responsibility. A reformed fiduciary duty might accordingly stipulate that the directors are under an obligation to conduct the business for profit, but that in so doing they must take account of affected interests (which might be specified).[98] The fear is often expressed that an expanded discretion of this kind would lead to a dangerous loss of control over management.[99] To the extent that the objection is simply that directors would be free to act in ways that are not designed to maximize shareholder wealth, that is, of course, the point of the change. As to loss of control, the objection assumes that the existing duty to maximize profits provides in any event a meaningful form of control over management discretion, but the view that this is so has been shown above to be seriously exaggerated.[100] More substantial problems concern not the dilution of legal control, but whether managers *can* be made more responsive to outside interests, and if

[97] It might, as in administrative law, be possible to show that the board had failed to consider relevant questions, but injunctive relief requiring the board to reconsider its decision seems likely to be futile.

[98] For a limited example see American Law Institute, *Principles of Corporate Governance: Analysis and Recommendations* Proposed Final Draft (1992), para 2.01 and accompanying commentary, and see the critical discussion in S. R. Munzer, *A Theory of Property* (1990), at 362–8.

[99] This, and the problem of the lack of enforceability of wider duties, is at the centre of the celebrated Berle-Dodd debate on the merits of departure from a duty expressed exclusively in terms of shareholder interests: see E. M. Dodd, 'For Whom are Corporate Managers Trustees?', (1932) 45 *Harv L Rev* 1145; A. A. Berle, 'For Whom Corporate Managers *Are* Trustees: A Note' (1932) 45 *Harv L Rev* 1365; J. L. Weiner, 'The Berle-Dodd Dialogue on the Concept of the Corporation', (1964) 64 *Colum L Rev* 1458. See also Sealy, 'Directors' "Wider" Responsibilities' (above, n. 93), at 175; F. H. Easterbrook and D. R. Fischel, *The Economic Structure of Corporate Law* (1991), at 38.

[100] See 92–6 above, and see L. L. Dallas, 'Two Models of Corporate Governance: Beyond Berle and Means', (1988) 22 *U Mich J L Ref* 19, at 104–5.

they can, whether the result will be a superior accommodation of interests or instead will reflect somewhat arbitrarily the variable disposition of power as between the company and different interest groups, and as between those interest groups themselves. Teubner is confident that '*procedural* fiduciary duties'—of 'disclosure, audit, justification, consultation and organization'— will enable the representatives of social interests to 'guarantee the rationality of the interest-weighing process'.[101] Far from sharing Berle's fears about 'the massing of group after group to assert their private claims by force or threat',[102] this approach celebrates the resulting dynamic: the aim is to transform 'external social problems' into 'internal political issues of the enterprise'.[103] The content and likely effectiveness of some of the procedural measures that might be adopted will now be considered.

Disclosure Requirements

The mere fact of being under a duty to disclose information is not in itself a reason for companies to change their behaviour. Rather, mandatory disclosure is a component in some more active process of control. Before examining these processes, however, two general observations about the role of disclosure of corporate social performance will be made. First, given the magnitude and pervasiveness of corporate power, it is arguable that in a society committed to democratic principles the presumption should be in favour of the maximum availability of information about company practices and impact. From the 'social enterprise' perspective adopted in Chapter 1, such information should be freely available unless there are good reasons to the contrary.[104] Even if making this information public were to have no effect on corporate behaviour, disclosure might still be justified, therefore, on the basis that in a mature society citizens have a right to know how power is exercised.[105] The cost of providing information cannot of course be ignored, but arguments against disclosure citing cost should be assessed with this general proposition as well as the other benefits from disclosure in mind. Second, social disclosure has value in balancing and supplementing purely financial indicators of company performance. Hirsch has pointed out that at the level of the economy as a whole, statistics on the gross national product are a misleading indicator of the extent to which society is enriched by economic activity because of their partial approach to the measurement of

---

[101] Teubner, 'Corporate Fiduciary Duties' (above, n. 78), at 167.

[102] Berle, 'For Whom Corporate Trustees *Are* Trustees: A Note' (above, n. 99), at 1368.

[103] (Above, n. 101), at 166.

[104] See R. B. Stevenson, *Corporations and Information: Secrecy, Access, and Disclosure* (1980), at 6–7.

[105] See *Company Law Reform* (above, n. 94): 'the bias must always be towards disclosure, with the burden of proof thrown on those who defend secrecy.' The proposals for the limited extension of disclosure contained in the document (see below) do not, however, fulfil this principle. It is, of course, hardly one that is applied in the UK in the case of government.

output. Thus he notes that, as well as recording the satisfaction of demand for goods and services,

In a more comprehensive view, satisfactions from particular forms of work, as well as from particular social or physical environments, also need to be assessed because they influence the value attached to input and therefore to net output. The same output produced under more pleasant working conditions, whether these comprise more interesting work processes or longer coffee breaks, ought to be registered as larger net output'.[106]

Figures for GNP are also misleading in that they fail to take account of the true costs of the recorded output, particularly in terms of the damage done to 'environmental assets' in the course of business operations.[107] A more comprehensive approach to costs and benefits would give a truer indication of the contribution of economic activity to welfare. Likewise, at the level of the individual enterprise, giving 'shareholders and the public the chance to judge companies' behaviour by social as well as financial criteria'[108] would allow a more accurate assessment of the value to society of corporate perform-ance.

Turning to the more specific role of disclosure as part of a process of corporate control, one way in which an obligation to disclose might increase responsibility has already been noted: the discipline of having to disclose information necessitates that companies first collect it, and the resulting improved information flow may cause managements to limit avoidable damage to third parties. More traditionally, it is the impact on decision makers of having to *reveal* information that has underlain disclosure policies.[109] The response may be essentially a voluntary one, as where management avoids conduct that would be embarrassing if publicized. Managers are, after all, likely to value their professional reputations and to be reluctant to have their personal failings exposed or to be seen to be associated with a company that is held in low public esteem. Alternatively, disclosure may induce a management response by facilitating some form of external control. Disclosure of material unfavourable to shareholder interests may, for example, result in direct pressure on management from institutional shareholders, or indirect pressure via the market for corporate control. A policy of compulsory disclosure designed to stimulate both self- and external control is evident in relation to a variety of issues of concern to shareholders. Thus disclosure is relied on to deter actionable misconduct (such as the

[106] F. Hirsch, *Social Limits to Growth* (1977), at 16.
[107] See D. Pearce, A. Markandya and E. B. Barbier, *Blueprint for a Green Economy* (1989), ch. 3.
[108] *Company Law Reform* (above, n. 94), para 12. The 'value added statement' is one way of making some progress in this direction: see R. Gray, D. Owen, and K. Maunders, *Corporate Social Reporting: Accounting and Accountability* (1987), at 44–5.
[109] A principal object of disclosure is also, of course, to assist shareholders in making investment decisions.

improper diversion of assets) and also to influence areas of management activity that are not otherwise easily reached by substantive legal controls. By providing a basis for comparison with the position in other companies disclosure may, for example, encourage restraint in setting the level of directors' remuneration (though this is not an area in which success has been conspicuous)[110] or exert pressure for improved economic performance by revealing low relative profitability.

A similar philosophy can be used to support a policy of social disclosure.[111] The social disclosure requirements currently contained in the Companies Act are very limited,[112] comprising a duty to disclose the company's policy on the employment of disabled persons,[113] information concerning arrangements for securing the safety and health of the company's employees,[114] and action taken to inform and consult the workforce on matters of concern to them as employees and to promote employee share schemes.[115] A belief that 'openness in company affairs is the first principle in securing responsible behaviour' underies recommendations in the 1973 White Paper, *Company Law Reform*,[116] for a more comprehensive disclosure framework. The subsequent Companies Bill proposed disclosure in relation to labour turnover, employment policy, and compliance with consumer law, but the Bill fell with the government in 1974. Perhaps the most ambitious and carefully worked-out programme of social disclosure proposed in this country was that put forward by Social Audit in 1973, partly in response to the White Paper.[117] Their recommenda-

[110] See Ch. 7 above.
[111] Cf. L. S. Sealy, *Company Law and Commercial Reality* (1984), at 21–9, who questions the value of the *existing* disclosure 'clutter'.
[112] The obligation to disclose political and charitable donations has more to do with the directors' stewardship role than with a policy of encouraging (discouraging?) donations, though the information revealed is of obvious public value: see C A 1985, s 234, and Sch 7, Part 1.
[113] C A 1985, s 234 and Sch 7, Part III. The Disabled Persons (Employment) Acts 1944 and 1958 impose a quota system, requiring employers to give priority in recruitment to registered disabled up to a quota of 3 per cent of the workforce.
[114] Provisions for disclosure in relation to health, safety, and welfare at work of employees have been inserted into companies legislation (see now Companies Act 1985, Sch 7, Part IV), but the necessary regulations to bring them into force have never been introduced. Health and safety disclosure was first recommended by the Robens Committee on Safety and Health at Work, Cmnd. 5034 (1972). The Companies Act provisions are a much-diluted version of the Robens suggestion that statistics on accidents, disease, and death at work be disclosed. A Private Member's Bill, requiring in a company's annual report disclosure *inter alia* of convictions for safety and environmental offences, failed in 1992: see H. Whitcomb, 'Corporate Accountability and the Environment', (1992) 142 *NLJ* 10.
[115] C A 1985, s 234 and Sch 7, Part V. There is no duty to do any of the things that must be reported on. A provision introduced by the Companies Act 1967 requiring companies to give information about exports has since been dropped, the cost of processing this information evidently not being justified by the export-stimulating effect of disclosing it.
[116] (Above, note 108), para 10. See the discussion in Gray et al., *Corporate Social Reporting* (above, n. 108), at 39–42.
[117] See 'The Case for a Social Audit' (1973) 1 *Social Audit* 4; Imberg and MacMahon, 'Company Law Reform', (1973) 2 *Social Audit* 3.

tions required detailed reporting on employment practices and industrial relations, consumer affairs, environmental issues, and defence contracting.

The rationale for such measures relies partly on 'shaming' the company into better performance, or more positively, on providing managers with an incentive to meet higher standards. The Accounting Standards Steering Committee, in the *Corporate Report*, for example, insists that '[m]anagements naturally respond to those indicators by which they consider their perform-ance is judged, and strive to achieve and present results accordingly. Special attention is bound to be given to those areas where the spotlight falls.'[118] This view seems optimistic, and social disclosure seems likely to have a more powerful effect where its function is to 'feed' external control mechanisms rather than encourage a largely voluntary response. But are there sanctioning mechanisms that can be brought to bear in relation to social issues equivalent to those that may be deployed where information about inadequate financial performance is revealed?

The group most obviously able to apply sanctions to management is the shareholders, who might in principle use the internal democratic and market controls available to them to attempt to secure improvements in the company's social profile, as well as its financial one. That they might do this is certainly plausible as regards anti-social behaviour that is also likely to depress profits, perhaps even where the effects will be mainly in the long term. The company's environmental impact is an obvious example, where adverse disclosures may imply significant clean-up costs and thus have a corresponding effect on share price.[119] There is not much reason to suppose that 'conventional' shareholders will respond to disclosures about the company's social record, where 'irresponsible' behaviour has no impact on profits, however, and especially where improvements would be likely to damage profitability. From the results of a small survey among institutional shareholders Social Audit concludes that most

see themselves as acting almost exclusively on behalf of, or for the benefit of their own shareholders, clients, supporters, or policy-holders—and feel bound to reflect this in their investment policies. The question of a separate responsibility to society for the performance of the companies invested in arises therefore only incidentally, if at all.[120]

[118] The Accounting Standards Steering Committee, *The Corporate Report* (1975), at 38. And see J. M. Renshall, 'Changing Perceptions behind the Corporate Report', (1976) 1 *Accounting, Organizations and Society* 105, at 108. The report itself makes recommendations for expanded reporting duties: for a discussion, see Gray et al., *Corporate Social Reporting* (above, n. 108), at 43–53. Note also Gray, *The Greening of Accountancy* (above, n. 79), at 78, on 'information inductance', i.e. the effect whereby 'information that an individual or group is required to report will influence the behaviour of that individual or group as the actors seek to produce actions which, when recorded by the information systems will appear benign.'

[119] The evidence on the extent to which investors are influenced by environmental considera-tions is inconclusive: see Gray, ibid. at 51–3. See also the discussion of investor responses to social disclosure in Gray et al., ibid. at 69–70.

[120] 'The Case for a Social Audit' (above, n. 117), at 9.

Strengthening the Constraints

This corresponds with the legal position as regards funds held in trust, where in general the overriding obligation is to act in the financial interests of the beneficiaries.[121]

Pressure for changed behaviour that goes beyond that required for long-term profit maximization is therefore likely to come only from ethical investment bodies or other organizations which are particularly sensitive to ethical issues, and from those who have acquired shares specifically for the purpose of campaigning for an alteration in company policy. There are now in this country a number of financial institutions, such as Unity Trust and the Friends Provident Stewardship Trust, prepared to invest only in businesses that satisfy certain ethical criteria, refusing to hold shares, for example, in companies that deal in tobacco or armaments, or which refuse to recognize trade unions. Organizations with particular ethical concerns arising from the nature of their membership or purpose, such as the British Medical Association and the Church Commissioners, have also been known to make investment decisions that reflect those concerns (selling shares in tobacco companies and selective disinvestment from South Africa, respectively).[122] More generally, the Ethical Investment Research and Information Service and the Pensions Investment Resource Centre exist to provide information to investors with an interest in social responsibility issues (in the latter case, local-authority pension funds) and to promote responsible investment.

Ethical investment strategies may take a number of different forms. One, as with the ethical funds mentioned above, is to refuse to invest in ethically unsound companies. This provides an important service to ethically concerned investors, giving them some assurance that their income is not derived from morally questionable activities. Whether such bodies can actually affect the policies of companies that they consider to be behaving unethically is dependent on the proportion of total investment funds that are under ethical management. It has been suggested that 10 per cent of the funds placed on Wall Street have ethical ties, which might be expected to have a depressive effect on the share price of proscribed companies.[123] Divesture of holdings in companies which fail to satisfy ethical criteria, as in the BMA and Church of England examples, is an alternative strategy.

---

[121] Except where the trust deed provides otherwise or all the beneficiaries agree to some other policy: *Cowan v Scargill* [1985] Ch 270. The position is different in respect of charitable trusts, where the trustees may choose not (or might be under an obligation not) to invest in companies whose objects conflict with the purpose of the charity, even though significant financial detriment might result: see *Harries v Church Commissioners for England* [1993] 2 All ER 300; P. Luxton, 'Ethical Investment in Hard Times', (1992) 55 *MLR* 587.

[122] See N. C. Smith, *Morality and the Market: Consumer Pressure for Corporate Accountability* (1990), at 175–6.

[123] Gray, *The Greening of Accountancy* (above, n. 79), at 52. The Social Investment Forum in the US claims to have the support of investors controlling $150 billion of assets in requiring companies to sign the (rather vague) 'Valdez Principles' on environmental responsibility, on pain of non- or dis-investment: ibid. at 76–7.

Disinvestment, if on a significant scale, might lower share price sufficiently to force a reconsideration of company policy, though as Herman has pointed out, price variations might well be cancelled out by non-ethical investors buying up the 'under-priced' securities.[124]

A different course is for ethical investors to make use of the democratic shareholder controls to attempt to bring pressure on management by way of attempts to remove directors, board nominations, or shareholder resolutions.[125] There are a number of celebrated examples of such tactics in the United States, the most prominent being 'Campaign G M', in which, among other things, an (unsuccessful) attempt was made to have three 'public-interest' directors elected to the board of General Motors.[126] Given the low levels of ethical investors' stakes and the customary lack of support from conventional investors, the significance of these efforts lies more in their ability to influence a company's behaviour by concentrating public attention on its record than in their direct effects, but as part of a broader strategy they may produce results.[127]

Parties who enter into contractual relationships with the company, notably consumers and employees,[128] are a second source of influence over management behaviour, and as with the shareholders, their influence might be increased with enhanced disclosure (not necessarily made through 'company law' channels or imposed by companies legislation). Thus mandatory disclosure of product information, for instance, the ingredients of processed food, not only enables customers to avoid products they consider harmful, but can also lead to a shift to the production of more favoured goods in response to the cumulative pressure from individual purchase decisions. Potentially, purchase behaviour can influence company policy on a much

---

[124] E. S. Herman, *Corporate Control, Corporate Power* (1981), at 269.

[125] Shareholders have the right to propose a resolution, and have notice of it circulated to the members, where between them they hold not less than one-twentieth of the total voting rights or represent at least 100 shareholders on whose shares an average of at least £100 has been paid up: CA 1985, s 376.

[126] See Herman, *Corporate Control, Corporate Power* (above, n. 124), at 265-7. For the history of such action in the US see J. W. Kuhn and D. W. Shriver, *Beyond Success: Corporations and Their Critics in the 1990s* (1991), at 54-67. On the attempt in the UK of Social Audit to gain shareholder support for two resolutions on social matters to be put to the AGM of Tube Investments, see (1974) 4 *Social Audit*: less than 5 per cent of shareholders supported the resolutions even being put, let alone their content.

[127] Stevenson, *Corporations and Information* (above, n. 104), at 139, notes that within three years of Campaign GM's resolutions, 'General Motors had elected to its board a black community leader, a woman, and an eminent scientist.' See also the account of the Nestlé Infant Formula Milk case in Kuhn and Shriver, *Beyond Success* (above, n. 126), at 216-36.

[128] Other contracting parties may also seek to influence the company's social performance, e.g. corporate customers may impose environmental standards on suppliers, and similarly lenders, who might find their loans secured on contaminated land or even be required to take over borrowers' environmental liabilities: see Gray, *The Greening of Accountancy* (above, n. 79), at 52-3. There are restrictions on the ability of local authorities to impose non-commercial obligations on contractors, e.g. relating to employment practices: Local Government Act 1988, ss 17-19.

broader range of issues than merely the nature of the product sold. Disclosure that opens up to the public the company's record on equal employment opportunities, working conditions in overseas subsidiaries, or testing on animals, for example, allows customers, if so minded, to exercise their 'consumer sovereignty' in relation to these questions as well as for more self-regarding purposes.[129] Without wishing to deny that purchase decisions can have significant effects, the influence of consumers should not, however, be exaggerated. In only weakly competitive markets the pressure to respond to consumer tastes is limited, and collective action problems are liable to undermine the inclinations of even altruistic consumers to make use of their purchasing power in order to 'vote' on company policies.[130] There are also considerable problems with the nature of the information that should ideally be provided and with the ability of consumers to interpret it. Raw social data will often be meaningless without detailed analysis and knowledge of context, making it difficult for consumers to distinguish 'good' suppliers or products from 'bad'.[131] Quantitative details of emissions, for example, obtain significance only with a background appreciation of the effects of the material emitted in the quantity and in the specific environment in which it is discharged. Further, as Herman points out, modifying objectionable conduct is not the only way of coping with possible consumer reactions to disclosure:

Corporate responses to disclosure of adverse information vary, from 'toughing it out', to making token gestures, to investing in image-making expenditures in lieu of substantive change. For example, the poor image of the polluter may be offset by stress on the fact that closing down polluting factories eliminates jobs.[132]

A second group able to exercise a measure of control over the company (generally, though not necessarily, in their own interests) through their contractual relationship with it is the employees. Information about the company's current financial state and prospects and proposals for the future is crucial if employees and their representatives are to bargain effectively. The Employment Protection Act 1975[133] currently imposes a duty on employers to disclose to recognized trade unions information needed for the purposes of collective bargaining.[134] The disclosure obligation is, however, of limited

[129] See Smith, *Morality and the Market* (above, n. 122), ch. 6.

[130] See 321–2 above.

[131] The Ecolabelling scheme is likely to be of some benefit in relation to environmental issues. The Ecolabelling Board Regulations 1992 (SI no. 2383) enable the Board to award labels to products which have a reduced adverse environmental impact during their whole life-cycle. The scheme is an EC initiative: see Council Regulation 880/92 (1992) OJ L99, p. 1.

[132] Herman, *Corporate Control, Corporate Power* (above, n. 124), at 278.

[133] S 17; see also *Disclosure of Information to Trade Unions for Collective Bargaining Purposes ACAS Code of Practice* (1977).

[134] The Industry Act 1975, ss 28–34, 37 (repealed) imposed disclosure obligations for the purposes of tripartite industrial planning.

scope and enforceability.[135] More fundamentally, the impact that collective bargaining can have on company policy depends on the issues that are regarded as suitable topics for negotiation (and, of course, the willingness of the employer to grant union recognition).[136] In this country bargaining is generally confined to the terms and conditions of employment, and does not, for example, extend to investment policy or other aspects of long-term strategy, which remain the exclusive prerogative of management. The statutory obligation to consult employee representatives about proposed redundancies, and potentially, other matters, and constitutional changes to give employees a role in the decision-making structure, will be considered separately below.

A third control mechanism that might be 'fed' by disclosure is what Boswell refers to as 'social monitoring'. Social monitors are 'bodies which evaluate, praise or criticize sectional units from the outside. Often they start out from legally disclosed data . . . They include consumer, environmental, and other pressure groups, academe, religious organizations, the media and, in terms of some of their work, public regulatory agencies.'[137] The functions that Boswell sees social monitors as performing are the collection and refining of publicly disclosed information which, in its raw state and without interpretation, may be overwhelming and confusing, and its supplementation through the 'forceful probing which is needed to break down typical institutional secrecies or even obstructions'.[138] By sifting and evaluating data social monitors are able to activate public opinion on issues of organizational performance and can themselves 'focus and represent a public opinion which would otherwise tend to be amorphous'.[139]

---

[135] See Lord Wedderburn, *The Worker and the Law* (3rd ed., 1986), at 291. See also Gray et al., *Corporate Social Reporting* (above, n. 108), ch. 9. Employees in Germany have more extensive information rights, covering 'the economic and financial situation of the enterprise, the production and investments program, changes in the organization, and other plans that could vitally affect employee's interests': K. J. Hopt, 'New Ways in Corporate Governance: European Experiments with Labor Representation on Corporate Boards', (1984) 82 *Mich Law Rev* 1338, at 1349. See also M. Dierkes, 'Corporate Social Reporting and Auditing: Theory and Practice', in Hopt and Teubner, *Corporate Governance and Directors' Liabilities* (above, n. 25), at 373, discussing the obligation in French law for companies to produce annual social balance sheets relating to employment issues, enabling unions to formulate a 'critique of business policy . . . [that may be integrated] into bargaining strategies with management'. And on this see also Gray et al., *Corporate Social Reporting* (above, n. 108), at 27–9. On the possibilities for using employee directors as a channel for communicating information to be used in collective bargaining, see 412–3 and generally, below.

[136] For current trends, see S. D. Anderman, *Labour Law: Management Decisions and Workers' Rights* (1992), at 229–31; Millward et al., *Workplace Industrial Relations in Transition: the ED/ESRC/PSI/ACAS Surveys* (1992), at 70–7.

[137] J. Boswell, *Community and the Economy: The Theory of Public Co-operation* (1990), at 117. For the theory of pressure group activity, in relation both to government and companies, see Smith, *Morality and the Market* (above, n. 122), ch 4.

[138] Boswell, ibid. See further, 382–3, below.

[139] Ibid.

Social monitoring can produce changes in company behaviour by a number of distinct means. One is that by drawing attention to actionable misconduct it may create pressure for enforcement, either in a particular case or generally, and publicizing social harm may lead to demands for a strengthening of the regulatory framework or other government action. Second, by processing and interpreting raw data social monitors can overcome some of the informational difficulties faced by would-be ethical purchasers, thereby making product markets a more effective mode of control.[140] A third factor on which Boswell lays particular stress is simply the force of public opinion. Managers undoubtedly view the company's possession of a favourable public image as a valuable asset to both the company and themselves, and by focusing public attention on aspects of corporate behaviour that may damage that image and by calling on managers to account personally for their conduct social monitors can impose pressure for change.

There are clearly weaknesses in the existing system of social monitoring, as well as room for doubt about its effectiveness in principle. There are limitations in coverage; Boswell asks, for instance, 'what regular, open, non-esoteric social monitoring is applied to banks, insurance companies or pension funds, not to mention foreign exchange markets, merger broking, or the portfolio investments of large financial institutions and multinational companies?'[141] And, because of the plurality of monitors in other areas, conflicting signals may be given out, limiting the guidance monitoring provides to managements and also letting companies off the hook in the resulting confusion. More fundamentally, as already noted, it is easy to overestimate the responsiveness of managements to public opinion, particularly where compliance costs are high, where relatively poor performance compared with other companies is difficult to establish, and where the company can postulate alternative social costs if it changes its behaviour in the way demanded. Notwithstanding these weaknesses, and granted that demonstrating the effects of social monitoring is problematical, social monitors seem capable of making an important impact on company behaviour, and as such it is desirable that attention be paid to their information needs. It may be noted in this connection that something of a social monitoring philosophy appears to underlie aspects of government and European Community policy with regard to the environment. The Environmental Protection Act 1990 provides for detailed disclosure on public registers of information relating to the company's

---

[140] This is the aim of the research organization, New Consumer. See R. Adams, J. Carruthers, and S. Hamil, *Changing Corporate Values: A Guide to Social and Environmental Policy and Practice in Britain's Top Companies* (1991), produced by New Consumer, and containing brief information on the record of a large number of consumer-goods companies in such areas as equal opportunities, marketing policy, Third-World relationships, and the environment.

[141] (Above, n. 137), at 120.

environmental performance.[142] This gives pressure groups, which are well organized and particularly active in the environmental field, access to information that will facilitate campaigning against poor performers. The Act also allows private prosecutions,[143] enabling such bodies to use the disclosed information to take action where the regulatory authorities fail to do so, and at the same time strengthening the leverage more generally of environmental pressure groups in relation to the companies they monitor.

The potential 'user groups' of disclosure have so far been considered, but very little has been said about the process of disclosure itself and the nature of the information to be disclosed. Technical questions are involved that cannot be gone into here, but it may be useful to take note of some of the key issues. A first point is that, if social disclosure is to be at all effective in meeting the objectives identified for it, disclosure must be on a mandatory basis. Concluding their survey of voluntary environmental disclosure by major UK companies Kirkman and Hope observe, for example, that '[t]he majority of the information provided was selective and almost solely concentrated on the positive aspects of a company's environmental performance. Most disclosures would appear to have been public relations driven, making it virtually impossible to derive a comprehensive picture of a company's environmental record.'[144] Self-evidently, to be useful disclosure must reveal bad as well as good news. Moreover, in order to facilitate the comparison of company performances it will usually be desirable for reporting to be on a standardized basis, as to both content and format.

The expansion of mandatory disclosure requirements demands a systematic approach to the identification of information needs and the development of methodologically sound performance indicators. Achievement in each of these respects varies between different subject areas. Dierkes notes that some target groups, such as consumers, are diffuse and ill-organized, with the result that their information requirements are inadequately articulated.[145] On the methodological issue he explains that the development of reliable and exact social indicators is still in its infancy in many areas, a particular weakness being the difficulty of measuring 'outputs rather than inputs, of determining the actual social impact of corporate activities',[146] the latter

[142] Environmental Protection Act 1990, ss 20–2, and see M. Purdue, 'Integrated Pollution Control in the Environmental Protection Act 1990: A Coming of Age of Environmental Law?', (1991) 54 *MLR* 534, at 548–9. For EC policy in this area see P. Sands, 'European Community Environmental Law: Legislation, the European Court of Justice and Common-Interest Groups', (1990) 53 *MLR* 685.

[143] E P A 1990, s 82. The registers are also of value in assisting civil enforcement.

[144] P. Kirkman and C. Hope, *Environmental Disclosure in UK Company Annual Reports* (1992), at 21.

[145] Dierkes, 'Corporate Social Reporting' (above, n. 135), at 367.

[146] Ibid. at 360. The approach to social reporting advocated by Gray et al., *Corporate Social Reporting* (above, n. 108), at 15, seems, to say the least, optimistic: 'each society must, as a whole, find a way to *uniquely identify the responsibilities that organizations must meet.* Then some way must be

depending on the specific context in which the company operates. That said, there are matters, such as the number of times the company has been prosecuted and the penalties imposed or the proportion of the company's workforce that is of minority ethnic origin,[147] that lend themselves to straightforward statistical presentation. A more complex area in which significant progress has nevertheless been made is environmental reporting. Under the pressure of legislation an increasing number of companies now conduct assessments of the environmental impact of their activities for internal management purposes, a consequence of which has been a growth in environmental consultancies and the development of sophisticated measurement and reporting techniques. The proposed EC Eco-Audit Scheme (participation in which is voluntary) will further standardize assessment procedures and requires detailed disclosure of the information collected.[148] Another aspect of the scheme is that the material disclosed must be validated by an accredited environmental auditor, working to a code of practice to be developed by the Commission. Some form of external check on all publicly disclosed information seems an essential attribute of an effective disclosure policy in any area. As Gray points out, 'there is considerable evidence to suggest that what an organization is *required* to report can have a significant influence on what it does—*if and only if* . . . the reported information can be considered to bear any reliable relationship with the events and things it purports to represent.'[149]

An alternative to the company itself publicly disclosing information is for an outside body to collect information about and report on the company. This is one of the potential activities of 'social monitors', and there have in fact been a number of experiments in this form of social reporting.[150] The best known are the investigations carried out by Social Audit Ltd in the 1970s, for example into Tube Investments[151] and Avon Rubber.[152] These resulted in wide-ranging statistical and narrative reports on such matters as employee relations, redundancies, pensions, race relations, overseas activities, and the environment. There have also been a number of reports produced by local authorities, chiefly on the externalities associated with plant

found to report, as objectively, truthfully and fairly as possible, the extent to which those responsibilities have been met' (emphasis added).

[147] Some companies collect this information voluntarily: see the description of the Ford Motor Company's equal-opportunities programme in D. Clutterbuck and D. Snow, *Working with the Community: A Guide to Corporate Social Responsibility* (1990), at 17–20.

[148] COM (92) 93 Final; OJ No C 104/5, April 24, 1992. Similarly, BS 7570 on Environmental Management Systems.

[149] Gray, *The Greening of Accountancy* (above, n. 79), at 105.

[150] See Gray et al. *Corporate Social Reporting* (above, n. 108), ch. 7; Social Science Research Council, *Advisory Panel on the Social Responsibilities of Business* (1976), at 8; Goyder, *The Just Enterprise* (above, n. 91), ch. 13.

[151] *Social Audit* vol. 1 no. 3, 1973/4.

[152] *Social Audit*, vol. 2 nos 3–4, 1976.

closures.[153] External reporting of this kind seems a promising way of increasing managerial circumspection and activating social pressure. Further investigation into the techniques external auditors might apply, methods of securing their independence and impartiality, and appropriate rights of access to information held by the company, therefore appears warranted.[154]

Mandatory Consultation

The technique of compulsory disclosure considered under the previous heading takes as given whatever means third parties may have for influencing company behaviour: the aim is simply to enhance the third parties' position by increasing their level of knowledge. Mandatory consultation, in contrast, while also requiring disclosure, creates a structured opportunity for the consultees to make their views known to management and to attempt to alter company policy. Mandatory consultation is an established feature of certain aspects of industrial relations, namely with regard to health and safety issues,[155] redundancies,[156] and transfers of the undertaking.[157] To take the example of redundancies, the employer is obliged to begin consultation with the appropriate trade union at the earliest opportunity, once the possibility of redundancies has been considered by the company. The employer must set out in writing, *inter alia*, the reasons for the proposal and the numbers and descriptions of the employees involved. The company must then consider the union's response and give reasons for rejecting any of its representations.[158] The proposed EC 'Vredeling' Directive,[159] if it is ever adopted, will

[153] See Gray et al. *Corporate Social Reporting* (above, n. 108), at 148–51.

[154] See Imberg and MacMahon, 'Company Law Reform' (above, n. 117), at 16: 'the most effective solution . . . would be to give the public a statutory right of access to all company information, except where there was a good case against: personnel records, trade secrets, and the like, would clearly need to be excluded.'

[155] Health and Safety at Work Act 1974, s 2; and see Wedderburn, *The Worker and the Law* (above, n. 132), at 291–4.

[156] Employment Protection Act 1975, ss 99–107, implementing the EC Directive on the Approximation of the Laws of the Member States Relating to Collective Redundancies (OJ 1975, L48/29). See Wedderburn, ibid. at 294–8; Anderman, *Labour Law* (above, n. 136), at 262–8.

[157] Transfer of Undertakings (Protection of Employment) Regulations 1981, implementing the Directive on Safeguarding Employees' Rights in the Event of Transfers of Undertakings (OJ 1977, L61/26). See Wedderburn, ibid. at 298–301.

[158] The remedy for failure to consult is a compensatory payment not exceeding 90 days' pay; the duty to consult cannot be enforced by court order.

[159] Amended Proposal for a Council Directive on Procedures for Informing and Consulting the Employees of Undertakings with Complex Structures, in Particular, Transnational Undertakings, OJ no C217 of 12.8.1983, p 3, Bull Supp 2/83. See generally C. Docksey, 'Information and Consultation of Employees: The United Kingdom and the Vredeling Directive' (1986) 49 *MLR* 281. A version of the draft may be revived in pursuance of the Social Charter: see Lord Wedderburn, *The Social Charter, European Company and Employment Rights: An Outline Agenda* (1990), at 37 and generally. See also Proposal for a Council Directive on the Establishment of a European Works Council in Community-scale Undertakings or Groups of Undertakings for the Purposes of Informing and Consulting Employees, COM (90) 581 final, OJ 15.2.91.

substantially expand the matters that must be made subject to consultation in 'complex undertakings', extending consultation backwards in the decision-making chain to a point before a redundancy proposal is formulated, and taking in any other management decisions that are liable to have important implications for the interests of the employees. A 'complex undertaking' is one in which there is a split between the place in which decisions are made and the place where employees actually work, for example, where the workers are employed by a subsidiary and decisions affecting them are made by the parent company management, possibly in another country. In such organizations the draft directive requires, first, that employees of subsidiaries be given information at least once a year that provides a clear picture of the position of the group as a whole, and also more specific information about the sector that concerns them directly.[160] Second, where the parent proposes to take a decision concerning the group or a subsidiary that is likely to have serious consequences for the subsidiaries' employees (e.g. closures, reorganizations, or changes in production methods consequent on the introduction of new technology), detailed information must be provided to the employees, who must be given 30 days to present their views and to consult with their immediate employer, during which time no decision can be made (in contrast with the UK redundancy provisions).

The discussion so far has been about consultation involving employees, but in principle consultation procedures could be extended to a wider range of interest groups, for example environmental or consumer bodies. As to the latter, 'consultative committees' might be established on an industry basis or in relation to individual companies, with consultation rights regarding significant price changes, for example, or safety issues or product development.[161] And Stone suggests that when 'the impact on some community of pulling up stakes is going to be significant, the law might well force high company officials to confront and negotiate 'in good faith' with community leaders'.[162]

What impact can consultation procedures be expected to have? As with any process that expands the cognitive base of decision-making, consultation has the potential to produce a superior accommodation of interests. Where, however, those in negotiation with the company encounter managerial intransigence the effects must surely be questionable. Provisions of this kind depend for their outcome on the bargaining power of the parties involved. In

---

[160] See Docksey, ibid. at 285–8. The information would not differ greatly from that currently provided to shareholders in accordance with the Companies Act.

[161] Cf. T. Prosser, 'Regulation of Privatized Enterprises: Institutions and Procedures', in L. Hancher and M. Moran (eds), *Capitalism, Culture, and Regulation* (1989) 135, at 137–8, describing the record of nationalized industry consumer councils as 'dismal', in part through the inadequacy of their information rights.

[162] Stone, *Where the Law Ends* (above, n. 48), at 220. See also Teubner, 'Corporate Fiduciary Duties' (above, n. 78), at 170–1, 173.

connection with consultation over proposed redundancies, for example, Anderman points out that

The periods of recession and high unemployment since 1979 have undermined the unions' bargaining strength and so exposed the weakness of the purely procedural legal duty to consult. Even when engaged in by the stronger unions, legally required consultations have often produced very little in the way of substantive modifications of employer decisions.[163]

The suggestion, furthermore, that consultation provisions should include an obligation to negotiate 'in good faith'[164] seems unlikely to be of much effect in compensating for any asymmetry in power that might exist between the parties. A duty to bargain in good faith should be distinguished from a duty to agree. The former duty is a feature of American industrial-relations law, imposing on employers and unions an obligation to meet and confer on terms and conditions of employment with a view to reaching an agreement, but the duty does not 'compel either party to agree to a proposal or require the making of a concession'.[165] It has been said of the duty that 'the chance of agreement is itself often advanced by requring good faith bargaining. Discussion is likely to disclose the parties' true positions, while the art of persuasion, when given a chance, may lead to an accommodation of seemingly irreconcilable views,'[166] but clearly if the employer is not prepared to move and the union lacks bargaining strength then the latter has no choice but to accept the position.[167] And even where a lack of good faith is established (as where, for example, a party unreasonably stalls the negotiations or takes prejudicial unilateral action in the course of them), if the only remedy is an enforced renegotiation no change in the substantive outcome is guaranteed. This is not to deny that good-faith obligations can be of value, but at best they can ensure only that affected interests are given an opportunity to influence the final decision; they do not alter the parties' relative positions of power.

[163] Anderman, *Labour Law* (above, n. 136), at 267. Wedderburn, *The Worker and the Law* (above, n. 135), comments that
most good employers buy out these statutory rights by making payments to employees thrown out of jobs for redundancy. Unions have made agreements that provide for continuous information, sometimes with guaranteed minimum notice or payments in lieu, and provisions on selection, retraining and redeployment. If the Act has had any success it has been in that function which is so difficult to prove: the stimulation of collective bargains, especially at the workplace, above its floor [references omitted].
[164] See n. 162 above. The draft Vredeling Directive requires consultation 'with a view to attempting to reach an agreement': art 4.3.
[165] National Labor Relations Act 1935, amended 1947 and 1959, s 8(d). An agreement to negotiate in good faith is not binding as a contract in English law on the ground that the obligation is too uncertain to be enforceable: *Walford v Miles* [1992] 2 WLR 174, HL, [1992] 1 All ER 453.
[166] H. H. Wellington, *Labor and the Legal Process* (1968), at 55.
[167] See P. Davies and Lord Wedderburn, 'The Land of Industrial Democracy', [1977] *ILJ* 197, at 205-6.

The more radical proposition of a duty going beyond one to negotiate in good faith and actually requiring the parties to agree would mean that an outside adjudicator would have to impose a solution where bargaining breaks down. This would provide an inducement for the parties themselves to reach agreement and might thus cause the company to make concessions that would not otherwise be forthcoming. Such an arrangement operates in Germany, where works councils (organized on both a plant and enterprise basis) have co-determination rights in relation to 'social issues' such as working hours, health and safety, and personnel questions.[168] Works councils also have the important right that where the company's management proposes a major change that will have an adverse effect on the employees, such as a plant closure or restructuring, management must agree with the works council a 'social plan' providing for the transfer of employees to alternative employment or the making of severance payments. If the parties cannot agree the issue goes to arbitration, and the company must then either accept the outcome of arbitration or cancel the proposed changes. Co-determination, giving the employees (and conceivably, other affected interests) 'an institutional position of power'[169] within the company has clearly a much greater potential for altering company behaviour than mere consultation.[170] Organized labour in this country has traditionally been opposed to works councils, seeing them as a rival to representation through the unions. It has been suggested however that this fear is exaggerated,[171] though in any case co-determination could be made to operate through union machinery. Co-determination that extends, at least in theory, to shaping company goals as well as managing the impact of company policy is considered in the next chapter.

Altering the Composition of the Board

Various proposals for reform of the board have been put forward over the past 30 years or so which broadly reflect the two models of responsibility discussed earlier. Put rather crudely, those based on the first model seek to give the company a 'conscience' by inserting individuals who possess that

---

[168] See F. Wooldridge, 'The System of Co-determination in Western Germany and its Proposed Reform', (1976) 5 *Anglo-American L Rev* 19, at 22–6.

[169] Davies and Wedderburn, 'The Land of Industrial Democracy' (above, n. 167), at 206.

[170] For the operation of German works councils in practice see L. Kissler, 'Co-determination Research in the Federal Republic of Germany: A Review', in C. J. Lammers and G. Széll, *International Handbook of Participation in Organizations*, vol. 1 (1989), 74, at 82–4. The proposed European Works Council Directive (see n. 159 above), providing for a works council in Community-scale undertakings at group management level, would have only information and consultation rights.

[171] See Wooldridge, 'The System of Co-determination in Western Germany' (above, n. 168), at 26: in Germany 'the union trustmen in the plant and the works council are interdependent bodies, which usually present a united front, and which together provide for a much greater degree of employee involvement and influence than either could achieve separately.'

faculty into the highest level of decision-making. The other type of reform aims to give the representatives of affected interests a direct input into company policy. Proposals of the first kind have been made mainly in the United States,[172] while those of the second have largely been of European origin, usually being concerned exclusively with the representation of labour.

Two of the best-known American proposals are those put forward by Stone and by Nader, Green, and Seligman. Stone's suggestion is for the appointment of 'general public directors' ('GPDs').[173] It is envisaged that GPDs would normally form a minority of the board; they would be nominated by a state agency, but appointment would require board approval, and the board would also have the power to remove them.[174] The candidates would include semi-retired executives and academics. Among the various functions of GPDs an important one would be to improve the inward flow of information, for instance by commissioning impact studies. These might be concerned not only with the usual safety and environmental factors, but might extend to any area where there was a possibility of harm to others: for example, industrial psychologists might be employed to measure the impact of planned productivity improvements on workers' emotional well-being.[175] Another role would be concerned with the out-flow of information, particularly to public authorities. Thus GPDs might be instrumental in disclosing early evidence that materials used in manufacturing pose a hazard to health, thereby increasing the speed of the regulatory response. More centrally with regard to strengthening the company's 'conscience', GPDs would perform a 'superego function', attempting to inject into its thinking an awareness of the interests of others and a willingness to consider alternatives to narrowly conceived self-interested action.

GPDs would certainly seem capable of invigorating the cognitive element of responsibility and might thus 'broaden the board's horizons [and] on occasion stimulate action not previously contemplated'.[176] This might lead to a welcome increase in profit-neutral or profit-enhancing responsibility, but it is unlikely in view of their minority status that GPDs would have much impact on what Stone calls 'class B behaviour', that is, behaviour that causes

---

[172] But not exclusively: see the material cited in Lord Wedderburn, 'Trust, Corporation and the Worker', (1985) 23 *Osgoode Hall L J* 203, at 223–4; Wedderburn, 'The Legal Development of Corporate Responsibility: For Whom Will Corporate Managers Be Trustees?', in Hopt and Teubner, *Corporate Governance and Directors' Liabilities* (above, n. 25), at 29–30. See also Goyder, *The Just Enterprise* (above, n. 92), at 69.

[173] Stone, *Where the Law Ends* (above, n. 48), ch. 15.

[174] See also E. J. Weiss 'Social Regulation of Business Activity: Reforming the Corporate Governance System to Resolve an Institutional Impasse', (1981) 28 *UCLA L Rev* 343, at 426–34, proposing that at least two-thirds of boards consist of members of a government-appointed 'National Directors Corps', but still elected by the shareholders.

[175] (Above, n. 173), at 168.

[176] V. Brudney, 'The Independent Director—Heavenly City or Potemkin Village?', (1982) 95 *Harv L Rev* 597, at 651.

harm to society, the avoidance of which would reduce profits in the long term, for example, the use of polluting, but lawful, processes, or the company's removal from a region in which it is a major employer. Given their minority position, the dependence of GPDs for their effectiveness on retaining the goodwill of management would probably also lead to a toning down of their policy proposals, since directors perceived to be too radical or as not having the company's financial interests at heart would find management especially unreceptive. Because GPDs would be drawn largely from the ranks of established businessmen and women, and bearing in mind that the board's right to veto appointments would inevitably lead to the screening out of potential boat-rockers,[177] it seems doubtful that those appointed would in any event see the company's responsibilities as extending much beyond compliance with law and the maintenance of reputation.

The proposals of Nader, Green, and Seligman involve the appointment not of general directors but of 'constituency' directors as a means of increasing responsibility.[178] The intention is not, however, that the directors should be elected by, or accountable to, the relevant affected interests. Rather, they would be appointed by the shareholders, this seemingly to avoid the risk of individual directors furthering the interests of the group they represent to the (excessive) detriment of the company's financial well-being and the interests of the other constituencies.[179] Correspondingly, the directors would have a duty 'to balance responsibility for representing a particular social concern against responsibility for the overall health of the enterprise'.[180] They would sit, in European terminology, on a supervisory board, the powers of which would include the selection and removal of the chief executive and the right to veto other senior appointments, and to approve or veto 'important executive business proposals'. The interests to be represented include employee welfare, consumer protection, environmental protection, and community relations, and there would also be directors with individual responsibility for shareholder rights, compliance with law, finances, purchasing and marketing, management efficiency, and planning and research. In this way 'each important public concern would be guaranteed at least one informed representative on the board.'[181]

Given their control over executive appointments and major policy issues the Nader constituency directors might seem capable of achieving more substantial results than Stone's GPDs, at least if they were prepared to

---

[177] Though at least they would not be initially selected by management, and hence would not be 'tied to the inside hosts by some sort of personal or business relationship': Herman, *Corporate Control, Corporate Power* (above, n. 124), at 48, and see the discussion of non-executive directors in Ch. 6 above.

[178] Nader, Green, and Seligman *Taming the Giant Corporation* (above, n. 87).

[179] Ibid. at 124.

[180] Ibid. at 125.

[181] Ibid. at 125.

collaborate in the face of management opposition. However, there must be even greater doubts than with the GPDs about the motivation of the individuals who would be likely to fill the constituency roles to impose significant constraints on management. Since the directors owe their positions to the shareholders rather than to the constituencies for which they are responsible they are hardly likely to be vigorous in attempting to curtail profits in the interests of affected groups.[182] Indeed, the institutionalization of this conflict between role and loyalty casts severe doubt on the coherence of the Nader group proposals. As Engel has pointed out:

the authors never adequately explain why shareholders in public corporations—who to date have shown little interest in anything but profits, and for the most part expend little energy on internal corporate affairs to further even that goal—should suddenly start choosing and ousting directors, whatever names we may give those directors, with an eye to the general social good.'[183]

While constituency directors might therefore have some success in channelling information about the organization's likely social impact into its decision-making processes and perhaps in suggesting minor modifications in policy to accommodate third-party interests, they cannot be expected to achieve a significant shift in corporate values.

We have seen that neither the Stone nor the Nader group proposals involve the direct representation on the board of affected interests by directors elected by, and accountable to, the interests concerned. The object of the reforms is rather to inject an other-regarding dimension into decision-making procedures, in furtherance of an aim of moralizing the enterprise. A major difficulty with this approach, however, is that if independent directors are to have a significant impact on company behaviour a set of relatively concrete substantive principles to guide their conduct seems to be required. The rationalization of social responsibility as a process concept is appropriate for purposes of analysis, but at the level of implementation, in the absence of such principles, it seems unlikely that independent directors will be capable of the coherent action necessary to deflect management from conventionally self-interested policies. The problem they face, as Schelling points out, is that 'there is often no source of reliable guidance, no acknowledged source of policy, no easy choice between the responsible and the selfish.'[184] In other

---

[182] The idea that 'those employees, consumers, racial or sex minorities, and local communities harmed by corporate depradations' (ibid. at 129) might protect their interests by becoming shareholders, is difficult to take seriously, even with Nader's proposals for nomination of directors by shareholder minorities and the 'passing through' of the voting rights of institutional shareholders to their underlying investors: see further the criticisms in A. F. Conrad, 'Reflections on Public Interest Directors', (1977) 75 *Mich L Rev* 941, at 956.

[183] D. L. Engel, 'An Approach to Corporate Social Responsibility', (1979) 32 *Stan L Rev* 1, at 91.

[184] Schelling, 'Command and Control' (above, n. 59), at 90. See also R. N. McKean, 'Economics of Trust, Altruism, and Corporate Responsibility', in E. S. Phelps, *Altruism, Morality and Economic Theory* (1975), at 38.

words, a set of substantive principles around which to organize the activities of independent directors, while necessary, is likely to prove elusive.

Board reform associated with the second model of responsibility seeks to avoid this difficulty by giving a voice within the institution to those affected by company activities, thereby enabling improved company policies to be emerge as the product of dialogue or bargaining.[185] Reform proposals may accordingly be founded on the principles of 'free dialogue', whereby a communicatively rational integration of interests is achieved,[186] or less ambitiously, they may be aimed at redirecting company policy through negotiation and compromise. By giving interest groups a decision-making role within the organizational structure some of the problems associated with influencing company behaviour from the outside, such as lack of information or weak bargaining position, might be overcome, thus supplementing and improving on other methods of implementing the second model. The most highly developed schemes, in both theory and practice, are those for employee representation. Representation at board level of purely private interests, for example, those of a bank or a major customer, are, of course, of long standing. The justification for an employee presence on the board is often not confined to the essentially 'self-regulatory' objective under consideration in this chapter, but reflects more the special status of employees as participants in the organization with interests that rank alongside those of the shareholders and with views that accordingly merit representation. To avoid repetition a discussion of the details of arrangements for employee representation will be confined to Chapter 12. Here, employee interests will be treated as merely one of a range of interests that might be protected by being represented in the decision-making structure.

Making operational the idea of interest group participation within the company gives rise to a number of practical problems. It might seem, first of all, at least ideally, that all groups on whom the company has a significant impact should be represented, since only in that way will a proper balancing of interests be achieved. But the effects of company policies are complex and almost infinite and securing representation for all affected groups will usually prove impossible. For example, as well as the communities in which the company's plants are located, which may be worldwide, should not the communities from which the company obtains its raw materials, or even from which its main suppliers obtain their materials, also be represented? On

---

[185] See e.g. H. Steinmann, 'The Enterprise as a Political System', in Hopt and Teubner, *Corporate Governance and Directors' Liabilities* (above, n. 25), 401; S. M. Beck, 'Corporate Power and Public Policy', in L. Bernier and A. Lajoie (eds), *Consumer Protection, Environmental Law and Corporate Power* (1985), 181, at 210–13; Dallas, 'Two Models of Corporate Governance' (above, n. 100), at 107–14.

[186] Steinmann, ibid.; and see J. Habermas, *The Theory of Communicative Action*, vol. 1, trans. T. McCarthy (1984).

the other hand, as Eisenberg has pointed out, there are some groups whose representation would be positively undesirable. Thus the fortunes of suppliers and immediate customers may be very much tied up with those of the company, but these are often themselves large companies. A mutual internal representation of interests would lead to a cartelization of business whose effects, Eisenberg argues, would be 'worse than the disease'.[187]

Representation of small (somehow defined) trading partners would not be open to that objection, but suggests a second problem, namely working out a suitable scheme of representation. A company may deal with hundreds of small suppliers, so they could not be represented individually, and since their interests may conflict (they might each want a larger share of the company's business) it is not clear how their interests could be jointly represented. An environmental representative seems a more plausible proposition, but problems arise again once it is recognized that environmental issues are multi-dimensional, with efforts to avoid one form of damage sometimes leading to another. For example, a decision not to site a factory in a rural location in order to save a natural habitat might result in its being built in a more urbanized area where it exacerbates poor air quality. Since environmental interests may be competitive as to location ('not in my backyard') or type of environmental impact, there are therefore potentially many different environmental constituencies that might each warrant separate representation. A further problem concerns the legitimacy of the claim of constituency directors to represent the various affected groups, given the difficulties in establishing practicable elective processes. With regard to consumers, for instance, the Bullock Committee observed that 'there is no recognisable consumer constituency . . . and therefore no way in which a guardian of consumer interests could be appointed to the board through representative machinery.'[188] This problem does not of course apply with respect to all groups: in relation to employees and the local community voting mechanisms already exist.[189]

[187] M. A. Eisenberg, *The Structure of the Corporation* (1976), at 21.

[188] *Report of the Committee on Industrial Democracy* (Cmnd. 6706, 1977), at 55–6. A possible way of resolving these legitimacy issues would be for the government to appoint directors with particular 'constituency' responsibilies: see e.g. T. M. Jones and L. D. Goldberg, 'Governing the Large Corporation: More Arguments for Public Directors', (1982) 7 *Academy of Management Rev* 603; Beck, 'Corporate Power and Public Policy' (above, n. 185), at 210, and the discussion in Herman, *Corporate Control, Corporate Power* (above, n. 124), at 289–92.

[189] Some of the other criticisms may also be misplaced or over-refined if the role of the outside directors is not seen as being to represent specific constituencies, but to help resolve the problems that arise in the relationship between the company and its environment. Thus in order to determine the composition of the board Steinmann recommends addressing the 'fundamental conflict situations' inherent in an economy involving a high degree of division of work. He identifies structural conflicts in a capitalist economy affecting consumers, workers, capital owners, and the 'public interest', indicating the need for representation in respect of each of these interests: 'The Enterprise as a Political System' (above, n. 185), at 411–15. See also Teubner, 'Corporate Fiduciary Duties' (above, n. 78), esp. at 164–5, 170.

Assuming that the interests to be represented and methods of selecting representatives could be resolved, it would be necessary to decide whether the outside directors should constitute a minority or a majority of the board overall. If they were a minority, the same reservations about the prospects for their reorientating company behaviour would apply as those expressed in relation to Stone's proposals. Nevertheless, representative, as opposed merely to 'public-spirited' directors, as in the latter and the Nader schemes, might at least have the advantage of injecting into company decision-making a more authentic understanding of the position of affected groups. Alternatively, the principal significance of board representation might be regarded as lying in improving such groups' access to information. For this purpose minority representation is likely to be sufficient, allowing interest groups to perform their more conventional role of imposing external pressure with increased effectiveness.

Majority 'constituency' board representation is potentially a quite different proposition. Making due allowance for the ability of inside management to select and structure information and hence to narrow the policy options apparently open to the board,[190] majority representatives, if prepared to work together, would seem to have the ability to alter company priorities. There is room for doubt, however, about just how representatives with potentially conflicting interests (e.g. jobs and the environment) would interrelate, about whether an attractive balancing of interests would be likely to result, and about the impact on the enterprise's primary economic goals. Thus, Chirelstein notes that

the proponents of interest-group control seem to assume that group representatives would consistently work with fellow board members toward publicly desirable ends or else that the processes of conflict and compromise would generally produce socially beneficial decisions. Whether they would or not is unknown, but it is easy to imagine situations in which the balancing process might scant important social interests because these were unrepresented or less well informed or because they lacked the bargaining strength to obtain concessions from the others.[191]

Herman for similar reasons questions whether multi-constituency representation would result in 'value choices that took better account of externalities and overall community long-run needs and preferences'.[192] He accordingly doubts that the impairment in operating efficiency that might ensue once corporate activity was no longer unified around the goal of profitable growth is a price worth paying. Certainly the programme outlined by Steinmann involving interest-group representatives, situated on a supervisory board, entering into a 'free dialogue' between themselves and with management

---

[190] See 419–20 below.
[191] M. A. Chirelstein, 'Corporate Reform Now', in McKie, *Social Responsibility and the Business Predicament* (above, n. 94) 41, at 71.
[192] Herman, *Corporate Control, Corporate Power* (above, n. 124), at 284.

with a view to reaching a consensus or 'rational agreement' on corporate plans submitted by the latter is an attractive one.[193] Whether the structural conditions for such an integrative dialogue, leading to the differentiation of 'good reasons from indefensible arguments,'[194] are capable of being met in practice, however, surely seems more questionable. And again, contrary to Steinmann's approach, it may be that lack of agreement about substantive principles will inhibit consistent or otherwise satisfactory outcomes.

Implementation

The third and final requirement for responsible corporate behaviour is the existence of mechanisms to ensure that the decisions and policies that flow from responsible decision-making processes are carried into effect. Particular difficulties arise in large and complex structures, since many policies, as distinct from 'one-off' decisions, will depend for their success on the cooper-ation of employees who may be physically and organizationally remote from top management, for example, in relation to environmental protection, health and safety at work, employment discrimination, and customer service. The circumstances of individual companies are too diverse to permit of generalized solutions, or solutions which could easily be externally mandated, though it might be hoped that companies with reformed decision-making processes would themselves select appropriate modes of implementation. There is in fact a degree of consensus about how policies adopted by top management might be projected downwards. It seems likely, for example, that values are most effectively transmitted throughout the organization where there is a manifest high-level commitment to the policies the company claims to espouse. Thus Burke and Hill suggest that while concern for the environment must become part of the portfolio of responsibilities of line managers, there must also be support from above, and this is 'unlikely to be adequate unless it includes the designation of a main board director with specific responsibility for improving environmental performance'.[195] Company codes of ethics also seen capable of playing a part here.[196] Another valuable technique is the setting of numerical performance targets, relating to the reduction of accidents, emissions, or customer complaints, for instance. Apart from signalling that the company is serious about the issues in question, where performance is measurable against prescribed standards the

[193] Steinmann, 'The Enterprise as a Political System' (above, n. 185). And see Hopt, 'New Ways with Corporate Governance' (above, n. 135), at 1358.

[194] Steinmann, ibid.

[195] T. Burke and J. Hill, *Ethics Environment and the Company: A Guide to Effective Action* (1990), at 20. See also Dawson et al. *Safety at Work: The Limits of Self-Regulation* (1988), at 89: 'the push to maintain a strong emphasis on health and safety at both the procedural and substantive levels has to come from within the management hierarchy.'

[196] See 284–6 above.

monitoring of compliance is facilitated and also the degree to which targets are met can be incorporated into the data by which individual employees are assessed. The results might then be reflected in remuneration, for example, putting an employee's contribution to the company's environmental performance on a par with performance measured by the more usual financial indicators.[197]

A reform that could be externally mandated is to require the company to appoint directors, independent of management, to police compliance with legal controls[198] and also with whatever extra-legal standards to which the company may be committed. This would be a role distinct from participation in the formulation of policy discussed above, and would not necessarily require the independent directors to be representatives of, or elected by, affected groups. They might carry out their functions by performing compliance audits, assisted by a staff of their own or by employing specialist consultants. Stone speaks of independent directors roaming through the organization identifying 'soft spots' and ensuring that remedial steps are taken. He suggests for example that if 'some area of product defect were suspected, a remedial plan might include placing a top quality-control person at a key production point', who would then report directly to the independent directors on progress made.[199] The directors might also perform a useful function as persons to whom whistle-blowers might safely disclose information.[200] The effectiveness of independent directors in securing compliance with legal and other standards will be affected by the calibre and degree of independence of the occupants of office, and their powers in relation to management. These issues will be addressed in the conclusion.

Conclusion

This section has considered a number of legal reforms to promote increased corporate responsibility. Some, such as additional disclosure and consultation obligations, involve new applications of existing techniques and would seem likely if implemented to achieve worthwhile, if perhaps modest, results. Others, notably alterations to the structure of the board, might bring about more substantial changes in behaviour, especially if they took the form of the

[197] Burke and Hill, ibid. at 19. ICI now links the pay of its managers to their performance in meeting environmental targets: see the *Financial Times*, 5 December 1990.

[198] In the case of illegal activity the directors might be given an obligation to make a report to the relevant outside agencies. Stone, *Where the Law Ends* (above, n. 48), at 164 suggests that information revealing a breach of the law should be turned over to public authorities only as a last resort, for fear of making it more difficult for the directors to gain access to potentially incriminating material.

[199] Ibid. at 163.

[200] For the law and practice of whistle-blowing, see M. Winfield, *Minding Your Own Business: Self-Regulation and Whistleblowing in British Companies* (1990).

appointment of constituency directors and these were put into a majority position. Such proposals face a number of practical problems, however, and just what the effects might be is unpredictable. A more limited, but less hazardous, board reform would be to require the appointment of independent directors whose function would be to monitor and enforce compliance with the law and the company's own social policies, as just considered in the previous section. Such a role could be added to the responsibilities of the proposed independent directors, recruited and supervised by a specialist nominating agency, that were discussed in Chapter 6. That is, as well as it being the duty of the directors to ensure the efficient operation of management and hence of the business, a duty could also be imposed requiring them to oversee the company's social performance. Independent directors could thus make a positive contribution to social responsibility through their enforcement role, and at the same time might make it possible to secure the efficient operation of the business while leaving room for executive management to pursue socially responsible objectives that might be incompatible with profit maximization. Though pressure for improved social performance under this arrangement would primarily come from outside the company, the monitoring of management could be sufficiently flexible to allow a constructive, rather than merely a grudging, response to that pressure.

The space for a constructive response could be expanded further if monitoring boards were relied on as a substitute for the constraining influence of the market for corporate control. Chapter 4 noted the disruptive social consequences of consummated take-overs, but the pressure to produce profits imposed by the market for control seems also to constitute an important restriction on the ability of managers to respect the interests of third parties in their normal conduct of the company's affairs. The relaxation of market pressure without the installation of an alternative source of discipline would be likely to have serious implications for efficiency. It was suggested in Chapter 6, however, that a genuinely independent, high-calibre monitoring board, because of informational advantages and lower transaction costs, might be able to discipline management more effectively than the market for control. Viewed from the perspective of this chapter, the monitoring board has the additional advantage over the market that it can discriminate between sub-profit-maximizing outcomes that result from shirking, extravagance, or waste on the one hand, and attempts to accommodate the legitimate interests of third parties on the other.[201] With monitoring boards in place, pressure from the market for control could be reduced by, for example, more stringent public controls on mergers, a more tolerant attitude

---

[201] There is evidence that existing boards in performing a monitoring role place a strong emphasis on the company's economic rather than its social performance: see A. Demb and F.-F. Neubauer, *The Corporate Board: Confronting the Paradoxes* (1992), at 44–5.

to take-over defences, or a requirement that the monitoring board, or the employees,[202] give their consent to a change in control.

A final issue concerns the mechanisms for appointing monitoring directors. If the independent directors, while having to be selected from the books of the nominating agency, still had to be elected by the shareholders, it would seem reasonable to expect them to adopt a comparatively narrow approach to their social role. They might seek to secure compliance with the law and prevent the company from engaging in socially damaging behaviour that is also harmful to long-term profits, such as the manufacture of dangerous products or involvement in major pollution incidents, but they would otherwise be likely to give priority to shareholder interests. In order to bring about a change in emphasis and to create a bigger space for social responsibility it would therefore seem necessary to design some alternative appointment procedure. One possibility is that directors nominated by the agency be elected not only by the shareholders, but also by the employees, and conceivably other groups, for example, the local community. The intention of this arrangement would not be that the directors should specifically represent the various groups, but simply that it should prevent an exclusively shareholder constituency from 'weeding out' directors who were perceived to be insufficiently committed to shareholder interests. With different groups each electing a proportion of the directors a more balanced board might be achieved.

[202] See e.g. 420–21 below.

12

The Democratic Imperative: Beyond Social Responsibility

Chapter 1 established the framework for this book by asking on what terms companies should be allowed to possess power. As the discussion has progressed it was noted how corporate power might be controlled not only through external regulation, leaving the profit goal intact, but also through regulation of the company's decision-making processes, designed to make companies take more account of third-party interests, that is, to exercise power with greater responsibility. Intervention to further the more traditional efficiency objective has also been considered. It seems possible (though to what extent is unclear) that some of the reforms examined, as well as achieving a more attractive balance between the performance of companies' economic functions and their social effects, might lead to a lessening or sharing of power. This might come about through increasing the social pressure to which businesses are subject or by facilitating interest-group participation in enterprise decision-making. It is hard to deny, however, that even if such developments were successful in tightening the limits on management freedom of action, companies would still retain a substantial discretion to make decisions that have broad economic, social, and political effects. For those who are concerned about the existence of centres of private power doubts about the legitimacy of the large public company would therefore be likely to persist.

The main purpose of this final chapter is to examine employee participation as a possible way of resolving these doubts. Chapter 11 discussed interest-group involvement in decision-making, including that of employees, as a means of softening the effects of profit-led policies. This analytical focus is, however, too narrow to encompass the full range of arguments for employee participation. Thus employees are often seen not merely as one of several 'outside' groups whose interests merit protection against too ruthless a pursuit of profits, but also as a special group with a claim to be regarded as 'insiders', with a right equal to that of the shareholders to demand that the company be run for their benefit. This perspective envisages a function for participation that extends beyond the requirements of social responsibility: the object of participation is not merely to constrain profit maximization, but to enforce an open-ended commitment to the furtherance of the interests of an employee, as well as a shareholder, constituency. Employee participation can be viewed therefore as a corrective to corporate power, responding to doubts about the legitimacy of the power that companies exercise over the lives of their workforces, and providing for the benefit of employees a practical means of broadening company goals.

While the introduction of participative arrangements may deal with a major facet of the problem of corporate power, it must be accepted that it by no means addresses all the objections to it. Employees are, after all, in one sense a 'private' group liable to act self-interestedly, and their representatives would be no more accountable to society as a whole than are managers owing responsibilities exclusively to shareholders.[1] One consequence is that employee participation would not reduce the need for safeguards to protect the interests of other groups of the kinds that were discussed in Chapter 11, or for conventional external regulatory controls. It is suggested that there is, nevertheless, a limited but important respect in which vesting power in employees might have positive effects extending beyond the employees themselves, namely in relation to community concerns.[2] Where employees have a say in investment or relocation decisions the economic well-being of the local community is likely to be better served than where these decisions are made entirely by distant boards or dispersed and remote investors. Similarly, employees might also be expected to show a greater sensitivity to the impact of commercial activity on the local physical environment, though there is no doubt scope here too for a conflict of interests between those who work in the enterprise and those who are otherwise affected by it. One response to the apparently limited capacity of employee participation to legitimate corporate power is to seek some alternative way of addressing that issue (see below). The response of other theorists, in contrast, is that participation in the form of 'co-determination' or 'joint regulation' does not go far enough in the direction of employee empowerment. For them, it is necessary to move away from capitalist forms of enterprise altogether and to establish in their place worker-controlled firms. Not only will the negation of the rights of capital remove a serious constraint on the scope for democracy

---

[1] This issue surfaces, e.g. in the debate between guild and state socialists at the beginning of this century, the latter arguing that worker control of autonomous enterprises would simply amount to 'worker capitalism': see R. Oakeshott, *The Case for Workers' Co-ops* (2nd ed., 1990, Basingstoke), ch. 4.

[2] And see R. A. Dahl, *A Preface to Economic Democracy* (1985), at 98 - 100 generally, and at 100:

> being far more numerous and closer to the average citizen than managers and owners, employees would be more representative of consumers and citizens. Whereas top managers are a minuscule proportion of the public and can more easily escape or absorb the social costs their decisions generate, employees are [a] much larger and more representative part of the public, as consumers, residents, and citizens. They are therefore more likely than managers to bear some of the adverse consequence of their decisions.

within the enterprise, but also, it is argued, it will help create a more just and genuinely participative society. An outline of the case for this more radical agenda will be sketched below.

Three other approaches to the problem of corporate power should be noted before we examine the arguments for employee participation in its different forms. A detailed analysis of them would take us too far from the central concerns of this book, but brevity of treatment is not meant to suggest that the approaches, either individually or in combination, do not merit serious attention. Perhaps the most obvious response to the problem of power is to attempt to dissipate it. Corporate power is an attribute of absolute size and market dominance and hence, if enterprises were reduced in scale, the ability of companies to exercise power might be substantially diminished. It has been pointed out that despite the vast size of enterprises, plants in the UK owned by the 100 largest firms employ on average less than 500 people.[3] Since in many industries the minimum plant size allowing efficient operation is considerably smaller than the average size of firms in the industry, the implication is that agglomerations of power could be broken up without sacrificing the benefits of large-scale production. As against this it must be acknowledged that there are also other economies associated with enterprise size, for example, in relation to financing, research and development, and marketing, and that these would be sacrificed if companies and groups of companies were dismantled in this way. The loss of these economies could to an extent be avoided if businesses were to enter into collaborative ventures, but it is not self-evident that the result would then be a significant reduction in power, at least to the extent that the firms involved ceased to be independent, competing units. And there may, conversely, be some disadvantages from an increase in competition, in that a degree of protection from the market is necessary if managers are to have the discretion to make decisions that are in the social interest but which are inconsistent with maximum profits. Breaking up enterprises may therefore bring benefits in terms of reducing market power and increasing the number of decision-making centres, but there are also countervailing factors to be taken into account.

A second approach is to address corporate power not through reform at the level of the company, but at the level of those who have control over capital. Previous chapters have indicated that shareholders in public companies typically intervene only to a very limited degree in the businesses in which they invest, but this need not inevitably be so. Furthermore, the controllers of capital (and capital is increasingly concentrated in the hands of a small number of institutions and their investment managers) exercise a

---

[3] D. Miller, *Market, State and Community: Theoretical Foundations of Market Socialism* (1989), at 12.

major influence over all aspects of the development of the economy. Through their decisions, for example, about whether to invest in equities or in property, or domestically or overseas, and their decisions about the sectors of the economy they will support and which individual firms, they have a massive impact on national economic well-being. Appointment of employee representatives as pension-fund trustees would be one way of opening up to wider influence and scrutiny funds' investment policies and decisions about how they should use their position as shareholders. Employee representation might be accompanied by a legal recognition that trustees were not bound to seek the maximum return on the assets under their control if they considered this to be contrary to the interests of those they represent. There is some existing experience of union representatives serving as trustees, but they have invariably been in a minority position and their presence seems to have had little practical effect.[4] Other possibilities include the creation of 'wage-earner funds', whereby a fixed percentage of company profits in the form of shares is distributed annually to funds organized on a national or regional basis for the benefit of employees.[5] This would in due course result in the funds accumulating controlling stakes in enterprises, with possible consequences for the policies those enterprises pursue, and would also bring about a more equal distribution of wealth and income. Proposals for 'democratizing' the control of capital need not be confined to pension funds, nor to employee representation. They could extend to all bodies having command over large capital stakes, and could involve other interest groups, for example local communities or environmental organizations. Multi-constituency representation would, however, seem likely to open up similar problems to those discussed in Chapter 11 in relation to constituency representation at the level of company boards.

A third approach to the problem of corporate power is to legitimate it through its absorption into the democratic process, that is, to subject companies to state control. State control in its most complete form of nationalization now has few friends, at least other than in relation to utilities and sometimes as a way of rescuing failed businesses. This is in large part because of the dismal economic performance of state-controlled industry in Eastern Europe. State control need not, however, be inevitably associated with central planning. Government-appointed directors might operate the enterprises under their control in response to market signals as in a capitalist economy, but rather than purely in the interests of profit, with due regard to the 'public interest' or whatever more specific social side-purposes might be

---

[4] See R. Minns, *Pension Funds and British Capitalism: the Ownership and Control of Shareholdings* (1980), ch. 5; T. Schuller, *Age, Capital and Democracy: Member Participation in Pension Scheme Management* (1986), ch. 4; T. Schuller, *Democracy at Work* (1985), ch. 5.

[5] The best-known proposal is the Swedish 'Meidner Plan', eventually implemented in a diluted form: see Dahl, *A Preface to Economic Democracy* (above, n. 2), at 125–8.

mandated by the state. State control need not therefore involve massive centralization and could in principle permit considerable enterprise autonomy. There would, however, undoubtedly be problems in making such arrangements work. In the limited example of nationalized industries in the UK Prosser explains how the initial intention that boards should pursue the 'public interest' at arm's length from government was undermined by the exigencies of macro-economic policy, and in any event that 'the idea of a self-defining "public interest" which could be discovered unproblematically by expert boards proved to be a will-o'-the-wisp'.[6] An alternative, more limited, model of state control is control exercised by way of a regulatory agency, involving a partial transfer of decision-making power from the company to the state. Such bodies, which have been created in this country in relation to privatized utilities and which have a much longer history in the United States,[7] might be established to supervise the operations of a broader range of industries, and with wider objectives than is currently the case of providing a surrogate for market forces in conditions of monopoly or near monopoly. Again, however, the problem is in identifying the public interest that regulatory agencies might protect and in making that idea operational. Furthermore, as with all modes of state control, while power may gain a formal legitimacy when exercised or constrained by the processes of the state, achieving a real increase in public participation or accountability is liable to prove problematical.

The response to the issue of private power that will be pursued here is to subject companies to a form of democratic control not by subsuming them within the machinery of the state, but instead through *internal* democratization, by way of employee participation or control. Section I will examine some of the main arguments in support of employee participation and the remainder of the chapter will discuss how different forms of participation might be put into practice. Section II will consider employee representation on the board as a means of securing 'co-determination' or 'joint regulation'. Section III will note developments in employee share ownership, that is, employee involvement not by way of direct participation in decision-making but by employees also becoming shareholders. The final section gives brief consideration to alternatives to the company, in which equity investors with control rights disappear altogether and the furtherance of employee interests within a fully participatory structure becomes the enterprise's explicit goal.

---

[6] T. Prosser, 'Regulation of Privatized Enterprises: Institutions and Procedures', in L. Hancher and M. Moran (eds), *Capitalism, Culture and Responsibility* (1989) 135, at 136.
[7] See C. Graham and T. Prosser, *Privatizing Public Enterprises* (1991), chs 6 and 7.

I THE CASE FOR EMPLOYEE PARTICIPATION

The debate about employee participation in industry has a long history and it is not intended to survey the full diversity of views here. A number of key themes will, however, be identified which bear on the issue of participation as a means of addressing the problem of power. The first argument points to the extent to which vital employee interests are affected by decisions made within the company, and questions the legitimacy of the making of those decisions, for example, about investment, technological change, and employment levels, without the participation of the employees affected. A recognition of the claim of employees to have an input into policy-making is at the centre of the philosophy expressed in the EC Green Paper on participation (prepared to stimulate discussion on the draft Fifth Directive in its early days),[8] which is worth quoting at length. The paper refers to:

the democratic imperative that those who will be substantially affected by decisions made by social and political institutions must be involved in the making of those decisions. In particular, employees are increasingly seen to have interests in the functioning of enterprises which can be as substantial as those of shareholders, and sometimes more so. Employees derive not only their income from enterprises which employ them, but they devote a large proportion of their daily lives to the enterprise. Decisions taken by or in the enterprise can have a substantial effect on their economic circumstances, both immediately and in the longer term; the satisfaction which they derive from work; their health and physical condition; the time and energy which they can devote to their families and to activities other than work; and even their sense of dignity and autonomy as human beings'.[9]

The paper goes on to argue that for sophisticated, industrial societies to maintain their democratic character it is essential that employees should have a degree of control over decisions that affect their interests, notwithstanding that their involvement may make decisions which are beneficial from a broad social and economic point of view, for example, decisions about restructuring the enterprise, more difficult.[10] The paper nevertheless envisages that over the long term participation will promote efficiency, through having a socially stabilizing effect and by avoiding confrontation. On the efficiency issue, the majority of the Bullock Committee on industrial democracy in this country were similarly of the view that the productivity of British industry would be increased by putting the relationship of capital and labour on a

---

[8] See below.
[9] Commission of the European Communities, *Employee Participation and Company Structure in the European Community* (1975), Bull Supp 8/75, at 9.
[10] Ibid. For a criticial examination of the view that co-determination is inefficient, since if it were not it would evolve spontaneously, see J. Gotthold, 'Codetermination and Property Rights Theory', in T. Daintith and G. Teubner (eds), *Contract and Organization: Legal Analysis in the Light of Economic and Social Theory* (1986), 244. See also Miller, *Market, State and Community* (above, n. 3), ch. 3 on the principle of market neutrality.

new basis. It was their view that by giving employee representatives a share in making strategic decisions affecting the future of the enterprise and allowing the workforce to take joint responsibility with shareholder representatives for the success and profitability of the business,[11] a more constructive dialogue would ensure.

Even if participation were likely to lead to a reduction in efficiency, for example, by slowing down the company's response to market or technological change, the case for it would not necessarily be undermined. The argument that employees should not be allowed to participate in decisions that affect their interests on the ground that participation will diminish economic efficiency is an argument to the effect that efficiency justifies the possession of power. This is an application of the wider justification for corporate power that was examined in Chapter 1, which holds that while the possession of power by companies may not be desirable in itself, it should be accepted as the price to be paid for efficient wealth creation. But it can be objected that the limitations on the ability of employees to shape their own destiny cannot be compensated for by increases in aggregate social wealth. Employees can never have complete control over the factors that affect their well-being since many of these are external to the enterprise. Nevertheless, managements enjoy a zone of discretion, for example, about how to respond to long-term changes in demand for the company's products, and it can be argued that employees should be allowed to participate in these decisions even though their involvement may have adverse economic effects. According to this view the contention that employees should be denied the right to participate on efficiency grounds should be rejected, because that right and the values that support it should be regarded as trumping general welfare considerations.[12] Employees should be treated as ends and not as means, as they are by the justification of corporate power in terms of social wealth.

The argument for participation so far considered is directed towards reforming the capitalist corporate enterprise rather than replacing it. There are, however, other, more radical arguments for participation that demand a different form of business association altogether. One such view contends that employees have a right of democratic self-government within enterprises. Dahl, for instance, has suggested that 'in a certain kind of human association, the process of government should as far as possible meet democratic criteria, because people involved in this kind of association possess a *right*, an inalienable right to govern themselves by the democratic process'.[13] Dahl argues

---

[11] *Report of the Committee of Inquiry on Industrial Democracy* (the Bullock Report, Cmnd. 6706, 1977), at 160. Cf. Oakeshott, *The Case for Workers' Co-ops* (above, n.1), ch. 1.

[12] For 'rights as trumps' see R. Dworkin, *Taking Rights Seriously* (2nd ed., 1978), at xi.

[13] Dahl, *A Preface to Economic Democracy* (above, n. 2), at 56–7, emphasis in original, and see chs 2 and 4 generally. See also M. Walzer, *Spheres of Justice* (1983), at 291–303; J. Cohen, 'The Economic Basis of Deliberative Democracy', in E. F. Paul, F. D. Miller and J. Paul (eds), *Socialism* (1989) 25.

that companies are a relevant form of 'human association' for this purpose, holding that the factors that justify democracy in governing the state, for example, the need to reach decisions that will be binding on all the members of society collectively, apply equally in relation to commercial enterprises. Democratic principles, furthermore, preclude those who are not subject to the firm's government from representation within it, thus denying providers of capital who do not also work in the enterprise any right of control. Structures for the co-determination of company policy by employee and shareholder representatives, supported by the argument considered above, clearly do not satisfy these principles. As Oakeshott points out, 'the essence of a democracy is precisely that all its members should be on the same footing in crucial matters such as the choice of leadership. If an enterprise is necessarily binary and two-sided that condition cannot strictly be met'.[14] As well as co-determination being democratic only in a restricted sense, under such arrangements the interests of capital will inevitably limit what can be achieved in terms of furthering employee interests. In addition, while co-determination introduces the possibility of some reallocation of profits as between shareholders and employees, the formal entitlement of the providers of capital to the firm's residual income is unaffected. To most advocates of worker control this appears unjust. Although (at least from a market socialist perspective) capital is entitled to a fixed return at the market rate, the surplus generated by the firm should be apportioned in accordance with labour contribution.

As mentioned earlier, the claimed advantages of a transformation from a capitalist economy to one composed of worker-controlled firms are not limited to the direct consequences for the workers concerned. Thus most proposals view worker control as an opportunity to create a more equal distribution of wealth and income. With regard to the latter, it has been pointed out that there are significantly lower differentials in rewards between managerial and other workers in existing worker-controlled firms, and it is argued that this would continue to be so if such firms were to become the dominant form of enterprise in the economy.[15] It is also claimed that a similar degree of equality could not be achieved in a capitalist economy through redistributive taxation, given the high returns to capital and managerial talent that appear to be necessary for the system to function effectively.[16] An important part of the case for a worker-controlled economy is therefore its ability to satisfy demands for a more just society. It is argued furthermore

---

[14] Oakeshott, *The Case for Workers' Co-ops* (above, n. 1), at 21.

[15] See Dahl, *A Preface to Economic Democracy* (above, n. 2), at 104–7; S. Estrin, 'Workers' Co-operatives: Their Merits and Their Limitations', in J. Le Grand and S. Estrin (eds), *Market Socialism* (1989), at 171–2.

[16] See Dahl, *A Preface to Economic Democracy* (above, n. 2), at 102–3; Miller, *Market, State and Community* (above, no. 3), at 14–15.

that greater economic equality is liable to be translated into greater political equality. Dahl, for example, maintains that differences between citizens in such matters as wealth, status, control over information, and access to political leaders, which are characteristic of capitalist economies, 'generate significant inequalities among citizens in their capacities and opportunities for participating as political equals in governing the state'.[17] The case for worker control usually envisages smaller-scale enterprises than current corporate groups, and so a dispersal of business power might be anticipated as well.

Arguments that reject the company as the dominant form of enterprise lie at the end of the spectrum that was introduced in Chapter 1, where it was asked on what terms companies should be allowed to possess power. The proposition considered first was that the social interest is best served when companies maximize their profits within the law. This was later modified by suggesting that profits should be sought within constraints designed to protect third-party and social interests additional to those imposed by external regulatory controls. This chapter has noted the argument that companies should no longer pursue the single goal of increasing shareholder wealth, but should serve jointly the interests of shareholders and employees. The case for worker-controlled firms holds that corporate enterprise, even with these modifications to the company's goal structure and representative arrangements, should be rejected, not least because an economy made up of worker-controlled firms would have advantages that cannot be obtained under capitalism. A book on company law is not the place in which to enter into the merits of this case in any detail. The issue of the relative efficiency of the worker-controlled firm does, however, warrant some attention.

Opponents of worker-controlled enterprises have put forward a number of reasons why they are likely to be significantly less efficient than capitalist equivalents. It is also argued on the other hand that worker-controlled firms may often be more efficient, for example, because the ending of the conflictual relationship with the owners of capital will engender a greater sense of teamwork, resulting in higher productivity.[18] Even if it could be shown that worker-controlled firms are inherently less efficient that capitalist firms, this would not, of course, as was the case also with the argument for co-determination, be dispositive of the question, since a higher priority may be afforded to the values that worker-controlled enterprises are intended to serve. But the

---

[17] See Dahl, *A Preface to Economic Democracy* (above, n. 2), at 54–5; emphasis omitted. See also ibid. 94–8, and C. Pateman, *Participation and Democratic Theory* (1970), ch. 3, arguing that participation within enterprises can act as a training ground for, and an encouragement towards, activity in the wider political sphere by fostering a sense of 'political efficacy'. It might thus contribute towards a more comprehensively participatory society by extending the scope of democracy and strengthening and stabilizing existing political institutions.

[18] See ibid. ch. 1.

efficiency issue is still an important one. If a worker-controlled economy would be significantly less productive than a capitalist economy this would be a serious drawback. Conversely, if there were likely to be no insuperable problems with efficiency, then the justification of corporate power in terms of the superior capacity of corporate enterprise to generate wealth would require a re-evaluation. Some of the reasons why worker-controlled firms might be considered to be less efficient than conventional companies will be examined in Section IV.

For completeness, a final argument for participation should be noted. It is more concerned with participation at 'grass-roots' level, in relation to such issues as the organization of work and working methods, than with participation at the level of the enterprise. The worker subject to control by a corporate hierarchy, it is argued, is deprived of opportunities for self-realization: he or she is excluded from the 'creation, development, and exercise of capacities and talents in cooperative association' that are taken to be central needs and aspirations of most human beings.[19] In the traditional employment relationship the employee is seen as being forced into a purely instrumental role. Thus in performing their functions at work employees are viewed merely as means of production: opportunities for personal development through work are subordinated to the demands of output. Participation in the sense of the personal involvement of the employee in, among other things, the selection of tasks, deciding how tasks are to be performed, setting the pace of work, and determining the mix of work and leisure, is advocated as a means of enabling the employee to overcome alienation and feelings of powerlessness and to develop a sense of self-worth. It has the potential to transform the employee's status as 'a subdued individual in the framework of hierarchical authority' and to 'promote the worker's human dignity, humanize the world of work . . . and control managerial domination'.[20]

In fact, in recent years many organizations have taken steps in the direction of increased employee autonomy, removing layers of hierarchy, broadening the range of issues that are left to employee discretion, and generally practising 'participative management' techniques in contrast to control through rules and strict supervision associated with the Taylorian

[19] See G. A. Dymski and J. E. Elliot, 'Capitalism and the Democratic Economy', in E. F. Paul et al. (eds), *Capitalism* (1989), 140, at 150. It is argued that the concept of self-realization requires not only control over the way a particular task is carried out, but also the ability to choose work that satisfies the needs of others, thus enabling the employee to work 'communally': see Miller, *Market, State and Community* (above, n. 3), ch. 8; J. Elster, 'Self-realization in Work and Politics: the Marxist Conception of the Good Life', in J. Elster and K. O. Moene (eds), *Alternatives to Capitalism* (1989), 127.

[20] G Teubner, 'Industrial Democracy through Law? Social Functions of Law in Institutional Innovations', in T. Daintith and G. Teubner (eds), *Contract and Organisation: Legal Analysis in the Light of Economic and Social Theory* (1986) 261, at 263.

model of industrial organization.[21] The motive for these developments is presumably not, however, to promote self-realization as an end in itself, but rather to increase efficiency. Participation is likely to have this effect by bringing about improvements in the sharing of knowledge and flexibility of response, savings on supervisory staff, and greater internalization of the company's objectives on the part of employees, thereby putting the company in a stronger position to meet increased international competition and demands for improvements in product quality, and to cope with technological change. While bringing benefits to employees in terms of increased job satisfaction, there are no doubt limits to the extent to which the requirements for self-realization will be met so long as the predominant concern is to achieve gains in productivity. With regard to the argument that this is as far as they *should* be met, it has been observed that this implies that it is desirable to give priority to 'consumption values' over 'production values'. That is, the argument supposes that increased output, ultimately to be enjoyed in the process of consumption, justifies limitations on the scope for self-realization in the process of production.[22] This supposition is contestable, since it can be argued that it relies on an arbitrarily selective conception of desirable social goods. Put slightly differently, the concept of efficiency employed to justify limiting the scope of participation, in recognizing only satisfactions arising from goods and services and not also from the process of production, is partial and hence defective. Whatever the merits of the rival views may be, ways in which employee self-realization might be increased will not be considered further here.[23] They involve detailed questions of internal organization rather than of the legal structure of the enterprise, though it is likely that whether or not businesses will pay attention to facilitating self-realization beyond the requirements of productivity will in fact depend on the scope for participation at enterprise level, to which we shall shortly turn.

Needless to say, the arguments in support of employee participation in its various forms are controversial. It is not intended to offer any concluded view, but enough has been said to provide an outline of the theoretical background to possible institutional reforms. Section II will now consider ways in which the corporate structure might be modified to permit employees to participate alongside shareholder representatives in the formulation of enterprise policy, with a view to giving employees a measure of control over the determinants of their economic well-being.

[21] See P. E. Tixier, 'The Labour Movement and Post-Rational Models of Organization: A French Case or a Trend in Western Societies?', in C. J. Lammers and G. Széll (eds), *International Handbook of Participation in Organizations*, vol 1 (1989) 26, at 27–30.
[22] See Elster, 'Self-Realisation in Work and Politics' (above, n. 19).
[23] For a description of methods of increasing employee 'autonomy and freedom over the way their working lives are ordered' see D. Elliot, *Conflict or Co-operation: The Growth of Industrial Democracy* (2nd ed., 1984), at 197–202.

II BOARD-LEVEL PARTICIPATION

This section is concerned with participation designed to enable employees to have a say in how the enterprise itself is run, that is, about such matters as investment, plant closures, or mergers and acquisitions, as distinct from 'social issues', such as immediate working conditions, holiday entitlements, or disciplinary matters. (The latter, which are, for example, also the subject of co-determination rights in Germany, exercised through works councils,[24] are in this country currently dealt with through collective bargaining, workplace consultation, or at the discretion of the employer.[25]) A number of preliminary points arise. First, for employee involvement to be able to influence enterprise policy it must be at the highest level in the organization and at other points at which strategic decisions are made. In other words, participation must be at the level of the board of the holding company, since it is here, at least formally, that the constraints within which individual divisions, subsidiaries, and plants must operate are determined. There must also be representation at other policy-making levels within the group, given that the constituent elements of the enterprise may enjoy considerable autonomy. Since the distribution of decision-making power varies considerably between groups, the precise structure of participation rights cannot be dictated by a statutory formula in advance. This difficulty can be overcome, however, as the Bullock Committee recommended, by the formulation by a reconstituted parent board of a policy on the levels at which employee representatives should sit.[26] Second, high-level participation will inevitably take a representative rather than a direct form. As such it may do little to diminish the individual employee's sense of powerlessness and subjugation to hierarchical control, though high-level participation may well present an opportunity for increasing the scope for self-realization beyond the limits imposed by the demands of productivity.[27] Finally, for participation to be effective in allowing more than marginal changes in policy in the interests of employees, it is clear that what is required, in Pateman's terminology, is 'full participation'.[28] Pateman draws a distinction between 'full participation' and 'partial participation'.

---

[24] See 386 above.

[25] For the incidence and subject-matter of consultation and the current scope of collective bargaining on non-pay issues, see Millward et al. *Workplace Industrial Relations in Transition: The ED/ESRC/PSI/ACAS Surveys* (1992), at 151–9 and 249–55 respectively.

[26] *The Bullock Report* (above, n. 11), at 133, para 21. The Committee also proposed representation on the board of parent companies of groups employing more than 2,000 in the UK, but in addition on the boards of all subsidiaries employing more than 2,000.

[27] Teubner, 'Industrial Democracy through Law?' (above, n. 20), at 263–4, has suggested that co-determination in Germany has achieved little in terms of individual participation, but that its function should be seen as being to make changes at the organizational level (in the distribution of power and corporate goals) rather than as a remedy for alienation.

[28] (Above, n. 17), ch. 4; see also n. 29. For a discussion of the effects of minority representation in several continental countries, see P. L. Davies, 'European Experience with

Partial participation exists in a situation in which A has an opportunity to influence B, but the final power to decide remains with B, as in a consultation procedure. There is full participation only where each party to a decision has equal power to determine the outcome.[29] As will be noted below, some of the proposals for participation and most of the existing arrangements for board representation on the Continent provide for only partial participation.[30]

There is currently little sign of any demand for board-level representation from organized labour in the UK, and most employers and the government are strongly opposed. The debate over the terms of the draft EC Fifth Directive has, however, kept the issue alive, though as will be seen shortly the current proposals include options for participation that do not involve board representation and which amount to no more than consultation. We will begin with a brief look at the high-water mark of participation proposals in this country, the Bullock Report, and continue with an examination of the Fifth Directive and what it might hold for the future.

The Bullock Report

Interest in employee participation at board level reached its high point in the UK with the appointment in 1975 of the Committee of Inquiry on Industrial Democracy, chaired by Lord Bullock, and its subsequent report.[31] Traditionally, trade unions had been opposed to 'collaborative' participation, viewing employer-employee relations as necessarily and fundamentally based on conflict, and fearing that an incorporation of worker representatives within company structures would weaken collective bargaining[32] and would have the effect of legitimating decisions contrary to employee interests, for example, about redundancies. In 1974, however, the TUC decided in favour of parity representation on large company boards, a change in policy which reflected the view that without direct access to top-level decision-making within the enterprise it would be impossible to extend the bargaining process to cover 'the strategic economic decisions upon which the very future of employment might depend ... the internal, corporate decisions which

Worker Representation on the Board', in E. Batstone and P. L. Davies, *Industrial Democracy: The European Experience* (1976), ch. 4. See also the discussion at 386–93 above.

[29] These two forms of participation should be distinguished from *pseudo participation*, which is a form of consultation whereby decisions already made are rendered more acceptable by creating a spurious impression that they are the result of participation: see Pateman, *Participation and Democratic Theory* (above, n. 17), at 68–9.

[30] e.g. in Sweden, where the primary object of representation is to give access to information: see Wedderburn, 'Trust, Corporation and the Worker' (1985) 23 *Osgoode Hall L J* 203, at 241–2 and see also n. 46 below.

[31] (Above, n. 11).

[32] See e.g. C. A. R. Crosland, *The Future of Socialism* (rev. ed., 1964), at 260–2, fearing a loss of union independence.

determined social priorities'.[33] Interest in the issue had also been sharpened by Britain's entry into the EEC in 1973, which made it necessary to consider attitudes towards proposals for worker participation contained in the draft Fifth Directive. The TUC conversion ensured that the issue was put onto the political agenda and the appointment of the Bullock Committee was the Labour government's response. The main recommendations of the majority of the committee (some of which are considered in more detail below) were that there should be a form of parity representation on a single-tier board in all enterprises with 2,000 or more employees in the UK, with the employees' representatives elected through the 'single channel' of union machinery within the enterprise. The report was greeted by industrial and City interests with outrage and alarm, the CBI in particular organizing a campaign of opposition. The unions, far from united in their support for the underlying idea of participation, were unwilling or unable to mount a strong defence. And the government, which in part shared the fears about union domination and was sensitive to the growing opposition, eventually brought forward compromise proposals involving a more gradual progress to only minority representation.[34] These fell with the Conservative election victory in 1979, and it is only the periodic reappearance of versions of the draft Fifth Directive that have kept the issue of board-level participation alive. As Wedderburn says, the pages of the Bullock Report now speak 'as if from another world'.[35]

The Draft Fifth Directive

The first draft of the Fifth Directive on the structure of public companies was published in 1972;[36] a revised text appeared in 1983,[37] and the latest proposed amendments to the draft in 1989[38] (the 'amended draft'). Adoption is still thought to be some years away, the length of the gestation period mainly reflecting opposition to the employee participation proposals, but also to the attempts to harmonize board structure more generally.[39] The

---

[33] Wedderburn, 'Trust, Corporation and the Worker', (above, n.30), at 242. For a discussion of the development of trade-union attitudes in the 1960s and seventies and the steps that led to the appointment of the Bullock Committee, see Elliot, *Conflict or Co-operation?* (above, n. 23), ch. 14.

[34] *Industrial Democracy* (Cmnd. 7231, 1978). Representation would have been by a third of the seats on a supervisory board. The company would also have been placed under a duty to consult a company-wide shop stewards committee on major issues such as investment, mergers, and take-overs, and expansion and contraction of the undertaking.

[35] Wedderburn, 'Trust, Corporation and the Worker' (above, n. 30), at 247.

[36] Official Journal 131, 13 December 1972.

[37] Document 1-862/81, 15 January 1982.

[38] These appear in DTI, *Amended Proposal for a Fifth Directive on the Harmonisation of Company Law in the European Community: A Consultative Document* (1990).

[39] See Ch. 6 above.

central theme of the proposals, at least at the outset, was that there was a need to move away from arrangements which were based on 'economic and social policies which saw employees' relationships with companies as essentially contractual', towards institutions which recognized that employees had interests in the functioning of enterprises 'as substantial as those of shareholders, and sometimes more so'.[40] It has been said that they reflect not 'necessarily a "socialist" perspective but one at which many different types of ideology arrived and with different emphases and accents'.[41] The aim was thus not to supplant the rights of capital, but to recognize the equal importance of the interests of the employees in the organization by granting them a full voice in decision making at the highest level. The latest proposals are no longer exclusively based on this co-determination philosophy, however, enabling member states to opt for a system which is merely one of consultation. Even so, such is the opposition of the British government to mandatory participation in any form that in a discussion document published in response to the amended draft comments on the participation aspects were not even invited.[42]

The draft now offers four participation options.[43] The first involves a two-tier board structure with employee representatives occupying at least a quarter, but not more than half, of the seats on the supervisory board, with provision to allow the outcome of a tied vote to be determined by a shareholder-appointed director, though this is not mandatory.[44] Alternatively, the board may, in addition to the shareholder- and employee-elected members, contain a number of 'neutral' members, not exceeding one-third of the other members.[45] Under this first option the supervisory board appoints the management board; the latter has an obligation to report to the supervisory board on the company's progress at three-monthly intervals and has a right to such other information from the management board as it may

[40] *Employee Participation and Company Structure in the European Community* (above, n. 9), at 9.

[41] Wedderburn, 'Trust, Corporation and the Worker' (above, n. 30), at 237.

[42] DTI *Amended Proposal for a Fifth Directive* (above, n. 38). The government believes that company management should '*inform* and *consult* employees about matters which affect them' on a voluntary basis: (para 4) emphasis added.

[43] The laws of member states would be required to make the adoption of one of the options compulsory by all companies (including subsidiaries) with 1,000 or more employees. Participation would not, however, be necessary where a majority of employees opposed it. See also the similar arrangements in the proposal for a Council Directive complementing the Statute for a European Company with regard to the involvement of employees in the European Company: COM(91) 174 final.

[44] As in the German system: see below. There is also provision to accommodate the Dutch system whereby the works council and shareholders' general meeting respectively may nominate directors for co-option to the supervisory board, with limited rights to veto appointments: see Davies, 'European Experience With Worker Representation on the Board' (above, n. 28), at 51–52.

[45] Thus permitting an arrangement along the lines of the Bullock Committee's '2X + Y' formula: see the Bullock Report (above, n. 11), ch. 9.

require. The second option is for a single-tier board, made up of executive and a majority of non-executive members, with similar employee representation arrangements as for the first option. In earlier drafts decisions on certain fundamental issues required the consent of the supervisory board, or in the case of the one-tier structure, could not be delegated to another body. These included closure or transfer of the undertaking or a substantial part of it and major changes in activities. In the latest version whether any issues must be reserved for decision by a body on which the employee representatives sit is now purely a matter for national law.

Under the third option, instead of an employee presence on the board there is provision for the creation of an employee representative body separate from the company's supervisory or management structure. This would have the right to receive periodic reports on the company's progress and other information necessary for the performance of its functions. The employee body would have to be consulted before each meeting of the board (the supervisory board, where the two-tier structure is adopted) and given the same information and documentation as the board receives. Consistent with the arrangements for representation at board level it would have no power of veto, though national law would be free to lay down that as regards specified matters (for example, closures), where the board did not agree with the opinion of the employee body it must give reasons for its disagreement. It should be noted that in practice even this limited obligation of consultation could be evaded, since the right to be consulted exists only in respect of matters that come before the board: the draft does not prevent issues of concern to employees from being delegated to some other body. The final option is for 'participation through collectively agreed systems'. This would require an agreement to be entered into between the company, or a body representing employers on the one hand and employee organizations on the other, which created participation rights that were at least equivalent to one of the other options set out above.

It is not clear what the provisions of the Directive in its final form will be, nor, of course, how the British government of the day would choose to implement them. Of the various arrangements currently offered, only parity board representation amounts to 'full participation' as defined by Pateman. With parity board membership employee representatives have at least in theory the ability to shape decisions through a process of agreement with the other board members by reason of their institutional position, whereas with anything less than equal representation, or where they merely have the right to be consulted, the extent to which the employees can affect the outcome depends on their pre-existing bargaining strength. This is not to deny that these forms of partial participation would improve the ability of employees to influence company decisions, but this would be chiefly by improving their access to information and broadening the range of issues about which the employees have the right to be heard. It is difficult to imagine parity representation being adopted in this country in the near future, or indeed the acceptance of mandatory employee representation on the board of any kind under the present government. A system of parity representation on supervisory boards is, however, an established feature in sections of German industry (where the two-tier board structure is compulsory), and it is worth examining what its impact, and the impact of employee board membership in other sectors falling short of parity representation, have been.[46]

The German Experience

Since the 1950s there has been parity representation on the supervisory boards of companies in the coal, iron, and steel industries (the so-called 'montan' industries), balanced by a 'neutral' director chosen by both groups. In the remainder of German companies the system is in effect one of minority employee representation. The position of employees outside the montan industries was strengthened in 1976,[47] when the proportion of worker directors on the supervisory board was increased from one-third to a half. However, in the event of deadlock the shareholder-elected chairman has a casting vote, and also the employee directors must include among them a representative of 'managerial workers', who is likely not to be a union member and to associate with shareholder, rather than general employee, interests.[48] These arrangements thus ensure that decision-making power ultimately remains in the hands of the representatives of the shareholders, a situation which, as has been noted, is expressly provided for in the Fifth Directive proposals.

The consensus is that parity representation in the montan industries has had little impact on the business policies of the companies involved. The Biedenkopf Commission, formed to investigate the effects of co-determination in anticipation of an extension of the parity principle, concluded that employee representatives had had little formative effect on business strategy, largely confining their attention to the social impact of policies devised by management, for example, in relation to potentially job-threatening overseas investment or plant closures.[49] While the presence of employee directors on the supervisory board had thus delayed the making or implementing of

[46] For a survey of employee representation on the board in other European countries, see Batstone and Davies, *Industrial Democracy* (above, n. 28).

[47] Mitbestimmungsgesetz 1976.

[48] See T. Hadden, 'Employee Participation — What Future for the German Model?', (1982) 3 *Co Law* 250, at 253.

[49] See *The Biendenkopt Report: Co-Determination in the Company, Report of the Commission of Experts*, trans. D. O'Niell (1970), pt III. See also K. J. Hopt, 'New Ways in Corporate Governance: European Experiments With Labor Representation on Corporate Boards', (1984) 82 *Mich L Rev* 1338, at 1354–6.

decisions while schemes to lessen the adverse impact of management policies on employees could be worked out, the Commission found that employee directors shared a commitment with the shareholder representatives to company efficiency and the profit objective. There was no evidence that co-determination had increased the power of the unions to the point that it presented a threat to managerial freedom of action. Similarly Davies, in his survey of the literature on the European experience with participation prepared for the Bullock Committee in 1976, notes that while worker representatives had shown great interest 'in influencing the social and person-nel aspects of board decisions', they had demonstrated much less 'in matters of general business policy', despite the obvious significance of decisions in the latter area to the employees' long-term interests.[50] It has been suggested that an important explanation for this is the ideology of the German trade-union movement and its unitary stance on industrial relations. Unions have not sought to redefine corporate objectives or to challenge management strategy, but rather to make use of board representation merely as a means of protecting traditional employee interests in pay, conditions, and job security, and even then, within the bounds of conventional ideas about profitability.[51] Board membership has not, therefore, been seen as an opportunity to take joint control of the company with the shareholder representatives and thus to influence the whole range of company policies, so much as a method of safeguarding narrowly conceived employee interests 'from the inside'. A further symptom of this has been the employee directors' failure to take an active interest in selecting the members of the management board, which would seem to offer considerable potential as a means of affecting a company's policy orientation. This evidence should, however, be taken in its context of a period of sustained growth and employment stability in the German economy, in which fewer hard choices between corporate and employee interests were likely to be required.

Apart from the modesty of union ambitions, it seems likely that the effects of parity representation have also been limited by the particular institutional arrangements adopted. First, the supervisory board is precisely that—it has no management powers or right to determine future strategy, and its consent to management proposals is necessary only where the company's constitution so provides. (Though in fact the common practice is to require supervisory approval for major investment decisions and organizational changes and in

[50] See Davies, 'European Experience with Worker Representation' (above, n. 28), at 65. See also D. Vagts, 'Reforming the "Modern" Corporation: Perspectives from the German', (1966) 80 *Harv L Rev* 23, at 64-76.

[51] Redundancies is an area in which major effects might have been expected. See however Batstone, 'Industrial Democracy and Worker Representation at Board Level: A Review of the European Experience' (above, n. 28), at 36, who notes that 'worker directors have rarely, if ever, pursued workers' interests to the extent of opposing closures, although they have ensured that social considerations are more fully recognized' (references omitted).

any case the technical division of powers significantly understates the scope for informal employee influence over management: see below). Second, all members of the supervisory board are under a duty to promote the interests of the enterprise. The content of this duty is not entirely settled; it is clear that the duty does not demand that worker directors must invariably subordinate the interests of the employees to the financial well-being of the company, and it is possible that it is wide enough to sanction any outcome that reflects a good-faith compromise of relevant interests.[52] Nevertheless, an emphasis on the interests of the company does not provide 'a comfortable theoretical setting for the activities of the employee representatives'[53] particularly as a director may be held liable for persuading the management board to act in a way detrimental to those interests.[54] Apart from inhibiting employee directors in carrying out their functions as members of the supervisory board, this duty is also a source of important restrictions on the freedom of employee directors to use their position to further employee interests by other means. The system of co-determination depends for its effectiveness on the interlocking roles of collective bargaining, works councils, and board representation. The variety of mechanisms tends to strengthen the influence of employees, rather than weaken it through division, in that more than one function is frequently combined in the same person and action may be coordinated through the trade unions. Thus an employee director may also sit on the works council and be a union member, and may be joined on the board by a national union official.[55] However, again subject to its precise meaning, the duty to further the interests of the enterprise limits the permissible information flow from the board to the other functions, and may also restrict the ability of representatives to participate in strike action against the company.[56] In that the influence of employee directors would appear to depend as much on their outside connections as on the powers flowing from their position as board members, these restrictions are likely to have a significant weakening effect. A final institutional limitation concerns the division of powers between the supervisory board and the general meeting. The latter body retains the rights, among others, to decide on increases in

---

[52] See F. Kübler, 'Dual Loyalty of Labor Representatives', in K. J. Hopt and G. Teubner (eds), *Corporate Governance and Directors' Liabilities* (1985) 429, at 433, 439–41; Hopt, 'New Ways in Corporate Governance' (above, n. 49), at 1360.

[53] Davies, 'European Experience with Worker Representation' (above, n. 28), at 68.

[54] Kübler, 'Dual Loyalty of Labor Representatives' (above, n. 52), at 433; see particularly the discussion of a hypothetical attempt by a union-nominated director to persuade the company not to invest overseas in order to save jobs at home in an *unrelated* company.

[55] Ibid. at 431–2; and see Hadden, 'Employee Participation' (above, n. 48), at 255. Under the 1976 Act two-thirds of the employee representatives are employees of the enterprise and the remainder may be outside union representatives, but in both cases elected by the workforce.

[56] Ibid. 434–8; and see S. Simitis, 'Workers' Participation in the Enterprise — Transcending Company Law?', (1975) 38 *MLR* 1, 12–4.

416 *The Democratic Imperative*

capital and dividends, thus reserving to the shareholders control over matters central to the company's future development.[57]

Notwithstanding these institutional barriers employee directors have, as noted, had some influence over company policy.[58] The limited functions of the supervisory board are much less of an obstacle to employee involvement than might appear. The practice has been for the employee representatives on the supervisory board to negotiate directly with the management board on a range of policy issues.[59] Whatever the formal role of the supervisory board, the parity position of employees on it means that management must take employee demands seriously, given that the supervisory board is responsible for appointing and renewing appointments of the executive directors. The employee directors also derive strength from management's need to secure the cooperation of the works council, and also the goodwill of the unions, both of which are likely to be imperilled by disagreement with the employee representatives on the board, particularly in view of the overlaps mentioned above.[60] These latter considerations also apply outside the montan industries, but here, given that the employee directors are effectively in only a minority position on the supervisory board, their bargaining position is considerably weaker, and it has been concluded that 'labour representatives on the supervisory boards of most of the enterprises which are subject to the 1976 co-determination law can exercise only a very narrow influence on their company's business policies'.[61]

German co-determination would thus seem to have brought benefits to employees, but they have chiefly been in moderating the impact of management-determined policies manifesting a traditional profit orientation. On the other hand, as Herman points out, 'the advantages of codetermination to *management* have been substantial'.[62] A result of bringing employee representatives within the decision-making structure seems to have been to make the labour leadership more accepting of management's position, and to facilitate a sympathetic presentation of that position to the workforce. And Kübler notes that integrating the representation of employees' interests into the process of corporate decision making may have been of value in resolving conflicts, that might have led to damaging strike action, not only between

[57] See Davies, 'European Experience with Worker Representation' (above, n. 28), at 68; P. L. Davies, 'Employee Representation on Company Boards and Participation in Corporate Planning', (1975) 38 *MLR* 254, at 260.
[58] And for a more sanguine view generally, see Teubner, 'Industrial Democracy Through Law' (above, n. 20).
[59] See L. Kissler, 'Co-determination Research in the Federal Republic of Germany: A Review', in Lammers and Széll, *International Handbook of Participation in Organizations* (above, n. 21) 74, at 85–6.
[60] See Davies, 'Employee Representation on Company Boards' (above, n. 57), at 268.
[61] Kissler, 'Co-determination Research in the Federal Republic of Germany' (above, n. 59), at 86.
[62] E. S. Herman, *Corporate Control, Corporate Power* (1981), at 286; emphasis added.

management and workers, but also conflicts, characteristic of high-technology industries, between different groups of workers.[63] In conclusion, board-level co-determination has therefore a favourable record with respect shielding employees from the full costs of industrial transition and in maintaining efficiency through the containment of conflict, but hardly one that reveals a major shift in power.

Strengthening Co-determination

If it were thought desirable to formulate arrangements that would lead to something closer to an equal sharing of power, what lessons can be learned from the German experience? A central issue concerns how employee and shareholder interests should be seen to interrelate, and how the role of employee representation fits into the perceived relationship. Joint regulation can be understood on the one hand as 'gradually reducing, perhaps even abolishing, the basic conflicts of interest in industry', or on the other as being based 'more squarely upon an inevitable continuation of social and industrial conflict'.[64] The perspective chosen affects one's view of how the co-determination idea should be institutionalized. German company law, as Simitis notes, has adopted a unitary or 'harmonistic'[65] perspective, seeking to resolve conflict but at the same time to contain the potentially destabilizing effect of employee board membership by requiring worker directors to operate within a framework dictated by the 'interests of the enterprise'. Subscribing to the view that a divergence of interests is inherent, Simitis argues that the imposition of such a duty merely suppresses the conflict between shareholder and employee interests, which in reality continue to differ, and the practical effect is to create a bias in company policy towards financial performance, notwithstanding equal employee representation.[66] For a significant shift in goals to take place, Simitis suggests therefore that the conflict of interests must be openly acknowledged: 'It is not the task of legal rules to conceal this conflict ... by constantly over-emphasising a community of interests which has never been exactly defined or by cultivating a purposely vague notion of

[63] Kübler, 'Dual Loyalty of Labor Representatives' (above, n. 52), at 442. Herman, ibid. at 287, also refers to improvements in morale and productivity, and see also Hopt, 'New Ways in Corporate Governance' (above, n. 49), at 1353–4, suggesting improved monitoring of management by worker directors, who may be more independent than traditional non-executive directors and have additional sources of information, e.g. from the works council and union machinery.

[64] Wedderburn, 'Trust, Corporation and the Worker' (above, n. 30), at 245, noting the existence of two differing tendencies within the majority of the Bullock Committee. Lord Wedderburn was a member of the Committee.

[65] Simitis, 'Workers' Participation in the Enterprise' (above, n. 56), at 19 n. 67.

[66] See also O. Kahn-Freund, 'Industrial Democracy', (1977) 6 *ILJ* 65, at 75–8, and 76–80 above.

the enterprise. Duties and responsibilities must ... be modelled on the commitment to basically different interests'.[67]

The alternative vision of joint regulation, responsive to these 'different interests', seeks to produce a framework conducive to 'conflictual partnership', that is, an arrangement in which the representatives of the employees and of the shareholders are able to bargain over company policy unencumbered by some transcendent notion of the interests of the enterprise.[68] Davies gives clear expression to this idea, commenting in relation to the UK that

If the proposal for worker directors stems in the first place from the inadequate reach of collective bargaining, then it may be more appropriate to see the worker-directors scheme as the carrying on of collective bargaining by other means. Thus, the supervisory board would be a place for negotiation between employee representatives and management over corporate planning.[69]

What is different about bargaining on the board from ordinary collective bargaining is of course that the outcome does not depend on the employees' 'bargaining strength', resting ultimately on the possibility of industrial action. As Davies explains, if the employee representatives hold half the seats on the board, they would have a veto over corporate planning until their consent was obtained. In order to be put into effect this alternative conceptualization of the co-determination process would seem to require, therefore, in addition to parity representation,[70] an explicit right for employee directors to further the interests of their constituency,[71] and also a right to an 'undisturbed communication' between the directors and the persons they represent.[72] It is not clear how important the precise legal setting is in determining the effectiveness of joint regulation (from the employees' point of view), in

[67] Simitis, 'Workers' Participation in the Enterprise' (above, n. 56), at 19. See also D. D. Prentice, 'Employee Participation in Corporate Government — A Critique of the Bullock Report', (1978) 56 *Can Bar Rev* 277, at 298.

[68] See P. L. Davies and Lord Wedderburn, 'The Land of Industrial Democracy', (1977) 6 *ILJ* 197, at 198–204. Wedderburn, 'Trust, Corporation and the Worker' (above, n. 30), at 245, describes this arrangement as 'transitional'.

[69] Davies, 'Employee Representation on Company Boards' (above, n. 28), at 272.

[70] This does not exclude the presence on the board of a third, 'neutral' element whose composition would be agreed by both sides (see e.g. the Bullock Committee's '2X + Y' formula, the Bullock Report (above, n. 11), ch. 9). As well as being a mechanism to avoid deadlock, the need to win the support of a disinterested group may act as a stimulus to constructive dialogue and be a source of alternative solutions.

[71] Davies and Wedderburn, 'The Land of Industrial Democracy' (above, n. 68), at 198–9, argue that despite some unfortunate 'incidental phraseology' (i.e. a reference to 'the best interests of the company'), this is the effect of the definition of directors' duties proposed by the Bullock Committee: (above, n. 11), at 84, para 38. The amended draft of the Fifth Directive is ambiguous, but seems to have unitary implications, art 10a para 2 providing that the directors shall 'carry out their functions in the interests of the company having regard in particular to the interests of its shareholders and employees'.

[72] See Simitis, 'Workers' Participation in the Enterprise' (above, n. 56), at 19. But see also 20 where he questions the coherence of strike action in relation to claims 'connected with the enterprise' in a situation in which employees are in a position of genuine joint control.

comparison, for example, with how employee directors see their role, but arrangements of this kind at least allow maximum freedom of action, and may help to shape role perceptions.

A feature of the German experience has been not only that employee directors have largely accepted the continuing predominance of the profit objective, but also that their stance has been reactive, rather than proactive: they have responded to a management-dictated agenda, and have not sought to initiate policy, for example, on investment and future strategy on which the interests of employees depend. A possible factor in this is the confinement of the employee directors to the supervisory board, and so the question arises of whether the scope for employee influence might be extended if the labour representatives operated within a single-tier structure. The view of the Bullock Committee on this issue was that the UK should not adopt the two-tier system, fearing that if the employee directors were situated on a supervisory board, removed from the management process, their ability to 'join in setting the framework of policy within which management operate and to influence decisions on major questions concerning investment, rationalisation, expansion and the like' would be inhibited.[73] As against this, the experience in the montan industries suggests that the formal division of responsibilities is of limited importance in practice, at least where the employees are in a parity position on the supervisory board and that board is responsible for appointing the executive directors. Further, where employees are placed on a unitary board the functions of the board are likely in reality to bifurcate, with the employee directors, lacking executive responsibilities, being somewhat removed from day-to-day decision-making. A two-tier structure may also have advantages in that the risk of disruption to the management function may be reduced where the employee directors sit on a supervisory board, particularly if the board is to be regarded as a 'place for negotiation'.

Of perhaps greater importance than the body on which the employee directors serve is ensuring that they have a meaningful opportunity to influence the decision-making process. The fact that the executive directors have an intimate involvement with the operation of the business inevitably gives them considerable informational advantages over the employee directors, and a corresponding ability convincingly to condemn as impracticable proposals of which they disapprove on other grounds. Given this imbalance it will often be open to management to manipulate the presentation of issues to less knowledgeable or expert board colleagues and hence to limit the apparent range of available policy choices. As Batstone has pointed out: 'management originate and formulate proposals. In doing so, they are able to "shape" problems in the manner they desire, taking aspects as given which others might see as crucial features of the issue and promoting what they see

---

[73] The Bullock Report (above, n. 11), at 75, para 10.

as important considerations to the detriment of others'.[74] The Bullock Committee was rightly concerned to ensure that important questions of policy were decided by the body on which the employees were represented, rather than by management below board level, and to that effect identified certain 'attributed functions', such as decisions about changes in capital structure or significant disposals, that were required to be determined by the board.[75] Provisions of this kind, while essential, cannot, however, prevent management from manipulating the way the issues and background facts are presented to the board. No easy solutions to this problem suggest themselves, though it is obviously important that the employee representatives should have relevant expertise and maximum access to information about the business.[76] The construction of a detailed alternative corporate strategy is also likely to be of value in allowing the employees to escape a management-imposed view of the company and its prospects and to broaden the terms of debate.[77]

An Alternative Forum for Co-determination

Leaving aside the absence of a political will to introduce employee participation at board level, the lack of union support is clearly an argument against the practicability of co-determination in the UK. As mentioned earlier, many trade unionists have in the past been ideologically opposed to involvement in the management of enterprises alongside the representatives of capital, and the union view has traditionally been that involvement in decision-making at enterprise level would inhibit collective bargaining over wages and compromise effective resistance lower down in the organization to plant closures or other measures that were contrary to the interests of employees. With these union reservations in mind McCarthy has suggested that a more promising line of development for the future might be co-determination not via the board but by means of an enterprise-wide joint council made up of management and employee representatives, separate from the company's own decision-making structure.[78]

[74] Batstone, 'Industrial Democracy and Worker Representation' (above, n. 28), at 19–20 (references omitted). See also R. E. Pahl and J. T. Winkler, 'The Economic Elite: Theory and Practice', in P. Stanworth and A. Giddens (eds) *Elites and Power in British Society* (1974) 102.

[75] The Bullock Report (above, n. 11), at 77–8, paras 16–8.

[76] The Bullock Report (above, n. 11), at 156–9, makes proposals for formal training.

[77] An example of such a strategy is the Lucas Aerospace Corporate Plan, which represented a union attempt radically to amend company policy in the interests of saving jobs and making 'socially useful' products. Despite receiving some critical acclaim for its ingenuity and technical competence it had little impact on the company. Had the plan been launched from a position on the board rather than by a shop stewards committee the results might conceivably have been different: for a full account see H. Wainwright and D. Elliot, *The Lucas Plan — A New Trade Unionism in the Making?* (1982).

[78] W. McCarthy, *The Future of Industrial Democracy*, Fabian Tract no. 526 (1988), at 6–11. See also, at 12–4, a suggested revision of the Bullock Committee proposals on representation through the 'single channel' of trade unions, given the recent decline in levels of unionization (on which

It is proposed that the employee representatives on such a body would have an extensive right to management information, a general right to be consulted in relation to matters affecting the workforce, and a right of co-determination in certain specified areas. In McCarthy's own view joint decision-making ought ideally 'to cover such questions as closures, take-overs and major changes in existing employment patterns—e.g. the use of contract labour'.[79] But he doubts that there would be general support for this degree of co-determination on the part of British unions, since it would in effect give the employee representatives a veto over 'the pace and degree of all significant management change', and be open as a result to objections similar to those to board-level participation. The virtue of the proposals is, however, that unlike participation at board level they allow employees to influence a select range of decisions rather than requiring participation in all decisions at the highest level of the enterprise, as, for example, with the Bullock proposals. They might on that account be more acceptable to the unions (and possibly employers). They have, futhermore, the considerable advantage of permitting a gradualist approach to participation. The area of co-determination might thus initially be limited to 'social' issues of the kind currently dealt with by the German works councils, with the possibility of expansion in the future in a more favourable climate. As such these outline proposals seem to offer constuctive possibilities for the response that might be made in this country to a finalized Fifth Directive.

The Limits of Co-determination

Co-determination in relation to the commercial policy issues ultimately favoured by McCarthy would seem in principle capable of ceding a significant degree of influence over enterprise decision-making to employees. How it would work out in practice, however, and whether if put into a position of joint responsibility in relation to key enterprise issues employee representatives would largely acquiesce in a management-dictated agenda, as appears to have been the case in Germany, can only be a matter for speculation. This section will conclude by noting some arguments to the effect that there are inherent limitations in co-determination as a vehicle for furthering employee interests and therefore that variations in the structural arrangements of joint regulation are likely to make only limited differences to its effectiveness.

On the basis of a study of employee participation in Germany and

see Millward et al., *Workplace Industrial Relations* (above, n. 25, ch 3). McCarthy also advocates a lowering of the enterprise size threshold for participation rights.

[79] Ibid. at 10. Joint decision-making in relation to take-overs would require further changes in company law, e.g. a right to be vested in the joint council to veto the appointment of a new board.

Norway, and also the experience with participation in the state-owned steel industry in the UK, Brannen et al. conclude that 'a process seems to take place in which workers' representatives' orientations take on a managerialist colouring, and in which their activities become increasingly supportive of management strategies and goals'[80] An explanation they advance for this phenomenon is that within hierarchical organizations the interests of the most powerful group assume the character of accepted values: 'the dominant vocabularies are those of the powerful'.[81] In other words, by becoming involved in enterprise decision-making employee representatives through a process of socialization come to share the outlook of management. Whether this is merely an inappropriate generalization from rather limited experience with co-determination or instead reflects an unavoidable truth is, however, unclear; it is arguable that the result would be not be replicated against the background of a more conflictual industrial-relations tradition. But it is contended further that in a capitalist economy there are in addition objective or structural constraints that shape the policies that a company may realistically adopt, and which therefore limit the contribution to policy that employee representatives are capable of making. The argument is thus that, within a capitalist economy, 'the logic of the market is central and profit necessarily assumes primacy as an objective. The board of the enterprise must then work within the logic of and the priorities of capitalism'.[82]

But this seems to ignore the discretion enjoyed by management in imperfectly competitive markets. As Teubner observes, it is this discretion that is the target of co-determination: 'labor gets "corrupted" in so far as labor representatives have to bend to economic constraints, but this is only true for decisions outside the room of discretion'.[83] The market may, therefore, set limits to what can be achieved by co-determination, but it does not prevent employees within those limits from redirecting company policy in their own interests. It must be acknowledged, however, that there are by definition internal as well as external bounds to co-determination. While co-determination may accordingly effect a significant redistribution of power within the company, there will inevitably be limits imposed by the demands of ownership on the extent to which enterprise goals can be reorientated in the interests of employees. It is dissatisfaction with these limits that 'generates pressure for a thorough overhaul of the relationship between capital and labour',[84] in other words, that creates a demand for new forms of enterprise

---

[80] P. Brannen, et al. *The Worker Directors: A Sociology of Participation* (1976), at 218. See this generally for a study of the short-lived experiment with board-level participation in steel, and similarly E. Batstone, A. Ferner, and M. Terry, *Unions on the Board* (1983), in relation to employee directors at the Post Office.

[81] Ibid. at 219.

[82] Ibid. at 219–20.

[83] Teubner, 'Industrial Democracy Through Law?' (above, n. 20), at 268–9.

[84] T. Schuller, *Democracy at Work* (1985), at 11–2.

in which the conflict between labour and capital is dissolved by removing the control rights of capital. Enterprises of this kind are the subject of Section IV. In the meantime developments in the distinctly less radical area of employee share ownership will be reviewed.

III EMPLOYEE SHARE OWNERSHIP

A second way of increasing employee influence in the company is by means of employee share ownership rather than direct participation in decision-making.[85] This route envisages no necessary changes in the institutions of company law or in the structure of the relationship between labour and capital. Rather, workers attain a dual capacity, becoming investors in the enterprise as well as its employees. The main aims of employee share ownership in practice have been to improve efficiency by providing employees with increased incentives and to encourage a sense of identity with the company (and to take advantage of tax subsidies), rather than to put employees into a shareholding position from which they can exert influence over management for their own ends. The object has been, in other words, to achieve financial participation rather than participation in decision-making. At least in principle, however, employee share ownership is capable of having control effects if employees hold a sufficient proportion of the company's equity.

Schemes to enable employees to share in the profits of the enterprises in which they work date from the middle of the nineteenth century.[86] Where these have involved employee shareholdings they have generally resulted in employees having only a small proportionate stake in the company, though there are a few celebrated examples of ownership of the entire enterprise being transferred to the employees.[87] From the 1970s governments have encouraged financial participation by providing tax incentives. Employee

[85] See J. Cornford, *A Stake in the Company: Shareholding, Ownership and ESOPs* (1990), at 17 and generally. Employees have, of course, substantial indirect interests in the shares of many companies, often including the one for which they work, by reason of membership of an occupational pension scheme. Employees have no effective control over the shareholdings in the fund, however, notwithstanding occasional employee representation on the board of trustees: see Minns, *Pension Funds and British Capitalism* (above, n. 4), ch. 5; Schuller, *Age, Capital and Democracy* (above, n. 4), ch. 4; Schuller, *Democracy at Work* (above, n. 77), ch. 5. For a discussion of the 'democratization' of capital through collective ownership in employee or 'wage-earner' funds, see n.5 above.

[86] See M. Poole, *The Origins of Economic Democracy: Profit-Sharing and Employee-Shareholding Schemes* (1989), at 8–14.

[87] The best known is the John Lewis Partnership, where in two settlements in 1929 and 1950 the whole of the voting capital was transferred to trustees to be held on behalf of the employees. The constitutional structure, however, limits the participation of employees in decision-making: see K. Bradley and S. Taylor, *Business Performance in the Retail Sector: The Experience of the John Lewis Partnership* (1992), chs 4 and 5.

shareholding has been considered worthy of state support in order to increase employee motivation and hence productivity[88] and to spread share ownership, not latterly with an egalitarian motive, but in order to promote 'popular capitalism' and the 'property-owning democracy'.[89] Government policy has also been influenced by the claimed macro-economic benefits of transforming existing pay arrangements by substituting for them a low fixed wage supplemented by profit-sharing (thus reducing the marginal cost of labour and increasing pay flexibility, resulting in higher levels of employment and greater employment stability, and thereby removing the inhibitions on enforcement of a rigorous anti-inflation policy).[90] The evidence on the impact of financial participation on enterprise performance is mixed, but in general it suggests positive effects on productivity.[91] These have tended to be small, though this may be reflective of the low proportion of employees' overall income that is derived at the present time from profit-sharing arrangements. As to the macro-economic argument, the assumptions on which it is based are subject to dispute,[92] though regardless of its validity profit-sharing is currently insufficiently widespread to have a significant macro-economic effect.[93]

A variety of employee share schemes attract tax advantages, both for the company and the employee, notably approved (by the Inland Revenue) profit-sharing schemes, save as you earn share option schemes, and discretionary share option schemes, introduced at different dates but now all consolidated in the Income and Corporation Taxes Act 1988.[94] Discretionary schemes are used in practice almost exclusively to provide benefits for directors and senior management, and these are operated by more than twice the number of companies operating all-employee schemes. Nevertheless in 1985 41 per cent of listed companies had at least one all-employee scheme, and it has been estimated that in 1988 more than two million employees

---

[88] See M. Uvalic, 'The Pepper Report: Promotion of Employee Participation in Profits and Enterprise Results in the Member States of the European Community', *Social Europe, Supplement 3/91* (1991), at 12–13. The report notes, at 13, that in some quarters the incentive effects 'are expected to be greater if employees are also involved in decision-making. The combination of employee financial participation *and* decisional participation is considered useful particularly in adjusting to a crisis, and hence a viable alternative to bankruptcy or costly subsidies to ailing concerns' (emphasis in original).

[89] Ibid. at 148–51; see also Schuller, *Democracy at Work* (above, n. 84), at 58–62.

[90] Ideas promoted by M. Wietzman and J. Meade: see the discussion in The Pepper Report (above, n. 88), at 13–15, and Cornford, *A Stake in the Company* (above, n. 85), at 35–7. These proposals explicitly exclude employee participation in decision making, which could lead to restrictive employment policies in order to increase the profit share of existing employees.

[91] The survey evidence is summarized in The Pepper Report, (above, n.88), at 161–5, and 186–8. The studies do not all compare like with like, some taking account of cash-based profit sharing as well as employee share ownership.

[92] See the material in n. 90 above.

[93] *Butterworths UK Tax Guide 1992–93* (1992), para 6.81–2.

[94] 'The Pepper Report' (above, n.88), at 151–61.

were involved in approved all-employee share schemes. Whatever the income and wealth effects of financial participation, however (and these too appear to be fairly small),[95] the impact of employee share ownership on control, which is the main concern here, is negligible. In one survey, for example, 56 per cent of respondent companies indicated that less than 1 per cent of their shares were held by employees, with only two companies approaching the 10 per cent limit set by the investment protection committees of the institutional investors on permissible holdings in employee schemes.[96] The picture is therefore one of employee share ownership having no significant effect in increasing employee influence over the companies in which they work.

A way in which the percentage holdings of employees might be raised is through the use of employee share ownership plans ('ESOPs'), which have operated in the United States since the 1970s but have been set up in this country only more recently and are still very few in number.[97] The details of ESOPs vary,[98] but in essence they involve the use of a trust, the employees' benefit trust ('EBT'), which buys shares in the company with funds provided either by the company itself or a third-party lender or both. Where the EBT uses borrowed funds the loan, which will be secured on the shares, is gradually paid off by a combination of contributions from the company, deductions from earnings, or dividend income. The shares are made available to employees via an employee share scheme in order to benefit from the tax exemptions, though they are not usually distributed until the loan has been discharged. The principle virtue of ESOPs in terms of building up a significant employee stake in the company is that they provide access to credit. As Cornford explains, 'employees cannot normally afford to buy shares on any substantial scale nor to borrow to do so either. The ESOP is a device which permits employees to borrow money to buy shares and to repay the borrowing from the future flow of income to which ownership of those shares entitles them'.[99] In addition, since ESOPs can buy shares on the market, they do not fall within the restrictions imposed by institutional investors on the issuing of new shares to employee schemes, though in fact

[95] See ibid. at 160–1.
[96] L. Baddon, et al. *People's Capitalism? A Critical Analysis of Profit-Sharing and Employee Share Ownership* (1989), at 65.
[97] See 'The Pepper Report' (above, n. 88), at 158–9.
[98] An ESOP may be a 'case-law' ESOP, or an Employee Share Ownership Plan or 'statutory ESOP' established under the Finance Act 1989, ss 66–74, and sch 5. Under the latter the company's contributions are deductible from profits for corporation tax purposes, but a number of requirements as to the nature of the scheme must be satisfied (e.g. a majority of the trustees must be employees, elected by the employees) which is said to make the statutory ESOP unattractive to employers: see Cornford, *A Stake in the Company* (above, n. 85), at 27–31. It has been established in any event that contributions to a caselaw ESOP are deductible (see *Bott (E) Ltd v Price* [1987] STC 100), thus making it possible to gain the benefits without the disadvantages of the statutory form.
[99] Cornford, *A Stake in the Company* (above, n. 85), at 13.

the institutions impose limits on the proportion of profits that may be contributed to an EBT with which many companies may feel constrained to comply.

In the United States it has been estimated that there are now over 10,000 ESOPs, covering 11 million employees.[100] Further, while in 1985 the median ESOP owned only 5 per cent of the company's equity, 19 per cent had acquired 25 per cent or more of the voting shares. These figures open up the possibility that in due course a significant number of US ESOPs will accumulate a majority interest in their companies,[101] and in themselves they suggest employee holdings which in aggregate are significant from a control point of view. It has been concluded, however, that 'very few ESOPs have to date exerted any substantial impact on the governance of their firms' with, for example, only 4 per cent of companies having an employee representative on the board, and, in the survey in question, no companies having majority employee board representation.[102] A number of factors appear to explain this. In the United States ESOP trusts in publicly traded companies are required to 'pass through' the voting rights attached to the shares they hold to the employees individually. The trustees, who are appointed by management, are entitled to vote unvoted shares at their discretion, however, and invariably support the board. The absence of employee representation may be explicable similarly by a tendency on the part of employees to adopt a pro-management position. Thus Herman suggests that employees may use their votes in support of the existing management as an expression of gratitude for what is perceived to be management largesse, and also because the employees with the most votes are those with the longest tenure, who are likely to have close ties to management.[103] These results are perhaps not surprising, given that companies establish ESOPs 'at their own initiative to suit their own ends'.[104] The experience with ESOPs in this country is as yet too slight to enable any conclusions to be drawn about their effects on company control and policy.

IV WORKER-CONTROLLED ENTERPRISES

It was noted in Section II that in companies subject to co-determination there are structural limitations to the ability of employee representatives to

[100] Ibid. at 13–14.
[101] R. Russell, 'Taking Stock of ESOPs', in Lammers and Széll, *International Handbook of Participation in Organizations* (above, n. 21) 50, at 55.
[102] Ibid.
[103] Herman, *Corporate Control, Corporate Power* (above, n. 62), at 151–2.
[104] Russell, 'Taking Stock of ESOPs' (above, n. 101), at 54. These ends include reducing the vulnerability of the company to take-over by placing a major share stake in friendly hands: see ibid.

determine policy, given the continued presence of counter-balancing share-holder representation. If these limitations are to be overcome it is necessary to remove the control rights of capital. Enterprises which meet this requirement—cooperatives—have long been a feature of the British economy. The defining characteristics of cooperatives are as follows, though in practice not all of them exhibit all the characteristics in the 'pure' form. The first is that voting rights are confined to members, that is, all those who work in the cooperative, and are allocated on the 'one person one vote' principle. Ultimate control over the enterprise is thus vested exclusively in the workforce. Second, profits or the residual income of the firm are attributable only to those who work in it, in accordance with their labour contribution. Capital used by the firm, whether provided by members or outsiders, is paid for at the market rate, but does not give a right to participate in profits. Accordingly, in the worker-controlled firm[105] labour hires capital, rather than the reverse as is the case in the conventional firm. The objection that in capitalist firms property owners exploit labour is therefore overcome.[106] The third right that must be allocated in all enterprises, in addition to control rights and rights to the residual income, is the right to the firm's net value, that is, its original endowment as increased or depreciated by subsequent trading. The practice in cooperatives varies in this respect. In firms conforming to the Industrial Common Ownership Movement ('ICOM') model rules the cooperative's assets are owned collectively. This means that the members have no divisible interest in the property employed in the cooperative and hence have no right, for example, to withdraw funds when they leave. Some co-operatives on the other hand (for example, those adopting the Co-opera-tive Producer Federation ('CPF') model) have rules that provide for severable property interests, allowing members to participate in the growth of the capital value of the enterprise.

The cooperative sector in this country is very small, with the majority of firms having only a handful of members, often in service industries and usually employing very low levels of capital.[107] Cooperative ventures exist on a more significant scale abroad, however, notably in France and Italy, and the Mondragon group of cooperatives in the Basque region of Spain is now well-known.[108] It is not intended to discuss the structure of cooperatives or other worker-controlled firms at length. The primary concern of this book is

[105] The term 'worker-controlled firm' will be used narrowly, to exclude e.g. firms with a conventional corporate structure in which all the shares happen to be held by employees. Here voting rights are attached to property rather than employment status, similarly the entitlement to profits.

[106] There are also likely to be narrower differentials in remuneration between different grades of worker than in conventional firms: see S. Estrin, 'Workers' Co-operatives: Their Merits and Their Limitations' (above, n. 15), at 171–2.

[107] See ibid. at 166–9; Oakeshott, *The Case for Workers' Co-ops* (above, n. 1), chs 5–7.

[108] See Oakeshott ibid. chs 8–11.

with conventional companies and the objectives that companies should pursue in capitalist economies. There will, however, be a brief discussion of the charge that worker-controlled firms are inherently inefficient, and therefore that a movement towards the democratization of the economy through the promotion of worker-controlled firms on a significantly larger scale would result in a serious loss of efficiency overall. This charge has been much disputed, or, at least, ways have been suggested by which the problems might be overcome. If the case for the existing form of corporate enterprise rests on its capacity to generate wealth, that case is clearly weakened if other forms of enterprise, whose democratic structure makes them attractive on that account, are not significantly less efficient. Three objections to worker-controlled firms on efficiency grounds will be considered, each suggesting that individual private ownership, lacking in this form of enterprise, plays a crucial role in securing the efficient operation of undertakings.

Controlling Shirking

The first argument is that worker-controlled firms are inefficient because they cannot provide adequate discipline to control shirking.[109] While it is in the interests of all the members for everyone to work hard, each individual member has an incentive not to pull his or her weight, since the gain to that member in terms of increased leisure or comfort will easily outweigh the individual financial loss that shirking involves. The argument is, therefore, that because all members will attempt to free ride on the efforts of others, worker-controlled enterprises will be less productive than equivalent conventional firms. As against this it has been suggested that shirking will be controlled in the workplace because members will recognize that their own self-interest dictates that they cooperate with others in order to induce reciprocal value-increasing behaviour and to avoid social sanctions, such as ostracism.[110] The imposition of sanctions necessitates a system of mutual monitoring to detect violations, however, and, since monitoring is not itself costless and brings only marginal benefits to the individual engaging in it, it is objected that a second-order free-rider problem will arise. The extent to which these rational choice speculations are likely to be borne out in practice is unclear, but a counter-argument may be noted to the effect that a system of mutual monitoring might actually be more efficient than hierarchical monitoring, in that peer-group surveillance might be expected to be more pervasive than supervision from above.[111]

---

[109] See A. Alchian and H. Demsetz, 'Production, Information Costs, and Economic Organization', (1972) 62 *Am Econ Rev* 777; B. Chiplin and J. Coyne, 'Property Rights, Industrial Democracy and the Bullock Report', in Chiplin and Coyne (eds), *Can Workers Manage?* (1977).

[110] See Elster and Moene, introduction, in *Alternatives to Capitalism* (above, n. 19), at 28–9.

[111] See Bradley and Taylor, *Business Performance in the Retail Sector* (above, n. 87), at 98.

The main response to the argument about shirking in worker-controlled enterprises, however, is that there is no reason why it should not be controlled in the same way as it is in conventional firms, that is, through a formal system of supervision. Other than in the very smallest organizations efficiency demands the delegation of substantial powers, including powers of supervision, to specialist management. This is not inconsistent with the cooperative ideal, so long as management is elected by and accountable to the workforce. But the counter-charge is then that supervision can be effective only where the supervisor has an incentive in the form of a right to the residual income generated by the business, that is, has rights of private ownership in the firm. Thus 'to minimize shirking behaviour . . . a bundle of property rights must be invested in the monitor . . . This bundle of rights defines the ownership of the traditional free-enterprise firm'.[112] The relevant bundle of rights is, by definition, missing in a worker-controlled firm.

The force of this contrast depends, however, on assumptions about the effectiveness of monitoring in the traditional enterprise. In companies of any size the residuary claimants - the shareholders—do not monitor the behaviour of individual employees, though they may monitor the performance of the enterprise as a whole. The notion is that by exerting pressure on management the shareholders set in motion a process whereby each level in the organizational hierarchy monitors the behaviour of the level below it, and hence ensures the productivity of each stage and ultimately of the entire workforce. However, as has been discussed earlier, shareholder monitoring and control, either where it relies on internal governance controls (which themselves suffer from free-riding problems) or on market mechanisms, is in practice consistent with high levels of managerial slack. Those responsible within the organization for eliminating shirking do not, in short, have an open-ended entitlement to profits, and those who do have that entitlement are able to control the former only imperfectly. This being so, it is not self-evident that managers accountable to and removable by a sovereign body of worker members (who also would have an open-ended right to profits) would be less effective in dealing with the shirking problem.

Allocative Efficiency

The argument that an economy composed of worker-controlled firms will be characterized by allocative inefficiency focuses on the idea that such firms have a different economic goal from the capitalist firm, and will accordingly be less responsive to market signals. The goal of cooperators is assumed to be

---

[112] Chiplin and Coyne (above, n. 109), at 25, quoted in G. M. Hodgson, *The Democratic Economy* (1984), at 140.

the maximization of their individual incomes, rather than the maximization of the profits of the enterprise. From this it follows that a worker-controlled firm will not be as responsive to rises in demand as an equivalent capitalist firm, because it will adopt a more restrictive policy towards increasing employment to meet that demand. The capitalist firm will raise employment where the marginal return from so doing exceeds the marginal cost. The co-operative, on the other hand, will take on more labour only so long as this has the effect of increasing the incomes of the existing members. This may be illustrated by an example.[113] Assume that a worker who could be hired for £50 will earn £51 for the co-operative. If workers doing the same job currently earn £55, the effect of taking the worker on, and paying him or her at the same rate,[114] will be to dilute the return to the existing members and so the firm has a disincentive to recruit. Thus, even though taking on an additional worker would produce a positive marginal return, since the effect would be to lower the incomes of the existing members expansion to the socially efficient level is unlikely to take place. An ameliorating factor is that the firm may react to the rise in demand by making production more capital-intensive, and hence the level of output may in due course approach the optimal one. This will occur, however, only if it is anticipated that the increase in demand will be sustained, and the process of adjustment is likely in any case to be slower than where increased demand is initially met by raising employment.[115]

The reply to this objection by supporters of cooperatives is that while worker-controlled enterprises may individually adopt restrictive employment policies and hence will be weakly responsive to changes in demand, this need not be the result at the level of the economy as a whole, since unmet demand will create profit opportunities that will provide the incentive for the introduction of additional capacity in the shape of new firms. As Estrin points out, however, apart again from the slowness of response, the problem then shifts to the relative difficulty of forming worker-controlled firms.[116] The entrepreneurial drive that brings new enterprises into being may be dulled where profits must be shared with fellow cooperators, and the additional

[113] Taken from Miller, *Market, State and Community* (above, n. 3), at 85.
[114] As Miller points out there will be a temptation to pay the employee at the market rate in the same way that a capitalist firm would. This would, however, be inconsistent with cooperative principles. These do not require that all employees be paid the same amount (which would prevent pay from acting as a signalling device to attract labour to its most productive use), but rather that the relationship between members be non-exploitative.
[115] A cooperative might alternatively respond to increased demand by reducing production, since increased demand will result in higher prices allowing incomes to be held constant at lower output. Cooperators will not be motivated strictly to maximize income, but overall welfare, and this is a function not only of income, but also duration and conditions of work: see Estrin, 'Workers Co-operatives' (above, n. 15), at 176.
[116] Ibid. at 177.

search costs involved in bringing together potential cooperators are also likely to restrict entry.

In addition to the inefficiencies associated with the creation and growth of worker-controlled firms, it should also be noted that a misallocation of resources may occur as a result of the reluctance of cooperatives to contract or close down once they have become uneconomic. The members may be tempted to continue in business out of a sense of loyalty or inertia when it is clear that they and the capital resources employed in the firm could be used more efficiently elsewhere. It has been suggested that solutions to these problems of enterprise formation, growth, and termination may lie in the creation of appropriate external financing bodies. The possibilities will be considered shortly below.

Investment

As well as being less responsive to market conditions than capitalist firms, cooperatives may, depending on their structure, have the separate drawback of a tendency to under-invest.[117] The root of this problem lies in the absence of individual ownership rights in the enterprise (this assumes that the cooperative's assets are owned collectively, rather than the members having individuated interests, as is permitted under the CPF rules). If the cooperators have no claims on the capital of the business (for example, a right to withdraw their 'share' when they leave), whether it is worthwhile from an individual point of view to invest in the assets of the enterprise will depend entirely on the income return on the investment during the period of membership. In contrast, in a capitalist firm an investment will result not only in increased income, but also an increase in the value of the firm, in which the owner will have a marketable interest. The effect of this is that the rate of return that must be expected before an investment will be considered worthwhile in a cooperative will be higher than that in a traditional firm.[118] The extent of the divergence depends on the time horizons of the cooperators—the longer they expect to stay with the cooperative the longer will be the period in which they will benefit from the investment, and hence the smaller will be the gap. This does make clear, however, that in cooperatives organized on the basis of collective ownership there is a divergence between the interests of the members and the wider social interest in securing an appropriate level of investment in the economy.

As mentioned, this problem is a consequence of the absence of individual

---

[117] See Miller (above, n. 3), at 85–90; Estrin, ibid. at 179–81.

[118] This problem might be overcome through external borrowing, but cooperatives experience difficulties in obtaining loan finance in a capitalist economy: see Miller, *Market, State and Community* (above, n. 3), at 88–90.

rights in the capital of the firm. It is avoided where the members each have an ownership stake that will appreciate as the firm invests, thus removing the pressure to distribute an excessive proportion of the firm's trading surplus as income. A compromise that takes account of this appears to be an important reason for the success of the Mondragon cooperatives. Capital is divided into a collectively owned component and a balance that is credited to individual members' capital accounts. The members make a contribution to capital on joining (part of which may be borrowed from the co-operative), and the amount returned on leaving will be increased (or reduced) to reflect the change in value of the firm. In this way the member is given an interest in the long-term future of the undertaking.[119]

A more radical solution to the problem of under-investment, and which seems better suited to situations in which very large amounts of capital are required, is that the members should not own the assets at all, either collectively or individually, but rather that capital should be hired from an outside provider. The investment problem would therefore be solved, it is argued, on the basis that in this system the cost of capital would simply be the market rate, in the same way that it is for a capitalist firm: the members would no longer be 'locking in' value in a collective asset that they are unable to realize. Accordingly, *ex hypothesi* they would decide to invest whenever the expected rate of return on the proposed investment was greater than the rate at which they could hire funds, which is the socially optimal position as well.[120] It has been suggested that external providers of capital could also play a vital role in forming and closing worker-controlled firms, performing the 'entrepreneurial function of spotting new profitable openings, and transferring resources from low to high productivity uses'[121] that is otherwise likely to be inadequately performed in an economy made up of worker-controlled firms. By regulating the entry and exit of firms into the economy these bodies would in addition, it is contended, be in a position to offset the problems of resource misallocation that result from the reluctance of cooperatives to expand employment sufficiently to meet increased demand, and to stay in business notwithstanding that their assets are under-employed.

[119] See Oakeshott, *The Case for Workers' Co-ops* (above, n. 1), at 190–4; Cornford, *A Stake in the Company* (above, n. 85), at 20–1.

[120] See Estrin, 'Workers' Co-operatives' (above, n. 15), at 185–92. A serious problem that would remain is that in the case of a capital-intensive cooperative, a small reduction in the cooperative's earnings would have a serious effect on the incomes of the members (a problem similar to high gearing in a company): see J. Meade, 'Labour Co-operatives, Participation and Value-Added Sharing', in A. Clayre (ed.), *The Political Economy of Co-operation and Participation* (1980) 89. The payment for capital need not, however, be regarded as a committment that must be met in all circumstances before the members could draw an income, i.e. fluctuations could be ironed out by flexibility on the part of the provider of capital. An inability to pay the cost of capital on a continuing basis would, however, be a sign that the cooperative should be terminated.

[121] Estrin, 'Workers' Co-operatives' (above, n. 15), at 187.

The nature of the bodies that would be charged with the responsibility of providing capital and of forming and overseeing the operation of worker-controlled firms is clearly of crucial importance to this scheme. Estrin envisages a large number of competitive, privately owned agencies (on the assumption that 'fundamental redistributive policies' have already been executed) lending funds on a basis that will maximize the profits of the agency, thereby ensuring that capital is employed in its most productive use.[122] But there are clearly other possibilities, including various forms of public ownership, one example involving a plurality of autonomous funding bodies organized on a regional basis. And mechanisms might be developed that would allow the distribution of funds in accordance with criteria that take account of objectives that would be excluded on a purely profit-maximizing approach, such as reducing sectoral or regional unemployment.[123]

Conclusion

Whether the arguments for worker-controlled firms are valid or not, the conversion of large companies to worker control is not currently on the political agenda. Cooperatives, at least in this country, seem likely for the foreseeable future to remain small in scale and to be confined to activities with low capital requirements. Any significant developments in worker participation in decision-making in larger organizations are more likely to take place within the context of the existing corporate form, though here too the prospects at present appear limited.

Looking back over the previous four chapters it seems appropriate to conclude with two points. The first is to stress the importance of finding improved methods of corporate governance. What is needed is mechanisms that will secure the efficient operation of the business, but which will not at the same time render management impervious to considerations other than maximum profits. Unless managers operate in a disciplinary framework that allows them to trade off profits in favour of third-party interests, other measures to increase responsibility are likely to have rather limited results. Some suggestions in outline about how such a framework might be constructed were considered at the end of Chapter 11, and there are various ways in which the input of employees could be combined with that framework, as noted in this chapter. The second point is that any changes designed to increase corporate social responsiveness that are liable to add significantly to companies' costs cannot in an increasingly global marketplace be safely introduced in one country. Whether the changes are in governance structures, or are measures to stimulate responsibility, or are more stringent

---

[122] Ibid. at 187–92.
[123] See Miller, *Market, State and Community* (above, n.3), at 309–12.

conventional regulatory controls, they will need to apply more widely if domestic economies are not to be disadvantaged in the face of international competition. In Europe, this emphasizes the importance of the social, in addition to the economic dimension of European collaboration.

Bibliography

Accounting Standards Board, *Operating and Financial Review* (London, 1992).

Accounting Standards Steering Committee, *The Corporate Report* (London, 1975).

Acton, Lord, *The History of Freedom and Other Essays* (London, 1907).

Adams, R., Carruthers, J., and Hamil, S., *Changing Corporate Values: A Guide to Social and Environmental Policy and Practice in Britains' Top Companies* (London, 1991).

Alchian, A. and Demsetz, H., 'Production, Information Costs, and Economic Organization', (1972) 62 *American Economic Review* 777.

Alexander, Lord, 'Investor Relations—Does the British System Work?', in National Association of Pension Funds, *Creative Tension?* (London, 1990), 1.

Alford, B.W.E., 'The Chandler Thesis—Some General Observations', in L. Hannah (ed.), *Management Strategy and Business Development* (London, 1976), 52.

Allied Research International, *The Views of Shareholders on Donations by Companies to Charity*, Report to the Charities Aid Foundation (London, 1985).

American Law Institute Corporate Governance Project, *Principles of Corporate Governance: Analysis and Recommendations* (Philadelphia, 1992).

Anderman, S.D., *Labour Law: Managerial Decisions and Workers' Rights* (London, 1992).

Anon.,'The Propriety of Judicial Deference to Corporate Boards', (1983) 96 *Harvard Law Review* 1894.

Arrow, K. J., 'Gifts and Exchanges', in E. S. Phelps, *Altruism, Morality and Economic Theory* (New York, 1975), 13.

Ashworth, A., *Principles of Criminal Law* (Oxford, 1991).

Association for Business Sponsorship of the Arts, *Annual Report 1989* (London, 1989).

—— *An Overall Total for Business Sponsorship of the Arts During 1990/91* (London, 1991).

Atiyah, P. S., *The Rise and Fall of Freedom of Contract* (Oxford, 1979).

Auditing Practices Board, *The Future Development of Auditing: A Paper to Promote Public Debate* (London, 1992).

Auditing Practices Committee, *The Auditor's Responsibility in Relation to Fraud, Other Irregularities and Errors* (London, 1990).

Axworthy, C. S., 'Corporate Directors—Who Needs Them?', (1988) 51 *Modern Law Review* 273.

Baddon, L. et al., *People's Capitalism? A Critical Analysis of Profit-Sharing and Employee Ownership* (London, 1989).

Baker, C. D., 'Disclosure of Directors' Interests in Contracts', [1975] *Journal of Business Law* 181.

Barry, N., *The Morality of Business Enterprise* (Aberdeen, 1991).

Batstone, E., 'Industrial Democracy and Worker Representation at Board Level: A Review of the European Experience', in E. Batstone and P. L. Davies, *Industrial Democracy: European Experience* (London, 1976), 9.

Batstone, E., Ferner, F., and Terry, M., *Unions on the Board* (Oxford, 1983).

Baumol, W. J., *Business Behavior, Value and Growth*, rev. ed. (New York, 1966).

—— 'Business Responsibility and Economic Behavior', in E. S. Phelps, (ed.), *Altruism, Morality and Economic Theory* (New York, 1975), 46.

—— '(Almost) Perfect Competition (Contestability) and Business Ethics', in W.J. Baumol, and S. A. B. Blackman, (eds.) *Perfect Markets and Easy Virtue: Business Ethics and the Invisible Hand* (Cambridge, Mass., 1991) .

Baxter, C., 'The True Spirit of *Foss v Harbottle*', (1987) 38 *Northern Ireland Legal Quarterly* 6.

Baysinger, B. D. and Butler, H. N., 'The Role of Corporate Law in the Theory of the Firm', (1985) 28 *Journal of Law and Economics* 179.

Bebchuk, L. A., 'The Case for Facilitating Tender Offers', (1982) 95 *Harvard Law Review* 1028.

—— 'The Debate on Contractual Freedom in Corporate Law', (1989) 89 *Columbia Law Review* 1395.

Beck, S. M., 'The Saga of Peso Silver Mines: Corporate Opportunity Reconsidered', (1971) 49 *Canadian Bar Review* 80.

—— 'Corporate Power and Public Policy', in I. Bernier and A. Lajoie (eds), *Consumer Protection, Environmental Law and Corporate Power*, Royal Commission on the Economic Union and Development Prospects for Canada, vol. 50 (Toronto, 1985), 181.

Beed, C. S., 'The Separation of Ownership from Control', (1966) 1 *Journal of Economic Studies* 29.

Bennett, D. M. J., 'The Ascertainment of Purpose when Bona Fides are in Issue— Some Logical Problems', (1989) 12 *Sydney Law Review* 5.

Berger, P. L., *The Capitalist Revolution* (Aldershot, 1987).

Bergman, D., *Deaths at Work: Accidents or Corporate Crime* (London, 1991).

Berle, A. A., 'Corporate Powers as Powers in Trust', (1931) 44 *Harvard Law Review* 1049.

—— 'For Whom Corporate Managers *Are* Trustees: A Note', (1932) 45 *Harvard Law Review* 1365.

—— *The 20th Century Capitalist Revolution* (New York, 1954).

—— *Power without Property* (London, 1960).

—— 'Modern Functions of the Corporate System', (1962) 62 *Columbia Law Review* 433.

Berle, A. A. and Means, G. C., *The Modern Corporation and Private Property* (New York, 1932, rev. ed. 1967).

Biendenkopt Report: *Co-determination in the Company, Report of the Committee of Experts*, trans. D. O'Neill (Belfast, 1970).

Bircher, P., 'Company Law Reform and the Board of Trade, 1929–1943', (1988) 18 *Accounting and Business Research* 107.

Birds, J. R., 'Proper Purposes as a Head of Fiduciary Duty', (1974) 37 *Modern Law Review* 580.

—— 'The Permissible Scope of Articles Excluding the Duties of Company Directors', (1976) 39 *Modern Law Review* 394.

—— 'Excluding the Duties of Directors', (1988) 8 *Company Lawyer* 31.

Bishop, J. W., 'Sitting Ducks and Decoy Ducks: New Trends in the Indemnification of Corporate Directors and Officers', (1966) 77 *Yale Law Journal* 1078.

Bishop, W. and Prentice, D. D., 'Some Legal and Economic Aspects of Fiduciary Remuneration', (1983) 46 *Modern Law Review* 289.

Black, B. S., 'Shareholder Passivity Reexamined', (1990) 89 *Michigan Law Review* 520.

—— 'Agents Watching Agents: The Promise of Institutional Investor Voice', (1992) 39 *UCLA Law Review* 811.

Blumberg, P. I., 'Limited Liability and Corporate Groups', (1986) 11 *Journal of Corporation Law* 573.

—— *The Law of Corporate Groups: The Substantive Law* (Boston, 1987).

Board of Trade, *The Savoy Hotel Ltd and the Berkeley Hotel Company Ltd: Investigation under Section 165(3) of the Companies Act 1948, Report of E. Milner Holland Q.C.* (London, 1954).

Boswell, J. S., *Business Policies in the Making: Three Steel Companies Compared* (London, 1983).

—— 'The Informal Social Control of Business in Britain, 1880 - 1939', (1983) 57 *Business History Review* 2.

—— *Community and the Economy: The Theory of Public Co-operation* (London, 1990).

Boswell, J. S. and Johns, B. R., 'Patriots or Profiteers? British Businessmen and the First World War', (1982) 11 *Journal of European Economic History* 2.

Boyle, A. J., 'The Private Law Enforcement of Directors' Duties', in K. J. Hopt and G. Teubner (eds), *Corporate Governance and Directors' Liabilities* (Berlin, 1985), 261.

—— 'The Judicial Review of the Special Litigation Committee: The Implications for the English Derivative Action after Smith v Croft', (1990) 11 *Company Lawyer* 3.

—— 'Barriers to Contested Takeovers in the European Community', (1991) 12 *Company Lawyer* 19.

—— 'Draft Fifth Directive: Implications for Directors' Duties, Board Structure and Employee Participation', (1992) 13 *Company Lawyer* 6.

—— (ed.), *Gore-Browne on Companies* 44th ed., (Bristol, 1986).

Bracewell-Milnes, J. B., *Are Equity Markets Short Sighted?: Short-termism and Its Critics*, Report for the Institute of Directors (London, 1987).

Bradley, C., 'Corporate Control: Markets and Rules', (1990) 53 *Modern Law Review* 170.

Bradley, I. C., *Enlightened Entrepreneurs* (London, 1986).

Bradley, K., and Taylor, S., *Business Performance in the Retail Sector: The Experience of the John Lewis Partnership* (Oxford, 1992).

Braithwaite, J. and Geis, G., 'On Theory and Action for Corporate Crime Control', (1982) 28 *Crime and Delinquency* 292.

Brannen, P. et al., *The Worker Directors: A Sociology of Participation* (London, 1976).

Bratton, W. W., 'The New Economic Theory of the Firm: Critical Perspectives from History', (1989) 41 *Stanford Law Review* 1471.

—— 'The "Nexus of Contracts" Corporation: A Critical Appraisal', (1989) 74 *Cornell Law Review* 407.

Brealey, R. A. and Myres, S. C., *Principles of Corporate Finance*, 4th ed., (New York, 1991).

Bronfenbrenner, M., 'The Consumer', in J. W. McKie (ed.), *Social Responsibility and the Business Predicament* (Washington, 1974).

Brudney, V., 'Dividends, Discretion and Disclosure', (1980) 66 *University of Virginia Law Review* 85.

—— 'The Independent Director—Heavenly City or Potemkin Village', (1982) 95 *Harvard Law Review* 597.

—— 'Corporate Governance, Agency Costs and the Rhetoric of Contract', (1985) 85 *Columbia Law Review* 1403.

Brudney, V. and Clark, R. C., 'A New Look at Corporate Opportunites', (1981) 94 *Harvard Law Review* 998.

Burke, T. and Hill, J., *Ethics, Environment and the Company: A Guide to Effective Action* (London, 1990).

Burnside, A., 'Overcoming Barriers to European M & A', (1992) 13 *Company Lawyer* 19.

Burridge, S. J., 'Wrongful Rights Issues', (1981) 44 *Modern Law Review* 40

Business in the Community, *Guidelines on Corporate Responsibility* (London, 1990).

Butler, H. N., 'The Contractual Theory of the Corporation', (1989) 11 *George Mason University Law Review* 999.

Butler, H. N. and Ribstein, L. E., 'Opting Out of Fiduciary Duties: A Response to the Anti—Contractarians', (1990) 65 *Washington Law Review* 1.

Butterworths *UK Tax Guide 1992/3* (London, 1992).

Buxbaum, R. M., 'Corporate Legitimacy, Economic Theory and Legal Doctrine', (1984) 45 *Ohio State Law Journal* 515.

Carlton, D. W. and Fischel, D. R., 'The Regulation of Insider Dealing', (1985) 14 *Stanford Law Review* 857.

Carty, J., 'Accounting for Takeovers', in A. Cosh et al., *Takeovers and Short-Termism in the UK*, IPPR Policy Paper no. 3 (London, 1990), 21.

Casson, M., *The Economics of Business Culture: Game Theory, Transaction Costs and Economic Performance* (Oxford, 1991).

Centre for Employment Initiatives, *Seconds Out* (London, 1988).

Chaiken, D., 'The Companies Act 1981 (3)', (1982) 3 *Company Lawyer* 115.

Chandler, A. D., *Strategy and Structure: Chapters in the History of American Industrial Enterprise* (Cambridge, Mass., 1962).

—— 'The Development of Modern Management Stucture in the US and UK', in L. Hannah (ed.), *Management Strategy and Business Development* (London, 1976), 24.

—— *The Visible Hand: The Managerial Revolution in American Business* (Cambridge, Mass., 1977) .

Channon, D. F., 'Corporate Evolution in the Service Industries', in L. Hannah (ed.), *Management Strategy and Business Development* (London, 1976), 213.

—— *Strategy and Structure of British Enterprise* (London, 1973).

Charities Aid Foundation, *Charity Trends*, 13th ed. (Tonbridge, 1990).

—— 15th ed. (Tonbridge, 1992).

Charkham, J., *Corporate Governance and the Market for Control* (London, 1989).

Chartered Institute of Management Accountants, *A Framework for Internal Control* (London, 1992).

Chayes, A., 'The Modern Corporation and the Rule of Law', in E. S. Mason (ed.), *The Corporation in Modern Society* (Cambridge, Mass., 1959), 25.

Cheffins, B. R., and Dine, J. M., 'Shareholder Remedies 1959: Lessons from Canada', (1992) 13 *Company Lawyer* 89.

Chew, P. K., 'Competing Interests in the Corporate Opportunity Doctrine', (1987) 67 *North Carolina Law Review* 435.

Chiplin, B. and Coyne, J., 'Property Rights, Industial Democracy and the Bullock Report', in B. Chiplin and J. Coyne (eds), *Can Workers Manage?* (London, 1977).

Chiplin, B. and Wright, M., *The Logic of Mergers* (London, 1987).

Chirelstein, M. A., 'Corporate Law Reform', in J. W. McKie (ed.), *Social Responsibility and the Business Predicament* (Washington, 1974), 52.

Christie, I. et al., *Profitable Partnerships: A Report on Business Involvement in the Community* (London, 1991).

Christie, M., 'The Director's Fiduciary Duty Not to Compete', (1992) 55 *Modern Law Review* 506.

Clark, R. C., 'Agency Costs Versus Fiduciary Duties', in J. W. Pratt and R. J. Zeckhauser (eds), *Principals and Agents: The Structure of Business* (Boston, 1985).

Clutterbuck, D. and Snow, D., *Working with the Community: A Guide to Corporate Social Responsibility* (London, 1990).

Coakley, J. and Harris, L., *The City of Capital* (Oxford, 1983).

Coase, R. H., 'The Nature of the Firm', (1937) ns 4 *Economica* 386.

—— 'The Problem of Social Cost', (1960) 3 *Journal of Economics* 1.

Coates, J. C., 'State Takeover Statutes and Corporate Theory: The Revival of an Old Debate', (1989) 64 *New York University Law Review* 806.

Coffee, J. C., 'No Soul to Damn: No Body to Kick: An Unscandalized Enquiry into the Problem of Corporate Punishment', (1981) 79 *Michigan Law Review* 386.

—— 'Regulating the Market For Corporate Control: A Critical Assessment of the Tender Offer's Role in Corporate Governance', (1984) 84 *Columbia Law Review* 1145.

—— 'Litigation and Corporate Governance: An Essay in Steering between Scylla and Charybdis', (1984) 52 *George Washington Law Review* 789.

—— 'Understanding the Plantiff's Attorney: the Implications of the Economic Theory for Private Enforcement of Law Through Class and Derivative Actions', (1986) 86 *Columbia Law Review* 669.

—— 'Shareholders Versus Managers: The Strain in the Corporate Web', in J. C. Coffee, L. Lowenstein, and S. Rose-Ackerman, (eds), *Knights, Raiders and Targets* (New York, 1988), 77.

—— 'No Exit? Opting Out, the Contractual Theory of the Corporation, and the Special Case of Remedies', (1988) 53 *Brooklyn Law Review* 919.

—— 'Liquidity Versus Control: The Institutional Investor as Corporate Monitor', (1991) 91 *Columbia Law Review* 1278.

Cohen, G. A., 'Nozick on Appropriation', (1985) 150 *New Left Review* 89.

Cohen, J., 'The Economic Basis of Deliberative Democracy', in E. F. Paul, F. D. Miller, and J. Paul (eds), *Socialism* (Oxford, 1989), 25.

Cohen, M. (ed.), *Ronald Dworkin and Contemporary Jurisprudence* (London, 1984).

Cohn, S. R., 'Demise of the Directors' Duty of Care: Judicial Avoidance of Standards Through the Business Judgement Rule', (1983) 62 *Texas Law Review* 591.

Coleman, J. L., *Markets, Morals and the Law* (Cambridge, 1988).

Coleman, J. S., 'Responsibility in Corporate Action: A Sociologists View', in K. J. Hopt and G. Teubner (eds), *Corporate Governance and Directors' Liabilities* (Berlin, 1985), 69.

Committee on Company Law Amendment (Cohen Committee), *Report* Cmnd. 6659 (London, 1945).

Committee on the Financial Aspects of Corporate Governance (Cadbury Committee), *Report* (London, 1992).

Committee on Safety and Health at Work (Robens Committee), *Report* Cmnd 5034, (London, 1972)

Committee to Review the Functioning of Financial Institutions, (Wilson Committee), *Report and Appendices*, Cmnd. 7939 (London, 1980).

Confederation of British Industry, *The Responsibilities of the British Public Company* (London, 1973).

—— *Company Responses to Unemployment, A Report by the Social Affairs Directorate* (London, 1981).

—— *Investing for Britain's Future: Report of the City/Industry Task Force* (London, 1987).

—— *Pension Fund Investment Management* (London, 1988).

—— *Waking Up to a Better Environment* (London, 1990).

Conrad, A. F., 'Reflections on Public Interest Directors', (1977) 75 *Michigan Law Review* 941.

—— 'Beyond Managerialism: Investor Capitalism?', (1988) 22 *University of Michigan Journal of Law Reform* 117.

Constable, J. and McCormick, R., *The Making of British Managers* (Corby, 1987).

Constitutional Reform Centre, *Company Donations to Political Parties: A Suggested Code of Practice* (London, 1985).

Cooke, C. A., *Corporation, Trust and Company* (Manchester, 1950).

Coopers & Lybrand, *Audit Committees: the Next Steps* (London, 1988).

Corkery, J. F., *Directors' Powers and Duties* (Melbourne, 1987).

Cornford, J., *A Stake in the Company: Shareholding, Ownership and ESOPs*, IPPR Economic Study no. 3 (London, 1990).

Cosh, A., 'The Remuneration of Chief Executives in the United Kingdom', (1975) 85 *Economic Journal* 75.

Cosh, A. et al., *Takeovers and Short-Termism in the UK* IPPR Policy Paper no. 3 (London, 1990).

—— 'Institutional Investment, Mergers and the Market for Corporate Control', (1989) 7 *International Journal of Industrial Economics* 73.

Council of Europe, *Liability of Enterprises for Offences*, Recommendation no. R (88) 18 (Strasbourg, 1990).

Craig, P. P., *Administrative Law*, 2nd ed. (London, 1989).

Cranston, R., *Regulating Business: Law and Consumer Agencies* (London, 1979).

—— 'Limiting Directors' Liability: Ratification, Exemption and Indemnification', [1992] *Journal of Business Law* 197.

Crosland, C. A. R., *The Future of Socialism*, revised ed. (London, 1964).

Cubbin, J. and Leech, D., 'The Effects of Shareholder Dispersion on the Degree of Control in British Companies: Theory and Measurement', (1983) 83 *Economic Journal* 351.

Cyert, R. M. and March, J. G., *A Behavioral Theory of the Firm* (Englewood Cliffs, N J, 1963).

Dahl, R. A., 'A Prelude to Corporate Reform', (1972) *Business and Society Review* 17.

—— *A Preface to Economic Democracy* (Cambridge, 1985).

Dahrendorf, R., *Class and Class Conflict in an Industrial Society* (London, 1959).

Daintith, T., 'Legal Research and Legal Values', (1989) 52 *Modern Law Review* 352.

Dallas, L. L., 'Two Models of Corporate Governance: Beyond Berle and Means', (1988) 22 *University of Michigan Journal of Law Reform* 19.

Danziger, Y. F., 'Remedial Defensive Tactics Against Takeovers', (1983) 4 *Company Lawyer* 3.

Davies, I. R. and Kelly, M., *Small Firms and the Manufacturing Sector*, Bolton Committee Research Report (London, 1973).

Davies, P., 'Employee Representation on Company Boards and Participation in Corporate Planning', (1975) 38 *Modern Law Review* 254.

—— 'Employee Experience with Worker Representation on the Board', in E. Batstone and P. L. Davies, *Industrial Democracy: European Experience* (London, 1976).

Davies, P. and Wedderburn, Lord, 'The Land of Industrial Democracy', [1977] *Industrial Law Journal* 197.

Dawson S. et al., *Safety at Work: The Limits of Self-Regulation* (London, 1988).

Demb, A. and Neubauer, F.-F., *The Corporate Board: Confronting the Paradoxes* (New York, 1992).

DeMott, D. A., 'Shareholder Litigation in Australia and the United States: Common Problems, Uncommon Solutions', (1987) 11 *Sydney Law Review* 259.

—— 'Beyond Metaphor: An Analysis of Fiduciary Obligation', [1988] *Duke Law Journal* 879.

—— 'Comparative Dimensions of Takeover Legislation' in J. C. Coffee, L. Lowenstein, and L. Rose-Ackerman (eds), *Knights, Raiders and Targets* (New York, 1988), 398.

Department of Employment, *Training in Britain: A Study of Funding, Activity and Attitudes* (London, 1989).

Department of Industry, 'The Importance of the "Top 100" Manufacturing Companies', (1976) *Economic Trends* no. 274, 85.

Department of Trade, *Report of the Company Law Committee* (The Jenkins Committee) Cmnd. 1749 (London, 1962).

—— *Report of the Committee of Enquiry on Industrial Democracy* (Bullock Committee), Cmnd. 6706 (London, 1977).

—— *Industrial Democracy*, Cmnd. 7231 (London, 1977).

Department of Trade and Industry, *Report on the Vehicle and General Insurance Co Ltd.* (London, 1972).

—— *Report on John Willmeet Automobiles Ltd* (London, 1973).

—— *Company Law Reform*, Cmnd. 5391 (London, 1973).

—— *Report on Rolls Royce Ltd.* (London, 1973).

—— *The Conduct of Company Directors*, Cmnd. 7037 (London, 1980).

—— 'Report on the Census of Production', *Business Monitor P A* 1002 (London, 1984).

—— *Mergers Policy: A Department of Trade and Industry Paper on the Policy and Procedures of Merger Control* (London, 1988).

—— *Barriers to Takeovers in the European Community: A Study by Coopers and Lybrand for the D.T.I.* (London, 1989).

—— *Companies in 1989–90* (London, 1990).

—— *Amended Proposal for a Fifth Directive on the Harmonisation of Company Law in the European Community: A Consultative Document* (London, 1990).

—— *Company Investigations: Government's Response to the Third Report of the House of Commons Trade and Industry Committee*, 1989–90 Session, Cm. 1149 (London, 1990).

—— *Barriers to Takeovers in the European Community: A Consultative Document* (London, 1990).

Department of Transport, *The Merchant Shipping Act 1894, mv Herald of Free Enterprise* (Sheen Report), (London, 1987).

—— *Investigation into the King's Cross Underground Fire* (Fennell Report), (London, 1988).

Devine, P. J. et al., *Introduction to Industrial Economics* 4th ed. (London, 1985).

Dewey, J., 'The Historic Background of Corporate Legal Personality', (1926) 35 *Yale Law Journal* 655.

Dias, R. W. N., *Jurisprudence*, 5th ed. (London, 1985).

Dierkes, M., 'Corporate Social Reporting and Auditing: Theory and Practice', in K. J. Hopt and G. Teubner (eds), *Corporate Governance and Directors' Liabilities* (Berlin, 1985), 69.

Directory of Social Change, *Company Giving News* (London, 1989).

Docksey, C., 'Information and Consultation of Employees: The Unitied Kingdom and the Vredeling Directive', (1986) 49 *Modern Law Review* 281.

Dodd, E. M., 'For Whom are Corporate Managers Trustees?', (1932) 45 *Harvard Law Review* 1145.

—— 'Is Effective Enforcement of the Fiduciary Duties of Corporate Managers Practicable?', (1935) 2 *University of Chicago Law Review* 194.

Donaldson, P. and Farquhar, J., *Understanding the British Economy* (London, 1988).

Donaldson, T., *Corporations and Morality* (Englewood Cliffs, NJ, 1982).

—— *The Ethics of International Business* (New York, 1989).

Dowie, M., 'Pinto Madness' in Hills, S. L. (ed.), *Corporate Violence: Injury and Death for Profit* (Totowa, 1987), 13.

Drury, R. R. and Xuereb, P. G. (eds), *European Company Laws: A Comparative Approach* (Aldershot, 1991).

Dubois, A. B., *The English Business Company after the Bubble Act, 1720–1800* (New York, 1938).

Dugdale, A. M., and Stanton, K. M., *Professional Negligence*, 2nd ed. (London, 1989).

Dworkin, R., *Taking Rights Seriously*, 2nd ed. (London, 1978).

—— 'Is Wealth a Value?', (1980) 9 *Journal of Legal Studies* 191.

—— *A Matter of Principle* (London, 1985).

Dymski, G. A. and Elliot, J. E., 'Capitalism and the Democratic Economy', in E. F. Paul et al. (eds), *Capitalism* (Oxford, 1989), 140.

Easterbrook, F. H. and Fischel, D. R., 'The Proper Role of a Target's Management in Responding to a Tender Offer', (1981) 94 *Harvard Law Review* 1161.

—— 'Corporate Control Transactions', (1982) 91 *Yale Law Journal* 698.

—— 'Limited Liability and the Corporation', (1985) 52 *University of Chigago Law Review* 89.

—— 'The Corporate Contract', (1989) 89 *Columbia Law Review* 1416.

—— *The Economic Structure of Corporate Law* (Cambridge, Mass., 1991).

Economist, The, 'Bosses' Pay', 1 February 1992, 22.

Edinburgh District Council, *Guinness PLC and the Scottish Economy* (Edinburgh, 1987).

Eisenberg, M. A., *The Structure of the Corporation: A Legal Analysis* (Boston, 1976).

—— 'Corporate Legitimacy, Conduct and Governance—Two Models of the Corporation', (1983) 17 *Creighton Law Review* 1.

—— 'The Structure of Corporation Law', (1989) 89 *Columbia Law Review* 1461.

Elkington, J., *The Environmental Audit: A Green Filter for Company Policies, Plants, Processes and Products* (London, 1990).

Elliot, J., *Conflict or Co-operation?: The Growth of Industrial Democracy* 2nd ed. (London, 1984).

Elster, J., 'Self-Realisation in Work and Politics: The Marxist Conception of a Good Life', in J. Elster and K. Moene, *Alternatives to Capitalism* (Cambridge, 1989), 127.

Engel, D. L., 'An Approach to Corporate Social Responsibility', (1979) 32 *Stanford Law Review* 1.

Estrin, S., 'Workers Co-operatives: their Merits and their Limitations', in J. Le Grand and S. Estrin (eds), *Market Socialism* (Oxford, 1989).

Etzioni, A., *The Moral Dimension: Towards a New Economics* (New York, 1988).

European Community, *Employee Participation and Company Structure in the European Community*, (1975) *Bull Supp* 8/75.

Evan, W. M. and Freeman, R. E., 'A Stakeholder Theory of the Modern Corporation: Kantian Capitalism', in T. L. Beauchamp and N. E. Bowie (eds), *Ethical Theory and Business*, 3rd ed. (Englewood Cliffs, NJ, 1988) 97.

Ewing, K. D., 'Company Political Donations and the Ultra Vires Rule', (1984) 47 *Modern Law Review* 57.

—— *The Funding of Political Parties in Britain* (Cambridge, 1987).

Fairburn, J. A., 'The Evaluation of Merger Policy in Britain', in J. A. Fairburn and J. A. Kay (eds), *Mergers and Merger Policy* (Oxford, 1989), 193.

Fairburn, J. A. and Geroski, P., 'The Empirical Analysis of Market Structure and Performance', in J. A. Fairburn and J. A. Kay (eds), *Mergers and Merger Policy* (Oxford, 1989).

Fama, E. F., 'Agency Problems and the Theory of the Firm', (1980) 88 *Journal of Political Economy* 288.

Fama, E. F. and Jensen, M. C., 'Separation of Ownership and Control', (1983) 26 *Journal of Law and Economics* 301.

Farrar, J. H., Furey, N. E. and Hannigan, B. M., *Farrar's Company Law* 3rd ed. (London, 1991).

Fidler, J., *The British Business Elite: Its Attitudes to Class, Status and Power* (London, 1981).

Field, S. and Jörg, N., 'Corporate Liability and Manslaughter: Should we be Going Dutch?', [1991] *Criminal Law Review* 156.

Financial Reporting Council, *The State of Financial Reporting* (London, 1991).

Finch, V. 'Company Directors: Who Cares about Skill and Care?', (1992) 55 *Modern Law Review* 179.

Finn, P. D., *Fiduciary Obligations* (Sydney, 1977).

Fischel, D. R., 'The Corporate Governance Movement', (1982) 35 *Vanderbilt Law Review* 1259.

Fisse, B., 'Recent Developments in Corporate Criminal Law and Corporate Liability to Monetary Penalties', (1990) 13 *University of New South Wales Law Journal* 1.

—— 'The Attribution of Criminal Liability to Corporations: A Statutory Model', (1991) 13 *Sydney Law Review* 277.

Fisse, B. and Braithwaite J., 'The Allocation of Responsibility for Corporate Crime: Individualism, Collectivism and Accountability', (1988) 11 *Sydney Law Review* 468.

Fitzgerald, R., *British Labour Management and Industrial Welfare 1846–1939* (London, 1988).

Florence, P. S., *Ownership, Control and Success of Large Companies* (London, 1961).

Foerschler, A., 'Corporate Criminal Intent: Toward a Better Understanding of Corporate Misconduct', (1990) 78 *California Law Review* 1287.

Fogarty, M., and Christie, I., *Companies and Communities* (London, 1990).

Ford, H. A. J., *Principles of Company Law*, 4th ed. (Sydney, 1986).

Foulkes, D., 'The Supervision of Companies—The Parliamentary Commissioner's Report', [1974] *Journal of Business Law* 23.

Francis, A., 'Company Objectives, Managerial Motivations and the Behaviour of Large Firms: An Empirical Test of the Theory of Managerial Capitalism', (1980) 4 *Cambridge Journal of Economics* 349.

—— 'Families, Firms and Financial Capital', (1980) 14 *Sociology* 1.

Franks, J. and Harris, R., *Shareholder Wealth Effects of Corporate Takeovers: the U.K. Experience 1955–85*, London Business School and University of North Carolina at Chapel Hill, Working Paper (1986).

—— 'Shareholder Wealth Effects of U.K. Takeovers: Implications for Merger Policy', in J. A. Fairburn and J. A. Kay (eds), *Merger and Merger Policy* (1989), 148.

Franks, J. and Mayer, C., 'Capital Markets and Corporate Control: A Study of France, Germany and the U.K.', (1990) 10 *Economic Policy* 191.

Freeman, R. E. (ed.), *Business Ethics: The State of the Art* (New York, 1991).

Fridman, G. H. L., *Law of Agency*, 6th ed. (London, 1990).

Friedman, M., *Capitalism and Freedom* (Chicago, 1962).

—— *An Economist's Protest* (Elen Ridge, 1972).

—— 'The Social Responsibility of Business is to Increase its Profits', in T. Beauchamp and N. Bowie, *Ethical Theory and Business* (Englewood Cliffs, NJ, 1988)

Frug, G. E., 'The Ideology of Bureaucracy in American Law', (1984) 97 *Harvard Law Review* 1276.

Furey, N. E., *The Companies Act 1989: A Practitioner's Guide* (Bristol, 1990).

Galbraith, J. K., *The New Industrial State*, 2nd ed. (Harmondsworth, 1972).

—— 'On the Economic Image of Corporate Enterprise' in R. Nader and M. Green (eds), *Corporate Power in America* (New York, 1973).

Gavis, A. C.; 'A Framework for Satisfying Corporate Directors' Responsibilities under State Nonshareholder Constituency Statutes: The Use of Explicit Contracts', (1990) 138 *University of Pennsylvania Law Review* 1451.

George, K., 'Do We Need A Merger Policy?', in J. A. Fairburn and J. A. Kay (eds), *Mergers and Merger Policy* (Oxford, 1989), 289.

Gilson, R. J., 'A Structural Approach to Corporations: The Case Against Defensive Actions in Tender Offers', (1981) 33 *Stanford Law Review* 819.

Gilson, R. J. and Kraakman, R., 'Reinventing the Outside Director: An Agenda for Institutional Investors', (1991) 43 *Stanford Law Review* 863.

Glasbeek, H. J., 'The Corporate Social Responsibilty Movement—The Latest in Maginot Lines to Save Capitalism', [1988] *Dalhousie Law Journal* 363.

Goldberg, G. D., 'Article 80 of Table A of the Companies Act 1948', (1970) 33 *Modern Law Review* 177.

Goodhart, D. and Grant, C., *Making the City Work*, Fabian Tract no. 528 (London, 1988).

Goodpaster, K. E., 'The Concept of Corporate Responsibility', (1983) 2 *Journal of Business Ethics* 1.

——— 'Ethical Imperatives and Corporate Leadership', in R. E. Freeman (ed.), *Business Ethics: The State of the Art* (New York, 1991), 89.

Gordon, J. N., 'The Mandatory Structure of Corporate Law', (1989) 89 *Columbia Law Review* 1549.

——— 'Corporations, Markets and Courts', (1991) 91 *Columbia Law Review* 1931.

Gotthold, J., 'Codetermination and Property Rights Theory', in T. Daintith and G. Teubner (eds.), *Contract and Organization: Legal Analysis in the Light of Economic and Social Theory* (Berlin, 1986), 244.

Gower, L. C. B., 'Corporate Control: The Battle for the Berkeley', (1955) 68 *Harvard Law Review* 1176.

——— *Review of Investor Protection Report: Part 1*, Cmnd. 9125 (London, 1984).

——— *Principles of Modern Company Law*, 4th ed. (London, 1979).

——— 5th ed. (London, 1992).

Goyder, G., *The Responsible Company* (Oxford, 1961).

——— *The Just Enterprise* (London, 1987).

Graham, C., 'Regulating the Company', in L. Hancher and M. Moran (eds), *Capitalism, Culture and Regulation* (Oxford, 1989).

Graham, C. and Prosser, T., *Privatizing Public Enterprises* (Oxford, 1991).

Grant, W., *Business and Politics in Britain* (Basingstoke, 1987).

Grantham, R., 'The Judicial Extension of Directors' Duties to Creditors', [1991] *Journal of Business Law* 1.

Gray, J., *Liberalism* (Milton Keynes, 1986).

Gray, R., *The Greening of Accountancy: The Profession After Pearce* (London, 1990).

Gray, R., Owen, D. and Maunders, K., *Corporate Social Reporting* (Hemel Hempstead, 1987).

Gregg, P., Machin S., and Szymanski, S., *The Disappearing Relationship between Directors' Pay and Corporate Performance*, LSE Centre for Economic Performance Working Paper no. 282 (London, 1992).

Gregory, R., 'The Scope of the Companies Act 1948, Section 205', (1982) 98 *Law Quarterly Review* 413.

Grossman, S. J. and Hart, O. D., 'Takeover Bids, the Free-rider Problem and the Theory of the Corporation', (1980) 11 *Bell Journal* 42.

Gwilliam, D., 'The Auditor's Responsibility for the Detection of Fraud', (1987) 3 *Professional Negligence* 5.

Habermas, J., *The Theory of Communicative Action*, trans T. McCarthy vol. 1 (Boston, 1984).

Hadden, T., *Company Law and Capitalism*, 2nd ed. (London, 1977).

——— 'Employee Participation—What Future for the German Model?', (1982) 3 *Company Lawyer* 250.

——— *The Control of Corporate Groups* (London, 1983).

——— 'Company Law', in P. Archer and A. Martin (eds), *More Law Reform Now* (Chichester, 1983), 21.

Halpern, P., Trebilcock, M. and Turnbull, S., 'An Economic Analysis of Limited

Liability in Corporation Law', (1980) 30 *University of Toronto Law Journal* 117.

Hancher, L. and Moran, M., 'Organizing Regulatory Space', in L. Hancher and M. Moran (eds), *Capitalism, Culture and Regulation* (Oxford, 1989), 272.

Handy, C., *The Making Of Managers* (London, 1987).

Hann, O., 'Takeover Rules in the European Community: An Economic Analysis of Proposed Takeover Guidelines and Already Issued Disclosure Rules', (1990) 10 *International Review of Law and Economics* 131.

Hannah, L., 'Takeover Bids in Britain before 1950: an Exercise in Business Pre-History', (1974) 16 *Business History* 65.

—— *Management Strategy and Business Development* (London, 1976).

—— *Inventing Retirement* (London, 1986).

—— *The Rise of the Corporate Economy*, 2nd ed. (London, 1983).

Hannah, L. and Kay, J. A., *Concentration in Modern Industry* (London, 1977).

Hansmann, N. and Kraakman, R., 'Toward Unlimited Shareholder Liability for Corporate Torts', (1991) 100 *Yale Law Journal* 1879.

Harrison, J.·F. C., *Robert Owen and the Owenites in Britain and America* (London, 1969).

Hart, H. L. A., 'Definition and Theory in Jurisprudence', (1954) 70 *Law Quarterly Review* 37

Hart, O., 'An Economist's Perspective of the Theory of the Firm', (1989) *Columbia Law Review* 1757.

Hartman, E. M., 'Donaldson on Rights and Corporate Obligations', in R. E. Freeman (ed.), *Business Ethics: The State of the Art* (New York, 1991), 163.

Harvey, B., Smith, S., and Wilkinson, B., *Managers and Corporate Social Policy: Private Solutions to Public Problems?* (London, 1984).

Hay, D. A. and Morris, D. J., *Industrial Economics and Organization: Theory and Evidence*, 2nd ed. (Oxford, 1991).

Hayek, F. A., *The Constitution of Liberty* (London, 1960).

—— 'The Corporation in a Democratic Society: In Whose Interest Ought It and Will It Be Run?', in H. I. Ansoff (ed.), *Business Strategy* (Harmondsworth, 1969), 266.

—— *Law, Legislation and Liberty*, complete ed. (London, 1982).

Hazen, T. L., 'Corporate Directors' Accountability: The Race to the Bottom—The Second Lap',(1987) 66 *North Carolina Law Review* 171.

Heald, M., *The Social Responsibilities of Business: Company and Community 1900–1960* (Cleveland, 1970).

Health and Safety Executive, *Deadly Maintenance* (London, 1985).

—— *Agricultural Blackspot* (London, 1986).

—— *Blackspot Construction* (London, 1988).

—— *Annual Reports*, 1988/89, 1989/90, (London, 1989 and 1990).

Held, D., *Models of Democracy* (Cambridge, 1987).

Helm, D., 'Mergers, Take-overs and the Enforcement of Profit Maximization', in J. A. Fairburn and J. A. Kay (eds), *Mergers and Merger Policy* (Oxford, 1989), 133.

Herman, E. S., *Corporate Control, Corporate Power* (Cambridge, 1981).

—— 'The Limits of the Market as a Discipline in Corporate Governance', (1984) 9 *Delaware Journal of Corporate Law* 530.

Herman, E. S. and Lowenstein, L., 'The Efficiency Effects of Hostile Takeovers', in J.

C. Coffee, L. Lowenstein, and S. Rose-Ackerman, (eds), *Knights, Raiders and Targets* (New York, 1988), 211.

Hessen, R., *In Defence of the Corporation* (Stanford, 1979).

Heydon, J. D., 'Directors' Duties and the Company's Interests', in P. D. Finn (ed.), *Equity and Commercial Relationships* (North Ryde, 1987).

Hicks, J., 'Limited Liability: the Pros and Cons', in A. Orhnial (ed.), *Limited Liability and the Corporation* (London, 1982), 11.

Hinsey, J., 'Business Judgment and the American Law Institute's Corporate Governance Project: the Rule, the Doctrine and the Reality', (1984) 52 *George Washington Law Review* 609.

Hirsch, F. *Social Limits to Growth* (Cambridge, Mass., 1977).

Hirschman, A. O., *Exit, Voice and Loyalty: Responses to Decline in Firms, Organizations and States* (Cambridge, Mass., 1970).

Hodgson, G. M., *The Democratic Economy* (Harmondsworth, 1984).

—— *Economics and Institutions* (Cambridge, 1988).

Hofstetter, K., 'Parent Responsibility for Subsidiary Corporations: Evaluating European Trends', (1990) 39 *International and Comparative Law Quarterly* 576.

Honoré, A., 'Ownership', in A. G. Guest (ed.), *Oxford Essays in Jurisprudence* (Oxford, 1961).

—— 'Property, Title, and Redistribution', in A. Honoré, *Making Law Bind* (Oxford, 1987).

Hopt, K. J., 'New Ways in Corporate Governance: European Experiments with Labor Representation on Corporate Boards', (1984) 82 *Michigan Law Review* 1338.

—— 'Self-Dealing and the Use of Corporate Opportunity and Information: Regulating Directors' Conflicts of Interest', in K. J. Hopt and G. Teubner (eds), *Corporate Governance and Directors' Liabilities* (Berlin, 1985).

Horn, E. J., *Management of Industrial Change in Germany* (Brighton, 1982).

Horn, N., Kötz, K. and Leser, H. G., *German Private and Commercial Law: An Introduction*, trans. T. Weir (Oxford, 1982).

Horwitz, M. J., 'The History of the Private/Public Distinction', (1982) 130 *University of Pennsylvania Law Review* 1423.

—— 'Santa Clara Revisited: The Development of Corporate Theory', (1985) 15 *West Virginia Law Review* 173 .

Hu, H. T. C., 'Risk, Time and Fiduciary Principles in Corporate Investment', (1990) 38 *Law Review* 277.

Hughes, A., 'The Impact of Merger: A Survey of Empirical Evidence for the U.K.', in J. A. Fairburn and J. A. Kay (eds), *Mergers and Merger Policy* (Oxford, 1989), 30.

Humble, J. and Johnson, M. A., *Corporate Social Responsibility: the Attitudes of European Business Leaders* (Brussels, 1978).

Hurst, J. W., *The Legitimacy of the Business Corporation* (Charlottesville, Va., 1970).

Imberg D., and MacMahon, P., 'Company Law Reform' (1973) 1 No. 2 *Social Audit* 3.

Innovation Advisory Board, *Innovation: City Attitudes and Practices* (London, 1990).

——— *Promoting Innovation and Long Termism* (London, 1990).

Institute of Business Ethics, *Company Philosophies and Codes of Business Ethics* (London, 1988).

——— *Business Ethics and Company Codes* (London, 1992).

Institute of Chartered Accountants of England and Wales, *Report of the Study Group on the Change in the Role of the Non-Executive Director* (London, 1991).

Institute of Directors, *A Code of Practice for the Non-Executive Director* (London, 1982).

——— *A New Agenda for Business* (London, 1987).

——— *Professional Development of and for the Board* (London, 1990).

Institutional Shareholders Committee, *The Role and Duty of Directors: A Statement of Best Practice* (London, 1991).

——— *Suggested Disclosure of Research and Development Expenditure* (London, 1992).

Instone, R., 'The Duty of Directors', [1977] *Journal of Business Law* 221.

International Chamber of Commerce, *Environmental Guidelines for World Industry* (London, 1990).

International Stock Exchange, *Admission of Securities to Listing*, rev. ed. (London, 1992).

Ireland, D., Grigg-Spall, I. and Kelly, D., 'The Conceptual Foundations of Modern Company Law', in P. Fitzpatrick and A. Hunt (eds), *Critical Legal Studies* (Oxford, 1987), 149.

Jackson, P. D., 'Management of U.K. Equity Portfolios', (May, 1987) *Bank of England Quarterly Bulletin* 457.

Jacobs, M., *The Green Economy: Environment, Sustainable Development and the Politics of the Future* (London, 1991).

Jenkinson, C. and Mayer, T., *Takeover Defence Strategies* (Oxford, 1991).

Jensen, M. C., 'Takeovers, Their Causes and Consequences', (1988) 2 *Journal of Economic Perspectives* 21.

——— 'Eclipse of the Public Corporation', (1989) 67 *Harvard Business Review* 61.

Jensen, M. C. and Meckling, M., 'Theory of the Firm: Managerial Behavior, Agency Costs and Ownership Structure', (1976) 3 *Journal of Financial Economics* 305

Jensen, M. C. and Murphy, K. J., 'Performance Pay and Top Management Incentives', (1990) 98 *Journal of Political Economy* 225.

——— 'C.E.O. Incentives—It's not how much you pay, but how', (1991) 69 *Harvard Business Review* 138.

Jensen, M. C. and Ruback, R., 'The Market for Corporate Control: The Scientific Evidence', (1983) 11 *Journal of Financial Economy* 5.

John, R. I., 'Relieving Directors from the Liabilities of Office: the Case for the Reform of Section 241, Corporations Law', [1992] *Companies and Securities Law Journal* 6.

Johns, R. I., *Company Community Involvement in the UK: An Independent Study* (Warwick, 1991).

Jones, G., 'Unjust Enrichment and the Fiduciary's Duty of Loyalty', (1968) 84 *Law Quarterly Review* 472.

Jones, T. M. and Goldberg, L. D., 'Governing the Large Corporation: More Arguments for Public Directors', (1982) 7 *Academy of Management Review* 603.

Kahn-Freund, O., 'Industrial Democracy', (1977) 6 *Industrial Law Journal* 65.

Kay, J. A., *The Role of Mergers*, Institute of Fiscal Studies Working Paper no. 94 (London, 1986).

Kaysen, C., 'The Social Significance of the Modern Corporation', (1957) 47 *American Economic Review* 311.

—— 'The Corporation: How Much Power? What Scope?', in E. S. Mason (ed.), *The Corporation in Modern Society* (Cambridge, Mass., 1959).

Kester, W. C., *Japanese Takeovers: the Global Contest for Corporate Control* (Boston, 1991).

King, D. S., 'Voluntary and State Provision of Welfare as Part of the Public-Private Continuum: Modelling the Shifting Involvements in Britain and the US', in A. Ware (ed.), *Charities and Government* (Manchester, 1989).

King, M. A., *Public Policy and the Corporation* (London, 1977).

Kirkman, P. and Hope, C., *Environmental Disclosure in UK Company Annual Reports* (Cambridge, 1992).

Kissler, L., 'Co-determination Research in the Federal Republic of Germany: A Review', in C. J. Lammers and G. Széll, *International Handbook of Participation in Organizations*, vol. 1 (Oxford, 1989), 74.

Klare, K. E., 'The Public/Private Distinction in Labour Law', (1982) 130 *University of Pennsylvania Law Review* 1358.

Knoeber, C. R., 'Golden Parachutes, Shark Repellants and Hostile Tender Offers', (1986) 76 *American Economic Review* 155.

Korn/Ferry International, *Board of Directors Study U.K.* (London, 1989 and 1991).

Kraakman, R., 'The Economic Functions of Corporate Liability', in K. J. Hopt and G. Teubner (eds), *Corporate Governance and Directors' Liabilities* (Berlin, 1985), 178.

Kübler, F., 'Dual Loyalty of Labor Representatives', in K. J. Hopt and G. Teubner (eds), *Corporate Governance and Directors' Liabilities* (Berlin, 1985), 429.

Kuehn, D. A., *Takeovers and the Theory of the Firm* (London, 1975).

Kuhn, J. W. and Shriver, D. W., *Beyond Success: Corporations and their Critics in the 1990s* (New York, 1991).

Labour Research Department, (1987) 76 *Labour Research* no. 1, 13.

—— (1988) 77 *Labour Research* no. 7, 7.

Ladd, J., 'Morality and the Ideal of Rationality in Formal Organizations', (1970) 54 *Monist* 488.

Larner, R. J., *Management Control and the Large Corporation* (New York, 1970).

Law Commission, *Working Paper no. 44: Codification of the Criminal Law—Criminal Liability of Corporations* (London, 1972).

—— *A Criminal Code for England and Wales*, Law Commission no. 177, (London, 1989).

Law Reform Commission (Canada), *Working Paper no. 16, Criminal Responsibility for Group Action* (Ottawa, 1976).

Lee, T. C., 'Limiting Corporate Directors' Liability: Delaware's section 102 (b) (7) and the Erosion of the Directors' Duty of Care', (1987) 136 *University of Pennsylvania Law Review* 239.

Leebron, D. W, 'Limited Liability, Tort Victims and Creditors', (1991) 91 *Columbia Law Review* 1565.

Leigh, L. H., *The Criminal Liability of Corporations in English Law* (London, 1969).

—— *The Control of Commercial Fraud* (London, 1982).

Levitt, T., 'The Dangers of Social Responsibility', in H. D. Marshall (ed.), *Business and Government: The Problem of Power* (Lexington, 1970).

Lindblom, C. E., 'Democracy and Economic Structure', in W. N. Chambers and R. H. Salisbury (eds), *Democracy Today: Problems and Prospects* (New York, 1962).

—— *Politics and Markets* (New York, 1977).

Lipsey, R. G., *An Introduction to Positive Economics*, 7th ed. (London, 1989).

Littlechild, S., 'Myths and Merger Policy', in J. A. Fairburn and J. A. Kay (eds), *Mergers and Merger Policy* (Oxford, 1989), 281.

Llewellyn, W., 'Management and Ownership in the Large Firm', (1969) 24 *Journal of Finance* 299.

Locke, J., *Two Treatises of Government* (London, 1690).

Lofthouse, S., 'Competition Policies as Take-over Defences', [1984] *Journal of Business Law* 320.

Lorenz, E. H., 'Neither Friends Nor Strangers: Informal Networks of Subcontracting in French Industry', in D. Gambetta (ed.), *Trust: Making and Breaking of Cooperative Relations* (Oxford, 1989).

Lowenstein L., 'Pruning Deadwood in Hostile Takeovers: A Proposal for Legislation', (1983) 83 *Columbia Law Review* 249.

Lowry, J. P., '"Poison Pills" in US Corporations—a Re-examination', [1992] *Journal of Business Law* 337.

Luhmann, N., *Funktion der Religion* (Frankfurt, 1977).

Lukes, S., 'Power and Authority', in T. Bottomore and R. Nisbet (eds.), *A History of Sociological Analysis* (London, 1979).

—— *Power: A Radical View* (London, 1974).

—— *Moral Conflicts and Politics* (Oxford, 1991).

Luxton, P., 'Ethical Investment in Hard Times', (1992) 55 *Modern Law Review* 587.

McCarthy, W., *The Future of Industrial Democracy* Fabian Tract no. 526 (London, 1988).

McChesney, F. S., 'Economics, Law and Science in the Corporate Field: A Critique of Eisenberg', (1989) 89 *Columbia Law Review* 1530.

McConnell, J. J. and Muscarella, C. J., 'Corporate Capital Expenditure Decisions and the Market Value of the Firm', (1985) 14 *Journal of Financial Economics* 399.

Mace, M. L., *Directors: Myth and Reality* (1971, Cambridge, Mass).

—— 'Directors: Myth and Reality—Ten Years Later', (1979) 32 *Rutgers Law Review* 293.

McEwin, R. I., 'Public Versus Shareholder Control of Directors', [1992] *Company and Securities Law Journal* 182.

McHugh, F. P., *Keyguide to Information Sources in Business Ethics* (London, 1988).

MacIntyre, A., *After Virtue: A Study in Moral Theory*, 2nd ed. (London, 1985).

McKean, R. N., 'Collective Choice', in J. W. McKie, *Social Reponsibility and the Business Predicament* (Washington, 1974), 109.

—— 'Economics of Trust, Altruism and Corporate Responsibility', in E. S. Phelps (ed.), *Altruism, Morality and Economic Theory* (New York, 1975), 29.

McLean, J. H., 'The Theoretical Basis of the Trustee's Duty of Loyalty', (1969) 7 *Alberta Law Review* 218.

McMahon, T. F., 'Models of the Relationship of the Firm to the Society', (1986) 5 *Journal of Business Ethics* 181

Main, B. and Johnston, J., 'Deciding Top Pay by Committee', (July, 1992) *Personnel Management* 32.

Manne, H. G., 'The "Higher" Criticism of the Modern Corporation', (1962) 62 *Columbia Law Review* 399.

—— 'Mergers and the Market for Corporate Control', (1965) 73 *Journal of Political Economy* 693.

—— 'In Defense of Insider Trading', (1966) 44 *Harvard Business Review* 133.

Manne, H. G. and Wallich, H. C., *The Modern Corporation and Social Responsibility* (Washington, 1972).

Manning, B., 'The Business Judgement Rule and the Directors' Duty of Attention: Time for Reality', (1984) 39 *Business Lawyer* 1477.

Manton, K., 'Funding the Arts in Seven Western Countries', in Charities Aid Foundation, *Charity Trends*, 13th ed. (Tonbridge, 1990), 108.

Marris, R., *The Economic Theory of 'Managerial' Capitalism* (London, 1964).

Marsh, H., 'Are Directors Trustees? Conflict of Interest and Corporate Morality', [1966] *Business Lawyer* 35.

Marsh, P., *Short-Termism on Trial* (London, 1990).

Marsh, D. and Locksey, G., 'Capital in Britain: Its Structural Power and Influence Over Policy' (1983) 6 *West European Politics* 36.

Mashaw, J. L., 'The Economic Context of Corporate Social Resonsibility', in K. J. Hopt and G. Teubner (eds), *Corporate Governance and Directors' Liability* (Berlin, 1985), 55.

Mason, E. S., 'The Apologetics of Managerialism', (1958) 31 *Journal of Business* 1.

Meade, J., 'Labour Co-operatives, Participation and Value-Added Sharing', in A. Clayre (ed.), *The Political Economy of Co-operation and Participation* (Oxford, 1980), 89.

Medawar, P., *The Social Audit Consumer Handbook: A Guide to the Social Responsibilities of Business to the Consumer* (London, 1978).

Meeks, G. and Whittington, G., 'Directors' Pay, Growth and Profitability', (1975) 24 *Journal of Industrial Economics* 1.

Meiners, R. E., Mofsky, J. S. and Tollison, R. D., 'Piercing the Veil of Limited Liability', (1979) 4 *Delaware Journal of Corporate Law* 351.

Meister, D. J., 'Criminal Liability for Corporations that Kill', (1990) 64 *Tulane Law Review* 919.

Melrose-Woodman, J. E. and Kverndal, I., *Towards Social Responsibility*, British Institute of Management, Management Survey Report no. 28 (London, 1976).

Metcalf, H., Pearson R., and Martin R., *Stimulating Jobs: The Charitable Role of Companies*, Institute of Manpower Studies Report no. 166 (Brighton, 1989).

Michelman, F. I., 'A Comment on Some Uses and Abuses of Economics in Law', (1979) 46 *University of Chicago Law Review* 307.

Midgley, K., *Companies and Their Shareholders—The Uneasy Relationship* (London, 1975).

Miliband, R., *The State in Capitalist Society* (London, 1969).

Miller, D., *Market, State and Community* (Oxford, 1989).

—— 'Why Markets?, in J. Le Grand and S. Estrin, *Market Socialism* (Oxford, 1989).

Miller, M., and Modigliani F., 'Dividend Policy, Growth and the Valuation of Shares', (1961) 34 *Journal of Business* 411.

Millon, D., 'Theories of the Corporation', [1990] *Duke Law Journal* 201.

—— 'Redefining Corporate Law', (1991) 24 *Indiana Law Review* 223.

Millward, N. et al., *Workplace Industrial Relations in Transition: the ED/ESRC/PSI/ ACAS Surveys* (Aldershot, 1992).

Minns, R., *Pension Funds and British Capitalism: The Ownership and Control of Shareholdings* (London, 1980).

Mishan, E. J., *The Costs of Economic Growth* (London, 1967).

Mitchell, N. J., *The Generous Corporation: A Political Analysis of Economic Power* (New Haven, 1989).

Mnookin, R. H., 'The Public Private Dichotomy: Political Disagreement and Academic Repudiation', (1982) 130 *University of Pennsylvania Law Review* 1429.

Moir, C., *The Acquisitive Streak* (London, 1986).

Moran, M., 'Investor Protection and the Culture of Capitalism', in L. Hancher and M. Moran (eds), *Capitalism, Culture and Regulation* (Oxford, 1989), 49.

Morris, D., 'Corporate Support for Charity', [1990] *Journal of Business Law* 495.

Morse, G. K., 'General Principle 7, The Law and Directors' Duties—The Consolidated Goldfields Affair', [1989] *Journal of Business Law* 427.

Munzer, S. R., *A Theory of Property* (Cambridge, 1990).

Musgrave, R., 'On Social Goods and Social Bads', in R. Marris (ed.), *The Corporate Society* (London, 1974), 251.

Nader, R., Green, M. and Seligman G., *Taming the Giant Corporation* (New York, 1976).

National Consumer Council, *Business Sponsorship of Teaching Material: Classroom Commercials* (London, 1986).

New Zealand Law Commission, *Company Law Reform and Restatement*, Report no. 9 (Wellington, 1989).

Nozick, R., *Anarchy, State and Utopia* (Oxford, 1974).

Nyman, S. and Silberston, A., 'The Ownership and Control of Industry', (1978) 30 *Oxford Economic Papers* 74.

Oakeshott, R., *The Case for Workers' Co-Ops*, 2nd ed. (London, 1990).

Office of Arts and Libraries, *Press Release*, 23 May 1990.

Olson, M., *The Logic of Collective Action: Public Goods and the Theory of Groups*, 2nd ed. (Cambridge, Mass., 1971).

—— 'On the Priority of Public Problems', in R. Marris (ed.), *The Corporate Society* (London, 1973), 294.

Pahl, R.E. and Winkler, J.T., 'The Economic Elite: Theory and Practice', in P. Stanworth and A. Giddens (eds), *Elites and Power in British Society* (London, 1974), 103.

Parkinson, J. E., 'The Modification of Directors' Duties', [1981] *Journal of Business Law* 335.

Parsons, T., *The Social System* (London, 1966).

Partridge, R. J. C., 'Ratification and the Release of Directors from Personal Liability', (1987) 46 *Cambridge Law Journal* 122.

Pateman, C., *Participation and Democratic Theory* (London, 1970).

Peacock, A. and Bannock, G., *Corporate Takeovers and the Public Interest* (Aberdeen, 1991).

Pearce, D., Markandya, A. and Barbier, E. B., *Blueprint for a Green Economy* (London, 1989).

Per Cent Club, *Annual Report 1989*.

Perkin, H. J., *The Rise of Professional Society: England since 1880* (London, 1989).

Perrow, C., *Complex Organizations: A Critical Essay* 3rd ed. (New York, 1986).

Phillips, D. M., 'Managerial Misuse of Property: The Synthesising Thread in Corporate Doctrine', (1979) 32 *Rutgers Law Review* 184.

—— 'Principles of Corporate Governance: A Critique of Part IV', (1984) 52 *George Washington Law Review* 653.

Plender, J., 'The Limits to Institutional Power', *Financial Times*, 22 May 1990, 20.
—— 'Takeovers and Short-termism in the U.K.', in A. Cosh et al., *Takeovers and Short-Termism in the UK*, IPPR Policy Paper no. 3 (London, 1990).
Polanyi, K., *The Great Transformation* (Boston, 1944).
Poole, M., *The Origins of Economic Democracy: Profit-Sharing and Employee-Shareholding Schemes* (London, 1989).
Pope, P. F. and Puxty, A. G., 'What is Equity: New Financial Instruments in the Interstices between the Law, Accounting and Economics', (1991) 54 *Modern Law Review* 889.
Porter, M. E., 'From Competitive Advantage to Economic Strategy', (1987) 65 *Harvard Business Review* 43.
Posner, R. A., 'Utilitarianism, Economics and Legal Theory', (1979) 8 *Journal of Legal Studies* 191.
—— *The Economics of Justice* (Cambridge, Mass, 1981).
—— 'An Economic Theory of the Criminal Law', (1985) 85 *Columbia Law Review* 1193.
—— *The Economic Analysis of Law*, 3rd ed. (Boston, 1986).
Prais, S. J., *The Evolution of Giant Firms in Britain* (Cambridge, 1976).
Prentice, D. D., 'Regal (Hastings) Ltd. v Gulliver— The Canadian Experience', (1967) 30 *Modern Law Review* 450.
—— 'Expulsion of Members from a Company', (1970) 33 *Modern Law Review* 700.
—— 'Employee Participation in Corporate Government— A Critique of the Bullock Report', (1978) *Canadian Bar Review* 277.
—— 'The Theory of the Firm: Minority Shareholder Oppression: Sections 459–461 of the Companies Act 1985', (1988) 8 *Oxford Journal of Legal Studies* 55.
—— 'Shareholder Actions: The Rule in Foss v Harbottle', (1988) 104 *Law Quarterly Review* 341.
Pro Ned, *Code of Practice on Non-Executive Directors* (London, 1987).
Prosser, T., 'Regulation of Privatized Enterprises: Institutions and Procedures', in L. Hancher and M. Moran, *Capitalism, Culture and Regulation* (Oxford, 1989).
Purdue, M., 'Integrated Pollution Control in the Environmental Protection Act 1990: A Coming of Age of Environmental Law?', (1991) 54 *Modern Law Review* 534.
Rabinowitz, L., *Weinberg and Blank on Takeovers and Mergers*, 5th ed. (London, 1989).
Ramsay, H., *1992—The Year of the Multinational? Corporate Behaviour, Industrial Restructuring and Labour in the Single Market* Warwick Papers in Industrial Relations no. 35 (Warwick, 1990).
Ramsay, I., 'Balancing Law and Economics: the Case of Partial Takeovers', [1992] *Journal of Business Law* 369.
Rawls, J., *A Theory of Justice* (Oxford, 1972).
Reagan, M. D., *The Managed Economy* (New York, 1963).
Rehnert, G. S., 'The Executive Compensation Contract: Creating Incentives to Reduce Agency Costs', (1985) 37 *Stanford Law Review* 1147.
Reid, G. L., *Efficient Markets and the Rationale of Takeovers* Hume Occasional Paper No. 22 (Aberdeen, 1990).
Renshall, J. M., 'Changing Perceptions Behind the Corporate Report', (1976) 1 *Accounting, Organizations and Society* 105.

Reynolds, F. M. B., *Bowstead on Agency*, 15th ed. (London, 1985).

Reynolds, J., *The Great Paternalist* (London, 1983).

Richardson, G., Ogus, A. and Burrows, P., *Policing Pollution: A Study of Regulation and Enforcement* (Oxford, 1982).

Richardson, J. J., *The Development of Corporate Responsibility in the U.K.* (Glasgow, 1983).

Rider, B. A. K., 'Burmah Oil Loses Claim against Bank of England', (1981) 2 *Company Lawyer* 220.

Rixon, F. G., 'Competing Interests and Conflicting Principles: An Examination of the Power of Alteration of Articles of Association', (1986) 49 *Modern Law Review* 446.

Roe, M. J., 'A Political Theory of American Corporate Finance', (1991) 91 *Columbia Law Review* 10.

Romano, R., 'Metapolitics and Corporate Law Reform', (1984) 36 *Stanford Law Review* 923.

Rose, H. B., and Newbould, G. D., 'The 1967 Takeover Boom', (Autumn, 1967) *Moorgate and Wall Street* 5.

Rostow, E. V., 'To Whom and for What Ends is Corporate Management Responsible?', in E. S. Mason (ed.), *The Corporation in Modern Society* (Cambridge, Mass, 1959), 64.

Rubner, A., *The Ensnared Shareholder: Directors and the Modern Corporation* (London, 1965).

Ryan, C.C., 'Yours, Mine and Ours: Property Rights and Individual Liberty', in J. Paul (ed.), *Reading Nozick* (Oxford, 1981).

Sands, P., 'European Community Environmental Law: Legislation, the European Court of Justice and Common-Interest Groups', (1990) 53 *Modern Law Review* 685.

Sands, P. and Alexander, D., 'Assessing the Impact', (1991) 141 *New Law Journal* 1487.

Sappideen, R., 'Fiduciary Obligations to Corporate Creditors', [1991] *Journal of Business Law* 365.

Sawyer, M. C., *The Economics of Industries and Firms* 2nd ed. (London, 1985).

Schelling, T. C., 'Command and Control', in J. W. McKie (ed.), *Social Responsibility and the Business Predicament* (Washington, 1974), 79.

Scherer, F. M., *Industrial Market Structure and Economic Performance*, 2nd ed.(Boston, 1980).

Schiller, H. I., *Culture Inc.: The Corporate Takeover of Public Expression* (New York, 1989).

Schlegelmilch, B. B. and Houston, J. E., *Company Codes of Ethics in Large U.K. Companies: An Empirical Investigation of Use, Content and Attitudes* (Edinburgh, 1988).

Schleifer, A. and Summers, L., 'Breach of Trust in Hostile Takeovers', in A. J. Auerbach (ed.), *Corporate Takeovers: Causes and Consequences* (Chicago, 1988), 33.

Schleifer, A. and Vishny R. W. , 'Value Maximization and the Acquisition Process', (1988) 2 *Journal of Economic Perspectives* 7.

Schmitthoff, C. M., 'Employee Participation and the Theory of Enterprise', [1975] *Journal of Business Law* 265.

Schuller, T., *Democracy at Work* (Oxford, 1985).

—— *Age, Capital and Democracy: Member Participation in Pension Scheme Management* (Aldershot, 1986).

Scott, J., *Corporations, Classes and Capitalism*, 2nd ed.(London, 1985).

Sealy, L. S., 'The Director as Trustee', [1967] *Cambridge Law Journal* 83.

—— 'Foss v Harbottle: A Marathon Where Nobody Wins', (1981) 40 *Cambridge Law Journal* 29.

—— *Company Law and Commercial Reality* (London, 1984).

—— 'Directors "Wider" Responsibilities— Problems Conceptual, Practical and Procedural', (1987) 13 *Monash University Law Review* 164.

—— 'Problems of Standing, Pleading and Proof in Corporate Litigation', in B. Pettet (ed.), *Company Law in Change* (London, 1987).

—— '"Bona Fides" and "Proper Purposes" in Corporate Decisions', (1989) 15 *Monash University Law Review* 265.

—— 'Reforming the Law on Directors' Duties', (1991) 12 *Company Lawyer* 175.

—— *Cases and Materials in Company Law*, 5th ed. (London, 1992).

Seligman, J., 'A Sheep in Wolf's Clothing: The American Law Institute Principles of Corporate Governance Project', (1987) 55 *George Washington Law Review* 325.

Sen, A., 'The Moral Standing of the Market', in E. F. Paul, F. D. Miller, and J. Paul (eds), *Ethics and Economics* (Oxford, 1985), 1.

Shenfield, B., *Company Giving* (London, 1969).

—— *Company Boards: Their Responsibilities to Shareholders, Employees and the Community* (London, 1971).

Simitis, S., 'Workers' Participation in the Enterprise—Transcending Company Law?', (1975) 38 *Modern Law Review* 1.

Simon, H. A., 'Theories of Decision-Making in Economic and Behavioral Sciences', (1959) 49 *American Economic Review* 253.

Simon, J., Powers C., and Gunneman, J., *The Ethical Investor: Universities and Corporate Responsibility* (New Haven, 1972).

Simon, W. H., 'Contract Versus Politics in Corporation Doctrine', in D. Kairys (ed.), *The Politics of Law: A Progressive Critique*, rev. ed. (New York, 1990).

Singer, J. W., 'The Reliance Interest in Property', (1988) 40 *Stanford Law Review* 611.

Slutsky, B. V., 'Canadian Rejection of the *Hogg v Cramphorn* "Improper Purposes" Principle: A Step Forward?', (1974) 37 *Modern Law Review* 457.

Smiley, R., 'Tender Offers, Transaction Costs and the Theory of the Firm', (1976) 58 *Review of Economics and Statistics* 22.

Smith, A., *An Inquiry into the Nature and Causes of the Wealth of Nations* (London, 1776).

Smith, J. C. and Hogan, B., *Criminal Law*, 7th ed. (London, 1992).

Smith, N. C., *Morality and the Market: Consumer Pressure for Corporate Accountability* (London, 1990).

Smith, R. J., 'Minority Shareholders and Corporate Irregularities', (1978) 41 *Modern Law Review* 147.

Social Audit, 'The Case For a Social Audit', (1973) 1 *Social Audit* 4.

Social Science Research Council, *Advisory Panel on the Responsibilities of Business* (London, 1976).

Stanworth P. and Giddens, A., 'The Modern Corporate Economy: Interlocking Directorships in Britain 1956–1970', (1975) 23 *Sociological Review* 5.

Steel, T., 'Defensive Tactics in Company Takeovers', (1986) 4 *Company and Securities Law Journal* 30.

Steiner, G. A. and Steiner, J. F., *Business, Government and Society: A Managerial Perspective*, 3rd ed. (New York, 1980).

Steinmann, H., 'The Enterprise as a Political System', in K. J. Hopt and G. Teubner (eds), *Corporate Governance and Directors' Liabilities* (Berlin, 1985), 401.

Stephen, F. H., *The Economics of Law* (London, 1988).

Stevenson, R. B., *Corporations and Information: Secrecy, Access and Disclosure* (Baltimore, 1980).

Stigler, G. J., 'Competition', (1968) 3 *International Encyclopedia of Social Science* 181.

Stokes, M., 'Company Law and Legal Theory', in W. Twining (ed.), *Legal Theory and the Common Law* (Oxford, 1986), 155.

Stone, C. D., *Where the Law Ends: The Social Control of Corporate Behaviour* (New York, 1975).

—— 'An Approach to Corporate Social Responsibility', (1979) 32 *Stanford Law Review* 1.

—— 'The Place of Enterprise Liability in the Control of Corporate Conduct', (1980) 90 *Yale Law Journal* 1.

—— 'Corporate Vices and Corporate Virtues: Do Public/Private Distinctions Matter?', (1982) *University of Pennsylvania Law Review* 1441.

—— 'Public Interest Representation: Economic and Social Policy Inside the Enterprise', in K. J. Hopt and G. Teubner (eds), *Corporate Governance and Directors' Liabilities* (Berlin, 1985), 122.

—— 'Corporate Social Responsibility: What it Might Mean, if it Were Really to Matter', (1986) 71 *Iowa Law Review* 557.

Stopford, J. M. and Turner, L. M., *Britain and the Multinationals* (Chichester, 1985).

Stout, L. A., 'The Unimportance of Being Efficient: an Economical Analysis of Stock Market Pricing and Securities Regulation', (1988) 87 *Michigan Law Review* 613.

Sullivan, G. R., 'Restating the Scope of the Derivative Action', (1985) 44 *Cambridge Law Journal* 236.

Sunday Times, 'Sterling Qualities on the Crest of a Wave', 7 December 1986.

Swift, J., 'Merger Policy: Certainty or Lottery', in J. A. Fairburn and J. A. Kay (eds), *Mergers and Merger Policy* (Oxford, 1989), 264.

'Symposium on the Theory of Public Choice', (1988) 74 *Virginia Law Review* 167.

Teubner, G., 'Substantive and Reflexive Elements in Modern Law', (1983) 17 *Law and Society Review* 239.

—— 'After Legal Instrumentalism? Strategic Models of Post-Regulatory Law', (1984) 12 *International Journal of Sociology of Law* 325.

—— 'Corporate Fiduciary Duties and their Beneficiaries: A Functional Approach to the Legal Institutionalization of Corporate Responsibility', in K. J. Hopt and G. Teubner (eds), *Corporate Governance and Directors' Liabilities* (Berlin, 1985), 149.

—— 'Industrial Democracy Through Law? Social Functions of Law in Institutional Innovations', in T. Daintith and G. Teubner (eds), *Contract and Organisation: Legal Analysis in the Light of Economic and Social Theory* (Berlin, 1986), 261.

Tixier, P. E., 'The Labour Movement and Post-Rational Models of Organization: A French Case or a Trend in Western Societies?', in C. J. Lammers and G. Széll, *International Handbook of Participation in Organizations*, vol. 1 (Oxford, 1989), 26.

Tobin, J., 'On the Efficiency of the Financial System', (July 1984) *Lloyds Bank Review*
1.

Touche Ross Corporate Finance, *The Performance Of Management: Buy-outs in the Longer
Term* (London, 1989).

Trebilcock, M. J., 'Liability of Company Directors for Negligence', (1969) 32 *Modern
Law Review* 499.

Tricker, R. I., *Corporate Governance: Practices, Procedures and Powers in British Companies
and Their Boards of Directors* (Aldershot, 1984).

Tunc, A., 'The French Commissaires aux Comptes', [1984] *Journal of Business Law*
279.

—— 'The Judge and the Businessman', (1986) 102 *Law Quarterly Review* 549.

Uvalic, M., 'The Pepper Report: Promotion of Employee Participation in Profits and
Enterprise Results in the Member States of the European Community', *Social
Europe, Supplement 3/91* (Florence, 1991).

Vagts, D. F., 'Reforming the 'Modern' Corporation: Perspectives from the German',
(1966) 80 *Harvard Law Review* 23.

—— 'Challenges to Executive Compensation: For the Markets or the Courts?',
(1983) 26 *Journal of Corporation Law* 231.

Veljanovski, C. G., 'The New Law–and–Economics: A Research Review', in A. I.
Ogus and C. G. Veljanovski (eds), *Readings in the Economics of Law and Regulation*
(Oxford, 1984), 12.

Vogl, F., *German Business after the Economic Miracle* (London, 1973)

Wainwright, H. and Elliot, D., *The Lucas Plan—a New Trade Unionism in the Making?*
(London, 1982).

Waldron, J., *The Right to Private Property* (Oxford, 1988).

Walker, B., 'Focus: Corporate Social Responsibility', (1992) 1 *Business Ethics: A
European Review* 29.

Walker, D. A., 'Some Perspectives for Pension Fund Managers', (1987) 27 *Bank of
England Quarterly Bulletin* 247.

Walzer, M., *Spheres of Justice* (Oxford, 1983).

Ware, A., 'Introduction, The Changing Relations between Charities and the State',
in A. Ware (ed.), *Charities and Government* (Manchester, 1989).

Webley, S., *Corporate Social Responsibility* (London, 1975).

—— *Company Philosophies and Codes of Business Ethics* (London, 1987).

—— *Business Ethics and Company Codes* (London, 1992).

Wedderburn, K. W., 'Shareholders' Rights and the Rule in *Foss v Harbottle*', [1957]
Cambridge Law Journal 194.

—— *Company Law Reform*, Fabian Tract no. 363 (London, 1965).

—— 'Control of Corporate Litigation', (1976) 39 *Modern Law Review* 327.

—— 'Derivative Actions and *Foss v Harbottle*', (1981) 44 *Modern Law Review* 202.

—— 'The Legal Development of Corporate Responsibility: For whom Will
Corporate Managers be Trustees?', in K. J. Hopt and G. Teubner (eds), *Corporate
Governance and Directors' Liabilities* (Berlin, 1985), 3.

—— 'The Social Responsibility of Companies', (1985) 15 *Melbourne University Law
Review* 4.

—— 'Trust, Corporation and the Worker', (1985) 23 *Osgoode Hall Law Journal* 203.

—— *The Worker and the Law*, 3rd ed. (Harmondsworth, 1986).

—— 'Control of Corporate Actions', (1989) 52 *Modern Law Review* 401.

—— *The Social Charter, European Company and Employment Rights: An Outline Agenda* (London, 1990).

Weiner, J. L., 'The Berle–Dodd Dialogue on the Concept of the Corporation', (1964) 64 *Columbia Law Review* 1458.

Weiss, E. J., 'Social Regulation of Business Activity: Reforming the Corporate Governance System to Resolve an Institutional Impasse', (1981) 28 *UCLA Law Review* 343.

Welling, B. L., *Corporate Law in Canada* (Toronto, 1984).

Wellington, H. H., *Labor and the Legal Process* (New Haven, 1968).

Wells, C., 'Manslaughter and Corporate Crime', (1989) 139 *New Law Journal* 488.

Whitcomb, H., 'Corporate Accountability and the Environment', (1992) 142 *New Law Journal* 10.

White, A. R., *Rights* (Oxford, 1984).

Wiener, M. J., *English Culture and the Decline of the Industrial Spirit* (Cambridge, 1981).

Williams, G., *Criminal Law: The General Part*, 2nd ed. (London, 1961).

—— *Textbook of Criminal Law*, 2nd ed. (London, 1983).

Williams, I. O., *The Firm of Cadbury 1831–1931* (London, 1931).

Williamson, O. E., *The Economics of Discretionary Behavior: Management Objectives in a Theory of the Firm* (Englewood Cliffs, NJ, 1964).

—— 'Economies as an Anti—Trust Defense: The Welfare Trade - Offs', (1968) 58 *American Economics Review* 18 .

—— 'Managerial Discretion, Organisational Form and the Multi-division Hypothesis', in R. Marris and A. Wood (eds), *The Corporate Economy* (London, 1971).

—— 'The Modern Corporation: Origins, Evolution, Attributes', (1981) 19 *Journal of Economic Literature* 1357.

—— *Economic Institutions of Capitalism* (New York, 1985).

Wilson, C., *The History of Unilever: Part 1* (London, 1954).

Wilson, G. K., *Business and Politics: A Comparative Introduction*, 2nd ed. (London, 1990).

Winfield, M., *Minding Your Own Business: Self-Regulation and Whistleblowing in British Companies* (London, 1990).

Winter, R.K., *Government and the Corporation* (Washington, 1978).

Wishart, D. A., 'Models and Theories of Directors' Duties to Creditors', (1991) 14 *New Zealand Universities Law Review* 323.

Wolff, C. C. P., 'Pre-emptive Rights versus Alternative Methods of Raising Equity on the London Stock Exchange', (1986) 80 *Investment Analyst* 3.

Wooldridge, F., 'The System of Co-Determination in Western Germany and its Proposed Reform', (1976) 5 *Anglo-American Law Review* 19.

Wright, M., Chiplin, B. and Coyne, J., 'The Market for Corporate Control: The Divestment Option', in J. A. Fairburn and J. A. Kay (eds), *Mergers and Merger Policy* (Oxford, 1989).

Xuereb, P. G., 'The Juridification of Industrial Relations through Company Law Reform', (1988) 51 *Modern Law Review* 156.

Zeitlin, M., 'Corporate Ownership and Control: The Large Corporation and the Capitalist Class', (1973–4) 79 *American Journal of Sociology* 1073.

Index

minority shareholders' action, *see* derivative
action
Mondragon co-operatives 427–8, 432
monitoring of management:
by banks 149–50
by courts 73 *et seq.*, 97–113, 132–6, 209,
224
by employees/workers 417 n., 428–9
by insurers 134
by managers 116–17
by non-executive directors 58, 174–6, 191–
9, 393–9
by shareholders 46–7, 105–6, 160, 167–74,
179, 214–17, 429
Monopolies and Mergers Commission 20 n.,
126 n., 158
Montan industries 413
multinationals 7–8

National Association of Pension Funds 169,
175 n.
nationalization 400–1
natural entity theory 26 n.
negligence:
see directors' duties; duty of care and skill;
duty of diligence
nexus of contracts 32, 53–4, 177–90, 203–5
and evolution of governance
structures 179–81, 183–90
and mandatory rules 181–3, 189
model of company defined 178
see also contract theory of the company
non-executive directors 58, 192–5, 218, 232
and corporate opportunities 232
duty of diligence 99
see also board of directors; independent
directors

objects clause 74, 273, 275–6, 278–9, 334
organizational slack 67–9
ownership control 59–63
ownership model 52–3, 76 n.

P. & O. 128 n.
pension funds 166–70, 400, 423 n.
see also institutional investors
Pensions Investment Resource Centre 376
Per Cent Club 291, 297
plant closures 17, 264, 306, 313, 327, 383–4,
408
political donations 275–7, 295–6, 344, 374 n.
positional conflict of interest, *see* conflict of
interest
power, concept of 8, 10
see also corporate power; market power
pre-emption rights 79 n., 137 n., 169 n.
privatization 149 n.

product market:
and consumer preferences 320–3
imperfections 10–12
and managerial discipline 114–16, 186
see also consumer sovereignty
profit maximization:
and the interests of shareholders 89–92
and the maximization of social wealth 41–
6, 260, 309–17, 322–3
meaning of 90, 93, 320
profit maximization within the law 42–3, 260,
266, 304, 324–30, 347, 405
Pro-Ned 193
proper purpose, duty to act for a, *see*
directors' duties
public choice theory 323
public interest:
company/management behaviour and
the 2, 41–4, 201–2, 304
and company law 21–5, 28–30, 42–3, 47–8,
75, 83, 91–2, 135, 237–9, 261–2, 335
meaning of 22, 401

Rank Organization 169
ratification:
and breach of duty of care 254–5
and fraud on the minority 254–6
and breach of proper purpose duty 139–40
meaning of 252–3
see also shareholder consent
redundancy 379, 414 n.
consultation about 383–4
see also plant closures
remuneration, directors of 114–16, 161 n.,
203, 218, 221–6, 231, 355, 374
and managerial motives 68
remuneration committee 58, 193, 218
residual rights theory 46–8, 266, 429
research and development 18–19, 128, 130–1,
399
risk, *see* directors
rule in *Foss* v. *Harbottle*
see Foss v. *Harbottle*, rule in

satisficing, *see* managerial goals
second best, problem of 310
self-dealing 200 *et seq.*, 252
see also directors; fiduciary duty; fiduciary
principle
separation of ownership and control 34–5, 53,
165, 177, 189, 200–1, 240
and corporate social responsibility 263–6
empirical evidence on effects of 71–2
financial control 62–3
location of control 56–63
management control 58–63
ownership control 59–63

Index